OAHU
HANDBOOK

OAHU
HANDBOOK

J.D. BISIGNANI

MOON
PUBLICATIONS, INC.

OAHU HANDBOOK

Please send all comments,
corrections, additions,
amendments, and critiques to:

**J.D. BISIGNANI
c/o MOON PUBLICATIONS
722 WALL STREET
CHICO, CA 95928 USA**

Published by
Moon Publications Inc.
722 Wall Street
Chico, California 95928 USA
tel. (916) 345-5473

Printed by
Colorcraft Ltd., Hong Kong

PRINTING HISTORY
First edition
July 1990

Library of Congress Cataloging in Publication Data

Bisignani, J.D., 1947-
  Oahu Handbook/J.D. Bisignani—1st ed.
  p. cm.
  Includes bibliographical references and index.
  ISBN 0-918373-49-2
  1. Oahu (Hawaii)—Description and travel—Guide-books I. Title
  DU628.03B57 1990
  919.69'3044—dc20   90-36698
  Printed in Hong Kong   CIP

Cover art: courtesy of Richard Fields Studios, Wailea, Maui.

Although the publishers have made every effort to ensure that the information was correct at the time of going to press, the publishers do not assume and hereby disclaim any liability to any party for any loss or damage caused by errors, omissions, or any potential travel disruption due to labor or financial difficulty, whether such errors or omissions result from negligence, accident, or any other cause.

WARNING: Nothing in this book is intended to be used for navigation. Mariners are advised to consult official sailing directions and nautical charts.

IS THIS BOOK OUT OF DATE?

In today's world, things change so rapidly that it's impossible for one person to keep up with everything happening in any one place. This is particularly true in Hawaii, where situations are always in flux. Travel books are like automobiles: they require fine tuning and frequent overhauls to keep in shape. Help us keep this book in shape! We require input from our readers so that we can continue to provide the best, most current information available. Please write to let us know about any inaccuracies, new information, or misleading suggestions. Although we try to make our maps as accurate as possible, errors do occur. If you have any suggestions for improvement or places that should be included, please let us know about them.

We especially appreciate letters from female travelers, visiting expatriates, local residents, and hikers and outdoor enthusiasts. We also like hearing from experts in the field as well as from local hotel owners and individuals wishing to accommodate visitors from abroad.

As you travel through the islands, keep notes in the margins of this book. Notes written on the spot are always more accurate than those put down on paper later. Send us your copy after your trip, and we'll send you a fresh one as a replacement. If you take a photograph during your trip which you feel might be included in future editions, please send it to us. Send only good slide duplicates or glossy black-and-white prints. Drawings and other artwork are also appreciated. If we use your photo or drawing, you'll be mentioned in the credits and receive a free copy of the book. Keep in mind, however, that the publisher cannot return any materials unless you include a self-addressed, stamped envelope. Moon Publications will own the rights on all material submitted. Address your letters to:

J.D. Bisignani
Moon Publications
722 Wall Street
Chico, CA 95928, USA

ACKNOWLEDGEMENTS

Writing the acknowledgements for a book is supercharged with energy. It's a time when you look forward, hopefully, to a bright future for your work, and a time when you reflect on all that has gone into producing it. Mostly it's a time to say thank you. Thank you for the grace necessary to carry out the task, and thank you to all the wonderful people whose efforts have helped so much along the way. To the following people, I offer my most sincere "thank you."

Firstly, to the Moon staff, professionals every one. As time has passed, and one book has followed another, they've become amazingly adept at their work, to the point where their mastery is a marvel to watch. Mark Morris and Taran March, my editors, whose eagle eyes inspect every page, oftentimes saving me from myself, and who make the book much more presentable after they're done buffing and polishing. Christa Jorgensen, who worked in the trenches transcribing over 3,000 pages of travel information. Asha Johnson, a true dynamo, who is typesetter, computer wiz, and "positive vibe person at large." Michelle Bonzey, who actually survived an entire two months as my secretary. Nancy Kennedy who fitted all the parts of the giant jigsaw puzzle matching text with maps, illustrations, photos, graphs, charts, and itsy-bitsy weirdnesses without losing her temper even one time. Louise Foote, map-maker *extraordinaire,* and her helper, Alex "Louise Jr." Foote who did the original maps in this book. Bob Race, who's taken over the map department and who revised each and every map, and whom we all can thank for pointing us in the right direction. Rick Johnson, who knows "where in the world" all the Moon books are, and who is chiefly responsible for keeping them on the bookstore shelves. Donna Galassi, director of sales, her assistant Bette Wells, and publicist Virginia Michaels who keep the Moon rising with every new order that they bring in the door. Cindy Fahey, bookkeeper, who, with some amazing fancy dancing, robs Peter to pay Paul and somehow makes them like it. My illustrators, Diana Lasich Harper, Louise Foote, Sue Strangio Everett, Mary Ann Abel, Debra Fau, Brian Bardwell, and Robert Race, contributing photographers David Stanley, Howard Lindeman, and R.J. Schallenberger, and cover artist Richard Fields, whose talents grace this book.

California State University at Chico professors Bob Vivian, George Benson, Ed Myles, and Ellen Walker, who provided me with quality interns from their respective departments of Journalism, Tourism, Geography, and English. The following student interns worked in the trenches transcribing, inputting, designing charts and graphs, and generally infusing my surroundings with positive energy: Caroline Schoepp, Maureen Cole, Suzanne Booth, Lee Wilkinson, Sally Price, Elena Wilkinson, Bret Lampman, Rich Zimmerman, Craig Nelson, Pat Presley, Leslie Crouch, Monica Moore, Annie Hikido, and Janeen Thomas.

I would also like to thank the following people for their special help and consideration: Dr. Greg Leo, an adventurer and environmentalist who has done remarkable field research and provided me with invaluable information about the unique flora and fauna of Hawaii; Roger Rose and Elisa Johnston of the Bishop Museum; Lee Wild, Hawaiian Mission Houses Museum; Marilyn Nicholson, State Foundation of Culture and the Arts; the Hawaii Visitors Bureau; Chris Tajeda, Tropical Car Rental; Keoni Wagner, Hawaiian Airlines; Jim and John Costello; Dr. Terry and Nancy Carolan; Sally Proctor of Aston Hotels; Renee Cochran and Will Titus, Colony Resorts; Linda Darling-Mann, Coco Palms Resort; Glenn Masutani, Hawaiian Pacific Resorts; Barbara Brundage, Dive Hawaii; Joel Rae, Judy Veirck, and Patti of Patti Cook Associates. To all of you, my deepest *aloha.*

CONTENTS

MAPS

CHARTS

MAP SYMBOLS

MAP LEGEND

FREEWAY
MAIN HIGHWAY
SECONDARY ROAD
JEEP TRAIL
FOOT TRAIL
(1) HIGHWAY NUMBER
WATER
MOUNTAIN

 LARGE TOWN OR CITY
O TOWN OR VILLAGE
o POINT OF INTEREST
● STATE OR BEACH PARK
HEIAU
▲ CAMPGROUND

All maps are oriented with north at the top of the map
unless otherwise indicated.

PHOTO AND ILLUSTRATION CREDITS

Photos
All photos that appear throughout the book are by the author except for: **Hawaii State Archives**—pages 19, 22, 25, 27, 32, 41, 46, 49, 51, 52, 53, 64, 68, 71, 78, 80, 106, 116, 148, 157, 183, 188, 192; **Howard Lindeman**—page 158; **Mission Houses Museum**—page 180.

Illustrations
Mary Ann Abel—pages 256, 271; **Brian Bardwell**—pages 131, 222, 281; **Sue Strangio Everett**—pages 86, 166, 169; **Debra Fau**—pages 328, 330; **Louise Foote**—pages 12, 13, 14, 16, 18, 44, 48, 72, 83, 127, 144, 145, 154, 155, 156, 173, 280, 327; **Diana Lasich Harper**—pages 5, 11, 15, 37, 38, 69, 70, 77, 79, 123, 124, 125, 139, 147, 168, 201, 216, 261, 305; **Bob Race**—pages 1, 131, 174, 217, 222, 262, 272, 281, 306, 320.

INTRODUCTION

It is the destiny of certain places on Earth to be imbued with an inexplicable magnetism, a power that draws people whose visions and desires combine at just the right moment to create a dynamism so strong that it becomes history. The result for these "certain places" is greatness . . . and Oahu is one of these.

It is difficult to separate Oahu from its vibrant metropolis, Honolulu, whose massive political, economic, and social muscle dominates the entire state, let alone its home island. But to look at Honolulu *as* Oahu is to look only upon the face of a great sculpture, ignoring the beauty and subtleness of the whole. Just the words "Honolulu, Waikiki, Pearl Harbor" conjure up visions common to people the world over. Immediately imaginations flush with palm trees swaying, a healthy tan, bombs dropping with infamy, and a golden moon rising romantically over coiled lovers on a white-sand beach.

Oahu is called the "Gathering Place," and to itself it has indeed gathered the noble memories of old Hawaii, the vibrancy of a bright-eyed fledgling state, and the brawny power so necessary for the future. On this amazing piece of land adrift in the great ocean, 800,000 people live; five times that number

visit yearly, and as time passes Oahu remains strong as one of those "certain places."

OVERVIEW

Oahu is partly a tropical garden, bathed by soft showers and sunshine, and swaying with a gentle but firm rhythm. You can experience this feeling all over the island, even in pockets of downtown Honolulu and Waikiki. However, its other side is brash—dominated by the confidence of a major American city perched upon the Pacific Basin whose music is a pounding staccato jackhammer, droning bulldozer, and mechanical screech of the ever-building crane. The vast majority of first-time and return visitors land at Honolulu International and spend at least a few days on Oahu, usually in Waikiki.

People are amazed at the diversity of experiences the island has to offer. Besides the obvious (and endless) beach activities are museums, botanical gardens, a fantastic zoo and aquarium, nightclubs, extravagant shows, free entertainment, cultural classes, theaters, sporting events, a major university, historical sights galore, an exotic cosmopolitan atmosphere, backcountry trekking, and

OAHU
(OVERVIEW)

KAUAI
NIIHAU
OAHU
MOLOKAI
MAUI
LANAI
KAHOOLAWE
HAWAII

ONLY MAIN TOWNS AND ROADS SHOWN

0   5 mi
0   5 km

© MOON PUBLICATIONS, INC.

Waikiki

an abundance of camping—all easily accessible via terrific public transportation. Finally, to sweeten the pot, Oahu can easily be the least expensive of the Hawaiian islands to visit.

Waikiki

Loosely, this world-famous beach is a hunk of land bordered by the **Ala Wai Canal** and running eastward to **Diamond Head.** Early last century these two golden miles were little more than a string of dirty beaches backed by a mosquito-infested swamp. Until 1901, when the Moana Hotel was built, only Hawaii's few remaining *ali'i* and a handful of wealthy *kamaaina* families had homes here. Now, over 125 hotels and condos provide more than 35,000 rooms, and if you placed a $20 bill on the ground, it would barely cover the land that it could buy!

This hyperactive area will delight and disgust you, excite and overwhelm you, but never bore you. Waikiki gives you the feeling that you've arrived *someplace.* Besides lolling on the beach and walking the gauntlet of restaurants, hotels, malls, and street merchants, you can visit the **Waikiki Aquarium** or **Honolulu Zoo.** Then, ever present Diamond Head, that monolith of frozen lava so symbolic of Hawaii, is a few minutes' drive and a leisurely stroll to its summit. Head eastward around the bulge passing exclusive residential areas and you quickly find a string of secluded beaches. Around this tip you pass **Koko Head Crater,** a trekker's haven, **Hanauma Bay,** an underwater conservation park renowned for magnificent family-class

snorkeling, **Sea Life Park,** an extravaganza of the deep, and the sleepy village of **Waimanalo Beach.** Nearby at **Bellow's Beach** is camping, where it's hard to believe the city's just 10 miles back.

Downtown Honolulu

Head for downtown and give yourself a full day to catch all the sights. It's as if a huge grappling hook, attached to the heart of a Mainland city, hauled it down to the sea. But don't get the idea that it's not unique, because it is! You'll find a delightful mixture of quaintly historic and future-shock new, exotic, and ordinary. The center is **Iolani Palace,** only royal palace in America, heralded by the gilded statue of Kamehameha I. In an easy walking radius is the **State Capitol** and attendant government buildings. Chrome and glass skyscrapers holding the offices of Hawaii's economically mighty shade small stone and wooden structures from last century: **Mission Houses Museum, Kawaiahao Church,** and **St. Andrew's Cathedral.**

Down at the harbor **Aloha Tower** greets the few passenger ships that still make port; nearby is the floating museum ship, *Falls of Clyde,* a nostalgic reminder of simpler times. Hotel Street takes you to old but not always venerable **Chinatown,** filled with alleyways housing tiny temples, herbalists, aromatic markets, inexpensive eateries, rough night spots, dives, and the strong, distinctive flavor of transplanted Asia.

If the hustle and bustle gets to be too much, head for **Foster Botanical Gardens.** Or hop a special London bus for the serenity of the

Bishop Museum and Planetarium, undoubtedly *the* best Polynesian cultural and anthropological museum in the world.

Pearl Harbor

Hawaii's only interstate, H-1, runs west of city center to Pearl Harbor. You can't help noticing the huge military presence throughout the area, and it becomes clear why Hawaii is considered the most militarized state in the Union. The attraction here, which shouldn't be missed, is the **USS *Arizona* Memorial.** The museum, visitors center, and tours, operated jointly by the U.S. Navy and the National Park Service, are both excellent and free.

Heading For The Hills

Behind the city is the **Koolau Range.** As you head for these beckoning hills, you can sidetrip over to the **University of Hawaii** and the **East West Center** while passing through Manoa Valley, epitome of the "good life" in Hawaii. Route 61 takes you up and over Nuuanu Pali to Oahu's windward side. En route you'll pass **Punchbowl,** an old crater holding some of the dead from WW II and the Korean and Vietnam wars in the **National Cemetery of the Pacific.**

As you climb, the road passes the **Royal Mausoleum,** final resting place for some of Hawaii's last kings, queens, and nobility. Then comes **Queen Emma's Summer Palace,** a Victorian home of gentility and lace. Next is **Nuuanu Pali,** where Kamehameha drove 16,000 Oahu warriors over the cliff, sealing his dominance of the island kingdom with their blood. The view is hauntingly beautiful, as the mountains drop suddenly to the coast of windward Oahu.

Windward Oahu

On the windward side, **Kailua** and **Kaneohe** have become suburban bedroom communities for Honolulu; this entire coast has few tourist accommodations, so it remains relatively uncrowded. The beaches are excellent, with beach parks and camping spots one after another, and the winds make this side off the island perfect for sailboarding. North of Kaneohe is **Valley of the Temples,** where a Christian cross sits high on a hill, and

Buddha rests calmly in **Byodo-In Temple.**

Just up Rt. 83, the coastal highway, comes **Waiahole,** Oahu's outback, where tiny farms and taro patches dot the valleys and local folks move with the slow beat of bygone days, then a quick succession of beaches, many rarely visited by more than a passing fisherman. **Punaluu Town** follows, offering some of the only accommodations along this coast, and a lovely walk to **Kahuwaa,** the Sacred Falls. In **Laie** is the **Polynesian Cultural Center,** operated by the Mormon Church. **Brigham Young University** is here too, along with a solid Mormon temple that's open to visitors.

Northern Tip

North Shore is famous for magnificent surf. From **Sunset Beach** to **Haleiwa,** world-class surfers come to be challenged by the liquid thunder of the **Banzai Pipeline** and **Waimea Bay.** Art shops, boutiques, tiny restaurants, and secluded hideaways line these sundrenched miles. At the far western end is **Dillingham Airfield** where you can take a glider or air tour of the island. The road ends with a very rugged jeep trail leading to **Kaena Point,** renowned for the most monstrous surf on the North Shore.

Northwest

The northwestern end of the island is the **Waianae Coast.** The towns of **Maili, Waianae,** and **Makaha** are considered the last domain of the locals of Oahu. This coastal area has escaped development so far, and it's one of the few places on the island where ordinary people can afford to live near the beach. Sometimes an attitude of resentment spills over against tourists; mostly though, lovely people with good hearts live here, who will treat you as nicely as you're willing to treat them.

World-class surfing beaches along this coast are preferred by many of the best-known surfers from Hawaii. Many work as lifeguards in the beach parks, and they all congregate for the annual surfing championships held in Makaha. Here is a perfect chance to mingle with the people and soak up some of the last real *aloha* left on Oahu.

THE LAND

When Papa, the Hawaiian earth mother, returned from vacationing in Tahiti, she was less than pleased. She had learned through a gossiping messenger that her husband, Wakea, had been playing around. Besides simple philandering, he'd been foolish enough to impregnate Hina, a lovely young goddess who bore him island children. Papa, scorned and furious, showed Wakea that two could play the same game by taking a handsome young lover, Lua. Their brief interlude yielded the man-child Oahu, sixth of the great island children. Geologically, Oahu is the second oldest main island after Kauai. It emerged from beneath the waves as hissing lava a few million years after Kauai, and cooled a little quicker than Papa's temper to form Hawaii's third largest island.

The modern geological theory concerning the formation of the Hawaiian Islands is no less fanciful than the Polynesian legends sung about their origins. Science maintains that 30 million years ago, while the great continents were being geologically tortured into their rudimentary shapes, the Hawaiian Islands were a mere ooze of bubbling magma 20,000 feet below the surface of the primordial sea. For millions of years this molten rock flowed up from fissures in the sea floor. Slowly, layer upon layer of lava was deposited until an island rose above the surface of the sea. The great weight then sealed the fissure, whose own colossal forces progressively crept in a southwestern direction, then burst out again and again to build the chain. At the same time the entire Pacific plate was afloat on the giant sea of molten magma, and it slowly glided to the northwest, carrying the newly formed islands with it.

In the beginning the spewing crack formed Kure and Midway islands in the extreme northwestern sector of the Hawaiian chain. This process continued for eons, and today more than 130 islands, islets, and shoals make up the Hawaiian Islands, stretching 1,600 miles across an expanse of the North Pacific. Some geologists maintain that the "hot spot" now primarily under the Big Island remains relatively stationary, and the 1,600-mile spread of the Hawaiian archipelago is only due to a northwest drifting effect of about three to five inches per year. Still, with the center of activity under the Big Island, Mauna Loa and Kilauea volcanos regularly add more land to the only state in the Union that is literally still growing. About 30 miles southeast of the Big Island is Loihi Sea Mount, waiting 3,000 feet below the waves. Frequent eruptions bring it closer and closer to the surface until one day it will emerge and become the newest Hawaiian island.

Land Facts

Oahu has a total land area of 608 square miles, and measured from its farthest points is 44 miles long by 30 miles wide. The 112-mile coastline holds the two largest harbors in the state, **Honolulu** and **Pearl.** The **Koolau Mountains** run north-south for almost the entire length of the island, dramatically creating windward and leeward Oahu. The **Koolau Range** is smaller, confined to the northwestern section of the island. It too runs north-south, dividing the **Waianae Coast** from the massive **Leilehua Plateau** of the interior. **Mount Ka'ala,** at 4,020 feet, in the northern portion of the Koolaus, is Oahu's highest peak. The huge Leilehua Plateau is still covered in pineapple and sugar cane, and lies between the two mountain ranges running all the way from Waialua on the north shore to Ewa, just west of Pearl Harbor. At its widest point, around Schofield Barracks, it's more than six miles across.

Oahu's most impressive natural features were formed after the heavy volcanic activity ceased and erosion began to sculpt the island. The most obvious is the wall-like cliffs of the **Pali**—mountain heads eroded by winds from the east, valleys cut by streams from the west. Perfect examples of these eroded valleys are **Nuuanu** and **Kalihi.** Other impressive examples are **Diamond Head, Koko Head,** and **Punchbowl,** three "tuff-cone" volcanos created after the heavy volcanic activity of early Oahu. A tuff cone is volcanic ash cemented together to form solid rock. Diamond Head is the most dramatic, formed after a minor eruption about 100,000 years ago and rising 760 feet from its base.

Oahu has the state's longest stream, **Kaukonahua,** which begins atop Puu Kaaumakua at 2,681 feet in the central Koolaus and runs westward for over 30 miles through the Leilehua Plateau. En route, it bypasses the **Wahiawa Reservoir** which, at 302 acres, forms the second largest body of fresh water in Hawaii. Oahu's tallest waterfalls are 80-feet **Kaliuwaa** (Sacred Falls), just west of Punaluu, and **Waihee Falls,** in the famous Waimea Park on the North Shore, that have a sheer drop of over 40 feet. Oahu's main water concern is that usage is outstripping supply, and major municipal water shortages are expected by the year 2000 unless conservation measures and new technology are employed.

Island Builders

The Hawaiians worshiped Madame Pele, the fire-goddess. Her name translates equally as "volcano," "fire pit," or "eruption of lava." When she was angry, she complained by spitting fire which cooled and formed land. Volcanologists say that the islands are huge mounds of cooled basaltic lava surrounded by billions of polyp skeletons which have formed coral reefs. The Hawaiian Islands are shield volcanos that erupt gently and form an elongated dome much like a turtle shell. Oahu, like the rest, is a perfect example of this. Once above the surface of the sea, the tremendous weight of lava seals the fissure below. Eventually the giant tube that carried lava to the surface sinks in on itself and forms a caldera, as evidenced at Hanauma Bay, the famous snorkeling spot on Oahu's southeast coast. More eruptions occur periodically, and they cover the already existing island like frosting on a titanic cake. Wind and water next take over and relentlessly sculpt the raw lava into deep crevices and cuts that become valleys. The once smooth pali of windward Oahu are now undulating green monoliths due to this process.

Lava

Lava flows in two distinct types, for which the Hawaiian names have become universal geological terms: *a'a* and *pa'hoehoe.* They're easily distinguished in appearance, but chemically they're the same. *A'a* is extremely rough and spiny, and will quickly tear up your shoes if you do much hiking over it. Also, if you have the misfortune to fall down, you'll immediately know why they call it *a'a*. *Pa'hoehoe* is billowy, ropey lava that looks like burned pancake batter and can mold itself into fantastic shapes. Examples of both are encountered on various hikes throughout Oahu. Other lava oddities that you may spot on Oahu are peridots, green gem-like stones called "Maui Diamonds," clear feldspar, and gray lichens covering the older flows known as "Hawaiian snow."

Rivers And Lakes

Oahu has no navigable rivers but there are hundreds of streams. The two largest are Kaukonahua Stream, which runs through central Oahu, and Waikele Stream, which drains the area around Schofield Barracks. A few reservoirs dot the island, like Wahiawa Reservoir and Nuuanu Pali Reservoir both excellent fresh water fishing spots (see p. 152), but there are no natural bodies of water on Oahu. Hikers should be aware of the uncountable streams and rivulets that can quickly turn from trickles to torrents, causing flash floods in valleys that were the height of hospitality only minutes before.

Tsunamis

Tsunami is the Japanese word for tidal wave. It ranks up there with the worst of them in causing horror in human beings. But if you were to count up all the people in Hawaii who have been swept away by tidal waves in the last 50 years, the toll wouldn't come close to those killed on bicycles in only a few Mainland cities in just five years.

A Hawaiian tsunami is actually a seismic sea wave generated by an earthquake that could easily have had its origins thousands of miles away in South America or Alaska. Some waves have been clocked at speeds up to 500 miles per hour. The safest place, besides high ground well away from beach areas, is out on the open ocean where even an enormous wave is perceived only as a large swell—a tidal wave is only dangerous when it is opposed by land. The worst tsunami to strike the islands in modern times occurred on April 1, 1946. The Hana Coast of windward east Maui bore the brunt with a tragic loss of many lives as entire villages were swept away.

Earthquakes

These rumblings are also a concern in Hawaii and offer a double threat because they cause tsunamis. If you ever feel a tremor and are close to a beach, get as far away as fast as possible. A few tremors are felt on Oahu, but the Big Island, because of its active volcanos, experiences hundreds of technical earthquakes, although 99% can only be felt on very delicate equipment. The last major quake occurred on the Big Island in late November 1975, reaching 7.2 on the Richter scale and causing many millions of dollars' worth of damage in the island's southern regions. The only loss of life occurred when a beach collapsed and two people from a large camping party were drowned. Oahu, like the rest of the state, has an elaborate warning system against natural disasters. You will notice loudspeakers high atop poles along many beaches and coastal areas; these warn of tsunamis, hurricanes, and earthquakes. They are tested at 11 a.m. on the first working day of each month. All island telephone books contain a civil defense warning and procedures section with which you should acquaint yourself. Note the maps showing which areas traditionally have been inundated by tsunamis, and what procedures to follow in case an emergency occurs.

THE CLIMATE

Oahu, like all the Hawaiian Islands, has equitable weather year-round with the average daily temperature about 80 degrees F. The mountainous interior experiences about the same temperatures as the coastal areas because of the small difference in elevation. However, the **Pali** is known for strong, chilly winds that rise up the mountainside from the coast. Precipitation is the biggest differentiating factor in the climate of Oahu. Generally, the entire leeward coast, from Makaha to Koko Head, is dry. Rain falls much more frequently and heavily in the Koolau Mountains and along the windward coast. Although rain can occur at any time of year, it is more plentiful in winter. Huge surf also pummels the North Shore during this period, closing off many beaches to the neophyte, but making them absolutely perfect for expert surfers. The maxim throughout the islands is "don't let rain spoil your day." If it's raining, simply move on to the next beach, or around to the other side of the island where it'll probably be dry. You can most often depend on the beaches of Waikiki and Waianae to be sunny and bright.

"So Good" Weather

The ancient Hawaiians had words to describe climatic specifics such as rain, wind, fog, and even snow, but they didn't have a general word for *weather*. The reason is that the weather is just about the same throughout the year and depends more on where you are on any given island than what season it is.

The Hawaiians did distinguish between *kau* (summer, May-Oct.) and *hoo'ilo* (winter, Nov.-April), but this distinction included social, religious, and even navigational factors, far beyond a mere distinction of weather variations.

The average daytime temperature throughout Hawaii is about 80 degrees F (26 degrees C), with the average January day registering 78 degrees, and the average August day raising the thermometer only seven degrees to 85. Nighttime temperatures drop less than 10 degrees. Elevation, however, does drop temperatures about three degrees for every 1,000 feet you climb. The lowest temperatures ever recorded in Hawaii were atop Haleakala in January 1961, when the mercury dropped well below freezing to a mere 11 degrees; the hottest day occurred in 1931 in the Puna District of the Big Island with a scorching (for Hawaii) 100 degrees.

The Trade Winds

One factor that keeps the Hawaiian temperatures both constant and moderate is the trade winds. These breezes are so reliable that the northeast sides of the islands are always referred to as "windward," regardless of where the wind happens to be blowing on any given day. You can count on the trades to be blowing on an average of 300 days per year: hardly missing a day during summer, and half the time in winter. They blow throughout the day, but are strong during the heat of the afternoon and weaken at night. Just when

WIND AND WAVES

SHORE   BREAKERS   SWELLS   CHOPS   RIPPLES   WIND

AVERAGE MAXIMUM/MINIMUM TEMPERATURE AND RAINFALL

Town		Jan.	Mar.	May	June	Sept.	Nov.
Honolulu	High	80	82	84	85	82	81
	Low	60	62	68	70	71	68
	Rain	4	2	0	0	0	4
Kaneohe	High	80	80	80	82	82	80
	Low	67	62	68	70	70	68
	Rain	5	5	2	0	2	5
Waialua	High	79	79	81	82	82	80
	Low	60	60	61	63	62	61
	Rain	2	1	0	0	1	3

N.B. Rainfall in inches; temperature in Fahrenheit

you need a cooling breeze, there they are, and when the temperature drops at night, it's as if someone turned down the giant fan.

The trade winds are also a factor in keeping down the humidity. They will suddenly disappear, however, usually in winter, and might not resume for a few weeks. The Tropic of Cancer runs through the center of Hawaii, yet its famed oppressively hot and muggy weather is joyfully absent. Honolulu, on the same latitude as sweaty Hong Kong and Havana, has only a 50-60 percent daily humidity factor.

Kona Winds

Kona means "leeward" in Hawaiian, and when the northeasterly trades stop blowing these southerly winds often take over, bringing in hot sticky air. To anyone from Hawaii, kona wind is euphemistic for bad weather. Luckily, they are most common from October to April, when they appear roughly half the time. The temperatures drop slightly during the winter so these hot winds are tolerable, and even useful for moderating the thermometer. In the summer they are awful, but luckily again they hardly ever blow during this season.

A "kona storm" is another matter. These subtropical low-pressure storms develop west of the Hawaiian Islands, and as they move east draw winds up from the south. Usual only in winter, they can cause considerable damage to crops and real estate. There is no real pattern to kona storms— some years they come every few weeks while in other years they don't appear at all.

Rain

Hardly a day goes by that it isn't raining somewhere on *all* the main islands. The islands have a windward (northeast, wet) and leeward (southwest, dry) side. It rains much more on the windward side, and much more often during winter than summer. (However, kona storms—because they come from the south—hit the islands' leeward sides most often.) Another important rain factor is the mountains, which act like water magnets. Moist winds gather around them and eventually build rain clouds. The ancient Hawaiians used these clouds and the reflected green light on their underbellies to spot land from great distances.

Precipitation mostly occurs at and below the 3,000-foot level; thus the upper slopes of taller mountains are quite dry. The average annual rainfall on the seas surrounding Hawaii is only 25 inches, while a few miles inland around the windward slopes of mountains it can be 250 inches! Conversely, the best beach weather is on the leeward sides: Kaanapali, Waikiki, Kailua-Kona, Poipu. They all sit in the "rain shadows" of interior mountains, and if it happens to be raining at one leeward beach, just move down the road to the next.

One more thing about Hawaiian rains—they aren't very nasty. Much of the time just a light drizzle, and they hardly ever last all day. Mostly localized to a relatively small area, you can oftentimes spot them by looking for the rainbows. Rain should never spoil your outings in Hawaii. Just "hang loose, brah," and follow the sunshine.

Bad Weather
With all this talk of ideal weather it might seem like there isn't any bad. Read on. When a storm does hit an island it can be bleak and miserable. The worst storms occur in the winter and often have the warped sense of humor to drop their heaviest rainfalls on areas that are normally quite dry. It's not unusual for a storm to dump more than three inches of rain an hour; this can go as high as 10, making Hawaiian rainfalls some of the heaviest on Earth.

Hawaii has also been hit with some walloping hurricanes in the last few decades. There haven't been many but they've been destructive. The vast majority of hurricanes originate far to the southeast off the coast of Mexico and Latin America. They mostly pass harmlessly south of Hawaii but some, swept along by kona winds, strike the islands. The most recent and destructive was Hurricane Ewa, which battered the islands in 1982. It had its greatest effect on Niihau, the Poipu Beach area of Kauai, and the leeward coast of Oahu. Ewa carried a destructive price tag of $200 million.

When To Go
The prime tourist season starts two weeks before Christmas and lasts until Easter. It picks up again with summer vacation in early June and ends once more in late August. If possible avoid Hawaii these times of year. Everything is usually booked solid and prices are inflated. Hotel, airline, and car reservations, which are a must, are often hard to coordinate. You can save between 10 and 50 percent and a lot of hassling if you go in the artificially created off-season, from September to early December, and mid-April (after Easter) till early June. You'll not only find the prices better, but the beaches, hikes, campgrounds, and even restaurants will be less crowded. The people will be happier to see you too.

FAUNA

Anyone who loves a mystery will be intrigued by the speculation about how plants and animals first came to Hawaii. Most people's idea of an island paradise includes swaying palms, dense mysterious jungles ablaze with wildflowers, and luscious fruits just waiting to be plucked. In fact, for millions of years these were raw and barren islands where no plants grew and no birds sang. Why? Because they are geological orphans that spontaneously popped up in the middle of the Pacific Ocean. The islands, more than 2,000 miles from any continental landfall, were therefore exempted from the normal ecological spread of plants and animals. Even the most tenacious travelers of the fauna and flora kingdoms would be sorely tried in crossing the mighty Pacific. Those that made it by pure chance found a totally foreign ecosystem. Luckily, the soil of Hawaii was virgin and rich, the competition from other plants or animals was nonexistent, and the climate was sufficiently varied and nearly perfect for most growing things.

The evolution of plants and animals on the isolated islands was astonishingly rapid. A tremendous change in environment, coupled with a limited gene pool, accelerated natural selection. For example, many plants lost their protective thorns and spines because there were no grazing animals or birds to destroy them. Many plants and birds became so specialized that they were not only limited to specific islands in the chain but to habitats that frequently encompassed a single isolated valley. It was as if after traveling so far and finding a niche they never budged again.

Pre-man Hawaii had no fruits, vegetables, palms, edible land animals, conifers, mangroves, or banyans. Flowers were relatively few. In a land where thousands of orchids now brighten every corner, there were only four native varieties, the least in any of the 50 states. Today, the original plants and animals have the highest rate of extinction anywhere on Earth. By the beginning of this century, native plants below 1,500 feet were almost completely extinct or totally replaced by introduced species.

The land and its living things have been greatly transformed by man and his agriculture. This inexorable process began when Hawaii was the domain of its original Polynesian settlers, then greatly accelerated when the land was inundated by Western man.

You would think that with Oahu's dense human population, little room would be left for animals. In fact, they are environmentally stressed, but they do survive. The interior mountain slopes are home to **wild pigs,** and a small population of **feral goats** survive in the Waianae Range. Migrating **whales** pass by, especially along the leeward coast where they can be observed from lookouts ranging from Waikiki to Koko Head. Half a dozen

pueo

introduced game birds are found around the island, but Oahu's real animal wealth is its indigenous birdlife.

Birds

The shores around Oahu, including those off Koko Head and Sand Island, but especially on the tiny islets of Moku Manu and Manana on the windward side, are home to thriving colonies of marine birds. On these diminutive islands it's quite easy to spot a number of birds from the **tern** family, including the white, gray, and sooty tern. All have a distinctive screeching voice, and an approximate wingspan of 30 inches. Part of their problem is that they have little fear of humans. Along with the terns are **shearwaters.** These birds have a normal wingspan of about 36 inches, and make a series of moans and wails, oftentimes while in flight. For some reason they're drawn to the bright lights of the city, where they fall prey to house cats and automobiles. Sometimes Moku Manu even attracts an enormous **Laysan albatross** with its seven-foot wingspan. **Tropicbirds** with their lovely streamer-like tails are quite often seen along the windward coast.

To catch a glimpse of exotic birds on Oahu you don't have to head for the sea or the hills. The city streets and beach parks are constantly aflutter with wings. Black **myna birds** with their sassy yellow eyes are common mimics around town. **Sparrows,** introduced to Hawaii through Oahu in the 1870s, are everywhere, while **munia,** first introduced as cage birds from Southeast Asia, have escaped and are generally found anywhere

around the island. Another escaped cage bird from Asia is the **bulbul,** a natural clown that perches on any likely city roost and draws attention to itself with loud calls and generally ridiculous behavior.

If you're lucky, you can also catch a glimpse of the *pueo* (Hawaiian Owl) in the mountainous areas of Waianae and the Koolaus. Also, along trails and deep in the forest from Tantalus to the Waianae Range you can sometimes see elusive native birds like the *elepaio, amakihi,* and the fiery red but very rare *i'iwi.*

Oahu also is home to a number of game birds mostly found in the dry upland forests. These include two varieties of **dove,** the **Japanese quail,** both the **green** and **ring-necked pheasant,** and Erkel's francolin. Hunting of these birds occurs year-round and information can be had by contacting the

Hawaiian stilt

Oahu branch of the Division of Forestry and Wildlife.

National Wildlife Refuges

Two areas at opposite ends of the island have been set aside as national wildlife refuges (NWR): **James Campbell NWR,** above the town of Kahuku on the extreme northern tip, and **Pearl Harbor NWR,** at the harbor entrance. Both were established in the mid '70s, and managed by the U.S. Fish and Wildlife Service. They serve mainly as wetland habitats for the endangered Hawaiian gallinule *(alae'ula),* stilt *(aeo)*, and coot *(alae ke'oke'o).* Clinging to existence, these birds should have a future as long as their nesting grounds remain undisturbed. These refuges also attract a wide variety of other birds, mostly introduced species such as **cattle egrets, herons,** a few species of **doves, munia, cardinals,** and the **common finch.**

Much of the area within the refuges are natural marshlands, but ponds, complete with water-regulating pumps and dikes, have been built. The general public is not admitted to these areas without permission from the refuge managers. For more information, and to arrange a visit, contact Refuge Manager, Hawaiian and Pacific Islands NWR, U.S. Fish and Wildlife Service, Federal Bldg., Room 5302, Box 50167, Honolulu, HI 96850.

FLORA

Hawaii's indigenous and endemic plants, flowers, and trees are both fascinating and beautiful, but unfortunately, like everything else that was native, they are quickly disappearing. The majority of flora found exotic by visitors was either introduced by the original Polynesians or later by white settlers. The Polynesians who colonized Hawaii brought foodstuffs, including coconut, banana, taro, breadfruit, sweet potato, yam, and sugar cane. They also carried along gourds to use as containers, *awa* to make a basic intoxicant, and the *ti* plant to use for offerings or to string into hula skirts. Non-Hawaiian settlers over the years have brought mangoes, papayas, passion fruit, pineapples, and all the other tropical fruits and vegetables associated with the islands. Also, most of the flowers, including protea, plumeria, anthuriums, orchids, heliconia, ginger, and most hibiscus have come from every continent on Earth. Tropical America, Asia, Java, India, and China have all contributed their most beautiful and delicate blooms. Hawaii is blessed with state parks, gardens, undisturbed rainforests, private reserves, and commercial nurseries that offer an exhaustive botanical survey. The following is just a sampling of common, native, and introduced flora that add the dazzling colors and exotic tastes to the landscape.

Native Trees

Koa and *ohia* are two native trees still seen on the main islands. Both have been greatly reduced by the foraging of introduced cattle and goats, and through logging and forest fires. The *koa,* a form of acacia, is Hawaii's finest native tree. It can grow to over 70 feet high and has a strong straight trunk which can measure more than 10 feet in circumference. The foliage is sickle shaped and produces an inconspicuous pale yellow flower. The *koa* does best in well-drained soil in deep forest

koa

ohia-lehua

Tropical Rainforests

When it comes to possessing a pure and diverse natural beauty, the U.S. is one of the finest pieces of real estate on Earth. As if purple mountains' majesty and fruited plains weren't enough, it even received a tiny living emerald of tropical rainforest. A tropical rainforest is where the Earth itself takes a breath and exhales pure sweet oxygen through its vibrant living green canopy. Located in the territories of Puerto Rico and the Virgin Islands, and in the state of Hawaii, these forests comprise only one-half of one percent of the world's total, and they must be preserved. The U.S. Congress passed two bills in 1986 designed to protect the unique biological diversity of its tropical areas, but their destruction has continued unabated.

The lowland rainforests of Hawaii, comprised mostly of native *ohia,* are being razed. Landowners slash, burn, and bulldoze them to create more land for cattle, agriculture—and most distressingly—for wood chips to generate electricity! Introduced wild boar gouge the forest floor, exposing sensitive roots and leaving tiny fetid ponds where mosquito larvae thrive. Feral goats that roam the forests are hoofed locusts that strip all vegetation within reach. Maui's Nature Conservancy Preserve in Waikamoi has managed to fence in a speck of this forest, keeping it safe from these animals for the time being.

areas, but scruffy specimens will grow in poorer soil. The Hawaiians used *koa* as the main log for their dugout canoes, and elaborate ceremonies were performed when a log was cut and dragged to a canoe shed. *Koa* wood was also preferred for paddles, spears, even surfboards. Today it is still considered an excellent furniture wood.

The *ohia* is a survivor and therefore the most abundant of all the native Hawaiian trees. Coming in a variety of shapes and sizes, it grows as miniature trees in wet bogs or as 100-foot giants on the cool dark slopes of higher elevations. This tree is often the first life in new lava flows. The *ohia* produces a tuft-like flower that resembles a natural pompon. Considered sacred to Pele, it was said that she would cause a rainstorm if you picked them without the proper prayers. The flowers were fashioned into a lei that resembled a feather boa. The strong hard wood was also used in canoe building, for *poi* bowls, and especially for temple images.

Almost half of the birds classified in the U.S. as endangered are from Hawaii, and almost all of these make their home in the rainforests. For example, Maui's rainforests have yielded the *poouli,* a new species of bird discovered only in 1974. Another forest survey in 1981 rediscovered the **Bishop's o'o,** a bird thought to be extinct at the turn of the century. We can only lament the passing of the rainforests that have already fallen to ignorance, but if this ill-fated destruction continues on the global level, we will soon be lamenting our own passing. We must nurture the rainforests that remain with the simple enlightenment to let them be.

HISTORY

THE ROAD FROM TAHITI

Until the 1820s, when New England missionaries began a phonetic rendering of the Hawaiian language, the past was kept vividly alive only by the sonorous voices of special *kahuna* who chanted the sacred *mele*. The chants were beautiful flowing word pictures that captured the essence of every aspect of life. These *mele* praised the land *(mele aina),* royalty *(mele ali'i),* and life's tender aspects *(mele aloha).* Chants were dedicated to friendship, hardship, and to favorite children. Entire villages sometimes joined together to compose a *mele*—every word was chosen carefully, and the wise old *kapuna* would decide if the words were lucky or unlucky. Some *mele* were bawdy or funny on the surface, but contained secret meanings, often with biting sarcasm, that ridiculed an inept or cruel leader. But the most important chants took the listeners back into the dim past, even before people lived in Hawaii. From these genealogies *(ko'ihonua),* the *ali'i* derived the right to rule, since these chants went back to the gods Wakea and Papa from whom the *ali'i* were directly descended.

The Kumulipo

The great genealogies, finally compiled in the late 1800s by order of King Kalakaua, were collectively known as *The Kumulipo, A Hawaiian Creation Chant,* basically a Polynesian account of Genesis. Other chants related to the beginning of this world, but *The Kumulipo* sums it all up and is generally considered the best. The chant relates that after the beginning of time, there is a period of darkness. The darkness, however, mysteriously brims with spontaneous life; during this period plants and animals are born, as well as Kumulipo, the man, and Po'ele, the woman. In the eighth chant darkness gives way to light and the gods descend to Earth. Wakea is "the sky father" and Papa is "the earth mother," whose union gives birth to the islands of Hawaii. First born is Hawaii, followed by Maui, then Kahoolawe. Apparently, Papa becomes bushed after three consecutive births and decides to vacation in Tahiti. While Papa is away recovering from postpartum depression and working on her tan, Wakea gets lonely, and takes Kaula as his second wife, who bears him the island-child of Lanai. Not fully cheered up, but getting the hang of it, Wakea takes a third wife, Hina, who promptly bears the island of Molokai. Meanwhile, Papa gets wind of these shenanigans, returns from Polynesia, and retaliates by taking up with Lua, a young and virile god, and soon gives birth to the island of Oahu. Papa and Wakea finally decide that they really are meant for each other and reconcile to conceive Kauai, Niihau, Kaula, and Nihoa. These two progenitors are the source from which all the *ali'i* ultimately traced their lineage, and from which they derived their god-ordained power to rule.

Basically, there are two major genealogical families: the **Nana'ulu,** who became the royal *ali'i* of Oahu and Kauai; and the **Ulu,** who provided the royalty of Maui and Hawaii. The best sources of information on Hawaiian myth and legend are Martha Beckwith's *Hawaiian Mythology,* and the monumental three-volume opus *An Account of the Polynesian Race* compiled by Abraham Fornander from 1878 to 1885. Fernander, after settling in Hawaii, married an *ali'i* from Molokai and had an illustrious career as a newspaper man, Maui circuit judge, and finally Supreme Court justice. For years Fornander sent scribes to every corner of the kingdom to listen to the elder *kupuna.* They returned with the firsthand accounts and he dutifully recorded them.

Polynesians

Since prehistory, Polynesians have been seafaring people whose origins cannot be completely traced. They seem to have come from Southeast Asia mostly through the gateway of Indonesia, and their racial strain pulls features from all three dominant races: white, negro, and mongoloid. They learned to navigate on tame narrow waterways along Indonesia and New Guinea, then fanned out eastward into the great Pacific. They sailed northeast to the low islands of Micronesia and southwest to Fiji, the New Hebrides (now called Vanuatu), and New Caledonia. Fiji is regarded as the "cradle of Polynesian cul-

ture"; carbon dating places humans there as early as 3,500 B.C. Many races blended on Fiji, until finally the Negroid became dominant and the Polynesians moved on. Wandering, they discovered and settled Samoa and Tonga, then ranged far east to populate Tahiti, Easter Island, and the Marquesas. Ultimately, they became the masters of the "Polynesian Triangle," which measures more than 5,000 miles on each leg, stretching across both the North and South Pacific studded with islands. The great Maori kingdom of New Zealand is the southern apex of the triangle, with Easter Island marking the point farthest east; Hawaii, farthest north, was last to be settled.

Migrations And Explorations

Ancient legends common throughout the South Pacific speak of a great Polynesian culture that existed on the island of Raiatea about 150 miles north of Tahiti. Here a powerful priesthood held sway in an enormous *heiau* in the Opoa district called Toputapuatea. Kings from throughout Polynesia came here to worship. Human sacrifice was common, as it was believed that the essence of the spirit could be utilized and controlled in this life; therefore the *mana* of Toputapuatea was great. Defeated warriors and common-

The Polynesians, attuned to every nuance in their environment, noticed that a migratory land bird called the golden plover arrived from the north every year. They reasoned that since the plover was not a seabird, there must be land to the north.

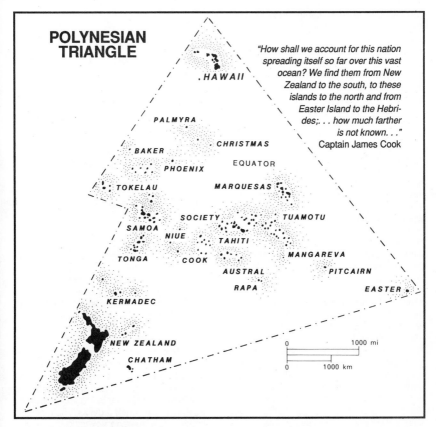

POLYNESIAN TRIANGLE

"How shall we account for this nation spreading itself so far over this vast ocean? We find them from New Zealand to the south, to these islands to the north and from Easter Island to the Hebrides;. . . how much farther is not known. . ."
Captain James Cook

HAWAII

PALMYRA

BAKER
CHRISTMAS
EQUATOR
PHOENIX
TOKELAU
MARQUESAS
SOCIETY
TUAMOTU
SAMOA
NIUE
TAHITI
TONGA
COOK
MANGAREVA
AUSTRAL
PITCAIRN
RAPA
EASTER
KERMADEC

NEW ZEALAND
CHATHAM

0   1000 mi

0   1000 km

ers were used as living rollers to drag canoes up onto the beach, while corpses were dismembered and hung in trees. The power of the priests of Opoa lasted for many generations, evoking trembling fear in even the bravest warrior just by the mention of their name. Finally, their power waned and Polynesians lost their centralized culture, but the constant coming and going from Raiatea for centuries sharpened the Polynesians' already excellent sailing skills and convinced them that the world was vast, and unlimited opportunities existed to better their lot.

Now explorers, many left to look for the "heavenly homeland to the north." Samoans called it *Savai'i;* Tongans *Hawai;* Rarotongans *Avaiki;* and Society Islanders *Havai'i.*

Others abandoned the small islands throughout Polynesia where population pressures exceeded the limits of natural resources, prompting famine. Furthermore, Polynesians were also very warlike among themselves; power struggles between members of a ruling family were common, as were marauders from other islands. So, driven by hunger or warfare, countless refugee Polynesians headed north. Joining them were a few who undoubtedly went for the purely human reason of wanderlust.

The Great Navigators
No one knows exactly when the first Polynesians arrived in Hawaii, but the great "deliberate migrations" from the southern is-

lands seems to have taken place between A.D. 500 and 800, though anthropologists keep pushing the date backward in time as new evidence becomes available. Even before that, however, it's reasonable to assume that the first people to set foot on Hawaii were probably fishermen, or perhaps defeated warriors whose canoes were blown hopelessly northward into unfamiliar waters; they arrived by a combination of extraordinary good luck and an uncanny ability to sail and navigate by the seat of their pants. With no instruments they could navigate, using the sun by day and the moon and rising stars by night. They could feel the water and determine direction by swells, tides, and currents. The movements of fish and cloud formations were also utilized to give direction. Since their arrival was probably an accident, they were unprepared to settle on the fertile but barren lands, having no stock animals, plant cuttings, or women. Forced to return southward, undoubtedly many lost their lives at sea, but a few wild-eyed stragglers must have made it home where they told tales of a paradise to the north where land was plentiful and the sea bounteous. This is affirmed by ancient navigational chants from Tahiti, Moorea, and Bora Bora, which passing from father to son revealed how to follow the stars to the "heavenly homeland in the north." Possibly a few migrations followed, but it's known that for centuries there was no real reason for a mass exodus, so the chants alone remained and eventually became shadowy legend.

From Where They Came

It's generally agreed that the first planned migrations were from the violent cannibal islands that Spanish explorers called the Marquesas, 11 islands in extreme eastern Polynesia. The islands themselves are harsh and inhospitable, breeding a toughness into these people which enabled them to withstand the hardships of long unsure ocean voyages and years of resettlement. Marquesans were a fiercely independent people whose chiefs could rise from the ranks because of bravery or intelligence. They must have also been a savage-looking lot. Both men and women tatooed themselves in com-

The canoe hull was a log shaped by masterly stone adze work. The sides were planks that were drilled and sewn together with fiber cord.

plex blue patterns from head to foot. The warriors carried massive, intricately designed ironwood war clubs and wore carved whaleteeth in slits in their earlobes which became stretched to the shoulders. They shaved the sides of their heads with sharks' teeth, tied their hair in two topknots that looked like horns, and rubbed their heavily muscled and tattooed bodies with scented coconut oils. Their cults worshiped mummified ancestors; the bodies of warriors of defeated neighboring tribes were consumed. They were masters at building great double-hulled canoes launched from huge canoe sheds. Two hulls were fastened together to form a catamaran, and a hut in the center provided shelter in bad weather. The average voyaging canoe was 60-80 feet long and could comfortably hold an extended family of about 30 people. These small family bands carried all the staples they would need in the new lands.

The New Lands

For five centuries the Marquesans settled and lived peacefully on the new land, as if Hawaii's *aloha* spirit overcame most of their fierceness. The tribes coexisted in relative harmony, especially since there was no competition for land. Cannibalism died out. There was much coming and going between Hawaii and Polynesia and new people came to settle for hundreds of years. Then, it appears that in the 12th century a deliberate exodus of warlike Tahitians arrived and subjugated the settled islanders. They came to conquer. This incursion had a terrific significance on the Hawaiian religious and social system. Oral tradition relates that a Tahitian priest, Paao, found the *mana* of the Hawaiian chiefs to be low, signifying that their gods were weak. Paao built a *heiau* at Wahaula on the Big Island, then introduced the warlike god Ku and the rigid *kapu* system through which the new rulers became dominant. Voyages between Tahiti and Hawaii continued for about 100 years and Tahitian customs, legends, and language became the Hawaiian way of life. Then suddenly, for no recorded or apparent reason, the voyages discontinued and Hawaii returned to total isolation. It remained forgotten for almost 500 years until the indomitable English seaman, Capt. James Cook, sighted Oahu on January 18, 1778, and stepped ashore at Waimea on Kauai two days later. At that time Hawaii's isolation was so complete that even the Polynesians had forgotten about it. On an earlier voyage, Tupaia, a high priest from Raiatea, had accompanied Capt. Cook as he sailed throughout Polynesia. Tupaia's knowledge of existing archipelagos throughout the South Pacific was vast, which he demonstrated by naming over 130 islands and drawing a map that included the Tonga group, the Cook Islands, the Marquesas, even tiny Pitcairn, a rock in far eastern Polynesia, where the mutinous crew of the *Bounty* found solace. In mentioning the Marquesas Tupaia said, *"he ma'a te ka'ata,"* which equals "food is man" or simply "cannibals!" But remarkably absent from Tupaia's vast knowledge was the existence of Easter Island, New Zealand, and Hawaii. The next waves of people to Hawaii would be white men, and the Hawaiian world would be changed quickly and forever.

THE WORLD DISCOVERS HAWAII

The late 18th century was an extraordinary time in Hawaiian history. Monumental changes seemed to happen all at once. First, Capt. James Cook, a Yorkshire farm boy, fulfilling his destiny as the all-time greatest Pacific explorer, found Hawaii for the rest of the world. For better or worse, it could no longer be an isolated Polynesian homeland. For the first time in Hawaiian history, a charismatic leader named Kamehameha emerged, and after a long civil war united all the islands into one centralized kingdom. The death of Capt. Cook in Hawaii marked the beginning of a long series of tragic misunderstandings between white man and native. When Kamehameha died, the old religious system of *kapu* came to an end, leaving the Hawaiians in a spiritual vortex. Many takers arrived to fill the void: missionaries after souls, whalers after their prey and a good time, traders and planters after profits and a home. The islands were opened and devoured like ripe fruit, as powerful nations, including Russia, Great Britain, France, and the United States, yearned to bring this strategic Pacific jewel under their own influence. The 19th century brought the demise of the Hawaiian people as a dominant political force in their own land and with it the end of Hawaii as a sovereign monarchy. An almost bloodless yet bitter military coup followed by a brief period of a Hawaiian Republic ended in annexation by the United States. As the U.S. became completely entrenched politically and militarily, a new social and eco-

Captain James Cook (Hawaii State Archives)

nomic order was founded on the plantation system. Amazingly rapid population growth occurred with the importation of plantation workers from Asia and Europe, which yielded a unique cosmopolitan blend of races like nowhere else on Earth. By the dawning of the 20th century, the face of old Hawaii had been altered forever; the "sacred homeland in the north" was hurled into the modern age. The attack on Pearl Harbor saw a tremendous loss of life and brought Hawaii closer to the U.S. by a baptism of blood. Finally, on August 21, 1959, after 59 years as a "territory," Hawaii officially became the 50th state of the Union.

Captain Cook Sights Hawaii

In 1776 Captain James Cook set sail for the Pacific from Plymouth, England, on his third and final expedition into this still vastly unexplored region of the world. On a fruitless quest for the fabled Northwest Passage across the North American continent, he sailed down the coast of Africa, rounded the Cape of Good Hope, crossed the Indian Ocean, and traveled past New Zealand, Tasmania, the Friendly Islands (where an unsuccessful plot was hatched by the *friendly* natives to murder him), and finally spotted Hawaii. On January 18, 1778 Capt. Cook's 100-foot flagship HMS *Resolution* and its 90-foot companion HMS *Discovery* sighted Oahu. Two days later, they sighted Kauai and went ashore at the village of Waimea on January 20, 1778. Though anxious to get on with his mission, Cook decided to make a quick sortie to investigate this new land and reprovision his ships. He did, however, take time to remark in his diary about the close resemblance of these new-found people to others he had encountered as far south as New Zealand, and marveled at their widespread habitation across the Pacific.

The first trade was some brass medals for a mackerel. Cook also stated that he never before met natives so astonished by a ship, and that they had an amazing fascination for iron which they called *toe,* Hawaiian for "adz." There is even some conjecture that a Spanish ship under one Capt. Gaetano had landed in Hawaii as early as the 16th century, trading a few scraps of iron that the Hawaiians valued even more than the Europeans valued gold. It was also noted that the Hawaiian women gave themselves freely to the sailors with the apparent good wishes of the island men. This was actually a ploy by the *kahfootuna* to test if the new whitecomers were gods or men—gods didn't need women. These sailors proved immediately mortal. Cook, who was also a physician, tried valiantly to keep the 66 men (out of 112) who had measurable cases of VD away from the women. The task proved impossible as women literally swarmed the ships; when Cook returned less than a year later, it was logged that signs of VD were already apparent on some natives' faces.

Cook was impressed with their swimming and with their well-bred manners. They had happy dispositions and sticky fingers, stealing any object made of metal, especially nails. The first item stolen was a butcher's cleaver. An unidentified native grabbed it, plunged overboard, swam to shore, and waved his booty in triumph. The Hawaiians didn't seem to care for beads and were not at all impressed with a mirror. Cook provisioned his ships by trading chisels for hogs, while common sailors gleefully traded nails for sex. Landing parties were sent inland to fill casks with fresh water. On one such excursion a Mr. Williamson, who was eventually drummed out of the Royal Navy for cowardice, unnecessarily shot and killed a native. After a brief stop on Niihau, the ships sailed away, but both groups were indelibly impressed with the memory of each other.

Cook Returns

Almost a year later, when winter weather forced Cook to return from the coast of Alaska, his discovery began to take on far-reaching significance. Cook had named Hawaii the "Sandwich Islands," in honor of one of his patrons, John Montague, the Earl of Sandwich. On this return voyage, he spotted Maui on November 26, 1778. After eight weeks of seeking a suitable harbor it was bypassed, but not before the coastline was duly drawn by Lt. William Bligh, one of Cook's finest and most trusted officers. (Bligh would find his own drama almost 10 years later as commander of the infamous HMS *Bounty*.) The *Discovery* and *Resolution* finally found a safe anchorage at Kealakekua on the Kona coast of the Big Island. It is very lucky for history that on board was Mr. Anderson, ship's chronicler, who left a handwritten record of the strange and tragic events that followed. Even more important were the drawings of John Webber, ship's artist, who rendered invaluable impressions in superb drawings and etchings. Other noteworthy men aboard were George Vancouver, who would himself lead the first British return to Hawaii after Cook's death and introduce many fruits, vegetables, cattle, sheep, and goats, and James Burney, who would become a longstanding leading authority on the Pacific.

The Great God Lono Returns

By all accounts Cook was a humane and just captain, greatly admired by his men. Unlike many other supremacists of that time, he was known to have a respectful attitude to any people he discovered, treating them as equals and recognizing the significance of their cultures. Not known as a violent man, he would use his superior weapons against natives only in an absolute case of self defense. His hardened crew had been at sea facing untold hardship for almost three years; returning to Hawaii was truly like reentering paradise.

A strange series of coincidences sailed with Cook into Kealakekua Bay on January 16, 1779. It was *makahiki* time, a period of rejoicing and festivity dedicated to the fertility god of the earth, Lono. Normal *kapu* days were suspended, and willing partners freely enjoyed each other sexually, along with dancing, feasting, and the islands' version of Olympic games. It was long held in Hawaiian legend that the great god Lono would return to Earth. Lono's image was a small wooden figure perched on a tall mast-like crossbeam; hanging from the crossbeam were long white sheets of *tapa*. Who else could Cook be but Lono, and what else could his ships with their masts and white sails be but his sacred floating *heiau*? This explained the Hawaiians' previous fascination with his ships, but to add to the remarkable coincidence, Kealakekua

Harbor happened to be considered Lono's private sacred harbor. Natives from throughout the land prostrated themselves and paid homage to the returning god. Cook was taken ashore and brought to Lono's sacred temple where he was afforded the highest respect. The ships badly needed fresh supplies and the Hawaiians readily gave all they had, stretching their own provisions to the limit. To the sailors' delight this included full measures of the *aloha* spirit.

The Fatal Misunderstandings

After an uproarious welcome and generous hospitality for over a month, it became obvious that the newcomers were beginning to overstay their welcome. During the interim a seaman named William Watman died, convincing the Hawaiians that the *haole* were indeed mortals, not gods. Watman was buried at Hikiau Heiau where a plaque commemorates the event to this day. Incidents of petty theft began to increase dramatically. The lesser chiefs indicated it was time to leave by "rubbing the Englishmen's bellies." Inadvertently many *kapu* were broken by the Englishmen, and once friendly relations became strained. Finally, the ships sailed away on February 4, 1779. After plying terrible seas for only a week, the foremast on the *Resolution* was badly damaged, and Cook sailed back into Kealakekua Bay, dragging the mast ashore on February 13th. The natives, now totally hostile, hurled rocks at the marines. Orders were given to load muskets with ball; firearms had previously only been loaded with shot and a light charge. Confrontations increased when some Hawaiians stole a small boat and marines set after them, capturing the fleeing canoe, which held an *ali'i* named Palea. The Englishmen treated him roughly; to the Hawaiians horror, they even smacked him on the head with a paddle. The Hawaiians then furiously attacked the marines who abandoned the small boat.

Cook Goes Down

Next the Hawaiians stole a small cutter from the *Discovery* that had been moored to a buoy and partially sunk to protect it from the sun. For the first time Capt. Cook became furious. He ordered Capt. Clerk of the *Discovery* to sail to the southeast end of the bay, and to stop any canoe trying to leave Kealakakua. Cook then made a fatal error in judgment. He decided to take nine armed marines ashore in an attempt to convince the venerable King Kalaniopuu to accompany him back aboard ship where he would hold him for ransom in exchange for the cutter. The old king agreed, but his wife prevailed upon him not to trust the *haole*. Kalaniopuu sat down on the beach to think while the tension steadily grew. Meanwhile, a group of marines fired upon a canoe trying to leave the bay and a lesser chief, Nookemai, was killed. The crowd around Cook and his men reached an estimated 20,000, and warriors outraged by the killing of the chief armed themselves with clubs and protective straw-mat armor. One bold warrior advanced on Cook and struck him with his *pahoa*. In retaliation Cook drew a tiny pistol lightly loaded with shot and fired at the warrior. His bullets spent themselves on the straw armor and harmlessly fell to the ground. The Hawaiians went wild. Lieutenant Molesworth Phillips, in charge of the nine marines, began a withering fire; Cook himself slew two natives. Overpowered by shear numbers, the marines headed for boats standing offshore, while Lt. Phillips lay wounded. It is believed that Capt. Cook, the greatest seaman ever to enter the Pacific, stood helplessly in knee-deep water instead of making for the boats because he could not swim! Hopelessly surrounded, he was knocked on the head, then countless warriors passed a knife around and hacked and mutilated his lifeless body. A sad Lt. King lamented in his diary, "Thus fell our great and excellent commander."

The Final Chapter

Captain Clerk, now in charge, settled his men and prevailed upon the Hawaiians to return Cook's body. On the morning of February 16th a grisly piece of charred meat was brought aboard: the Hawaiians, according to their custom, had afforded Cook the highest honor by baking his body in an underground oven to remove the flesh from the bones. On the 17th a group of Hawaiians in a canoe taunted the marines by brandishing Cook's hat. The Englishmen, strained to the limit and thinking that Cook was being desecrated, finally broke. Foaming with blood-lust, they leveled their cannon and muskets on shore and shot anything that moved. It is believed that Kamehameha the Great was wounded in this flurry, along with four *ali'i* and 25 *makaainana* (commoners). Finally on February 21, 1779, the bones of Capt. James Cook's hands, skull, arms, and legs were returned

"The Death of Captain Cook," by John Webber, ship's artist on Cook's third Pacific exploration, c. 1779 (Hawaii State Archives)

and tearfully buried at sea. A common seaman, one Mr. Zimmerman, summed up the feelings of all who sailed under Cook when he wrote, "...he was our leading star." The English sailed next morning after dropping off their Hawaiian girlfriends who were still aboard.

Captain Clerk, in bad health, carried on with the fruitless search for the Northwest Passage. He died and was buried at the Siberian village of Petropavlovisk. England was at war with upstart colonists in America, so the return of the expedition warranted little fanfare. The *Resolution* was converted into an army transport to fight the pesky Americans; the once proud *Discovery* was reduced to a convict ship ferrying inmates to Botany Bay, Australia. Mrs. Cook, the great captain's steadfast and chaste wife, lived to the age of 93, surviving all her children. She was given a stipend of 200 pounds per year, and finished her days surrounded by Cook's mementos, observing the anniversary of his death to the very end by fasting and reading from the Bible.

THE UNIFICATION OF OLD HAWAII

Hawaii was already in a state of political turmoil and civil war when Cook arrived. In the 1780s the islands were roughly divided into three kingdoms: venerable Kalaniopuu ruled Hawaii and the Hana district of Maui; wily and ruthless warrior-king Kahekili ruled Maui, Kahoolawe, Lanai, and later Oahu; and Kaeo, Kahekili's brother, ruled Kauai. War ravaged the land until a remarkable chief, Kamehameha, rose and subjugated all the islands under one rule. Kamehameha initiated a dynasty that would last for about 100 years, until the independent monarchy of Hawaii forever ceased to be. To add a zing to this brewing political stew, Westerners and their technology were beginning to come in ever increasing numbers. In 1786, Capt. La-Perouse and his French exploration party landed in what's now LaPerouse Bay, near Lahaina, foreshadowing European attention. In 1786 two American captains, Portlock and Dixon, made landfall in Hawaii. Also, it was known that a fortune could be made on the fur trade between the great Northwest and Canton, China; stopping in Hawaii could make it all feasible. After this was reported, the fate of Hawaii was sealed.

Hawaii under Kamehameha was ready to enter its "golden age." The social order was medieval, with the *ali'i* as knights, owing their military allegiance to the king, and the serf-like *makaainana* paying tribute and working the lands. The priesthood of *kahuna* filled the posts of advisors, sorcerers, navigators, doctors, and historians. This was Polynesian Hawaii at its apex. But like the uniquely Hawaiian silversword, the old culture blossomed, and as soon as it did, it began to wither. Ever since, all that was purely Hawaiian has been supplanted by the relentless foreign influences that began bearing down upon it.

Young Kamehameha

Kamehameha was a man noticed by everyone; there was no doubt he was a force to be reckoned with. He had met Capt. Cook when the *Discovery* unsuccessfully tried to land at Hana on Maui. While aboard, he made a lasting impression, distinguishing himself from the multitude of natives swarming the ships by his royal bearing. Lt. James King, in a diary entry, remarked that Kamehameha was a fierce-looking man, almost ugly, but that he was obviously intelligent, observant, and very good-natured. Kamehameha received his early military training from his uncle Kalaniopuu, the great king of Hawaii and Hana, who fought fierce battles against Alapai, the usurper who stole his hereditary lands. After regaining Hawaii, Kalaniopuu returned to his Hana district and turned his attention to conquering all of Maui. During this period young Kamehameha distinguished himself as a ferocious warrior and earned himself the nickname of "the hard-shelled crab," even though old Kahekili, Maui's king, almost annihilated Kalaniopuu's army at the sand hills of Wailuku.

When the old king neared death he passed on the kingdom to his son Kiwalao. He also, however, empowered Kamehameha as the keeper of the family war god, Kukailimoku: Ku of the Bloody Red Mouth, Ku the Destroyer. Oddly enough, Kamehameha had been born not 500 yards from Ku's great *heiau* at Kohala, and had heard the chanting and observed the ceremonies dedicated to this fierce god from his first breath. Soon after Kalaniopuu died, Kamehameha found himself in a bitter war that he did not seek against his two cousins, Kiwalao and his brother Keoua, with the island of Hawaii at stake. The skirmishing lasted nine years until Kamehameha's armies met the two brothers at Mokuohai in an indecisive battle in which Kiwalao was killed. The result was a shaky truce with Keoua, a much embittered enemy. During this fighting, Kahekili of Maui conquered Oahu, where he built a house of the skulls and bones of his adversaries as a reminder of his omnipotence. He also extended his will to Kauai by marrying his half brother to a high-ranking chieftess of that island. A new factor would be needed to resolve this stalemate of power—the coming of the *haole*.

The Olowalu Massacre

In 1790 the American merchant ship *Ella Nora*, commanded by Yankee captain Simon Metcalfe, was looking for a harbor after its long voyage from the Pacific Northwest. Following a day behind was the *Fair American*, a tiny ship manned by Metcalfe's son Thomas and a crew of five. Metcalfe, perhaps by necessity, was a stern and humorless man who would broach no interference. While anchored at Olowalu, a beach area about five miles east of Lahaina, some natives slipped close in their canoes and stole a small boat, killing a seaman in the process. Metcalfe decided to trick the Hawaiians by first negotiating a truce and then unleashing full fury upon them. Signaling he was willing to trade, he invited canoes of innocent natives to visit his ship. In the meantime, he ordered that all cannon and muskets be readied with scatter shot. When the canoes were within hailing distance, he ordered his crew to fire at will. Over 100 people were slain; the Hawaiians remembered this killing as "the day of spilled brains." Metcalfe then sailed away to Kealekakua Bay and in an unrelated incident succeeded in insulting Kameiamoku, a ruling chief, who vowed to annihilate the next *haole* ship that he saw.

Fate sent him the *Fair American* and young Thomas Metcalfe. The little ship was entirely overrun by superior forces. In the insuing battle, the mate, Isaac Davis, so distinguished himself by open acts of bravery that his life alone was spared. While harbored at Kealekakua, Metcalfe sent John Young to reconnoiter. Kamehameha, learning of the capture of the *Fair American,* detained Young so he could not report, and Metcalfe, losing patience, marooned his own man and sailed off to Canton. (Metcalfe never learned of the fate of his son Thomas, and was later killed with another son while trading with the Indians along the Pacific coast.) Kamehameha quickly realized the significance of his two captives and the *Fair American* with its brace of small cannon. He appropriated the ship and made Davis and Young trusted advisors, eventually raising them to the rank of chief. They would all play a significant role in the unification of Hawaii.

Kamehameha The Great

Later in 1790, supported by the savvy of Davis and Young and the cannon from the *Fair American* which he mounted on carts, Kamehameha invaded Maui using Hana as his power base. The island defenders under Kalaniekupule, son of Kahekili who was lingering on Oahu, were totally demoralized, then driven back into the death-trap of Iao Valley. There, Kamehameha's forces annihilated them. No mercy was expected and none given, although mostly commoners were slain with no significant *ali'i* falling to the victors. So many were killed in this sheer-walled, inescapable valley that the battle was called *"ka pani wai"* which means "the damming of the waters"...literally with dead bodies. While Kamehameha was fighting on Maui, his old nemesis Keoua was busy running amuk back on Hawaii, again pillaging Kamehameha's lands. The great warrior returned home flushed with victory, but in two battles could not subdue Keoua. Finally, Kamehameha had a prophetic dream in which he was told that Ku would lead him to victory over all the lands of Hawaii if he would build

Kamehameha I as drawn by Louis Choris, ship's artist for the Von Kotzebue expedition, c. 1816, supposedly the only time that Kamehameha sat to have his portrait rendered (Hawaii State Archives)

a *heiau* to the war god at Kawaihae. Even before the temple was finished, old Kahekili attempted to invade Waipio, Kamehameha's stronghold. But Kamehameha summoned Davis and Young, and with the *Fair American* and an enormous fleet of war canoes defeated Kahikili at Waimanu. Kahekili had no choice but to accept the indomitable Kamehameha as the king of Maui, although he himself remained the administrative head until his death in 1794.

Now only Keoua remained in the way and he would be defeated not by war, but by the great *mana* of Ku. While Keoua's armies were crossing the desert on the southern slopes of Kilauea, the fire goddesss Pele trumpeted her disapproval and sent a huge cloud of poisonous gas and mud-ash into the air. It descended upon and instantly killed the middle legions of Keoua's armies and their families. The footprints of this ill-fated army remain to this day outlined in the mud-ash as clearly as if they were deliberately encased in wet cement. Keoua's intuition told him that the victorious *mana* of the gods had swung to Kamehameha and that his own fate was sealed. Kamehameha sent word that he

wanted Keoua to meet with him at Ku's newly dedicated temple in Kawaihae. Both knew that Keoua must die. The old nemesis came riding proudly in his canoe, gloriously outfitted in the red and gold feathered cape and helmet signifying his exalted rank. When he stepped ashore he was felled by Kamehameha's warriors and his body was ceremoniously laid upon the altar along with 11 others who were slaughtered and dedicated to Ku, of the Maggot-Dripping Mouth.

Increasing Contact

By the time Kamehameha had won the Big Island, Hawaii was becoming a regular stopover for numerous ships seeking the lucrative sandalwood trade with China. In February 1791, Capt. George Vancouver, still seeking the Northwest Passage, returned to Kealekakua where he was greeted by a throng of 30,000. The captain at once recognized Kamehameha, who was wearing a Chinese dressing gown that he had received in tribute from another chief who in turn had received it directly from the hands of Cook himself. The diary of a crewmember, Thomas Manby, relates that Kamehameha, missing his front teeth, was more fierce-looking than ever as he approached the ship in an elegant double-hulled canoe sporting 46 rowers. The king invited all to a great feast prepared for them on the beach. Kamehameha's appetite matched his tremendous size. It was noted that he ate two sizable fish, a king-size bowl of *poi*, a small pig, and an entire baked dog. Kamehameha personally entertained the Englishmen by putting on a mock battle in which he deftly avoided spears by rolling, tumbling, and catching them in mid-air, all the while hurling his own a great distance. The English reciprocated by firing cannon bursts into the air, creating an impromptu fireworks display. Kamehameha requested from Vancouver a full table setting with which he was provided, but his request for firearms was prudently denied. The captain did, however, leave beef cattle, fowl, and breeding stock of sheep and goats. The ship's naturalist, Archibald Menzies, was the first *haole* to climb Mauna Kea; he also introduced a large assortment of fruits and vegetables. The Hawaiians were cheerful, outgoing, and showed remorse when they indicated that the remainder of Cook's bones had been buried at a temple close to Kealekakua. John Young, by this time firmly entrenched into Hawaiian society, made no request to sail away with Vancouver. During the next two decades of Kamehameha's rule, the French, Russians, English, and Americans discovered the great whaling waters off Hawaii, and their increasing visits shook and finally tumbled the ancient religion and social order of *kapu*.

Finishing Touches

After Keoua was laid to rest it was only a matter of time till Kamehameha consolidated his power over all of Hawaii. In 1794 the old warrior Kahekili of Maui died, and gave Oahu to his son Kalanikupule, while Kauai and Niihau went to his brother Kaeo. Warring between themselves, Kalanikupule was victorious, though he did not possess the grit of his father nor the great *mana* of Kamehameha. He had previously murdered a Capt. Brown who had anchored in Honolulu and seized his ship the *Jackall*. With the aid of this ship, Kalanikupule now determined to attack Kamehameha. However, while en route, the sailors regained control of their ship and cruised to the Big Island to inform and join with Kamehameha. An army of 16,000 was raised and sailed for Maui, where they met only token resistance, destroyed Lahaina, pillaged the countryside, and vanquished Molokai in one bloody battle. The war canoes next sailed for Oahu and the final showdown. The great army landed at Waikiki, and though defenders fought bravely, giving up Oahu by the inch, they were steadily driven into the surrounding mountains. The beleagured army made its last stand at Nuuanu Pali, a great precipice in the mountains behind present-day Honolulu. Kamehameha's warriors mercilessly drove the enemy into the great abyss. Kalanikupule, who hid in the mountains, was captured after a few months and sacrificed to Ku, The Snatcher of Lands, thereby ending the struggle for power. Kamehameha put down a revolt on Hawaii in 1796 and the king of Kauai, Kaumuali, accepting the inevitable, recognized Kamehameha as supreme ruler

without suffering the hopeless ravages of a needless war. Kamehameha, for the first time in Hawaiian history, was the undisputed ruler of all the islands of "the heavenly homeland in the north."

Kamehameha's Rule

Kamehameha was as gentle in victory as he was ferocious in battle. His rule lasted until his death on May 8, 1819, under which Hawaii enjoyed a peace unlike the warring islands had ever known before. The king moved his royal court to Lahaina, where in 1803 he built the "Brick Palace," the first permanent building of Hawaii. The benevolent tyrant also enacted the "Law of the Splintered Paddle." This law, which protected the weak from the exploitation of the strong, had its origins when, many years before, a brave defender of a small overwhelmed village broke a paddle over Kamehameha's head and taught the chief—literally in one stroke—about the nobility of the common man.

However, just as Old Hawaii reached its "golden age," its demise was at hand. The relentless waves of *haole* both innocently and determinedly battered the old ways into the ground. With the foreign ships came prosperity and fanciful new goods after which the *ali'i* lusted. The *makaaina* were worked mercilessly to provide sandalwood for the China trade. This was the first "boom" economy to hit the islands, but it set the standard of exploitation that would follow. Kamehameha built an observation tower in Lahaina to watch for ships, many of which were his own, returning laden with riches from the world at large. In the last years of his life Kamehameha returned to his beloved Kona coast where he enjoyed the excellent fishing renowned to this day. He had taken Hawaii from the darkness of warfare into the light of peace. He died true to the religious and moral *kapu* of his youth, the only ones he had ever known, and with him died a unique way of life. Two loyal retainers buried his bones after the baked flesh had been ceremoniously stripped away. A secret burial cave was chosen so that no one could desecrate the remains of the great chief, thereby absorbing his *mana*. The tomb's whereabouts remains unknown, and *the great Queen Kaahumanu, by ship's artist Louis Choris from the Otto Von Kotzebue expedition c. 1816 (Hawaii State Archives)*

disturbing the dead remains one of the strictest *kapu* to this day. "The Lonely One's" kingdom would pass to his son, Liholiho, but true power would be in the hands of his beloved but feisty wife Kaahumanu. As Kamehameha's spirit drifted from this Earth, two forces sailing around Cape Horn would forever change Hawaii: the whalers and the missionaries.

MISSIONARIES AND WHALERS

The year 1819 is of the utmost significance in Hawaiian history. It marked the death of Kamehameha, the overthrow of the ancient *kapu* system, the arrival of the first "whaler" in Lahaina, and the departure of Calvinist missionaries from New England determined to convert the heathen islands. Great changes began to rattle the old order to its foundations. With the *kapu* system and all of the ancient gods abandoned (except for the fire goddess Pele of Kilauea), a great void permeated the souls of the Hawaiians. In the coming decades Hawaii, also coveted by Russia, France, and England, was finally consumed by America. The islands had the first American school, printing press, and newspaper *(The Polynesian)* west of the Mississippi. Lahaina, in its heyday, became the world's greatest whaling port, accommodating over 500 ships during its peak years.

The Royal Family

Maui's Hana District provided Hawaii with one of its greatest queens, Kaahumanu, born in 1768 in a cave within walking distance of Hana Harbor. At the age of 17 she became the third of Kamehameha's 21 wives and eventually the love of his life. At first she proved to be totally independent and unmanageable, and was known to openly defy her king by taking numerous lovers. Kamehameha placed a *kapu* on her body and even had her attended by horribly deformed hunchbacks to curb her carnal appetites, but she continued to flaunt his authority. Young Kaahumanu had no love for her great, lumbering, unattractive husband, but (even Capt. Vancouver was pressed into service as a marriage counselor) in time she learned to love him dearly. She in turn became his favorite wife, although she remained childless throughout her life. Kamehameha's first wife was the supremely royal Keopuolani, who so outranked even him that the king himself had to approach her naked and crawling on his belly. Keopuolani produced the royal children Liholiho and Kauikeaouli, who became King Kamehameha II and III, respectively. When Kamehameha I died in 1819 he appointed Liholiho his successor, but he also had the wisdom to make Kaahumanu the *kuhina nui* or queen regent. Initially, Liholiho was weak and became a drunkard. Later he became a good ruler, but he was always supported by his royal mother Keopuolani and by the ever-formidable Kaahumanu.

Kapu Is Pau

Kaahumanu was greatly loved and respected by the people. On public occasions, she donned Kamehameha's royal cloak and spear: so attired and infused with the king's *mana,* she demonstrated that she was the real leader of Hawaii. For six months after Kamehameha's death, Kaahumanu counseled Liholiho on what he must do. The wise *kuhina nui* knew that the old ways were *pau* ("finished") and Hawaii could not hope to function in a rapidly changing world under the *kapu* system. In November 1819, Kaahumanu and Keopuolani prevailed upon Liholiho to break two of the oldest and most sacred *kapu:* to eat together with women and to allow women to eat previously forbidden foods, such as bananas and certain fish. Kaahumanu sat with Liholilho, heavily fortified with strong drink, and attended by other high-ranking chiefs and a handful of foreigners, they ate in public. This feast became known as *Ai Noa* ("free eating"), and as the first morsels passed her lips the ancient gods of Hawaii tumbled. Throughout the land revered *heiau* were burned and abandoned and the idols knocked to the ground. Now the people had nothing but their own weakened inner selves to rely on. Nothing and no one could answer their prayers; their spiritual lives were empty and in shambles.

Missionaries

In October 1819 the brig *Thaddeus* left Boston carrying 14 missionaries bound for Hawaii. On April 4, 1820 they landed at Kailua on the Big Island where Liholiho had moved the royal court. The reverends Bingham and Thurston went ashore and were granted a one-year trial missionary period by King Liholiho. They established themselves on Hawaii and Oahu and from there began the transformation of Hawaii. The missionaries were men of God, but also practical-minded Yankees. They brought education, enterprise, and most importantly, unlike the transient seafarers, a commitment to stay and build. In 1823, Rev. Richards established the first mission in Lahaina, a village of about 2,300 inhabitants.

Rapid Conversions

The year 1823 also marked the death of Keopuolani, who was given a Christian burial. Setting the standard by accepting Christianity, a number of the *ali'i* had followed the queen's lead. Liholiho had sailed off to England where he and his wife contracted measles and died. Their bodies were returned by the British in 1825, on the HMS *Blonde* captained by Lord Byron, cousin of *the* Lord Byron. During these years, Kaahumanu allied herself with Rev. Richards and together they wrote Hawaii's first code of laws based upon the Ten Commandments. Foremost was the condemnation of murder, theft, brawling, and the desecration of the Sabbath by work or play. The early missionaries had the best of intentions, but like all zealots were blinded by the singlemindedness that was also their greatest ally. The destruction of the native beliefs they felt to be abominations was not surgically selective. *Anything* native was felt to be inferior, and they set about to wipe out all traces of the old ways. In their rampage they reduced the Hawaiian culture to ashes, plucking self- will and determination from the hearts of a once proud people. More so than the whalers, they terminated the Hawaiian way of life.

The Early Seamen

A good portion of the common seamen of the early 19th century were the dregs of the Western world. Many a whoremongering drunkard had awoken from a stupor and found himself on the pitching deck of a ship, discovering to his dismay that he had been "pressed into naval service." For the most part these sailors were a filthy, uneducated, lawless rabble. Their present situation was dim, their future hopeless, and they would live to be 30 if they were lucky and didn't die from scurvy or a thousand other miserable fates. They snatched brief pleasure in every port, and jumped ship at every opportunity, especially in an easy berth like Lahaina. They displayed the worst elements of Western culture—which the Hawaiians naively mimicked. In exchange for *aloha* they gave drunkeness, sloth, and insidious death by disease. By the 1850s the population of native Hawaiians tumbled from the estimated 300,000 reported by Capt. Cook in 1778 to barely 60,000. Common conditions such as colds, flu, venereal disease, and sometimes small pox and cholera decimated the Hawaiians, who had no natural immunities to these foreign ailments. By the time the missionaries arrived, *hapahaole* children were common in Lahaina streets. The earliest lawless opportunists had come seeking sandalwood after first filling their holds with furs from the Pacific Northwest. Aided by *ali'i* hungry for manufactured goods and Western finery, they raped Hawaiian forests of this fragrant wood so coveted in China. Next, droves of sailors came in search of the whales. The whalers, decent men at home, left their morals back in the Atlantic and lived by the slogan "no conscience east of the Cape." The delights of Hawaii were just too tempting for most.

Two Worlds Tragically Collide

The 1820s were a time of confusion and soul-searching for the Hawaiians. When Kamehameha II died the kingdom passed to Kauikeaouli (Kamehameha III), who made his life-long residence in Lahaina. The young king was only nine years old when the title passed to him, but his power was secure because Kaahumanu was still a vibrant *kuhina nui*. The young prince, more so than any other, was raised in the cultural confusion of the times. His childhood was spent during the very cusp of the change from old ways to new, and he was often pulled in two directions by vastly differing beliefs. Since he was royal born, according to age-old Hawaiian tradition he must mate and produce an heir with the highest ranking *ali'i* in the kingdom. This natural mate happened to be his younger sister, the Princess Nahienaena. To the old Hawaiian advisors, this arrangement was perfectly acceptable and encouraged. To the increasingly influential missionaries, incest was an unimaginable abomination in the eyes of God. The problem was compounded by the fact that Kamehameha III and Nahien-

Kamehameha III

aena were drawn to each other and were deeply in love. The young king could not stand the mental pressure imposed by conflicting worlds. He became a teenage alcoholic too royal to be restrained by anyone in the kingdom, and his bouts of drunkenness and womanizing were both legendary and scandalous. Meanwhile, Nahienaena was even more pressured because she was a favorite of the missionaries, baptized into the church at age 12. She too vacillated between the old and the new. At times a pious Christian, at others she drank all night and took numerous lovers. As the prince and princess grew into their late teens, they became even more attached to each other and hardly made an attempt to keep their relationship from the missionaries. Whenever possible, they lived together in a grass house built for the Princess by her father.

In 1832, the great Kaahumanu died, leaving the king on his own. In 1833, at the age of 18, Kamehameha III announced that the "regency" was over and that all the lands in Hawaii were his, personally, and that he alone was the ultimate law. Almost immediately, however, he decreed that his half sister Kinau would be "premier," signifying that he would leave the actual running of the kingdom in her hands. Kamehameha III fell into total drunken confusion, until one night he attempted suicide. After this episode he seemed to straighten up a bit and mostly kept a low profile. In 1836, Princess Nahienaena was convinced by the missionaries to take a husband. She married Leleiohoku, a chief from the Big Island, but continued to sleep with her brother. It is uncertain who fathered the child, but Nahienaena gave birth to a baby boy in September 1836. The young prince survived for only a few hours, and Nahienaena never recovered from her convalescence. She died in December 1836, and was laid to rest in the mausoleum next to her mother, Keopuolani, on the royal island in Mokuhina Pond, still in existence in modern-day Lahaina. After the death of his sister, Kamehameha III became a sober and righteous ruler. Oftentimes seen paying his respects at the royal mausoleum, he ruled longer than any other king until his death in 1854.

The Missionaries Prevail

In 1823, the first mission was established in Lahaina under the pastorage of Rev. Richards and his wife. Within a few years, many of the notable ali'i had been, at least in appearance, converted to Christianity. By 1828 the cornerstones for Wainee Church, the first stone church on the island, were laid just behind the palace of Kamehameha III. The struggle between missionaries and whalers centered around public drunkenness and the servicing of sailors by local native girls. The normally god-fearing whalers had signed on for perilous duty that lasted up to three years, and when they anchored in Lahaina they demanded their pleasure. The missionaries were instrumental in placing a curfew on sailors and prohibiting native girls from boarding ships, which had become customary. These measures certainly did not stop the laiasons between sailor and wahine, but

it did impose a modicum of social sanction and tolled the end of the wide-open days. The sailors were outraged; in 1825 the crew from the *Daniel* attacked the home of the meddler, Rev. Richards. A year later a similar incident occurred. In 1827, confined and lonely sailors from the whaler *John Palmer* fired their cannon at Rev. Richards' newly built home.

Slowly the tensions eased, and by 1836 many sailors were regulars at the Seamen's Chapel, adjacent to the Baldwin Home. Unfortunately, even the missionaries couldn't stop the pesky mosquito from entering the islands through the port of Lahaina. The mosquitos arrived in 1826, from Mexico, aboard the merchant *Wellington*. They were inadvertently carried as larvae in the water barrels and democratically pestered everyone in the islands from that day forward regardless of race, religion, or creed.

Lahaina Becomes A Cultural Center

By 1831, Lahaina was firmly established as a seat of Western influence in Hawaii. That year marked the founding of Lahainaluna School, the first *real* American school west of the Rockies. Virtually a copy of a New England normal school, it attracted the best students, both native and white, from throughout the kingdom. By 1834, Lahainaluna had an operating printing press publishing the islands' first newspaper, *The Torch of Hawaii,* starting a lucrative printing industry centered in Lahaina that dominated not only the islands but also California for many years.

An early native student was David Malo. He was brilliant and well educated, but more importantly, he remembered the "old ways." One of the first Hawaiians to realize his native land was being swallowed up by the newcomers, Malo compiled the first history of pre-contact Hawaii and the resulting book, *Hawaiian Antiquities,* became a reference masterpiece which has yet to be eclipsed. David Malo insisted that the printing be done in Hawaiian, not English. Malo is buried in the mountains above Lahainaluna where, by his own request, he is "high above the tide of foreign invasion." By the 1840s, Lahaina was firmly established as the "whaling capital of the world"; the peak year 1846 saw 395 whaling ships anchored here. A census in 1846 reported that Lahaina was home to 3,445 natives, 112 permanent *haole,* 600 sailors, and over 500 dogs. The populace was housed in 882 grass houses, 155 adobe houses, and 59 relatively permanent stone and wooden framed structures. Lahaina would probably have remained the islands' capital, had Kamehameha III not moved the royal capital to the burgeoning port of Honolulu on the island of Oahu.

Foreign Influence

By the 1840s Honolulu was becoming the center of commerce in the islands; when Kamehameha III moved the royal court there from Lahaina the ascendant fate of the new capital was guaranteed. In 1843, Lord Paulet, commander of the warship *Carysfort,* forced Kamehameha III to sign a treaty ceding Hawaii to the British. London, however, repudiated this act and Hawaii's independence was restored within a few months when Queen Victoria sent Admiral Thomas as her personal agent of good intentions. The king memorialized the turn of events by a speech in which he uttered the phrase, *"Ua mau ke ea o ka aina i ka pono,"* ("The life of the land is preserved in righteousness"), now Hawaii's motto. The French used similar bullying tactics to force an unfavorable treaty on the Hawaiians in 1839; as part of these heavy-handed negotiations they exacted a payment of $20,000, and the right for Catholics to enjoy religious freedom in the islands. In 1842 the U.S. recognized and guaranteed Hawaii's independence without a formal treaty, and by 1860 over 80 percent of the islands' trade was with America.

The Great *Mahele*

In 1840 Kamehameha III ended his autocratic rule and instituted a constitutional monarchy. This brought about the Hawaiian Bill of Rights, but the most far-reaching change was the transition to private ownership of land. Formerly, all land belonged to the ruling chief who gave wedge-shaped parcels called *ahupua'a* to lesser chiefs to be worked for

him. The commoners did all the real labor, their produce heavily taxed by the *ali'i.* The fortunes of war, the death of a chief, or the mere whim of a superior could force a commoner off his land. The Hawaiians, however, could not think in terms of "owning" land. No one could *possess* land, one could only *use* land, and its *ownership* was a strange foreign concept. (As a result, naive Hawaiians gave up their lands for a song to unscrupulous traders, which remains an integral unrectified problem to this day.) In 1847 Kamehameha III and his advisers separated the lands of Hawaii into three groupings: crown land (belonging to the king), government land (belonging to the chiefs), and the people's land (the largest parcels). In 1848, 245 *ali'i* entered their land claims in the *Mahele Book,* assuring them ownership. In 1850 the commoners were given title in fee simple to the lands they cultivated and lived on as tenants, not including house lots in towns. Commoners without land could buy small *kuleana* (farms) from the government at 50 cents per acre. In 1850, foreigners were also allowed to purchase land in fee simple, and the ownership of Hawaii from that day forward slipped steadily from the hands of its indigenous people.

KING SUGAR

The sugar industry began at Hana, Maui, in 1849. A whaler named George Wilfong hauled four blubber pots ashore and set them up on a rocky hill in the middle of 60 acres he had planted in sugar. A team of oxen turned "crushing rollers" and the cane juice flowed down an open trough into the pots, under which an attending native kept a roaring fire burning. Wilfong's methods of refining were crude but the resultant high-quality sugar turned a neat profit in Lahaina. The main problem was labor. The Hawaiians, who had made excellent whalers, were basically indentured workers. They became extremely disillusioned with their contracts, which could last up to 10 years. Most of their wages were eaten up by manufactured commodities sold at the company store, and it didn't take long

Women of many ethnic backgrounds worked the plantations at the turn of the century.

for them to realize that they were little more than slaves. At every opportunity they either left the area or just refused to work.

Imported Labor

The **Masters and Servants Act of 1850,** which allowed importation of laborers under the contract system, ostensibly guaranteed an endless supply of cheap labor for the plantations. Chinese laborers were imported, but were too enterprising to remain in the fields for a meager $3 per month. They left as soon as opportunity permitted, and went into business as small merchants and retailers. In the meantime, Wilfong had sold out, releasing most of the Hawaiians previously held under contract, and his plantation fell into disuse. In 1860 two Danish brothers, August and Oscar Unna, bought land at Hana to raise sugar. They solved the labor problem by importing Japanese laborers who were extremely hard-working and easily managed. The workday lasted 10 hours, six days a week, for a salary of $20 per month with housing and medical care thrown in. Plantation life was very structured with stringent rules governing even bedtimes and lights out. A worker was fined for being late or for smoking on the job. Even the Japanese couldn't function under these circumstances, and im-

provements in benefits and housing were slowy gained.

Sugar Grows

The demand for "Sandwich Island Sugar" grew as California was populated during the gold rush, and increased dramatically when the American Civil War demanded a constant supply. The only sugar plantations on the Mainland were small plots confined to the Confederate states, whose products would hardly be bought by the Union and whose fields, later in the war, were destroyed. By the 1870s it was clear to the planters, still mainly New Englanders, that the U.S. was their market; they tried often to gain closer ties and favorable tariffs. The Americans also planted rumors that the British were interested in annexing Hawaii; this put pressure on the U.S. Congress to pass the long-desired **Reciprocity Act,** which would exempt sugar from import duty. It finally passed in 1875, in exchange for U.S. long-range rights to the strategic naval port of Pearl Harbor, among other concessions. These agreements gave increased political power to a small group of American planters, whose outlooks were similar to the post-Civil War South where a few powerful whites were the virtual masters of a multitude of dark-skinned laborers. Sugar was now big business and the Hana District alone exported almost 3,000 tons per year. All of Hawaii would have to reckon with the "sugar barons."

Changing Society

The sugar plantation system changed life in Hawaii physically, spiritually, politically, and economically. Now boatloads of workers came not only from Japan, but from Portugal, Germany, and even Russia. The white-skinned workers were most often the field foremen (luna). With the immigrants came new religions, new animals and plants, unique cuisines, and a plantation language known as pidgin or da kine. The Orientals mainly, but also portions of all the other groups including the white plantation owners, intermarried with Hawaiian girls. A new class of people properly termed "cosmopolitan" but more familiarly and aptly known as "locals" was emerging. These were the people of multiple race backgrounds who couldn't exactly say *what* they were but it was clear to all just *who* they were. The plantation owners became the new "chiefs" of Hawaii who could carve up the land and dispense favors. The Hawaiian monarchy was soon eliminated.

A KINGDOM PASSES

The fate of Lahaina's Wainee Church through the years has been a symbol of the political and economic climate of the times. Its construction heralded the beginning of missionary dominance in 1828. It was destroyed by a tornado or "ghost wind" in 1858, just when whaling began to falter. The previously dominant missionaries began losing their control to the merchants and planters. In 1894, Wainee Church was burned to the ground by Royalists supporting the besieged Queen Liliuokalani, then was rebuilt with a grant from H.P. Baldwin in 1897 while Hawaii was a republic ruled by the sugar planters. It wasn't until 1947 that Wainee was finally completed and remodeled.

The Beginning Of The End

Like the Hawaiian people themselves, the Kamehameha dynasty in the mid-1800s was dying from within. King Kamehameha IV (Alexander Liholiho) ruled from 1854 to 1863; his only child died in 1862. He was succeeded by his older brother Kamehameha V (Lot Kamehameha) who ruled until 1872. With his passing the Kamehameha line ended. William Lunalilo, elected king in 1873 by popular vote, was of royal, but not Kamehameha, lineage. He died after only a year in office, and being a bachelor left no heirs. He was succeeded by David Kalakaua, known far and wide as "The Merry Monarch." He made a world tour and was well received wherever he went. He built Iolani Palace in Honolulu and was personally in favor of closer ties with the U.S., helping push through the Reciprocity Act. Kalakaua died in 1891 and was replaced by his sister Lydia Liliuokalani, last of the Hawaiian monarchs.

The Revolution

When Liliuokalani took office in 1891 the native population was at a low of 40,000 and she felt that the U.S. had too much influence over her homeland. She was known to personally favor the English over the Americans. She attempted to replace the liberal constitution of 1887 (adopted by her pro-American brother) with an autocratic mandate in which she would have much more political and economic control of the islands. When the McKinley Tariff of 1890 brought a decline in sugar profits, she made no attempt to improve the situation. Thus, the planters saw her as a political obstacle to their economic growth; most of Hawaii's American planters and merchants were in favor of a rebellion. She would have to go! A central spokesman and firebrand was Lorrin Thurston, a Honolulu publisher who, with a central core of about 30 men, challenged the Hawaiian monarchy. Although Liliuokalani rallied some support and had a small military potential in her personal guard, the coup was ridiculously easy—it took only one casualty. Capt. John Good shot a Hawaiian policeman in the arm and that did it. Naturally, the conspirators could not have succeeded without some solid assurances from a secret contingent in the U.S. Congress as well as outgoing President Benjamin Harrison who favored Hawaii's annexation. Ma-

Queen Liliuokalani

rines from the *Boston* went ashore to "protect American lives," and on January 17, 1893, the Hawaiian monarchy came to an end.

The provisional government was headed by Sanford B. Dole who became president of the Hawaiian Republic. Liliuokalani actually surrendered not to the conspirators but to U.S. Ambassador John Stevens. She believed that the U.S. government, which had assured Hawaiian independence, would be outraged by the overthrow and would come to her aid. Actually, incoming President Grover Cleveland *was* outraged and Hawaii wasn't immediately annexed as expected. When queried about what she would do with the conspirators if she were reinstated, Liliuokalani said that they would be hung as traitors. The racist press of the times, which portrayed the Hawaiians as half-civilized blood-thirsty heathens, publicized this widely. Since the conspirators were the leading citizens of the land, the queen's words proved untimely. In January 1895, a small, ill-fated counterrevolution headed by Liliuokalani failed, and she was placed under house arrest in Iolani Palace. Forced to abdicate her throne, officials of the Republic insisted that she use her married name (Mrs. John Dominis) to sign the documents. She was also forced to swear allegiance to the new Republic. Liliuokalani went on to write *Hawaii's Story* and also the lyric ballad *Aloha O'e*. She never forgave the conspirators and remained to the Hawaiians "queen" until her death in 1917.

Annexation

The overwhelming majority of Hawaiians opposed annexation and desired to restore the monarchy. But they were prevented from voting by the new Republic because they couldn't meet the imposed property and income qualifications—a transparent ruse by the planters to control the majority. Most *haoles* were racist and believed that the "common people" could not be entrusted with the vote because they were childish and incapable of ruling themselves. The fact that the Hawaiians had existed quite well for 1,000 years before the white man even reached Hawaii was never considered. The Philippine theater of the Spanish-American War also prompted annexation. One of the strongest proponents was Alfred Mahon, a brilliant naval strategist who, with support from Theodore Roosevelt, argued that the U.S. military must have Hawaii to be a viable force in the Pacific. In addition, Japan, flushed with victory in its recent war with China, protested the American intention to annex, and in so doing prompted even moderates to support annexation in fear that the Japanese themselves coveted the prize. On July 7, 1898, President McKinley signed the annexation agreement, and this "tropical fruit" was finally put into America's basket.

MODERN TIMES

Hawaii entered the 20th century totally transformed from what it had been. The old Hawaiian language, religion, culture, and leadership were all gone. Western dress, values, education, and recreation were the norm.

Native Hawaiians were now unseen citizens who lived in dwindling numbers in remote areas. The plantations, new centers of social order, had a strong Oriental flavor; more than 75 percent of their work force was Asian. There was a small white middle class, an all-powerful white elite, and a single political party ruled by that elite. Education, however, was always highly prized, and by the turn of the century all racial groups were encouraged to attend school. By 1900, almost 90 percent of Hawaiians were literate (far above the national norm) and schooling was mandatory for all children between ages six and 15. Intermarriage was accepted, and there was a mixing of the races like nowhere else on Earth. The military became increasingly important to Hawaii. It brought in money and jobs, dominating the island economy. The Japanese attack on Pearl Harbor, which began U.S. involvement in World War II, bound Hawaii to America forever. Once the islands had been baptized by blood, the average Mainlander felt that Hawaii was American soil. A movement among Hawaiians to become part of the Union began to grow. They wanted a real voice in Washington, not merely a voteless delegate as provided under their territory status. Hawaii became the 50th state in 1959 and the jumbo jet revolution of the 1960s made it easily accessible to growing numbers of tourists from all over the world.

Military History

A few military strategists realized the importance of Hawaii early in the 19th century, but most didn't recognize the advantages until the Spanish-American War. It was clearly an unsinkable ship in the middle of the Pacific from which the U.S. could launch military operations. Troops were stationed at Camp McKinley, at the foot of Diamond Head, the main military compound until it became obsolete in 1907. Pearl Harbor was first surveyed in 1872 by General Schofield. Later a military base named in his honor, Schofield Barracks, was a main military post in central Oahu. It first housed the U.S. 5th Cavalry in 1909 and was heavily bombed by the Japanese at the outset of WW II. Pearl Harbor, first dredged in 1908, was officially opened on December 11, 1911. The first warship to enter was the cruiser *California*. Ever since, the military has been a mainstay of island economy. Unfortunately, there has been long-standing bad blood between locals and military personnel. Each group has tended to look down upon the other.

Honolulu Star-Bulletin 1st EXTRA

8 PAGES—HONOLULU, TERRITORY OF HAWAII, U. S. A., SUNDAY, DECEMBER 7, 1941—8 PAGES ✦ PRICE FIVE CENTS

WAR !

(Associated Press by Transpacific Telephone)
SAN FRANCISCO, Dec. 7.— President Roosevelt announced this morning that Japanese planes had attacked Manila and Pearl Harbor.

OAHU BOMBED BY JAPANESE PLANES

SIX KNOWN DEAD. 21 INJURED, AT EMERGENCY HOSPITAL

The Honolulu Star Bulletin *banner headline announces the beginning of U.S. involvement in WW II on Sunday, December 7, 1941.*

Pearl Harbor Attack

On the morning of December 7, 1941, the Japanese carrier *Akagi,* flying the battle flag of the famed Admiral Togo of the Russo-Japanese War, received and broadcast over its PA system island music from Honolulu station KGMB. Deep in the bowels of the ship a radio man listened for a much different message, coming thousands of miles from the Japanese mainland. When the ironic poetic message "east wind rain" was received, the attack was launched. At the end of the day, 2,325 U.S. servicemen and 57 civilians were dead; 188 planes were destroyed; 18 major warships were sunk or heavily damaged; and the U.S. was in the war. Japanese casualties were ludicrously light and the ignited conflict would rage for four years until Japan, through Nagasaki and Hiroshima, was vaporized into total submission. At the end of hostilities, Hawaii would never again be considered separate from America (see p. 266 for more details).

Statehood

A number of economic and political reasons explain why the ruling elite of Hawaii desired statehood, but simply, the vast majority of people who lived there, especially after WW II, considered themselves Americans. The first serious mention of making "The Sandwich Islands" a state was in the 1850s under President Franklin Pierce, but wasn't taken seriously until the monarchy was overthrown in the 1890s. For the next 50 years statehood proposals were made repeatedly to Congress, but there was stiff opposition, especially from the southern states. With Hawaii a territory, an import quota system beneficial to mainland producers could be enacted on produce, especially sugar. Also, there was prejudice against creating a state in a place where the majority of the populace was not white. This situation was illuminated by the infamous Massie Rape case of 1931 (see p. 55), which went down as one of the greatest miscarriages of justice in American history. During WW II, Hawaii was placed under martial law, but no serious attempt to intern the Japanese population was made, as in California. There were simply too many Japanese, who went on to gain respect of the American people by their outstanding fighting record during the war. Hawaii's own 100th Batallion became the famous 442nd Regimental Combat Team which gained notoriety by saving the Lost Texas Batallion during the Battle of the Bulge, and went on to be *the* most decorated battalion in all of WW II. When these GIs returned home, *no one* was going to tell them that they were not loyal Americans. Many of these AJAs (Americans of Japanese Ancestry) took advantage of the GI Bill and received higher education. They were from the common people, not the elite, and they rallied grass-roots support for statehood. When the vote finally occurred, approximately 132,900 voted in favor of statehood with only 7,800 votes against. Congress passed the Hawaii State Bill on March 12, 1959, and on August 21, 1959, President Eisenhower announced that Hawaii was officially the 50th state.

GOVERNMENT

The only difference between the government of the state of Hawaii and other states is that it's "streamlined," and in theory more efficient. There are only two levels of government: the state and the county. With no town or city governments to deal with, considerable bureaucracy is eliminated.

Hawaii, in anticipation of becoming a state, drafted a constitution in 1950 and was ready to go when statehood came. Politics and government are taken seriously in the "Aloha State," which consistently turns in the best national voting record per capita. For example, in the first state elections 173,000 of 180,000 registered voters voted—a whopping 94 percent of the electorate. In the election to ratify statehood, hardly a ballot went uncast, with 95 percent of the voters opting for statehood. The bill carried every island of Hawaii except for Niihau, where, coincidentally, the majority of people (total population 250 or so) are of relatively pure Hawaiian blood. The U.S. Congress passed the "Hawaii State Bill" on March 12, 1959, and on August 21, 1959, President Eisenhower proclaimed Hawaii the 50th state. The present governor is John Waihee III, first Hawaiian governor in the United States. Mr. Waihee has held this office since 1986.

Oahu has been the center of government for about 150 years, since King Kamehameha III permanently established the royal court there in the 1840s. In 1873-74, King David Kalakaua built Iolani Palace as the central showpiece of the island kingdom. Liliuokalani, the last Hawaiian monarch, lived after her dethronement in the nearby residence, Washington Place. While Hawaii was a territory, and for a few years after it became a state, the palace was used as the capitol building, the governor residing in Washington Place. Modern Oahu, besides being the center of state government, governs itself as the **City and County of Honolulu.** The county not only covers the entire island of Oahu, but all the far-flung Northwest Islands,

HOUSE DISTRICTS

KAUAI
49

OAHU
42
49
41
43
38
39
40
35
10-34, 44-48
37
36
HONOLULU

HONOLULU CITY & COUNTY: 10-49

SENATORIAL DISTRICTS

22
OAHU
21
19
20
6-17, 23, 24
18
HONOLULU

HONOLULU CITY
& COUNTY: 6-24
N.B. ALSO INCLUDES
NORTHWESTERN ISLANDS

© MOON PUBLICATIONS, INC.

except for Midway, which is under federal jurisdiction.

State Representation

Oahu has four times as many people as the other islands combined. Nowhere is this more evident than in the representation of Oahu in the state House and Senate. Oahu claims 19 of the 25 state senators, and 39.7 of the 51 state representatives. (The 0.7 state representative covers the split district of the north Waianae area of Oahu, and the north shore of Kauai chips in with the remainder 0.3 of the representative.) These lopsided figures make it obvious that Oahu has plenty of clout, especially Honolulu urban districts, which elect more than 50 percent of Oahu's representatives.

Frequent political battles ensue, since what's good for the city and county of Honolulu isn't always good for the rest of the state. More often than not, the political moguls of Oahu, backed by huge business interests, prevail. The Oahu state senators are overwhelmingly Democratic, except for three Republicans, all from the Honolulu urban districts. State representation is similar: only nine are Republicans, all from urban Honolulu or the suburban communities around Kailua.

ECONOMY

Hawaii's mid-Pacific location makes it perfect for two primary sources of income: tourism and the military. Tourists come in anticipation of endless golden days on soothing beaches, while the military is provided with the strategic position of an unsinkable battleship. Each economic sector nets Hawaii about $4 billion annually, which should keep flowing smoothly and increasing into the foreseeable future. These revenues mostly remain aloof from the normal ups and downs of the mainland U.S. economy. Together they make up 60 percent of the islands' income, and both attract either gung-ho enthusiasts or rabidly negative detractors. The remaining 40 percent comes in descending proportions from manufacturing, construction, and agriculture (mainly sugar and pineapples). As long as the sun shines and the balance of global power requires a military presence, the economic stability of Hawaii is guaranteed.

Economically, Oahu dwarfs the rest of the islands combined. It generates income from government spending, tourism, and agriculture. A huge military presence, an international airport that receives the lion's share of visitors, and unbelievably, half of the state's best arable lands keep Oahu in the economic catbird seat. The famous "Big Five" all maintain their corporate offices in downtown Honolulu, from which they oversee vast holdings throughout Hawaii and the Mainland. Located in about the same spots as when their founders helped to overthrow the monarchy, things are about the same as then, except that they're going strong, while the old royalty of Hawaii has vanished.

TOURISM

"The earthly paradise! Don't you want to go to it? Why, of course!" This was the opening line of *The Hawaiian Guide Book* by Henry Whitney which appeared in 1875. In print for 25 years, it sold for 60 cents during a time when a roundtrip sea voyage between San Francisco and Honolulu cost $125. The technique is a bit dated, but the human desires remain the same: some of us seek paradise, all seek escape, some are drawn to play out a drama in a beautiful setting. Tourists have been coming to Hawaii ever since steamship service began in the 1860s. Until WW II, luxury liners carried the financial elite on exclusive voyages to the islands. By the 1920s 10,000 visitors a year were spending almost $5 million dollars—cementing the bond between Hawaii and tourism.

A $25,000 prize offered by James Dole of pineapple fame sparked a trans-Pacific air race in 1927. The success of the aerial daredevils who answered the challenge proved that commercial air travel to Hawaii was feasible. Two years later, **Hawaiian Air** was offering regularly scheduled flights between all of the major islands. By 1950 airplanes had captured over 50 percent of the transportation market, and ocean voyages were relegated to "specialty travel," catering to the elite. By 1960 the large airbuses made their debut; 300,000 tourists arrived on eight designated airlines. The Boeing 747 began operating in 1969. These enormous planes could carry hundreds of passengers at reasonable rates, so travel to Hawaii became possible for the average-income person. In 1970, two million arrived, and by 1980 close to four million passengers arrived on 22 international air carriers. The first hotel in Honolulu was the **Hawaiian,** built in 1872. It was predated by **Volcano House,** which overlooked Kilauea Crater on the Big Island and was built in 1866. The coral-pink **Royal Hawaiian,** built in 1927, is Waikiki's graciously aging grand dame, a symbol of days gone by. As late as the 1950s it had Waikiki Beach almost to itself. Only 10,000 hotel units were available in the islands in 1960; today there are over 60,000, and thousands of condos as well.

The flow of visitors to Oahu has remained unabated ever since tourism outstripped sugar and pineapples in the early 1960s, becoming Hawaii's top moneymaker. Of the nearly five million people that visit the state yearly, two-thirds stay on Oahu; almost all the rest, en route to the Neighbor Islands, at least pass through. Hotels directly employ over 15,000 workers, half the state's total, not including all the shop assistants, waiters and waitresses, taxi drivers, and everyone else needed to ensure a carefree vacation. Of Hawaii's 60,000 hotel rooms, Oahu claims 34,000. The visitor industry generates over $2 billion of yearly revenue, and this is only the amount that can be directly related to the hotel and restaurant trades. With the flow of visitors seemingly endless, Oahu has a bright economic future.

Tourists: Who, When, And Where

Tourism-based income outstripped pineapples and sugar by the mid-'60s and the boom was on. Long-time residents could even feel a physical change in air temperature: many trees were removed from Honolulu to build parking lots, and reflected sunlight made Honolulu much hotter and at times unbearable. Even the trade winds, known to mod-

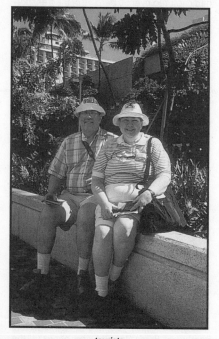

tourista

erate temperatures, were not up to that task. So many people from the outlying farming communities were attracted to work in the hotels that there was a *poi* famine in 1967. But for the most part, islanders knew that their economic future was tied to this "non-polluting industry."

Most visitors (75 percent) are Americans, and the largest numbers come from the West Coast. Sun-seeking refugees from frigid Alaska, however, make up the greatest proportional number, according to population figures. The remaining arrivals are in descending order from Japan, Canada, Australia, and England. Europe, as a whole, sends proportionately less visitors than North America or Asia, while the least amount come from South America. The Japanese market is constantly growing and by the year 1990 over a million Japanese visitors per year are expected. This is particularly beneficial to the tourist market because the average Western tourist spends about $90 per day, while his Japanese counterpart spends just over $200 per day. However, they stay only about five days, shorter than the typical visit. Up until very recently the Japanese traveled only in groups and primarily stayed on Oahu. Now the trend is to travel independently, or come with a group and then peel off, with a hefty percentage heading for the Neighbor Islands.

The typical visitor is slightly affluent, about 35, with 20 percent more women than men. The average age is a touch higher than most vacation areas because it reflects an inflated proportion of retirees heading for Hawaii, especially Honolulu, to fulfill a lifelong "dream" vacation. A typical stay lasts about 12 days, down from a month in the 1950s; a full 50 percent are repeat visitors. On any given day there are about 70,000 travelers on Oahu, 15,000 on Maui, and about 7,000 each on Kauai and Hawaii. Molokai and Lanai get so few that the figures are hardly counted. In 1964 only 10 percent of the islands' hotel rooms were on the Neighbor Islands, but by 1966 the figure jumped to 25 percent, with more than 70 percent of tourists opting to visit the Neighbor Islands. Today four out of 10 hotel rooms are on the Neighbor Islands and that figure should reach 50 percent shortly.

Waikiki growing rice, c. 1920 (Hawaii State Archives)

The overwhelming number of tourists are on package tours, and the largest number of people congregate in Waikiki, which has a 74-percent average hotel occupancy rate and attracts 2½ times as many visitors as the Neighbor Islands together. Obviously, Waikiki is still most people's idea of paradise. Those seeking a more intimate experience can have it with a 20-minute flight from Oahu or a direct flight to Hilo (Hawaii) and now Maui and Kauai.

Joaquin Miller, the 19th-century poet of the Sierra said, "I tell you my boy, the man who has not seen the Sandwich Islands, in this one great ocean's warm heart, has not seen the world." The times have certainly changed, but the sentiments of most visitors to Hawaii remain consistently the same.

Tourism-related Problems

Tourism is both boon and blight to Hawaii. It is the root cause of two problems: one environmental, the other socioeconomic. The environmental impact is obvious and best described in the lament of songstress Joni Mitchell's "They paved paradise and put up a parking lot." Simply, tourism can draw too many people to an area and overburden it. In the process, it stresses the very land and destroys the natural beauty that attracted people in the first place. Tourists come to Hawaii for what has been called its "ambient

resource": a balanced collage of indulgent climate, invigorating waters, intoxicating scenery, and exotic people all wrapped up neatly in one area which can both soothe and excite at the same time. It is in the best interest of Hawaii to preserve this "resource."

Most point to Waikiki as a prime example of development gone mad. It is super-saturated, and amazingly enough, hotel owners themselves are now trying to keep development in check. Two prime examples of the best and the worst development can be found on Maui's south shore at Kihei and Wailea, less than five miles apart. In the late '60s Kihei experienced a development-inspired "feeding frenzy" that made the real sharks offshore seem to be about as dangerous as Winnie the Pooh. Condos were slapped up as fast as cement would dry and their architecture was as inspired as a stack of shoe boxes. They lined the coast renowned for its beauty, wiping out the view in the process. Anyone who had the bucks built, and now Kihei looks like a high-rise, low-income, federally funded housing project. You can bet those who made a killing building here don't live here.

Just down the road, Wailea is a model of what development could and should be. The architecture is tasteful, low-rise, unobtrusive, and done with people and the preservation of the scenery in mind. It's obviously more exclusive, but access points to the beaches are open to everyone and the view is still there for all to enjoy. It points the way for the development of the future.

Changing Lifestyle

Like the land, humans are stressed by tourism. Local people, who once took the "Hawaiian lifestyle" for granted, become displaced and estranged in their own land. Some areas, predominantly along gorgeous beaches that were average- to low-income communities, are now overdeveloped with prices going through the roof. The locals are not only forced to move out, but often must come back as service personnel in the tourist industry and cater to the very people who displaced them. At one time the psychological blow was softened because, after all, the newcomers were merely benign tourists who would stay a short time, spend a wad of money, and leave.

Today, condos are being built and a different sort of visitor is arriving. Many condo owners are in the above-average income bracket: well-educated businesspeople and professionals. The average condo owner is a Mainlander who purchases one as a second or retirement home. These people are not islanders and have a tough time relating to the locals, who naturally feel resentment. Moreover, since they don't *leave* like normal tourists, they use all community facilities, find those special nooks and crannies for shopping or sunbathing that were once exclusively the domain of locals, and have a say as voters in community governments. The islanders become more and more disenfranchised. Many believe that the new order instigated by tourism is similar to what has always existed in Hawaii: a few from the privileged class being catered to by many from the working class. In a way it's an extension of the plantation system, but instead of carrying pineapples, most islanders find themselves carrying luggage, cocktails, or broiled fish. One argument, however, remains undeniable: whether it's people or pineapples, one has to make a living. The days of a little grass shack on a sunny beach aren't gone; it's just that you need a wallet full of credit cards to afford one.

THE MILITARY

Hawaii is the most militarized state in the Union: all five services are represented. Camp H.M. Smith, overlooking Pearl Harbor, is the headquarters of CINCPAC (Commander in Chief Pacific), which is responsible for 70 percent of the Earth's surface, from California to the east coast of Africa and to both poles. The U.S. military presence dates back to 1887, when Pearl Harbor was given to the Navy as part of the "Sugar Reciprocity Treaty." The sugar planters were given favorable "duty-free" treatment for their sugar, while the U.S. Navy was allowed exclusive rights to one of the best harbors in the Pacific. In 1894, when the monarchy was being overthrown by the sugar planters, the USS *Boston* sent a contingency of Marines ashore to "keep order," which really amounted to a show of force, backing the revolution. The Spanish-American War saw U.S. troops billeted at Camp McKinley at the foot of Diamond Head, and Schofield Barracks opened to receive the 5th Cavalry in 1909. Pearl Harbor's flames ignited WW II and there has been no looking back since then.

About 60,000 military personnel are stationed in Hawaii, with a slightly higher number of dependents. The Navy and Marines combined have the most personnel with about 36,000, followed by the Army's 17,000, 6,000 in the Air Force, and 1,000 or so Coast Guard members. Besides this, 20,000 civilian support personnel account for 65 percent of all federal jobs in Hawaii. The combined services are one of the largest landholders with over 242,000 acres, accounting for six percent of Hawaiian land. The two major holdings are the 100,000-acre Pohahuloa Training Area on Hawaii and 100,000 acres on Oahu, which is a full 26 percent of the entire island. The Army controls 71 percent of the military lands, followed by the Navy at 25 percent, and the remainder goes to the Air Force and a few small installations to the Coast Guard.

Pearl Harbor Yards,
Joseph Strauss
missile destroyer

The Military Has No Aloha

Not everyone is thrilled about the strong military presence in Hawaii. Two factions, native Hawaiians and anti-nuclear groups, are downright angry. Radical contingencies of native Hawaiian-rights groups actually consider Hawaii to be an independent country, besieged and "occupied" by the U.S. government. They date their loss of independence to Liliuokalani's overthrow in 1894. The vast majority of ethnic Hawaiians, though they consider themselves Americans, are concerned with loss of their rightful homelands, with no financial reparation, and a continuing destruction and disregard for their traditional religious and historical sites. A long list of grievances is cited by native Hawaiian action groups, but the best and clearest example is the controversy over the sacred island, Kahoolawe, which is used as a bombing target by the Navy.

The second controversy raised by the military presence focuses on Hawaii as a nuclear target. The ultimate goal of the anti-nuclear protestors is to see the Pacific, and the entire world, free from nuclear arms. They see Hawaii as a big target that the international power merchants on the Mainland use as both pawn and watchdog. There is no doubt that Hawaii is a nuclear time bomb/powderkeg and the anti-nuke groups say that if war breaks out the Hawaiian Islands will be reduced to cinders. The military naturally counters that a strong Hawaii is a deterrent to nuclear war and that Hawaii is not only a powerful offensive weapon, but one of the best-defended regions of the world. Unfortunately, when you are on an island there is no place to go: like a boxer in a ring, you can run, but you can't hide.

Anyone interested in the nuclear controversy can contact any of the following organizations: cAtholic Action of Hawaii, 1918 University Ave., Honolulu, HI 96822; U.S. Nuclear Free Pacific Network, 942 Market St., Rm. 711, San Francisco, CA 94102; or *Kahuliau* ("an independent newspaper focusing on Hawaii and Pacific issues"), Box 61337, Honolulu, HI 96822.

AGRICULTURE

You'd think that with all the people living on Oahu, coupled with the constant land development, there'd hardly be any room left for things to grow. But that's not the case. The land is productive, though definitely stressed. It is startling that in downtown Honolulu and Waikiki, so many trees have been removed to build parking lots that the asphalt becomes overheated from the lack of shade, allowing temperatures, once moderated by the trade winds, to rise demonstrably.

Changing times and attitudes led to a "poi famine" that hit Oahu in 1967 because very few people were interested in the hard work of farming this staple. However, with half the state's best arable land, Oahu manages to produce a considerable amount of sugar cane, pineapples, and the many products of diversified agriculture. Sugar lands account for 33,000 acres, most owned by the James Campbell Estate, located around Ewa, north and west of Pearl Harbor, with some acreage around Waimea and Waialua on the north shore. Pineapples cover 11,500 acres, with the biggest holdings in the Leilehua Plateau belonging to Dole, a subsidiary of Castle and Cooke. In the hills, entrepreneurs raise *pakalolo,* which has become the state's most productive cash crop. Oahu is also a huge agricultural consumer, demanding more than four times as much vegetables, fruits, meats, and poultry to feed its citizens and visitors than the remainder of the state combined.

THE "BIG FIVE"

Until statehood, Hawaii was ruled economically by a consortium of corporations known as "the Big Five": **C. Brewer and Co.,** sugar, ranching, and chemicals, founded 1826; **Theo. H. Davies & Co.,** sugar, investments, insurance, and transportation, founded 1845; **Amfac Inc.** (originally H. Hackfield Inc.—a German firm that changed its name and ownership during the anti-German sentiment of WW I to American Factors), sugar, insurance, and land development, founded 1849; **Castle and Cooke Inc.,** (Dole) pineapple, food packing, and land development, founded 1851; and **Alexander and Baldwin Inc.,** shipping, sugar, and pineapple, founded 1895. This economic oligarchy ruled Hawaii with a velvet glove and a steel grip.

With members on all important corporate boards, they controlled all major commerce, including banking, shipping, insurance, hotel development, agriculture, utilities, and wholesale and retail merchandising. Anyone trying to buck the system was ground to dust, finding it suddenly impossible to do business in the islands. The Big Five were made up of the islands' oldest and most well-established

haole families; all included bloodlines from Hawaii's own nobility and *ali'i.* They looked among themselves for suitable husbands and wives, so breaking in from the outside even through marriage was hardly possible. The only time they were successfully challenged prior to statehood was when Sears, Roebuck and Co. opened a store on Oahu. Closing ranks, the Big Five decreed that their steamships would not carry Sears's freight. When Sears threatened to buy its own steamship line, the Big Five relented.

Actually, statehood, and more to the point, tourism, broke their oligarchy. After 1960 too much money was at stake for Mainland-based corporations to ignore. Eventually the grip of the Big Five was loosened, but they are still enormously powerful and richer than ever, though unlike before, they don't control everything. Now their power is land. With only five other major landholders, they control 65 percent of all the privately held land in Hawaii.

YOUNG SUGARCANE

LAND OWNERSHIP

OAHU
380,800 ACRES

STATE
FEDERAL
HAWAIIAN HOMES
SMALL PRIVATE
LARGE PRIVATE

© MOON PUBLICATIONS, INC.

LAND OWNERSHIP

Landwise, Hawaii is a small pie, and its slices are not at all well divided. Of 6,425 square miles of land, the six main inhabited islands make up 98 percent. (This figure does not include Niihau, which is privately owned by the Robinson family and inhabited by the last remaining pure-blooded Hawaiians, nor does it include Kahoolawe, the uninhabited Navy bombing target just off Maui's south shore.) Of the 4,045,511 acres that make up the inhabited islands, 36 percent is owned by the state, 10 percent by the federal government, and the remaining 54 percent is in private hands. But only 40 owners with 5,000 or more acres own 75 percent of all private lands.

Moreover, only 10 private concerns own two-thirds of these lands. To be more specific, Castle and Cooke Inc. owns 99 percent of Lanai, while 40-60 percent of Maui, Oahu, Molokai, Kauai, and Hawaii are owned by less than a dozen private parties. The largest private landowner is the Kamehameha Schools/Bishop Estate, which recently lost a Supreme Court battle that allows the state of Hawaii to acquire privately owned land for "the public good."

More than in any other state, Hawaii's landowners tend to lease land instead of selling it, and many private homes are on rented ground. Many feel that with land prices going up all the time, only the very rich land developers will be able to purchase, and the "people" of Hawaii will become even more land-poor.

"The land and industries of Hawaii are owned by old families and large corporations, and Hawaii is only so large."

—Jack London

Hawaii State Archives

PEOPLE

Nowhere else on Earth can you find such a kaleidoscopic mixture of people. Every major race is accounted for, and over 50 ethnic groups are represented throughout the islands, making Hawaii the most racially integrated state in the Union. Its population of one million includes 120,000 permanently stationed military personnel and their dependents, and it's the only state where whites are not the majority. About 60 percent of the people living in Hawaii were born there, 25 percent were born on the mainland U.S., and 15 percent of the people are foreign-born.

The population of Hawaii has been growing steadily in recent times, but it fluctuated wildly in times past. In 1876 it reached its lowest ebb, with only 55,000 permanent residents in the islands. This was the era of large sugar plantations, and their constant demand for labor was the primary cause for the importation of various peoples from around the world, which is what led to Hawaii's so racially integrated society. WW II saw Hawaii's population swell from 400,000 just prior to the war to 900,000 during the war. Naturally, 500,000 were military personnel who left at war's end, but many returned to settle after getting a taste of island living.

Of the one million people in the islands today, 800,000 live on Oahu, with over half of these living in the Honolulu Metropolitan Area. The rest of the population is distributed as follows: 93,000 on Hawaii, with 36,000 living in Hilo; 63,000 on Maui, with the largest concentration, 23,000, in Wailuku/Kahului; 40,000 on Kauai, including 230 pure-blood Hawaiians on Niihau; Molokai with 6,000; and Lanai with just over 2,000. The population density, statewide, is 156 people per square mile, slightly less than California's 183 people per square mile. The population is not at all evenly distributed, with Oahu claiming about 1,600 people per square mile, and Maui the second-most densely populated island with only 105 people per square mile. City dwellers outnumber those living in the country by four to one.

For most visitors, regardless of where they've come from, Oahu (especially Honolulu) will be the first place they've ever encountered such an integrated multiracial society. Various countries may be cosmopolitan, but nowhere will you meet so many individuals from such a diversity of ethnic groups, and mixes of these groups. You could be driven to your hotel by a Chinese-Portuguese cab driver, checked in by a Japanese-Hawaiian clerk, served lunch by a Korean waiter, serenaded by a Hawaiian-Italian-German musician, while an Irish-English-Filipino-French chambermaid tidies your room. This racial symphony is evident throughout Hawaii, but it's more apparent on Oahu, where the large population creates more opportunity for a racial hodgepodge. The warm feeling you get almost immediately upon arrival is that everyone belongs.

Population Figures

Oahu's 800,000 residents account for 80 percent of the state's population. All these people are on an island comprising only 10 percent of the state's land total. Sections of Waikiki can have a combined population of permanent residents and visitors as high as 90,000 per square mile, making cities like Tokyo, Hong Kong, and New York seem quite roomy by comparison. The good news is that Oahu *expects* all these people and knows how to accommodate them comfortably.

About 400,000 people live in greater Honolulu, generally considered the built-up area from Ewa to Koko Head. The next most populous urban centers after Honolulu are the Kailua-Kaneohe area with about 100,000 residents, followed by Pearl City and Waipahu with a combined total of about 75,000 or so. With all of these people, and such a finite land resource, real estate on the island is sky-high. A typical one-family home sells for $180,000, while a condo averages about $110,000. And for plenty of prime real estate, these figures would barely cover the down payment!

So where is everybody? Of the major ethnic groups you'll find the Hawaiians clustered around Waianae and on the windward coast near Waiahole; the whites tend to be in Wahiawa, around Koko Head, in Waikiki, and in Kailua-Kaneohe; those of Japanese ancestry prefer the valleys heading toward the Pali, including Kalihi, Nuuanu, and Tantalus; Filipinos live just east of the airport, in downtown Honolulu, around Barbers Point, and in Wahiawa; the Chinese are in Chinatown and around the Diamond Head area. Of the minor ethnic groups the highest concentration of blacks is in the Army towns around Schofield Barracks; Samoans live along with the Hawaiians in Waianae and the windward coastal towns, though the heaviest concentration is in downtown Honolulu not far from Aloha Tower; Koreans and Vietnamese are scattered here and there, but mostly in Honolulu.

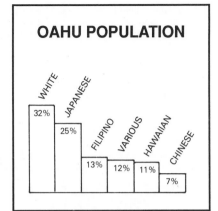

OAHU POPULATION

WHITE 32%
JAPANESE 25%
FILIPINO 13%
VARIOUS 12%
HAWAIIAN 11%
CHINESE 7%

THE HAWAIIANS

The study of the native Hawaiians is ultimately a study in tragedy because it ends in their demise as a viable people: when Capt. Cook first sighted Hawaii in 1778, there were an estimated 300,000 natives living in perfect harmony with their ecological surroundings; within 100 years a scant 50,000 demoralized and dejected Hawaiians existed almost as wards of the state. Today, although 115,000 people claim varying degrees of Hawaiian blood, experts say that less than 1,000 are pure Hawaiian, and this is stretching the point.

It's easy to see why people of Hawaiian lineage could be bitter over what they have lost, being strangers in their own land now, much like American Indians. The overwhelming majority of "Hawaiians" are of mixed heritage, and the wisest take the best from all worlds. From the Hawaiian side comes simplicity, love of the land, and acceptance of people. It is the Hawaiian legacy of *aloha* that remains immortal and adds that special elusive quality that *is* Hawaii.

Polynesian Roots

The Polynesians' original stock is muddled and remains an anthropological mystery, but it's believed that they were nomadic wanderers who migrated from both the Indian subcontinent and Southeast Asia through Indonesia, where they learned to sail and navigate on protected waterways. As they migrated they honed their sailing skills until they could take on the Pacific, and as they moved, they absorbed people from other cultures and races until they had coalesced into what we now know as Polynesians.

Abraham Fornander, still considered a major authority on the subject, wrote in his 1885 *Account of the Polynesian Race* that he believed the Polynesians started as a white (Aryan) race, which had been heavily influenced by contact with the Cushite Chaldeo-Arabian civilization. He estimated their ar-

The ali'i wore magnificent feathered capes that signified their rank. The noblest colors were red and yellow, provided by specialized hunters who snared and plucked just the right birds.

rival in Hawaii at A.D. 600, based on Hawaiian genealogical chants. Modern science seems to bear this date out, although it remains skeptical on his other surmises. According to others, the intrepid Polynesians who actually settled Hawaii are believed to have come from the Marquesas Islands, 1,000 miles southeast of Hawaii. The Marquesans were cannibals known for their tenacity and strength, attributes that would serve them well.

The Caste System

Hawaiian society was divided into rankings by a strict caste system determined by birth, and from which there was no chance of escaping. The highest rank was the *ali'i*, the chiefs and royalty. The impeccable genealogies of the *ali'i* were traced back to the gods themselves, and the chants *(mo'o ali'i)* were memorized and sung by professionals (called *ku'auhau)* who were themselves *ali'i*. Ranking passed from both father and mother and custom dictated that the first mating of an *ali'i* be with a person of equal status.

A *kahuna* was a highly skilled person whose advice was sought before any major project was undertaken, such as building a house, hollowing a canoe log, or even offering a prayer. The *mo'o kahuna* were the priests of Ku and Lono, and they were in charge of praying and following rituals. They were very powerful *ali'i* and kept strict secrets and laws concerning their various functions.

Besides this priesthood of *kahuna*, there were other *kahuna* who were not *ali'i* but commoners. The two most important were the healers *(kahuna lapa'au)*, and the black magicians *(kahuna ana'ana)*, who could pray a person to death. The *kahuna lapa'au* had a marvelous pharmacopeia of herbs and spices that could cure over 250 diseases common to the Hawaiians. The *kahuna ana'ana* could be hired to cast a love spell over a person or cause his untimely death. They seldom had to send out a reminder of payment!

The common people were called the *maka'ainana*, "the people of land"—the farmers, craftsmen, and fishermen. The land that they lived on was owned by the *ali'i*, but they were not bound to it. If the local *ali'i* was cruel or unfair, the *maka'ainana* had the right to leave and reside on another's lands. The *maka'ainana* mostly loved their local *ali'i* much like a child loves a parent, and the feeling was reciprocal. *Maka'ainana* who lived close to the *ali'i* and could be counted on as warriors in times of trouble were called *kanaka no lua kaua*, "a man for the heat of battle." They were treated with greater favor than those who lived in the backcountry, *kanaka no hii kua*, whose lesser standing opened them up to discrimination and cruelty. All *maka'ainana* formed extended families called *ohana* and they usually lived on the same section of land, called *ahuapua'a*. Those farmers who lived inland would barter their produce with the fishermen who lived on the shore, and thus all shared equally in the bounty of the land and sea.

A special group called *kauwa* was a landless, untouchable caste confined to living on reservations. Their origins were obviously Polynesian, but they appeared to be descendants of castaways who had survived and become perhaps the aboriginals of Hawaii before the main migrations. It was *kapu* for anyone to go onto *kauwa* lands, and doing so meant instant death. If a human sacrifice was needed, the *kahuna* would simply summon a *kauwa*, who had no recourse but to mutely comply. To this day, to call someone *kauwa*, which now supposedly only means servant, is still considered a fight-provoking insult.

Kapu And Day-to-day Life
There were occasional horrible wars, but mostly the people lived a quiet and ordered life based on a strict caste society and the *kapu* (taboo) system. Famine was known but only on a regional level, and the population was kept in check by birth control, crude abortions, and the distasteful practice of infanticide, especially of baby girls. The Hawaiians were absolutely loving and nurturing parents under most circumstances, and would even take in an adopted *hanai* (child or oldster), a lovely practice that lingers to this day.

A strict division of labor existed among men and women. Men were the only ones permitted to have anything to do with taro: this foodstuff was so sacred that it had a greater *kapu* than man himself. Men pounded poi and served it to the women. Men also were the fishermen and the builders of houses, canoes, irrigation ditches, and walls. Women tended to other gardens and shoreline fishing, and were responsible for making tapa

Ship's artist Jacques Arago depicts the harsh verdict delivered to a kapu *breaker, c. 1819 (Hawaii State Archives)*

cloth. The entire family lived in the common house called the *hale noa*.

Certain things were *kapu* between the sexes. Primarily, women could not enter the *mua* (man's house) nor could they eat with men. Certain foods such as pork and bananas were forbidden to women, and it was *kapu* for a man to have intercourse before going fishing, engaging in battle, or attending a religious ceremony. Young boys lived with the women until they underwent a circumcision rite called *pule ipu*. After this was performed, they were required to keep the *kapu* of men.

Ali'i could also declare a *kapu*, and often did so. Certain lands or fishing areas were temporarily made *kapu* so that they could revitalize. Even today, it is *kapu* for anyone to remove all the *opihi* (a type of limpet) from a rock. The great King Kamehameha I even placed a *kapu* on the body of his notoriously unfaithful child bride, Kaahumanu. It didn't work! The greatest *kapu (kapu moe)* was afforded to the highest ranking *ali'i*: anyone coming into their presence had to prostrate themselves. Lesser ranking *ali'i* were afforded the *kapu noho:* lessers had to sit or kneel in their presence. Commoners could not let their shadows fall upon an *ali'i* or enter their house except through a special door. Breaking a *kapu* meant immediate death.

Fatal Flaws

Less than 100 years after Capt. Cook's arrival, King Kalakaua found himself with only 48,000 Hawaiian subjects, down more than 80 percent. Wherever the king went, he would beseech his people, *Hooulu lahui,* "Increase the race," but it was already too late. It was as if nature herself had turned her back on these once proud people. Many of their marriages were barren and in 1874 when only 1,400 children were born, a full 75 percent died in infancy. The Hawaiians sat around and could do nothing as their race faded from existence.

The Causes Of Decline

The ecological system of Hawaii has always been exceptionally fragile and this included its people. When the white man came he

Aloha *still shows.*

found a great people who were large, strong, and virile, but when it came to fighting off the most minor diseases they proved as delicate as hothouse flowers. To exacerbate the situation, the Hawaiians were totally uninhibited toward sexual intercourse between willing partners, and they engaged in it openly and with abandon. Unfortunately, the sailors who arrived were full of syphilis and gonorrhea. The Hawaiian women brought these diseases home and, given the nature of Hawaiian society at the time, they spread like wildfire. By the time the missionaries came in 1820 and helped to halt the unbridled fornication, they estimated the native population at only 140,000, less than half of what it had been only 40 years since initial contact! In the next 50 years measles, mumps, influenza, and tuberculosis further ravaged the people. Hawaiian men were excellent sailors and it's estimated that during the whaling years, at least 25 percent of all able-bodied Hawaiian men sailed away, never to return.

But the *coup de grâce* that really ended the Hawaiian race, as such, was that all racial newcomers to the islands were attracted to the Hawaiians and the Hawaiians were in turn attracted to them. With so many interracial marriages, the Hawaiians literally bred themselves out of existence. By 1910, there were still twice as many full-blooded Hawaiians as mixed-bloods, but by 1940 mixed-blooded

Hawaiians were the fastest-growing group, and full-blooded the fastest declining.

Hawaiians Today

Many of the Hawaiians who moved to the cities became more and more disenfranchised. Their folk society stressed openness and a giving nature, but downplayed the individual and the ownership of private property. These cultural traits made them easy targets for the users and schemers until they finally became either apathetic or angry. Most surveys reveal that although Hawaiians number only 12 percent of the population, they account for almost 50 percent of the financially destitute families, and similarly, about half of arrests and illegitimate births. Niihau, a privately owned island, is home to about 250 pure-blood Hawaiians, representing the largest concentration of them, per capita, in the islands. The Robinson family, which owns the island, restricts visitors to invited guests only.

The second largest concentration is on Molokai, where 2,700 Hawaiians, living mostly on 40-acre *kuleana* of Hawaiian Homes Lands, make up 45 percent of that island's population. The majority of mixed-blood Hawaiians, 80,000 or so, live on Oahu, where they are particularly strong in the hotel and entertainment fields. People of Hawaiian extraction are still a delight to meet, and anyone so lucky as to be befriended by one long regards this friendship as the highlight of his travels. The Hawaiians have always given their *aloha* freely to all the peoples of the world, and it is we who must acknowledge this precious gift.

THE CHINESE

Next to Yankees from New England, the Chinese are the oldest migrant group in Hawaii, and their influence has far outshined their meager numbers. They brought to Hawaii, along with their individuality, Confucianism, Taoism, and Buddhism, although many have long since become Christians. The Chinese population at 57,000 makes up only six percent of the state's total, and the majority (52,000) reside on Oahu. As an ethnic group they account for the least amount of crime, the highest per capita income, and a disproportionate number of professionals.

Many believed that the devastating Chinatown fire of 1900 was deliberately allowed to burn in order to displace the Chinese population of Honolulu. (Hawaii State Archives)

The First Chinese

No one knows his name, but an unknown Chinese man is credited with being the first person in Hawaii to refine sugar. This Oriental wanderer tried his hand at crude refining on Lanai in 1802. Fifty years later the sugar plantations desperately needed workers, and the first Chinese brought to Hawaii under the newly passed Masters and Servants Act were 195 coolies from Amoy who arrived in 1852. These conscripts were contracted for three to five years and given $3 per month plus room and board. This was for 12 hours a day, six days a week, and even in 1852 these wages were the pits. The Chinese almost always left the plantations the minute their contracts expired. They went into business for themselves and promptly monopolized the restaurant and small shop trades.

The Chinese Niche

Although almost all people in Hawaii considered all Chinese the same, they were actually quite different. The majority came from Kwangtung Province in southern China. They were two distinct ethnic groups: the Punti made up 75 percent of the immigrants, and the Hakka made up the remainder. In China, they remained separate from each other, never mixing; in Hawaii, they mixed out of necessity. For one, hardly any Chinese women came over at first, and the ones who followed were at a premium and gladly accepted as wives, regardless of ethnic background. The Chinese were also one of the first groups who willingly intermarried with the Hawaiians, from whom they gained a reputation for being exceptionally caring husbands.

The Chinese accepted the social order and kept a low profile. For example, during the turbulent labor movements of the 1930s and '40s in Hawaii, the Chinese community produced not one labor leader, radical intellectual, or left-wing politician. When Hawaii became a state, one of the two senators elected was Hiram Fong, a racially mixed Chinese. Since statehood, the Chinese community has carried on business as usual as they continue to rise both economically and socially.

THE JAPANESE

Most scholars believe that (inevitably) a few Japanese castaways floated to Hawaii long before Capt. Cook arrived, and might have introduced iron, which the islanders seemed to be familiar with before the white men arrived. The first official arrivals were ambassadors sent by the Japanese shogun to negotiate in Washington; they stopped en route at Honolulu in March 1860. But it was as plantation workers that the Japanese were brought to the islands. A small group arrived in 1868, and mass migration started in 1885.

indentured Japanese plantation workers and mounted overseer

In 1886, because of famine, the Japanese government allowed farmers mainly from southern Honshu, Kyushu, and Okinawa to emigrate. Among these were members of Japan's little-talked-about untouchable caste, called *eta* or *burakumin* in Japan and *chorinbo* in Hawaii. They gratefully seized this opportunity to better their lot, an impossibility in Japan. The first Japanese migrants were almost all men. Between 1897 and 1908 migration was steady, with about 70 percent men and 30 percent women arriving. Afterwards, migration slowed because of a "Gentlemen's Agreement," a euphemism for racism against the "yellow peril." By 1900 there were over 60,000 Japanese in the islands, constituting the largest ethnic group.

AJAs, Americans Of Japanese Ancestry

Parents of most Japanese children born before WW II were *issei* (first generation), who considered themselves apart from other Americans and clung to the notion of "We Japanese." Their children, the *nisei* or second generation, were a different matter altogether. In one generation they had become Americans, and they put into practice the high Japanese virtues of obligation, duty, and loyalty to the homeland, and that homeland was now unquestionably America. After Pearl Harbor was bombed, the FBI kept close tabs on the Japanese community, and the menace of the "enemy within" prompted the decision to place Hawaii under martial law for the duration of the war. It has since been noted that not a single charge of espionage or sabotage was ever reported against the Japanese community in Hawaii during the war.

AJAs As GIs

Although Japanese had formed a battalion during WW I, they were insulted by being considered unacceptable as American soldiers in WW II. Some American-Japanese volunteered to serve in labor battalions, and because of their flawless work and loyalty, it was decided to put out a call for a few hundred volunteers to form a combat unit. Over 10,000 signed up! AJAs formed two distinguished units in WW II: the 100th Infantry Battalion, and later the 442nd Regimental

The Japanese GIs returned as "our boys."

Combat Team. They landed in Italy at Salerno and even fought from Guadalcanal to Okinawa. They distinguished themselves by becoming *the* most decorated unit in American military history.

The AJAs Return

Many returning AJAs took advantage of the G.I. Bill and received college educations. The "Big Five" Corporations (see p. 44) for the first time accepted former AJA officers as executives and the old order was changed. Many Japanese became involved with Hawaiian politics and the first elected to Congress was Daniel Inouye, who had lost an arm fighting in WW II. Hawaii's past governor, George Ariyoshi, elected in 1974, was the country's first Japanese-American ever to reach such a high office. Most Japanese, even as they climb the economic ladder, tend to remain Democrats.

Today, one out of every two political offices in Hawaii is held by a Japanese-American. In one of those weird quirks of fate, it is now the Hawaiian Japanese who are accused by other ethnic groups of engaging in unfair political practices—nepotism and reverse discrimination. Many of these accusations against AJAs are undoubtedly motivated by jealousy, but the AJAs' record with social fairness issues is not without blemish; true to their custom of family loyalty, they do stick together.

There are now 240,000 people in Hawaii of Japanese ancestry, one-quarter of the state's population. They are the least likely of any ethnic person in Hawaii to marry outside of their group—especially the men— and they enjoy a higher-than-average standard of living.

CAUCASIANS

White people have a distinction from all other ethnic groups in Hawaii: they are all lumped together as one. You can be anything from a Protestant Norwegian dockworker to a Greek Orthodox shipping tycoon, but if your skin is white, in Hawaii, you're a *haole*. What's more, you could have arrived at Waikiki from Missoula, Montana, in the last 24 hours, or your *kamaaina* family can go back five generations, but again, if you're white, you're a *haole*.

The word *haole* has a floating connotation that depends upon the spirit in which it's used. It can mean everything from a derisive "honky" or "cracker" to nothing more than "white person." The exact Hawaiian meaning is clouded, but some say it meant "a man of no background," because white men couldn't chant a genealogical *kanaenae* telling the Hawaiians who they were. *Haole* then became euphemised into "foreign white man" and today, simply "white person."

White History
Next to Hawaiians themselves, white people have the oldest stake in Hawaii. They've been there as settlers in earnest since the missionaries of the 1820s, and were established long before any other migrant group. From last century until statehood, old *haole* families owned and controlled everything, and although they were generally benevolent, philanthropic, and paternalistic, they were also racist. They were established *kamaaina* families, many of whom made up the boards of the Big Five Corporations, or owned huge plantations and formed an inner social circle that was closed to the outside. Many managed to find mates from among close family acquaintances.

Their paternalism, which they accepted with grave responsibility, at first only extended to the Hawaiians, who saw them as replacing their own *ali'i*. Orientals were considered "primarily as instruments of production." These supremacist attitudes tended to drag on in Hawaii until quite recent times. They are today responsible for the sometimes sour relations between white and nonwhite people in the islands. Today, all individual white people are resented to a certain degree because of these past acts, even though they personally were in no way involved.

White Plantation Workers
In the 1880s the white landowners looked around and felt surrounded and outnumbered by Orientals, so they tried to import white people for plantation work. None of their schemes seemed to work out. Europeans were accustomed to a much higher wage scale and better living conditions than were provided on the plantations. Although only workers and not considered the equals of the ruling elite, they still were expected to act like a special class. They were treated preferentially, which meant higher wages for the same job performed by an Oriental. Some of the imported workers included: 600 Scandinavians in 1881; 1,400 Germans from 1881-85; 400 Poles from 1897-98; and 2,400 Russians, from 1909-12. Many proved troublesome, like the Poles and Russians who staged strikes after only months on the job.

Many quickly moved to the Mainland. A contingency of Scots, who first came as mule skinners, did become successful plantation managers and supervisors. The Germans and Scandinavians were well received and climbed the social ladder rapidly, becoming professionals and skilled workers.

The Depression years, not as economically bad in Hawaii as in the continental U.S., brought many Mainland whites seeking opportunity, mostly from the South and the West. These new people were even more racist toward brown-skinned people and Orientals than the *kamaaina haoles,* and they made matters worse. They also competed more intensely for jobs. The racial tension generated during this period came to a head in 1932 with the infamous "Massie Rape Case."

The Massie Rape Case

Thomas Massie, a naval officer, and his young wife Thalia attended a party at the Officers Club. After drinking and dancing all evening, they got into a row and Thalia rushed out in a huff. A few hours later, Thalia was at home, confused and hysterical, claiming to have been raped by some local men. On the most circumstantial evidence, Joseph Kahahawai and four friends of mixed ethnic background were accused. In a highly controversial trial rife with racial tensions, the verdict ended in a hung jury.

While a new trial was being set, Kahahawai and his friends were out on bail. Seeking revenge, Thomas Massie and Grace Fortescue, Thalia's mother, kidnapped Joseph Kahawai with a plan of extracting a confession from him. They were aided by two enlisted men assigned to guard Thalia. While questioning Joseph, they killed him and attempted to dump his body in the sea but were apprehended. Another controversial trial—this time for Mrs. Fortescue, Massie, and the accomplices—followed. Clarence Darrow, the famous lawyer, sailed to Hawaii to defend them. For killing Kahahawai, these people served *one hour* of imprisonment in the judge's private chambers. The other four, acquitted with Joseph Kahahawai, maintain innocence of the rape to this day. Later, the

Massies divorced, and Thalia went on to become a depressed alcoholic who took her own life.

The Portuguese

The last time anyone looked, Portugal was still attached to the European continent, but for some anomalous reason the Portuguese weren't considered *haoles* in Hawaii for the longest time. About 12,000 arrived from 1878 to 1887 and another 6,000 came between 1906 and 1913. Accompanied during this period by 8,000 Spanish, they were considered one and the same. Most of the Portuguese were illiterate peasants from Madeira and the Azores, and the Spanish hailed from Andalusia. They were very well received, and because they were white but not *haole* they made a perfect "buffer" ethnic group. Committed to staying in Hawaii, they rose to be skilled workers—the *"luna* class" on the plantations. They, however, de-emphasized education and became very racist toward Orientals, regarding them as a threat to their job security.

By 1920 the 27,000 Portuguese made up 11 percent of the population. After that they tended to blend with the other ethnic groups and weren't counted separately. Portuguese men tended to marry within their ethnic group, but a good portion of Portuguese women married other white men and became closer to the *haole* group, while another large portion chose Hawaiian mates and grew further away. Although they didn't originate pidgin English (see "Language"), the unique melodious quality of their native tongue did give pidgin that certain lilt it has today. Also, the ukulele ("jumping flea") was closely patterned after the *cavaquinho,* a Portuguese stringed folk instrument.

The White Population

Today all white people together make up the largest racial, if not ethnic, group in the islands at 33 percent (about 330,000) of the population. There are heavy white concentrations throughout Oahu especially in Waikiki, Kailua-Kaneohe, and around Pearl City. The white population is the fastest growing in the islands, because most people resettling in *carver at International Market Place, Waikiki*

Hawaii are white Americans predominantly from the West Coast.

FILIPINOS AND OTHERS

The Filipinos who came to Hawaii brought high hopes of making a fortune and returning home as rich heroes: for most it was a dream that never came true. Filipinos had been American nationals ever since the Spanish-American War of 1898, and as such weren't subject to immigration laws that curtailed the importation of Oriental workers at the turn of this century. The first to arrive were 15 families in 1906, but a large number came in 1924 as strikebreakers. The majority were illiterate peasants called *Ilocanos* from the northern Philippines, with about 10 percent Visayans from the central cities. The Visayans were not as hard-working or thrifty, but were much more sophisticated. From the first, Filipinos were looked down upon by all the other immigrant groups, and were considered particularly uncouth by the Japanese. They put the least amount of value on education of any group, and even by 1930 only about half could speak rudimentary English, the majority remaining illiterate. They were billeted in the worst housing, performed the most menial jobs, and were the last hired and first fired.

One big difference with Filipinos was that they had no women to marry, so they clung to the idea of returning home. In 1930 there were 30,000 men and only 360 women. This hopeless situation led to a great deal of prostitution and homosexuality; many of these terribly lonely bachelors would feast and drink on weekends and engage in their gruesome but exciting pastime of cockfighting on Sundays. When some did manage to find wives, their mates were inevitably part Hawaiian. Today, there are still plenty of old Filipino bachelors who never managed to get home, and the Sunday cockfights remain a way of life.

The Filipinos constitute 14 percent of Hawaii's population (140,000) with almost 90 percent living on Oahu. Many visitors to Hawaii mistake Filipinos for Hawaiians because of their dark skin, and this is a minor irritant to both groups. Some streetwise Filipinos even claim to be Hawaiians, because being Hawaiian is "in" and goes over well with the tourists, especially the young women tourists. For the most part, these people are hard-working, dependable laborers who do tough work for little recognition. They still remain low man on the social totem pole and have not yet organized politically to stand up for their rights.

Other Groups

About 10 percent of Hawaii's population is made up of a conglomerate of small ethnic groups. Of these, the largest is Korean with 14,000 people. About 8,000 Koreans came to Hawaii from 1903 until 1905, when their own government halted emigration. During the same period about 6,000 Puerto Ricans arrived, but they have become so assimilated that only 4,000 people in Hawaii today consider themselves Puerto Rican. There were also two attempts made last century to import other Polynesians to strengthen the dying Hawaiian race, but they were failures. In 1869 only 126 central Polynesian natives could be lured to Hawaii, and from 1878 to 1885 2,500 Gilbert Islanders arrived. Both groups became immediately disenchanted with Hawaii. They pined away for their own islands and departed for home as soon as possible.

Today, however, 12,000 Samoans have settled in Hawaii, and with more on the way they are the fastest growing minority in the state. For unexplainable reasons, Samoans and native Hawaiians get along extremely poorly and have the worst racial tensions and animosity of any groups. The Samoans ostensibly should represent the archetypical Polynesians that the Hawaiians are seeking, but it doesn't work that way. Samoans are criticized by Hawaiians for their hot tempers, lingering feuds, and petty jealousies. They're clannish and often are the butt of "dumb" jokes. This racism seems especially ridiculous, but that's the way it is.

Just to add a bit more exotic spice to the stew, there are about 10,000 blacks, a few thousand American Indians, and a smattering of Vietnamese refugees.

LANGUAGE

Hawaii is America and people speak English there, but that's not the whole story. If you turn on the TV to catch the evening news, you'll hear "Walter Cronkite" English, unless of course you happen to tune in a Japanese-language broadcast designed for tourists from that country. You can easily pick up a Chinese-language newspaper, or groove to the music on a Filipino radio station, but let's not confuse the issue. All your needs and requests at airports, car rental agencies, restaurants, hotels, or wherever you happen to travel will be completely understood, as well as answered, in English. However, when you happen to overhear "islanders" speaking, what they're saying will sound somewhat familiar, but you won't be able to pick up all the words, and the beat and melody of the language will be noticeably different.

Hawaii, like New England, the deep South, and the Midwest, has its own unmistakable linguistic regionalism. All the ethnic peoples who make up Hawaii have enriched the English spoken there with words, expressions, and subtle shades of meaning that are commonly used and understood throughout the islands. The greatest influence on English has come from the Hawaiian language itself, and words such as aloha, hula, and muumuu are familiarly used and understood by most Americans.

Other migrant peoples, especially the Chinese, Japanese, and Portuguese, influenced the local dialect to such an extent that the simplified plantation lingo that they spoke has become known as "pidgin." A fun and enriching part of the "island experience" is picking up a few words of Hawaiian and pidgin. English is the official language of the state, business, education, and perhaps even the mind; but pidgin is the language of the people, the emotions, and life, while Hawaiian remains the language of the heart and the soul.

PIDGIN

The dictionary definition of pidgin is: a simplified language with a rudimentary grammar used as a means of communication between people speaking different languages. Hawaiian pidgin is a little more complicated than that. It had its roots during the plantation days of last century when white owners and *luna* had to communicate with recently arrived Chinese, Japanese, and Portuguese laborers. It was designed as a simple language of the here and now, and was primarily con-

CAPSULE PIDGIN

The following are a few commonly used words and expressions that should give you an idea of pidgin. It really can't be written properly, merely approximated, but for now, *"Brah, study da' kine an' bimbye you be hele on, brah! O.K.? Lesgo."*

an' den—and then? big deal; so what's next; how boring

bimbye—after a while; bye and bye. "Bimbye, you learn pidgin."

blalah—brother, but actually only refers to a large, heavy-set, good-natured Hawaiian man

brah—all the bros in Hawaii are brahs; brother; pal. Used to call someone's attention. One of the most common words used even among people who are not acquainted. After a fill-up at a gas station, a person would say "Tanks, brah."

cockaroach—steal; rip off. If you really want to find out what *cockaroach* means, just leave your camera on your beach blanket when you take a little dip.

da' kine—a catchall word of many meanings that epitomizes the essence of pidgin. *Da' kine* is easily used as a euphemism for pidgin and is substituted whenever the speaker is at a loss for a word or just wants to generalize. It can mean: you know? watchamacallit; of that type.

geev um—give it to them; give them hell; go for it. Can be used as an encouragement. If a surfer is riding a great wave, the people on the beach might yell, "Geev um, brah!"

hana ho—again. Especially after a concert the audience shouts "hana ho" (one more!).

hele on—right on! hip; with it; groovy

howzit?—as in "howzit brah?" what's happening? how is it going? The most common greeting, used in place of the more formal "How do you do?"

hu hu—angry! "You put the make on the wrong da' kine wahine brah, and you in da' kine trouble, if you get one big Hawaiian blalah plenty hu hu."

kapu—a Hawaiian word meaning forbidden. If *kapu* is written on a gate or posted on a tree it means "No trespassing." *Kapu*-breakers are still very unpopular in the islands.

lesgo—Let's go! Do it!

li'dis an' li'dat—like this or that; a catchall grouping especially if you want to avoid details; like, ya' know?

lolo buggah—stupid or crazy guy (person). Words to a tropical island song go, "I want to find the lolo who stole my pakalolo."

mo' bettah—real good!; great idea. An island sentiment used to be, "mo' bettah you *come* Hawaii." Now it has subtly changed to, "mo' bettah you *visit* Hawaii."

ono—number one! delicious; great; groovy. "Hawaii is ono, brah!"

pakalolo—literally "crazy smoke"; marijuana; grass; reefer. "Hey, brah! Maui-wowie da' kine ono pakalolo."

pakiki head—stubborn; bull-headed

pau—a Hawaiian word meaning finished; done; over and done with. *Pau hana* means end of work or quitting time. Once used by plantation workers, now used by everyone.

stink face—basically frowning at someone; using facial expression to show displeasure. Hard looks. What you'll get if you give local people a hard time.

swell head—burned up; angry

talk story—spinning yarns; shooting the breeze; throwing the bull; a rap session. If you're lucky enough to be around to hear *kapuna* (elders) "talk story," you can hear some fantastic tales in the tradition of old Hawaii.

tita—sister, but only used to describe a fun-loving, down-to-earth country girl

waddascoops—what's the scoop? what's up? what's happening?

cerned with the necessary functions of working, eating, and sleeping. It has an economical noun-verb-object structure (not necessarily in that order).

Hawaiian words make up most of pidgin's non-English vocabulary. There is a good smattering of Chinese, Japanese, Samoan, and the distinctive rising inflection is provided by the melodious Mediterranean lilt of the Portuguese. Pidgin is not a stagnant language. It's kept alive by hip new words introduced by people who are "so radical," or especially by slang words introduced by teenagers. It's a colorful English, like "jive" or "ghettoese" spoken by American blacks, and is as regionally unique as the speech of Cajuns from Louisiana's bayous. *Maka'ainana* of all socioethnic backgrounds can at least understand pidgin. Most islanders are proud of it, while some consider it a low-class jargon. The Hawaiian House of Representatives has given pidgin an official sanction, and most people feel that it adds a real local style and should be preserved.

Pidgin Lives

Pidgin is first learned at school, where all students, regardless of background, are exposed to it. The pidgin spoken by young people today is "fo' real" different from that of their parents. It's no longer only plantation talk, but has moved to the streets and picked up some sophistication. At one time there was an academic movement to exterminate it, but that idea died away with the same thinking that insisted on making left-handed people write with their right hand. It is strange, however, that pidgin has become the unofficial language of Hawaii's grass-roots movement, when it actually began as a white owners' language which was used to supplant Hawaiian and all other languages brought to the islands.

Although hip young *haoles* use it all the time, it has gained some of the connotation of being the language of the nonwhite locals, and is part of the "us against them" way of thinking. All local people, *haole* or not, do consider pidgin their own island language, and don't really like it when it's used by *malihini* (newcomers). If you're in the islands

long enough, you don't have to bother learning pidgin; it'll learn you. There's a book sold all over the islands called *Pidgin to da Max,* written by (you guessed it) a *haole* from Nebraska named Doug Simonson. You might not be able to understand what's being said by locals speaking pidgin (that's usually the idea), but you should be able to *feel* what's being meant.

HAWAIIAN

The Hawaiian language sways like a palm tree in a gentle wind. Its words are as melodious as a love song. Linguists say that you can learn a lot about people through their language: when you hear Hawaiian you think of gentleness and love, and it's hard to imagine the ferocious side so evident in Hawaii's past. With many Polynesian root words

THE ALPHABET.

VOWELS.		SOUND.	
	Names.	Ex. in Eng.	Ex. in Hawaii.
A a	---â	as in *father*,	la—sun.
E e	--- a	— *tete*,	hemo—cast off.
I i	--- e	— *marine*,	marie—quiet.
O o	--- o	— *over*,	ono—sweet.
U u	--- oo	—*rule*,	nui—large.

CONSONANTS.	Names.	CONSONANTS.	Names.
B b	be	N n	nu
D d	de	P p	pi
H h	he	R r	ro
K k	ke	T t	ti
L l	la	V v	vi
M m	mu	W w	we

The following are used in spelling foreign words:

F f	fe	S s	se
G g	ge	Y y	yi

1

cover page of the first Hawaiian primer

that are easily traced to Indonesian and Malayan, it's evident that Hawaiian is from this same stock. The Hawaiian spoken today is very different from old Hawaiian. Its greatest metamorphosis occurred when the missionaries began to write it down in the 1820s. There is a movement to reestablish the Hawaiian language, and courses in it are offered at the University of Hawaii. Many scholars have put forth translations of Hawaiian, but there are endless, volatile disagreements in the academic sector about the real meanings of Hawaiian words. Hawaiian is no longer spoken as a language except on Niihau, and the closest tourists will come to it is in place names, street names, and in words that have become part of common usage, such as aloha and *mahalo*. A few old Hawaiians still speak it at home and there are sermons in Hawaiian at some local churches. Kawaiahao Church in downtown Honolulu is the most famous of these. (See the Glossary for lists of commonly used Hawaiian words.)

Wiki Wiki Hawaiian

Thanks to the missionaries, the Hawaiian language is rendered phonetically using only 12 letters. They are the five vowels, a-e-i-o-u, sounded as they are in Italian, and seven consonants, h-k-l-m-n-p-w, sounded exactly as they are in English. Sometimes "w" is pronounced as "v," but this only occurs in the middle of a word and always follows a vowel. A consonant is always followed by a vowel, forming two-letter syllables, but vowels are often found in pairs or even triplets. A slight oddity about Hawaiian is the "glottal stop." This is merely an abrupt break in sound in the middle of a word such as "oh-oh" in English, and is denoted with an apostrophe ('). A good example is *ali'i* or even better, the Oahu town of **Ha'iku**, which actually means "abrupt break."

Pronunciation Key

For those unfamiliar with the sounds of Italian or other Romance languages, the vowels are sounded as follows:

A—in stressed syllables, long *a* as in "Ah" (that feels good!). For example, Haleakala

(Hah lay ah kah lah.) Unstressed syllables get a short "a" as in "again" or "above." For example, Kamehameha (**Ka**me**ha**me**ha**).

E—short **e** as in p**e**n or d**e**nt (Hal**e**). Long **e** sounded as "ay" as in sw**ay** or d**ay**. For example the Hawaiian goose (**Ne ne**) is a "nay nay," not a "knee knee."

I—a long **i** as in s**ee** or w**e** (Hawa**ii** or pal**i**).

O—round **o** as in n**o** or **o**h (k**o**a, or **OnO**).

U—round **u** like "d**o**" or "st**ew**."(kap**u**, or p**u**na).

Diphthongs

There are also eight vowel pairs known as "diphthongs" (ae-ai-ao-au-ei-eu-oi-ou). These are the sounds made by gliding from one vowel to another within a syllable. The stress is placed on the first vowel. In English, examples would be s**oi**l and **eu**phoria. Common examples in Hawaiian are l**ei** (lay) and *h**ei**au*.

Stress

The best way to learn which syllables are stressed in Hawaiian is just by listening closely. It becomes obvious after a while. There are also some vowel sounds that are held longer than others and these can occur at the beginning of a word such as the first "a" in *aina* or in the middle of a word like the first "a" in *lanai*. Again, it's a matter of tuning your ear and paying attention. No one is going to give you a hard time if you mispronounce a word. It's good, however, to pay close attention to the pronunciation of street and place names because many Hawaiian words sound alike and a misplaced vowel here or there could be the difference in getting to where you want to go and getting lost.

CAPSULE HAWAIIAN

The list on the following pages is merely designed to give you a "taste" of Hawaiian and to provide a basic vocabulary of words in common usage which you are likely to hear. Becoming familiar with them is not a strict necessity, but they will definitely enhance your experience and make it more congenial when talking with local people. You'll soon notice that many islanders spice their speech with certain words, especially when they're speaking "pidgin," and you too can use them just as soon as you feel comfortable. You might even discover some Hawaiian words that are so perfectly expressive that they'll become a regular part of your vocabulary. Many Hawaiian words have actually made it into the English dictionary. Place names, historical names, and descriptive terms used throughout the text may not appear in the lists below, but will be cited in the glossary at the back of the book. Also see "Pidgin," "Food," and "Getting Around" for applicable Hawaiian words and phrases in these categories. The definitions given are not exhaustive, but are generally considered the most common.

BASIC VOCABULARY

a'a—rough clinker lava. *A'a* has become the correct geological term to describe this type of lava found anywhere in the world.

ae—yes

akamai—smart; clever; wise

ali'i—a Hawaiian chief or nobleman

aloha—the most common greeting in the islands. Can mean both hello and goodbye, welcome or farewell. It also can mean romantic love, affection or best wishes.

aole—no

hale—house or building; often combined with other words to name a specific place such as Haleakala ("House of the Sun"), or Hale Pai at Lahainaluna, meaning "printing house"

hana—work; combined with *pau* means end of work or quitting time

haole—a word that at one time meant foreigner, but now means a white person or Caucasian. Many etymological definitions have been put forth, but none satisfy everyone. Some feel that it signified a person without a background, because the first white men could not chant their genealogies as was common to Hawaiians.

hapai—pregnant. Used by all ethnic groups when a *keiki* is on the way.

hapa—half, as in a mixed-blooded person being refered to as *hapa haole*

heiau—a traditional Hawaiian temple. A platform made of skillfully fitted rocks, upon which structures were built and offerings made to the gods

holomuu—an ankle-length dress that is much more fitted than a muumuu, and which is often worn on formal occasions

hoolaulea—any happy event, but especially a family outing or picnic

hoomalimali—sweet talk; flattery

hu hu—angry; irritated; mad

huli huli—barbecue, as in *huli huli* chicken

hula—a native Hawaiian dance where the rhythm of the islands is captured in swaying hips and the stories told by lyrically moving hands

hui—a group; meeting; society. Often used to refer to Chinese businessmen or familiy members who pool their money to get businesses started.

imu—underground oven filled with hot rocks and used for baking. The main cooking feature at a luau, used to steam-bake the pork and other succulent dishes. Traditionally the tending of the *imu* was for men only.

ipo—sweetheart; lover; girl or boyfriend

kahuna—priest; sorcerer; doctor; skillful person. *Kahuna* had tremendous power in old Hawaii which they used for both good and evil. The *Kahuna ana'ana* was a feared individual because he practiced "black magic" and could pray a person to death, while a *Kahuna lapa'au* was medical practitioner bringing aid and comfort to the people.

kalua—means roasted underground in an *imu*. A favorite island food is *kalua* pork.

kamaaina—a child of the land; an old-timer; a longtime island resident of any ethnic background; a resident of Hawaii or native son. Oftentimes, hotels and airlines offer discounts called *"kamaaina* rates" to anyone who can prove island residency.

kane—means man, but is actually used to signify a husband or boyfriend. Written on a door, it means "Men's Room."

kapu—forbidden; taboo; keep out; do not touch

kapuna—a grandparent or old-timer; usually means someone who has gained wisdom. The statewide school system now invites *kapuna* to talk to the children about the old ways and methods.

kaukau—slang word meaning food or chow; grub. Some of the best eating in Hawaii is from *"kaukau* wagons," which are trucks from which plate lunches and other morsels are sold.

keiki—child or children; used by all ethnic groups. "Have you hugged your *keiki* today?"

kokua—help. As in "Your *kokua* is needed to keep Hawaii free from litter."

kona wind—a muggy subtropical wind that blows from the south and hits the leeward side of the islands. It usually brings sticky hot weather, and is one of the few times when air-conditioning will be appreciated.

lanai—veranda or porch. You'll pay more for a hotel room if it has a lanai with an ocean view.

lei—a traditional garland of flowers or vines. One of Hawaii's most beautiful customs. Given at any auspicious occasion, but especially when arriving or leaving Hawaii.

limu—varieties of edible seaweed gathered from the shoreline. It makes an excellent salad, and is used to garnish many island dishes—a favorite at luaus.

lomilomi—traditional Hawaiian massage; also, a vinegared salad made up of raw salmon, chopped onions, and spices

lua—the toilet; the head; the bathroom

luau—a Hawaiian feast featuring poi, *imu* baked pork and other traditional foods. A good luau provides some of the best gastronomical delights in the world.

mahalo—thanks; thank you. *Mahalo nui* means big thanks or thank you very much.

mahu—a homosexual; often used derisively like "fag" or "queer"

makai—toward the sea; used by most islanders when giving directions

malihini—what you are if you have just arrived: a newcomer; a tenderfoot; a recent arrival

manauahi—free; gratis; extra

manini—stingy; tight. A Hawaiianized word taken from the name of Don Francisco *Marin,* who was instrumental in bringing many fruits and plants to Hawaii. He was known for never sharing any of the bounty from his substantial gardens on Vineyard Street in Honolulu; therefore his name came to mean stingy.

mauka—toward the mountains; used by most islanders when giving directions

mauna—mountain. Often combined with other words to be more descriptive, as in Mauna Kea ("White Mountain").

moana—the ocean; the sea. Many businesses and hotels as well as place names have *moana* as part of their name.

muumuu—the garment introduced by the missionaries to cover the nakedness of the Hawaiians. A "Mother Hubbard," a long dress with a high neckline that has become fashionable attire for almost any occasion in Hawaii.

ohana—a family; the fundamental social division; extended family. Now used to denote a social organization with "grassroots," as in the "Save Kahoolawe Ohana."

okolehau—literally "iron bottom"; a traditional booze made from *ti* root; *okole* means your "rear end" and *hau* means iron, which was descriptive of the huge blubber pots that it was made in. Also, if you drink too much it'll surely knock you on your *okole*.

ono—delicious; delightful; the best. *Ono ono* means "extra or absolutely" delicious.

opu—belly; stomach

pa'hoehoe—smooth ropey lava that looks like burnt pancake batter. *Pa'hoehoe* is now the correct geological term used to describe this type of lava found anywhere in the world.

pakalolo—"crazy smoke"; marijuana; grass; smoke; dope

pali—a cliff; precipice. Hawaii's geology makes them quite common. The most famous are the *pali* of Oahu where a major battle was fought.

paniolo—a Hawaiian cowboy. Derived from the Spanish *espaniola*. The first cowboys brought in during the early 19th century were Mexicans from California.

pau—finished; done; completed. Often combined into *pau hana,* which means end of work or quitting time.

pilau—stink; smells bad; stench

pilikia—trouble of any kind, big or small; bad times

pono—righteous or excellent

poi—a glutinous paste made from the pounded corn of taro which, slightly fermented, has a light sour taste. Purplish in color, it is a staple at luaus, where it is called one-, two-, or three-finger poi, depending upon its thickness.

puka—a hole of any size. *Puka* is used by all island residents and can be employed when talking about a tiny *puka* in a rubber boat or a *puka* (tunnel) through a mountain.

punee—bed; narrow couch. Used by all ethnic groups. To recline on a *punee* on a breezy lanai is a true island treat.

pupule—crazy; nuts; out of your mind

pu pu—an appetizer; a snack; hors d'oeuvres; can be anything from cheese and crackers to sushi. Oftentimes, bars or nightclubs offer them free.

tapa—a traditional paper cloth made from beaten bark. Intricate designs were stamped in using beaters, and color was added with natural dyes. The tradition was lost in Hawaii, but is now making a comeback, and provides some of the most beautiful folk art in the islands.

tutu—grandmother; granny; older woman. Used by all as a term of respect and endearment.

ukulele—*uku* means "flea" and **lele** means "jumping," thus ukelele means "jumping flea," which was the way the Hawaiians perceived the quick finger movements on the banjo-type Portuguese folk instrument called a *cavaquinho*. The ukulele quickly became synonymous with the islands.

wahine—young woman; female; girl; wife. Used by all ethnic groups. When written on a door means "Women's Room."

wai—fresh water; drinking water

wela—hot. *Wela kahao* is a "hot time" or "making whoopee."

wiki—quickly; fast; in a hurry. Often seen as *wiki wiki* ("very fast"), as in "Wiki wiki Messenger Service."

USEFUL PHRASES

Aloha ahiahi—Good evening.
Aloha au ia oe—I love you!
Aloha kakahiaka—Good morning.
aloha nui loa—much love; fondest regards
Hauoli la hanau—Happy Birthday.

Hauoli makahiki hau—Happy New Year.
komo mai—please come in; enter; welcome
Mele Kalikimaka—Merry Christmas.
okole maluna—bottoms up; salute; cheers; kampai

RELIGION

The Lord saw fit to keep His island paradise secret from mankind for a few million years, but once we finally arrived we were awfully thankful. Hawaii sometimes appears like a floating tabernacle; everywhere you look there's a church, temple, shrine, or *heiau*. The islands are either a very holy place, or there's a powerful lot of sinning going on that would require so many houses of prayer. Actually, it's just America's "right to worship" concept fully employed . . . in microcosm. All the peoples who came to Hawaii brought their own form of devotion. The Polynesian Hawaiians praised the primordial creators, Wakea and Papa, from whom their pantheon of animistically inspired gods sprang. Obviously to a modern world these old gods would never do. Unfortunately for the old gods, there were simply too many of them, and belief in them was looked upon as mere superstition, the folly of semicivilized pagans. So the famous missionaries of the 1820s brought Congregational Christianity and the "true path" to heaven.

Inconveniently, the Catholics, Mormons, Reformed Mormons, Adventists, Episcopalians, Unitarians, Christian Scientists, Lutherans, Baptists, Jehovah's Witnesses, Salvation Army, and every other major and minor denomination of Christianity that followed in their wake brought their own brand of enlightenment and never quite agreed with each other. The Chinese and Japanese migrants came and established all the major sects of Buddhism, Confucianism, Taoism, and Shintoism. Allah is praised, the Torah is chanted in Jewish synagogues, and nirvana is available at a variety of Hindu temples. If the spirit moves you, a Hare Krishna devotee will be glad to point you in the right direction and give you a free flower for only a dollar or two. If the world is still too much with you, you might find peace at a Church of Scientology, or meditate at a Kundalini Yoga institute, or perhaps find relief at a local assembly of Baha'i. Anyway, rejoice, because in Hawaii you'll not only find paradise, but you might even find salvation.

HAWAIIAN BELIEFS

The Polynesian Hawaiians worshipped nature. They saw its forces manifested in a multiplicity of forms to which they ascribed godlike powers, and daily life was based on this animistic philosophy. Handpicked and specially trained storytellers chanted the exploits of the gods. These ancient tales, kept alive in a special oral tradition called *moolelo*, were recited only by day. Entranced listeners encircled the chanter; in respect for the gods and in fear of their wrath, they were forbidden to move once the tale was begun. This was serious business where a man's life could be at stake. It was not like the telling of *kaao*, which were simple fictions, tall tales, and yarns of ancient heroes, merely related for amusement and to pass the long nights. Any object, animate or inanimate, could be a god. All could be infused with mana, especially a dead body, or a respected ancestor.

Ohana had personal family gods called *amakua* whom they called on in times of danger or strife. There were children of gods called *kupua* who were thought to live among men and were distinguished either for their beauty and strength or for their ugliness and terror. It was told that processions of dead *ali'i*, called "Marchers of the Night," wandered through the land of the living and unless you were properly protected it could mean death if they looked upon you. There were simple ghosts known as *akua lapu* who merely frightened people. Forests, waterfalls, trees, springs, and a thousand forms of nature were the manifestations of *akua li'i*, "little spirits" who could be invoked at any time for help or protection. It made no difference who or what you were in old Hawaii, the gods were ever-present and they took a direct and active role in your life.

Behind all of these beliefs was an innate sense of natural balance and order. It could be interpreted as positive-negative, yin-yang, plus-minus, life-death, light-dark, whatever, but the main idea was that everything had its opposite. The time of darkness when only the gods lived was *po*. When the great gods descended to the Earth and created light, this was *ao* and man was born. All of these *moolelo* are part of the *Kumulipo*, the great chant that records the Hawaiian version of creation. From the time the gods descended and touched Earth at Ku Moku on Lanai, where the genealogies were kept. Unlike the Bible, these included the noble families of female *ali'i* as well as males.

Note: For more information regarding life in pre-contact Hawaii please see p. 15.

THE STRIFES OF MAUI

Of all the heroes and mythological figures of Polynesia, Maui is the best known. His "strifes" are like the great Greek epics, and they make excellent tales of daring that elders loved to relate to youngsters around the evening campfire. Maui was abandoned by his mother, Hina of Fire, when he was an infant. She wrapped him in her hair and cast him upon the sea where she expected him to die; he lived and returned home to become her favorite. She knew then that he was a

Kukailimoku, Kamehameha's war god, was 30 inches tall. Fashioned from feathers, it presented a horrible sight with its gaping mouth of dog's teeth and was reputed to utter loud cries while battle was being waged.

born hero and had strength far beyond that of ordinary mortals. His first exploit was to lift the sky. In those days the sky hung so low that men had to crawl around on all fours. Then a seductive young woman approached Maui and asked him to use his great strength to lift the sky. In fine heroic fashion, the big boy agreed, if the beautiful woman would euphemistically "give him a drink from her gourd." He then obliged her by lifting the sky, and he might even have made the earth move for her once or twice.

More Land

The territory of man was small at that time. Maui decided that more land was needed, so he conspired to "fish up islands." He descended into the land of the dead and petitioned an ancestress to fashion him a hook out of her jawbone. She obliged, and created the mythical hook, *Manai ikalani*. Maui then secured a sacred *alae* bird that he intended to use for bait and bid his brothers to paddle him far out to sea. When he arrived at the deepest spot, he lowered *Manai ikalani* baited with the sacred bird, and his sister, Hina of the Sea, placed it into the mouth of "Old One Tooth," who held the land fast to the bottom of the waters. Maui then exhorted his brothers to row, but warned them not to look back. They strained at the oars with all their might and slowly a great land mass arose. One brother, overcome by curiosity, looked back, and when he did so, the land shattered into all of the islands of Polynesia.

Further Exploits

Maui still desired to serve mankind. People were without fire, the secret of which was held by the sacred *alae* birds, who learned it from Maui's far distant mother. Hina of Fire gave Maui her burning fingernails, but he oafishly kept dropping them into streams until all had fizzled out and he had totally irritated his generous progenitor. She pursued him, trying to burn him to a cinder; Maui chanted for rain to put out her scorching fires. When she saw that they were all being quenched she hid her fire in the barks of special trees and informed the mud hens where they could be found, but

first made them promise never to tell men. Maui knew of this and captured a mud hen, threatening to wring its scrawny, traitorous neck unless it gave up the secret. The bird tried trickery and told Maui first to rub together the stems of sugar cane, then banana and even taro. None worked, and Maui's determined rubbing is why these plants have hollow roots today.

Finally, with Maui's hands tightening around the mud hen's gizzard, the bird confessed that fire could be found in the *hau* tree and also the sandalwood, which Maui named *ili aha* ("fire bark") in its honor. He then rubbed all the feathers off the mud hen's head for being so deceitful, which is why their crowns are featherless today.

The Sun Is Snared

Maui's greatest deed, however, was in snaring the sun and exacting a promise that it would go slower across the heavens. The people complained that there were not enough daylight hours to fish or farm. Maui's mother could not dry her tapa cloth because the sun rose and set so quickly. She asked her son to help. Maui went to his blind grandmother, who lived on the slopes of Haleakala and was responsible for cooking the sun's bananas, which he ate every day in passing. She told him to personally weave 16 strong ropes with nooses out of his sister's hair. Some say these came from her head, but other versions insist that it was no doubt Hina's pubic hair that had the power to hold the sun-god. Maui positioned himself with the rope, and as each of the 16 rays of the sun came across Haleakala, he snared them until the sun was defenseless and had to bargain for his life. Maui agreed to free him if he promised to go more slowly. From that time forward the sun agreed to move slowly and Haleakala ("The House of the Sun") became his home.

HEIAU AND IDOLS

A *heiau* is a Hawaiian temple. The basic *heiau* was a masterly built and fitted rectangular stone wall that varied in size from as large as a basketball court to the size of a football field. Once the restraining outer walls were built, the interior was backfilled with smaller stones and the top dressing was expertly laid and then rolled, perhaps with a log, to form a pavement-like surface. All that remains of Hawaii's many *heiau* are the stone platforms. The buildings upon them, made from perishable wood, leaves, and grass, have long since disappeared.

Some *heiau* were dreaded temples where human sacrifices were made. Tradition says that this barbaric custom began at Wahaula Heiau on the Big Island in the 12th century and was introduced by a ferocious Tahitian priest named Paao. Other *heiau,* such as Puuhonua o Honaunau, also on the Big Island, were temples of refuge where the weak, widowed, orphaned, and vanquished could find safety and sanctuary.

Idols

All the people worshipped gods who took the form of idols fashioned from wood, feathers, or stone. The eyes were made from shells and until these were inlaid, the idol was dormant. The hair used was often human hair, and the arms and legs were usually flexed. The mouth was either gaping or formed a wide figure-eight lying on its side, and more likely than not, it was lined with glistening dog teeth. There were small figures made of woven basketry that were expertly covered with feathers. Red and yellow were favorite colors which were taken from specific birds by men whose only work was to roam the forests in search of them.

Ghosts

The Hawaiians had countless superstitions and ghost legends, but two of the more interesting involve astral travel of the soul, and the "death Marchers of the Night." The soul, *uhane,* was considered by Hawaiians to be totally free and independent of its body, *kino.* The soul could separate, leaving the body asleep or very drowsy. This disincorporated soul *(hihi'o)* could visit people, and was considered quite different from a *lapu,* an ordinary spirit of a dead person. A *kahuna* could

immediately recognize if a person's *uhane* had left his body, and a special wreath was placed upon his head to protect him and to facilitate reentry. If a person was confronted by an apparition, he could test to see if it was indeed dead or still alive by placing leaves of an *ape* plant upon the ground. If the leaves tore when they were walked upon, the spirit was merely human, but if they remained intact it was a ghost. Also, you could sneak up and startle the vision and if it disappeared it was a ghost, or if no reflection of the face appeared when it drank water from an offered calabash, it was also a ghost. Unfortunately, there were no instructions to follow once you had determined that you indeed had a ghost on your hands. Maybe it was better not to know! Some people would sprinkle salt and water around their houses, but this only kept away evil spirits, not ghosts.

There are also many stories of *kahuna* restoring a soul to a dead body. First they had to catch it and keep it in a gourd. They then placed beautiful tapa and fragrant flowers and herbs about the body to make it more enticing. Slowly, they would coax the soul out of the gourd, which reentered the body through the big toe.

Death Marchers

One inexplicable phenomenon that many people attest to is *ka huakai o ka po,* "Marchers of the Night." This march of the dead is fatal if you gaze upon it, unless one of the marchers happens to be a friendly ancestor who will protect you. The peak time for "the march" is from 7:30 p.m. till 2 a.m. The marchers can be dead *ali'i* and warriors, the gods themselves, or the lesser *amakua.* When the *amakua* march there is usually chanting and music. *Ali'i* marches are more somber. The entire procession, lit by torches, oftentimes stops at the house of a relative and might even carry them away. When the gods themselves march, there is often thunder, lightning, and heavy seas. The sky is lit with torches, and they walk six abreast, three gods and three goddesses. If you get in the way of a march, remove your clothing and prostrate yourself. If the marching gods or

William Alexander preaching on Kauai. Drawing by A. Agate, c. 1840 (Hawaii State Archives)

amakua happen to be ones to which you prayed, you might be spared. If it's a march of the *ali'i* you might make it if you lie face upward and feign death. If you *do* see a death march, the last thing that you'll worry about is lying naked on the ground and looking ridiculous.

MISSIONARIES ONE AND ALL

In Hawaii, when you say "missionaries," it's taken for granted you're referring to the small and determined band of Congregationalists who arrived aboard the brig *Thaddeus* in 1820, and the follow-up groups called "companies" or "packets" that reinforced them. They were sent from Boston by the American Board of Commissioners for Foreign Missions (ABCFM), which learned of the supposed sad and godless plight of the Hawaiian people through returning sailors and especially through the few Hawaiians who had come to America to study.

The person most instrumental in bringing the missionaries to Hawaii was a young man named Opukahaia. He was an orphan befriended by a ship's captain and taken to New England, where he studied theology. Obsessed with the desire to return home and save his people from certain damnation, his accounts of life in Hawaii were published and widely read. These accounts were directly responsible for the formation of the Pioneer Company to the Sandwich Islands Missions in 1819. Unfortunately, Opukahaia died in New England from typhus the year before they left.

"Civilizing" Hawaii

The first missionaries had the straightforward task of bringing the Hawaiians out of paganism and into Christianity and civilization. They met with terrible hostility—not from the natives, but from the sea captains and traders who were very happy with the open debauchery and wanton whoremongering that was status quo in the Hawaii of 1820. Many direct confrontations between these two factions even included the cannonading of missionaries' homes by American sea captains, who were denied the customary visits of island women, thanks to meddlesome "do-gooders." The most memorable of these incidents involved "Mad Jack" Percival, the captain of the USS *Dolphin,* who bombed a church in Lahaina to show his rancour. In actuality, the truth of the situation was much closer to the sentiments of James Jarves, who wrote, "The missionary was a far more useful and agreeable man than his Catholicism would indicate; and the trader was not so bad a man as the missionary would make him out to be." The missionaries' primary aim might have been conversion, but the most fortuitous by-product was education, which raised the consciousness of every Hawaiian, regardless of his religious affiliation. In 40 short years Hawaii was considered a civilized nation well on its way into the modern world, and the American Board of Missions officially ended its support in 1863.

Non-Christians

By the turn of the century, both Shintoism and Buddhism, brought by the Japanese and Chinese, were firmly established in Hawaii. The first official Buddhist temple was Hongpa Hongwanji, established on Oahu in 1889. All the denominations of Buddhism account for 17 percent (170,000 parishioners) of the island's religious total, and there are about 50,000 Shintoists. The Hindu religion has perhaps 2,000 adherents, and about the same number of Jewish people live throughout Hawaii, with only one synagogue, Temple Emanuel, on Oahu. The largest number of people in Hawaii (300,000) remain unaffiliated, and about 10,000 people are in new religious movements and lesser-known faiths such as Baha'i and Unitarianism.

Ti plants are always found around heiau, where their leaves are still used to wrap stones as simple offerings to the gods.

ARTS AND CRAFTS

Referring to Hawaii as "paradise" is about as hackneyed as you can get, but when you combine it into "artists' paradise" it's the absolute truth. Something about the place evokes art (or at least personal expression) from most people. The islands are like a magnet: they not only draw artists to them, but they draw art *from* the artists. The list of literary figures who have visited Hawaii and had something inspirational to say reads like a freshman survey in literature: William Henry Dana, Herman Melville, Mark Twain, Robert Louis Stevenson, Jack London, Somerset Maugham, Joaquin Miller, and of course, James Michener.

The inspiration comes from the astounding natural surroundings. The land is so beautiful yet so raw; the ocean's power and rhythm is primal and ever-present; the riotous colors of flowers and fruit leap from the deep-green jungle background. Crystal water beads and pale mists turn the mountains into mystic temples, while rainbows come riding on the crests of waves. The stunning variety of faces

begging to be rendered appears as if all the world sent a local delegation to the islands. And in most cases it did! Inspiration is everywhere, as is art, good or bad.

Sometimes the artwork is overpowering in itself and in its sheer volume. Though geared to the tourist's market of cheap souvenirs, there is hardly a shop in Hawaii that doesn't sell some item that falls into the general category of "art." You can find everything from carved monkey-face coconut shells to true masterpieces. The Polynesian Hawaiians were master craftsmen, and their legacy still lives in a wide variety of woodcarvings, basketry, and weavings. The hula is art in swaying motion, and the true form is rigorously studied and taken very seriously. There is hardly a resort area that doesn't offer the "bump and grind" tourist's hula and even these revues are accompanied by proficient local musicians. Nightclubs offer "slack key" balladeers and island music made on ukuleles, and Hawaii's own steel guitars spill from many lounges.

Vibrant fabrics, which catch the spirit of the islands, are rendered into muumuus and *aloha* shirts at countless local factories. They're almost a mandatory purchase! Pottery, heavily influenced by the Japanese, is well developed at numerous kilns. Local artisans fashion delicate jewelry from coral and olivine, while some ply the whaler's legacy of etching on ivory, called scrimshaw. There is a fine tradition of quilt-making, flower art in leis, and street artists working in everything from airbrush to glass. The following is an overview; for local offerings please see "Shopping" in the travel chapters.

ARTS OF OLD HAWAII

Since everything in old Hawaii had to be fashioned by hand, almost every object was either a work of art or at least a highly refined craft. With the "civilizing" of the natives, most of the "old ways" disappeared, including the old arts and crafts. Most authentic Hawaiian art exists only in museums, but with the resurgence of Hawaiiian *roots,* many old arts are being revitalized, and a few artists are becoming proficient.

Magnificent Canoes

The most respected artisans in old Hawaii were the canoe makers. With little more than a stone adze and a pump drill, they built canoes that could carry 200 people and last for generations—sleek, well proportioned, and infinitely seaworthy. The main hull was usually a gigantic *koa* log, and the gunwale planks were minutely drilled and sewn to the sides with sennit rope. Apprenticeships lasted for years, and a young man knew that he had graduated when one day he was nonchalantly asked to sit down and eat with the master builders. Small family-sized canoes with outriggers were used for fishing, and perhaps carried a spear rack; large oceangoing double-hulled canoes were used for migration and warfare. On these, the giant logs had been adzed to about two inches thick. A mainsail woven from pandanus was mounted on a central platform, and the boat was steered by two long paddles. The hull was dyed with plant juices and charcoal, and the entire village helped launch the canoe in a ceremony called "drinking the sea."

Carving And Weaving

Wood was a primary material, and craftsmen turned out well-proportioned and distinctive calabashes. Made mostly from *koa,* the luster and intricate grain was brought out with hand rubbing. Temple idols were a major product of woodcarving, and a variety of stone artifacts, including poi pounders, mirrors, fish sinkers, and small idols were turned out.

Hawaiians became the *best* basket makers and mat weavers in all of Polynesia. *Ulana* (mats) were made from *lau hala* (pandanus) leaves. Once split, the spine was

carvings and weavings of old Hawaii (Hawaii State Archives)

short feather capes for men of rank

removed and the leaves stored in large rolls. When needed they were soaked, pounded, and then fashioned into various floor coverings and sleeping mats. Intricate geometrical patterns were woven in, and the edges were rolled and well fashioned. Coconut palms were not used to make mats in old Hawaii, but a wide variety of basketry was made from the aerial root, *ie'ie*. The shapes varied according to use. Some were tall and narrow, some were cones, others were flat like trays, while many were woven around gourds and calabashes.

A strong tradition of weaving and carving has survived in Hawaii, and the time-tested material of *lau hala* is still the best, although much is now made from coconut fronds. You can purchase anything from beach mats to a woven hat and all share the qualities of strength, lightness, and air flow.

Feather Work

This highly refined art was only found on the islands of Tahiti, New Zealand, and Hawaii, while the fashioning of feather helmets and idols was unique to Hawaii alone. Favorite colors were red and yellow, which came only in a very limited number on a few birds such as the *o'o, i'iwi, mamo,* and *apapane.* Professional bird hunters in old Hawaii paid their taxes to *ali'i* in prized feathers. The feathers were fastened to a woven net of *olona* cord and made into helmets, idols, and beautiful flowing capes and cloaks. These resplendent garments were made and worn only by men, especially during battle when a fine cloak became a great trophy of war. Featherwork was also employed in the making of *kahili* and leis, which were highly prized by the noble *ali'i* women.

Tapa Cloth

Tapa, cloth made from tree bark, was common throughout Polynesia and was a woman's art. A few trees such as the *wauke* and *mamaki* produced the best cloth, but a variety of other barks could be utilized. First the raw bark was pounded into a felt-like pulp and beaten together to form strips. The beaters had distinctive patterns that also helped to make the cloth supple. They were then decorated by stamping, using a form of block printing, and dyed with natural colors from plants and sea animals, in shades of gray, purple, pink, and red. They were even painted with natural brushes made from pandanus fruit, with an overall gray color made from charcoal. The tapa cloth was sewn together to make bed coverings, and fragrant flowers and herbs were either sewn or pounded in to produce a permanent fragrance. tapa cloth is still available today, but the Hawaiian methods have been lost, and most comes from other areas of Polynesia.

First Western Artists

When Capt. Cook made first contact in 1778, the ship's artists immediately began recording things Hawaiian. John Webber and James Clevely made etchings and pen-and-ink drawings of Hawaiian people, structures, *heiau* and everyday occurences that struck them as noteworthy or peculiar. William Ellis, ship's surgeon, also a fair hand at etching, was attracted to portraying native architecture. These three left a priceless and faithful record of what Hawaii was like at the moment of contact. Louis Choris, ship's artist with Otto Von Kotzebue in 1816, painted early portraits of King Kamehameha and Queen Kaahumanu, the two grandest figures in Hawaii's history. Jacques Arago, aboard the *Uranie* with the French Captain de Freycinet in 1819, recorded some gruesome customs of punishment of *kapu* breakers, and made many drawings of island people. Robert Dampier, who sailed on the *Blonde,* the ship that returned King Liholiho's body from England, recorded one of the earliest landscapes of Honolulu, a site which has continued to be depicted on film by more tourists than almost any other city on Earth. These early artists merely set a trend that continues unabated to this day; artists endeavour to "capture" Hawaii, and they do so with every artistic medium avilable.

Modern Masters
Countless artists working at all levels of accomplishment try to match their skills to the vigor and beauty of the islands. Some have set the standards, and their names have become synonymous with Hawaiian art. Heading this list of luminaries are Huc Luquiens, Madge Tennent, Tadashi Sato, Jean Charlot, and John Kelly. Madge Tennent (1889-1972) was an Englishwoman who came to Hawaii via Samoa after spending years in South Africa and New Zealand. She worked in oils that she applied liberally and in bold strokes. Enamored with the people of Hawaii, her portraits are of a race striking in appearance and noble in character. Her works, along with those of other island artists, are displayed at the Tennent Art Foundation, on the slopes of Punchbowl on Oahu.

Huc Luquiens, former chairman of the Art Department at the University of Hawaii, was a master at etching, and was especially accomplished in dry point. His works, mainly island landscapes, are displayed in the Hawaiiana Collection of the Honolulu Academy of Arts. Maui-born Tadashi Sato, a superbly accomplished muralist, has produced such famous mosaics as the 30-foot "Aquarius" at the State Capitol in Honolulu, and the 60-foot "Portals of Immortality" at the Maui Memorial Gymnasium in Lahaina.

Frenchman Jean Charlot perfected his mural art in Mexico before coming to Hawaii in 1949. He is renowned for his frescoes and became a well-known art critic and the grand old man of Hawaiian art. He died in 1979 at the ripe old age of 90. John M. Kelly was in love with Hawaiian women; his etchings of them are both inspired and technically flawless. Kelly was infinitely patient, rendering his subjects in the minutest detail.

These artists are the "Big Five of Hawaiian Art"; their accomplishments should be seen as an "artistic gauge" of what Hawaii can inspire in an artist. By observing their works you can get an instant "art course" and a comparative view of the state of the arts in Hawaii.

Contemporary Artists
The crop of new artists making their mark always seems to be bounteous and their works, heavily influenced by the "feeling of Hawaii," continue to be superb. Every island has art galleries, co-ops, or unofficial art centers. One of the finest groups of island artists can be found at the **Sunday Art Mart,** which recently changed its official name to **Artists of Oahu, Sunday Exhibit.** It's located along the "fence" of the Honolulu Zoo fronting Kapiolani Park. These artists, along with others around the island, will be discussed in their respective travel chapters, so check. The following list of artists, with a short description of their work, is by no means exhaustive. It merely shows the wide range of artwork available.

Richard Fields, a former Californian, now lives on Maui. The fascinating beauty of the *aina* is his inspiration that he depicts in his supra-realistic paintings of birds, mountains, clouds, flowers, and waterfalls. Richard creates his rich renditions using a mixed media of airbrush, acrylic, india ink, and stencils. His works are as striking and as inspiring as the ever-changing beauty of the islands.

Robert Nelson is a Maui artist who superbly transmits the integrated mystical life of land and sea. His watercolors are often diffused with the strange filtered light found beneath the waves. A conservationist, he has often depicted the gentle frolicking life of the whales that visit Hawaiian waters.

Bill Christian is a master of scrimshaw, which he renders on slate. He also produces fine oil paintings of the sea and old salts. A world-class artist, his works are displayed at art galleries on Maui as well as in the Smith-

Hawaiian maiden by John Costello

sonian and the New Bedford Massachusetts Whaling Museum.

Pegge Hopper is often compared with Madge Tennent. She works in bold colors and strokes. Her subject matter is islanders, especially the delicacy and inner strength of women. Her works are displayed at various galleries, especially on Maui and Oahu, and are often available in limited-edition serigraphs.

John Costello, an Oahu artist, specializes in pointalism to capture the waves, women, and flora of Hawaii in a sensitive and mystical way. He co-owns and operates Kaala Art and Rainbow Island T's with his brother, Jim, in Haleiwa on North Shore Oahu. John's work as well as local artists' are showcased in their small shop.

Alapai Hanapi is a traditionalist sculptor who tries to recreate the motifs of his Hawaiian ancestors. He works in wood and stone with tools that he fashions himself. His driving force is "cultural awareness" and through his art he tells of the old ways. He

lives simply with his wife and three daughters near an old fishpond on eastern Molokai. His work is known for its simplicity and is available at art shows periodically held throughout the islands.

Al Furtado is a freelance artist working in Honolulu. He specializes in capturing the movement of Hawaiian dance. His depictions are often larger than life with a strong sense of vitality and motion.

Daniel Wang was born in Shanghai where he learned the art of Chinese watercolors. Although born deaf and mute, he speaks loudly, clearly and beautifully through his art. Daniel has a special technique in which the palm of his hand becomes his artistic tool. He feels that he can transmit intense inner emotions directly from his body to the canvas.

The following is a potpourri of distinguished artists displayed at various galleries around the islands. Any work bearing their name is authentic island art considered to be superior by fellow artists. William Waterfall, photographer (see p. 219); Satoru Abe, sculptor; Ruthadell Anderson, weaver; Betty Tseng Yuho Ecke, *dsui* painter; Claude Horan, sculptor, ceramics; Erica Karawina, stained glass; Ron Kowalke, painter; Ben Norris, painter; Louis Pohl, printmaker; Mamoru Sato, sculptor; Tadashi Sato, painter; Reuben Tam, painter; Jean Williams, weaver; John Wisnosky, painter; John Young, painter.

ARTS TO BUY

Wild Hawaiian shirts or bright muumuus, especially when worn on the Mainland, have the magical effect of making wearers "feel" like they're in Hawaii, while at the same time eliciting spontaneous smiles from passersby. Maybe it's the colors, or perhaps it's just the "vibe" that signifies "party time" or "hang loose," but nothing says Hawaii like alohawear does. There are more than a dozen fabric houses in Hawaii turning out distinctive patterns, and many dozens of factories creating their own personalized designs. Oftentimes these factories have attached retail outlets, but in any case you can find hundreds of shops selling alohawear. Aloha shirts were the brilliant idea of a Chinese merchant in

ART INFORMATION

Organization	Address and Telephone	Remarks
Arts Council of Hawaii	Box 50225 Honolulu, HI 96850 tel. 524-7120	A citizens' advocacy group for the arts providing technical assistance and information. Publishes the *Cultural Climate* newsletter covering the arts of Hawaii. Includes a calendar of events, feature articles, and editorials. Membership fee, $15, includes newsletter, nonmembers, $.50 per issue.
Bishop Museum	1355 Kalihi St. Box 19000-A Honolulu, HI 96819 tel. 847-3511	World's best museum covering Polynesia and Hawaii; exhibits, galleries, archives, demonstrations of Hawaiian crafts, and a planetarium. On premises, Shop Pacifica has books and publications on Hawaiian art and culture. Shouldn't be missed. See p. 192.
Contemporary Museum of Art	2411 Makiki Heights Rd. tel. 526-1322	Focuses on exhibitions rather than collections, although works by David Hockney are on permanent display. Changing exhibits reflect different themes in contemporary art. Under the direction of Fritz Frauchinger. Open Monday through Saturday, 10 a.m.-4 p.m., noon-4 p.m. Sunday, closed Tuesday, admission $3.
East-West Center Learning Institute	Burns Hall 4076 1777 East-West Rd. Honolulu, HI 96848 tel. 948-8006	At U of H campus. Dedicated to the sharing, exhibiting, and appreciation of arts, culture, and crafts from throughout Asia and the Western world. Their free bi-monthly Centerviews includes an event calendar and tropical editorials on the Pacific. See p. 190.
East West Journal	1633 Kapiolani Blvd. Honolulu, HI 96814	Yearly guide to exhibition galleries featuring the work of locally renowned artists.
Hawaii Craftsmen	Box 22145 Honolulu, HI tel. 523-1974	Increases awareness of Hawaiian crafts through programs, exhibitions, workshops, lectures, and demonstrations.
Honolulu Academy of Arts	900 S. Beretania St. Honolulu, HI 96814 tel. 538-3693	Collects, preserves, and exhibits artworks. Offers public art education programs related to their collections, plus tours, classes, lectures, films, and a variety of publications. See p. 194.

Honolulu Symphony Society	1000 Bishop St. Honolulu, HI 96813 tel. 537-6171	Provides professional-level music, primarily symphonic and concerts.
Pacific Handcrafters Guild	Box 15491 Honolulu, HI 96818 tel. 923-5726	Focuses on developing and preserving handicrafts in Hawaii and the Pacific. Sponsors four major craft fairs annualy.
State Foundation on Culture and the Arts	335 Merchant Street Room 202 Honolulu, HI 96813 tel. 548-4145	Preserves Hawaii's cultural and artistic heritage. Publishes *Hawaii Cultural Resource Directory,* listing art organizations, galleries, councils, co-ops, and guilds. Very complete.
University of Hawaii at Manoa Art Gallery	2535 The Mall Honolulu, HI 96822 tel. 948-6888	Showcase for contemporary artwork. Theme changes periodically. See p. 190.

Honolulu, who used to hand-tailor them and sell them to the tourists who arrived by ship in the glory days before WW II. They were an instant success. Muumuus or "Mother Hubbards" were the idea of missionaries, who were appalled by Hawaiian women running about *au naturelle* and insisted on covering their new Christian converts from head to foot. Now the roles are reversed, and it's Mainlanders who come to Hawaii and immediately strip down to as little clothing as possible.

Alohawear
At one. time exclusively made of cotton, or from man-made yet naturally based rayon, these materials were and still are the best for any tropical clothing. Beware, however: polyester has slowly crept into the market! No material could possibly be worse than polyester for the island climate, so when buying your alohawear make sure to check the label for material content. Muumuus now come in various styles and can be worn for the entire spectrum of social occasions in Hawaii. Aloha shirts are still basically cut the same as always, but the patterns have undergone changes, and apart from the original flowers and ferns, modern shirts might depict an island scene, giving the impression of a silk-screen painting. A basic good-quality muumuu or aloha shirt starts at about $25 and is

guaranteed to be worth its price in good times and happy smiles. The connoisseur might want to purchase *The Hawaiian Shirt, Its Art and History,* by R. Thomas Steele. It's illustrated with more than 150 shirts that are now considered works of art by collectors the world over.

Scrimshaw
This art of etching and carving on bone and ivory has become an island tradition handed down from the times of the old whaling ships. Although scrimshaw can be found throughout Hawaii, the center remains in the old whaling capital of Lahaina. Here along Front Street are numerous shops specializing in scrimshaw. Today, pieces are carved on fossilized walrus ivory that is gathered by Eskimos and shipped to Hawaii. It comes in a variety of shades from pure white to mocha, depending upon the mineral content of the earth in which it was buried. Elephant ivory or whale bone is no longer used because of ecological considerations, but there is a "gray market" in Pacific walrus tusks. Eskimos can legally hunt the walrus. They then make a few minimal scratches on the tusks which technically qualifies them to be "Native American art," and free of most governmental restrictions. The tusks are then sent to Hawaii as art objects, but the superficial scratches are immediately removed and the ivory is reworked

by artisans. Scrimshaw is made into everything from belt buckles to delicate earrings and even into coffee-table centerpieces. The prices can go from a few dollars up into the thousands.

Woodcarvings

One Hawaiian art that has not died out is woodcarving. This art was extremely well developed among the old Hawaiians and they almost exclusively used *koa* because of its density, strength, and natural luster. It was turned into canoes, woodware, and furniture for the *ali'i*. Koa is becoming increasingly scarce, but many items are still available, though costly. Milo and monkeypod are also excellent woods for carving and have largely replaced *koa*. You can buy tikis, bowls, and furniture at numerous shops. Countless inexpensive carved items are sold at variety stores, such as little hula girls or salad servers, but most of these are imported from Asia or the Philippines and can be bought at any variety store.

Weaving

The minute you arrive in Hawaii you should shell out $2 for a woven beach mat. This is a necessity, not a frivolous purchase, but it definitely won't have been made in Hawaii. What is made in Hawaii is *lau hala*. This is traditional Hawaiian weaving from the leaves *(lau)* of the pandanus *(hala)* tree. These leaves vary greatly in length, with the largest over six feet, and they have a thorny spine that must be removed before they can be worked. The color ranges from light tan to dark brown. The leaves are cut into strips from one-eighth to one inch wide and are then employed in weaving. Any variety of items can be made or at least covered in *lau hala*. It makes great purses, mats, baskets, and table mats.

Woven into a hat, it's absolutely superb but should not be confused with a palm-frond hat. A *lau hala* hat is amazingly supple and even when squashed will pop back into shape. A good one is expensive ($25) and with proper care will last for years. All *lau hala* should be given a light application of mineral oil on a monthly basis, especially if it's exposed to the

sun. For flat items, iron over a damp cloth and keep purses and baskets stuffed with paper when not in use. Palm fronds also are widely used in weaving. They, too, are a great natural raw material, but not as good as *lau hala*. Almost any item, such as a beach bag, woven from palm makes a good authentic yet inexpensive gift or souvenir, and are available in countless shops.

Gift Items

Jewelry is always an appreciated gift, especially if it's distinctive, and Hawaii has some of the most original. The sea provides the basic raw materials of pink, gold, and black coral, and it's so beautiful that it holds the same fascination as gemstones. Harvesting the coral is very dangerous work. The Lahaina beds off Maui have one of the best black coral lodes in the islands, but unlike reef coral these trees grow at depths bordering the outer limits of a scuba diver's capabilities. Only the best can dive 180 feet after the black coral, and about one diver per year dies in pursuit of it. Conservationists have placed great pressure on the harvesters of these deep corals, and the state of Hawaii has placed strict limits and guidelines on the firms and divers involved.

Pink coral has long been treasured by man. The Greeks considered it a talisman for good health, and there's even evidence that it has been coveted since the Stone Age. Coral jewelry is on sale at many shops throughout Hawaii and the value comes from the color of the coral and the workmanship.

Puka (shells with little naturally occurring holes) and *opihi* shells are also made into jewelry. Many times these items are very inexpensive, yet they are authentic and great purchases for the price. Hanging macrame planters festooned with seashells are usually quite affordable and sold at roadside stands along with shells.

Hawaii produces some unique food items that are appreciated by most people. Various-sized jars of macadamia nuts and butters are great gifts, as are tins of rich, gourmet-quality Kona coffee, the only coffee produced in the U.S. Guava, pineapple, passion fruit, and mango are often gift-boxed into assortments of jams, jellies, and spicy chutneys. And for that special person in your life, you can bring home island fragrances in bottles of perfumes and colognes in the exotic odors of gardenia, plumeria, and even ginger. All of the above items are reasonably priced, lightweight, and easy to carry.

HULA AND LEIS

Hawaiian hula was never performed in grass skirts; tapa or *ti*-leaf skirts were worn. Grass skirts came to Hawaii from the Gilbert Islands, so if you see grass or cellophane skirts in a "hula revue," you'll know that it's not traditional. Hula, like all artforms, has its own highly specialized techniques. A dancer has to learn how to control every part of his or her body, including the facial expressions, which become very important and help to set the mood. The hands are extremely important and provide instant background scenery. For example, if the hands are thrust outwardly in an aggressive manner, this can be a battle; if they sway gently overhead, they refer to the gods or the early time of creation. They can easily become rain or clouds or the sun, sea, or moon. You must watch the hands to get the gist of the story, but the best comeback

to this advice was the classic wisecrack, "You watch the parts you like, and I'll watch the parts I like."

Swaying hips, depending upon their motion, can be a long walk, a canoe ride, or sexual intercourse. The foot motion can portray a battle, a walk, or any kind of movement or conveyance. The overall effect is multidirectional synchronized movement.

The correct chanting of the *mele* is an integral part of the performance. These story-chants, combined with the various musical instruments that accompany the dance, make the hula very much like opera, and are especially similar in the way the tale is unfolded.

Language Of The Lei

Every major island of Hawaii is symbolized by its own lei, made from a distinctive flower, shell, or fern. Each island has its own official color as well, which doesn't necessarily correspond to the color of the island's lei. Oahu, *The Gathering Place,* is symbolized by yel-

man from the Sandwich Islands dancing (Hawaii State Archives)

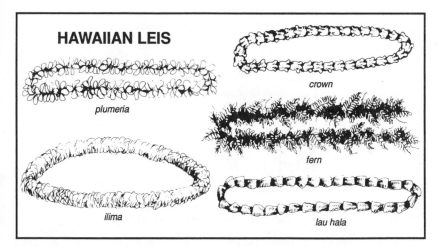

HAWAIIAN LEIS

plumeria

crown

fern

ilima

lau hala

low, the color of the tropical sun. Its flower is the delicate *ilima,* which resembles hibiscus, and ranges in color from pastel yellow to a burnt orange. The blooms are about as large as a silver dollar and leis made from *ilima* were at one time reserved only for the *ali'i,* designating them as a royal flower.

THAT GOOD OLD ISLAND MUSIC

The missionaries usually take a beating when it's recounted how much Hawaiian culture they destroyed while civilizing the natives. However, they seemed to have done one thing right. They taught the Hawaiians the diatonic musical scale and immediately opened a door filled with latent and superbly harmonious talent. Before the missionaries, the Hawaiians knew little about melody. Though sonorous, their *mele* were repetitive chants where the emphasis was placed on historical accuracy and not on "making music." The Hawaiians, in short, didn't *sing.* But within a few years of the missionaries' arrival, they were belting out good old Christian hymns and one of their favorite pastimes became group and individual singing.

Early in the 1800s, Spanish *vaqueros* from California were imported to teach the Hawaiians how to be cowboys. With them came guitars and moody ballads. The Hawaiian *paniolos* (cowboys) quickly learned both how

to punch cows and to croon away the long lonely nights on the range. Immigrants that came along a little later in the 19th century, especially from Portugal, helped create a Hawaiian-style music. Their biggest influence was a small four-stringed instrument called a *braga* or *cavaquinho.* One owned by Augusto Dias was the prototype of a home-grown Hawaiian instrument that became known as the *ukulele.* "Jumping flea," the translation of ukuelele, is an appropriate name devised by the Hawaiians when they saw how nimble the fingers were as they "jumped" over the strings.

The Merry Monarch, King Kalakaua, and Queen Liliuokalani were both patrons of the arts who furthered the Hawaiian musical identity at the turn of the century. Kalakaua revived the hula and was also a gifted lyricist and balladeer. He wrote the words to "Hawaii Pono," which became the national anthem of Hawaii and later the state anthem. Liliuokalani wrote the hauntingly beautiful "Aloha Oe," which is often pointed to as the "spirit of Hawaii" in music. Detractors say that its melody is extremely close to the old Christian hymn, "Rock Beside the Sea," but the lyrics are so beautiful and perfectly fitted that this doesn't matter.

Just prior to Kalakaua's reign a Prussian bandmaster, Capt. Henri Berger, was invited to head the fledgling Royal Hawaiian Band, *bandmaster Henri Berger and the Royal Hawaiian Band (Hawaii State Archives)*

which he turned into very respectable orchestra lauded by many visitors to the islands. Berger was open-minded and learned to love Hawaiian music. He collaborated with Kalakaua and other island musicians to incorporate their music into a Western format. He headed the band for 43 years until 1915, and was instrumental in making music a serious pursuit of talented Hawaiians.

Popular Hawaiian Music

Hawaiian music has a unique twang, a special feeling that says the same thing to everyone that hears it: "Relax, sit back in the moonlight, watch the swaying palms as the surf sings a lullaby." This special sound is epitomized by the bouncy ukulele, the falsetto voice of Hawaiian crooners, and by the smooth ring of the "steel" or "Hawaiian" guitar. The steel guitar is a variation that was originated by Joseph Kekuku in the 1890s. Stories abound of how Joseph Kekuku devised this instrument; the most popular versions say that Joe dropped his comb or pocket knife on his guitar strings and liked what he heard. Driven by the faint rhythm of an inner sound, he went to the machine shop at the Kamehameha School and turned out a steel bar for sliding over the strings. To complete the sound he changed the cat-gut strings to steel and raised them so they wouldn't hit the frets. *Voilà!*—Hawaiian music as the world knows it today.

The first melodious strains of **slack-key guitar** can be traced back to the time of Kamehameha III, when Spanish cowboys (the forerunners of Hawaiian *paniolos*) from California were brought to the kingdom to run the wild cattle that had grown steadily in numbers ever since killing them was made *kapu* by Kamehameha I. The white man's gift had become a menace, growing in numbers to the point where they were even attacking grass houses for fodder. The Spanish cowboys roped, branded, and corralled them, and living up to the cowboy image, would pass lonesome nights on the range singing and playing their guitars. The Hawaiians, who made excellent cowboys, and their ears, recently tuned by the missionaries, picked up the melodies accompanied by the strange new instrument, and quickly *Hawaianized* them. The Spanish had their way of tuning the guitar, and played difficult and aggressive music that did not sit well with Hawaiians, who were much more gentle and casual in their manners.

Hawaiians soon became adept at making their own music. At first, one person played the melody, but it lacked fullness. There was no body to the sound. So, as one *paniolo* fooled with the melody, another soon learned to play bass, which added depth. But, a player was often alone, and by experimenting learned that he could get the right hand going with the melody, and at the same time could play the bass note with the thumb to improve the sound. Singers also learned that they could "open tune" the guitar to match their rich voices.

Due to *kahunamism,* Hawaiians believed that knowledge was sacred, and what is sacred should be treated with utmost respect, which meant keeping it secret, except from sincere apprentices. Guitar playing became a personal artform whose secrets were closely guarded, handed down only to family members, and only to those who showed ability and determination. When old-time slack-key guitar players were done strumming, they loosened all the strings so that no one could figure out how they had it tuned. If they were playing, and some folks came by that were interested and weren't part of the family, the Hawaiians stopped what they were doing, put the guitar down, and put their foot on it across the strings to wait for the person to go away. As time went on, more and more Hawaiians began to play slack key, and a common repertoire emerged.

An accomplished musician could easily figure out the simple songs, once they had figured out how the family had tuned the guitar. One of the most popular tunings was the "open G." Old Hawaiian folks called it the "taro patch tune." Different songs came out, and if you were in their family and were interested in the guitar, they took the time to sit down and teach you. The way they taught was straightforward, and a test of your sincereity at the same time. The old master would start to play. They just wanted you to listen, get a feel for the music, not any more than that. You brought your guitar and *listened*. When you felt it, you played it, and the knowledge was transferred. Today, only a handful of slack-key guitar players know how to play the classic tunes classically. The best-known and perhaps greatest slack-key player was Gabby Pahinui, with The Sons of Hawaii. He passed away recently, but left many recordings behind. A slack-key master still singing and playing is Raymond Kane. Raymond now teaches a handful of students his wonderful and haunting music. Not one of his students are from his own family, and most are *haole* musicians trying to preserve the classical method of playing.

Hawaiian music received its biggest boost from a remarkable radio program known as "Hawaii Calls." This program sent out its music from the Banyan Court of the Moana Hotel from 1935 until 1975. At its peak in the mid-1950s, it was syndicated on over 700 radio stations throughout the world. Ironically, Japanese pilots heading for Pearl Harbor tuned in island music as a signal beam. Some internationally famous classic tunes came out of the '40s and '50s. Jack Pitman composed "Beyond the Reef" in 1948; over 300 artists have recorded it and it has sold well over 12 million records. Other million-sellers include: "Sweet Leilani," "Lovely Hula Hands," "The Crosseyed Mayor of Kaunakakai," "The Hawaiian Wedding Song."

By the 1960s, Hawaiian music began to die. It was just too corny for those turbulent years. Hawaiian music was too light, belonging to the older generation and the good times that followed WW II. One man was instrumental in keeping Hawaiian music alive during this period. Don Ho, with his Tiny Bubbles, became the token Hawaiian musician of the '60s and early '70s. He's persevered long enough to become a legend in his own time, and his Polynesian Extravaganza still packs them in six nights a week in Honolulu. Al Harrington, "The South Pacific Man," has another Honolulu "big revue" that draws large crowds. Of this type of entertainment, perhaps the most Hawaiian is Danny Kaleikini, who entertains his audience with dances, Hawaiian anecdotes, and tunes on the traditional Hawaiian nose flute.

The Beat Goes On

Beginning in the mid-'70s, islanders began to assert their cultural identity. One of the unifying factors was the coming of age of "Hawaiian" music. It graduated from the "little grass shack" novelty tune and began to include sophisticated jazz, rock, and contemporary rhythms. Accomplished musicians whose roots were in traditional island music began to highlight their tunes with this distinctive sound. The best embellish their arrangements with ukuleles, steel guitars, and traditional percussion and melodic instruments. Some excellent modern recording artists have become island institutions. The local people say that you know if the Hawaiian harmonies are good if they give you "chicken skin."

Each year special music awards, Na Hoku Hanohano, or Hoku for short, are given to distinguished island musicians. The following are recent Hoku winners considered by their contemporaries to be among the best in Hawaii. If they're playing while you're there, don't miss them. They include: **Brothers Cazimero**, whose *Island in Your Eyes,* won Best Contemporary Hawaiian Album. The Brothers are blessed with beautiful harmonic voices, but they are becoming increasingly commercial. **Krush**, whose *More and More,* won the Hoku for "Best Contemporary Album"; **The Peter Moon Band**, contemporary but 100 percent quality with a strong traditional sound. **Karen Keawehawai'i**, whose "With Love, Karen" won the Hoku for "Best Female Vocalist," has a sparkling voice and can be very funny when the mood strikes her. **Henry Kapono**, formerly of Cecelio and Kapono, keeps a low profile but is an incredible performer and excellent songwriter. His shows are noncommercial and very special. **Cecelio** is now teamed up with **Maggie Herron;** the two are hot together and have a strong following in Honolulu. **The Makaha Sons of Niihau** captured the Hoku for Best Traditional Hawaiian Album, and Best Group. Their sound, led by Israel Kamakawiwoole, is the best. They shouldn't be missed. **The**

Beamer Brothers are excellent performers, and can be seen at various nightspots.

Some top-notch newcomers that are gaining popularity are: Ledward Kaapana; Mango; Oliver Kelly; Ka'eo; Na Leo Pilimehana, whose "Local Boys" recently won a Hoku for Best Single; Freitas Brothers; Brickwood Galuteria, who won a double Hoku for Best Male Vocalist and Most Promising Artist; and Third Road Delite.

Classical And Chamber Music

A wide assortment of classical and chamber music is offered in Hawaii. The following organizations sponsor concerts throughout the year: Chamber Music Hawaii, 905 Spencer St., No. 404, Honolulu, HI 96822 (tel. 531-6617); Classical Guitar Society of Hawaii, 1229 D. Waimanu, Honolulu, HI 96814 (tel. 537-6451); The Ensemble Players Guild, Box 50225, Honolulu, HI 96850 (tel. 735-1173); Hawaii Concert Society, Box 663, Hilo, HI 96721 (tel. 935- 5831); Honolulu Symphony Society, 1000 Bishop St., Suite 901, Honolulu, HI 96813 (tel. 537-6171); Kauai Concert Assoc., 5867 Haaheo Pl., Kapaa, HI 96746 (tel. 822-7593); Maui Philharmonic Society, 2274 S. Kihei Rd., Kihei, HI 96753 (tel. 879-2962).

SHOPPING

You can't come to Oahu and *not* shop. Even if the idea of it doesn't thrill you, the lure of almost endless shops offering every imaginable kind of merchandise will sooner or later tempt even the most "big-waste-of-time" mumbler through their doors. So why fight it? And if you're the other type, who feels as though a day without shopping is like being marooned on a deserted island, have no fear of rescue, because everywhere on the horizon is "a sale, a sale!"

You can use "much much more" as either an aspersion or a tribute when describing Oahu, and nowhere does this qualifier fit better than when describing its shopping. Over a dozen major and minor shopping centers and malls are in Honolulu and Waikiki alone! Population centers around the island, including those in the interior, the South Shore, windward shore, and North Shore, all have shopping centers in varying degrees—at the very least, a parking lot rimmed with a half-dozen shops that can provide immediate necessities.

On the Neighbor Islands, a major shopping mall is usually found only in the island's main city, with mom'n' pop stores and small superettes taking up the slack. On Oahu, you've got these too, but you're never very far from some serious shopping centers. The tourist trade fosters the sale of art and artifacts, jewelry and fashions, and numerous boutiques selling these are strung around the island like a shell necklace. Food costs, in supermarkets, tend to be reasonable because Oahu is the main distribution center, and with all the competition, prices in general seem to be lower on the islands. If your trip to Hawaii includes a stop on Oahu, do most of your shopping here, because of the cutrate prices and much greater availability of goods. When most Hawaiians go on a shopping spree, they head for Oahu.

The following listings are general; refer to "Shopping" in the travel sections for listings of specific shops, stores, and markets.

Honolulu Shopping Centers

Since it serves as the main terminal for The-Bus, you could make a strong case that **Ala Moana Shopping Center** (see p. 213), under considerable renovation, is the heart of shopping on Oahu. At one time billed as the largest shopping center in the country, today it settles for being the largest in the state, with its hundreds of stores covering 50 acres. It's on Ala Moana Blvd., just across from the Ala Moana Beach Park. **The Ward Warehouse** (see p. 214) is just a few blocks west of the Ala Moana Center, at 1050 Ala Moana Blvd. The **Ward Center** (see p. 215) on Ala Moana across from Ward Warehouse, is a relatively new shopping center that's gaining a reputation for some exclusive shops.

shell macrame

Waikiki Shopping

Shopping in Waikiki (see p. 257) is as easy as falling off a surfboard. In two or three blocks of Kuhio and Kalakaua avenues are no less than seven shopping centers. If that's not enough, there are hundreds of independent shops, plus plenty of street vendors. Main shopping centers include **Royal Hawaiian Shopping Center,** the **Waikiki Shopping Plaza,** and the **International Market Place,** an open-air shopping bazaar across from the Moana Hotel at 2330 Kalakaua Ave., open daily from 9 a.m. until the vendors get tired at night.

The **Hyatt Regency Shopping Center** is located on the first three floors of the Hyatt Regency Hotel, at 2424 Kalakaua Ave., tel. 922-5522. The **King's Village** is at 131 Kaiulani Ave., the **Waikiki Trade Center** is on the corner of Seaside and Kuhio avenues, and the **Rainbow Bazaar** is a unique mall located at the Hilton Hawaiian Hotel, at 2005 Kalia Road.

Around The Island

Heading east from Waikiki on Rt. 72, the first shopping opportunity is the **Niu Shopping Center** on your left, about four miles before Hanauma Bay. The **Time Supermarket** is known for good prices. Also on the left is the **Koko Marina Shopping Center** (see p. 279), just before Hanauma Bay, with a Liberty House, a few art galleries, and **Foodland Supermarket. Kailua** and **Kaneohe** bedroom communities have shopping malls. Numerous shops are found along the North Shore from Haleiwa to Waimea, including surf, art, boutiques, and plenty of fast food and restaurants. The **Pearlridge Shopping Center** (see p. 270) in Pearl City at the corner of the Kamehameha Hwy. and Waimano Home Rd. is a full shopping complex with over 90 stores. The **Waianae Mall** (see p. 326) at 86-120 Farrington Hwy. serves the Waianae coast with a supermarket, drugstore, fast foods, and sporting goods.

Sundries

ABC has over a dozen mini-marts in and around Waikiki. Their prices are generally high, but they do have some good bargains on suntan lotions, sunglasses, and beach mats. The cheapest place to buy **film** is at **Sears, Woolworth's,** and **Longs Drugs.** All have good selections, cheap prices, and stores all over the island. **Francis Camera Shop** in the Ala Moana Center, tel. 946-2879, is extremely well stocked with accessories. For a large selection of military surplus and camping goods try the **Big 88** at 330 Sand Island Access Rd., tel. 845-1688.

If gadgetry fascinates you, head for **Shirokiya Department Store** at the Ala Moana and Pearlridge centers and in Waikiki. Besides everything else, they have a wonderful selection of all the jimjicks and doohickeys that Nippon has to offer. The atmosphere is somewhat like a trade fair. Those who can't imagine a tour with anything on their feet but Birkenstock can have their tootsies accommodated, but they won't be entirely happy. If you get a sole blowout, **Birkenstock Footprints** at Ala Moana Center, tel. 531-6014, will resole them for $14, but they want a full week to do it. For one-day service, they'll refer you to a shoemaker, **Joe Pacific** at the Ala Moana Center, tel. 946-2998, but he wants a toe-twisting $25 for the service!

Bookstores

Oahu has plenty of excellent bookstores. In Honolulu, try the **Honolulu Book Shops,** with three locations at the Ala Moana Center, tel. 941-2274, in downtown Honolulu at 1001 Bishop St., tel. 537-6224, and at the Pearlridge Center, tel. 487-1548. **Waldenbooks** is at the Pearlridge Center, tel. 488-9488, Kahala Mall, tel. 737-9550, and Waikiki Shopping Plaza, tel. 922-4154. For a fine selection of Hawaiiana try the **Bishop Museum and Planetarium Bookshop,** at the Bishop Museum, 1525 Bernice St., tel. 847-3511, and at the **Mission Houses Museum** in downtown Honolulu at 553 S. King St., tel. 531-0481.

Three women, Rachel McMahan, Janice Beam, and Kathryn Decker, have shopped their fingers to the bone for you and have written a small but definitive book entitled *The Shopping Bag.* It lists and describes shops all over Oahu from art supplies to toys and sporting goods.

Arts And Crafts

The following are a few of Oahu's many art shops and boutiques, just to get you started. An excellent place to find original arts and crafts at reasonable prices is along **The Fence** surrounding the Honolulu Zoo fronting Kapiolani Park. Island artists come here every weekend from 10 a.m.-4 p.m. to display and sell their artwork. The **Honolulu Academy of Arts** at 900 S. Beretania, open Tues. to Sat. 10 a.m.-4:30 p.m., Sun. 1-5 p.m., is not only great to visit (free), but has a fine gift shop that specializes in Asian art.

The same high-quality and authentic handicrafts are available in both the **Hawaiian Mission Houses Museum** and **Bishop Museum** gift shops (see "Bookstores" above). For Oriental art try **Gallery Mikado** and **Garakuta-Do,** both in Waikiki's Eaton Square Complex. **Ka'ala Art,** tel. 637-7533, in Haleiwa (see p. 317) is a great one-stop shop for fine arts, pop art, and handicrafts, all by aspiring island artists. Also in Haleiwa, the **Fettig Art Gallery,** tel. 637-4933, is the oldest gallery on the North Shore, featuring works by Beverly Fettig and other island artists. The **Punaluu Gallery,** tel. 237-8325, is the oldest gallery on the windward coast. It's been there over 30 years and is now operated by candle maker extraordinaire Scott Bechtol.

Flea Markets And Swap Meets

These are the cheapest places to find treasures. Two operate successfully on Oahu and have a regular following. **Aloha Flea Market,** tel. 732-2437, is at Aloha Stadium every Wed., Sat., and Sun. from 7.a.m.-3 p.m. It's the biggest flea market on Oahu, selling everything from bric-a-brac to real heirlooms and treasures. **Kam Swap Meet,** tel. 488-5822, Kam Drive-In Theater, 98-850 Moanalua Rd., Pearl City, is open Wed., Thurs., Sat., and Sun. mornings. Regular stall holders to housewives cleaning out the garage offer great fun and bargains.

FESTIVALS, HOLIDAYS, AND EVENTS

In addition to all the American national holidays, Hawaii celebrates its own festivals, pageants, ethnic fairs, and a multitude of specialized exhibits. They occur throughout the year, some particular to only one island or locality, while others such as Aloha Week and Lei Day are celebrated on all the islands. Some of the smaller local happenings are semi-spontaneous, so there's no *exact* date when they're held. These are some of the most rewarding, because they provide the best times to have fun with the local people. Check local newspapers and the free island magazines for exact dates of some events.

The following events and celebrations are either particular to Oahu, or they're celebrated here in a special or different way. This central island has more festivities and events than all the others, and these times provide great social opportunities for meeting people. Everyone is welcomed to join in the fun, and most times the events are either free, or nominally priced. There's no better way to enjoy yourself while vacationing than by joining in with a local party or happening.

JANUARY

January 1: *Hauoli Makahiki Hou*. Start the New Year off right by climbing to the top of Koko Crater on Oahu. A great way to focus on the limitless horizons of the coming year and a great hangover remedy. See the HVB for details. Or continue the party with the **Sunshine Music Festival** rock concert at Diamond Head Crater.

January 2: **Queen Emma Museum Open House.** This is Queen Emma's birthday, and the public is invited to visit her summer home and view a well-preserved collection of her personal belongings. Call 595-6291.

First Saturday: Watch the old pigskin get booted around in the **Hula Bowl Game**, Aloha Stadium, Honolulu. Annual college all-star football classic. Call Aloha Stadium, 488-7731.

Mid-January to early February: **The Narcissus Festival** in Honolulu's Chinatown starts with the parade and festivities of Chinese New Year. Lion dances in the street, fireworks, beauty pageant, and a coronation ball. For details call Welton Won at 533-3181.

Late January: **Robert Burns Night** at the Ilikai Hotel, Honolulu. Scots from Canada and mainland U.S. celebrate the birthday of Scotland's poet Robert Burns. Louis Macphee, tel. 488-3839.

Cherry Blossom Festival in Honolulu. can begin in late January and last through March. Japanese cultural and trade show, tea ceremony, flower arranging, queen pageant, and coronation ball. Call Ray Urabetel, 847-3763, and check newspapers and free tourist magazines for dates and times of various Japanese cultural events.

FEBRUARY

Early February: **NFL Pro Bowl**. Aloha Stadium, Honolulu. Annual all-star football game offering the best from both conferences. Aloha Stadium, tel. 488-7731.

Punahou School Carnival, Honolulu. Arts, crafts, and a huge rummage sale at one of Hawaii's oldest and most prestigious high schools. Great ethnic foods and you'd be surprised at what Hawaii's oldest and most established families donate to the rummage sale. Call Yvonne Brown, 944-5752.

The Hawaiian Open International Golf Tournament, in Honolulu at Waialae Country Club. $500,000 prize money lures the best PGA golfers to this tournament, which is beginning its second decade. Call Chester Kahapea, 836-0060.

Mid-February: **Haleiwa Sea Spree** on Oahu's North Shore. Surfing championships, outrigger canoe races, and ancient Hawaiian sports, topped off by an around-the-island bicycle race. Competitions last four days.

Late February-early March: **Buffalo's Annual Big Board Surfing Classic** at Makaha Beach, Oahu. Features the best of the classic board riders. A real cultural event complete with entertainment, crafts, and food. A two-day event held the last weekend in February and again on the first weekend in March.

MARCH

Remember **Buffalo's Big Board Classic** and the **Carole Kai Bed Race** down Kalakaua Ave. in Waikiki and a free concert at the Waikiki Shell the night before. There's a race and appearances by Hawaii's name entertainers in this fun-filled charity fund-raiser. Call 732-2835.

Hawaiian Song Festival and Song Composing Contest. Kapiolani Park Bandstand in Waikiki. Determines the year's best Hawaiian song. Presented by top-name entertainers. Call 521-9815.

Emerald Ball. An elegant affair sponsored by the Society of the Friendly Sons of St. Patrick which features dinner and dancing by a big-name band. Also, the Saint Patrick's Day Parade. Kalakaua Ave. Waikiki. Call 471-0006.

Kamehameha School Annual Song Contest. Blaisdell Center Arena, Honolulu. Competition among secondary-grade students of Hawaiian ancestry. Kamehameha Schools, tel. 842-8211.

Late March: **Hawaiian Highland Gathering**, Honolulu. A gathering of the clans for Scottish games, competition, Scottish foods, highland dancing, and pipe bands. Great Scotsmen with kilts and leis too. Richardson's Field, Pearl Harbor, Oahu. 523-5050.

Annual Hawaiian Festival of Music. A musical competition between visiting Mainland bands and local bands, with categories in swing, marching bands, and madrigals. Everyone, especially the spectators, can't help being winners. Call, 637-6566.

APRIL

Early April: **Easter Sunday**. Sunrise Service at the National Memorial Cemetery of The Pacific, Punchbowl Crater, Honolulu.

Annual Hawaiian Festival of Music. Waikiki Shell, Honolulu. A grand and lively music competition of groups from all over the islands and the Mainland. A music lover's smorgasbord offering everything from symphony to swing and all in between. Call 637-6566.

April 8: **Wesak or Buddha Day**. The closest Sunday to April 8, celebrates the birthday of Gautama Buddha. Ornate offerings of tropical flowers at temples throughout Hawaii. Great sunrise ceremonies at Kapiolani Park, Honolulu. Mainly Japanese in their best *kimono*. Flower festival pageant and dance programs in all island temples.

Mid-April: **Aloha Basketball Classic**, Blaisdell Center Arena, Honolulu. Top college seniors are invited to Hawaii to participate in charity games made up of four teams. Blaisdell Center, tel. 527-5400.

MAY

May 1: **Lei Day**. May Day to the rest of the world, but in Hawaii red is only one of the colors when everyone wears a lei. Festivities throughout Hawaii with special goings-on at Kapiolani Park, Waikiki.

Early May: **Pacific Handcrafters Guild Fair**, at Ala Moana Park, Honolulu. An opportunity to see the "state of the arts" in Hawaii. Some of the islands' finest craftsmen in one spot selling their creations. Call 538-7227.

Late May: **Memorial Day**. Special military services held at Honolulu, National Memorial Cemetery of the Pacific on the last Monday in May. Call 546-3190.

50th State Fair, at Aloha Stadium, Honolulu. Agricultural exhibts, downhome cooking, entertainment, and produce. Lasts four weekends. Call 536-5492.

JUNE

Early June: **Mission Houses Museum Fancy Fair**, Houolulu. A top-notch collection of Hawaii's best artists and craftsmen. A great chance to browse and buy. Also, foods and entertainment. Call 531-0481.

June 11: **King Kamehameha Day** is a Hawaiian state holiday honoring Kamehameha the Great, Hawaii's first and greatest universal king. Lei-draping ceremony at King Kamehameha statue and parades complete with floats and pageantry featuring a ho'olaule'a (street party) in Waikiki. Civic Center, downtown Honolulu.

Mid-June: **Annual King Kamehameha Traditional Hula And Chant Competition**. Brigham Young University, Laie.

Annual Hawaiian Festival of Music, Waikiki Shell, Honolulu. A repeat of the April festivities, but no less of a music lover's delight as local and Mainland bands compete in genres from symphony to swing.

Late June: **Annual Japan Festival**, dances and festivities in Honolulu at Kapiolani Park and the Blaisdell Center. Also, bon odori, the Japanese festival of departed souls, which features dances and candle- lighting ceremonies at numerous Buddhist temples throughout the islands. A special bon odori festival is offered at Haleiwa Jodo Mission, Haleiwa, Oahu. These festivities change yearly and can be held anytime from late June to early August.

JULY

Early: **Tin Man Triathlon**, Honolulu. Over 1,000 triathletes gather to swim 800 meters, bike 25 miles and finish with a 10,000-meter (6.2 miles) run around Diamond Head and back to Kapiolani Park in Waikiki. call 533-4262.

Pan Am Clipper Cup Series. Boats from ports around the world sail to Oahu to navigate a series of triangles off Waikiki, along with one nonstop race from Ala Wai Harbor to Molokai, and an around-the-state nonstop race.

Trans Pacific Yacht Race, from Los Angeles to Honolulu during odd-numbered years. Yachties arrive throughout the month and converge on the Ala Wai Yacht Basin, where "party" is the password. They head off for Hanalei Bay, Kauai, to begin the year's yachting season.

Hawaiian Islands Tall Ships Parade, July 4, Oahu. Tall-masted ships from throughout the islands parade from Koko Head to Sand Island and back to Diamond Head. A rare treat and taste of days gone by.

Mid-July: **Prince Lot Hula Festival**, Honolulu. A great chance for visitors to see authentic hula from some of the finest hula halau in the islands. Moanalua Gardens, tel. 839-5334.

Annual Ukulele Festival, Kapiolani Park Bandstand, Waikiki. Hundreds of ukulele players from throughout the islands.

Pacific Handcrafters Fair, Thomas Square, Honolulu. A chance to see the "state of the arts" all in one locality. Browse, buy, and eat ethnic foods at various stalls.

Late July: International Sailboard Championship Invitational held of Diamond Head. Watch the amazing "aquabatics" as sailboarders run before the wind on their amazing one-man crafts.

AUGUST

Early August: **Honolulu Zoo Day,** Waikiki. A day of family fun where "kids" of all ages get a close-up look at the animals and a day of entertainment.

Hula Festival, Kapiolani Park, Waikiki. Recent hula graduates from Honolulu's Summer Fun classes perform hulas they have learned. All ages and some amazing bodily gyrations.

Late August: **Hawaiian Open State Tennis Championships**, Honolulu. Held at various courts around town offering substantial prizes. Don Andrews, tel. 923-9727.

Queen Liliuokalani Keiki Hula Competition, Kamehameha Schools, Honolulu. Children ages 5-12 compete in a hula contest. Caution: "Terminal Cuteness."

SEPTEMBER

Early September: **Waikiki Rough Water Swim**, Honolulu. A two-mile open-ocean swim from Sans Souci Beach to Duke Kahanamoku Beach. Open to all ages and ability. Contact Gen Linuma, tel. 547-6410.

Late September: **Aloha Week**. There are major festivities on all of the islands, as everyone celebrates Hawaii's own "intangible quality," *aloha*. There are parades, luaus, historical pageants, balls, and various other entertainment. The spirit of *aloha* is infectious and all are welcomed to join in. Check local papers and tourist literature for happenings near you. Downtown parades attract thousands, and even parking lots do their bit by charging a $1 flat fee during these festival times. The savory smells of ethnic foods fill the air from a multitude of stands, and the Honolulu Symphony performs at the Blaisdel Center, while free concerts are given at the Wakiki Shell.

Molokai To Oahu Canoe Race. Women (men in October) in Hawaiian-stlye canoes race from a remote beach on Kauai to Fort DeRussy in Honolulu. In transit they must navigate the rough Kaiwi Channel.

OCTOBER

Early October: **Pacific Handcrafters Guild**, Ala Moana Center Gallery, Honolulu. A fall show of the best works of Handcrafters Guild members. Perfect for early-bird and unique Christmas shopping.

Makahiki Festival, Waimea Falls Park, Oahu. Features Hawaiian games, crafts, and dances, reminiscent of the great Makahiki celebrations of ancient Hawaii. On an 800-acre tropical preserve.

Molokai To Oahu Canoe Race. Men (women in Sept.) navigate Hawaiian-style canoes across the rough Kaiwi Channel from a remote beach on Molokai to Fort DeRussy, Honolulu. Contact Fred Hemmings, tel. 926-0611.

Oktoberfest. Where else would you expect to find German oom-pah bands, suc-

Aloha Week

culent wienerschnitzels, *und* beer, than in Honolulu. At the Budweiser Warehouse, 99-877 Iwaena St., Halawa Park, from noon until 10 p.m.

Mid-October: **Pan Am International Rugby Club Tournament**. Odd-numbered years. Watch the boys from throughout Oceania smash, clash, and collide in this rough and tumble sport. Queen Kapiolani Park, Honolulu. Contact Dick Gooch, tel. 836-6741.

Annual Orchid Plant And Flower Show. Hawaii's copious and glorious flowers are displayed. Blaisdell Center Exhibition Hall, Honolulu. Blaisdell Center, tel. 527-5400.

Late October: **Bishop Museum Festival**. A superb time to visit the world's best museum on Polynesia and Hawaii. Arts, crafts, plants, and tours of the museum and planetarium. A full day for the family, with special "back room" exhibits open to the public which are usually not seen. Bishop Museum, Honolulu. Bishop Museum tel. 847-3511.

NOVEMBER

Early November: **Ho'Olaulea in Waianae**, Wainae, Oahu. The military lets down its hair and puts on a display accompanied by top entertainers, food, and music in this very ethnic area. All-day event. Army Community Relations, tel. 438-9761.

November 11: **Veterans Day Parade**. National Holiday. A parade from Fort DeRussy to Queen Kapiolani Park, Waikiki. American Legion, tel. 949- 1140.

Christmas in November: **Mission Houses Museum Annual Christmas Fair**. Quality items offered by Hawaii's top craftsmen in an open-air bazaar. Call 531-0481.

Late November: **Hawaiian Pro-Surfing Championships**. The best surfers in the world come to the best surfing beaches on Oahu. Wave action determines sites except for Men's Masters which is always held at Banzai Pipeline, North Shore, Oahu. Big money and national TV coverage. Call 521- 8555.

Artists Of Hawaii Annual Exhibition. The best works of Hawaii's contemporary fine artists. The Honolulu Academy of Arts, Honolulu, Oahu, tel. 538-3693.

DECEMBER

Early December: **Hawaii International Film Festival**, East-West Center, Honolulu. The best art films from the East, West, and Oceania. Call 944-7203.

Christmas celebrations: **Kamehameha Schools Christmas Concert**, Blaisdell Center Concert Hall, Honolulu, Oahu. Call 842-8211.

Pacific Handcrafters Guild Christmas Fair, Thomas Square, Honolulu. The best by the best, just in time for Christmas. Open air. Pacific Handcrafters, tel. 538-7227.

Mid-December: **Annual Honolulu Marathon**. An institution in marathon races. One of the best-attended and very prestigious races in the country, where top athletes from around the world turn out to compete. Call 734-7200.

Annual Rainbow Classic. Invitational tournament of collegiate basketball teams. Blaisdell Center Arena, Honolulu, Oahu. Call 948- 7523.

Aloha Bowl Game. Collegiate football. Aloha Stadium, Honolulu, tel. 488-7731.

PERFORMING ARTS EVENTS

The following offer top-notch performances at various times throughout the year: **Honolulu Symphony**, tel. 537-6191; **Hawaii Opera Theatre**, tel. 521-6537; **Honolulu Community Theatre**, tel. 734-0274; **Hawaii Performing Arts Company Theatre**, tel. 988-6131.

GETTING THERE

With the number of visitors each year approaching six million, and double that number of travelers just passing through, Hawaii is one of the easiest places in the world to get to . . . by plane. About 10 large U.S. airlines (and other small ones) fly to and from the islands; about the same number of foreign carriers, mostly from Asia and Oceania, touch down on a daily basis. In 1978 airlines were "deregulated." In 1984, the reign of the Civil Aeronautics Board (CAB), which controlled exactly which airlines flew where and how much they could charge, ended. Routes, prices, and schedules were thrown open to free competition. Airlines that had previously monopolized preferred destinations found competitors prying loose their strangleholds. Thus, Hawaii is now one of the most hotly contested air markets in the world. The competition between carriers is fierce, and this makes for "sweet deals" and a wide choice of fares for the money-wise traveler. It also makes for pricing chaos. It's impossible to give airline prices that will hold true for more than a month, if that long. But it's comforting to know that flights to Hawaii are cheaper today than they have been in years, and mile for mile are one of the best travel bargains in the industry. What's really important is to be familiar with the alternatives at your disposal, so you can make an informed travel selection. Now more than ever you should work with a sharp travel agent who's on your side.

Brief Airline History

On May 20-21, 1927, the people of the world were mesmerized by the heroic act of Charles Lindbergh, The Lone Eagle, as he safely piloted his sturdy craft, *The Sprit of St. Louis,* across the Atlantic. With the Atlantic barrier broken, it took only four days for Jim Dole, of pineapple fame, to announce an air race from the West Coast to Hawaii. He offered the same first prize of $25,000 that Lindbergh had claimed, and to sweeten the pot he offered $10,500 for second place. The **Dole Air Derby** applied only to civilian flights, though the military was already at work attempting the Pacific crossing.

In August 1925, a Navy flying boat took off from near San Francisco, piloted by Commander John Rodgers. The seaplane flew without difficulty across the wide Pacific's expanse, but ran out of gas just north of the Hawaiian Islands and had to put down in a stormy sea. Communication devices went dead and the mission was given up as lost. Heroically, Rodgers and his crew made crude sails from the wing's fabric and sailed the plane to within 12 miles of Kauai, where they were spotted by an incredulous submarine crew. On June 28, 1927, Army Lieutenants Maitland and Hegenberger successfully flew a Fokker tri-motor land plane, *The Bird of Paradise,* from Oakland to Oahu in just under 26 hours.

On July 14, 1927, independent of the air derby, two indomitable pilots, Smith and Bronte, flew their *City of Oakland* from its namesake to a forced landing on the shoreline of Molokai. On August 16, 1927, eight planes lined up in Oakland to start the derby. The first to take off was the *Woolaroc,* piloted by Art Goebel and Bill Davis. It went on to win the race and claim the prize in just over 26 hours. Second place went to the appropriate-

PACIFIC CROSSROADS

© MOON PUBLICATIONS, INC.

ly named *Aloha,* crewed by Martin Jensen and Paul Schluter, coming in two hours behind the *Woolaroc.* Unfortunately, two planes were lost in the crossing and two more in the rescue attempt, which accounted for 12 dead. However, the race proved that flying to Hawaii was indeed feasible.

WINGS TO HAWAII

There are two categories of airlines that you can take to Hawaii: **domestic,** meaning American-owned, and **foreign**-owned. An American law, penned at the turn of the century to protect American shipping, says "only" an American carrier can transport you to and from two American cities. In the airline industry, this law is still very much in effect. It means, for example, that if you want a round-trip San Francisco/Honolulu, you *must* fly on a domestic carrier, such as United or Pan Am. If, however, you are flying San Francisco to Tokyo, you are at liberty to fly a "foreign" airline such as Japan Air Lines, and you may even have a stopover in Hawaii, but you must continue on to Tokyo or some other foreign city and cannot fly JAL back to San Francisco. Canadians have no problem flying Canadian Pacific roundtrip from Toronto to Honolulu because this route does not connect two American cities, and so it is with all foreign travel to and from Hawaii. Travel agents all know this, but if you're planning your own trip be aware of this fact and know that if you're flying roundtrip it must be on a domestic carrier.

Kinds Of Flights

The three kinds of flights are the "milk run," direct, and nonstop. Milk runs are the least convenient. On these, you board a carrier, say in your home town, fly it to a gateway city, change planes and carriers, fly on to the West Coast, change again, and then fly to Hawaii. They're a hassle—your bags have a much better chance of getting lost, you waste time in airports, and to top it off, they're not any cheaper. Avoid them if you can.

On direct flights you fly from point A to point B without changing planes; it doesn't mean that you don't land in between. Direct flights

do land usually once to board and deplane passengers, but you sit cozily on the plane along with your luggage and off you go again. Nonstop is just that, but can cost a bit more. You board and when the doors open again you're in Hawaii. All nonstop flights from the West Coast gateway cities are "God willing," because there is only the Pacific in between!

Travel Agents

At one time people went to a travel agent the same way they went to a barber or beautician . . . loyally sticking with one. Most agents are reputable professionals who know what they're doing. They should be members of the American Society of Travel Agents (ASTA) and licensed by the Air Traffic Conference (ATC). Most have the inside track on the best deals, and they'll save you countless hours calling 800 numbers and listening to elevator music while on hold. Unless you require them to make very special arrangements, their services are free—the airlines and hotels that they book you into pay their commission.

If you've done business with a travel agent in the past, and were satisfied with the services and prices, by all means stick with him or her. If no such positive rapport exists, then shop around. Ask friends or relatives for recommendations; if you can't get any endorsements go to the Yellow Pages. Call two or three travel agents to compare prices. Make sure to give them equal information and be as precise as possible. Tell them where and when you want to go, how long you want to stay, class you want to travel, and any special requirements. Write down their information. It's amazing how confusing travel plans can be when you have to keep track of flight numbers, times, prices, and all the preparation info. When you compare, don't look only for the cheapest price. Check for convenience in flights, amenities of hotels, and any other fringe benefits that might be included. Then make your choice of agent; if he or she is willing to give you individualized service, stick with them from this point on.

Agents become accustomed to offering the same deals to many clients because they're familiar with making the arrangements and they worked well in the past. Sometimes these are indeed the best, but if they don't suit you, don't be railroaded into accepting them. Any good agent will work with you. After all, it's your trip and your money.

Package Tours

As an independent traveler, practical package deals that include flight, car, and lodging only are OK. Agents put these together all the time and they just might be the best, but if they don't suit you make arrangements separately. A package tour is totally different. On these you get your hand held by an escort, eat where they want you to eat, go where they want you to go, and watch Hawaii slide by past the window of your bus. For some people, especially older folks or groups, this might be the way, but everyone else should avoid them. You'll see Hawaii best on your own, and if you want a tour you can arrange one there, often cheaper. Once arrangements have been made with your travel agent, make sure to take all receipts and letters of confirmation (hotel, car) with you to Hawaii. They probably won't be needed, but if they are, nothing will work better in getting results.

Fares

There are many categories of airline fares, but only three generally apply to the average traveler: 1st class, coach, and excursion (APEX). Traveling **1st class** seats you in the front of the plane, gives you free drinks and movie headsets, a wider choice of meals, more legroom, and access to VIP lounges if they exist. There are no restrictions, payment penalties on advance booking, minimum stays, or rebooking return flights.

Coach, the way that most people fly, is totally adequate. You sit in the plane's main compartment behind 1st class. Your seats are comfortable, but you don't have as much legroom or such a wide choice of meals. Movie headsets and drinks cost you a few dollars, but that's about it. **Coach** offers many of the same benefits as 1st class and costs about 30 percent less. You can buy tickets up to takeoff; you have no restrictions on minimum or maximum stays; you receive liberal stopover privileges, and you can cash in your return ticket or change your return date with no penalties.

Excursion or **advance payment excursion (APEX)** fares are the cheapest. You are accommodated on the plane exactly the same as if you were flying coach. There are, however, some restrictions. You must book and pay for your ticket in advance (seven to 14 days). At the same time, you must book your return flight, and under most circumstances can't change either without paying a penalty. Also, your stopovers are severely limited and you will have a minimum/maximum stay period. Only a limited number of seats on any one plane are set aside for APEX fares, so book as early as you can. Also, if you must change travel plans, you can go to the airport and get on as a standby passenger using a discounted ticket even if the airline doesn't have an official standby policy. There's always the risk that you won't get on but you do have a chance, as well as priority over an actual standby customer.

Standby is exactly what its name implies: you go to the airport and wait around to see if any flights going to Hawaii have an empty seat. You can save some money, but cannot have a firm itinerary or limited time. Since Hawaii is such a popular destination standbys can wait days before catching a plane. A company called **Stand Bys Ltd.** offers an up-to-the-minute newsletter and an 800 number which gives you information on charter flights that haven't sold out. The service costs $45 per year, but you can save from 15-60 percent on most tickets. Write Stand Bys Ltd., 26711 Northwestern Hwy., Southfield, MI 48034 tel. (313) 352-4876.

Active and retired **military personnel** and their dependents are offered special fares on airlines and in military hostels. An excellent resource book listing all of these special fares and more is *Space-A*, ($11.75 for book and first-class postage), available from Military Travel News, P.O. Box 9, Oakton, VA 22124. Plenty of money-saving tips.

Charters

Charter flights were at one time only for groups or organizations that had memberships in travel clubs. Now they're open to the general public. A charter flight is an entire plane or a "block" of seats purchased at a quantity discount by a charter company and then sold to customers. Because they are bought at wholesale prices, charter fares can be the cheapest available. As in package deals, only take a charter flight if it is a "fly only," or perhaps includes a car. You don't need one that includes a guide and a bus. Most importantly, make sure that the charter company is reputable. They should belong to the same organizations (ASTA and ATC) as most travel agents. If not, check into them at the local chamber of commerce.

More restrictions apply to charters than any others. You must pay in advance. If you cancel after a designated time, you can be penalized severely or lose your money entirely. You cannot change departure or return dates and times. However, up to 10 days before departure the charter company is legally able to cancel, raise the price by 10 percent, or change time and dates. They must return your money if cancellation occurs, or if changed arrangements are unacceptable to you. Mostly they are on the up and up and flights go smoothly, but there are horror stories. Be careful. Be wise. Investigate!

Tips

Flights from the West Coast take about five hours; you gain two hours over Pacific Standard Time when you land in Hawaii. From the East Coast it takes about 11 hours and you gain five hours over Eastern Standard Time. Try to fly Monday through Thursday, when flights are cheaper and easier to book. Pay for your ticket as soon as your plans are firm. If prices go up there is no charge added, but merely booking doesn't guarantee the lowest price. Make sure that airlines, hotels, and car agencies get your phone number too, not only your travel agent's, in case any problems with availability arise (travel agents are often closed on weekends. It's not necessary, but it's a good idea to call and reconfirm flights 24-72 hours in advance.

First-row (bulkhead) seats are good for people who need more leg room, but bad for watching the movie. Airlines will give you special meals (vegetarian, kosher, low cal, low salt) often at no extra charge, but you must notify them in advance. If you're "bumped" from an overbooked flight, you're entitled to a comparable flight to your destination within one hour. If more than an hour elapses, you get denied-boarding compensation which goes up proportionately with the amount of time you're held up. Sometimes this is cash or a voucher for another flight to be used in the future. You don't have to accept what the airlines offer on the spot, if you feel they aren't being fair.

Traveling With Children

Fares for children two-12 are 50 percent of the adult fare; children under two not occupying a seat travel free. If you're traveling with an infant or active toddler, book your flight well in advance and request the bulkhead seat or first row in any section and a bassinet if available. Many carriers have fold-down cribs with restraints for baby's safety and comfort. Toddlers appreciate the extra space provided by the front-row seats. Be sure to reconfirm and arrive early to assure getting this special seating. On long flights you'll be glad that you took these extra pains.

Although most airlines have coloring books, puppets, etc., to keep your child busy, it's always a good idea to bring your own. These can make the difference between a pleasant flight and a harried ordeal. Also, remember to bring baby bottles, formula, diapers, and other necessities as many airlines may not be equipped with exactly what you need. Make all inquiries ahead of time so you're not caught unprepared.

Baggage

You are allowed two free pieces of luggage and a carry-on bag. The two main pieces can weigh up to 70 pounds each with an extra charge levied for extra weight. The largest can have an overall added dimension (height plus width plus length) of 62 inches and the second at 55 inches. Your carry-on must fit under your seat or in the overhead storage compartment. Purses and camera bags are not counted as carry-ons and may be taken aboard. Surfboards and bicycles are about

$15 extra. Although they make great mementos, remove all previous baggage tags from your luggage; they can confuse handlers. Attach a sturdy holder with your name and address on the handle, or use a stick-on label on the bag itself. Put your name and address inside the bag, and the address where you'll be staying in Hawaii if possible. Carry your cosmetics, identification, money, prescriptions, tickets, reservations, change of underwear, camera equipment, and perhaps a change of shirt or blouse in your carry-on.

Visas
Entering Hawaii is like entering anywhere else in the U.S. Foreign nationals must have a current passport and proper visa. An ongoing or return air ticket as well as sufficient funds for the proposed stay in Hawaii are also requirements of foreign nationals by U.S. Immigration. Canadians do not need a visa or passport, but must have proper identification such as passport, driver's license, or birth certificate.

OAHU ARRIVALS

The old adage of "all roads leading to Rome" applies almost perfectly to Oahu, though instead of being cobblestones, they're sea lanes and air routes. Except for a handful of passenger ships still docking at Honolulu Harbor, and some limited nonstop flights to Maui and the Big Island, all other passengers to and from Hawaii are routed through **Honolulu International Airport.** These flights include direct flights to the Neighbor Islands, which means stopping over at Honolulu International and continuing on the same plane, or more likely changing to an inter-island carrier whose fare is included in the original price of the flight.

Honolulu International Airport
The state's only international airport is one of the busiest in the entire country, with hundreds of flights to and from cities around the world arriving and departing daily. In a routine year, over 15 million passengers utilize this facility. The two terminals (directions given as you face the main entranceway) are: the main terminal, accommodating all international and Mainland flights, with a small wing at the far-left end of the ground floor for a few commuter airlines; and the inter-island terminal in a separate building at the far right end of the main terminal.

The ground floor of the **main terminal** is mostly for arriving passengers, and contains the baggage claim area, lockers and long-

© MOON PUBLICATIONS, INC.

term storage, car rental agencies, and international and domestic arrival doors which are kept separate. The second floor is for departing passengers, with most activity centered here, including ticket counters, shops, lounges, baggage handlers, and the entrance to most of the gates. From both levels you can board taxis and TheBus to downtown Honolulu and Waikiki.

International carriers usually park on the right side of the main terminal and use gates 26 through 31, while gates six through 31, on the left, are used by domestic carriers. The peak hours for the airport are 7-11 a.m. and 5-7 p.m.

The **inter-island terminal** services flights aboard Hawaiian, Aloha, and Mid-Pacific Airlines to and from Honolulu. It has its own snack bars, car rental booths, transportation to and from the city, lounges, information windows, and restrooms. It is only a leisurely five minutes stroll between the two terminals, which is fine if you don't have much baggage; if you do, there are plenty of shuttles every few minutes. If you are at the small commuter airlines terminal at the opposite end of the complex, shuttles ($.50) come regularly, but if you need one in a hurry just ask at the ticket booths there to summon one for you.

Services, Information, Tips

The main **information booth** is located on the second level just near the central escalators. Besides general information, they have good maps of the airport, Oahu, Honolulu, and Waikiki. Also, inquiry booths lined up along the ground level and at the inter-island terminal are friendly and helpful, but not always stocked with as many maps as the main information booth.

The **lost and found** is located on the ground level of the main terminal, and at the inter-island terminal. The **post office** is across the street from the main entranceway toward the inter-island terminal.

Lockers are located on both levels of the main terminal and at the inter-island terminal, with a **baggage storage room** only on the ground floor of the main terminal. Locker rental is $1 for a 24-hour period, with a refundable $5 key deposit. You can rent lockers

for a month or longer, but you must prepay and leave a deposit. The baggage storage accepts no personal checks, no prepayments, and no pets or perishables. You *must* have your claim ticket to retrieve your belongings. The service is well run, efficient, and unfriendly.

Money can be a hassle at the airport, especially getting change, which is a downright rip-off, and very bad public relations for visitors. Unfortunately, no one will give you change, putting you at the mercy of $1 bill-change machines located throughout the airport. These machines happily dispense $.85 for every $1 you put in, so if you want to make a phone call, or the like, you're out of luck. The snack bars will only change money for you with a purchase. For a state that prides itself on the *aloha* spirit and depends on good relations with its visitors, this is a ridiculously poor way of greeting people, or giving them a last impression before they return home. The **foreign currency exchange** is on the second floor of the main terminal along the concourse behind the United ticket window. Here, and at a few smaller exchanges on the ground floor, the charge is one percent per transaction on foreign currency, and the same on traveler's cheques no matter where they're from, with a minimum charge of $1.50.

To refresh and relax, you might visit the **Shower Tree,** on the second floor behind the United counter, next to the hairdresser. You can have a shower for $7.50, which includes soap, towel, shampoo, deodorant, and hairdryers; an eight-hour sleep in a private little room and a shower for $18.72; or a rest at $3 per hour. If this seems a bit pricy, just use the public bathrooms for a quick wash, then choose any one of three small gardens near the central concourse to take a little nap. If you're there just for a short snooze, airport security won't bother you.

Airport Transportation

Car rental agencies are lined up at booths on the ground floor of both terminals. Many courtesy phones for car rental agencies not at the airport are located in and around the baggage claim area; call for free vans to pick you up and take you to their nearby facility. This procedure even saves the hassle of maneuvering through heavy airport traffic— you usually wait at the island in the middle of the road just outside the baggage claim area. Make sure to specify the number of the area where you'll wait.

If you're driving to the airport to pick up or drop off someone, you should know about **parking.** If you want to park on the second level of the parking garage for departures, you must either take the elevator up to the fourth floor, or down to ground level, and from there cross the pedestrian bridge. There's no way to get across on levels two and three.

Public transportation to downtown Honolulu, especially Waikiki, is abundant. Moreover, some hotels have courtesy phones near the baggage claim area; if you're staying there, they'll send a van to fetch you. Current charges for taxis, vans, TheBus, and limos are posted just outside the baggage claim area, so you won't have to worry about being overcharged. **Taxis** to Waikiki cost about $15, not counting bags. **Grayline** runs a small bus or van to Waikiki for about $5 with no baggage charge. Also, a number of vans and motorcoaches leave from the central island in the roadway just outside the baggage claim. They charge $5, but a wait of up to 45 minutes for one is not out of the ordinary. Moreover, they drop passengers at hotels all over Waikiki, so if you're not one of the first stops by chance, it could be an hour or so after reaching Waikiki before you're finally deposited at your hotel.

Terminal Transportation, tel. 926-4747, offers hotel pick-up and a ride to the airport, including two standard pieces of luggage, for $5 adult, $2 child. **Em's Airport Shuttle,** tel. 545-1266, offers similar service from Waikiki every half-hour from 6 a.m.-10 p.m. Or call **Airport Transportation,** tel. 261-7880 or 923-5700, adults $5, children 5-11 $2. They'll pick you up at a Waikiki hotel and bring you to the airport or vice versa.

You can take **TheBus** (#8 and #20) to Waikiki via the Ala Moana Terminal, from which you can get buses all over the island. If you're heading north pick up buses 20, 51, or 52 just outside the airport. TheBus only

costs $.60 (exact change), but you are allowed only one carry-on bag that must be small enough to be held on your lap. Drivers are sticklers on this point.

DOMESTIC CARRIERS

The following are the major domestic carriers to and from Hawaii. The planes used are primarily DC-10s and 747s, with a smaller 727 flown now and again. A list of the "gateway cities" from which they fly direct and nonstop flights is given, but "connecting cities" are not. All flights, by all carriers, land at Honolulu International Airport except for limited direct flights to Maui and Hawaii. Only the established companies are listed. Entrepreneurial small airlines, such as the now defunct Hawaii Express, pop up now and again and specialize in dirt-cheap fares. There is a hectic frenzy to buy their tickets and business is great for a while, but then the established companies lower their fares and the gamblers fold.

Hawaiian Air
One of Hawaii's own domestic airlines has entered the Mainland market. They operate a daily flight from Los Angeles and San Francisco to Honolulu, with periodic flights from Anchorage, Las Vegas, Portland, and Seattle. The "common fare" ticket price includes an ongoing flight to any of the Neighbor Islands, and if leaving from Hawaii, a free flight from a Neighbor Island to the link-up in Honolulu. Hawaiian Air's trans-Pacific schedule features flights between Honolulu and points in the South Pacific nearly every day: flights depart for Pago Pago, American Samoa, half continuing on to Apia, Western Samoa, the rest to Tonga, with additional flights to New Zealand, Guam, Tahiti, and Rarotonga. Hawaiian Air offers special discount deals with Dollar rental cars and select major island hotels. Contact Hawaiian Air at (800) 367-5320.

United Airlines
Since their first island flight in 1947, United has become top dog in flights to Hawaii. Their Mainland routes connect over 100 cities to Honolulu. The main gateways are direct

flights from San Francisco, Los Angeles, San Diego, Seattle, Portland, Chicago, New York, Denver, and Toronto. They also offer direct flights to Maui from San Francisco, Los Angeles, and Chicago, and from Los Angeles to the Big Island. United offers a number of packages, including flight and hotel on Oahu, and flight, hotel, and car on the neighboring islands. They interline with Aloha Airlines and deal with Hertz rental cars. They're the "big guys" and they intend to stay that way—their packages are hard to beat. Call (800) 241-6522.

American Airlines
Offers direct flights to Honolulu from Los Angeles, San Francisco, Dallas, and Chicago. They also fly from Los Angeles and San Francisco to Maui, with a connection in Honolulu. Call (800) 433-7300.

Continental
Flights from all Mainland cities to Honolulu go via Los Angeles and San Francisco. Also available are direct flights from Australia and New Zealand to Honolulu. Call (800) 525-0280 or (800) 231-0856 for international information.

Northwest Orient
Northwest flies from Los Angeles, San Francisco, and Portland via Seattle. There are onward flights to Tokyo, Osaka, Okinawa, Manila, Hong Kong, Taipei, and Seoul. Call (800) 225-2525.

Delta Airlines
In 1985, Delta entered the Hawaiian market; when it bought out Western Airlines its share became even bigger. They have nonstop flights to Honolulu from Dallas/Ft. Worth, Los Angeles, San Francisco, and San Diego, and now flights to Kahului, Maui, via Los Angeles or Honolulu. Call (800) 221-1212.

Pan Am
Pan Am's flights to Honolulu from New York, Miami, San Francisco, San Diego, and other Mainland cities all go through Los Angeles. Onward flights go to major Asian cities. Call (800) 843-8687.

America West
America West started as a regional carrier in Arizona making milk runs between Phoenix and Los Angeles. In November 1989, it entered the Hawaii market. Fares are comparable to the larger airlines and will allow Midwesterners to fly to either Phoenix or Las Vegas, and then straight on to Honolulu from there. They're flying brand-new 747s, and as an employee-owned airline have made an excellent reputation for service, friendliness, and on-time scheduling. For information call (800) 247-5692.

INTER-ISLAND CARRIERS

The only effective way for most visitors to travel between the Hawaiian islands is by air (also see Inter-island Ferry p.102). Luckily, Hawaii has excellent air transportation that boasts one of the industry's safest flight records. The three airlines following all have competitive prices with inter-island flights at about $55 o/w. You can also save money (about $15) if you **take the first or last daily scheduled flight.** This offer usually applies only to flights to and from Honolulu, but check as policy often changes. Another alternative is to **purchase a booklet of six flight vouchers.** You save about $7 per ticket, and they are transferable. Just book a flight as normal and present the filled-in voucher to board the plane. Perfect for families or groups of friends, and they can be purchased at any ticket office or at Honolulu International.

Hawaiian Air, tel (800) 882-8811 statewide, (800) 367-5320 on the Mainland, offers the largest number of daily flights to and from all Neighbor Islands. From Honolulu to Kauai, 26 nonstop flights go from 5:40 a.m. to 8 p.m.; to Maui flights begin at 5:40 a.m. with one every 20 minutes or so until 8:05 p.m., also regularly scheduled flights to Kapalua, West Maui Airport; to Hilo flights every 40 minutes from 5:50 a.m. to 6:55 p.m. and to Kona from 5:55 a.m. to 6:45 p.m. Also, daily flights to Lanai and Molokai. **Aloha Airlines**, (800) 367-5250, connects Oahu to Kauai, Maui, and both Kona and Hilo on Hawaii. Aloha's routes to Kauai are: from Honolulu, 22 non-

INTER-ISLAND AIR ROUTES

PRINCEVILLE
LIHUE
KAUAI
PORT ALLEN
OAHU
38 MIN
27 MIN
HONOLULU INTERNATIONAL
KALAUPAPA
MOLOKAI
MŌLOKAI
27 MIN
41 MIN
KAHULUI
18 MIN
LANAI
LANAI
15 MIN
13 MIN
HANA
28 MIN
MAUI
UPOLU POINT
35 MIN
WAIMEA-KOHALA
15 MIN
GENERAL LYMAN FIELD (HILO)
KE-AHOLE
23 MIN
HAWAII

● MAJOR AIRPORT WITH FULL FACILITIES
○ SECONDARY AIRPORT

0 ——— 30 mi
0 ——— 40 km

© MOON PUBLICATIONS, INC.

stop flights from 5:40 a.m. until 6:10 p.m.; to Maui, about 30 flights daily, with one departing every 20 minutes or so from 5:40 a.m. to 8:15 p.m.; to Kona, about 20 flights daily from 5:40 a.m. to 7:00 p.m.; and to Hilo, 12 flights from 5:50 a.m. to 7:00 p.m.

Aloha Island Air (formerly Princeville Airways), tel. (800) 323-3345 on the Mainland, is a commuter airline operating flights to and from Princeville Airport on Kauai's north shore. Flying comfortable 18-passenger Twin Otter De Havilland aircraft, they connect the resort community of Princeville with airports on all the islands. Part of their schedule offers seven daily nonstop flights from Honolulu starting at 6 a.m. and ending at 5:15 p.m. Flights to and from all Neighbor Island airports leave regularly throughout the day. Flights from Kapalua, West Maui, come four times a day, 9:10 a.m. until 3:35 p.m., all with one stop; from Kahului, Maui, they run from 8:35 a.m. until 3:30 p.m., all with two stops; and from Hana, Maui, three times daily from 8:10 a.m. until 2:45 p.m., all with three stops. Additional flights come from

Lanai at 9:05 a.m. and 4:10 p.m., and from Kamuela, Hawaii, at 7:30 a.m. and 1:40 p.m., all going through Honolulu.

FOREIGN CARRIERS

The following carriers operate throughout Oceania but have no U.S. flying rights. This means that in order to vacation in Hawaii using one of these carriers, your flight must originate or terminate in a foreign city. You can have a stopover in Honolulu with a connecting flight to a Neighbor Island. For example, if you've purchased a flight on Japan Air Lines from San Francisco to Tokyo, you can stop in Hawaii, but you then must carry on to Tokyo. Failure to do so will result in a stiff fine, and the balance of your ticket will not be refunded.

Canadian Airlines International
Nonstop flights from Canada to Honolulu originate in Vancouver, Toronto, and Calgary; nonstop Pacific flights go to Fiji, Auckland,

and Sydney, with connecting flights to other Pacific cities. Call (800) 426-7007.

Air New Zealand
Flights link New Zealand, Australia, and Fiji with Los Angeles via Honolulu. Also offered is a remarkable APEX fare from Los Angeles to New Zealand, with stops in Honolulu and Fiji, and a Super Pass fare that lets you stop in eight cities between Los Angeles and Australia. Occasionally, other special fares are offered. Call (800) 262-1234 for current information.

Japan Air Lines
The Japanese are the second largest group, next to Americans, to visit Hawaii. JAL flights to Honolulu originate in Tokyo, Nagoya, and Osaka. There are no JAL flights between the Mainland and Hawaii. Call (800) 525-3663.

All Nippon Airways
Flights from Tokyo via Honolulu and Los Angeles to San Francisco. Occasional charter flights are offered from Tokyo to Honolulu. Call (800) 235-9262 for current information.

Philippine Airlines
Flights to and from Los Angeles and San Francisco to Manila via Honolulu. Connections in Manila to most Asian cities. Call (800) 435-9725.

Qantas
Daily flights from San Francisco and Los Angeles to Sydney via Honolulu. Stopovers are possible in Fiji and Tahiti. Call (800) 622-0850.

China Airlines
They maintain routes from Los Angeles to Taipei with stopovers in Honolulu and Tokyo possible, but they are not available year-round. Connections from Taipei to most Asian capitals. Call (808) 652-1428.

Korean Air
Some of the least expensive flights to Asia. Flights leave only from Los Angeles, stopping in Honolulu, with either a direct flight to Seoul or a stopover in Tokyo. Connections to many Asian cities. Call (800) 421-8200.

Singapore Airlines
Flights to and from San Francisco and Los Angeles to Singapore via Honolulu and either Hong Kong or Taipei. Free stopovers for seven-day advance-purchase tickets. Call (800) 742-3333.

Air Tungaru
Limited flights from Kiribati to Honolulu via Christmas Island and Tarawa. In Hawaii, call 735-3994.

Air Nauru
The South Pacific's richest island offers flights throughout Polynesia, including most major islands, with connections to Japan, Taipei, Hong Kong, Manila, Singapore, and Australia. In Hawaii, call 531-9766.

TRAVEL BY SHIP

At one time Hawaiians lined the pier in Honolulu waiting to greet the cruise ships bringing visitors. It was the only way to get to Hawaii, but these days are long gone. Now only one American company and a few foreign lines make the crossing.

American Hawaii Cruises
This American cruise ship company operates two 800-passenger ships, the SS *Independence,* and the SS *Constitution.* Primarily, these ships offer similar seven-day itineraries that circumnavigate and call at the four main islands. Their price ranges from an inside "thrifty cabin" at $1095 to a luxury suite for $3695. Children under 16 are often given special rates, and cruise free from June to September when they share a cabin with their parents. You come aboard in Honolulu after arriving by plane arranged by American Hawaii Cruises. Each ship is a luxury seagoing hotel and gourmet restaurant; swimming pools, driving ranges, tennis courts, health clubs, movies, and nightclubs are all part of

American Hawaiian Cruises' SS Independence

the amenities. For details contact: American Hawaii Cruises, 550 Kearny St., San Francisco, CA 94108, tel. (800) 227-3666, from Canada call collect (415) 392-9400.

Alternatives

Other companies offering varied cruises are **P&O Lines**, which operates the *Sea Princess* through the South Pacific, making port at Honolulu on its way from the West Coast once a year.

Royal Cruise Line out of Los Angeles, or Auckland alternatively, sails the *Royal Odyssey,* which docks in Honolulu on its South Pacific and Orient cruise, from $2200 to $4000.

The **Nauru Pacific Line** offers freighter/-passenger service from San Francisco to Micronesia via Honolulu, six-week intervals year-round.

The **Holland America Line** sails the *Rotterdam* on its 108-day Grand Circle cruise, departing Fort Lauderdale, passing around South America, and calling at Honolulu as it heads for Asia. Prices are from $20,000 to $70,000. Call (800) 426-0327.

Society Expeditions offers a 42-day cruise throughout the South Pacific departing from Honolulu. Fares are from $3000 to $9000. Tel. (800) 426-7794.

Information

Most travel agents can provide information on the above cruise lines. If you're really interested in traveling by ship contact: **Freighter Travel Club of America,** Box 12693, Salem, Oregon U.S.A.; or **Ford's Freighter Travel Guide,** Box 505, 22151 Clarendon St., Woodland Hills, CA U.S.A.

Inter-island Ferry

From time to time ferry companies have operated in Hawaii, but very stiff competition generated by the airline industry and the notoriously rough waters of the Hawaiian channels have combined to scuttle their opportunity for success. A new company has opened, making daily runs between Oahu (Honolulu), Molokai (Kaunakakai), and Maui (Lahaina) aboard their 118-foot vessel *The Maui Princess.* The boat, a converted oil-platform-personnel carrier from Louisiana, has been reoutfitted for Hawaii and includes a sun deck and hydraulic stabilizers which take some of the roll out of the rocky crossing. In effect, it's still a work boat, carrying workers from Molokai to Lahaina, along with some light cargo.

As beautiful as the Hawaiian Islands are from the air, this is a wonderful opportunity to have an experience from sea level. You depart, leaving behind Aloha Tower, *the* symbol of Hawaii from bygone days, and cruise past Diamond Head en route to Kaunakakai and then across the Lahaina Roads to Maui. The crossing from Oahu is the roughest, while going with the current and wind from Maui and Molokai to Oahu is much easier. The cabin is comfortable with air-conditioning, and the crew, all local people, play guitar, ukulele, and sing old island tunes, helping to raise everyone's spirits. The majority of the people riding the shuttle are islanders, so if you're looking for a colorful and cultural experience, this is one of the best opportunities. The snack bar serves burgers and sandwiches for under $2, while beer is only $1.50 and the very stiff mixed drinks are around $2.

Be advised, however, that a few problems have to be lashed down before everything is ship-shape. No transport shuttle is provided to get you to Pier 8, just between Aloha Tower and the *Falls of Clyde,* from where the *Maui Princess* embarks in Honolulu. If you have a rental car, you'll have to drop off your baggage first, return your car and then make it back to Pier 8 by bus, taxi, or rely on the kindness of the car companies to give you a lift (don't count on it if they are busy!). Once at Pier 8, the boarding entrance is through the huge parking garage at dock level. Look to your left for the large sign inside the garage. When you arrive in Lahaina you are met about 300 yards offshore by the *Lin Wa,* a

sister ship usually used as a local tourist cruiser. Since Lahaina Harbor is so small, the *Maui Princess* cannot enter. Passengers and luggage are offloaded *at sea* as the crews perform some amazing feats of balance, handling all manner of cargo between the pitching, yawing boats.

Upon arrival in Lahaina, prearrange a pickup by the car companies (most have offices in nearby Kaanapali) or you'll be stranded. The *Maui Princess* is often late and the car companies close by 6:30 p.m., another logistical problem. The trip is tough, but it adds a realness of arriving on an island that you don't get from a plane. Fares are Oahu-Maui $42, Oahu-Molokai $21, Molokai-Maui $21, children half price. Bicyclists will be especially happy, because no extra fee is charged to transport your wheels. For information and reservations call (800) 833-5800, or on Oahu 533-6899, Molokai 553-5736, Maui 661-5857.

TOUR COMPANIES

Many tour companies advertise packages to Hawaii in large city newspapers every week. They offer very reasonable airfares, car rentals, and accommodations. Without trying, you can get roundtrip airfare from the West Coast and a week in Hawaii for $400 using one of these companies. The following companies offer great deals, and have excellent reputations. This list is by no means exhaustive.

Council Travel Services

These full-service budget-travel specialists are a subsidiary of the nonprofit Council on International Educational Exchange, and the official U.S. representative to the International Student Travel Conference. They'll custom-design trips and programs for everyone from senior citizens to college students. Bona fide students have extra advantages, however, including the availability of the International Student Identification Card (CISC), which often gets you discount fares and entrance fees. Groups and business travelers are also welcome. However, they deal with Hawaii mainly as a stopover en

---

**MAUI PRINCESS
SAILING SCHEDULE**

For information and reservations:
on Molokai call 553-5736
on Maui call 661-5857
on Oahu call 533-6899
Mainland toll-free (800) 533-5800

Depart:	Kaunakakai, Molokai	5:45 am
Arrive:	Lahaina, Maui slip 3	7:00 am
Depart:	Lahaina, Maui slip 3	7:15 am
Arrive:	Kaunakakai, Molokai	8:30 am
Depart:	Kaunakakai, Molokai	8:45 am
Arrive	Honolulu, Oahu pier 8	11:45 am
Depart:	Honolulu, Oahu pier 8	12:15 pm
Arrive:	Kaunakakai, Molokai	3:45 pm
Depart:	Kaunakakai, Molokai	4:00 pm
Arrive:	Lahaina, Maui slip 3	5:15 pm
Depart:	Lahaina, Maui slip 3	5:30 pm
Arrive:	Kaunakakai, Molokai	6:45 pm

route to Asia. For full information, write to the main offices at Council Travel Services, 919 Irving St., #102, San Francisco, CA 94122, tel. (415) 566-6222. Other offices are in Austin, Berkeley, Boston, Long Beach, Los Angeles, Miami, New York, Portland, San Diego, and Seattle.

Student Travel Network
You don't have to be a student to avail yourself of their services. Their main office is at 2500 Wilshire Blvd. #920, Los Angeles, CA 90057, tel. (213) 380-2184. In Honolulu at 1831 S. King St., Honolulu, HI 96826, tel. 942-7755. STN also maintains offices in San Diego, San Francisco, and Northridge, California, Toronto, and Vancouver, as well as throughout Australia and Europe.

Nature Expeditions International
These quality tours have nature as the theme. Trips are 15-day, four-island natural history expeditions, with the main emphasis on plants, birds, and geology. Their guides are experts in their fields and give personable and attentive service. Operations are temporarily suspended, but plans are to revive these trips in 1990. Contact Nature Expeditions International at 474 Willamette, Box 11496, Eugene, OR 97440 for current status, tel. (503) 484-6529.

SunTrips
This California-based tour and charter company sells vacations all over the world. They're primarily a wholesale company, but will work with the general public. SunTrips often works with Air America when flying to Hawaii, and has special arrangements with Tropical Rent-a-Car and various hotel/condos. Contact SunTrips, 100 Park Center, Box 18505, San Jose, CA 95158, tel. (800) 662-9292, 941-2697 in Honolulu.

Pacific Outdoor Adventures
This truly remarkable tour company operated by John Grey and Bob Wilson offers the best in nature tours. The emphasis is on the outdoors with hiking, camping, and kayaking central. These professional guides go out of

their way to make your trip totally enjoyable and safe. Their specially designed kayaks are seaworthy in all conditions and for all ability levels. They focus on giving you a fun-filled "edutainment" adventure, where you can immerse yourself in the local culture, geography, and natural wonder of the areas visited. Although based in Hawaii with a full schedule of trips to the outer islands, Pacific Outdoor Adventures heads for fantastic and little-visited destinations throughout the Pacific. Prices are absolutely unbeatable for the experience offered and arrangements for packages can be made that include everthing from airfare to accommodations and gourmet meals. For a full list of itineraries contact Pacific Outdoor Adventures at P.O. Box 61609, Honolulu, HI 96839, tel. (808) 988-3913, toll-free (800) 52-KAYAK. If an unforgettable outdoor adventure is your goal, you can't go wrong!

Ocean Voyages is a unique company offering seven- and 10-day itineraries aboard a variety of yachts in the Hawaiian Islands. The yachts, equipped to carry from two to 10 passengers, ensure individualized sail training. The vessels sail throughout the islands, exploring hidden bays and coves, and berthing at different ports as they go. This opportunity is for anyone who wishes to see the islands in a timeless fashion, thrilling to sights experienced by the first Polynesian settlers and Western explorers. For rates and information contact Ocean Voyages, 1709 Bridgeway, Sausalito, CA 94965, tel. (415) 332-4681.

Island Holiday Tours
An established Hawaii-based company that offers flights with American and United, and rental cars through Budget. Arrangements can also be made for tours, luaus, helicopter rides, etc., on all islands. Contact Island Holiday Tours, 2255 Kuhio Ave., Honolulu, HI 96815, tel. (800) 448-6877.

Pleasant Hawaiian Holidays
A California-based company specializing in Hawaii. Arrangements are made for flights, accommodations, and transportation only. At 2404 Townsgate Rd., West Lake Village, CA 91361, tel. (800) 242-9244.

Unique Outdoor Tours/Experiences

Sierra Club Trips take nature lovers to Hawaii who are interested in an outdoor experience. Various trips include hikes over Mauai's Haleakala, a kayak trip along the Na Pali coast of Kauai, or a family camping spree in Kauai's Kokee region. All trips are led by experienced guides and are open to Sierra Club members only ($33 per year to join). For information contact the Sierra Club Outing Dept., 730 Polk St., San Francisco, CA 94109, tel. (415) 776-2211.

Earthwatch allows you to become part of an expeditionary team dedicated to conservation and the study of the natural environment. An expedition might be the study of dolphins in Kewalo Basin Marine Mammal Laboratory, or observing the ubiquitous mongoose from an observation hut high atop Mauna Kea. Basically, you are an assistant field researcher and your lodgings can be a dorm room at the University of Hawaii, and your meals can come from a remote camp kitchen. Fees vary and are tax deductible. If you are interested in this learning experience, contact Earthwatch, 680 Mt. Auburn St., Box 403-P, Watertown, MA 02272, tel. (617) 926-8200.

Hawaii State Archives

GETTING AROUND

Touring Oahu is especially easy, since almost every normal (and not so normal) mode of conveyance is readily available. You can rent anything from a moped to a pedicab, and the competition is very stiff, which helps keep prices down. A few differences separate Oahu from the other islands. To begin with, Oahu has a model public transportation system called TheBus—not only efficient, but very inexpensive. Also, Oahu is the only island that has a true expressway system, though along with it came rush hour and traffic jams. A large part of Oahu's business is processing people, even if it's only to send them on to another island! The agencies operating these businesses on the island are masters at moving people down the road. With the huge volume of tourists that visit every year, it's amazing how smoothly it works. The following is a cross section of what's available and should help you to decide how you want to get around. Have fun! Also see p. 225 for more information about getting around in Waikiki.

CAR RENTALS

Does Hawaii really have more rental cars than pineapples? Oahu's Yellow Pages have eight pages of listings for car rental agencies; there are over 40 firms on Maui, a few dozen on the Big Island, 20 or so on Kauai, Molokai has a handful, and even Lanai has one or two. You can rent anything from a 60-passenger Scenic-cruiser to a 60-cc moped. Even so, if you visit the islands during a peak tourist frenzy without reserving your wheels in advance, you'll be marooned at the airport.

There's a tremendous field of cars and agencies from which to choose and they're cheaper than anywhere else in America. Special deals come and go like tropical rain showers; swashbuckling price-slashings and come-ons are common all over the rental car market. A little knowledge combined with some shrewd shopping around can save you a bundle. And renting a car is the best way to see the islands if you're going to be there for a limited time. Outside of Oahu, it simply isn't worth hassling with the poor public transportation system, or relying on your thumb.

Car Rental Categories

When you arrive at any of Hawaii's airports, you'll walk the gauntlet of car rental booths and courtesy phones shoulder to shoulder along the main hallways. Of the three categories of car rental agencies in Hawaii, each has its own advantage. The first category is the big international firms like National, Hertz, Avis, and Budget. These big guys are familiar, easy to work with, sometimes offer special fly/drive deals with airlines, and live up to their promises. If you want your rental experience to be hassle-free, they're the ones. Also, don't be prejudiced against them just because they're so well known; sometimes they offer the best deal.

Hawaii has spawned a good crop of statewide car rental agencies such as Tropical, Robert's, and Holiday Hawaii. These companies and their cars are also reliable, easy to book through a travel agent, and give good service. Their bargain prices and special deals make it worthwhile to price them. The third category is the local entrepreneurial rental agencies. Their deals and cars can range, like rummage-sale treasures, from great finds to pure junk. Some, like Hawaii Rent a Car, El Cheapo, and Molokai U Drive, are reliable and good. These companies have the advantage of being able to cut deals on the spot. If nothing is moving from their lot on the day you arrive, you might get a real bargain. Unfortunately, mixed in this category is a hodgepodge of fly-by-nights. Some of these are small, but adequate, while others are a rip-off. Their cars are bad, their service is worse, and they have more hidden costs than a Monopoly board.

Agencies

A Hawaii-based company with an excellent reputation is **Tropical Rent a Car,** tel. 836-1176, Waikiki tel. 949-2002, (800) 367-5140 nationwide, (800) 352-3923 from Neighbor Islands. Being based in Hawaii, they can take care of any problem on the spot without hassle. Tropical's personnel go out of their

way to make your rental go smoothly by adding that "*aloha* touch." Prices are very competitive, and they can put you into anything from an economy car with no a/c, to a convertible, Cadillac, or European sports car.

National is one of the best, airport location at 2965 N. Nimitz Hwy., tel. 836-2655, in Waikiki at 2160 Kalakaua Ave., tel. 922-6461, or toll-free at (800) 227-7368. **Avis,** at the airport, tel. 836-5531, in Waikiki at tel. 836-5543, or (800) 331-1212; **Hertz,** with 11 locations around the island plus at the airport, tel. 836-2511, or toll-free (800) 654-8200.

Budget, at the airport, tel. 836-1700; for locations in Waikiki, call central reservations at 922-3600, or toll-free (800) 527-0700.

Smaller but good firms include: **Sears,** accepting Sears credit cards, central reservations tel. 922-3805; **Thrifty,** airport tel. 836-2388, Waikiki tel. 923-7383, toll-free (800) 367-2277; **Aloha Funway Rentals,** airport tel. 834-1016, Waikiki tel. 942-9696; **Holiday,** airport tel. 836-1974, Waikiki tel. 926-2752.

Cheaper firms offer bargain rates and older cars. Many of these rent without a major credit card, but require a stiff deposit. Sometimes they even rent to those under 21, but you'll have to show reservations at a major hotel. Some where you usually make out all right are: **Mal-Mat,** at 1111 Kapiolani Blvd., tel. 533-3986; **Alpert's Used Car Rentals,** tel. 955-4370; **Hawaii Discount,** tel. 536-1861; **AAA Rents,** 524-8060.

If you're after a luxury car or a convertible try: **Convertibles Honolulu,** tel. 595-6170; and **Convertible Rentals,** featuring Mustangs, tel. 923-4131.

Requirements

A variety of requirements are imposed on the renter by car agencies, but the most important clauses are common. Some of the worst practices being challenged are: no rentals to people under 25 and over 70, and no rentals to military personnel or Hawaiian residents! Before renting, check that you fulfill the requirements. Generally, you must be 21, although some agencies rent to 18-year-olds, while others still require you to be 25. You must possess a valid driver's license, with licenses from most countries accepted, but to be safe if you are not American, get an International Driver's License. You should have a major credit card in your name. This is the easiest way, though some companies take a deposit, but it will be very stiff. It could easily be $50 per day on top of your rental fees and sometimes much more, and a credit check on the spot, complete with phone calls to your employer and bank, may be required. If you damage the car, charges will be deducted from your deposit, and the car company itself determines the extent of the damages. Some companies will not rent you a car without a major credit card in your name, no matter how much of a deposit you are willing to leave.

When To Rent

On this one, you'll have to make up your own mind, because it's a "bet" that you can either win or lose big. But it's always good to know the odds before you plop down your money. You can reserve your car in advance when you book your air ticket, or play the field when you get there. If you book in advance, you'll obviously have a car waiting for you, but the deal that you made is the deal that you'll get—it may or may not be the best around. On the other hand, if you wait you can oftentimes take advantage of excellent on-the-spot deals. Obviously, however, you're betting that cars are available. You might be totally disappointed, and not be able to rent a car at all, or you might make a honey of a deal.

If you're arriving during the peak seasons of Christmas, Easter, and late summer vacation, *absolutely book your car in advance.* They are all accounted for during this period,

and even if you can find a junker from a fly-by-night, they'll price-gouge you mercilessly. If you're going off-peak, you stand a good chance of getting the car you want, at the price you want. It's generally best to book ahead, but the majority of car companies have free 800 numbers (listed below). At least call them for an opinion of your chances of getting a car when you intend to arrive.

Rates

If you pick up a car rental brochure at a travel agent, notice that the price for Hawaii rentals are about the lowest in the U.S. The two rate options for renting are **mileage,** or **flat rate.** A third type, mileage/minimum, is generally a bad idea unless you plan to do some heavy-duty driving. Mileage rate costs less per day, but you are charged for every mile driven. Mileage rates are best if you drive less than 30 miles per day—but even on an island that isn't much! The flat rate is best with a fixed daily rate and unlimited mileage. With either rate, you buy the gas; don't buy the cheapest because the poor performance from low octane eats up your savings.

Discounts of about 10-15 percent for weekend, weekly, and monthly rates are available. It's sometimes cheaper to rent a car for the week even if you're only going to use it for five days. Both weekly and monthly rates can be split between neighboring islands, but this will only apply if the firm has inter-island offices, and this usually eliminates the small local guys. Extra costs are assessed if you drop off the car at a different spot from where you rented it; a common one is a Hilo pickup and a Kona dropoff on the Big Island. Don't be surprised if some car companies want an extra fee if you drop your Waikiki rental at the Honolulu Airport, even if they have a facility there.

Warning: If you keep your car beyond your contract, you'll be charged the highest daily rate unless you notify the rental agency beforehand. Don't keep your car longer than the contract without notifying the company. They are *quick* to send out their repossession specialists. You might find your car gone, a warrant for your arrest, and an extra charge. A simple courtesy call notifying them of your intentions saves a lot of headaches and hassle.

What Wheels To Rent

The super-cheap rates on the eye-catcher brochures refer to subcompact standard shifts. The price goes up with the size of the car and with an automatic transmission. Like options on a new car, the more luxury, the more you pay. If you can drive a standard shift, get one! They're cheaper to rent and operate. Because many Hawaiian roads are twisty affairs, you'll appreciate the down-shifting ability and extra control of a standard shift. AM/FM radios are good to have for entertainment, and for getting weather and surf conditions. If you have the choice, take a car with cloth seats instead of sticky vinyl.

The average price of a subcompact, stand-ard shift, without air conditioning is $25 per day with a weekly rate of $90 (add about $8 per day—$50 per week—for an automatic) but rates vary widely. Luxury cars are about $10 a day more with a comparable weekly rate. Most of the car companies, local and national, offer special rates and deals. If you fly Hawaiian Air on their Mainland service or inter-island, you can get a car with Tropical or Holiday for less than $15 per day. Budget sometimes runs fly/drive specials with United and Western, and Hertz has a truly "Afford-able Hawaii" package that gives you an ex-cellent weekly rate if you meet the prerequi-sites. These deals fluctuate too rapidly to give any hard and fast information except that they are common, so make sure to inquire. Also, peak periods have "black outs" where normal good.deals no longer apply.

Insurance

Before signing your car rental agreement, you'll be offered "insurance," for around $8 per day. Since insurance is already built into the contract (don't expect the rental agency to point this out), what you're really buying is a waiver on the deductible ($500-$1000), in case you crack up the car. If you have in-surance at home, you will almost always have coverage on a rental car, including your nor-mal deductible, but not all policies are the same, so check with your agent. Also, if you

haven't bought their waiver, and you have a mishap, the rental agencies will put a claim against your major credit card on the spot for the amount of deductible, even if you can prove that your insurance will cover. They'll tell you to collect from your insurance be-cause they don't want to be left holding the bag on an across-the-waters claim. If you have a good policy with a small deductible, it's hardly worth paying the extra money even if you do have a claim against you; you'll eventually recover it, but if your own policy is inadequate, buy the insurance. Also, most major credit cards offer complimentary car rental insurance as a repayment for using their cards to rent the car. Simply call the toll-free number of your credit card company to see if this service is included.

Driving Tips

Protect your children as you would at home with car seats. Their rental prices vary con-siderably: Alamo offers them free of charge; National charges $3 per day; Hertz needs 48 hours' notice; Dollar gives them free but they're not always available at all locations; and, almost all the agencies can make ar-rangements if you give them enough notice. Check before you go and if all else fails, bring one from home.

There are few differences between driving in Hawaii and on the Mainland. Just remem-ber that many people on the roads are tour-ists and can be confused about where they're going. Since many drivers are from some-where else, there's hardly a "regular style" of driving in the islands. A farmer from Iowa accustomed to poking along on back roads can be sandwiched between a frenetic New Yorker who's trying to drive over his roof and a super-polite but horribly confused Japa-nese tourist who normally drives on the left.

In Hawaii, drivers don't honk their horns except to say hello, or in an emergency. It's considered rude, and honking to hurry some-one might earn you a knuckle sandwich. Ha-waiian drivers reflect the climate: they're re-laxed and polite. Oftentimes, they'll brake to let you turn left when they're coming at you. They may assume you'll do the same, so be ready, after a perfunctory turn signal, for a driver to turn across your lane. The more rural the area, the more apt this is to happen.

It may seem like common sense, but remember to slow down when you enter the little towns strung along the circle-island route. You have the tendency to bomb along on the highway and flash through these towns, missing some of Oahu's best scenery. Also, rural children expect *you* to be watchful, and will assume that you are going to stop for them when they dart out into the crosswalks.

The **H-1 and H-2 Freeway** throw many Mainlanders a Polynesian "screwball." Accustomed to driving on super highways, Mainlanders assume that these are the same. They're not. Oahu's super highways are much more twisted, turned, and convoluted than most Mainland counterparts. Subliminally they look like a normal freeway, except that they've been tied into a Hawaiian knot. There are split-offs, crossroads, and exits in the middle of the exits. Stay alert and don't be lulled into familiar complacency.

B-Y-O Car

Unless you'll be in Hawaii for a bare minimum of six months, and spending all your time on one island, don't even think about bringing your own car. It's an expensive proposition and takes time and plenty of arrangements. From California, it costs at least $600 to Honolulu, with an additional $100 to any other island. It would be better to buy and sell a car there, or lease for an extended period to save on rental costs. If you want to bring your own car write for information to: Director of Finance, Division of Licenses, 1455 S. Beretania St., Honolulu, HI 96814.

Four-wheel Drives

If you're into 4WDs try: **Odyssey Rentals,** tel. 947-8036; **United Car Rental,** tel. 922-4605; or **Aloha Funway Rentals,** tel. 834-1016.

BICYCLES AND MOPEDS

Peddling around Oahu can be both fascinating and frustrating. The roads are well paved, but the shoulders are often torn up. Traffic in

great views with only half the flats to worry about

and around Honolulu is horrifying, and the only way to avoid it is by leaving very early in the morning. TheBus has no facilities for transporting your bike out of town, so an early departure is your only alternative. Once you leave the city, traffic, especially on the secondary interior roads, isn't too bad. Unfortunately, all of the coastal roads are heavily trafficked. Instead of a delicate road bike, you're better off renting a **cruiser** or **mountain bike** which allow for the sometimes poor road conditions and open up the possibilities of off-road biking. Even experienced mountain bikers should be careful on Oahu trails, which are often extremely muddy and rutted. Peddling around Waikiki, although congested, is usually safe, and a fun way of seeing the sights. Always lock your bike, and take your bike bag.

For info on biking on Oahu, contact **Hawaii Bicycling League,** Box 4403, Honolulu, HI 96813. This nonprofit corporation sponsors rides all over Oahu almost every weekend. Nonmembers are always welcome. The rides are multiple-level ability and are listed in the Hawaii Bicycling League's monthly newsletter, *Spoke-n-Words*. If you're into cycling and want a unique look at Oahu, don't miss these rides. Also see p. 113.

For bicycle rentals try: good old **Aloha Funway Rentals,** tel. 942-9696; **The Bike Way,** at 655 Kapiolani Blvd., tel. 538-7433. For sales and repairs try: **The Bike Shop,** featuring Fuji, Mongoose, and Schwinn, at 1149 S. King St., tel. 531-7071; **McCully Bicycle,** featuring Specialized, Miyata, and Takara, at 1018 McCully St., tel. 955- 6329; and **The Bike Way,** featuring Bianchi and Univega, at 655 Kapiolani, tel. 538-7433.

Motorcycles and mopeds are available from: **Aloha Funway Rentals,** tel. 942-9696; **Continental Rent a Bike,** 923-7533; **Sunshine Moped Rentals,** tel. 923-6083; and **Odyssey Rentals,** tel. 947-8036. Also see Waikiki, p. 226.

PUBLIC TRANSPORTATION

TheBus

If Dorothy and her mates had TheBus to get them down the Yellow Brick Road, she might have chosen to stay in Oz and forget about Kansas. TheBus, TheBus, ThewonderfulBus is the always-coming, slow-moving, go-everywhere friend of the budget traveler. Operated by Mass Transit Lines (MTL) Inc., it could serve as a model of efficiency and economy in any city of the world. What makes it all the more amazing is that it all came together by chance, beginning as an emergency service in 1971. These brown, yellow, and orange coaches go up and down both the windward and leeward coasts, through the interior, while passing through all of the major and most of the minor towns in between, and most often stopping near the best sights.

The **direction** in which TheBus travels is posted after the number and the name of the town. They are designated as EB (eastbound toward Diamond Head) and WB (westbound towards the airport). The **fare** is only $.60, paid in exact change upon entering. Even putting a $1 bill into the box and not expecting change is unacceptable. Students under age 19 and over six are charged $.25, while kids under five who can sit on their parent's lap aren't charged at all. Adult **monthly bus passes,** good at any time and on all routes, are $15, students $7.50, and senior citizens

over age 65 travel free. But they (seniors) must furnish proof of age and the processing period takes three to four weeks. Passes are available at Foodland and Emjay stores, Pioneer Federal Banks, 7-eleven convenience stores, all city halls, U. of Hawaii (adult passes only), and at the MTL Bus Pass office at 725 Kapiolani Boulevard.

Transfers are free and are issued upon request when entering TheBus, but you can only use them for ongoing travel in the same direction, and on a different line (numbered bus). They are also timed and dated. For example, you can take #8 from Waikiki to the Ala Maona Terminal, get off and do some fast shopping, then use your transfer on #20 to continue on to Pearl Harbor.

Circling the island is a terrific way to see the sights and meet people all along the way. The circle route takes about four hours if you stay on, but you can use the transfer system to give yourself a reasonable tour of the sights that strike your fancy. The **circle-island** bus is #52, but remember that there are two #52s, going in different directions. The buses are labeled: **#52 Wahiawa Kaneohe,** going inland to Wahiawa, north to Haleiwa, along the north shore, down the windward coast to Kaneohe and back over the Pali to Honolulu; **#52 Kaneohe Wahiawa,** following the same route but in the opposite direction. If you'll be taking this bus to Pearl Harbor, be absolutely sure to take #52 Wahiawa Kaneohe, because if you took the other, you'd have to circle the entire island before arriving at Pearl!

Get full information on TheBus by writing to **MTL Inc.,** TheBus, 1585 Kapiolani St., Honolulu 96813, tel. 942-3702, or by visiting the information booth at the Ala Moana Terminal, where you can pick up fliers and maps. An excellent, inexpensive little guide is *Hawaii Bus and Travel Guide* by Milly Singletary, available in most bookstores. The following are some popular destinations and their bus numbers, all originating from the Ala Moana Terminal: **Airport,** #8 Airport, #20; **Arizona Memorial, Pearl Harbor,** numbers 20, 50, 51, 52 Wahiawa, (not #52 Kaneohe); **Bishop Museum,** #2 School; **Chinatown,** numbers 1, 2, 3, 4, 6, 8, 9, 11, 12, 50, 52

Wahiawa; **Fisherman's Wharf,** #8 Airport, #20, #52 Kaneohe; Hanauma Bay, numbers 1, 57, beach bus weekends; **Honolulu (downtown),** numbers 1, 2, 3, 4, 9, 11, 12; **Pali Lookout,** not serviced; **Polynesian Culture Center,** both #52s, then a shuttle; **Queen Emma Palace,** #4; **Sea Life Park,** #57; **Waikiki Beach,** numbers 2, 4, 8, 14, 20.

A special "beach bus," an old battered green clunker, operates from June through August and runs from Waikiki to Waimanalo Beach, stopping at Hanauma Bay and Sandy Beach. It has racks for surfboards and leaves every hour (11 a.m. to 4 p.m.) from the corner of Monsarrat and Kalakaua avenues.

Taxis

The law says that taxis are not allowed to cruise around looking for fares, so you can't hail them. But they do and you can, and most policemen have more important things to do than monitor cabs. Best is to summon one from your hotel or a restaurant. All are radiodispatched, and they're usually there in a flash. The fares, posted on the taxi doors, are set by law and are fair, but still expensive for the budget traveler. The rates do change, but expect about $1.50 for the flag fall, and then $.25 for each additional one-sixth mile. The airport to Waikiki is about $15. You pay extra for bags.

Of the many taxi companies, some with good reputations are: **SIDA,** a cooperative of owner-drivers, at tel. 836-0011; **Aloha State Taxi,** tel. 847-3566; **Charley's,** tel. 955-2211; **Discount Taxi,** 841- 033. If you need some special attention like a Rolls-Royce limo, try: **Silver Cloud Limousines,** tel. 941-2901; for the handicapped and people in wheelchairs, **Handicabs,** tel. 524-3866. For **Pedicabs,** see p. 225.

HITCHHIKING

Hitchhiking varies from island to island, both in legality and method. On Oahu, hitchhiking is legal, and you use the tried-and-true style of facing traffic and waving your thumb. But you can only hitchhike from bus stops! Not many people hitchhike and the pickings are reasonably easy, but TheBus is only $.60 for

anywhere you want to go and the paltry sum that you save in money is lost in "seeing time." It's semilegal (the police don't bother you) to hitch on Kauai and Hawaii. Remember that Hawaii is indeed a "big" island; be prepared to take some time getting from one end to the other. Though on Lanai and Molokai hitching is illegal, hardly any policemen are to be seen. If they stop, it will probably be just to warn you, but note that the traffic is light on both islands.

On Maui, thumbing a ride is illegal and the police will hassle you. You must learn a new and obviously transparent charade to hitch successfully. Basically: thumb at your side, stand by the road, face traffic, and smile. Everyone knows you're hitching, but that's the game. You will get a ride eventually, but in comparison to the amount of traffic going by it isn't easy. Two things against you: many of the people are tourists and don't want to bother with hitchhikers, and many locals don't want to bother with nonlocal hitchhikers. When you do get a ride, most of the time it will be from a *haole* who is either a tourist on his own or a recent island resident. If you are just hitchhiking along a well-known beach area, perhaps in your bathing suit and obviously not going far, you can get a ride more easily. Women should exercise caution like everywhere else in the U.S., and avoid hitchhiking alone.

SIGHTSEEING TOURS

Guided land tours are much more of a luxury than a necessity on Oahu. Because of the excellent bus system and relatively cheap rental cars, you spend a lot of money for a narration and to be spared the hassle of driving. If you've come in a group and don't intend on renting a car, they also may be worth it. Sea cruises and air tours are equally luxurious, but provide glimpses of this beautiful island you'd normally miss. The following partial list of tour companies should get you started.

Note: For all activities, including snorkeling, scuba, all water sports, horseback riding, parasailing, golf, tennis, etc., please refer to "Sports And Recreation."

Land Tours

If you're going to take a land tour, you must have the right attitude, or it'll be a disaster. Your tour leader, usually driving the van or bus, is part instructor, comedian, and cheerleader. There's enough "corn" in his jokes to impress an Iowa hog. On the tour, you're expected to become part of one big happy family, and most importantly, to be a good sport. Most guides are quite knowledgeable about Oahu and its history, and they honestly try to do a good job. But they've done it a million times before, and their performance can be as stale as week-old bread. The larger the tour vehicle and the shorter the miles covered, the worse it is likely to be. If you still want a tour, take a full-day jaunt in a small van: you get to know the other people and the guide, who'll tend to give you a more in-depth presentation. Tips are cheerfully accepted. Also, be aware that some tours get kickbacks from stores and restaurants they take you to, where you don't always get the best bargains. Most companies offer free hotel pickup and delivery. Lunch or dinner is not included unless specified, but if the tour includes a major tourist spot like Waimea Falls Park or the Polynesian Culture Center, admission is usually included.

About eight different tours offered by most companies are variations on the same theme; since the prices are regulated, the cost is fairly uniform. The more popular are the **circle-island tour,** including stops at Diamond Head, Hanauma Bay, the windward and north shores, Waimea Falls, and perhaps the Mormon Temple and Dole Pineapple Plantation, for about $40, and half for children. A **night tour** to the Polynesian Culture Center, including admission and dinner show, costs $50. **Picnic tours,** and tours to **Byodo-In Temple,** go for around $35. Tours to **Punchbowl** and the *Arizona* **Memorial** are around $20. A small tour worth considering is the **snorkel and swim** at Hanauma Bay, including transport to this underwater park, about four hours exploring, and your snorkel gear, for under $15.

Some reputable companies include: **Akamai Tours,** tel. 922-6485; **Polynesian Adventure Tours,** tel. 922-0888; **Robert's**

Hawaii Tours, tel. 947-3939, and **Gray Line Hawaii Ltd.,** tel. 922-5094 (large coaches accommodating 30 or more as well as smaller vans); **Transhawaiian Tours,** tel. 735-6467; **Charley's Tours,** tel. 955-3381; **E. Noa Tours,** 941-6608; and **Four Wheel Drive Tours,** tel. 623-7021 (touring the rough road to Kaena Point).

The following are special tours that you should seriously consider. **Walking Tour of Chinatown,** tel. 533-3181, by the Chinese Chamber of Commerce, leaves every Tues. at 9:30 a.m. from in front of their offices at 42 N. King Street. You get a narrated three-hour tour of Chinatown for about $3, and an optional Chinese lunch for around $4. **Walking Tour of Honolulu, the 1800s,** tel. 531-0481, is a two-hour tour led by a very knowledgeable volunteer from the Mission Houses Museum, who is probably a member of the Cousin's Society and a descendant of one of the original Congregationalist missionaries to Hawaii. You're led on a wonderfully anecdoted walk through the historical buildings of central Honolulu for only $4 for the tour alone, and $7 if you combine it with a museum tour, every Wed. and Fri. at 9:30 a.m., beginning from TheBus stop in front of the Capitol.

Ka'ao o Honolulu (stories of Honolulu) is an interpretive walking tour of the city's past. Run by Kapiolani Community College, Office of Community Services, adults $5, children five-six $2, students and seniors $4, tel. 739-9211. The tours are thematic and change regularly, but expect topics like "The Revolution of 1893," "The lighter side of old Honolulu," and the very popular "Ghosts of Honolulu." Master storyteller Glen Grant hosts many of the tours. Reserve!

Oahu By Bicycle

Free rides and tips for cycling are offered by the **Hawaiian Bicycling League** (see p. 110). Also, **Island Bicycle Adventures,** 569 Kapahulu Ave., Honolulu, HI 96815, tel. 734-0700 or (800) 233-2226, offers guided rides on Oahu, Maui, and the Big Island. These tours are led by Ken Reilly, Roberta Baker, and Frank and Laura Smith, all effective cycling instructors. They run three extensive tours: Maui Magic, five days touring Maui,

$495; Hawaii Highlights, 10 days on the Big Island, $795, Oahu Explorer, a two-day leisurely circuit, $159. Good-quality KHS 12-speeds are provided at an additional $10 per person per day. Helmets, insurance, and all accommodations and meals are included in the price. Write for full details to the above address.

Oahu By Air

When you soar above Oahu, you realize just how beautiful this island actually is, and considering that the better part of a million people live in this relatively small space, it's amazing just how much undeveloped land still exists in the interior and even along the coast. The following are some air tours worth considering. Remember that small, one- or two-plane operations come and go as quickly as cloudbursts. They're all licensed and regulated for safety, but if business is bad, the propellers stop spinning.

Novel air tours are offered from Dillingham Airfield, up on the northwest section of Oahu, a few miles down the Farrington Hwy. from Waialua. Up here you can soar silently above the coast with **Glider Rides,** tel. 677- 3404, an outfit offering one- or two-passenger piloted rides infinitely more exciting than the company's name. A plane tows you aloft and you circle in a five-mile radius with a view that can encompass 80 miles on a clear day. The rides are available daily, first-come, first-served, from 10 a.m. to 5 p.m. Cost is around $40 single, $60 double, and flights, depending upon air currents, last about 20 minutes (see p. 308).

Surf Air Tours, tel. 637-7003, offers plane rides along the North Shore for a reasonable $49 per person that last a half-hour, while a one-hour cirlce-island tour costs $79. The aircraft are very dependable Cessna 172s or 206s, and the pilots narrate while positioning the plane so that you can take some good photos. The operation is professional but lowkey, like taking a spin with a guy in his private plane.

Islands in the Sky is a one-day flying extravaganza that covers all the main islands except the Big Island, offered by the most reputable island-based airline, **Hawaiian Air,** tel. 537-5100. For about $200 they fly you to the seven islands, and include a breakfast, lunch, and ground excursion to Hana on Maui and the Fern Grotto on Kauai. It's a long full day, and one to remember.

Panorama Air Tours, tel. 836-2122 or (800) 367-2671, have tailor-made tours of Oahu and an all-encompassing "flightsee Hawaii tour" similar to Hawaiian Air's for about the same price. They fly smaller two-engined aircraft, and include the Big Island, Maui, and Kauai with a ground stop on each.

Helicopter companies rev up their choppers to flightsee you around the island, starting at $50 for a short trip over Waikiki. Prices rise from there as you head for the North Shore. Chopper companies include: **Hawaii Pacific Helicopters,** tel. 836-1561; **Kenai Air Hawaii,** one of the oldest and most reputable companies in the islands, tel. 836-2071; and Royal Helicopters, tel. 941-4683.

Sails And Dinner Cruises

If you're taking a tour at all, your best bet is a sail or dinner cruise. They're touristy, but a lot of fun, and actually good value. Many times money-saving coupons for them are found in the free tourist magazines, and plenty of street buskers in Waikiki give special deals. The latter are mostly on the up and up, but make sure that you know exactly what you're getting. Most of these cruises depart from the Kewalo Basin Marina, near Fisherman's Wharf, at 5:30 p.m. and cruise Waikiki toward Diamond Head before returning about two hours later. On board are a buffet, open bar, live entertainment, and dancing. Costs vary but expect to spend about $40-50 per person. For cruises to Pearl Harbor and the *Arizona Memorial* see p. 267, and snorkeling and fishing charters, p. 146.

Some of the better dinner sails and cruises follow. **Jada Yacht Charters**, tel. 955-0722, sail sister ships *Jada I* and *Jada II,* usually in tandem. Double-masted and with classic lines, they are the sharpest boats off Waikiki. Jada Charters takes you on a real sail, not a

dinner sail, Waikiki

booze cruise where you stuff yourself on fried-to-death teriyaki chicken. They disembark from Ke'ehi Harbor, and will send a van to shuttle you from Waikiki. **Royal Hawaiian Holidays** is a tour-booking company that can get you on a variety of cruises from a lunch to dinner sail. Prices are as low as $28, tel. 926-0623. The *Manu Kai* of the Hyatt Regency, tel. 922- 9292, ext. 75145, takes hotel guests and the general public for a snorkel, sail, or cocktail cruise aboard this lovely 35-footer. **Aikane Catamarans**, tel. 522-1533, is an established company with a number of

boats sporting a thatched roof and Polynesian Revue. **Windjammer Cruises**, tel. 521-0036, sails a three-deck, 285-foot, four-masted fake sailing ship called the *Rella Mae* from Kewalo Basin. It looks good, but the sails are only for show. If you're sitting on Waikiki Beach and you see a rainbow-colored sail, it belongs to **Rainbow Cruises**, tel. 955- 3348. **Paradise Cruise**, tel. 536-3641, sails the *Pearl Kai* from Kewalo Basin on an evening sunset cruise. **Royal Hawaiian Cruises**, tel. 672-4141, boasts one of the least expensive cruises at $26, which includes a dinner, full bar, Polynesian revue, and dancing.

For something different try the **No Booze Cruise**, tel. 944-8033, sailing from Hula Kai Pier no. 11 aboard the *Adventure V* at 5:15 p.m. on Friday evening, and offers worship on the water on Sundays at 7:40 a.m. Live Christian music, soft drinks, and popcorn. Small fee on Friday and donation on Sunday. The **International Society for Krishna Consciousness** offers free rides on its *Jaludata,* along with free love feasts on Sunday at 4:30 p.m. For information, *Hare Krishna, hare rama,* call 595-3947. The *Ani Ani* belongs to **Glass Bottom Boats Hawaii**, tel. 537-1958, doing one-hour cruises along Waikiki; three cruises in the morning and three in the afternoon run on the hour, beginning at 9:30 a.m. and 1:30 p.m. Cost is under $10.

If you think that Oahu is beautiful topside, just wait until you see it below the waves. **Atlantis Submarines**, tel. 522-1710, cost about $50, departs from the Hilton Hawaiian Village, where you board the Hilton Rainbow Catamaran that ferries you to the waiting sub. Once aboard, you're given a few instructions and then it's "run silent, run deep, run excited." The sub is amazingly comfortable. Seats are arranged so that everyone gets a prime view through the large windows, and the air is amazingly fresh. A thrill of a lifetime.

by Alphonse Pellion, c. 1819 (Hawaii State Archives)

ACCOMMODATIONS

The innkeepers of Oahu would be personally embarrassed if you couldn't find adequate lodging on their island. So long as Oahu has to suffer the "slings and arrows" of development gone wild, at least you can find all kinds, qualities, and prices of places in which to spend your vacation. Of the nearly 60,000 rooms available in Hawaii, 35,000 are on Oahu, 30,000 of them in Waikiki alone! Some accommodations are living landmarks, historical mementos of the days when only millionaires came by ship to Oahu, dallying as if it were their own private hideaway. When the jumbo jets began arriving in the early '60s, Oahu, especially Waikiki, began to build frantically. The result was hotel skyscrapers that grew faster than bamboo in a rainforest. These monoliths, which offered the "average family" a place to stay, marked a tremendous change in social status of visitors to Oahu. The runaway building continued unabated for two decades, until the city politicians, supported by the hotel keepers themselves, cried "Enough!" and the activity finally slowed down.

Now a great deal of money is put into refurbishing and remodeling what's already built. Visitors can find breathtakingly beautiful hotels that are the best in the land next door to more humble inns that can satisfy most anyone's taste and pocketbook. On Oahu, you may not get your own private beach with swaying palms and hula girls, but it's easy and affordable to visit one of the world's most exotic and premier vacation resorts. The following is merely an overview of the accommodations available on Oahu. For details and listings of specific accommodations, refer to the "Accommodations" section in the travel chapters.

What, Where, And How Much

At almost anytime of year, bargains, plenty of them, include **fly/drive/stay deals,** or any combination thereof, designed to attract visitors while keeping the prices down. You don't even have to look hard to find roundtrip airfare, room, and rental car for a week from the West Coast, all for around $500 based on double occupancy. Oahu's rooms are found in all sorts of hotels, condos, and private homes. Some venerable old inns along **Waikiki Beach** were the jewels of the city when only a few palms obscured the views of Diamond Head. However, most of Waikiki's hotels now are relatively new high-rises. In Waikiki's **Five-star** hotels, prices for deluxe accommodations, with all the trimmings, run about $150-200 per night.

But a huge inventory of rooms go for half that amount and less. If you don't mind being one block from the beach, you can easily find nice hotels for $30-40. You can even find these prices in hotels on the beach, though most tend to be a bit older and heavily booked by tour agencies. You, too, can get a room in these, but expect the staffs to be only perfunctorily friendly, and the hotels to be a bit worn around the edges. Waikiki's side streets also hold many apartment-hotels that are, in effect, condos. In these you get the benefit of a full kitchen for under $50. Stays of a week or more bring further discounts.

Central Honolulu has few acceptable places to stay except for some no-frills hotels in and around Chinatown. Bad sections of Hotel Street have dives frequented by winos and prostitutes, not worth the hassle for the few dollars saved. Some upscale hotels around Ala Moana put you near the beach, but away from the heavy activity of Waikiki. For those passing through, a few **overnight-style** hotels are near the airport.

The remainder of the island, outside Waikiki, was mostly ignored as far as resort development was concerned. In the interior towns, and along the south and most of the windward coasts, you'll be hard pressed to find a room because there simply aren't any. Even today, only a handful of hotels are found on the leeward coast, mostly around **Makaha.** The area has experienced some recent development with a few condos and some full resorts going up, but it remains mostly undeveloped. **Windward Oahu** does have established resorts especially at Turtle Bay, Laie, and Punaluu, but most of the lodging there is in rentable beach houses, and tiny, basic inns.

To round things off, there is a network of **bed and breakfast** homes, YM/WCAs, youth hostels, elderhostels, and summer sessions complete with room and board at the U. of Hawaii (see "Honolulu Accommodations" for details). Oahu also offers plenty of spots to pitch a tent at both state and county campgrounds.

HOTELS

Types Of Hotel Rooms

Even with the wide variety of other accommodations available, most visitors, at least first-timers, tend to stay in hotels. At one time, hotels were the only places to stay, and characters like Mark Twain were berthed at Kilauea's rude Volcano House, while millionaires and nobility sailed for Waikiki where they stayed in luxury at the Moana Hotel or

Hilton Hawaiian Village

Royal Hawaiian, which both still stand as vintage reminders of days past.

Today, there are 60,000 hotel rooms statewide, and every year more hotels are built and older ones renovated. They come in all shapes and sizes, from 10-room family-run affairs to high-rise giants. Most readily available and least expensive is a bedroom with bath, the latter sometimes being shared in the more inexpensive hotels. Some hotels also offer a studio, a large sitting room that converts to a bedroom; suites, a bedroom with sitting room; and apartments that have a full kitchen plus at least one bedroom. Kitchenettes are often available, and contain a refrigerator, sink, and stove usually in a small corner nook, or fitted together as one space-saving unit. Kitchenettes cost a bit more, but save a bundle by allowing you to prepare some of your own meals. To get that vacation feeling while keeping costs down, eat breakfast in, pack a lunch for the day, and go out to dinner. If you rent a kitchenette, make sure all the appliances work as soon as you arrive. If they don't, notify the front desk immediately, and if the hotel will not rectify the situation ask to be moved or for a reduced rate. Hawaii has cockroaches (see p. 158), so put all food away.

Hotel Rates

Every year Hawaiian hotels welcome in the New Year by hiking their rates by about 10 percent. A room that was $30 this year will be $33 next year, and so on. Hawaii, because of its gigantic tourist flow and tough competition, offers hotel rooms at universally lower rates than most developed resort areas around the world. Package deals, especially to Waikiki, almost throw in a week's lodging for the price of an air ticket. The basic daily rate is geared toward double occupancy; singles are hit in the pocketbook. Single rates are cheaper than doubles, but never as low as half the double rate; the most you get off is 40 percent. **Weekly and monthly** rates will save you approximately 10 percent off the daily rate. Make sure to ask because this information won't be volunteered. Many hotels will charge for a double and then add an additional charge ($3 to $25) for extra persons. Some hotels, not always the budget ones, let

you cram in as many as can sleep on the floor with no additional charge, so again, ask. Others have a policy of **minimum stay,** usually three days, but their rates can be cheaper. A tax of **nine percent** is levied on all rooms!

Hawaii's **peak season** runs from just before Christmas until after Easter, and then again in early summer. Rooms are at a premium, and peak-season rates are an extra 10 percent above the normal daily rate. Oftentimes they'll also suspend weekly and monthly rates during peak season. The **off-peak** season is in late summer and fall, when rooms are easy to come by and most hotels offer lower rates. Here, subtract about 10 percent from the normal rate.

In Hawaiian hotels you always pay more for a good view. Terms vary slightly, but usually "ocean front" means your room faces the ocean and mostly your view is unimpeded. "Ocean view" is slightly more vague. It could be a decent view, or it could require standing on the dresser and craning your neck to catch a tiny slice of the sea sandwiched between two skyscrapers. Rooms are also designated and priced upward as **standard, superior, and deluxe.** As you go up, this could mean larger rooms with more amenities, or can merely signify a better view.

Plenty of hotels offer the **family plan,** which allows children under a certain age to stay in their parents' room free, if they use the existing bedding. If another bed or crib is required, there is an additional charge. Only a limited number of hotels offer the **American plan,** in which breakfast and dinner are included with the night's lodging. In many hotels, a refrigerator and a heating unit to make coffee and tea are provided free.

Paying, Deposits, And Reservations

The vast majority of Hawaiian hotels accept foreign and domestic traveler's cheques, personal checks preapproved by the management, foreign cash, and most major credit cards. Reservations are always the best policy, and they're easily made through travel agents or directly by contacting the hotel. In all cases, bring documentation of your confirmed reservations with you in case of a mix-up.

Deposits are not always required to make reservations, but they do secure them. Some hotels require the first night's payment in advance. Reservations without a deposit can be legally released if the room is not claimed by 6 p.m. Remember, too, that letters "requesting reservations" are not the same as "confirmed reservations." In letters, include your dates of stay, type of room you want, and price. Once the hotel answers your letter, "confirm" your reservations with a phone call or follow-up letter and make sure that the hotel sends you a copy of the confirmation. All hotels and resorts have **cancellation requirements** for refunding deposits. The time limit on these can be as little as 24 hours before arrival to a full 30 days. Some hotels require full **advance payment** for your length of stay, especially during peak season or during times of crowded special events such as the Merrie Monarch Festival in Hilo. Be aware of the time required for a cancellation notice *before* making your reservation deposit, especially when dealing with advance payment.

If you have confirmed reservations, especially with a deposit, and there is no room for you, or one that doesn't meet prearranged requirements, you should be given the option of accepting alternate accommodations. You are owed the difference in room rates if there is any. If there is no room whatsoever, the hotel is required to find you one at another comparable hotel and refund your deposit in full.

Amenities

All hotels have some of them, and some hotels have all of them. Air-conditioning is available in most, but under normal circumstances you won't need it. Balmy trade winds provide plenty of breezes, which flow through louvered windows and doors in many hotels. Ceiling fans are better than the air conditioning. TVs are often included in the rate, but not always. In-room phones are provided, but a service charge is usually tacked on, even for local calls. Swimming pools are very common, even though the hotel may sit right on the beach. There is always a restaurant of some sort, a coffee shop or two, a bar, cocktail lounge, and sometimes a sundries shop.

Some hotels also offer tennis courts or golf courses either as part of the premises or affiliated with the hotel; usually an "activities desk" can book you into a variety of daily outings. Plenty of hotels offer laundromats on the premises, and hotel towels can be used at the beach. Bellhops get about $1 per bag, and maid service is free, though maids are customarily tipped $1-2 per day and a bit more if kitchenettes are involved. Parking is free. Hotels can often arrange special services like babysitters, all kinds of lessons, and often special entertainment activities. A few even have bicycles and some snorkeling equipment to lend. They'll receive and send mail for you, cash your traveler's cheques, and take messages.

CONDOMINIUMS

The main qualitative difference between a condo and a hotel is in amenities. At a condo, you're more on your own. You're temporarily renting an apartment, so there won't be any bellhops and rarely a bar, restaurant, or lounge on the premises, though many times you'll find a sundries store. The main lobby, instead of having that grand entrance feel of many hotels, is more like an apartment house entrance, although there might be a front desk. Condos can be efficiencies (one big room), but mostly they are one- or multiple-bedroom affairs with a complete kitchen. Reasonable housekeeping items should be provided: linens, all furniture, and a fully equipped kitchen. Most have TVs and phones, but remember that the furnishings provided are all up to the owner. You can find brand-new furnishings that are top of the line, right down to garage sale bargains. Inquire about the furnishings when you make your reservations. Maid service might be included on a limited basis (for example, once weekly), or you might have to pay extra for it.

The method of paying for and reserving a condo is just about the same as for a hotel. However, requirements for deposits, final payments, and cancellation charges are much stiffer than in hotels. Make absolutely sure you fully understand all of these requirements when you make your reservations.

Manoa Valley Inn

Condos usually require a minimum stay, although some will rent on a daily basis, like hotels. Minimum stays when applicable are often three days, but seven is also commonplace, and during peak season, two weeks isn't unheard of. Swimming pools are common, and depending on the "theme" of the condo, you can find saunas, weight rooms, jacuzzis, and tennis courts. Rates are about 10-15 percent higher than comparable hotels, with hardly any difference between doubles and singles. A nominal extra is charged for more than two people, and condos can normally accommodate four to six guests. You can find clean, decent condos for as little as $200 per week, all the way up to exclusive apartments for well over $1000. Their real advantage is for families, friends who want to share, and especially long-term stays where you will always get a special rate. The kitchen facilities save a great deal on dining costs, and it's common to find units with their own mini-washers and dryers. Parking space is ample for guests, and like hotels, plenty of stay/drive deals are offered. You'll find condos all over Hawaii, but they're particularly prevalent on Maui.

Hotel/Condominium Information
The best source of hotel/condo information is the **Hawaii Visitors Bureau**. While planning your trip, either visit one nearby or write to them in Hawaii. (Addresses are given in the "Hawaii Visitors Bureau" section of the Introduction.) Request a copy of their free and current *Member Accommodation Guide*. This handy booklet lists all the hotel/condo members of the HVB, with addresses, phone numbers, facilities, and rates. General tips are also given.

BED AND BREAKFAST

Bed and breakfasts are hardly a new idea. The Bible talks of the hospitable hosts who opened the gates of their homes and invited the wayfarer in to spend the night. Bed and breakfasts (B&Bs) have a long tradition in Europe, and were commonplace in Revolutionary America. Now, lodging in a private home called a bed and breakfast is becoming increasingly fashionable throughout America, and Hawaii is no exception. Not only can you visit Oahu, you can "live" there for a time with a host family and share an intimate experience of daily life.

Points To Consider
The primary feature of bed and breakfast homes is that every one is privately owned, and therefore uniquely different from every other. The range of B&Bs is as wide as the living standards in America. You'll find every-

thing from semi-mansions in the most fashionable residential areas to little grass shacks offered by a downhome fisherman and his family. This means that it's particularly important for the guest to choose a host family with whom their lifestyle is compatible.

Unlike a hotel or a condo, you'll be living *with* a host and most likely his or her family, although your room will be private, with private baths and separate entranceways being quite common. You don't just "check in" to a bed and breakfast. In Hawaii you go through agencies (listed below) which act as a go-between, matching host and guest. Write to them and they'll send you a booklet with a complete description of the bed and breakfast, its general location, the fees charged, and a good idea of the lifestyle of your host family. With the reservations application they'll include a questionnaire that will basically determine your profile: are you single? have children? smoker? etc., as well as arrival and departure dates and all pertinent particulars.

Since bed and breakfasts are run by individual families, the times that they will accept guests can vary according to what's happening in their lives. This makes it imperative to write well in advance: three months is good; earlier is too long and too many things can change. Four weeks is about the minimum time required to make all necessary arrangements. Expect a minimum stay (three days is common) and a maximum stay. Bed and breakfasts are not long-term housing, although it's hoped that guest and host will develop a friendship and future stays can be as long as both desire.

B&B Agencies

One of the most experienced agencies, **Bed And Breakfast Honolulu Statewide,** at 3242 Kaohinanai Dr., Honolulu, HI 96817, tel. 595-7533, or (800) 288-4666, owned and operated by Marylee and Gene Bridges, began in 1982. Since then, they've become masters at finding visitors the perfect accommodation to match their desires, needs, and pocketbook. Their repertoire of guest homes offers more than 400 rooms, with half on Oahu, and the other half scattered around the state. Accommodations from Marylee and Gene are more personally tailored than a hotel room. When you phone, they'll match your needs to their computerized in-house guidelines. B&B Honolulu Statewide also features bargain package deals for inter-island fly/car rentals. If you have special needs and are coming during peak season, reserve up to four months in advance; normal bookings are perfect with two-month's lead time. But, don't count them out if you just show up at the airport. Rooms can't be guaranteed, but they'll do their best to find you a place to stay.

Another top-notch B&B agency is **Bed and Breakfast Hawaii,** operated by Evelyn Warner and Al Davis. They've been running this service since 1978, and their reputation is excellent. B&B Hawaii has a membership fee of $10 yearly. For this they mail you their "Directory of Homes," a periodic "hot sheet" of new listings, and all pertinent guest applications; add $1 handling. Write Bed and Breakfast Hawaii, Box 449, Kapaa, HI 96746. Phone info and reservations at (808) 822-7771.

Bed and Breakfast Maui Style is the oldest B&B agency operating on Maui. The friendly host, Jeanne Rominger, can arrange a stay on Maui as well as on any of the other islands, including Molokai. Accommodations range from a room in a private home to one-bedroom apartments. Write Bed and Breakfast Maui Style, P.O. Box 886, Kihei, HI 96753, tel. 879- 7865.

Other well-known agencies are: **Go Native Hawaii,** who will send you a directory and all needed information by writing to their Mainland address at P.O. Box 13115, Lansing, MI 48901, or in Hawaii at 130 Puhili St., Hilo, HI 96720. Go Native will also accept collect calls from travelers already in Hawaii at (808) 961-2080. **Pacific Hawaii Bed And Breakfast** at 970 N. Kalaheo, Suite A218, Kailua 96734, tel. 262-6026 or (800) 999-6026, lists homes throughout the state, but especially around Kailua/Kaneohe on Oahu's upscale windward coast. Three specializing in beachfront villas, luxury condominiums, and exclusive estates are **Villas of Hawaii,** 4218 Waialae Ave., Suite 203, Honolulu 96816, tel. 735-9000; **All Islands B&B,** at 823 Kainui, Kailua HI 96734, tel. 263-2342, or (800) 542-0344, is owned and operated by Ann Carlin and Peggy Frazier. This newest and most energetic agency, with over 300 host homes, prides itself on personalized attention; **Premier Connections of Hawaii,** at 1993 S. Kihei Rd, Suite 209, Kihei, Maui, HI 96753; and **Vacation Locations Hawaii,** P.O. Box 1689, Kihei, HI 96753, tel. 874-0077. Information on B&Bs can also be obtained from the **American Board of Bed and Breakfast Assn.,** Box 23294, Washington, D.C. 20026.

OTHER ACCOMMODATIONS

Home Exchanges

One other method of staying in Hawaii, open to homeowners, is to offer the use of your home in exchange for use of a home in Hawaii. This is done by listing your home with an agency that facilitates the exchange and publishes a descriptive directory. To list your home and to find out what is available, write Vacation Exchange Club, 12006 111 Ave., Youngtown, AZ 85363; or Interservice Home Exchange, Box 87, Glen Echo, MD 20812.

For **camping** information, see "Camping And Hiking" below.

FOOD AND DRINK

Hawaii is a gastronome's Shangri-La, a sumptuous smorgasbord in every sense of the word. The varied ethnic groups that have come to Hawaii in the last 200 years have brought their own special enthusiasm and culture, and lucky for all, they didn't forget their cook pots, hearty appetites, and exotic taste buds.

The Polynesians who first arrived found a fertile but barren land. Immediately they set about growing their taro, coconuts, and bananas, and raising chickens, pigs, fish, and even dogs, though these were reserved for the nobility. The harvests were bountiful and the islanders thanked the gods with the traditional feast called the luau. The underground oven, the *imu*, baked most of the dishes, and participants were encouraged to feast while relaxing on straw mats and enjoying the hula and various entertainments. The luau is as popular as ever, and a treat that's guaranteed to delight anyone with a sense of eating adventure.

The missionaries and sailors came next and their ships' holds carried barrels of ingredients for the puddings, pies, dumplings, gravies, and roasts—the sustaining "American foods" of New England farms. The mid-1800s saw the arrival of boatloads of Chinese and Japanese peasants, who wasted no time making rice instead of bread the staple of the islands. The Chinese added their exotic spices, creating complex Szechuan dishes as well as workingmen's basics like chop suey. The Japanese introduced *shoyu*, sashimi, boxed *(bento)* lunches, delicate tempura, and rich, filling noodle soups. The Portuguese brought their luscious Mediterranean dishes with tomatoes and peppers surrounding plump spicy sausages, nutritious bean soups, and mouthwatering sweet treats like *malasadas* and *pao dolce* (sweet bread). Koreans carried crocks of zesty *kimchi,* and quickly fired up barbecue pits for *pulgogi,* a traditional marinated beef cooked over an open fire. Filipinos served up their tarty *adobo* stews of fish, meat, or chicken in a rich sauce of vinegar and garlic.

Recently, Thai and Vietnamese restaurants have been offering their irresistible dishes side by side with fiery burritos from Mexico and elegant cream sauces from France. The ocean breezes of Hawaii not only cool the skin, but on them waft some of the most delectable aromas on Earth, to make the taste buds thrill and the spirit soar.

THE CUISINES OF HAWAII

Hawaiian foods, oldest of all island dishes, are wholesome, well prepared, and delicious. All you have to do on arrival is notice the size of some of the local boys (and women) to know immediately that food to them is indeed a happy and serious business. An oft-heard island joke is that "local men don't eat until they're full, they eat until they're tired." Many Hawaiian dishes have become standard fare at a variety of restaurants, eaten one time or another by anyone who spends time in the islands. Hawaiian food in general is called *kaukau*, cooked food is *kapahaki*, and something broiled is called *kaola*. Any of these prefixes on a menu will let you know that Hawaiian food is served. Usually inexpensive, they'll definitely fill you and keep you going.

Traditional Favorites

In old Hawaii, although the sea meant life, many more people were involved with cultivating beautifully tended garden plots of taro, sugar cane, breadfruit, and various sweet potatoes *(uala)* than fishing. They husbanded pigs and barkless dogs *(ilio)*, and prized *moa* (chicken) for their feathers and meat, but found eating the eggs repulsive. Their only farming implement was the *o'o*, a sharpened hardwood digging stick. The Hawaiians were the best farmers of Polynesia, and the first thing they planted was taro, a tuberous root that was created by the gods at the same time as man. This main staple of the old Hawaiians was made into poi. Every luau will have poi, a glutinous purple paste made from pounded taro root. It comes in liquid consistencies referred to as "one-, two-, or three-finger poi." The fewer fingers you need to eat it, the thicker it is. Poi is one of the most nutritious carbohydrates known, but people unaccustomed to it find it bland and tasteless, although some of the best, fermented for a day or so, has an acidic bite. Poi is made to be

eaten *with* something, but locals who love it pop it in their mouths and smack their lips. However, those unaccustomed to it will suffer constipation if they eat too much.

A favorite popular desert is *haupia,* a custard made from coconut. *Limu* is a generic term for edible seaweed, which many people still gather from the shoreline and eat as a salad or mix with ground *kukui* nuts and salt as a relish. A favorite Hawaiian snack is *opihi,* small shellfish (limpets) that cling to rocks. People gather them, always leaving some on the rocks for the future. Cut from the shell and eaten raw by all peoples of Hawaii, as testament to their popularity they sell for $150 per gallon in Honolulu.

A general term that has come to mean *hors d'oeuvres* in Hawaii is *pu pu*. Originally the name of a small shellfish, now everyone uses the term for any "munchy" that's considered a finger food. A traditional liquor made from *ti* root is *okolehao*. It literally means "iron bottom," reminiscent of the iron blubber pots used to ferment it.

TROPICAL FRUITS AND VEGETABLES

Some of the most memorable taste treats from the islands require no cooking at all: the luscious tropical and exotic fruits and vegetables sold in markets and roadside stands, or found just hanging on trees, waiting to be

common banana

picked. Make sure to experience as many as possible. The general rule in Hawaii is that you are allowed to pick fruit on public lands, but it should be limited to personal consumption. The following is a sampling of some of Hawaii's best produce.

Bananas

No tropical island is complete without them. There are over 70 species in Hawaii, with hundreds of variations. Some are for peeling and eating while others are cooked. A "hand" of bananas is great for munching, back packing, or just picnicking. Available everywhere—and cheap.

Avocados

Brought from South America, avocados were originally cultivated by the Aztecs. They have a buttery consistency and a nutty flavor. Hundreds of varieties in all shapes and colors are available fresh year-round. They have the highest fat content of any fruit next to the olive.

Coconuts

What tropical paradise would be complete without coconuts? Indeed, these were some of the first plants brought by the Polynesians. When children were born, coconut trees were planted for them so they'd have fruit throughout their lifetime. Truly tropical fruits, they know no season. Drinking nuts are large and green, and when shaken you can hear the milk inside. You get about a quart of fluid from each. It takes skill to open one, but a machete can handle anything. Cut the stem end flat so that it will stand, then bore a hole into the pointed end and put in a straw or hollow bamboo. Coconut water is slightly acidic and helps to balance alkaline foods. Spoon meat is a custard-like gel on the inside of drinking nuts. Sprouted coconut meat is also an excellent food. Split open a sprouted nut, and inside is the yellow fruit, like a moist sponge cake. "Millionaire's salad" is made from the heart of a coconut palm. At one time an entire tree was cut down to get to the heart, which is just inside the trunk below the fronds and is like an artichoke heart except that it's about the size of a watermelon. In a downed tree, the heart stays good for about two weeks.

breadfruit

Breadfruit

This is a staple of the islands that provides a great deal of carbohydrates, but many people find the baked, boiled, or fried fruit bland. It grows all over the islands and is really thousands of little fruits growing together to form a ball.

Mangoes

These are some of the most delicious fruits known to humans. They grow wild all over the islands; the ones on the leeward sides of the islands ripen from April to June, while the ones on the windward sides can last until October. They're found in the wild on trees up to 60 feet tall, and the problem is to stop eating them once you start!

Papayas

This truly tropical fruit has no real season but is mostly available in the summer. They grow on branchless trees and are ready to pick as soon as any yellow appears. Of the many varieties, the "solo papaya," meant to be eaten by one person, is the best. Split them in half, scrape out the seeds, and have at them with a spoon.

Passion Fruit

Known by their island name of *lilikoi,* they make excellent juice and pies. They're a small yellow fruit (similar to lemons but smooth-skinned) mostly available in summer and fall, and many wild ones grow on vines, waiting to be picked. Slice off the stem end, scoop the seedy pulp out with your tongue, and you'll know why they're called "passion fruit."

Guavas

These small round yellow fruits are abundant in the wild where they are ripe from early summer to late fall. Considered a pest—so pick all you want. A good source of vitamin C, they're great for juice, jellies, and desserts.

Macadamia Nuts

The king of nuts was brought from Australia in 1892. Now it's the state's fourth-largest agricultural product. Available roasted, candied, or buttered.

Litchis

Called nuts but really a small fruit with a thin red shell. They have a sweet and juicy white flesh when fresh, and appear like nuts when dried.

Potpourri

As well as the above, you'll find pineapples, oranges, limes, kumquats, thimbleberries, and blackberries, as well as carambolas, wild cherry tomatoes, and tamarinds.

FISH AND SEAFOOD

Anyone who loves fresh fish and seafood has come to the right place. Island restaurants specialize in seafood, and it's available everywhere. Pound for pound, seafood is one of the best dining bargains on Oahu. You'll find it served in every kind of restaurant, and often the fresh catch-of-the-day is proudly displayed on ice in a glass case. The following is a sampling of the best.

Mahi Mahi

This excellent eating fish is one of the most common and least expensive in Hawaii. It's referred to as a "dolphin," but is definitely a fish and not a mammal at all. *Mahi mahi* can weigh 10-65 pounds; the flesh is light and moist. This fish is broadest at the head. When caught it's a dark olive color, but after a while the skin turns iridescent—blue, green, and yellow. Can be served as a main course, or as a patty in a fish sandwich.

A'u

This true island delicacy is a broadbill swordfish or marlin. It's expensive even in Hawaii because the damn thing's so hard to catch. The meat is moist and white and truly superb. If it's offered on the menu, order it. It'll cost a bit more, but you won't be disappointed.

Ono

Ono means "delicious" in Hawaiian so that should tip you off to the taste of this wahoo, or king mackerel. *Ono* is regarded as one of the finest eating fishes in the ocean, and its white flakey meat lives up to its name.

Manini

These five-inch fish are some of the most abundant in Hawaii and live in about 10 feet of water. They school and won't bite a hook but are easily taken with spear or net. Not often on a menu, but they're favorites with local people who know best.

Ulua

This member of the crevalle jack family ranges between 15 and 100 pounds. Its flesh is white and has a steak-like texture. Delicious and often found on the menu.

Uku

This is a gray snapper that's a favorite with local people. The meat is light and firm and grills well.

Ahi

A yellowfin tuna with distinctive pinkish meat. A great favorite cooked, or uncooked in sushi bars.

Moi

This is the Hawaiian word for "king." This fish has large eyes and a shark-like head. Considered one of the finest eating fishes in Hawaii, it's best during the autumn months.

Seafood Potpourri

Some other island seafood found on the menu include *limu,* edible seaweed; *opihi,* a small shellfish (limpet) that clings to rocks

HAWAIIAN GAME FISH

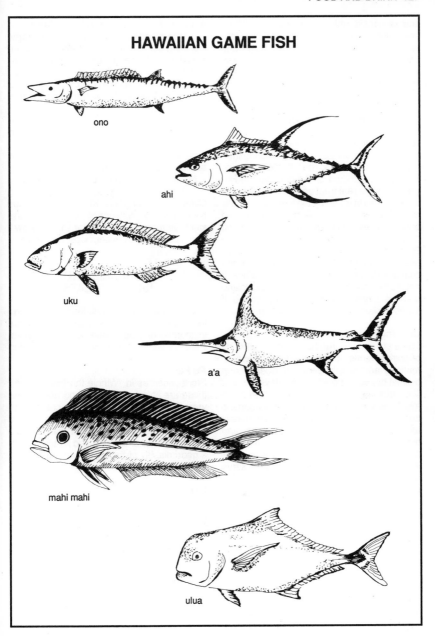

ono

ahi

uku

a'a

mahi mahi

ulua

and is considered one of the best island delicacies, eaten raw; *aloalo,* like tiny lobsters; crawfish, plentiful in taro fields and irrigation ditches; *ahipalaka,* albacore tuna; various octopuses (squid or calamari); and shark of various types.

ISLAND DRINKS

To complement the fine dining in the islands, the bartenders have been busy creating their own tasty concoctions. The full range of beers, wines, and standard drinks is served in Hawaii, but for a real treat you should try some mixed drinks inspired by the islands. A locally brewed beer is Primo. At one time brewed only in Hawaii, it's also made on the Mainland now. It's a serviceable American brew in the German style, but like others, it lacks that full, hearty flavor of the European beers. Kona coffee is the only coffee grown in America. It comes from the Kona District of the Big Island and it is a rich, aromatic, truly fine coffee. If it's offered on the menu, have a cup.

Drinking Laws

There are no state-run liquor stores; all kinds of spirits, wines, and beers are available in markets and shops, generally open during normal business hours, seven days a week. The drinking age is 21, and no towns are "dry." Legal hours for serving drinks depend on the type of establishment. Hours generally are: hotels, 6 a.m. to 4 a.m.; discos, and nightclubs where there is dancing, 10 a.m. to 4 a.m.; bars, lounges where there is no dancing, 6 a.m. to 2 a.m. Most restaurants serve alcohol, and in many that don't, you can bring your own.

Exotic Drinks

To make your experience complete, you must order one of these colorful island drinks. Most look very innocent because they come in pineapples, coconut shells, or tall frosted glasses. They're often garnished with little umbrellas or sparklers, and most have enough fruit in them to give you your vitamins for the day. Rum is used as the basis of many

of them. It's been an island favorite since it was introduced by the whalers of last century. Here are some of the most famous: Mai tai, a mixture of light and dark rum, orange curaçao, orange and almond flavoring, and lemon juice; Chi Chi, a simple concoction of vodka, pineapple juice and coconut syrup, a real sleeper because it tastes like a milk shake; Blue Hawaii, vodka and blue curaçao; Planter's Punch, light rum, grenadine, bitters, and lemon juice—great thirst quencher. Singapore Sling is a sparkling mixture of gin, cherry, brandy and lemon juice.

Maui Lager is a new, premium, all-natural beer brewed in Wailuku at the Pacific Brewing Company by brothers Klaus and Aloysius Klink. The nonpasteurized beer follows the strict German Reinheitsgebot ("Purity Law") which calls for only water, hops, and yeast.

MUNCHIES AND ISLAND TREATS

Certain "finger foods," fast foods, and island treats are unique to Hawaii. Some are a meal in themselves, but others are just snacks. Here are some of the best and most popular.

Pu Pu

Pronounced as in "Winnie the Pooh Pooh," these are little finger foods and hors d'oeuvres. They're everything from crackers to cracked crab. Often, they're given free at lounges and bars and can even include chicken drumettes, fish kebabs, and tempura. With a good display of them you can have a free meal.

Crackseed

A sweet of Chinese origin, these are preserved and seasoned fruits and seeds. Some favorites include coconut, watermelon, pumpkin seeds, mango, and papaya. Different tasting, they take some getting used to, but make great "trail snacks." Available in all island markets. Also look for dried fish (cuttlefish) on racks, usually near the crackseed. These are nutritious and delicious and make a great snack.

Shave Ice

This real island institution makes the Mainland "snow cone" melt into insignificance. Special machines literally shave ice to a fluffy consistency. It's mounded into a paper cone and you choose from dozens of exotic island syrups that are generously poured over it. You're given a straw and a spoon, and just slurp away.

Malasadas And *Pao Dolce*

Two sweets from the Portuguese. *Malasadas* are holeless donuts and *pao dolce* is sweet bread. They're sold in island bakeries and they're great for breakfast or just as a treat.

Lomi Lomi Salmon

This is a salad of salmon, tomatoes, and onions with garnish and seasonings. Often accompanies "plate lunches" and is featured at buffets and luaus.

MONEY-SAVERS

Only one thing is better than a great meal: a great meal at a reasonable price. The following are island institutions and favorites that will help you to eat well and keep prices down.

Kaukau Wagons

These are lunch wagons, but instead of being slick stainless-steel jobs, most are old delivery trucks converted into portable kitchens. Some say they're a remnant of WW II, when workers had to be fed on the job; others say the meals they serve took their inspiration from the Japanese *bento,* a boxed lunch. You'll see them parked along beaches, in city parking lots, or on busy streets. Usually a line of local people will be placing their orders, especially at lunchtime, a tip-off that they serve a delicious, nutritious island dish for a reasonable price. They might have a few tables, but basically they serve food to go. Most of their filling meals are about $3.50, and they specialize in the "plate lunch."

Plate Lunch

This is one of the best island standards. These lunches give you a sampling of au-

Those really determined to save money can always try this!

thentic island food and can include teriyaki chicken, *mahi mahi, lau lau,* and *lomi lomi* salmon, among others. They're served on paper or styrofoam plates, are packed to go, and usually cost less than $3.50. Standard with a plate lunch is "two-scoop rice," a generous dollop of macaroni salad, or some other salad. A full meal, they're great for keeping down food costs and for making an instant picnic. Available everywhere from *kaukau* wagons to restaurants.

Saimin

Special "saimin shops," as well as restaurants, serve this hearty Japanese-inspired noodle soup on their menu. Saimin is a word unique to Hawaii. In Japan, these soups would either be called *ramin* or *soba,* and it's as if the two were combined into saimin. These are large bowls of noodle soup, in a light broth with meat, chicken, fish, or vegetables stirred in. They cost only a few dollars and are big enough for an evening meal. The best place to eat saimin is in a little local hole-in-the-wall shop, run by a family.

Tips

Even some of the island's best restaurants in the fanciest hotels offer "early bird specials"—the regular menu dinners offered to diners who come in before the usual dinner hour, which is approximately 6 p.m. You pay as little as half the normal price, and can dine in luxury on some of the best foods. Often advertised in the "free" tourist books, coupons for reduced meals might also be included: two for one, or limited dinners at a much lower price. Just clip them out.

Food Shopping

Around the island plenty of mom 'n' pop grocery stores provide fertile ground for a cultural exchange, but they're expensive. Oahu's large supermarkets include **Times, Safeway, Foodland,** and **Star Markets.** Preference is highly individual, but Times has a good reputation for fresh vegetables and good prices. Japanese **Holiday Mart** has stores around the island. They've got some bargains in their general merchandise departments, but because they try to be everything, their food section suffers, especially the fruits and vegetables.

A **Floating Farmer's Market** appears at different times and places around Honolulu. For example, on Wednesday mornings from 9:45 to 10:45 a.m., it's across the street from the main library at 478 S. King St., in downtown Honolulu. The vendors are mostly Filipino, who drive up in small battered trucks and sell wonderful fresh vegetables from their home plots at very reasonable prices. Big

shots who bring in fruits and vegies from California and the like have been trying to weed these little guys out. The Honolulu Dept. of Parks regulates the time and place for the market, and you can get information at tel. 527-6060.

Chinatown offers the **People's Open Market** at the Cultural Plaza, located at the corner of Mauna Kea and Beretania streets. Besides produce, you'll find fresh fish, meats, and poultry; the **Oahu Fish Market** is in the heart of Chinatown along King Street. The shops are run-down but clean, and sell everything from octopus to *kimchi.*

Health Food Stores

Brown rice and tofu eaters can keep that special sparkle in their eyes with no problem on Oahu—some excellent health food stores. Most have a snack bar where you can get a delicious and nutritious meal for bargain prices (see "Food" in the various travel sections.) **Down to Earth,** 2525 S. King St., tel. 947-7678, is an old standby where you can't go wrong; great stuff at great prices. **Kokua Co-op Natural Foods And Grocery Store,** at the corner of S. Beretania and Isenberg, tel. 941-1921 is open to the public Mon.-Sat. 9 a.m-8 p.m. Sun. 10 a.m.-7 p.m. Full service store with organic and fresh produce, cheese, milk, juices, bulk foods, and breads. **Celestial Natural Foods,** at the Haleiwa Shopping Plaza on the North Shore, tel. 637-6729, is also top-notch. **Kailua Health Foods** at 124 Oneawa in Kailua, tel. 261-0353, is small but well stocked, especially with detoxification products. **Vim and Vigor** is a small chain of health food stores with locations around the island; the main one is at the Ala Moana Center, tel. 955-3600, and others at Pearlridge Center and the Kahala and Kamehameha centers.

CAMPING AND HIKING

Few people equate visiting Oahu with camping. The two seem mutually exclusive, especially when you focus on the mystique of Waikiki, and the dominance of a major city like Honolulu. But between state, county, and private campgrounds, and even a military reserve or two, you have about 20 spots to choose from all over the island. Camping on Oahu, however, is a little different from camping on the Neighbor Islands, which are simply more amenable to camping. In an island state, they're considered "the woods, the sticks, the backcountry," and camping seems more acceptable there.

Although totally legal to camp, and done by both visitors and residents, Oahu's camping problems are widely divergent, with social and financial implications. When the politically powerful tourist industry thinks of visitors, it imagines people sitting by a hotel pool, drinking mai tais, and dutifully spending money! Campers just won't cooperate in parting with their quota of dollars, so there's not much impetus to cater to their wants and needs. Moreover, Honolulu is an international city that attracts both the best and worst kinds of people. The tourist industry, supported by the civil authorities, has a mortal dread that low-

lifers, loafers, and bums will ensconce themselves on Oahu's beaches. This would be disastrous for Oahu's image! Mainland cities, not so dependent upon tourism, can obviously be more tolerant of their citizens who have fallen through the social net. So in Oahu they keep a close eye on the campgrounds, enforcing the rules, controlling the situation. The campgrounds are patrolled, adding a measure of strictness along with a measure of security. Even decent people can't bend the rules and slide by a little, where they normally might on the Neighbor Islands.

An odd inherent social situation adds to the problem. Not too long ago, the local people either lived on the beach or used them extensively, oftentimes for their livelihood. Many, especially fishermen and their families, would set up semipermanent camps for a good part of the year. You can see the remnants of this practice at some of the more remote and ethnically claimed campgrounds. As Oahu, much more than the Neighbor Islands, felt the pressures of growing tourism, beachfront property became astronomically expensive. Local people had to relinquish what they thought of as their beaches. The state and county, in an effort to keep some beaches public and there-

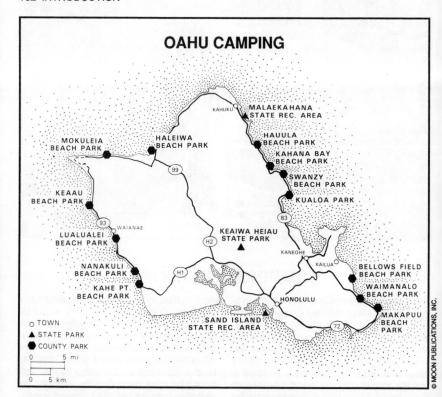

OAHU CAMPING

MALAEKAHANA STATE REC. AREA

KAHUKU

HAUULA BEACH PARK

MOKULEIA BEACH PARK

HALEIWA BEACH PARK

KAHANA BAY BEACH PARK

SWANZY BEACH PARK

KEAAU BEACH PARK

99

KUALOA PARK

93 WAIANAE

83

KEAIWA HEIAU STATE PARK

H2

LUALUALEI BEACH PARK

KANEOHE

NANAKULI BEACH PARK

KAILUA

H1

BELLOWS FIELD BEACH PARK

KAHE PT. BEACH PARK

WAIMANALO BEACH PARK

HONOLULU

MAKAPUU BEACH PARK

○ TOWN
▲ STATE PARK
⬣ COUNTY PARK

0   5 mi
0   5 km

SAND ISLAND STATE REC. AREA

72

© MOON PUBLICATIONS, INC.

fore undeveloped, created **beach parks.** This ensured that all could use the beaches forever, but it also meant that their access would be governed and regulated.

Local people, just like visitors, must follow the rules and apply for camping permits limited by the number of days that you can spend in any one spot. Out went the semipermanent camp and with it, for the local people, the idea of *our* beach. Now, you have the same rights to camp in a spot that may have been used, or even owned, in past generations, by the family of dark-skinned people next to you. They feel dispossessed, infringed upon, and bitter. And you, especially if you have white skin, can be the focus of this bitterness. This situation, although psychologically understandable, can be a monumental drag. Of course, not all island people have this attitude, and chances are very good that nothing

negative will happen. But you must be aware of underlying motivations so that you can read the vibes of the people around your camp spot.

If all of these "problems" haven't made you want to pull up your tent stakes and head into a more congenial sunset, you can have a great and inexpensive time camping on Oahu. All of this is just the social climate that you *may* have to face, but most likely, nothing unpleasant will happen, and you'll come home tanned, relaxed, and singing the praises of the great outdoors on Hawaii's capital island.

State Parks

Oahu boasts 23 state parks and recreation areas. The majority offer a beach for day use, walks, picnicking, toilets, showers, and pavilions. A few of these, including some very important *heiau,* along with **Washington Place,** the state capitol, **Iolani Palace, the Royal Mausolem,** and **Diamond Head** are designated as state monuments. Three state parks offer tent camping: **Sand Island State Park,** just a few minutes from downtown Honolulu; **Keaiwa State Park,** in the interior on the heights above Aiea; and **Malaekahana State Park,** a mile north of Laie on the windward coast.

Oahu state parks close their gates and parking lots at night. Those *not* offering camping are open from 7 a.m.-8 p.m., from May 1 to September 30, closing during the remainder of the year at 6:30 p.m. To camp at the three designated parks, you must acquire a permit (free) from Dept. of Forestry, Division of State Parks, 1151 Punchbowl St., Honolulu 96813, tel. 548-7455. Office hours are 8 a.m.-4:15 p.m. Oahu campsite permit reservations can be made no earlier than the fifth Wednesday before the first day of camping, but *must* be made at least one week in advance by writing a letter including your name, address, phone number, number of persons in your party, type of permit requested, and duration of your stay. The permits can be picked up on arrival with proof of identification.

On Oahu campsites are at a premium and people line up at 8 a.m. on the 1st-floor breezeway on the Beretania Street side of the issuing office, just outside the double glass doors, where you are given a number on a first-come first-served basis. After this go to the third floor where the office is located. **Note!** Camping is allowed *only* from 8 a.m. Friday to 8 a.m. Wednesday with the other two days shut down, supposedly for regrowth. Camping is allowed for only five consecutive days in any one month, and don't forget a parking permit for your vehicle, which must remain within the locked park gates at night. *Alooohaaa!*

County Parks

The city and county of Honolulu has opened 13 (changes periodically) of its 65 beach parks around the island to tent camping, and most allow trailers and RVs. These are the parks at which you're more likely to encounter hassles. A free permit is required, and camping is allowed for one week from Friday at 8 a.m. until the following Wednesday at 8 a.m., at which time your campsite must be vacated (no camping Wednesday and Thursday evenings). These campsites are also at a premium, but you can write for reservations and pick up your permits on arrival with proper identification. For information and reservations write or visit City and County of Honolulu, Dept. of Parks and Recreation, 650 S. King St., Honolulu, HI 96813, tel. 523-4525. Permits are also available from the satellite city halls around the island.

Note that all of the beach parks are closed during designated months (they differ from park to park) throughout the year. This is supposedly for cleaning, but really it's to reduce the possibility of squatters moving in. Make sure, if you're reserving far in advance, that the park will be open when you arrive! Don't count on the Parks and Recreation Department informing you!

Camping Gear And Rentals

If you've come without camping gear and wish to purchase some try: **War Surplus,** 97-719 Kamehameha Hwy., Pearl Ridge, tel. 456-5075; **The Bike Shop,** 1149 S. King St., tel. 531-7071; for rentals, **Omar the Tentman,** 1336 Dillingham Blvd., tel. 841-1057.

HIKING

The best way to leave the crowds of tourists behind and become intimate with the beauty of Oahu is to hike it. Although the Neighbor Islands receive fewer visitors, a higher percentage of people hike them than Oahu. Don't get the impression that you'll have the island to yourself, but you will be amazed at how open and lovely this crowded island can be. Some cultural and social hikes can be taken without leaving the city, like a stroll through Waikiki and a historical walking tour of downtown Honolulu and Chinatown. But others—some mere jaunts, others quite strenuous—are well worth the time and effort.

Remember that much of Oahu is privately owned, and you must have permission to cross this land, or you may be open to prosecution. Usually private property is marked by signs. Another source that might stomp your hiking plans with their jungle boots is the military. A full 25 percent of Oahu belongs to Uncle Sam, and he isn't always thrilled when you decide to play in his back yard. Some of the finest walks (like to the summit of Mt. Kaala) require crossing military lands, much of which has been altered by very unfriendly looking installations. Always check and obey any posted signs to avert trouble. The following listings are by no means all-inclusive, but should help you to choose a trail that seems interesting and is within your ability level.

Diamond Head

The most recognized symbol of Hawaii, this is the first place you should head for a strikingly beautiful panorama of Waikiki and greater Honolulu. Called Leahi, ("Casting Point") by the Hawaiians, it was named Diamond Head after a group of wild-eyed English sailors espied what they thought to be diamonds glistening in the rocks. Hawaii had fulfilled so many other dreams, why not a mountain of diamonds?! Unfortunately, the glimmer was caused by worthless calcite crystals. No fortune was made, but the name stuck.

To get there, follow Kalakaua Avenue south from Waikiki until it leads into Diamond Head Road, then quickly a sign points you to Diamond Head Crater. Pass through a tunnel and into the heavily militarized section in the center of the crater; the trail starts here. Although the hike is moderate, you should bring along water, flashlight (a must), and binoculars if you have them. Run by the Division of State Parks, the park is open daily from 6 a.m. to 6 p.m. A sign at the beginning describes the rigors you'll encounter, and informs that the trail is seven-tenths of a mile long and was built to the 760-foot summit of Leahi Point in 1908 to serve as a U.S. Coast Artillery Observation Station. It was heavily fortified during WW II, and part of the fun is exploring the old gun emplacements and tunnels built to link and service them.

Though only 10 minutes from Waikiki, wildflowers and chirping birds create a peaceful setting. When you come to a series of cement and stone steps, walk to a flat area to the left to find an old winch that hauled the heavy building materials to the top. Here's a wide panorama of the sea, and Koko Head, and notice too that atop every little hillock is an old gun emplacement. Next comes a short but dark (flashlight!) tunnel and immediately a series of 99 steps. You can avoid the steps by taking the trail to the left, but the footing is slippery and there are no guard rails. Following the steps is a spiral staircase that leads down into a large gun emplacement, through which you walk and come to another tunnel. If you haven't brought a flashlight, give your eyes a few minutes to adjust; there's enough light to make it. Once on top, another stairway and ladder takes you to the very summit.

Judd Trail

This is an excellent trail to take to experience Oahu's "jungle" while visiting the historic and picturesque **Nuuanu Pali.** From Honolulu take H-1 and turn onto Rt. 61, the Pali Highway. Turn right onto the Old Pali Highway, then right again onto Nuuanu Pali Drive. Follow it for just under a mile to Reservoir No. 2 spillway. The trail begins on the ocean side of the spillway and leads through fragrant eucalyptus and a dense stand of picture-perfect Norfolk pines. It continues through the forest reserve and makes a loop back to the starting point. En route you pass **Jackass Ginger Pool.** In the immediate area are "mud slides," where you can take a ride on a makeshift toboggan of *pili* grass, *ti* leaves, or a piece of plastic, if you've brought one. This activity is rough on your clothes, and even rougher on your body. The wet conditions after a rain are perfect. Afterward, a dip in Jackass Pool cleans the mud and refreshes at the same time. Continue down the trail to observe wild ginger, guava, and *kukui,* but don't take any confusing side trails. If you get lost head back to the stream and follow it until it intersects the main trail.

Tantalus And Makiki Valley Trails

Great sightseeing and hiking can be combined when you climb the road atop Tantalus. A range of trails in this area offer magnificent

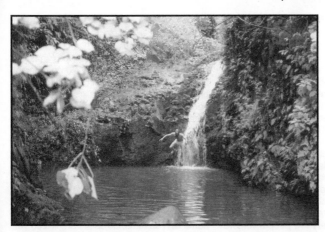

After a hike into the interior, refresh yourself with a dip in the pool of Maunawili Falls.

views. A few roads lead up Tantalus, but a good one heads past Punchbowl along Puowaina Drive; just keep going until it turns into Tantalus Drive. The road switchbacks past some incredible homes and views until it reaches the 2,013-foot summit, where it changes its name to Round Top Drive, then heads down the other side.

The best place to start is at the top of Tantalus at the **Manoa Cliff Trailhead,** where a number of intersecting trails give you a selection of adventure. Once on Round Top Drive, pass a brick wall with the name Kalaiopua Road imbedded in the stonework, and continue until you pass Forest Ridge Way, right after which is a large turnout on both sides of the road near telephone pole no. 56. To the right is the beginning of half-mile-long **Moleka Trail,** which offers some excellent views and an opportunity to experience the trails in this area without an all-day commitment. The trails are excellently maintained, often by the local Sierra Club. Your greatest hazard here is mud, but in a moment you're in a lovely stand of bamboo, and in 10 minutes the foliage parts onto a lovely panorama of Makiki Valley and Honolulu in the background. These views are captivating, but remember to have "small eyes"—check out the varied-colored mosses and fungi, and don't forget the flowers and fruit growing around you.

A branch trail to the left leads to Round Top Drive, and if you continue the trail splits into three: the right is the **Makiki Valley Trail** that cuts across the valley starting at a Boy Scout camp on Round Top Drive and ending atop Tantalus; **Ualakaa Trail** branches left and goes for another half mile, connecting the Makiki Valley Trail with Puu Ualakaa State Park; straight ahead is the **Makiki Branch A Trail,** which descends for one-half mile, ending at the Division of Forestry Baseyard at the bottom of the valley.

On the mountainside of the Manoa Cliffs Trailhead is the **Connector Trail.** This pragmatic-sounding trail does indeed connect the lower trails with **Manoa Cliffs Trail,** skirting around the backside of Tantalus and intersecting the **Puu Ohia Trail,** which leads to the highest point on Tantalus and the expected magnificent view.

Maunawili Falls Trail

Maunawili Falls is on the other side of Nuuanu Pali, near Maunawili Town. This trail offers adventure into Oahu's jungle, with a rewarding pool and falls at the end. At the third red light as you head down the windward side of the Pali Highway, make a right onto Auloa Road. In a few hundred yards, take the left fork onto Maunawili Road and follow it toward the mountains through a residential area. Turn right onto Aloha Oe Drive, follow it to the end, and make a right on Maleko Road. Take this to the end of the cul-de-sac. To the right is a wooden fence and walkway. A sign says "Private," so don't tresspass; instead go under the fence and start up what looks like a jeep trail, but soon becomes a walking path. In 400 yards, at three telephone poles, the trail splits into three branches. Go straight ahead downhill until you intersect a trail that leads right along the creek. This trail is very muddy, but worth it. Follow it for about 15 minutes until you come to Maunawili Falls—deep enough to dive in. You can also see an upper falls. Above them is an open field perfect for an overnight camp. To the left a path leads past a small banana plantation, along an irrigation ditch cut into the mountainside, paralleled by a wooden walkway. Very few people venture into this safe but fascinating area.

Hauula Loop Trails

Built by the Workers Civilian Conservation Corps (WCCC) during the Depression, these manicured trails run up and down two ridges and deep into an interior valley, gaining and loosing height as they switchback through the extraordinary jungle canopy. The **Gulch and Papali trails,** branches of the Hauula Loop Trail, start from the same place. The Hauula Trail is wide with good footing. There're a few stream crossings, but it's not muddy even after a heavy rain, which can shut down the Sacred Falls Trail just a few miles north. The hard-packed trail, covered in a soft carpet of ironwood needles, offers magnificent coastal views once you reach the heights, or you can look inland into verdant gulches and gulleys (valleys).

You'll be passing through miniature eco-systems very reminiscent of the fern forests on the Big Island, but on a much smaller scale. The area flora is made up of ironwoods, passion fruit, thimbleberries, *ohia,* wild orchids, and fiddlehead ferns. To get there, head for Hauula on coastal Rt. 83 (Kam Hwy.) and just past the 7-eleven Store, between mile markers 21-22, look inland for Hauula Homestead Road. Take it for a minute until you see the well-marked sign leading to the trails.

Sacred Falls

On coastal Rt. 83, between Hauula and Punaluu (mile marker 22-23), an HVB Warrior points you to Sacred Falls. Note that you *cannot* drive to the falls. An old commercial venture put out this misinformation, which persists to this day. The walk is a hardy stroll, so you'll need jogging shoes, not thongs. The area becomes a narrow canyon, and the sun sets early; don't start out past 3 p.m., especially if you want a dip in the stream. The trail was roughed up by Hurricane Ewa, and a sign along it says "Danger. Do not go past this point." Ignore it! The walking is a little more difficult but safe.

The area's Hawaiian name was Kaliuwaa ("Canoe Leak") and although the original name isn't as romantic as the anglicized version, the entire area was indeed considered sacred. En route, you pass into a very narrow valley where the gods might show disfavor by dropping rocks onto your head. Notice many stones wrapped with a *ti* leaf. This is an appeasement to the gods, so they're not tempted to brain you. Go ahead, wrap a rock; no one will see you! You hear the falls dropping to the valley floor. Above you the walls are 1,600 feet high, but the falls drop only 90 feet or so. The pool below is ample for a swim, but the water is chilly and often murky. A number of beautiful picnic spots are on the large flat rocks.

North Oahu Treks

Some of the hiking in and around northwest Oahu is quite difficult. However, you should take a hike out to **Kaena Point.** You have two choices: you can park your car at the end of the road past Dillingham Airfield on the north coast and hike in; or you can park your car at the end of the road past Makua on the Waianae coast and hike in. Both are about the same distance, and both are hardy but not difficult. The attraction of Kaena Point is huge surf, sometimes 30 feet high. The trail is only two miles, from each end, and few people come here except some local fishermen.

Peacock Flat is a good family-style trail that offers primitive camping. Follow Rt. 93

toward Dillingham Airfield and just before getting there turn left onto a dirt road leading toward the Kawaihapi Reservoir. If you want to camp, you need permits from the Division of Forestry and a waiver from the Mokuleia Ranch, tel. 637-4241, which you can get at their office, located at the end of a dirt road just before the one leading to Kawaihapi Reservoir. They also provide instructions and a key to get through two locked gates before reaching the trailhead, if you decide to go in from that end. Heading through the Mokuleia Forest Reserve, you can camp anywhere along the trail, or at an established but primitive campground in Peacock Flat. This area is heavily used by hunters, mostly after wild pig.

Dupont Trail takes you to the summit of Mt. Kaala, highest point and by far the most difficult hike on the island. The last mile is downright dangerous, and has you hanging on cliff edges, with the bottom 2,000 feet below! This is not for the average hiker. Follow Rt. 930 to Waialua, make a left at Waialua High School onto a cane road, and follow it to the second gate, about 1½ miles. Park there. You need a hiking permit from the Division of Forestry and a waiver from the Waialua Sugar Company, tel. 637-3521. Atop Kaala, although the views are magnificent, you'll also find a mushroom field of FAA satellite stations.

INFORMATION AND EQUIPMENT

Hiking Groups And Information

The following organizations can provide information on wildlife, conservation, and organized hiking trips. **Hawaiian Trail and Mountain Club,** Box 2238, Honolulu 96804, meets behind Iolani Palace on Saturdays at 10 a.m., and Sundays at 8 a.m. Their hikes are announced in the *Honolulu Star Bulletin*'s "Pulse of Paradise" column. **Hawaii Audubon Society** can be reached at Box 22832, Honolulu 96822. **Sierra Club,** 1212 University Ave., Honolulu 96826, tel. 946-8494, can provide you with a packet describing Hawaii's trails, charted by island, along with their physical characteristics and information on obtaining maps and permits. The packet costs $3, postage paid. Write the Division of Forestry, 1151 Punchbowl St., Room 325, Honolulu, HI 96813, tel. 548-2861, and ask for a copy of their *Island of Oahu Recreation Map*. It gives good information on hiking, camping, and hunting with a description of most trails.

Equipment

Like everything else you take to Hawaii, your camping and hiking equipment should be lightweight and durable. Camping equipment size and weight should not cause a problem with baggage requirements on airlines: if it does, it's a tip-off that you're hauling too much. One odd luggage consideration you might make is to bring along a small **styrofoam cooler** packed with equipment. Exchange these for food items when you get to Hawaii; if you intend to car camp successfully and keep food prices down, you'll definitely need a cooler. You can also buy one on arrival for only a few dollars. You'll need a lightweight **tent,** preferably with a rainfly and a sewn-in floor. This will save you from getting wet and miserable, and will keep out mosquitoes, cockroaches, ants, and the few stinging insects on Oahu.

Sleeping bags are a good idea, although you can get along at sea level with only a blanket. Down-filled bags are necessary for Haleakala, Mauna Kea, Mauna Loa, or any high-elevation-camping—you'll freeze without one. **Campstoves** are needed because there's very little wood in some volcanic areas, it's often wet in the deep forest, and open fires are often prohibited. If you'll be car camping, take along a multiburner stove, and for trekking, a backpacker's stove will be necessary. The grills found only at some campgrounds are popular with many families that go often to the beach parks for an open-air dinner. You can buy a very inexpensive charcoal grill at many variety stores throughout Hawaii.

It's a great idea to take along a **lantern.** This will give added safety for car campers. Definitely take a **flashlight,** replacement batteries, and a few small **candles.** A complete **first-aid kit** can be the difference between life and death, and is worth the extra bulk. Hikers, especially those leaving the coastal areas, should take **rain gear**, a plastic ground cloth, utility knife, compass, safety whistle, mess kit, water purification tablets, canteen, nylon twine, and waterproof matches. You can find plenty of stores that sell, and a few stores that rent, camping equipment; see the Yellow Pages under "Camping Equipment," and "Shopping" in the following travel chapters.

Safety

There are two things in Hawaii that you must keep your eye on to remain safe: humans and nature. The general rule is, the farther you get away from towns, the safer you'll be from human-induced hassles. If possible, don't hike or camp alone, especially if you're a woman. Don't leave your valuables in your tent, and always carry your money, papers, and camera with you. (See "Theft.") Don't tempt the locals by being overly friendly or unfriendly, and make yourself scarce if they're drinking. While hiking, remember that many trails are well maintained, but trailhead markers are often missing. The trails themselves can be muddy, which can make them treacherously slippery and oftentimes knee-deep. Always bring food because you cannot, in most cases, forage from the land. Water in most streams is biologically polluted and will give you bad stomach problems if you drink it without purifying it first, either through boiling or with tablets. For your part, please don't use the streams as a toilet.

Precautions

Always tell a ranger or official of your hiking intentions. Supply an itinerary and your expected route, then stick to it. Twilight is short in the islands, and night sets in rapidly. In June sunrise and sunset are around 6 a.m. and 7 p.m., in December these occur at 7 a.m. and 6 p.m. If you become lost at night, stay put, light a fire if possible, and stay as dry as you

can. If lost, walk on ridges and avoid the gulches, which have more obstacles and make it harder for rescuers to spot you.

Hawaii is made of volcanic rock which is brittle and crumbly. Never attempt to climb steep *pali* (cliffs). Every year people are stranded and fatalities have occurred on the *pali*. Be careful of elevation sickness, especially on Haleakala, Mauna Loa, and Mauna Kea. The best cure is to head down as soon as possible.

Heat can cause you to lose water and salt. If you become woozy or weak, rest, take salt, and drink water as you need it. Remember, it takes much more water to restore a dehydrated person than to keep hydrated; take small frequent sips. Be mindful of flash floods. Small creeks can turn into raging torrents with upland rains. Never camp in a dry creek bed. Fog is only encountered at the 1,500- to 5,000-foot level, but be careful of disorientation. Generally, stay within your limits, be careful, and enjoy yourself.

Guide Books

For a well-written and detailed hiking guide complete with maps, check out the *Hiking Hawaii Series* (a book for each island, plus a general book for all the islands) by Robert Smith, published by Wilderness Press, 2440 Bancroft Way, Berkeley, CA 94704. Another book by the same company is *Hawaiian Camping* by Shirley Rizzuto. Geared toward family camping, it's adequate for basic information and listing necessary addresses, but at times it's limited in scope.

Topographical And Nautical Charts

For in-depth topographical maps, write **U.S. Geological Survey,** Federal Center, Denver, CO 80225. In Hawaii, a wide range of topographical maps can be purchased at **Trans-Pacific Instrument Co.,** 1406 Colburn St., Honolulu, HI 96817, tel. 841-7538. For nautical charts, write **National Ocean Service,** 6501 Lafayette Ave., Riverdale, MD 20737-1199, tel. (301) 436-6990.

SPORTS AND RECREATION

Oahu is a playground for young and old with sports, games, and activities galore. Everyone can find something they enjoy, and most activities are free, relatively cheap, or once-in-a-lifetime thrills that are worth the money. The sea is the ideal playground. You can swim, snorkel, scuba, surf, fish, sail, canoe, kayak, sailboard, bodysurf, parasail, cruise, or merely stroll along the shore picking shells or exploring tidepools.

If it can be ridden, sailed, glided, flown, bounced, smashed with a racquet, struck with a club, bat, or foot, or hooked with the right bait, you'll find it on Oahu. And lots of it! The pursuit of fun is serious business here, and you can find anything, sportswise, that you ever dreamed of doing. The island offers tennis and golf, along with plenty of horseback riding, hiking, hunting, and freshwater fishing. Spectator sports like baseball, basketball, polo, and especially football are popular. Whatever your desire or physical abilities may be, there'll be some activity that strikes your fancy.

One of the best tonics for relaxation is to play hard at something you thoroughly enjoy, so you're deliciously tired and fulfilled at day's end. For you this might be hooking onto an 800-pound marlin that'll test you to the limit, or perhaps just giving yourself to the sea and floating on gentle waves. Hawaii is guaranteed to thrill the young, invigorate the once-young, put a twinkle in your eye and a bounce in your step.

GOLF

With 24 private, public, and military golf courses scattered around such a relatively small island, it's a wonder that it doesn't rain golf balls. At present 15 links are open to the public, ranging from modest nine-holers to world-class courses whose tournaments attract the biggest names in golf today. Prices range from a token $2 up to $40 or more. Legendary courses like the super-exclusive **Waialae Country Club** charge upwards of $20,000 membership fees, and have a reputation for such magnificently smooth greens that some of the snobbier members would rather stroke them than the mink upholstery in their Rolls-Royces. An added attraction of playing Oahu's courses is that you get to walk around on some of the most spectacular and manicured pieces of real estate on the island. Some afford sweeping views of the coast, like

GOLF COURSES OF OAHU

COURSE	PAR	YARDS	FEES WEEKDAY	CART
Ala Wai Golf Course 404 Kapahulu Ave. HI 96851 tel. 296-4653	70	6065	$8	$5.50
Bay View Golf Center 45-285 Kaneohe Bay Dr. Kaneohe, HI 96744 tel. 247-0451	54	2231	$5	$1
Hawaii Country Club Kunia Rd. Kunia, HI 96759 tel. 621-5654	71	5664	$17	Incl.
Hawaii Kai Championship Golf Course 8902 Kalanianaole Hwy. Honolulu, HI 96825 tel. 395-2358	72	6350	$40	Incl.
Hawaii Kai Executive Golf Course 8902 Kalanianaole Hwy. Honolulu, HI 96825 tel. 395-2358	55	2433	$9	$6
Honolulu Country Club 1690 Ala Puunalu St. Honolulu, HI 96818 tel. 833-4541	73	6808	$35	Incl.
Kahuku Golf Course * x P.O. Box 143, Kahuku, HI 96731 tel. 293-5842	35	2699	$2	
Makaha Valley Country Club 84-627 Makaha Valley Rd. Waianae, HI 96792 tel. 695-7111	71	6369	$30	Incl.
Mid Pacific Country Club 266 Kaelepulu Dr. Kailua, HI 96734 tel. 261-9765	72	6812	$100	$20
Mililani Golf Club 95-176 Kualelani Ave. Mililani, HI 96789 tel. 623-2222	72	6815	$45	Incl.
Moanalua Golf Club * 1250 Ala Aolani St. Honolulu HI 96819 tel. 839-2411	36	2972	$12.50	$9
Oahu Country Club 150 Country Club Rd. Honolulu, Hi 96817 tel. 595-3256	71	6000	$50	Incl.
Olomana Golf Links 41-1801 Kalanianaole Hwy. Waimanalo, HI 96795 tel. 259-7926	72	6081	$23.50	$10

GOLF COURSES OF OAHU (cont.)

COURSE	PAR	YARDS	FEES WEEKDAY	CART
Pali Golf Course 45-050 Kamehameha Hwy. Kaneohe, HI 96744 tel. 261-9784	72	6493	$8	$5.50
Pearl Country Club 98-535 Kanonohi St. Aiea, HI 96701 tel. 487-3802	71	6924	$28	Incl.
Sheraton Makaha Resort and Country Club P.O. Box 896 Makaha Valley Rd. Waianae, HI 96792 tel. 695-9544	72	7091	$85	Incl.
Ted Makalena Golf Course 93059 Waipio Point Access Rd., Waipahu HI 96796 tel. 296-7888	71	5976	$8	$11
Turtle Bay Hilton and Country Club P.O. Box 187, Kahuku, HI 96731 tel. 293-8811	72	7036	$65	$9.50
Waialae Country Club x• 4997 Kahala Ave. Honolulu, HI 96816 tel. 734-2151	72	6529	$30	$8

*N.B. *= 9-hole course x=no club rentals •=guests only*

the **Hawaii Kai Championship Course,** while others, like the **Pali Golf Course,** have a lovely mountain backdrop, or, like Waikiki's **Ala Wai Golf Course,** are set virtually in the center of all the downtown action.

The **Hawaiian Open Invitational Golf Tournament** held in late January or February at the Waialae Country Club brings the world's best golfers. Prize money is close to $1 million, and all three major TV networks cover the event. This is usually the only opportunity the average person gets to set foot on this course.

Military personnel, or those with military privileges, are welcome to golf at a number of courses operated by all four branches of the service. Calling the respective bases provides all necessary information.

Those who can't find their way to the links on their own might enjoy the services of **Alii**

Golf, tel. 735-0060, or **Kato's Golf Tours,** tel. 947-3010; both take you to a number of island courses and provide carts, greens fees, clubs, shoes, and roundtrip transportation as part of their services. For the rest, the preceding chart should help you tee off.

TENNIS

Grease up the old elbow because Oahu boosts over 168 county-maintained tennis courts. Get a complete list of them by writing a letter of inquiry and enclosing a SASE to the Dept. of Parks and Recreation, Tennis Division, 3908 Paki Ave., Honolulu, HI 96815, tel. 923-7927. Also, plenty of hotel and private courts are open to the public for a fee, though a few hotels limit play to guests only. The following chart is a partial listing of what's available.

TENNIS COURTS OF OAHU

COUNTY COURTS

Under the jurisdiction of the Department of Parks and Recreation, 3908 Paki Avenue, Honolulu, HI 96815. Telephone 923-7927. Courts listed are in Waikiki and main towns only. There are approximately 30 additional courts around the island.

Location	Name of Court	No. of Courts	Lighted
Aiea	Aiea Recreation Center	2	Yes
Ewa	Ewa Beach Community Park	4	Yes
Kahala	Kahala Recreation Center	2	No
Kailua	Kailua Recreation Center	8	Yes
Kaimuki	Kaimuki Recreation Center	2	Yes
Kalakaua	Kalakaua Recreation Center	4	Yes
Kaneohe	Kaneohe District Park	6	No
Keehi	Keehi Lagoon courts	12	No
Koko Head	Koko Head District Park	6	Yes
Maunawili	Maunawili Park	2	Yes
Pearl City	Pearl City Recreation Center	2	Yes
Sunset Beach	Sunset Beach Neighborhood Park	2	Yes
Wahiawa	Wahiawa Recreation Center	4	Yes
Waialua	Waialua Recreation Center	4	Yes
Waianae	Waianae District Park	8	Yes
Waikiki	Ala Moana Park	10	Yes
Waikiki	Diamond Head Tennis Center	7	No
Waikiki	Kapiolani Tennis courts	4	Yes
Waimanalo	Waimanalo District Park	4	No
Waipahu	Waipahu Recreation Center	4	Yes

HOTEL AND PRIVATE COURTS THAT ARE OPEN TO THE PUBLIC

Location	Name of Court	No. of Courts	Lighted
Honolulu	Hawaiian Regent Hotel (fee)	1	No
Honolulu	Ilikai Hotel, The Westin (fee)	7	Yes
Honolulu	King Street courts (fee)	4	Yes
Honolulu	Waikiki Malia Hotel (fee for non-guests)	1	No
Kailua	Windward Tennis Club (fee)	5	Yes
Waianae	Makaha Resort (fee)	4	Yes

SCUBA AND SNORKELING

If you think that Oahu is beautiful above the sea, wait until you explore below. The warm tropical waters and coral growth make it a fascinating haven for reef fish and aquatic plantlife. You'll soon discover that Hawaiian waters are remarkably clear, with excellent visibility. Fish in every fathomable color parade by. Lavender clusters of coral, red, and gold coral trees and over 1,500 different types of shells carpet the ocean floor. In some spots (like Oahu's Hanauma Bay) the fish are so accustomed to humans that they'll eat bread from your hand. In other spots, lurking moray eels add the special zest of danger. Sharks and barracuda pose less danger than scraping your knee on the coral or being driven against the rocks by a heavy swell. There are enormous but harmless sea bass and a profusion of sea turtles. All this awaits below Hawaii's waters.

Oahu has particularly generous underwater vistas open to anyone donning a mask and fins. Snorkel and dive sites, varying in difficulty and challenge, are accessible from the island. Sites can be totally hospitable, where families and first-time snorkelers can have an exciting but safe frolic, or accessible only to the experienced diver. All over the island are dive shops from which you can rent or buy all equipment, and where dive boats and instruction on all levels can be arranged. Particular spots are listed under "Beaches and Parks" in the travel sections, but some well-known favorites are Hanauma Bay, Black Point off Diamond Head, the waters around Rabbit Island, Sharks Cove on the North Shore, Wanalua Bay between Koko and Diamond Heads (good for green sea turtles), Magic Island near Ala Moana Beach Park, and some sunken ships and planes just off the Waianae coast.

Scuba

If you're a scuba diver you'll have to show your C Card before local shops will rent you gear, fill your tanks, or take you on a charter dive. Plenty of outstanding scuba instructors will give you lessons towards certification, and they're especially reasonable because of the stiff competition. Prices vary, but you can take a three- to five-day semiprivate certification course, including all equipment, for about $275 (instruction book, dive tables, logbook extra charge). Divers unaccustomed to Hawaiian waters should not dive alone regardless of their experience. Most opt for dive tours to special dive grounds guaranteed to please. These vary also, but an *accompanied* single-tank dive where no boat is involved goes for about $65. For a single-tank boat dive, expect to spend $75. There are special charter dives, night dives, and photography dives. Most companies pick you up at your hotel, take you to the site, and return you home. Basic equipment costs $20-30 for the day, and most times you'll only need the top of a wetsuit.

Scuba Rentals

The following full-service dive shops charge around $65 for an introductory dive, $75 for a one-tank boat dive, and around $275 for a three- to five-day certification course. Dive shops with a good reputation include: **Waikiki Diving,** at 1734 Kalakaua, and at 420 Nahua, tel. 922-7188, do PADI certification. No snorkeling tours, but they rent snorkeling equipment at $6 for 24 hours. Certification courses costs $300. Open-water dive for beginners from shore is $50 one dive, $75 two dives. Try **Steve's Diving Adventures,** 1860 Ala Moana Blvd., tel. 947-8900; **South Sea Aquatics,** 1050 Ala Moana Blvd; tel. 538-3854; **Hawaiian Divers,** 2344 Kam Hwy., tel. 845-6644; **American Dive Oahu,** 3648 Waialae Ave., tel. 732-2877 is a full-service dive shop offering certification, shore and boat dives, and snorkeling adventures.

Surf and Sea, tel. 637-9887, is a complete dive shop on the North Shore in Haleiwa. **Aaron's Dive Shop,** at 602 Kailua Rd., Kailua, tel. 261-1211, open Mon.-Fri 8-8, Sat. till 6, Sun. till 5, is a full-service dive shop. Snorkel outfit $7 for 24 hours. They have a four-day scuba certification course for $300, PADI. Introductory dive on boat about $75, off the beach is $75 but you get two dives. **Leeward Dive Center,** 87-066 Farrington Hwy., Maili, tel. 696-3414, (800) 255-1574,

REEF FISH

Achilles tang

Hawaiian lionfish

red-lipped parrotfish

moorish idol

manta ray

mottled moray

Potter's angelfish

lagoon
humu

trumpetfish

uhu

manini

blue-spotted
cowfish

threadfin buterflyfish

saddleback
wrasse

bluestripe butterflyfish

offers PADI and NAUI courses for $300. Introductory dives are $65, boat dives $65 for two tanks, $70 night dives. **Aloha Dive Shop,** at Koko Marina (on the way to Haunama Bay), tel. 395-5922, does it all from snorkeling to boat dives. Excellent rates.

Snorkeling

Scuba diving takes expensive special equipment, skills, and athletic ability. Snorkeling in comparison is much simpler and enjoyable to anyone who can swim. In about 15 minutes you can be taught the fundamentals of snorkeling—you really don't need formal instructions. Other snorkelers or dive shop attendants can tell you enough to get you started. Because you can breathe without lifting your head, you get great propulsion from the fins and hardly ever need to use your arms. You can go for much greater distances and spend longer in the water than if you were swimming. Experienced snorkelers make an art of this sport and you too can see and do amazing things with a mask, snorkel, and flippers. Don't, however, get a false sense of invincibility and exceed your limitations.

exploring the reefs of Oahu

Snorkel Rental Equipment And Tours

Those interested can buy or rent equipment in dive shops and in department stores. Sometimes condos and hotels have snorkeling equipment free for their guests, but if you have to rent it, don't do it from a hotel or condo, but go to a dive shop where it's much cheaper (see above). Expect to spend $5-8 a day for mask, fins, and snorkel. Many boats will take you out snorkeling or diving. Prices range from $40 (half day, four hours) to $70 (full day, eight hours); check "Getting Around—Sightseeing Tours" for many of the boats that do it all, from deep-sea fishing to moonlight cruises. A hotel's "activities center" can arrange these excursions for no extra charge. The following are outfits where you can rent equipment and/or take excursions (also see "Scuba" above). Do yourself a favor and wash all the sand off rented equipment. Most shops irritatingly penalize you $1 if you don't. All want a deposit, usually $30, that they put on a credit card slip and tear up when you return. Underwater camera rentals are

now normal at most shops, and go for around $10-12 including film (24 shots), but not developing. Happy diving!

Hanauma Bay is a wonderful place to begin snorkeling, but it's very crowded. A number of outfits sponsor snorkel excursions to this underwater park. This is one of those times where you might consider going with a tour, and not on your own—it's cheap, and you don't have to worry about parking. A tour shouldn't cost any more than $15, and sometimes as little as $12 for a half day, including hotel pick-up and return, all snorkeling equipment, a beach mat, fish food, corrective lenses, vests, sometimes a complimentary soft drink, and free use of an underwater camera. Naturally, you're stuffed on a bus, and a normal tour lasts about three hours. If you go early in the morning, usually around 7 a.m., the bay will be much less crowded, and you can even save a few more dollars. The free tourist literature often has coupons that reduce these prices further! Hanauma Bay snorkeling tour operators include: **Pacific In-**

HAWAIIAN SHELLS

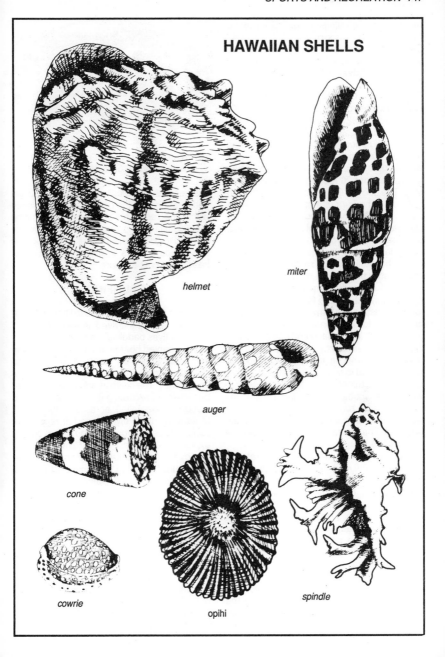

helmet

miter

auger

cone

spindle

cowrie

opihi

terlude, tel. 848-0949; **Hawaii Snorkeling,** tel. 944-2846; **Budget Snorkel,** tel. 947-2447; **Seashore Snorkeling,** tel. 395-8947; **Tommy's Tours,** tel. 944-8828; **Paradise Snorkeling Adventures,** tel. 923-7766.

Snuba Tours Of Oahu

No that's not a typo. **Snuba,** at 2233 Kalakaua Ave., B-205A, Suite 1271, Honolulu, HI 96815, tel. 922-7762, offers a hybrid sport that is half snorkeling and half scuba diving. You have a regulator, a weight belt, mask, and flippers, and you're tethered to scuba tanks that float 20 feet above you on a seasled. The unofficial motto of Snuba is "secure but free. "The idea is that many people become anxious diving under the waves encumbered by tanks and all the scuba apparatus. Snuba frees you. You would think that being tethered to the sled would slow you down, but actually you're sleeker and can make better time than a normal scuba diver. The sled is made from industrial-strength polyethylene and is 2½ feet wide by 7½ feet long, consisting of a view window, and a belly in the sled for location of the scuba tank. If you get tired, just surface and use it as a raft. Snuba was invented by Mike Stafford of Placerville, California, as an aid to disabled people who wished to scuba. He got the idea from modern gold miners in the Mother Lode area who set a scuba tank on the side of the riverbank and run an air line down to the water to look for gold nuggets wedged under boulders. The first raft came off the assembly line in 1988.

Mick Riegel, the owner and operator of Snuba of Oahu, is one of the first to open a commercial venture in this newest of underwater sports. Mick conducts two morning tours, and one afternoon tour daily. From Monday through Friday, the dive spot of choice is at Hanauma Bay, but on weekends and holidays no commercial activity is allowed at the bay, so on those days, the morning surf report dictates the dive spot. Snuba will send its van to fetch you, and will return you to your hotel after the dive. The morning tour at $49.95 is designed for the beginner, and lasts 30 minutes under water. You are given instruction, and two people are

by ship's artist Francis Olmsted, c. 1840
(Hawaii State Archives)

assigned as "buddies" on one sled. You get your first taste of the underwater experience within the reef. The afternoon dive costing $59.95 lasts one hour underwater, and you're allowed to go beyond the reef. On weekends and holidays tours include picnics on the beach and cost $5 more.

SURFING

Surfing is a sport indigenous to Hawaii. When the white man first arrived he was astonished to see natives paddling out to meet the ships on long carved boards, then gracefully riding them into shore on crests of waves. The Hawaiians called surfing *he'enalu* (to "slide on a wave"). The newcomers were fascinated by this sport, recording it on engravings and woodcuts marvelled at around the world. Meanwhile, the Polynesians left records of surfing as petroglyphs and in *mele* of surfing exploits of times past. A local Waikiki beachboy by the name of Duke Kahanamoku won a treasure box full of gold medals for swimming at the Olympic Games of 1912, and thereafter became a celebrity who toured the Mainland and introduced surfing to the modern world. Surfing later became a lifestyle spread far and wide by the songs of the Beach Boys in the '60s. Now surfing is a spor enjoyed around the world complete with championships, movies, magazines, and advanced board technology.

It takes years of practice to become good but with determination, good swimming abi ity, and a sense of balance you can learn th fundamentals in a short time. At surf shop all around the island you can rent a board for very reasonable prices. The boards of the ancient *ali'i* were up to 20 feet long and weighed over 150 pounds, but today's board is made from ultralight foam plastic covered in fiberglass. They're about six feet long and weigh 12 pounds or so. Innovations occur every day in surfing, but one is the changeable "skeg" or rudder allowing you to surf in variable conditions.

The sport of surfing is still male-dominated, but women champions have been around for years. The most famous surfing beaches in the world are Sunset Beach and the Bonzai Pipeline on North Shore Oahu. Every year the nationally televised Pro-Tour Surfing Championship is held there, usually in late November and December. It's only a matter of time before surfing becomes an Olympic sport.

One of the most brilliant books ever written on surfing is *Surfing, The Ultimate Pleasure,* by Leonard Lueras and designed by Fred Bechlen. Published by Workman Publishing of New York, a copy can be found at almost every surf shop.

All the Hawaiian islands have incredibly good surfing conditions, but Oahu is best. Conditions here are perfect for rank beginners up to the best in the world. Waikiki's surf is predictable, and just right to start on, while the Banzai Pipeline and Waimea Bay on the North Shore have some of the most formidable surfing conditions on Earth. Makaha Beach in Waianae is perhaps the best all-around surfing beach, frequented by "living legends" in this most graceful sport.

If there is such a thing as "the perfect wave," Oahu's waters are a good place to look for it. Summertime brings rather flat action all around the island, but the winter months are a totally different story, with monster waves on the North Shore, and heavy surf at times even in the relative calm of Waikiki. *Never* surf without asking about local conditions, and remember that "a fool and his surfboard, and maybe his life, are soon parted." See pp. 87, 90 for local and international surfing competitions on Oahu.

Lessons? A number of enterprises in Waikiki offer beach services. Often these concessions are affiliated with hotels, and almost all hotel activities desks can arrange surfing lessons for you. An instructor and board go for about $15 per hour. A board alone is half the price, but as in skiing, a few good lessons to start you off are well worth the time and money. Some reputable surfing lessons along Waikiki are provided by: Outrigger Hotel, 2335 Kalakaua Ave. tel. 923-0711; Hilton Hawaiian Village, 2005 Kalia Rd., tel. 949-4321; Halekulani Hotel, 2199 Kalia Rd., tel. 923-2311; Big Al Surfing School, 2210 Kalia Rd., tel. 923-4375. Also check near the huge rack of surfboards along Kalakaua Ave., just near Kuhio Beach at the Waikiki Beach Center, where you'll find a number of beachboy enterprises at competitive rates. Fort DeRussy Beach Services, tel. 941-7004, is another good one, and in Haleiwa on the North Shore, try Surf and Sea, tel. 637-9887.

SAILBOARDING

The fastest growing water sport, both in Hawaii and around the world, is sailboarding. Many people call this relatively new sport "windsurfing," after the name of one of the most famous manufacturers of sailboards. A combination of surfing and sailing, the equipment is a rather large and stable surfboard mounted with a highly maneuverable sail. If it sounds difficult, most people find it slightly easier than surfing because you're mobilized by the wind and not at the mercy of the waves. You don't have to "read" the waves as well as a surfer, and like riding a bicycle, as long as you keep moving, you can hold your balance. Unlike male-dominated surfing, women, too, are excellent at sailboarding. Kailua Bay has perfect conditions for this sport, and you can go there any day to see sailboarders skimming the waves with their multihued sails displayed like proud peacocks.

Sailboarding Lessons And Rentals

Far and away the most famous sailboarding beach on Oahu is Kailua Beach Park on the windward coast (see p. 284.) Daily, a flotilla of sailboarders glide over its smooth waters, propelled by the always blowing breezes. Along the shore and in town a number of

sailboards at Kealia Beach

enterprises build, rent, and sell sailboards. There is also sailboarding along the North Shore (see p. 318 for rentals there). Commercial ventures are allowed to operate along Kailua Beach only on weekdays and weekend mornings, but weekend afternoons and holidays are *kapu!* Here are some of the best.

Aloha Windsurfing, tel. 926-1185, sets up along the beach. Group lessons and board rentals are $35 for three hours, or $47 for five hours. Transportation from Waikiki including all-day rental is $57, or $47 for rental only. They also rent kayaks at $10/first hour and $5 for each additional hour.

The **Froome Boating Company,** tel. 261-2961, at 789 Kailua Rd., on the corner of Kailua Road and the Pali Hwy. just as you're entering town, rents sailboards. They'll put it on the roof of your car with a rack provided. It's $29 for four hours, $35 for the day, $40 for 24 hours, full week $130. They also rent kayaks and wave skis, half day $25, full day

$30, 24 hours $35. Hobies rent from $60 half day to $350 for the week for a 14-footer; a 16-footer is $80 half day, $400 week. Hobie Cat lessons available.

Kailua Sailboard Company, 130 Kailua Rd., tel. 262-2555, open 8:30 a.m.-5 p.m. daily, is a full-service sailboard store. Rentals are $27 per day (24 hours), half day $20, longer term available. Beginning group lessons are $35 for a three-hour session. During the week they have equipment right at the beach so you don't have to have a car to transport it. Weekends they provide a push cart, or a roof rack at no additional charge. They also have boogie boards for $7.50/day, wave skis $15/day, and two-person kayaks at $35.

Naish Hawaii, 160 Kailua Rd. (just off the beach), tel. 261-6067, and 155 A Hamakua Dr., tel. 262-6068, open 9-5 daily, are very famous makers of custom boards, production boards, sails, hardware, accessories, and repairs. At the beach store they also have T-shirts, bathing suits, beach accessories, hats, and slippers. The other location is the showroom. Naish is the largest and oldest sailboarding company in Hawaii. One of the major priorities of the Kailua Road store, known as the Naish Windsurfing School, is giving lessons. Early-bird specials from 8:30-10 a.m. are one person $25, two people $39; basic lessons for one person throughout the day is $35 for four hours including equipment. There's also a kids' clinic weekdays from 4-6 p.m. Naish has an excellent reputation as the biggest and the best.

MORE WATER SPORTS

Thrill Craft

Those into **jet-skiing** might try **Offshore Sports Hawaii,** tel. 395-3434, at the Koko Marina Shopping Center, near Hanauma Bay. Upstairs on the water side of the Koko Marina is **American Sports Ltd.,** tel. 395-5319, which offers jet-skiing, snorkeling, and can book you into parasailing and scuba diving as well. Their special deal is jet-skiing, plus snorkeling, plus lunch (French fries or a Japanese *bento* if you prefer) for $49. **Waikiki Beach Services,** tel. 924-4941, rents jet skis along Waikiki. Their rates are $40 for one

1. Wahiawa pond (J.D. Bisignani)   **2.** Kawainui Canal, Kailua (J.D. Bisignani)
3. water lilies (J.D. Bisignani)

1. Waikiki skyline (J.D. Bisignani)   **2.** Royal Hawaiian Hotel (J.D. Bisignani)

1. Byodo-In (J.D. Bisignani)   **2.** the moody Pali from Kailua-Kaneohe (J.D. Bisignani)

1. windsurfing Oahu (J.D. Bisignani) **2.** roadside fruitstand, Waiahole (J.D. Bisignani)

2

1. and 2. hula dancers, Waimea Falls Park (J.D. Bisignani)

1. Hawaiian gallinule (R.J. Shallenberger) **2.** orchid (J.D. Bisignani)

hour, or $60 for two people on one ski for one hour. If you like water-skiing, **Suyderhoud's Water Ski Center,** tel. 395-3777, also at the Koko Marina Shopping center, can provide all your equipment, rentals, and lessons. Also see "Sailboarding Lessons And Rentals" above since many of those companies also rent other water equipment.

Go Bananas Hawaii, 740 Kapapulu, tel. 737-9514, open 9-6 daily, is into kayaks, wave skis, and water toys. They run day tours and overnight tours but don't like to rent to beginners. But you can go for a guided day tour with at least three people at $30 per head. The store also sells aqua socks for walking on the reef, books, soaps, sunglasses, and T-shirts. Also see **Pacific Outdoor Adventures** (p. 104) and "Sailboarding Rentals" (p. 149) for more companies renting kayaks, Hobie Cats, and a variety of marine equipment.

Boogie Boards

If surfing or sailboarding are a bit too much for you, try a boogie board—a foam board about three feet long that you lie on from the waist up. You can get tremendous rides on boogie boards with the help of flippers for maneuverability. You can learn to ride in minutes and it's much faster, easier, and more thrilling than bodysurfing. Boogie boards are for sale all over the island and are relatively cheap. You can rent one from a dive or surf shop for a couple bucks, or buy your own for $35-70. The most highly acclaimed boogie-boarding beach on Oahu is Sandy Beach. It also has the dubious distinction of being the most dangerous beach in Hawaii, with more drownings, broken backs, and broken necks than anywhere in the state. Waikiki is tame and excellent for boogie boarding, while Waimanalo Beach (p. 278) is more for the intermediate boarder.

Rental Gear

Sea Wind and Surf Shop in the 400 block of Royal Hawaiian Ave. rents surfboards, boogie boards, and snorkel sets from 8 a.m.-10 p.m. A surfboard is $8 for the day, boogie boards $6, snorkel set $5. They're a full-service shop where you can buy clothing as well. **Titou Rental Shop,** tel. 923-3627, in the

Outrigger East Hotel along Kuhio Ave. is open 8 a.m.-5 p.m. daily. They rent snorkel gear, boogie boards—cheapest is $7.50 for 24 hours—and surfboards. Surfboards are $15 a day. Snorkel package is $5.50 for 24 hours, $11 for three days. They don't give surfing lessons, but can arrange them. Also see "Scuba And Snorkeling," and "Sailboarding" for more info.

OTHER SPORTS

Horseback Riding

A different and delightful way to see Oahu is from the back of a horse. A few outfits operating trail rides on different parts of the island include: **Gunstock's Ranch,** tel. 488-1593, offering rides over the ranch grounds on the North Shore; **Kualoa Ranch,** tel. 531-8531, by reservation only, on north windward Oahu; **Turtle Bay Hilton,** tel. 293-8693, on the North Shore, non-guests welcome; **Koko Crater Stables,** tel. 395-2682, with rides into Koko Head crater.

Hang Gliding And Parasailing

For a once-in-a-lifetime treat try **Aloha Parasail,** tel. 521-2446. Strapped into a harness complete with lifejacket, you're towed aloft to glide effortlessly over the water. Aloha Parasail has free hotel pickup. **Skyrider,** tel. 924-4941, straps you into a specially equipped chair big enough for two, with a two-way radio and you-control-the-height mechanism.

For those with a very adventurous spirit and a lot of guts, **Tradewinds Hang Gliding,** tel. 396-8557, provides quality instruction in the guaranteed thrill of hang gliding. Beginning lessons on easy slopes $40, advanced with instructor $75. Happy landings!

Spectator Sports

Oahu is home to a number of major sporting events throughout the year. Many are "invitationals" that bring the cream of the crop from both collegiate and professional levels (see pp. 86-90). Here are the major sports happenings on the island.

Football is big in Hawaii. The University of Hawaii's Rainbows play during the normal collegiate season at Aloha Stadium near

Pearl Harbor. In early January, the **Hula Bowl** brings together two all-star teams from the nation's collegiate ranks. You can hear the pads crack in February, when the NFL sends its best players to the **Pro Bowl.**

Basketball is also big on Oahu. The University of Hawaii's Rainbow Warriors play at the **Neal S. Blaisdell Center,** in Honolulu at 777 Ward Street. Mid-April sees some of the nation's best collegiate hoopballers make up four teams to compete in the **Aloha Basketball Classic.**

You can watch the Islanders of the Pacific Coast League play **baseball** during the regular season at Aloha Stadium. Baseball goes back well over 100 years in Hawaii, and the Islanders receive extraordinary fan support.

Watersport festivals include surfing events, usually from November through February. The best-known are: the **Hawaiian Pro Surfing Championships;** the **Duke Kahanamoku Classic; Buffalo's Big Board Classic;** and the **Haleiwa Sea Spree,** featuring many ancient Hawaiian sports. You can watch some of the Pacific's most magnificent yachts sail into the **Ala Wai Yacht Basin** in mid-July, completing their run from Los Angeles in the annual **Trans Pacific Yacht Race.**

GONE FISHING

Hawaii has some of the most exciting and productive "blue waters" in all the world. You'll find a statewide sport-fishing fleet made up of skippers and crews who are experienced professional anglers. You can also fish from jetties, piers, rocks, and from shore. If rod and reel don't strike your fancy, try the old-fashioned throw net, or take along a spear when you go snorkeling or scuba diving. There's nighttime torch fishing that requires special skills and equipment, and freshwater fishing in public areas. Streams and irrigation ditches yield introduced trout, bass, and catfish. While you're at it, you might want to try crabbing for Kona and Samoan crabs, or working low-tide areas after sundown, hunting octopus, a tantalizing island delicacy. See "Hawaiian Game Fish Chart, p. 127.

Deep-sea Fishing

Most game-fishing boats work the blue waters on the calmer leeward sides of the islands. Some skippers, carrying anglers who are accustomed to the sea, will also work the much rougher windward coasts and island channels where the fish bite just as well. Trolling is the preferred method of deep-sea fishing; this is done usually in waters of between 1,000-2,000 fathoms (a fathom is six feet). The skipper will either "area fish," which means running in a crisscrossing pattern over a known productive area, or "ledge fish," which involves trolling over submerged ledges where the game fish are known to feed. The most advanced marine technology, available on many boats, sends sonar bleeps searching for fish. On deck, the crew and anglers scan the horizon in the age-old Hawaiian tradition—searching for seabirds clustered in an area, feeding on the very baitfish pursued to the surface by the huge and aggressive game fish. "Still fishing," or "bottom fishing" with hand lines, yields some tremendous fish.

One of the most famous fishing spots in Hawaii are the **Penguin Banks** off the west coast of Molokai and the south coast of Oahu. "Chicken Farm" at the southern tip of the Penguin Banks is great trolling waters for marlin and *mahi mahi.* The calm waters off the Waianae coast of Oahu, from Barber's Point to Kaena Point, yield marlin and *ahi.*

Charter Boats

The charter boats of Hawaii come in all shapes and sizes, but they are all manned by professional, competent crews and captains intimately knowledgeable of Hawaiian waters. Prices vary but expect to spend $60-80 on a "share basis." The average number of fishermen per boat is six, and most boats rent all day for $300-400. You can also arrange half days, and bigger boats with more anglers cost as little as $40 per person. All tackle from 30 to 130 pounds is carried on the boats and is part of the service. Oftentimes soft drinks are supplied, but usually you carry your own lunch.

It is customary for the crew to be given any fish that are caught, but naturally this doesn't apply to trophy fish; the crew is also glad to cut off some steaks and fillets for your personal use. Honolulu's Kewalo Basin, only a few minutes from Waikiki, has the largest fleet of charter boats. Pokai Bay also has a fleet, and many charter boats sail out of Kaneohe Bay.

The vast majority of Oahu's fleet moors in **Kewalo Basin,** in Honolulu Harbor along Ala Moana Boulevard next to Fishermen's Wharf. The boat harbor is a sight in itself, and if you're contemplating a fishing trip, it's best to head down there the day before and yarn with the captains and returning fishermen. This way you can get a feel for a charter to suit you best.

Charter organizations include: **Island Charters,** tel. 536-1555; **Happy Time Charters,** tel. 329-9530; **Sport Fishing Hawaii,** tel. 536-6577, with the largest fleet of all. Many private boats operating out of Kewalo Basin include: *Tina Rei,* tel. 536-5018; *Alii Kai,* tel. 521-3969; *Kahuna Kai,* tel. 235-6236; *Fish Hawk,* tel. 531-8338; *Pacific Blue,* tel. 487-8448; *Sea Verse,* tel. 521-8829.

A few boats operate out of **Pokai Bay,** in Waiane on the northern leeward coast. One of the best is the *Kamalii Kai Too,* operated by Capt. Jim Hilton, tel. 696-7264. A few boats are even berthed in Haleiwa on the North Shore. One with an excellent reputation is the *Haole Queen,* tel. 637-5189, skippered by Lester Walls. Another good boat is the *Stacy-K,* with Capt. Bill Mattox, tel. 637-7060.

The Game Fish

The most thrilling game fish in Hawaiian waters is marlin, generically known as "billfish" or *a'u* to the locals. The king of them is the blue marlin, with record catches well over 1,000 pounds. There're also striped marlin and sailfish, which often go over 200 pounds. The best times for marlin are during spring, summer, and fall. The fishing tapers off in January and picks up again by late February. "Blues" can be caught year-round, but, oddly enough, when they stop biting it seems as though the striped marlin pick up. Second to

the marlin are tuna. *Ahi* (yellowfin tuna) are caught in Hawaiian waters of depths of 100-1,000 fathoms. They can weigh 300 pounds, but between 25 and 100 pounds is common. There's also *aku* (skipjack tuna) and the delicious *ono,* which average between 20 and 40 pounds.

Mahi mahi is another strong, fighting, deep-water game fish abundant in Hawaii. These delicious fish can weigh up to 70 pounds. Shore fishing and baitcasting yield *papio,* a jack tuna. *Akule,* a scad (locally called *halalu,)* is a smallish schooling fish that comes close to shore and is great to catch on light tackle. *Ulua* are shore fish and can be found in tidepools. They're excellent eating, average two to three pounds, and are taken at night or with spears.

O'io are bonefish that come close to shore to spawn. They're caught by baitcasting and bottom fishing with cut bait. They're bony, but they're a favorite for fish cakes and *poki. Awa* is a schooling fish that loves brackish water. It can get up to three feet long, and is a good fighter. A favorite for throw netters, it's even raised commercially in fishponds. Besides these there are plenty of goatfish, mullet, mackerel, snapper, various sharks, and even salmon. For Hawaiian game fish, see p. 127.

Freshwater Fishing

Due to Hawaii's unique geology, only a handful of natural lakes and rivers are good for fishing. The state maintains two public freshwater fishing areas on Oahu. The **Wahiawa Public Fishing Area** is 300 acres of fishable waters in and around the town of Wahiawa. It's basically an irrigation reservoir used to hold water for cane fields. Species regularly caught here are large and smallmouth bass, sunfish, channel catfish, *tucunare,* oscar, carp, snakehead, and Chinese catfish. The other area is the **Nuuanu Reservoir no. 4,** a 25-acre restricted watershed above Honolulu in the Koolau Mountains. It's open for fishing only three times per year in May, August, and November. Fish caught here are tilapia and Chinese catfish.

Hawaii has only one native freshwater game fish, the *o'opu.* This gobie is an oddball

FRESHWATER FISH

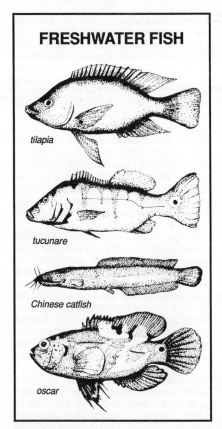

tilapia

tucunare

Chinese catfish

oscar

with fused ventral fins. They grow to be 12 inches and are found on all islands, especially Kauai. Introduced species include largemouth and smallmouth bass, bluegills, catfish, *tucunare,* oscar, carp, and tilapia. The only trout to survive is the rainbow, found only in the streams of Kauai. The *tucunare* is a tough, fighting, good-tasting gamefish introduced from South America, similar to the oscar, from the same region. Both have been compared to bass, but are of a different family.

Tilapia are from Africa and have become common in Hawaii's irrigation ditches. They're "mouth breeders" and the young will take refuge in their parents' protective jaws

even a few weeks after hatching. Snakehead are eel-like fish that inhabit the reservoirs and are great fighters. Channel catfish can grow to over 20 pounds and bite best after sundown. There're also carp, and with their broad tail and tremendous strength, they're the poor man's gamefish. All of these species are best caught with light spinning tackle, or with a bamboo pole and a trusty old worm.

Fishing Rules
Fishing licenses (freshwater needed only) are good from July 1 to June 30. Licenses cost $7.50 for nonresidents, $3.50 for tourists, good for 30 days, $3.75 for residents and military personnel, $1.50 for children between nine and 15 years old, and free to senior citizens. Licenses are obtained from Division of Conservation and Resources Enforcement (Oahu, tel. 548-8766) or from most sporting goods stores. For free booklets and information write Division of Aquatic Resources, 1151 Punchbowl St., Honolulu, HI 96813. All gamefish may be taken year-round, except trout. Trout, only on Kauai, may be taken for 16 days commencing on the first Saturday of August. Thereafter, for the remainder of August and September, trout can be taken only on Sat., Sun., and state holidays.

HUNTING

Most people don't think of Hawaii as a place for hunting, but actually it's quite good. Seven species of introduced game animals are regularly hunted, and 16 species of game birds. Not all species of game animals are open on all islands, but every island offers hunting. Please refer to "Sports" in the travel chapters for full details on hunting on particular islands.

General Hunting Rules
Hunting licences are mandatory to hunt on public, private, or military land anywhere in Hawaii. They're good for one year beginning July 1, and cost $7.50 residents, $15 nonresident, senior citizens free. Licenses are available from sporting goods stores and from the

feral pig

various offices of the Division of Forestry and Wildlife (see below). This government organization also sets and enforces the rules, so contact them with any questions. Generally hunting hours are from a half hour before sunrise to a half hour after sunset. At times, there are "checking stations," where the hunter must check in before and after hunting.

Rifles must have greater than a 1,200-foot-pound muzzle velocity. Shotguns larger than .20 gauge are allowed, and muzzleloaders must have a .45 caliber bore or larger. Bows must have a minimum draw of 45 pounds for straight bows and 30 pounds for compounds. Arrows must be broadheads. Dogs are permitted only with some birds and game, and smaller caliber rifles and shotguns are permitted with their use, along with spears and knives. Hunters must wear orange safety cloth on front and back no smaller than a 12-inch square. Certain big-game species are hunted only by lottery selection; contact the Division of Forestry and Wildlife two months in advance. Guide service is not mandatory, but is advised if you're unfamiliar with hunting in Hawaii. You can hunt on private land only with permission, and you must possess a valid hunting license. Guns and ammunition brought into Hawaii must be registered with the chief of police of the corresponding county within 48 hours of arrival.

Information

Hunting rules and regulations are always subject to change. Also, environmental considerations often change bag limits and seasons. Make sure to check with the Division of Forestry and Wildlife for the most current information. Request "Rules Regulating Game Bird Hunting, Field Trails and Commercial Shooting Preserves," "Rules Regulating Game Mammal Hunting," and "Hunting in Hawaii." Direct inquiries to: Dept. of Land and Natural Resources, Division of Forestry and Wildlife Office, 1151 Punchbowl St., Honolulu 96813, tel. 548-2861; on Maui, 54 S. High St., P.O. Box 1015, Wailuku, 96793, tel. 244-4352; on Hawaii, Box 4849, Hilo 96720, tel. 961-7221; on Lanai, 338 8th St., Lanai City 96763, tel. 565-6688; on Kauai, 3060 Eiwa St., Box 1671, Lihue 96766, tel. 245-4444; on Molokai, Puu Kapeelua Ave., Hoolehua 96729, tel. 553-5415.

Game Animals

All game animals on Hawaii have been introduced. Some are adapting admirably and becoming well entrenched, while the existence of others is still precarious. **Axis deer** originated in India and were brought to Lanai and Molokai, where they're doing well. The small herd on Maui is holding its own. Their unique flavor makes them one of the best wild meats, and they're hunted on Molokai and Lanai in March and April, by public lottery. **Feral pigs** are escaped domestic pigs that have gone wild and are found on all islands except Lanai. The stock is a mixture of original Polynesian pigs and all that came later. Hunted with dogs and usually killed with a spear or long knife, pig hunting is not recommended for the timid or tenderhearted. These beasts' four-inch tusks and fighting spirit make them tough and dangerous. **Feral goats** come in a variety of colors. Found on all islands except Lanai, they have been known to cause erosion and are considered a pest in some areas, especially on Haleakala. Openly hunted on all islands, their meat when done properly is considered delicious.

Black-tailed deer come from the Rocky Mountains. Forty were released on Kauai in 1961; the herd is now stabalized at around 400 and they're hunted in October by public lottery. **Mouflon sheep** are native to Corsica and Sardinia. They do well on Lanai and on the windswept slopes of Mauna Loa and

Gambel's quail

Mauna Kea, where they're hunted at various times by public lottery. **Feral sheep** haunt the slopes of Mauna Kea and Mauna Loa from 7,000 to 12,000 feet. They travel in flocks and destroy vegetation. It takes determination and a good set of lungs to bag one, especially with a bow and arrow. **Pronghorn** on Lanai,

feral cattle on the Big Island, and **rock wallaby,** from Australia, who now make their home on Oahu, are not hunted.

Game Birds

A number of game birds are found on most of the islands. Bag limits and hunting seasons vary, so check with the Division of Forestry and Wildlife for details. **Ring-necked pheasant** are one of the best game birds, and found on all the islands. The **kalij pheasant** from Nepal is found only on the Big Island, where the **green pheasant** is also prevalent; some are found on Oahu and Maui. **Francolins,** gray and black, from India and the Sudan, are similar to partridges. They are hunted on all islands with dogs and are great roasted. There are also **chukar** from Tibet, found on the slopes of all islands; a number of **quail,** including the **Japanese and California** varieties; **doves;** and the **wild Rio Grande turkey** which is found on all islands except Kauai and Oahu (although a few of the "featherless variety" have been known to walk the streets of Waikiki).

Feral goats have over-populated and become pests. They roam from coast to mountaintop, depleting vegetation and causing considerable erosion.

HEALTH AND WELL-BEING

In a recent survey published by *Science Digest,* Hawaii was cited as the healthiest state in the Union to live in. Indeed, Hawaiian citizens live longer than anywhere else in America: men to 74 years on average and women to 78. Lifestyle, heredity, and diet help with these figures, but Hawaii is still an oasis in the middle of the ocean, and germs just have a tougher time getting there. There are no cases of malaria, cholera, or yellow fever. Because of a strict quarantine law, rabies is also nonexistent. On the other hand, tooth decay, perhaps because of the wide use of sugar and the enzymes present in certain tropical fruits, is 30 percent above the national average.

With the perfect weather, a multitude of fresh-air activities, soothing negative ionization from the sea, and a generally relaxed and carefree lifestyle, everyone feels better there. Hawaii is just what the doctor ordered: a beautiful natural health spa. That's one of the main drawing cards. The food and water are perfectly safe, and the air quality is the best in the country.

Handling The Sun
Don't become a victim of your own exuberance. People can't wait to strip down and lie on the sand like a beached whale, but the tropical sun will burn you to a cinder if you're silly. The burning rays come through easier in Hawaii because of the sun's angle, and you don't feel them as much because there's always a cool breeze. The worst part of the day is from 11 a.m. until 3 p.m. You'll just have to force yourself to go slowly. Don't worry; you'll be able to flaunt your best souvenir, your golden Hawaiian tan, to your green-with-envy friends when you get home. It's better than showing them a boiled lobster body with peeling skin! If your skin is snowflake white, 15 minutes on the first day is plenty. Increase by 15-minute intervals every day, which will allow you a full hour per side by the fourth day. Have faith; this is enough to give you a deep golden, uniform tan.

Haole Rot
A peculiar condition caused by the sun is referred to locally as *haole* rot. It's called this because it supposedly affects only white people, but you'll notice some dark-skinned people with the same condition. Basically, the skin becomes mottled with white spots that refuse to tan. You get a blotchy effect, mostly on the shoulders and back. Dermatologists have a fancy name for it, and they'll give you

a fancy prescription with a fancy price tag to cure it. It's common knowledge throughout the islands that Selsun Blue Shampoo has some ingredient that stops the white mottling effect. Just wash your hair with it and then rub the lather over the affected areas, and it should clear up.

Bugs

Everyone, in varying degrees, has an aversion to vermin and creepy crawlers. Hawaii isn't infested with a wide variety, but it does have its share. Mosquitos were unknown in the islands until their larvae stowed away in the water barrels of the *Wellington* in 1826 and were introduced at Lahaina. They bred in the tropical climate and rapidly spread to all the islands. They are a particular nuisance in the rainforests. Be prepared, and bring a natural repellent like citronella oil, available in most health stores on the islands, or a commercial product available in all groceries or drug stores. Campers will be happy to have mosquito coils to burn at night as well.

Cockroaches are very democratic insects. They hassle all strata of society equally. They breed well in Hawaii and most hotels are at war with them, trying desperately to keep them from being spotted by guests. One comforting thought is that in Hawaii they aren't a sign of filth or dirty housekeeping. They love the climate like everyone else, and it's a real problem keeping them under control. Many hotels post a little card in each room instructing you to call the desk if you spot a roach; they'll be happy to charge up to your room and annihilate it. Of a number of different roaches in Hawaii, the ones that give most people the jitters are big bombers over two inches long. Roaches are after food crumbs and the like, and very infrequently bother with a human. Be aware of this if you rent a room with a kitchenette or condo. If you are in a modest hotel and see a roach, it might make you feel better to know that the millionaire in the $600-a-night suite probably has them too. Bring your own spray if you wish, call the desk if you see them, or just let them be.

WATER SAFETY

Hawaii has one very sad claim to fame: more people drown here than anywhere else in the world. Moreover, there are dozens of yearly victims of broken necks, backs, and scuba and snorkeling accidents. These statistics shouldn't keep you out of the sea, because it is indeed beautiful, benevolent in most cases, and a main reason to go to Hawaii. But if you're foolish, the sea will bounce you like a basketball and suck you away for good. The best remedy is to avoid situations you can't handle. Don't let anyone dare you into a situation that makes you uncomfortable. "Macho men" who know nothing about the power of the sea will be tumbled into a Cabbage Patch doll in short order. Ask lifeguards or

This "denizen of the deep" is much more afraid of you than you are of him.

beach attendants about conditions, and follow their advice. If local people refuse to go in, there's a good reason. Even experts get in trouble in Hawaiian waters. Some beaches, such as Waikiki, are as gentle as a lamb and you would have to tie an anchor around your neck to drown there. Others, especially on the north coasts during the winter months, are frothing giants.

While beachcombing, or especially when walking out on rocks, never turn your back to the sea. Be aware of undertows (the waves drawing back into the sea). They can knock you off your feet. Before entering the water, study it for rocks, breakers, reefs, and riptides. Riptides are powerful currents, like rivers in the sea, that can drag you out. Mostly they peter out not too far from shore, and you can often see their choppy waters on the surface. If caught in a "rip," don't fight to swim directly against it; you'll lose and only exhaust yourself. Swim diagonally across it, while going along with it, and try to stay parallel to the shore. Don't waste all your lung power yelling, and do rest by floating.

When bodysurfing, never ride straight in; come to shore at a 45-degree angle. Remember, waves come in sets. Little ones can be followed by giants, so watch the action awhile instead of plunging right in. Standard procedure is to duck under a breaking wave. You can even survive thunderous oceans using this technique. Don't try to swim through a heavy froth and never turn your back and let it smash you. Don't swim alone if possible, and obey all warning signs. Hawaiians want to entertain you and they don't put up signs just to waste money. The first rule is, "If in doubt, stay out."

Yikes!

Sharks live in all the oceans of the world. Most mind their own business and stay away from shore. Hawaiian sharks are well fed—on fish—and don't usually bother with unsavory humans. If you encounter a shark, don't panic! Never thrash around because this will trigger their attack instinct. If they come close, scream loudly. Portuguese men-o-war put out long floating tentacles that sting if they touch you. Don't wash it off with fresh water,

as this will only aggravate it. Hot salt water will take away the sting, as will alcohol, the drinking or rubbing kind, after-shave lotion, and meat tenderizer (MSG), which can be found in any supermarket or Chinese restaurant. Coral can give you a nasty cut, and it's known for causing infections because it's a living organism. Wash the cut immediately and apply an antiseptic. Keep it clean and covered, and watch for infection.

Poisonous sea urchins, such as the lacquer-black *wana,* can be beautiful creatures. They are found in shallow tidepools and can only hurt you if you step on them. Their spines will break off, enter your foot and, burn like blazes. There are cures. Vinegar and wine poured on the wound will stop the burning. If not available, the Hawaiian method is urine. It might be ignominious to have someone pee on your foot, but it'll put the fire out. The spines will disintegrate in a few days, and there are generally no long-term effects.

Hawaiian reefs also have their share of moray eels. These creatures are ferocious in appearance, but will never initiate an attack. You'll have to poke around in their holes while snorkeling or scuba diving to get them to attack. Sometimes this is inadvertent on the diver's part, so be careful where you stick your hand while underwater.

HAWAIIAN FOLK MEDICINE AND CURES

Hawaiian folk medicine is well developed, and its cures for common ailments have been used effectively for centuries. Hawaiian *kahuna* were highly regarded for their medicinal skills, and Hawaiians were by far some of the healthiest people in the world until the coming of the Europeans. Many folk remedies and cures are used to this day and, what's more, they work. Some of the most common plants and fruits that you'll encounter provide some of the best remedies. When roots and seeds and special exotic plants are used, the preparation of the medicine is as painstaking as in a modern pharmacy. These prescriptions are exact and take an expert to prepare. They should never be prepared or administered by

KUKUI (CANDLENUT)

Reaching heights of 80 feet, the kukui (candlenut) was a veritable department store to the Hawaiians, who made use of almost every part of this utilitarian giant. Used as a cure-all, its nuts, bark, or flowers were ground into potions and salves and taken as a general tonic, applied to ulcers and cuts as an effective antibiotic, or administered internally as a cure for constipation or asthma attacks. The bark was mixed with water and the resulting juice was used as a dye in tattooing, tapa cloth-making, canoe painting, and as a preservative for fishnets. The oily nuts were burned as a light source in stone holders, and ground and eaten as a condiment called inamona. Polished nuts took on a beautiful sheen and were strung as leis. Lastly, the wood itself was hollowed into canoes and used as fishnet floats.

wounds is made from the skins of ripe bananas. Peelings have a powerful antibiotic quality and contain vitamins A, B, and C, phosphorous, calcium, and iron. The nectar from the plant was fed to babies as a vitamin juice. Breadfruit sap is used for healing cuts and as a moisturizing lotion. Coconut is used to make moisturizing oil, and the juice was chewed, spat into the hand, and used as a shampoo. Guava is a source of vitamins A, B, and C. Hibiscus has been used as a laxative.

Kukui nut oil is a gargle for sore throats, a laxative, and the flowers are used to cure diarrhea. *Noni* reduces tumors, diabetes, high blood pressure, and the juice is good for diarrhea. Sugar cane sweetens many concoctions, and the juice of toasted cane was a tonic for sick babies. Sweet potato is used as a tonic during pregnancy, and juiced as a gargle for phlegm. Tamarind is a natural laxative, and contains the most acid and sugar of any fruit on Earth. Taro has been used for lung infections, thrush, and as suppositories. Yams are good for coughs, vomiting, constipation, and appendicitis.

HELP FOR THE HANDICAPPED

A handicapped or physically disabled person can have a wonderful time in Hawaii; all that's needed is a little pre-planning. The following is general advice that should help with your planning.

Commission On The Handicapped
This commission was designed with the express purpose of aiding handicapped people. They are a source of invaluable information and distribute self-help booklets free of charge. Any handicapped person heading to Hawaii should write first or visit their offices on arrival. For a "Handicapped Travelers Guide" to four of the islands, write or visit the head office at: Commission on the Handicapped, Old Federal Bldg., 335 Merchant St., no. 215, Honolulu, HI 96813, tel. 548-7606; on Maui, 54 High St., Wailuku, Maui, HI 96793, tel. 244-4441; on Kauai, Box 671, Lihue, Kauai, HI 96766, tel. 245-4308; on Hawaii, Box 1641, Hilo, HI 96820, tel. 935-7257.

an amateur. For hospitals, doctors, and conventional medical help see p. 169

Common Curative Plants
Arrowroot, for diarrhea, is a powerful narcotic used in rituals and medicines. The pepper plant *(Piper methisticum)* is chewed and the juice is spat into a container for fermenting. Used as a medicine in urinary tract infections, rheumatism, and asthma, it also induces sleep and cures headaches. A poultice for

General Information

The key for a smooth trip is to make as many arrangements ahead of time as possible. Here are some tips concerning transportation and accommodations. Tell the companies concerned of the nature of your handicap in advance so that they can make arrangements to accommodate you. Bring your medical records and notify medical establishments of your arrival if you'll be needing their services. Travel with a friend or make arrangements for an aide on arrival (see below). Bring your own wheelchair if possible and let airlines know if it is battery-powered; boarding inter-island carriers requires steps. No problem. They'll board you early on special lifts, but they must know that you're coming. Many hotels and restaurants accommodate disabled persons, but always call ahead just to make sure.

Oahu Services

At Honolulu International, parking spaces are on the fourth floor of the parking garage near the elevator closest to the inter-island terminal. The **Wiki Wiki Bus** to town has steps. **Medical Services,** 24 hours, Honolulu County Medical Society, tel. 536-6988; airport medical services at tel. 836-3341; visitor information at tel. 836-6417. For getting around, the City of Honolulu has a free curb-to-curb service for disabled persons, called **Handi-Van.** You must make arrangements for a pass 24 hours in advance. For a free handicapped bus pass for disabled but ambulatory people, write Handi-Van Pass, or Handicapped Bus Pass, 650 S. King St., Honolulu 96813, tel. 524-4626. A private special taxi company is **Handi-Cabs of the Pacific** in Honolulu at tel. 524-3866. **Avis** will rent cars with hand controls, tel. 836-5511. **Grant Wheelchair and Repair of Honolulu,** tel. 533-2794, will do just that and outfit cars with hand controls.

For **medical equipment** the following Honolulu establishments rent all kinds of apparatus: **AAA Medical,** tel. 538-7021; **Abbey Rents,** tel. 537-2922; **Medical Supplies,** tel. 845-9522; **Honolulu Orthopedic,** tel. 536-6661. For **medical support and help** the following provide nurses, companions, and health aides—all require advance notice. **Hawaii Center for Independent Living,** tel. 537-1941; **Travel-Well International,** tel. 689-5420; **Voluntary Action Center,** tel. 536-7234.

THE HEAVY STUFF

Though the small towns and villages are as safe as you can find anywhere in America, Hawaii isn't all good clean fun. Wherever there's a constant tourist flow, a huge military presence, and high cost of living, there will be those people that mama warned you about. Most of the heavy night action occurs in Waikiki around Kuhio and Kalakaua avenues, and on Chinatown's Hotel Street (see pp. 219 and 252). Something about the *vibe* exudes sexuality. The land is raw and wild, and the settings are intoxicating. All those glistening bodies under the tropical sun, and the carefree lifestyle are super-conducive to you know what! It's long been known as a great place for boy meets girl, or whomever, but there is also "play for pay" if you want it.

Hawaii's sugar and pineapple industries started to flag in the last decade and people had to do something to make ends meet. More than a few began to grow *pakalolo* (marijuana), now counted as one of the biggest cash crops in Hawaii. The *pakalolo* (literally "crazy smoke") is first-rate, and will knock your purple socks off. Theft and minor assaults can be a problem, but they're usually not violent or vicious as in some Mainland cities. Mostly, it's locals with a chip on their shoulder and little prospects, who will ransack your car or make off with your camera. A big Hawaiian or local guy will be obliged to flatten your nose if you look for trouble, but mostly it will be sneak thieves out to make a fast buck.

You can go two ways on the "sleaze" scene in Hawaii: ignore it and remain aloof and never see any; or, look for and find it with no trouble. The following is neither a condemnation nor an endorsement of how you should act and what you should do. It's merely the facts and the choice is up to you.

Prostitution—The Way It Was

Ever since the first ship arrived in 1778, Hawaii has known prostitution. At that time, a sailor paid for a woman for the night with one iron nail. Funny, today they'll take a plastic card. Prostitution, rampant until the missionaries arrived in 1819, was indeed a major cause of the tragic population decline of the Hawaiian race. The tradition carried on into this century. Iwilei was a notorious red-light district in Honolulu at the turn of the century. The authorities, many of whom were clientele, not only turned a blind eye to this scene, but semilegalized it. A policeman was stationed inside the "stockade" and police rules were listed on the five entrances. The women were required to have a weekly VD checkup from the Board of Health, and without a current disease-free certificate they couldn't work. Iwilei was even considered by some to be an attraction: when Somerset Maugham passed through the islands in 1916 on his way to Russia as a spy for England, he was taken here as if on a sightseeing tour. The long-established military presence in Hawaii has also helped to keep prostitution a flourishing business. During WW II, troops were entertained by streetwalkers, houses of prostitution, and at dance halls. The consensus of the military commanders is that prostitution is a necessary evil, needed to keep up the morale of the troops.

The Scene Today

The two areas notorious for prostitution today are Kuhio and Kalakaua avenues in Waikiki, which are geared toward the tourist, and Hotel Street in downtown Honolulu, for servicemen and a much rougher trade. All sorts of women solicit on Kuhio and Kalakaua avenues—whites, blacks, and Asians—but the majority are young white women from the Mainland. They cruise along in the old-fashioned style, meeting your eyes and giving you the nod. As long as they keep walking the police won't roust them. They talk business on the street, and then take their john to a nearby backstreet hotel, where he'll be required to pay for the room. Prices vary with the services sought. Rock bottom is $75 for

a 15-minute "slam bam." The room might cost another $15.

The prostitutes on Waikiki number about 300, and are very easy to find, mostly hanging out across the street from the police station on Kalakaua. Oh! Those brazen hussies! Or, in front of the Hyatt, as if standing in front of a classy hotel will make them a class act. There was a great influx when Los Angeles cracked down for the 1984 Olympics, and Honolulu inherited many of her displaced streetwalkers. Most hookers prefer Japanese clientele, followed by the general tourist, and lastly, the always-broke serviceman. In the terse words of one streetwalker queried about the preference for Japanese, she said, "They're small, clean, fast, and they pay a lot." Sounds like a streetwalker's dream! If anyone in Waikiki can speak Japanese, a hooker can.

Most are not *equal opportunity employees*. Western guys, whether white or black, don't stand much of a chance. They are after the Japanese in a sort of crazy payback. The Japanese fish American waters, and the "pros" of Waikiki hook big Japanese fish. A Honolulu policemen on his Kuhio Avenue beat said, "I can't do anything if they keep walking. It's a free country. Besides, I'm not here to teach anyone morals. . . . Last week a john "fell" out of an eight-story window and a prostitute was found with her throat slit. . .

I'm just on the front lines fighting herpes and AIDS. Just fighting herpes and AIDS, man." The average guy won't have any hassles with a Waikiki prostitue. Mostly it's a straightforward business transaction, but unlike the days of Iwilei there is absolutely no official control or testing for VD.

Chinatown's Hotel Street (see p. 219) is as rough as guts. The girls are shabby, the bars and strip joints are shabbier, and the vibe is heavy. Prices are cheaper, but if you visit a Hotel Street hooker, you'd be well advised to wear a condom and a scuba diving wet suit for protection. Women can find male prostitutes on most of the beaches of Honolulu and Waikiki. Mostly these transactions take place during the day. Although many men make a legitimate living as "beach boys" instructing in surfing and the like, many are really prostitutes. It's always up to the woman to decide how far her "lessons" proceed.

Massage Parlors, Etc.

Besides streetwalkers, Honolulu and some of the Neighbor Islands have their share of massage parlors, escort services, and exotic dance joints. Most are in Honolulu, and some will even fly their practitioners to the Neighbor Islands if necessary. For massage parlors and "escort services" you can let your fingers do the walking—through 14 pages in the Honolulu Yellow Pages alone. Oddly enough, the "massage" listing is preceded by one for "marketing" and followed by one for "meat." Many legitimate massage practitioners in Hawaii can offer the best therapeutic massages in a variety of disciplines, including *shiatsu, lomi lomi,* and Swedish. Unfortunately, they share the same listings with the other kind of massage parlors. If the Yellow Pages listing reads something like "Fifi's Playthings—We'll rub it day or night, wherever it is," this should tip you off. Usually they offer escort services too, for both men and women. The initial cost is about $50 to have an "escort" come to your hotel. Once there, this young man or woman will negotiate his or her own deal for services (about $75). This protects the escort service business, because if you happen to be an undercover vice officer, the "escort" takes the rap and not the business, since of course they had no idea of what was really going on.

Honolulu also has a number of exotic dance clubs, many along Kapiolani Boulevard. Basically, they're strip joints with an extra twist. The dancers themselves are very attractive white women who have been brought over from the Mainland. They can easily make $100 per night dancing, and the majority are not prostitutes, although money, if it's enough, always talks. Their act lasts for three songs, and gets raunchier as it goes. They start off like the girl next door in a prom dress, and wind up writhing naked on the floor, gyrating to some imaginary phallic stimulus. If you invite a dancer to have a drink, it'll cost you $10, but it will be a real drink. This gets you nothing but conversation. The patron's drinks aren't as inflated as the scene would suggest, and some think it a bargain for the price of one drink to have a naked woman bumping and grinding just five feet away. Working the sexually agitated male crowd are women who can best be described as "lap sitters." They're almost always older Korean women who've been through the mill. They'll charge you $5 for a fake drink called *niko hana* ("nothing"), and then try to entice you over to a dark corner table, where they'll chisel $20 more, for all you can manage, or are brave enough to do, in a dark corner of a nightclub. Their chief allies are dim lights and booze. See pp. 219 and 254.

ILLEGAL DRUGS

The use and availability of illegal, controlled, and recreational drugs are about the same in Hawaii as throughout the rest of America. Cocaine constitutes the fastest-growing recreational drug, and it's available on the streets of the main cities, especially Honolulu. Although most dealers are small-time, the drug is brought in by organized crime. The underworld here is mostly populated by men of Asian descent, and the Japanese *yakuza* is said recently to be displaying a heightened involvement in Hawaiian organized crime. Cocaine trafficking fans out from Honolulu.

A new drug menace hitting the Honolulu streets is known as "ice." Ice is smokable methamphetamine that will wire a user for up to 24 hours. The high lasts longer, and is cheaper, than cocaine or its derivative, "crack". Users become quickly dependent, despondent, and violent because ice robs them of their sleep, along with their dignity. Its use is particularly prevalent among late-night workers. Many of the violent deaths in Honolulu have been linked to the growing use of ice.

However, the main drug available and commonly used in Hawaii is marijuana, which is locally called *pakalolo*. There are also three varieties of psychoactive mushrooms that contain the hallucinogen psilocybin. They grow wild but are considered illegal controlled substances.

Pakalolo Growing

About 20 years ago, mostly *haole* hippies from the Mainland began growing pot in the more remote sections of the islands, such as Puna on Hawaii and around Hana on Maui. They discovered what legitimate planters had known for 200 years: plant a broomstick in Hawaii, treat it right, and it'll grow. *Pakalolo*, after all, is only a weed, and it grows in Hawaii like wildfire. The locals quickly got into the act when they realized that they, too, could grow a "money tree." As a matter of fact, they began resenting the *haole* usurpers, and a quiet and sometimes dangerous feud has been going on ever since. Much is made of the viciousness of the backcountry "growers" of Hawaii. There are tales of booby traps and armed patrols guarding their plants in the hills, but mostly it's a cat and mouse game between the authorities and the growers. If you, as a tourist, are tramping about in the forest and happen upon someone's "patch," don't touch anything. Just back off and you'll be OK. Pot has the largest monetary turnover of any crop in the islands, and as such, is now considered a major source of agricultural revenue. There are all kinds of local names and varieties of pot in Hawaii, the most potent

being "Kona Gold," "Puna Butter," and "Maui Wowie." Actually, these names are all becoming passé. You can ask a likely person for pot, but mostly dealers will approach you. Their normal technique is to stroll by, and in a barely audible whisper say, "Buds?"

Hawaiian *pakalolo* is sold slightly differently than on the Mainland. The dealers package it in heat-sealed "Seal-a-Meal" plastic bags. The glory days are over, and many deals, especially on the streets of Honolulu, are rip-offs.

THEFT AND HASSLES

From the minute you sit behind the wheel of your rental car you'll be warned about not leaving valuables unattended and locking your car up tighter than a drum. Signs warning about theft at most major tourist attractions help to fuel your paranoia. Many hotel rooms offer coin- operated safes, so you can lock your valuables away and be able to relax while getting sunburned. Stories abound about purse snatchings and surly locals who are just itching to give you a hard time. Well, they're all true to a degree, but Hawaii's reputation is much worse than the reality. In Hawaii you'll have to observe two golden laws: if you look for trouble, you'll find it; and, a fool and his camera are soon parted.

Theft

The majority of theft in Hawaii is of the "sneak thief" variety. If you leave your hotel door unlocked, a camera sitting on the seat of your rental car, or valuables on your beach towel, you'll be inviting a very obliging thief to pad away with your stuff. You have to learn to take precautions, but they won't be anything like those employed in rougher areas like South America or Southeast Asia, just normal American precautions.

If you must walk alone at night, stay on the main streets in well-lit areas. Always lock your hotel door and windows and place all valuable jewelry in the hotel safe. When you leave your hotel for the beach, there is absolutely no reason to carry all your traveler's cheques, credit cards, or a big wad of money. Just take what you'll need for drinks and lunch. If you're uptight about leaving any money in your beach bag, just stick it in your bathing suit or bikini. American money is just as negotiable if it is damp. Don't leave your camera or portable stereo on the beach unattended. Ask a person nearby to watch them for you while you go for a dip. Most people won't mind at all, and you can repay the favor.

While sightseeing in your shiny new rental car, which immediately brands you as a tourist, again, don't take more than what you'll need for the day. Why people leave a camera sitting on the seat of their car is a mystery! Many people lock valuables away in the trunk, but remember that most good car thieves can "jimmy" it as quickly as you can open it with your key. If you must, for some reason, leave your camera or valuables in your car, lock them in the trunk or consider putting them under the hood. Thieves usually don't look there and on most modern cars, you can only pop the hood with a lever on the inside of the car. It's not failsafe, but it's worth a try.

Campers face special problems because their entire scene is open to thievery. Most campgrounds don't have any real security, but who, after all, wants to fence an old tent or a used sleeping bag? Many tents have zippers that can be secured with a small padlock. If you want to go trekking and are afraid to leave your gear in the campgrounds, take a large green garbage bag with you. Transport your gear down the trail and then walk off through some thick brush. Put your gear in the garbage bag and bury it under leaves and other light camouflage. That's about as safe as you can be. You can also use a variation on this technique instead of leaving your valuables in your rental car.

Hassles

Another self-perpetuating myth about Hawaii is that "the natives are restless." An undeniable animosity exists between locals, especially those with some Hawaiian blood, and haole. Fortunately, this prejudice is directed mostly at the "group" and not at the "in-dividual." The locals are resentful against those haoles who came, took their land, and relegated them to second-class citizenship. They realize that this is not the average tourist and they can tell what you are at a glance. Tourists usually are treated with understanding and are given a type of immunity. Besides, Hawaiians are still among the most friendly, giving, and understanding people on Earth.

Haole who live in Hawaii might tell you stories of their children having trouble at school. They could even mention an unhappy situation at some schools called "beat-up-a-haole" day, and you might hear that if you're a haole it's not a matter of if you'll be beaten up, but when. Truthfully, most of this depends upon your attitude and your sensitivity. The locals feel infringed upon, so don't fuel these feelings. If you're at a beach park and there is a group of local people in one area, don't crowd them. If you go into a local bar and you're the only one of your ethnic group in sight, you shouldn't have to be told to leave. Much of the hassle involves drinking. Booze brings out the worst prejudice on all sides. If you're invited to a beach party, and the local guys start getting drunk, make this your exit call. Don't wait until it's too late.

Most trouble seems to be directed toward white men. White women are mostly immune from being beaten up, but they have to beware of the violence of sexual abuse and rape. Although plenty of local women marry white men, it's not a good idea to try to pick up a local girl. If you're known in the area and have been properly introduced, that's another story. Also, girls out for the night in bars or discos can be approached if they're not in the company of local guys. If you are with your bikini-clad girlfriend, and a bunch of local guys are, say, drinking beer at a beach park, don't go over and try to be friendly and ask, "What's up?" You, and especially your girlfriend, just might find out. Maintain your own dignity and self-respect by treating others with dignity and respect. Most times you'll reap what you sow.

WHAT TO TAKE

It's a snap to pack for a visit to Oahu. Everything is on your side. The weather is moderate and uniform on the whole, and the style of dress is delightfully casual. The rule of thumb is to pack lightly: few items, and light clothing both in color and weight. What you'll need will depend largely on your itinerary and your desires. Are you drawn to the nightlife, the outdoors, or both? If you forget something at home, it won't be a disaster. You can buy everything you'll need in Hawaii. As a matter of fact, Hawaiian clothing, such as muumuus and *aloha* shirts, are some of the best purchases you can make, both in comfort and style. It's quite feasible to bring only one or two changes of clothing with the express purpose of outfitting yourself while there. Prices on bathing suits, bikinis, and summer wear in general are quite reasonable.

Matters Of Taste
A grand conspiracy in Hawaii adhered to by everyone—tourist, traveler, and resident—is to "hang loose" and dress casually. Best of all, alohawear is just about all you'll need for virtually every occasion, and for comfort. The classic muumuu is large and billowy, and aloha shirts are made to be worn outside of the pants. The best of both are made of cool cotton. Rayon is a natural fiber that isn't too bad, but polyester is hot, sticky, and not authentic. Not all muumuus are of the "tent persuasion." Some are very fashionable and form-fitted with peek-a-boo slits up the side, down the front, or around the back. *Holomuus* are muumuus fitted at the waist with a flowing skirt to the ankles. They are not only elegant, but perfect for "stepping out."

In The Cold And Rain
Two occasions for which you'll have to consider dressing warm are visiting the top of mountains, and going for boat rides where wind and ocean sprays are a factor. You can conquer both with a jogging suit (sweat suit) and a featherweight, water-resistant windbreaker. If you're intending to visit Maui's Haleakala, or Mauna Kea and Mauna Loa on the Big Island, it'll be downright chilly. Your jogging suit with a hooded windbreaker/raincoat will do the trick for all occasions. If you're going to camp or trek, you should add another layer, the best being a woolen sweater. Wool is the only fiber that retains most of its warmth-

giving properties even if it gets wet. If your hands get cold, put a pair of socks over them. Tropical rain showers can happen at any time, so you might consider a fold-up umbrella; but the sun quickly breaks through and the warming winds blow.

Shoes

Dressing your feet is hardly a problem. You'll most often wear zoris (rubber thongs) for going to and from the beach, leather sandals for strolling and dining, and jogging shoes for trekking and sightseeing. A few discos require leather shoes, but it's hardly worth bringing them just for that. If you plan on heavy-duty trekking, you'll definitely want your hiking boots. Lava, especially *a'a*, is murderous on shoes. Most backcountry trails are rugged and muddy, and you'll need those good old lug soles for traction. If you plan moderate hikes, you might want to consider bringing rubberized ankle supports to complement your jogging shoes. Most drug stores sell them, and the best are a rubberized sock with toe and heel cut out.

Specialty Items

Following is a list of specialty items that you might wish to consider bringing along. They're not necessities but most will definitely come in handy. A pair of binoculars really enhances sightseeing—great for watching birds, sweeping panoramas, and almost a necessity if you're going whalewatching. A folding Teflon-bottomed travel iron makes up for cotton's one major shortcoming, wrinkles, and you can't always count on hotels having irons. Nylon twine and miniature clothespins are handy for drying garments, especially bathing suits. Commercial and hotel laundromats abound, but many times you'll get by with hand washing a few items in the sink. A transistor radio/tape recorder provides news, weather, entertainment, and can be used to record impressions, island music, and a running commentary for your slide show. Hair dryer: although the wind can be relied on to dry, it leaves a bit to be desired in the styling department.

An inflatable raft for riding waves, along with flippers, mask and snorkel, can easily be bought in Hawaii, but don't really weigh that much or take up much space in your luggage. If you'll be camping, trekking, or boating with only sea water available for bathing, take along "Sea Saver Soap," available from good sporting goods stores. This special soap will lather in sea water and rinse away the sticky salt residue with it.

For The Camper

If you don't want to take it with you, all necessary camping gear can be purchased or rented while in Hawaii. Besides the above, you should consider taking the following: frame backpack or the convertible packs that turn into suitcases, daypack, matches in a waterproof container, all-purpose knife, mess kit, eating utensils, flashlight (remove batteries), candle, nylon cord, and sewing kit (dental floss works as thread). Take a first-aid kit containing band-aids, all-purpose antiseptic cream, alcohol swabs, tourniquet string, cotton balls, elastic bandage, razor blade, Telfa pads, and a small mirror for viewing private nooks and crannies. A light sleeping bag is good, although your fleecy jogging suit with a ground pad and covering of a light blanket or even your rain poncho will be sufficient. Definitely bring a down bag for mountainous areas, and in a film container pack a few nails, safety pins, fish hooks, line, and bendable wire. Nothing else does what these do and they're all handy for a million and one uses. (See also p. 137.)

Basic Necessities

As previously mentioned, you really have to consider only two modes of dressing in Hawaii: beachwear and casual clothing. The following is designed for the midrange traveler carrying one suitcase or a backpack. Remember there are laundromats and you'll be spending a considerable amount of time in your bathing suit. Consider the following: one or two pairs of light cotton slacks for going out and about, and one pair of jeans for trekking; two or three casual sundresses—muumuus are great; three or four pairs of shorts for beachwear and for sightseeing; four to five short-sleeved shirts or blouses and one long-sleeved; three or four colored and printed T-shirts that can be worn anytime from trekking to strolling; a beach cover-up with the short terrycloth-type being the best; a brimmed hat for rain and sun—the crushable floppy type is great for purse or daypack; two or three pairs of socks are sufficient, nylons you won't need; two bathing suits, nylon ones dry quickest; plastic bags to hold wet bathing suits and laundry; five to six pairs of underwear; towels (optional, because hotels provide them, even for the beach); a first-aid kit, pocket size is sufficient; suntan lotion, insect repellent; a daypack or large beach purse; and don't forget your windbreaker, and perhaps a shawl for the evening and a universal jogging suit.

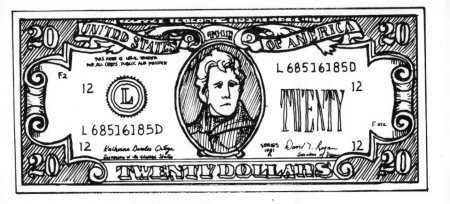

INFORMATION AND SERVICES

Emergency And Health

Police, fire, and ambulance can be summoned from anywhere on Oahu by calling **911**. Reach the **Coast Guard** for search and rescue at tel. 536-4336 and the **Life Guard Service** at tel. 922-3888.

Full-service hospitals include: **Queen's Hospital,** 1301 Punchbowl St., Honolulu, tel. 538-9011; **Kaiser Foundation,** 1697 Ala Moana Blvd., Honolulu, tel. 949-5811.

Medical services and clinics include: **Doctors Emergency and Medical Services,** 1860 Ala Moana Blvd., tel. 943-1111, for emergencies and "house calls" to your hotel, 24 hours a day; in Waikiki call 926-4777, at Hyatt Regency Hotel, the Reef Tower Hotel, and the Hyatt Regency. House calls and office visits 24 hours a day seven days a week. Call 923- 9966 for Japanese speaking doctors. **Medi-Mart,** Waikiki, Royal Hawaiian Shopping Center, Bldg. A, Room 401, tel. 922-2335, open 9 a.m.-6 p.m.; **Waikiki Health Center,** 277 Ohua Ave., tel. 922-4787, for low-cost care including pregnancy and confidential VD testing, open 9 a.m-8 p.m. Mon. to Thurs., until 4:30 p.m. Fri., until 2 p.m. Saturday. For dental referral call **Dentist Information Bureau** at tel. 536-2135, 24-hour service. You can get a free **blood pressure** check at the fire station in Waikiki, corner of Paki and Kapahulu streets, daily 9 a.m.-5 p.m.

Pharmacies around the island include: **Outrigger Pharmacy,** in Waikiki Outrigger Hotel, 2335 Kalakaua Ave., tel. 923-2529; **Kuhio Pharmacy,** at the corner of Kuhio and Nahua, tel. 923-4466, is full-service; **Longs Drugs,** in Honolulu at the Ala Moana Shopping Center, tel. 941-4433, and at the Kaneohe Shopping Center, tel. 235-4511; **Pay 'n' Save** at 86-120 Farrington Hwy., Waianae, tel. 696-6387.

For **alternative health care** try: **Acupuncture Clinic,** Waikiki Medical Bldg., 305 Royal Hawaiian Ave. Rm. 208, tel. 923-6939, open Mon. to Fri. 9 a.m.-4 p.m.; **Honolulu School of Massage,** 1750 Kalakaua Ave., tel. 942-8552, open 10 a.m.-6 p.m., with some later hours; **Ed Hoopai** is an excellent masseur whose motto is "You're in good hands," tel. 926-9045, at 250 Lewers St., second floor of the Outrigger Village Hotel, the suite above the pool. He deals basically in headaches, neck and shoulders, and lower backs. Half-hour for neck and shoulder or back is $22, one hour for full body is $36. Open Mon.-Sat. 9 a.m.-6 p.m. and by appointment. **Colon Therapy of Hawaii,** 122 Oneawa St. Kailua, tel. 261-4511, detoxification and massage administered by Alcyone.

Chiropractic care: Chiropractic Referral Service, 700 Bishop St., tel. 521-5784, offers free information and referral to qualified chiropractors. **Chiropractic Dial-a-Tape** has taped messages for what ails, call tel. 737-1111; on the leeward side is **Dr. Tom Smith,** 1222 Oneawa St., Kailua, tel. 261-4511, limited hours.

The "HVB Warrior" is posted alongside the roadway, marking sites of cultural and historical importance.

Visitor Information
A complete listing of **Hawaii Visitors Bureau** offices appears on p. 171. The **Japanese Chamber of Commerce** has special information on things Japanese, tel. 949-5531; the **Chinese Chamber of Commerce** offers information and tours on Chinatown, tel. 533-3181. **State Foundation on Culture and Arts,** 335 Merchant St. Rm. 202, tel. 548-4657, dispenses information on what's happening culturally on Oahu. For general information, or if you have a hassle, try the **Office of Information and Complaints,** tel. 523-4385 or 523-4381.

Reading Material
Besides a number of special-interest Chinese, Japanese, Korean, Filipino, and military newspapers, two major dailies are published on Oahu. The *Honolulu Advertiser,* tel. 525-8000, is the morning paper, and the *Honolulu Star Bulletin,* tel. 525-8000, is the evening paper. They combine to make a Sunday paper. A money-saving paper is the *Pennysaver,* tel. 521-9886, featuring classified ads on just about anything. Call for distribution points.

Don't miss out on the **free tourist literature** available at all major hotels, shopping malls, the airport, and stands along Waikiki's streets. They all contain up-to-the-minute information on what's happening, and a treasure trove of free or reduced-price coupons for various attractions and services. Always featured are events, shopping tips, dining and entertainment, and sightseeing. The main ones are: *This Week Oahu,* the best and most complete; *On the Go, Hawaii,* general information about the island attractions; *Waikiki, On the Go,* focusing mostly on Waikiki; *Spotlight Hawaii,* with good sections on dining and sightseeing. Two free tabloids, *Waikiki Beach Press* and *Island News,* offer entertainment calendars and feature stories of general interest to visitors. *Oahu Drive Guide,* handed out by all the major car rental agencies, has some excellent tips and orientation maps. Especially useful to get you started from the airport.

For **bookstores,** see p. 85.

Post Offices And Libraries
Many small post offices are found in various towns around the island. The main post office in downtown Honolulu is at 3600 Aolele St., tel. 422-0770; in Waikiki at 330 Saratoga Rd., tel. 941-1062; in Kailua at 335 Hahani, tel. 262-7205; in Waianae at 86-015 Farrington Hwy., tel. 696-4032; in Haleiwa at 66-437 Kam Hwy., tel. 637-5755; in Wahiawa at 115 Lehua, tel. 621-8496.

Oahu's libraries include: Hawaii State Library, in Honolulu at 478 S. King St., tel. 548-4775; Kailua Library, 239 Kuulei Rd., tel. 261-4611; Library for the Blind and Physically Handicapped, 402 Kapahulu Ave., tel. 732-7767; Waikiki branch next door, at 400 Kapahulu, tel. 732-2777.

Weather And Surf Conditions
For a weather report call 836-0234; for surfing conditions, call 836-1952; for Hawaiian waters report, tel. 836-3921.

Helpful Numbers
Arizona Memorial, tel. 922-1626; **Babysitting services,** tel. 923-8337, in Waikiki at 922-5575; **Bishop Museum,** tel. 922-1626; **Council of Churches,** tel. 521-2666; **Dept. of Agriculture,** plants, produce, regulations,

etc., tel. 836-1415; **directory assistance,** tel. 1-411; Honolulu Harbor, daily ship arrival recording, tel. 537-9260; **Honolulu International Airport,** tel. 836-1411/6431; **Time,** tel. 983-3211; **Whale watch,** tel. 922-1626.

HAWAII VISITORS BUREAU OFFICES

Hawaii
The main HVB administration office is at Waikiki Business Plaza, 2270 Kalakaua Ave., Suite 801, **Honolulu,** HI 96815, tel. 923-1811. On Maui, 380 Dairy Rd., **Kahului,** HI 96732, tel. 244-9141. On Kauai, 3016 Umi St., **Lihue,** HI 96799, tel. 245-3971. Hawaii has two branches: Hilo Plaza, 180 Kinoole St., Suite 104, **Hilo,** HI 96720, tel. 961-5797, and 75-5719 W. Alii Dr., **Kailua-Kona,** HI 96740, tel. 329-7787. HVB also operates a number of information works at the airport in Honolulu.

North America
441 Lexington Ave., Room 1407, **New York,** NY 10017, tel. (212) 986-9203. 1511 K St. N.W., Suite 415, **Washington, D.C.** 20005, tel. (202) 393-6752. 180 N. Michigan Ave. Suite 1031, **Chicago,** IL 60601, tel. (312) 236-0632. Central Plaza, 3440 Wilshire Blvd. Room 502, **Los Angeles,** CA 90010, tel. (213) 385-5301. Suite 450, 50 California St., **San Francisco,** CA 94111, tel. (415) 392-8173.

Canada
4915 Cedar Crescent, Delta, B.C., Canada V4M 1J9.

United Kingdom
C/o First Public Relations Ltd., 16 Bedford Sq., London WC 1B 3JH, England.

Australia
C/o Walshes World, 92 Pitt St., Sydney, N.S.W. 2000.

Asian Offices
Japan, 630 Shin Kokusai Bldg., 4-1 Marunouchi 3-chome, Chiyoda-ku, Tokyo 100; **Indonesia,** c/o Pacific Leisure, Jalan Prapatan 32, Jakarta; **Hong Kong,** c/o Pacific Leisure, Suite 904, Tung Ming Bldg., 40 Des Voeux Rd., Central Hong Kong; **Philippines,** c/o Philippine Leisure Inc., Interbank Bldg., 111 Paseo de Roxas, Makati, Metro Manila; **Korea,** c/o Bando Air, Room 1510, Ankuk Insurance Bldg., 87, 1-ka, Eulchi-ro, Chung Ku, Seoul 100; **Singapore,** c/o Pacific Leisure, #03- 01 UOL Bldg., 96 Somerset Rd., Singapore 0923; **Thailand,** c/o Pacific Leisure, 542/1 Ploenchit Rd., Bangkok; other offices are found through Pacific Leisure in **Kuala Lumpur, Penang,** and **Taipei.**

MONEY AND FINANCES

Currency
U.S. currency is among the drabbest in the world. It's all the same size and color; those unfamiliar with it should spend some time getting acquainted so that they don't make costly mistakes. U.S. coinage in use is: $.01, $.05, $.10, $.25, $.50, and $1 (uncommon); paper currency is $1, $2 (uncommon), $5, $10, $20, $50, $100. Bills larger than $100 are not in common usage.

Banks
Full-service banks tend to open slightly earlier than Mainland banks, at 8:30 a.m. Monday through Friday. Closing is at three p.m., except for late hours on Friday when most banks remain open until 6 p.m. Of most value to travelers, banks sell and cash traveler's cheques, give cash advances on credit cards, and exchange and sell foreign currency.

Traveler's Cheques
Traveler's cheques are accepted throughout Hawaii at hotels, restaurants, car rental agencies, and in most stores and shops. However, to be readily acceptable they should be in American currency. Some larger hotels that often deal with Japanese and Canadians will accept their currency. Banks accept foreign-currency traveler's cheques, but it'll mean an extra trip and inconvenience.

Credit Cards
More and more business is transacted in Hawaii using credit cards. Almost every form

THE METRIC SYSTEM

1 inch = 2.54 centimeters (cm)
1 foot = .304 meters (m)
1 mile = 1.6093 kilometers (km)
1 km = .6214 miles
1 fathom = 1.8288 m
1 chain = 20.1168 m
1 furlong = 201.168
1 acre = .4047 hectares (ha)
1 sq km = 100 ha
1 sq mile = 59 sq km
1 ounce = 28.35 grams
1 pound = .4536 kilograms (kg)
1 short ton = .90718 metric ton
1 short ton = 2000 pounds
1 long ton = 1.016 metric tons
1 long ton = 2240 pounds
1 metric ton = 1000 kg
1 quart = .94635 liters
1 US gallon = 3.7854 liters
1 Imperial gallon = 4.5459 liters
1 nautical mile = 1.852 km

To compute centigrade temperatures, subtract 32 from Fahrenheit and divide by 1.8. To go the other way, multiply centigrade by 1.8 and add 32.

of accommodations, shop, restaurant, and amusement accepts them. For renting a car they're almost a must. With "credit card insurance" readily available, they're as safe as traveler's cheques and sometimes even more convenient. Don't rely on them completely because there are some establishments that won't accept them, or perhaps won't accept the kind that you carry.

OTHER PRACTICALITIES

Telephone: All-Hawaii Area Code 808

Like everywhere else in the U.S., long-distance rates go down at 5 p.m. and again at 11 p.m. until 8 a.m. the next morning. From Friday at 5 p.m. until Monday morning at 8 a.m. rates are cheapest. Local calls from public telephones (anywhere on the same island is a local call) cost 25 cents. Calling between islands is a toll call, and the price depends on when and from where you call and for how long you speak. Emergency calls are always free. The area code for the entire state of Hawaii is 808. For directory assistance: local, 1-411; inter-island, 1-555-1212; Mainland, 1-area code- 555-1212; toll free, (800) 555-1212.

Time Zones

There is no "daylight saving time" observed in Hawaii. When daylight saving time is not observed on the Mainland, Hawaii is two hours behind the West Coast, four hours behind the Midwest, and five hours behind the East Coast. Hawaii, being just east of the international date line, is almost a full day behind most Asian and Oceanic cities. Hours behind these countries and cities are: Japan, 19 hours; Singapore, 18 hours; Sydney, 20 hours; New Zealand 22 hours; Fiji 22 hours.

Electricity

The same electrical current is in use in Hawaii as on the U.S. Mainland and is uniform throughout the islands. The system functions on 110 volts, 60 cycles of alternating current (AC). Appliances from Japan will work, but there is some danger of burnout, while those requiring the normal European current of 220 will not work.

Distance, Weights, And Measures

Hawaii, like all of the U.S., employs the "English method" of measuring weights and distances. Basically, dry weights are in ounces and pounds; liquid measures are in ounces, quarts, and gallons; and distances are measured in inches, feet, yards, and miles. The metric system, based on units of 10, is known but is not in general use. The preceding conversion charts should be helpful.

HONOLULU

Honolulu is *the* most exotic city in America. It's not any one attribute that makes this so; it's a combination of things. Honolulu's like an ancient Hawaiian goddess who can change her form at will. At one moment you see a black-eyed beauty, swaying provocatively to a deep and basic rhythm, and in the next a high-tech scion of the computer age sitting straight-backed behind a polished desk. The city is the terminus of "manifest destiny," the end of America's relentless westward drive, until no more horizons were left. Other Mainland cities are undoubtedly more historic, cultural, and perhaps, to some, more beautiful than Honolulu, but none come close to having all of these features in the same overwhelming combination. The city's face, though blemished by high-rises and pocked by heavy industry, is eternally lovely. The Koolau Mountains form the background tapestry from which the city emerges; the surf gently foams along Waikiki; the sun hisses fire-red as it drops into the sea, and Diamond Head beckons with a promise of tropical romance.

In the center of the city, skyscrapers rise as silent, unshakable witnesses to Honolulu's economic strength. In glass and steel offices, businesspeople wearing conservative three-piece uniforms are clones of any found on Wall Street. Below, a fantasia of people live and work. In nooks and crannies are an amazing array of arts, shops, and cuisines. In a flash of festival the streets become China, Japan, Portugal, New England, old Hawaii, or the Philippines.

New England churches, royal palaces, bandstands, tall-masted ships, and coronation platforms illustrate Honolulu's history. And what a history! You can visit places where in a mere twinkle of time past, red-plumed warriors were driven to their death over an impossibly steep *pali,* or where the skies were alive with screaming Zeros strafing and bombing the only American city threatened by a foreign power since the War of 1812. In hallowed grounds throughout the city lie the bodies of fallen warriors. Some are entombed in a mangled steel sepulcher below the waves, others from three wars rest in a natural bowl of bereavement and silence. And a nearby royal mausoleum holds the remains of those who were "old Hawaii."

Honolulu is the pumping heart of Hawaii. The state government and university are here. So are botanical parks, a fine aquarium and zoo, a floating maritime museum, and the world's foremost museum on Polynesia. Art flourishes like flowers, as do professional and amateur entertainment, extravaganzas, and local and world-class sporting events. But the city isn't all good clean fun. The seedier side includes "girlie" shows, raucous GI bars, street drugs, and street people. But somehow this blending and collision of East and West, this hodgepodge of emotionally charged history, this American city superimposed on a unique Pacific setting works well as Honolulu, the "Sheltered Harbor" of man and his dreams.

SIGHTS

The best way to see Honolulu is to start from the middle and fan out on foot for the inner city. You can *do* downtown in one day, but the sights of greater Honolulu require a few days to see them all. It's a matter of opinion where the center of downtown Honolulu actually is, but the King Kamehameha Statue in front of Aliiolani Hale is about as central as you can get, and a perfect landmark from which to start. If you're staying in Waikiki, leave your rental car in the hotel garage and take The-Bus (# 2) for downtown sightseeing.

Parking And Transportation, Downtown Honolulu

If you can't bear to leave your car behind, head for Aloha Tower. When you get to where you can see the Aloha Tower off the S. Nimitz Hwy., look for a sign pointing you left to "Piers 4 and 11, Aloha Tower." Enter to find plenty of parking. The traffic is not as congested here and the large lot is open 24 hours, at $.50 per hour, with a four-hour maximum on the meter. Bring change, as none is available. You might have to come back and feed the meter again if you want to go as far as Chinatown, but this will be plenty of time for the local attractions which are well within walking distance.

For various sights outside the downtown area, your rental car is fine. Some shuttles running out to the *Arizona* Memorial are more expensive than TheBus ($.60), but so convenient that they're worth the extra few coins. The **Waikiki Trolley,** tel. 526-0112, conducts tours throughout the downtown area. For $10 adults, $5 children, you can ride it all day long. It looks like a trolley but it's a bus that's been ingeniously converted.

DOWNTOWN HONOLULU

The **Statue of King Kamehameha** is at the junction of King and Mililani streets. Running off at an angle is **Merchant Street,** the oldest thoroughfare in Honolulu, and you might say its "the beginning of the road to modernity." The statue is much more symbolic of Kamehameha's strength as a ruler and unifier of the Hawaiian Islands than as a replica of the man himself. Of the few drawings of Kamehameha that have been preserved, none is necessarily a good likeness. Kamehameha was a magnificent leader and statesman, but by all accounts not very good-looking. This statue is one of three. The original, lost at sea

KAMEHAMEHA I

near the Falkland Islands en route from Paris where it was bronzed, was later recovered, but not before insurance money was used to cast this second one. The original is in the town of Kapaau, in the Kohala District of the Big Island, not far from where Kamehameha was born, but although they supposedly came from the same mold, they somehow seem quite different. The third stands in Washington, D.C., dedicated when Hawaii

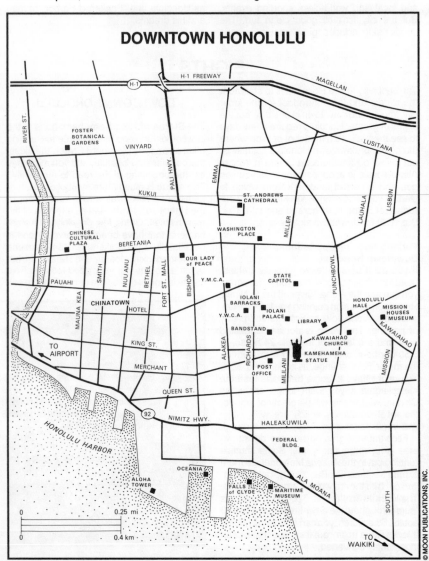

DOWNTOWN HONOLULU

© MOON PUBLICATIONS, INC.

Iolani Palace, the only royal residence in America

became a state. The Honolulu statue was dedicated in 1883, as part of King David Kalakaua's coronation ceremony. Its black and gold colors are striking, but it is most magnificent on June 11, King Kamehameha Day, when 18-foot leis are draped around the neck and the outstretched arms.

Behind Kamehameha stands **Aliiolani Hale,** now the State Judiciary Building. This handsome structure, designed by an Australian architect and begun in 1872, was originally commissioned by Kamehameha V as a palace, but was redesigned as a general court building. It looks much more grand than Iolani Palace across the way. Kamehameha V died before it was finished, and it was officially dedicated by King Kalakaua in 1874. Less than 20 years later, on January 17, 1893, at this "hall of justice," the first proclamation by the Members of the Committee of Safety was read, stating that the sovereign nation of Hawaii was no more, and that the islands would be ruled by a provisional government.

Iolani Palace

As you enter the park-like palace grounds, notice the emblem of Hawaii in the center of the large iron gates. They're often draped with simple leis of fragrant *maile*. The quiet grounds are a favorite strolling and relaxing place for many government workers, especially in the shade of a huge banyan, purportedly planted by Kalakaua's wife, Kapiolani. The building, with its glass and ironwork imported from San Francisco, and its Corinthian columns, is the only royal palace

in America. Iolani ("Royal Hawk") Palace, begun in 1879 under orders of King Kalakaua, was completed in December 1882 at a cost of $350,000. It was the first electrified building in Honolulu, and had a direct phone line to the Royal Boat House.

Non-Hawaiian island residents of the day thought it a frivolous waste of money, but here poignant scenes and profound changes rocked the Hawaiian islands. After nine years as king, Kalakaua built a **Coronation Stand** that temporarily sat in front of the palace, (now off to the left). In a belated ceremony, Kalakaua raised a crown to his head and placed one on his queen, Kapiolani. During the ceremony, 8,000 Hawaiians cheered, while Honolulu's foreign, tax-paying businessmen boycotted. On August 12, 1898, after only two Hawaiian monarchs, Kalakaua and Liliuokalani (his sister), had resided in the palace, the American flag was raised up the flagpole following a successful coup that marked Hawaii's official recognition by the U.S. as a territory. During this ceremony, loyal Hawaiian subjects wept bitter tears, while the businessmen of Honolulu cheered wildly.

Kalakaua, later in his rule, was forced to sign a new constitution that greatly reduced his own power to little more than figurehead status. He traveled to San Francisco in 1891, where he died. His body was returned to Honolulu and lay in state in the palace. His sister, Liliuokalani, succeeded him; she attempted to change this constitution and gain the old power of Hawaii's sovereigns, but the businessmen revolted and the monarchy fell.

*Washington Place,
Honolulu*

Iolani Palace then became the main executive building for the provisional government, with the House of Representatives meeting in the throne room and the Senate in the dining room. It served in this capacity until 1968.

Iolani Palace is open to one-hour **guided tours only,** Wed. to Sat. 9 a.m.- 2:15 p.m.; $4 adults, $1 children, with no children under five admitted. They're popular so make reservations at least a day in advance. Tickets are sold at a window at the Barracks, open Tues. to Sat. 8:30 a.m.- 2:15 p.m. The Palace shop is open 8:30 a.m.-3:30 p.m. Tues.-Saturday. For information and reservations call 522-0832.

Palace Grounds

Kalakaua, known as the "Merry Monarch," was credited with saving the hula. He also hired Henri Burger, first Royal Hawaiian Bandmaster, and together they wrote "Hawaii Pono," the state anthem. Many concerts were given from the Coronation Stand, which became known as the **Royal Bandstand.** Behind it is **Iolani Barracks** (Hale Koa), built in 1870 to house the Royal Household Guards. When the monarchy of Hawaii fell to provisional government forces in 1893, only *one* of these soldiers was wounded in a pathetic show of strength. The barracks were moved to the present site from nearby land on which the State Capitol was erected.

To the right behind the palace are the **State Archives.** This modern building, dating from 1953, holds records, documents, and vintage photos. A treasure trove to scholars and those tracing their genealogy, it is worth a visit by the general public to view the old photos on display. Free, open Mon. to Fri. 7:45 a.m.- 4:30 p.m. Next door is the **Hawaii State Library,** housing the main branch of this statewide system. As in all Hawaii state libraries, you are entitled to a card on your first visit, and are then eligible to take out books. The central courtyard is a favorite lunch spot for many of the government workers. Some of the original money to build the library was put up by Andrew Carnegie. For information call 548-4775.

Government Buildings

Liliuokalani was deposed and placed under house arrest in the palace for nine months. Later, after much intrigue that included a visit to Washington, D.C., to plead her case and an aborted counterrevolution, she sadly accepted her fate and moved to nearby **Washington Place.** This solid-looking structure fronts Beretania Street and was originally the home of sea captain John Dominis. It was inherited by his son John Owen Dominis, who married a lovely young Hawaiian aristocrat, Lydia Kapaakea, who became Queen Liliuokalani. She lived in her husband's home, proud but powerless, until her death in 1917.

Washington Place is now the official residence of the governor of Hawaii.

To the left of Washington Place is **St. Andrew's Cathedral.** Built in 1867 as an Anglican church, many of its stones and ornaments were shipped from England; Hawaii's monarchs worshipped here, and the church is still very much in use. To the right is the **War Memorial.** Erected in 1974, it replaced an older memorial to the people who perished in WW II. A courtyard and benches are provided for quiet meditation.

Directly in front is the magnificent **Hawaii State Capitol,** built in 1969 for $25 million. The building itself is a metaphor for Hawaii: the pillars surrounding it are palms, the reflecting pool is the sea, and the cone-shaped rooms of the Legislature represent the volcanoes of Hawaii. It's lined with rich koa wood from the Big Island, and is further graced with woven hangings and murals, with two gigantic, four-ton replicas of the State Seal hanging at both entrances. The inner courtyard has a 600,000-tile mosaic, "Aquarius," rendered by island artist Tadashi Sato, and on one side is a poignant sculpture of **Father Damien of the Lepers.** The state Legislature is in session January to March, and opens with dancing, music, and festivities at 10 a.m. on the third Wednesday in January, public invited. Peek inside, then take the elevator to the fifth floor for outstanding views of the city.

MISSION HOUSES MUSEUM

This living museum, on King Street across from Kawaiahao Church (oldest in Honolulu), is a complex including two main houses, a printing house annex, a library and a fine, inexpensive gift shop. It's operated by the **Hawaiian Mission Children's Society** (or Cousins' Society), whose members serve as guides and hosts. Many are direct descendants, or spouses of descendants, of the Congregationalist missionaries who built these structures. Tours are conducted Tues.-Sat. 9 a.m.-4 p.m., Sun. 12-4 p.m., closed Mondays. Guided tours of the Frame House 9:30 a.m.-3 p.m.; $3.50 admission, tel. 531-0481. The museum hosts Hawaii's only **living history program.** Volunteers, all adept at acting, dress up in fashions of the period and assume the roles of missionaries in 1830 Honolulu. Feel free to interact and ask questions, but remember that they stay in character, so the answers may surprise you. Saturdays only from 10 a.m.-3 p.m., admission for adults $3.50.

Construction

If you think that precut modular housing is a new concept, think again. The first structure that you enter is the **Frame House,** the oldest wooden structure in Hawaii. Precut in Boston, it came along with the first missionary packet in 1819. Since the interior frame was left behind and didn't arrive until Christmas Day, 1820, the missionary families lived in thatched huts until it was erected. Finally the Chamberlain family occupied it in 1821. Many missionary families used it over the years, with as many as four households occupying this small structure at the same time. This is where the Christianizing of Hawaii truly began.

The missionaries, being New Englanders, first dug a cellar. The Hawaiians were very suspicious of the strange hole, convinced that the missionaries planned to store guns and arms in this "fort." Though assured to the contrary, King Liholiho, anxious to save face and prove his omnipotence, had a cellar dug near his home twice as deep and large. This satisfied everyone.

Notice the different styles, sizes, and colors of bricks used in the structures. Most of the ships of the day carried bricks as ballast. After unloading cargo, the captains either donated or sold the bricks to the missionaries, who incorporated them into the structures. A common local material was coral stone: pulverized coral was burned with lime to make a rudimentary cement, which was then used to bind cut-coral blocks. The pit that was used for this purpose is still discernible on the grounds.

Kitchen

The natives were intrigued with the missionaries, whom they called "long necks" because of their high collars. The missionaries, on the other hand, were a little more wary of their "charges." The low fence around the *left to right: Frame House, Printing House, Chamberlain House (courtesy Mission Houses Museum)*

complex was symbolic as well as utilitarian. The missionaries were obsessed with keeping their children away from Hawaiian children, who at first ran around naked and played many games with overt sexual overtones. Almost every evening a small cadre of Hawaiians would assemble to peer into the kitchen to watch the women cook, which they found exceedingly strange because their *kapu* said that *men* did the cooking. In the kitchen, actually an attached cookhouse, the woodburning stove kept breaking down. More often than not, the women used the fireplace with its built-in oven. About once a week, they fired up the oven to make traditional New England staples like bread, pies, cakes, and puddings. The missionaries were dependent on the Hawaiians to bring them fresh water. Notice a large porous stone through which they would filter the water to remove dirt, mud, and sometimes brackishness.

The Hawaiians were even more amazed when the entire family sat down to dinner, a tremendous deviation from their beliefs that separated men and women when eating. When the missionaries assembled to dine or meet at the "long table," the Hawaiians silently stood at the open door to watch the evening soap opera. The unnerved missionaries eventually closed the door and cut two windows into the wall, which they could leave

opened but draped. The long table took on further significance. The one you see is a replica. When different missionaries left the islands, they, like people today, wanted a souvenir. For some odd reason, they elected to saw a bit off the long table. As years went by, the table got shorter and shorter until it was useless.

Residents

The house was actually a duplex. Although many families lived in it, two of the best known were the Binghams and the Judds. Much of the furniture here was theirs. Judd, a member of the third missionary company, assumed the duties of physician to all the missionaries and islanders. He often prescribed alcohol of different sorts to the missionary families for a wide variety of ailments; many records remain of these prescriptions, but not one record of complaints from his patients. The Binghams and Judds got along very well, and entertained each other and visitors, most often in the Judds' parlor because they were a little better off. The women would often congregate here to do their sewing, which was in great demand, especially by members of the royal household. Until the missionary women taught island girls to sew, providing clothing for Hawaii's royalty was a tiresome and time-consuming obligation.

The missionaries were self-sufficient, and had the unbounded energy of youth, as the average age was only 25. The husbands often built furniture for their families. Reverand Bingham, a good craftsman, was pressed by Queen Kaahumanu to build her a rocking chair after she became enamored of one made for Mrs. Bingham. The queen weighed almost 400 pounds, so building her a suitable chair was no slim feat! Still, the queen could only use it in her later years when she'd lost a considerable amount of weight. After she died, the Bingham's asked for it to be returned, and it sits in their section of the house. Compare Bingham's chair to another in the Judds' bedroom, jury-rigged by a young missionary husband from a captain's chair. An understatement, found later in his diary, confirmed that he was not a carpenter.

When you enter the Judds' bedroom, note how small it is, and consider that two adults and five children slept here. As soon as the children were old enough, they were sent back to the Mainland for schooling, no doubt to relieve some of the congestion. Also notice that the windows were fixed, in the New England style, and imagine how close it must have been in these rooms. The Binghams' bedroom is also small, and not as well furnished. Bingham's shaving kit remains, and is inscribed with "The Sandwich Isles." In the bedroom of Mary Ward, a missionary woman who never married, notice that the roof was raised to accommodate her canopy bed.

Another famous family that lived in the complex were the Cookes. When the missionary board withdrew its support, the Cookes petitioned them to buy the duplex, which was granted. Shortly thereafter, Mr. Cooke, who had been a teacher, formed a partnership with one Mr. Castle, and from that time forward Castle and Cooke grew to become one of Hawaii's oldest and most powerful corporations. The largest building in the compound is **The Chamberlain House.** This barn-like structure was completed in 1831 and used as a warehouse and living quarters for Levi Chamberlain's family. Goods were stored in most of the structure, while the family occupied three modest rooms.

Printing House
The missionaries decided almost immediately that the best way to convert the natives was to speak to them in their own language, and to create a written Hawaiian language which they would teach in school. To this end, they created the **Hawaiian alphabet,** consisting of 12 letters, including the five vowels and seven consonants. In addition, to disseminate the doctrines of Christianity, they needed books, and therefore a printing press. On the grounds still stands the Printing House, built in 1841 but first used as annex bedrooms by the Hall family. The original printing house, built in 1823, no longer exists. In the Printing House is a replica of the Ramage press brought from New England, first operated by Elijah Lewis. He returned to the Mainland when he was 24, and soon died of TB, but not before he had earned the distinction of being the first printer west of the Rockies. Here were printed biblical tracts, textbooks, or anything that the king or passing captains were willing to pay to have printed. Although it took eight hours of hard work to set up one page to be printed, it is estimated that in the 20 years the press operated under the missionaries, over seven million pages were produced.

Gift Shop
While on the grounds make sure to visit the bookstore and gift shop. It's small but has an excellent collection of Hawaiiana, and some very inexpensive but quality items, such as *tapa* bookmarks for only $.25, and an outstanding collection of Niihau shellwork, considered the finest in Hawaii. The shelves hold tasteful items like woodcarvings, bread boards, hats, weavings, chimes, flags of old Hawaii, and stuffed pillows with classic Hawaiian quilt motifs. Also a good collection of Hawaiian dolls, for kids and adults. Between the bookstore and the research library are restrooms. Also, consider a **Walking Tour of Honolulu,** offered by the museum, that guides you through downtown Honolulu for two hours, hitting all the historic sights with an extremely knowledgeable narration by one of the museum's guides (see p. 113). For

further information write Hawaiian Mission Children's Society, 553 S. King St., Honolulu, HI 96813, tel. 531- 0481.

KAWAIAHAO CHURCH

This church, so instrumental in Hawaii's history, is the most enduring symbol of the original missionary work in the islands. A sign welcomes you and bids the blessing, "Grace and peace to you from God our Father." The church was constructed from 1836 until 1842 according to plans drawn up by Hiram Bingham, its minister. Before this, at least four grass shacks of increasing size stood here. One was destroyed by a sailor who was reprimanded by Rev. Bingham for attending services while drunk; the old sea dog returned the next day and burned the church to the ground. Kawaiahao ("Water of Hao") Church is constructed from over 14,000 coral blocks quarried from offshore reefs. In 1843, following Restoration Day, when the British returned the Hawaiian Islands to sovereignty after a brief period of imperialism by a renegade captain, King Kamehameha III here uttered the profound words in a thanksgiving ceremony that were destined to become Hawaii's motto, *"Ua mau ke ea o ka aina i ka pono,"* "The life of the land is preserved in righteousness."

Other noteworthy ceremonies held at the church were the marriage of King Liholiho and his wife Queen Emma, who bore the last child born to a Hawaiian monarch. Unfortunately, little Prince Albert died at the age of four. On June 19, 1856, Lunalilo, the first king elected to the throne, took his oath of office in the church. A bachelor who died childless, he always felt scorned by living members of the Kamehameha clan, and refusing to be buried with them at the Royal Mausoleum in Nuuanu Valley, he is buried in a tomb in the church's cemetery. Buried along with him is his father, Charles Kanaina, and nearby lies the grave of his mother, Miriam Kekauluohi. In the graveyard lies Henri Burger, and many members of the Parker, Green, Brown and Cooke families, early missionaries to the islands. Liliuokalani's body lay in state in the church before it was taken to the Royal Mausoleum. A jubilation service was held in the church when Hawaii became a state in 1959. Kawaiahao holds beautiful Christmas services with a strong Polynesian and Hawaiian flavor. Hidden away in a corner of the grounds is an unobtrusive adobe building, remains of a schoolhouse built in 1835 to educate Hawaiian children.

HAWAII MARITIME CENTER

The development of this center is a wonderful concept whose time has finally come. It's amazing that a state and former nation, whose discovery and very birth are so intimately tied to the exploration, navigation, and exploitation of the sea, has never had a center dedicated exclusively to these profoundly important aspects of its heritage. Now the Hawaii Maritime Center, at Pier 7, Honolulu Harbor, Honolulu, HI 96813, tel. 523-6151, is exactly that . . . and it needs your support as a visitor. The center, along with its museum in the **Kalakaua Boathouse**, now consists of three attractions: Aloha Tower, the beacon of hospitality welcoming people to Hawaii for six decades; the classic, and last remaining, fully rigged, four-masted *Falls of Clyde* floating

1. anthurium (J.D. Bisignani)   **2.** You should have seen the frog! (J.D. Bisignani)

1. north coast, windward Oahu (J.D. Bisignani) **2.** the rainbow connection (J.D. Bisignani)

1. Punchbowl Crater (J.D. Bisignani)   **2.** Hanauma Bay Beach Park (David Stanley)
3. Kaneohe Bay (J.D. Bisignani)

1. the Pali Highway (Dr. Janos Balogh) **2.** Diamond Head (J.D. Bisignani)

1. seaside vista, windward Oahu (J.D. Bisignani)   **2.** Waikiki sunset (J.D. Bisignani)

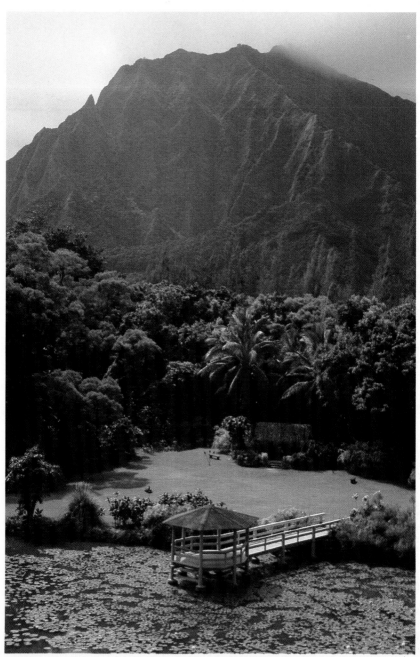

the *pali* from the Haiku Restaurant (J.D. Bisignani)

museum; and the reproduction of a Hawaiian sailing canoe, *The Hokule'a,* that recently sailed back in time using ancient navigational methods to retrace the steps of Hawaii's Polynesian explorers. Take bus #8 or 20 from Waikiki and you're deposited just in front. Admission $6, all attractions. Open 9 a.m.-5 p.m. every day.

The Kalakaua Boathouse

The main building of the center is the two-storied Kalakaua Boathouse. Behind is Coasters, an American standard restaurant (see p. 206), and an area called Kalakaua Park, a garden and observation area perfect for lunch. Eighty-one steps lead to the "crow's nest," and "widow's walk," with great views of the harbor and city.

Upon entering you find a glass case filled with trophies and memorabilia from the days of King Kalakaua. His words have a sadly prophetic ring. "Remember who you are. Be gracious, but never forget from whence you came for this is where your heart is. This is the cradle of your life." Notice the phones installed throughout the capital in 1887, a few years before California had electricity. Kalakaua had previously installed telephones between his boathouse and the palace in 1878, just two years after Bell's invention. The bottom floor of the center recalls ancient fishing methods, and the traditional division of land and sea resouces among the people.

Another fascinating display traces the development of surfing through the ages, from original boards, more like seagoing canoes at 18 feet long, until the modern debut of the fiberglass board. Spot a vintage album of *Surfin Safari* by The Beach Boys. Here, too, is a land-surfing sled used for games during the Makahiki Festival. It measures six inches wide and 10-14 feet long. Trails to accommodate it were up to a mile long. Built on steep hills, they were paved in stone, layered with earth and topped with slippery grass. Once launched there was no stopping until the bottom. Yippee!

One corner of the museum is dedicated to tattooing, Polynesian and Western. It shows traditional tattoos worn by both men and women, and then how the Western style be-

King David Kalakaua (Hawaii State Archives)

came more popular, as Hawaii was a main berth for sailors, who sported these living souvenirs from around the world. **Mail buoys** sounds uninteresting, but these tidbits of old Hawaiiana, still alive today, are fascinating. Fashioned from gaily painted metal cans, passing ships, mainly from Peru and Equador, still radio Honolulu Harbor that they are dropping one. Someone, anyone, who heard the message, would fetch them. Inside are little gifts for the finder, who takes the enclosed mail and sends it on its way.

The second floor is dedicated to the discovery of Hawaii, both by the Polynesians and Westerners. Through ledgers, histories, and artifacts, it traces original discovery, Western discovery, the death of Capt. Cooke, and the roll of the sea otter pelt which brought the first whalers and traders after sandalwood. The whaling section is dripping with blood and human drama. Look at the old harpoons and vintage film footage. Yes, film footage, and photos. A remarkable display is of schrimshaw from the whaling days. Sailors would be at sea for five to seven years, and would have untold hours to create beauty in what were dismal conditions. Suspended from the ceiling are replicas of double-hulled sailing canoes. One corner is a replica of H. Hatfield and Co., a whaling supply store of the era. The rear of the second floor shows steamships that cruised between Hawaii, Japan, and the East coast, a nature exhibit of weather, marinelife, and volcanoes, and an auditorium with a video on the climatic conditions in Hawaii.

Aloha Tower

When this endearing and enduring tourist cliché was built in 1926 for $160,000, the 184-foot, 10-story tower was the tallest structure on Oahu. As such, this landmark, with clocks embedded in all four walls, and emblazoned with the greeting and departing word, *Aloha,* became the symbol of Hawaii. Before the days of air transport, ocean liners would pull up to the pier to disembark passengers at the foot of the tower, and on these "Steamer Days," festive well-wishers from throughout the city would gather to greet and lei the arriving passengers. The Royal Hawaiian Band would even turn out to welcome the guests ashore.

When you take the escalator up from the parking area, notice the huge U.S. Customs rooms that at one time processed droves of passengers. Today, the crowds are gone and the tower is quiet. Only a few harbormasters on the top floor oversee the comings and goings of cargo ships. When you enter the tower a sign claims that you can only get to the observation area on the top floor by elevator. You can walk up to the ninth floor if you want, but to get to the very top does necessitate taking the elevator, which has the dubious distinction of being one of the first elevators in Hawaii. Once atop the tower, you get the most remarkable view of the harbor and the city. A high-rise planned for just next door will surely ruin the view, but many people with good sense, and luckily with some clout, are fighting this project. A remarkable feature of the vista is the reflections of the city and the harbor in many of the steel and reflective

glass high-rises. It's as if a huge mural were painted on them. The tower is open free of charge, daily from 8 a.m.-9 p.m.

The *Falls Of Clyde*

This is the last fully rigged, four-masted ship afloat on any of the world's oceans. She was saved from being scrapped in 1963 by a Seattle bank that was attempting to recoup some money on a bad debt. The people of Hawaii learned of her fate and spontaneously raised money to have the ship towed back to Honolulu Harbor. The *Falls of Clyde* was always a worker, never a pleasure craft. It served the Matson Steamship Company as a cargo and passenger liner from 1898 until 1920. Built in Glasgow, Scotland, in 1878, she was converted in 1906 to a sail-driven tanker; a motor aboard was used mainly to move the rigging around. After 1920, she was dismantled, towed to Alaska and became little more than a floating oil depot for fishing boats. Since 1968, the *Falls of Clyde* has been a floating museum, sailing the imaginations of children and grownups to times past, and in this capacity has perhaps performed her greatest duty.

The *Hokule'a*

The newest and perhaps most dynamic feature of the center is the *Hokule'a*. This authentic recreation of a traditional double-hulled sailing canoe captured the attention of the world when in 1976 it made a 6,000-mile roundtrip voyage to Tahiti. Piloted by Mau Piailug, a Caroline Islander, only ancient navigational techniques guided it successfully on its voyage. This attempt to relive these ancient voyages as closely as possible included eating traditional provisions only—*poi,* coconuts, dried fish, and bananas. Toward the end of the voyage some canned food had to be broken out!

Modern materials such as plywood and fiberglass were used, but by consulting many petroglyphs and old drawings of these original craft, the design and lines were kept as authentic as possible. The sails, made from a heavy cotton, were the distinctive crab-claw type. In trial runs to work out the kinks and choose the crew, she almost sank in the treacherous channel between Oahu and Kauai and had to be towed in by the Coast Guard. But the *Hokule'a* performed admirably during the actual voyage. The experiment was a resounding technical success, but it was marred by bad feelings between members of the crew who argued and drew racial boundary lines. Both Hawaiian and white crew members found it impossible to work as a team, thereby mocking the canoe's name, "Star of Gladness." The tension was compounded by the close quarters of more than a dozen men living on an open deck only nine feet wide by 40 feet long. The remarkable navigator Piailug refused to return to Hawaii with the craft and instead sailed back to his native island.

The *Hokule'a,* sponsored by the Polynesian Sailing Society, will make Pier seven its home berth when not at sea. This double-hulled canoe, a replica of the ones that Captain Cook found so remarkable, should fascinate you too.

Nearby Attractions

Two other attractions in the area are not part of the Hawaii Maritime Museum: in fact they're the antithesis of what this fine museum stands for. One is a monstrosity of a dinner boat called the *Relame,* an old flat-bottomed ferry whose four-masts were added for effect. If ever the sails were unfurled, it'd roll around like a drunken tub-of-lard on roller skates. Also berthed close by is the *Oceania* Floating Restaurant. This barge, towed all the way from Hong Kong to Honolulu Harbor in 1972, is billed as the world's largest floating restaurant. It would best be described as "modern Oriental rococo." Unlike the *Relame,* the structure is just bizarre enough to make it interesting. Businesses seem to come and go here, and at the moment the *Oceania* has an empty hold.

PALI HIGHWAY

Cutting across Oahu from Honolulu to Kailua on the windward coast is Rt. 61, better known as the Pali Highway. Before getting to the famous Nuuanu Pali Lookout at the very crest of the Koolau Mountains, you can spend a full and enjoyable day sightseeing. Stop en route at Punchbowl's National Memorial Cemetery, followed by an optional side trip to the summit of Tantalus for a breathtaking view of the city (see p. 134). You can also visit the **Royal Mausoleum** in the vicinity. Take the H-1 Freeway to Vineyard Boulevard (exit 22), cross the Pali Hwy. to Nuunau Avenue and follow it to the mausoleum. If you continue up Nuuanu Avenue, it intersects the Pali Hwy. in a minute or two, but you'll have passed the Punchbowl turnoff. This small chapel, built in 1865 by Kamehameha IV, holds the bodies of most of the royal family who died after 1825. Their bodies were originally interred elsewhere but were later moved here. The mausoleum at one time held 18 royal bodies but became overcrowded, so they were moved again to little crypts scattered around the grounds. Few tourists visit this serene place open weekdays from 8 a.m-4 p.m., tel. 536-7602.

About two miles past the Punchbowl turn-off, heading up the Pali Hwy. (exit 21-B off H-1), an HVB Warrior points you to the **Walker Home** across from Nuuanu Congregational Church. It's famous for its gardens, and at one time visitors were welcome to come and tour them for a fee. It's hard to tell if this is still happening. The gates are open and no signs tell you to keep out, but an unsmiling housekeeper backed by a steely-eyed German shepherd make you want to wave from your car and keep rolling. Next comes Queen Emma's Summer Palace (see following) and the Daijingu Temple, a Baptist college, and a Catholic church. It seems as though these sects were vying to get farther up the hill to be just a little closer to heaven.

A sign, past Queen Emma's Palace, points you off to **Nuuanu Pali Drive.** Take it! This few-minutes' jog off the Pali Hwy. (which it rejoins) takes you through some wonderful scenery. Make sure to bear right as soon as you pull off and not up the Old Pali Hwy., which has no outlet. Immediately the road is canopied with trees, and in less than half a mile there's a bubbling little waterfall and a pool. The homes in here are grand, and the entire area gives a park-like effect. One of the nicest little roads that you can take while

GREATER HONOLULU

TO KANEOHE

TO PEARL CITY

TO KAILUA
PALI HWY.
61

LIKELIKE HWY.
63

78
PUULOA RD
MOANALUA RD
MIDDLE ST
RD

KALIHI
KAPALAMA
SCHOOL ST.
LILIHA
PAUOA
NUUANU

BISHOP MUSEUM
KING ST
VINEYARD
DILLINGHAM BLVD
KALIHI ST

90
92

NIMITZ HWY.
CHINATOWN
BETHEL
BISHOP

PACIFIC HEIGHTS
TANTALUS DR.
MAKIKI HEIGHTS
MAKIKI HTS. DR.
NEHOA
WILDER
PIIKOI
WARD
QUEEN ST

STATE CAPITOL

H-1
PENSACOLA
PUNCHBOWL

ROUND TOP DR.
PUNAHOU ST.
MANOA
University of Hawaii

MAUNALANI HEIGHTS

ST. LOUIS HEIGHTS

MANOA RD.
OAHU AVE.
METCALF
UNIVERSITY
KING
McCULLEY
KAPIOLANI BLVD.
KEEAUMOKU

MOILIILI
KAIMUKI

WAIALAE AVE.
LUNALILO
DATE ST.
H-1

ALA WAI CANAL
ALAWAI BLVD.
LEWERS
KALIA
KALAKAUA
Waikiki Beach

KAPAHULU
PAKI
MONSARRAT AVE.
DIAMOND HEAD RD
18th

KAHALA
KAHALA AVE.
KAHALA HILTON
KEALAOLU
KILANEA

KAANANAOE HWY
72
TO WAIMANALO

DIAMOND HEAD

ALOHA TOWER
HONOLULU HARBOR
SAND ISLAND ACCESS RD.
SAND ISLAND STATE PARK
Ala Moana Shopping Ctr
ALA MOANA HWY.
KEWALO BASIN
Ala Wai Yacht Harbor
ALA WAI BASIN

KEEHI LAGOON
LAGOON DR.
HONOLULU AIRPORT
TO PEARL HARBOR
90

1 mi
1 km
0
0

N.B. ONLY MAIN ROADS SHOWN

© MOON PUBLICATIONS, INC.

looking around, this side trip wastes no time at all.

Queen Emma's Summer Palace

This summer home is more the simple hideaway of a well-to-do family than a grand palace. The 3,000-square-foot interior has only two bedrooms and no facilities for guests. The first person to put a house on the property was John George Lewis. He purchased the land for $800 from a previous owner by the name of Henry Pierce, and then resold it to John Young II. The exterior has a strong New England flavor, and indeed the house was prefabricated in Boston. The simple square home, surrounded by a *lanai,* was built from 1843 to 1847 by John Young II, Queen Emma's uncle. When he died, she inherited the property and spent many relaxing days here, away from the heat of Honolulu, with her husband King Kamehameha IV. Emma used the home little after 1872, and following her death in 1885 it fell into disrepair.

Rescued from demolition by the Daughters of Hawaii in 1913, it was refurbished and has operated as a museum since 1915. The Palace, at 2913 Pali Hwy., tel. 595-3167, is open daily 9 a.m.-4 p.m., admission $4, children under 12 $.50. Although it's just off the Pali Highway, the one and only sign comes up quickly, and many visitors pass it by. If you pass the entranceway to the Oahu Country Club just across the road, you've gone too far.

As you enter, notice the tall *kahili,* symbols of noble rank in the entranceway, along with *lau hala* mats on the floor, which at one time were an unsurpassed speciality of Hawaii. Today they must be imported from Fiji or Samoa. The walls are hung with paintings of many of Hawaii's kings and queens, and in every room are distinctive Hawaiian artifacts, such as magnificent feather capes, fans, and *tapa* hangings.

The furnishings have a very strong British influence. The Hawaiian nobility of the time were enamored with the British. King Kamehameha IV traveled to England when he was 15 years old; he met Queen Victoria, and the two become good friends. Emma and Kame-

Prince Albert

hameha IV had the last child born to a Hawaiian king and queen on May 20, 1858. Named Prince Albert after Queen Victoria's consort, he was much loved but died when he was only four years old on August 27, 1862. His father followed him to the grave in little more than a year. The king's brother, Lot Kamehameha, a bachelor, took the throne but died very shortly thereafter, marking the end of the Kamehameha line; after that, Hawaii elected her kings. Prince Albert's canoe-shaped cradle is here, made in Germany by Wilhelm Fisher from four different kinds of Hawaiian wood. His tiny shirts, pants, and boots are still laid out, and there's a lock of his hair, and one from Queen Emma. In every room there are royal memorabilia. The royal bedroom displays a queen-size bed covered with an exquisite pink and purple *tapa* bedspread. There's vintage Victorian furniture, and even a piano built in London by Collard and Collard. A royal cabinet made in Berlin holds porcelains, plates, and cups. After Queen Emma died, it stood in Charles R. Bishop's drawing room but was later returned. The grounds are beautifully manicured, and the house is surrounded by shrubbery and trees, many of which date from when the royal couple lived here. Restrooms are around back.

Walk around back past the basketball court and keep to the right. Soon you'll see a modest little white building. Look for a rather thick and distinctive rope hanging across the entranceway. This is the Shinto temple **Dai Jingu**. It's not nearly as spectacular as the giant trees in this area, but it is authentic and worth a quick look.

The Daughters of Hawaii have added a gift shop around back, which is open the same hours as the palace. It's small but packed with excellent items like greeting cards, leis, travel guidebooks, beverage trays (reproductions of the early Matson Line menus), little Hawaiian quilt pillows, needlepoint, wraparounds from Tahiti, T-shirts with Queen Emma's Summer Palace logo, and Niihau shellwork, the finest in Hawaii.

Nuuanu Pali Lookout

This is one of those extra-benefit places where you get a magnificent view without any effort at all. Merely drive up the Pali Hwy. to

engraving of Hawaii's unique pali by Barthelme Lauvergne, c. 1836. (Hawaii State Archives)

the well-marked turnout and park. Rip-offs happen, so take all valuables. Before you, if the weather is accommodating, an unimpeded view of windward Oahu lies at your feet. Nuuanu Pali ("Cool Heights") lives up to its name; the winds here are chilly, extremely strong, and funnel right through the lookout. You definitely need a jacket or windbreaker. On a particularly windy day just after a good rainfall, various waterfalls tumbling off the *pali* will actually be blown uphill! A number of roads, punched over and through the *pali* over the years, are engineering marvels. The famous "carriage road" built in 1898 by John Wilson, a Honolulu boy, for only $37,500, using 200 laborers and plenty of dynamite, was truly amazing. Droves of people come here, many in huge buses, and they all go to the railing to have a peek. Even so, by walking down the old road built in 1932 that goes off to the right, you actually get private and better views. You'll find the tallest point in the area, a huge needle-like rock. The wind is quieter here.

Nuuanu Pali figures prominently in Hawaii's legend history. It's said, not without academic skepticism, that Kamehameha the Great pursued the last remaining defenders of Oahu to these cliffs in one of the final battles fought to consolidate his power over all of the islands in 1795. If you use your imagination, you can easily feel the utter despair and courage of these vanquished warriors as they were driven ever closer to the edge. Mercy was not shown nor expected. Some jumped to their deaths rather than surrender, while others fought until they were pushed over. The estimated number of casualties varies considerably, from a few hundred to a few thousand, while some believe that the battle never happened at all. Compounding the controversy are stories of the warriors' families, who searched the cliffs below for years, and supposedly found bones of their kinsmen, that they buried. The Pali Lookout is romantic at night, with the lights of Kailua and Kaneohe in the distance, but the best nighttime view is from Tantalus Drive, where all of Honolulu lies at your feet.

Punchbowl Cemetery

PUNCHBOWL, NATIONAL CEMETERY OF THE PACIFIC

One sure sign that you have entered a place of honor is the hushed and quiet nature that everyone adopts without having to be told. That's the way it is the moment that you enter this shrine. The Hawaiian name, Puowaina ("Hill of Sacrifice"), couldn't have been more prophetic. Punchbowl is the almost perfectly round crater of an extinct volcano that holds the bodies of nearly 25,000 men and women who fell fighting for the United States, from the Spanish-American War to Vietnam. At one time, Punchbowl was a bastion of heavy cannon and artillery trained on Honolulu Harbor to defend it from hostile naval forces. In 1943 Hawaii bequeathed it to the federal government as a memorial; it was dedicated in 1949, when the remains of an unknown serviceman killed during the attack on Pearl Harbor were the first interred.

As you enter the main gate, a flagpole with the Stars and Stripes unfurled is framed in the center of a long sweeping lawn. A roadway lined with monkeypods adds three-dimensional depth to the impressionistic scene, as it leads to the steps of a marble, altar-like monument in the distance. The eye has a continuous sweep of the field, as there are no elevated tombstones, just simple marble slabs lying flat on the ground. The field is dotted with trees, including eight banyans, a special tree and symbolic number for the many Buddhists buried here. Brightening the scene are plumeria and rainbow shower trees, often planted in Hawaiian graveyards because they produce flowers year-round as perennial offerings from the living to the dead when they can't personally attend the grave. All are equal here; the famous, like Ernie Pyle, the stalwart who earned the Congressional Medal of Honor, and the unknown who died alone and unheralded on muddy battlefields in Godforsaken jungles. To the right, just after you enter is the office, open Mon. to Fri. 9 a.m.-5 p.m. with brochures and restrooms. Tour buses, taxis, and limousines are lined up here. Don't leave valuables in your car.

The Monument

Like a pilgrim, you climb the steps to the monument, where on both sides marble slabs seem to whisper the names of the 20,000-plus servicemen, all MIAs whose bodies were never found but whose spirits are honored here. The first slabs on the right are for the victims of Vietnam, on the left are those from WW II, and you can see that time is already weathering the marble. They lie together, as they fought and died . . . men, boys, lieutenants, captains, private soldiers, infantry-men, sailors . . . from everywhere in America. "In proud memory . . . this memorial has been erected by the United States of America."

At the monument itself, built in 1966, is a chapel and in the middle is a statue of a woman, a woman of peace, a heroic woman of liberty. Around her on the walls are etched maps and battles of the Pacific War whose names still evoke passion: Pearl Harbor, Wake, Coral Sea, Midway, Iwo Jima, the Gilbert Islands, Okinawa. Many of the visitors are Japanese. Many of Hawaii's war dead are also Japanese. Four decades ago we battled each other with hatred and malice. Today, on bright afternoons we come together with sad-dened hearts to pay reverence to the dead.

To get to Punchbowl take the H-1 Freeway to Rt. 61, the Pali Highway, and exit at 21B. Immediately get to the right, where a sign points you to Punchbowl. You'll make some fancy zigzags through a residential area, but it's well marked and you'll come to Puowaina Street, which leads you to the main gate. Make sure to notice landmarks going in, be-cause as odd as it sounds, no signs lead you back out and it's easy to get lost.

UNIVERSITY OF HAWAII

You don't have to be a student to head for the University of Hawaii, Manoa Campus. For one, it houses the **East-West Center,** which was incorporated in 1975 and officially sepa-rated from the university; here nations from Asia and the Pacific present fascinating dis-plays of their homelands. Also, Manoa Valley itself is one of the loveliest residential areas on Oahu. To get to the main campus follow the H-1 Freeway to exit 24B (University Avenue). Don't make the mistake of exiting at the Uni-versity's Makai Campus. Follow University Avenue to the second red light, Dole Avenue, and make a right onto campus. Stop immedi-ately at one of the parking lots and get a parking map! Parking restrictions are strictly enforced, and this map not only helps to get you around, but saves you from fines or hav-ing your car towed away. Parking is $.50 an hour, even for visitors, so think about taking TheBus, which services this area quite well.

Student Center
Make this your first stop. As you mount the steps, notice the idealized mural of old Ha-waii: smiling faces of contented natives all doing interesting things. Inside is the **Infor-mation Center,** which dispenses info not only about the campus, but also about what's happening socially and culturally around town. They even have lists of cheap restau-rants, discos, and student hangouts. Next door are typewriters available to nonstudents at $2 per day. The food in the cafeteria is institutional but cheap, and has a Hawaiian twist. The best place to eat is at the **Manoa Gardens** in the Hemingway Center, where you can get a tasty stir-fry or good vegetarian dishes for $3.50 and up.

The **University Bookstore** is excellent, open Mon. to Fri. 8:15 a.m.- 4:15 p.m., Sat. 8:15-11:45 a.m. The bookstore is worth com-ing to for its excellent range of specialty items, like language tapes, and its extensive assort-ment of travel guidebooks. The **University Art Gallery** is on the third floor, and is worth a look. Free! The exhibits change regularly. Next to the gallery is a lounge filled with overstuffed chairs and big pillows, where you can kick back and even take a quick snooze. This is not a very social campus. By 4:30 or 5 p.m. the place is shut up and no one is around. Don't expect students gathered in a common reading room, or the activity of so-cial and cultural events. When school lets out at the end of the day, people simply go home.

East-West Center
Follow Dole Avenue to East-West Road and make a left. Free tours, Wednesdays only at 1:30 p.m., originate from Imin Center-Jeffer-son Hall opposite Kennedy Theater. For more info contact the Friends of the East-West Center, 1777 East-West Rd., Honolulu, HI 96848, tel. 944-7691. The Center's 21 acres were dedicated in 1960 by the U.S. Congress to promote better relations between the countries of Asia and the Pacific with the U.S. Many nations, as well as private companies and individuals, fund this institution of coop-erative study and research. John Burn's Hall's main lobby dispenses information on what's happening, along with self-guiding maps. Imin

Bishop Museum

Center-Jefferson Hall, fronted by Chinese lions, has a serene and relaxing Japanese garden behind, complete with a little rivulet and a teahouse named Jakuan, "Cottage of Tranquility." The murals inside are excellent, and it also contains a large reading room with relaxing couches.

The impressive Thai Pavilion was a gift from the king of Thailand, where it was built and sent to Hawaii to be reconstructed. This 23-ton, solid teak sala is a common sight in Thailand. The Center for Korean Studies (not part of the East-West Center) is also outstanding. A joint venture of Korean and Hawaiian architects, its inspiration was taken from the classic lines of Kyongbok Palace in Seoul. Most of the buildings are adorned with fine artworks: tapa hangings, murals, calligraphy, paintings, and sculpture. The entire center is tranquil, and along with the John F. Kennedy Theater of Performing Arts just across the road, is indeed fulfilling its dedication as a place of sharing and learning, culture and art.

BISHOP MUSEUM
(STATE MUSEUM OF NATURAL
AND CULTURAL HISTORY)

This group of stalwart stone buildings holds the greatest collection of historical relics and scholarly works on Hawaii and the Pacific in the world. Referring to itself as a "museum to instruct and delight," in one afternoon walking through its halls you can educate yourself about Hawaii's history and people and enrich your trip to the islands tenfold.

Officially named Bernice Pauahi Bishop Museum, its founding was directly connected to the last three royal women of the Kamehameha Dynasty. Princess Bernice married Charles Reed Bishop, a New Englander who became a citizen of the then-independent monarchy in the 1840s. The princess was a wealthy woman in her own right, with lands and an extensive collection of "things Hawaiian." Her cousin, Princess Ruta Keeikolani, died in 1883, and bequeathed Princess Bernice all of her lands and Hawaiian artifacts. Together, this meant that Princess Bernice owned about 12 percent of all Hawaii! Princess Bernice died less than two years later, and left all of her land holdings to the **Bernice Pauahi Bishop Estate,** which founded and supported the Kamehameha School, dedicated to the education of Hawaiian children. (Though this organization is often confused with the Bishop Museum, they are totally separate. The school shared the same grounds with the museum, but none of the funds from this organization were, or are, used for the museum.) Bernice, left her personal property, with all of its priceless Hawaiian artifacts, to her husband, Charles. Then, when Queen Emma, her other cousin, died the following year, she too desired Charles Bishop to combine her Hawaiian artifacts with the already formidable collection and establish a Hawaiian museum.

True to the wishes of these women, he began construction of the museum's main building on December 18, 1889, and within a few years the museum was opened. In 1894, after 50 years in Hawaii, Bishop moved to San Francisco where he died in 1915. He is still regarded as one of Hawaii's most generous philanthropists. In 1961, a science wing and planetarium were added, and two dormitory buildings are still used from when the Kamehameha School for Boys occupied the same site.

Getting There

To get there, take exit 20A off the H-1 Freeway, which puts you on Rt. 63, the Likelike Highway. Immediately get into the far right lane. In only a few hundred yards, turn onto Bernice Street, where you'll find the entrance. Or, exit H-1 onto Hofftailing Street, Rt. 61, exit 20B. Keep your eyes peeled for a clearly marked but small sign directing you to the museum. TheBus # 2 (School-Middle Street) runs from Waikiki to Kapalama Street, from which you walk two blocks.

Admission And Information

The museum is located at 1525 Bernice St., Honolulu, HI 96817, tel. 847- 3511, and is open seven days per week from 9 a.m.-5 p.m. The official entrance has been changed. It's now at the new building just near the planetarium, not at the old lava stone building. Admission is $5.95 adults, six and younger free, but some exhibits and the planetarium are closed to children under six. It's sometimes best to visit on weekends because many weekdays bring teachers and young students who have more enthusiasm for running around than checking out the exhibits. Food, beverages, smoking, and flash photography are all strictly prohibited in the museum. The natural light in the museum is dim, so if you're into photography you'll need super-fast film (400 ASA performs only marginally). Before leaving the grounds make sure to visit **Atherton Halau,** where a hula is performed Mon. through Sat. at 10:15 a.m. and 2 p.m. Throughout the week, the hall

offers demonstrations in various Hawaiian crafts like lei-making, featherwork, and quilting. The **planetarium** opens up its skies daily at 11 a.m. and 2 p.m.

There are special nighttime shows and family discount days offered, call 847-3511 for details. The snack shop has reasonable prices, and **Shop Pacifica,** the museum bookstore and boutique, has a fine selection of materials on Hawaii and the Pacific, and some authentic and inexpensive souvenirs. The **museum cafe** has a limited menu with dishes like Hawaiian fruit salad for $3.50, hamburger, $2.85, teriyaki burger, $2.65, and snacks like chili dogs, muffins, chips, and drinks.

Exhibits

It's easy to become overwhelmed at the museum, so just take it slowly. The number of exhibits is staggering: over 100,000 artifacts, almost 20 million(!) specimens of insects, shells, fish, birds, and mammals, plus an extensive research library, photograph collection, and fine series of maps. The main gallery is highlighted by the rich tones of *koa,* the showpiece being a magnificent staircase. Get a map at the front desk that lists all of the halls, along with a description of what theme is found in each, and a suggested route to

Princess Bernice (Hawaii State Archives)

Fort DeRussy tank

follow. The following are just a potpourri of the highlights that you'll discover.

To the right of the main entranceway is a fascinating exhibit of the old Hawaiian gods. Most are just called "wooden image" and date from the early 19th century. Among them are: Kamehameha's war-god, Ku; the tallest Hawaiian sculpture ever found, from Kauai; an image of a god from a temple of human sacrifice; and lesser gods, personal *amakua* that controlled the lives of Hawaiians from birth until death. You wouldn't want to meet any of them in a dark alley! Outside, in what's called the **Hawaiian Courtyard,** are implements used by the Hawaiians in everyday life, as well as a collection of plants that have all been identified. The first floor of the main hall is perhaps the most interesting because it deals with old Hawaii. Here are magnificent examples of *kahili,* feathered capes, plumed helmets . . . all the insignia and regalia of the *ali'i.* A commoner sits in a grass shack, a replica of what Capt. Cook might have seen.

Don't look up! Over your head is a 55-foot sperm whale hanging from the ceiling. It weighed over 44,000 pounds alive. You'll learn about the ukulele, and how vaudevillians spread its music around the world. Hula-skirted damsels from the 1870s peer provocatively from old photos, bare-breasted and with plenty of "cheesecake." Tourists bought these photos even then, although the grass skirts they're wearing were never a part of old Hawaii but were brought by Gilbert Islanders. See authentic hula instruments like a "lover's whistle," a flute played through the nose, and a musical bow, the only stringed pre-European Hawaiian instrument.

Don't miss the *koa* wood collection. This accomplished artform produced medicine bowls, handsome calabashes, some just simple home bowls, and others reputed to be the earthly home of the wind goddess, and had to be refitted for display in Christianized Iolani Palace. A model *heiau* tells of the old religion, and the many strange *kapu* that governed every aspect of life. Clubs used to bash in the brains of *kapu*-breakers are next to benevolent little stone gods, the size and shape of footballs, that protected humble fishermen from the sea. As you ascend to the upper floors, time becomes increasingly closer to the present. The missionaries, whalers, merchants, laborers, and Westernized monarchs have arrived. Yankee whalers from New Bedford, New London, Nantucket, and Sag Harbor appear determined and grim-faced as they scour the seas, harpoons at the ready. Great blubber pots, harpoons, and figureheads are preserved from this perilous and unglamorous life. Bibles, thrones, the regalia of power and of the new god are all here.

MUSEUMS, GALLERIES, GARDENS, AND TOURS

Military Museums

The museum at **Battery Randolph,** with the hulks of tanks standing guard, is one long corridor where you feel the strength of the super-thick reinforced walls of this once-active gun emplacement. Located at Fort DeRussy, on the corner of Kalia and Saratoga roads, free guided tour, open Tues.-Sun. 10 a.m.-4:30 p.m., tel. 543-2687. The U.S. Battery Randolph once housed two 14-inch coast artillery rifles meant to defend Honolulu and Pearl harbors. The architecture is typical of the Taft Period forts constructed between 1907 and 1920. The battery is listed in the National Register of Historic Places. Upon entering is a shop dedicated to *things military,* flying jackets to wall posters. Walk the halls to learn the military history of Hawaii traced as far back as Kamehameha I. Here are rifles, swords, and vintage photos of Camp McKinley, a turn-of-the-century military station in the shadow of Diamond Head.

A side room holds models of artillary used to defend Waikiki from times when Battery Randolph was an active installation. One room shows how the guns worked in a method called "disappearing guns." The gun would raise up and fire and then disappear. The recoil of the gun would lock it back in position, and after it was reloaded a 50-ton counterweight would pop it up ready to fire. The explosive sound would rattle the entire neighborhood so they were seldom test-fired.

Exhibits show the fledgling days of Army aviation in Hawaii when on July 13, 1913, 14 officers began a military flying school. There are beautiful models of military equipment, especially one of an old truck unit. Then comes the ominous exhibit of "Rising Japan" with its headlong thrust into WW II. Hawaii, grossly overconfident, felt immune to attack because of the strong military presence. Photos from the '30s and '40s depict the carefree lifestyle of visiting celebrities like Babe Ruth and Shirley Temple, which ended abruptly on Dec. 7, 1941 in the wreckage of Pearl Harbor.

An entire room is dedicated to the Pearl Harbor attack and is filled with models of Japanese planes, aircraft carriers, and real helmets and goggles worn by the Zero pilots. Most interesting are the slice-of-life photos of Hawaii mobilized for war: defense workers, both men and women, sailors, soldiers, entertainers, street scenes. Pamphlets from the time read, "Know Your Enemies," and there's a macabre photo of people gathered at a stadium to see the demonstration of the devasting effect of flame throwers that would be employed upon the Japanese enemy. Bob Hope is here entertaining the troops,

while a 442nd Regimental Battle Flag bears testament to the most decorated unit in American history, comprised mostly of *nisei* Japanese from Hawaii. Then come photos and exhibits from the soul-wrenching conflicts in Korea and Vietnam. Finally a room, like a whispering tomb, tells of the heroics of Hawaiian soldiers who have been awarded the Congressional Medal of Honor, almost all posthumously.

Make sure to go outside to the upper level exhibit where you'll see one of the old guns still pointing out to sea, which seems incongruous with sunbathers just below on the quiet and excellent stretch of beach. On the upper deck are depth charges, torpedoes, and shells, along with a multimedia slide show. Your eyes will take a few minutes to refocus to the glorious sunshine of Waikiki after the cold gloom of the bunker. Perhaps our hearts and souls could refocus as well.

Honolulu Academy Of Arts

This museum has a brilliant collection of classic and modern art, strongly emphasizing Asian artwork. James Michener's outstanding collection of Japanese *ukiyoe* is here. The story goes that an unfriendly New York cop hassled him on his way to donate it to a New York City museum, while a Honolulu officer was the epitome of *aloha* when Michener was passing through, so he decided that his collection should reside here. This collection is currently displayed about six months per year, but a decision has been made to display it year-round. Magnificent Korean ceramics, Chinese furniture, Japanese prints, along with Western masterworks from the Greeks to Picasso make the academy one of the most rounded art museums in America. Some collections are permanent while others change, so the museum remains dynamic no matter how many times you visit.

Enjoy the magnificent building and grounds as well as the glorious artwork. It's a perfect building designed by architect Bertrum Goodhugh and benefactor Mrs. Charles Montague expressly as a museum. The design is a combination of East and West with a Hawaiian roof and thick white stucco walls reminiscent of the American Southwest.

Enter through the foyer and pass to the courtyard that gets you away from the hustle and bustle of downtown. Great for a little respite from noise. Pass through double French doors to the thick white-walled galleries that create a perfect atmosphere for displaying fine works of art. Discover delights like Paul Gauguin's *Two Nudes on a Tahitian Beach,* Whistler's *Arrangement in Black No. 5,* John Singer Sargent's *Portrait of Mrs. Thomas Lincoln Hansen Jr.* An entire wing is dedicated to religious art, while another holds furniture from medieval Europe. The courtyards are resplendent with statuary from the 6th century A.D. and a standing figure from Egypt, circa 2500 B.C. The Hawaiian climate is perfect for preserving artwork.

Stop at the **Academy Shop,** specializing in art books, museum repros, Hawaii out-of-prints, jewelry, notebooks, and post cards, open 1-4 Tues.-Sat., 1-5 Sunday. The **Garden Cafe,** open 11:30 a.m.-1 p.m. Tues.-Fri., Thursday supper at 6:30 p.m., is in a garden under a canopy. They have a light but terrific menu, and besides, a trip to the Academy demands a luncheon in the cafe. For menu and details see p. 207.

Museum hours are Tues.-Sat. 10 a.m.-4:30 p.m., Sun. 1-5 p.m., closed Monday. Free, donations only. Guided tours are conducted at 11 a.m. Tues., Wed., Fri., Sat., and at 1 p.m. on Thurs. and Sunday. The Academy of Arts is at 900 S. Beretania St. (TheBus # 2), opposite Thomas Square, tel. 538-1006.

The Contemporary Museum

Under the direction of Fritz Frauchinger, at 2411 Mikiki Heights Rd., tel. 526-1322, the museum welcomes you with two coppergreen gates that are sculptures themselves. This open and elegant structure, the former Spalding House, has yielded six galleries, a shop, and an excellent gourmet restaurant (see p. 207). Acquired through the generosity of the *Honolulu Advertiser's* stockholders, it was donated to the museum as a permanent home in 1988. Surrounding it are three magnificent acres sculpted into Oriental gardens perfect for strolling and gazing at the sprawl of Honolulu far below. The focus is on exhibitions, not collections, although works by David Hockney are on permanent display. Always changing exhibits reflect different themes in contemporary art. Open Mon.-Sat. 10 a.m.-4 p.m., Sun. noon-4 p.m., closed Tues., admission $3.

Tennent Art Foundation

At 201-203 Prospect St., on the *ewa* slope of Punchbowl, the foundation is open Tues. through Sat. 10 a.m.- noon, and Sun. 2-4 p.m., tel. 531-1987. Free. There is a library and the walls hold the paintings of Madge Tennent, one of Hawaii's foremost artists, as well as many other contemporary works. It's beautiful and quiet and worth a visit.

Foster Botanical Gardens

Fifteen acres of exotic trees, many of which have been growing in this manicured garden for over 100 years, at one time this was the private estate of Dr. Hillebrand, physician to the royal court, who brought many of the seedlings from Asia. Two dozen of these trees enjoy lifetime protection by the state. At 180 N. Vineyard St., tel. 531-1939, open daily 9 a.m.-4 p.m., free, self-guiding brochures. Guided tours Mon., Tues., and Wed. at 1:30 p.m. Many nature hikes on Oahu and the Neighbor Islands are sponsored by the gardens.

Manoa Road

Leading past the University of Hawaii into Manoa Valley is a lovely residential area. En route you pass **Punahou School,** one of the oldest and most prestigious high schools in Hawaii. Built in 1841 from lava rock, children of the missionary families of wealthy San Franciscans attended, getting the best possible education west of the Rockies. Manoa Road turns into Oahu Avenue. **Waioli Tea Room,** 3016 Oahu Ave., owned and operated by the Salvation Army, is a small park; their snack bar features fresh-baked pastries and serves lunch daily from 11 a.m.- 2 p.m. Also featured here is the **Little Grass Shack** transported from Waikiki that Robert Louis Stevenson supposedly lived in. Visit the chapel with its distinctive stained-glass windows. Waioli Tea Room is open daily except Monday, from 8 a.m.-3:30 p.m., luncheon served from 11 a.m.-2 p.m. Reservations, tel. 988-2131.

The Dole Cannery Square

Look for the giant pineapple rising 200 feet into the air. A landmark of Honolulu, it was built in Chicago and erected here in 1928. It is still used as a reservoir and holds 100,000 gallons of water that's piped throughout the Dole Cannery, whose outer buildings were transformed in 1988 to a mini-mall which complements the ongoing Dole Cannery Tour. Located at 650 Iwilei Rd., tel. 548-4837, 45-minute tours are conducted daily from 9 a.m.- 5 p.m., with the last departing at 3 p.m. Admission $5, children under 12 free. Free parking is provided if you take your car, but ride the **Pineapple Transit,** tel. 523-DOLE, a van that runs from 8:30 a.m.- 3:30 p.m., stopping at many Waikiki hotels, $.50 one way. Upon entering the atrium area, look high on the walls to see reproductions of Dole Pineapple can labels. They're pop art, and convey a feeling of simpler times past. Here also is the **Food Court,** providing snacks, salads, sandwiches, and soups for a quick lunch.

The tour itself begins with a stereophonic slide show that instructs on the development of pineapple in Hawaii. Plenty of memorabilia and vintage photos help create a sense of the past. You're then conducted right into the factory where workers are busy packing the fruit, and where you learn the process of how it makes it to the kitchen table. Observe the newest generation of the marvelous Ginaca machine, first built in 1913 by Henry Ginaca, a draftsman hired by James Dole to modernize the industry. This whirring wonder can peel, core, cut, slice, and dice 100 fruits per minute. Within 20 minutes of reaching the machine, the canned fruit's ready for the grocer's shelf. After the tour, you're taken to a tasting room where you're offered complimentary . . . guess what?

On the second floor you'll find a cluster of shops laid out as traditional storefronts and featuring items made in Hawaii. Stop at the **Dole Logo Shop** for a T-shirt with a replica of a vintage pineapple can label, along with hats, gift items, and glassware all bearing the Dole logo. The **Island Moo Moo Works,** popular with local people, has racks of affordable muumuus and alohawear. The **Jungle Jerky Shop** has jerky of all sorts and sells stuffed animals, all life-size, as well as cotton cloth flowers. New shops like **Mamo Howell** and **Island Princess** will add elegance with their fashions, or you can take care of your sweet tooth at **Sharyn's Hawaiian Island Cookies.** One of the nicest shops is the **Village Beach Shop.** They're a complete resort-wear store with plenty of muumuus, sandals, and even boogie boards to choose from. They have a fine selection of T-shirts with gold designs by Ericka Paeis, a very creative and distinctive designer in the crowded field of Hawaiian T-shirts.

Paradise Park

These 13 acres of lush tropical plants explode in the 160 inches of annual rainfall that cascades into this farthest section of Manoa Valley. Magnificent blooms compete with the wild plumage of 50 species of exotic birds. You first walk into a giant bird cage laced with paths. The birds perform circus acts at scheduled intervals; some could easily win a spot with Barnum and Bailey for their tricks. This is purely make-believe Hawaii, good for a few hours of family fun. The Chuck Machado Luau is held here on Sunday evenings, and Henri Hawaii's Restaurant, on the premises, has good food at not too inflated prices at 3737 Manoa Rd., tel. 988-6686. Admission is $7.95 adults, $5.95 children, open daily 9:30 a.m.-5:30 p.m., allow two to three hours to see the entire park. Drive or take TheBus, # 8-Paradise Park, from Ala Moana Center. Also, a special tour bus from Waikiki is available.

Moanalua Gardens

Those private gardens of the Damon Estate, at 1352 Pineapple Pl., tel. 839-5334, were given to the original owner by Princess Bernice Bishop in 1884. Just off the Moanalua Freeway, and open to the public, these gardens are not heavily touristed, a welcome respite from the hustle and bustle of the city. Some magnificent old trees include a Buddha tree from Ceylon and a monkeypod called "the most beautifully shaped tree" in the world by *Ripley's Believe It or Not*. The Moanalua Foundation also sponsors walks deep into Moanalua Valley for viewing the foliage of "natural Hawaii." The free guided walks begin at 9 a.m. usually on weekends; make arrangements by calling 839-5334.

HONOLULU BEACHES AND PARKS

The beaches and parks listed here are found in and around Honolulu's city limits. World-famous Waikiki has its own entire section (see p. 231). The good thing about having Waikiki so close is that it lures most bathers away from other city beaches, which makes them less congested. The following list contains most of Honolulu's beaches, ending at Fort DeRussy Beach Park, just a few hundred yards from where the string of Waikiki's beaches begin. Also see "Aiea", p. 266.

Sand Island State Recreation Area
As you enter this 140-acre park by way of the Sand Island Access Road, clearly marked off the Nimitz Highway, you pass through some ugly real estate—scrapyards, petrochemical tanks, and other such beauties. Don't get discouraged, keep going! Once you cross the metal bridge, a favorite fishing spot for local people, and then pass the entrance to the U.S. Coast Guard base, you enter the actual park, 14 acres landscaped with picnic and playground facilities. Follow the road into the park; pass two observation towers that have been built in the middle of a grassy field from where you get an impressive view of Honolulu, with Diamond Head making a remarkable counterpoint. The park is excellently maintained, with pavilions, cold-water showers, walkways, and restrooms. For day use only; the park closes at 6:30 p.m. The camping area is usually empty (state permit required, see p. 133). The sites are out in the open, but a few trees provide some shade.

Unfortunately, you're under one of the main glide paths for Honolulu International Airport. Many local people come to fish, and the surfing is good, but the beaches for snorkeling and swimming are fair at best. Some of the beach area is horrible, piled with broken stone, rubble, and pieces of coral. However, if you follow the road past the tower and park in the next lot, turn right and follow the shore up to a sandy beach. The currents and wave action aren't dangerous, but remember that this part of the harbor receives more than its share of pollutants. For delicious and inexpensive plate lunches, make sure to stop at Penny's just next door to Dirty Dan's Topless Go-Go Bar on your way down the access road (see pp. 207 and 212).

La Mariana Yacht Sailing Club
This small marina at 50 Sand Island Access Road is a love song in the middle of an industrialized area. The marina is Annette La Mariana Nahinua's labor of love that has remained true since 1955. You can read her fantastic story on the menu of the marina's **Hideaway Restaurant** (p. 208), which is the only real restaurant on Sand Island. In 1955 this area was forgotten, forsaken, and unkempt. Ms. Nahinua, against the forces of nature, and the even more unpredictable and devastating forces of bureaucracy, took this land and turned it into a yacht harbor. The main tools were indefatigable determination, God listening to her prayers, and a shovel and rake. It's one of the last enclaves of old Hawaii, a place to come for dinner, a drink, or just to look at the boats. The nighttime bartender, Mr. Lee, is friendly but stoic after decades of seeing and hearing it all. Annette, the founder, is now a little gray-haired woman, a motherly type in Birkenstocks, who lives right here above the Hideaway. In the daytime she wanders around spreading her magic while talking to old salts or new arrivals.

The marina is adjacent to an open waterway, which means that you don't have to pay for anchorage. It comes under the old "rights of sailors" to find a free port in which to berth. This unique setup has created an atmosphere in which a subculture of people have built subsistence shacks on the little islands that dot the bay. Some also live on old scows, shipshape yachts, or on very imaginative homemade crafts, afloat and semi-afloat on this tranquil bay. Many are disillusioned and disenfranchised Vietnam vets who have become misanthropes. You'll see the Stars and Stripes flying from their island hooches. Others are yachties who disdain being land-lubbers, while others are poor souls who have fallen through the social net. La Mariana is a unique statement of personal freedom in a city where unique statements are generally not tolerated.

Kakaako (Point Panic) Beach Park

This small facility was carved out of a piece of land donated by the University of Hawaii's Biomedical Research Center. Next to Kewalo Basin Harbor, follow Ahuii Street, off Ala Moana Boulevard. You'll come to some land-scaped grounds with a cold-water shower and a path leading to the bathing area. Kewalo Basin, developed in the '20s to hold Honolulu's tuna fleet, is home to many char-ter boats. If you're lucky, you may even spot a manta ray which are known to frequent these waters. This area is poor for swimming, known for sharks, but great for bodysurfing. Unfortunately, novices will quickly find out why it's called Point Panic. A long seawall with a sharp dropoff runs the entire length of the area. The wave action is perfect for riding, but all wash against the wall. Beginners stay out! The best reason to come here is for the magnificent and unobstructed view of the Waikiki skyline and Diamond Head.

Ala Moana Park

Ala Moana ("Path to the Sea") Beach Park is by far Honolulu's best. Most visitors congre-gate just around the bend at Waikiki, but residents head for Ala Moana, the place to soak up the local color. During the week, this beautifully curving white-sand beach has plenty of elbow room. Weekends bring fami-lies that come for every water sport Oahu offers. The swimming is great, with manage-able wave action, plenty of lifeguards, and even good snorkeling along the reef. Board riders have their favorite spots, and bodysurf-ing is excellent. The huge area has a number of restrooms, food concessions, tennis courts, softball fields, a bowling green, and parking for 500 cars. Many Oahu outrigger canoe clubs practice in this area, especially in the evening; it's great to come and watch

them glide along. A huge banyan grove pro-vides shade and strolling if you don't fancy the beach, or you can bring a kite to play aloft with the trade winds. Ala Moana Park stretches along Ala Moana Avenue, between the Ala Wai and Kewalo Basin boat harbors. It's across from the Ala Moana Shopping Center, so you can rush right over if your credit cards start melting from the sun.

Aina Moana ("Land from the Sea") **Rec-reation Area** used to be called Magic Island because it was reclaimed land. It is actually the point of land stretching out from the eastern edge of Ala Moana, and although it has a different name, appears to be part of Ala Moana. All the beach activities are great here, too.

Kahanamoku Beach

The stretch of sand in front of the Hilton Hawaiian Village is named after Hawaii's most famous waterman, Duke Kahanamoku. The man-made beach and lagoon were com-pleted in 1956. A system of pumps pushes water into the lagoon to keep it fresh. The swimming is great, and plenty of concessions offer surfboards, beach equipment, and cata-maran cruises.

Fort DeRussy Beach

This is the last beach before reaching the Waikiki beaches proper. You pass through right-of-way of Fort DeRussy military area where you'll find restrooms, picnic facilities, volleyball courts, and food and beverage con-cessions. Lifeguard service is provided by military personnel—no duty is too rough for our fighting men and women! A controversy has raged for years between the military and developers who covet this valuable piece of land. The government has owned it since the turn of the century, and has developed what once was wasteland into the last stretch of non-cement, non-high-rise piece of real estate left along Waikiki. Since the public has access to the beach, and since Congress voted a few years back that the lands cannot be sold, it'll remain under the jurisdiction of the military. **Battery Randolph,** on the mili-tary grounds, is open to the public as a mili-tary museum.

ACCOMMODATIONS

The vast majority of Oahu's hotels are strung along the boulevards of Waikiki. Most are neatly clustered, bounded by the Ala Wai Canal, and run eastward to Diamond Head. These hotels will be discussed in the Waikiki section. The remainder of greater Honolulu has few hotels, but what do exist are some of Oahu's cheapest. Most are clean, no-frills establishments, with a few others at the airport, or just off the beaten track.

Oahu's YM/WCAs And YH

Oahu has a number of YM/WCAs from which to choose, and the only official youth hostel in the state. They vary as far as private room and bath are concerned, facilities offered, and prices. Expect to pay about $30 s with a shared bath, and about $32.50 d with a private bath.

The **YMCA Central Branch** (men only) at 401 Atkinson Dr., Honolulu, 96814, tel 941-3344, is the most centrally located and closest to Waikiki. You can call ahead, but there are no reservations, no curfew, no visitors after 10 p.m.; it has an outside pool, singles, doubles, and private baths. This Y is located just across from the eastern end of Ala Moana Park, only a 10-minute walk to Waikiki.

YMCA Nuuanu (men only), 1441 Pali Hwy., Honolulu 96813, tel. 536-3556, just near the intersection of S. Vineyard Blvd., is a few minutes' walk from downtown Honolulu. You'll find a modern, sterile facility with a pool, shared and single rooms, and private or communal showers; reservations accepted.

Armed Services YMCA, open to military personnel and civilians, both men and women, at 250 S. Hotel St., Honolulu, tel. 524-5600. No reservations, but a pool, single and double rooms, plenty of sporting facilities, and child care!

YMCA Atherton Branch, 1810 University Ave., Honolulu, tel. 946-0253. Near U of Hawaii, men and women students are given preferential treatment. Dormitory style, no recreational facilities. Cheapest in town, but there's a three-night minimum, and a one-time membership fee.

YWCA Fernhurst, 1566 Wilder Ave., Honolulu 96822, tel. 941-2231, just off Manoa Rd., across from the historical Punahou School. Singles and doubles with shared bath, women only. Weekly rates. Breakfast and dinner included (except Sunday) for low price. Doors closed at 11 p.m., but the night guard will admit later arrivals. Limited reservations depending on availability with deposit. Women can stay for up to one year, and many women from around the world add an international flavor.

The only official American Youth Hostel in Hawaii (more listed under Waikiki) is the **Honolulu International Youth Hostel,** 2323 A Seaview Ave., Honolulu, HI 96822, tel. 946-0591, located near the University of Hawaii. This YH is always busy, but will take reservations. AYH members with identity cards are given priority, but nonmembers are accepted on a space-available day-by-day basis. For information and reservations write to the manager, and include SASE and a night's lodging deposit. For information and membership cards write American Youth Hostels, 1332 I St., N.W., Suite 895, Washington, D.C. 20005.

Elderhostel, 100 Bolyston St., Suite 200, Boston, MA 02116, offers noncredit courses at Hawaii Loa College, Oahu. For people 60 years and older. Fees begin at $175 and include course, room, and board.

University Of Hawaii

Two six-week summer sessions beginning late May and in early July are offered to bona fide students of accredited universities at the University of Hawaii at Manoa, Oahu. Reasonable rates in residence halls (mandatory meals) and in apartments on campus; special courses with emphasis on Polynesian and Asian culture and languages, including China and Japan. Unbeatably priced tours and outings to points throughout the islands for students and the general public at the Summer Session Activities Office. For information, catalog, and enrollment, write Summer Session Office, University of Hawaii, 2500 Dole St.,

Manoa Valley Inn

alog, and enrollment, write Summer Session Office, University of Hawaii, 2500 Dole St., Krauss Hall 101, Honolulu, HI 96822, tel. 944-1014 or 949-0771.

Moderate/Expensive Hotels

The **Kobayashi Hotel** at 250 N. Beretania St., Honolulu, HI 96817, tel. 536-2377, is in Chinatown, and its an old standby as an inexpensive but clean hotel. It's away from all the Waikiki action, and the spartan, linoleumed rooms rent for under $37. Plenty of travelers pass through here, and the hotel's restaurant serves authentic Japanese food at moderate prices.

The **Nakamura Hotel** is a little bit more *uptown* both price- and location-wise. It's at 1140 S. King St., Honolulu, HI 96814, tel. 537-1951. The rooms are well-appointed, carpeted, and have large bathrooms. Some a/c rooms face busy King Street; the *mauka* side rooms are quieter, with plenty of breezes to keep you cool. Often you can find a room at this meticulously clean hotel when others are booked out, only because it's out of the mainstream.

The **Pagoda Hotel,** 1525 Rycroft St., Honolulu, HI 96814, tel. (800) 367-6060, on Oahu 941-6611, behind Ala Moana Park between Kapiolani Blvd. and S. King Street. Because this hotel is away from the "action," you get very good value for your money. Rooms with kitchenettes start at about $55, with two-bedroom suites at around $90. All rooms have TV, a/c, parking, swimming pool, and well-known Pagoda Restaurant.

Another in the same category is the **Hawaii Dynasty Hotel,** at 1830 Ala Moana Blvd., tel. 955-1111. Rooms here are clean, decent, away from the action, and reasonably priced.

The **Ala Moana Americana,** 410 Atkinson Dr., Honolulu, HI 96814, tel. (800) 228-3278, on Oahu 955-4811, is another hotel where you're just off the Waikiki strip. It's located just behind Ala Moana Park between Ala Moana and Kapiolani boulevards, with a walking ramp connecting it directly with the Ala Moana Shopping Center. Rooms start at $90 and go up to around $250 for a two-bedroom suite (six people). There's a/c, TV, swimming pools, an all-night coffee shop, and the Summit Supper Club on the top of this 36-story hotel.

Manoa Valley Inn

The Manoa Valley Inn, at 2001 Vancouver Dr. Honolulu, HI 96822, tel. 947-6019, (800) 634-5115 offers a magnificent opportunity to lodge in turn-of-the-century elegance. Formerly the John Guild Inn, this bed and breakfast was completely restored in 1982 and is listed on the National Register of Historic Places. Innkeeper Marianne Schultz offers a double bed with a shared bath, including continental breakfast, at a very reasonable $80, or a private suite for $145.

After registering in the main foyer, turn right into what was the dining room. Here is a handcrafted pool table with a thick slate botcontinental breakfasts that are prepared in the kitchen just behind. In the morning, the aroma of fresh-brewed coffee wafts up the stairs. The breakfast selections are bran muffins, croissants, little sticky buns, fresh fruit of the season, and hand-squeezed juices. The daily and Sunday newspapers lie around. Pick one and sink into the billowy cushions of a wicker chair on the lava-rock-colonnaded back porch. Both inside and out, you'll find coffee tables surrounded by overstuffed chairs and, nearby, decanters of port and sherry and dishes filled with chocolates. Every evening, wine and gourmet cheese, along with crackers and fresh fruits, are presented. All complimentary to guests.

The original structure was a very modest, two-story, box-like home. It was situated on seven acres, but the demand for land by growing Honolulu has whittled it down to the present half acre or so. The grounds are well-kept, but small, so don't expect sweeping grand lawns. The original owner was Milton Moore, an Iowa lumberman. He sold it to John Guild in 1919, a secretary to Alexander and Baldwin, who basically created the structure that you see today. The home went through several owners and even did a stint as a fraternity house. It ended up as low-priced apartment units until it was rescued and refurbished by Rick Ralston, the owner of Crazy Shirts and one of Hawaii's successful self-made men, a patron of arts and antiques. He outfitted the house from his warehouse of antiques with furnishings not original to the house, but true to the period. The original structure was built in 1915. In 1919 the third floor was added, along with the back porch. A cottage with a white on white theme offers seclusion and privacy away from the main house.

Climb the wide wooden staircase. Upstairs, each room has a slightly different theme. There's the John Guild Suite, the only suite in the house with a sitting room. Inside recline on a velvet couch while perusing old books on Hawaiian commerce, or even flipping through the 1940 phone book. In the bedroom is a king-size bed, with a carved headboard, matching side tables, and two stained-glass lamps. Enter the bathroom to find a separate bathtub and shower, and everything in marble. This is a real bathtub, designed for you to immerse yourself in a full recling position.

The rooms are air-conditioned in the same way as the day they were built, beautiful breezes through open windows. That's what Manoa Valley is known for.

FOOD

The restaurants mentioned below are outside of the Waikiki area, although many are close, even within walking distance. Others are located near Ala Moana, Chinatown (see p. 220), downtown, and the less touristed areas of greater Honolulu. Some are first-class restaurants; others, among the best, are just roadside stands where you can get a satisfying plate lunch. The restaurants are listed according to price range and location, with differing cuisines mixed in each range. Besides the sun and surf, it's the amazing arrays of food found on Oahu that makes the island extraordinary.

SHOPPING CENTER DINING

Ala Moana Shopping Center

The following are all located at the Ala Moana Shopping Center, which has recently undergone a full face lift. Most are located in the **Makai Food Court,** a huge central area where you can inexpensively dine on dishes from San Francisco to Tokyo. Counter-style restaurants serve island favorites, reflecting the multiethnic culinary traditions from around the Pacific. You take your dish to a nearby communal dining area, which is great for people-watching. The **China House** is open daily for lunch and dinner, tel. 949-6622. This enormous dining hall offers the usual selection of Chinese dishes, but is famous for its dim sum (served 11 a.m. to 2 p.m.); you pick and choose bite-sized morsels from carts.

La Cocina, open daily for lunch and dinner, tel. 949-9233, serves Mexican food for under $5 with complimentary chips and salsa. Dining facilities and takeout service. Less spicy offerings to suit American tastes.

Michel's Baguette, first floor ocean side. Open weekdays from 7 a.m.-9 p.m., Sat. till 5:30 p.m., Sun. 8 a.m.-5 p.m., tel. 946-6888. They specialize in French bread, pastries, and croissants baked on the premises. A good selection of tasty soups, salads, and sandwiches. A change from the ordinary burger.

Patti's Chinese Kitchen, first floor facing the sea, tel. 946-5002, has all the ambience

you'd expect from a cafeteria-style Chinese fast-food joint, plus lines about a block long. But don't let either discourage you. The lines move incredibly quickly, and you won't get gourmet food, but it's tasty, plentiful, and cheap. The "Princess-Queen Special" is steamed rice, fried rice or noodles, a chow mein plus, two entrees like sweet and sour pork, or a chicken dish—for around $3. The Queen is the same, but add an entree—under $4. You can even have four entrees, which fills two large paper plates. The princesses who eat this much food aren't tiny-waisted damsels waiting for a rescuing prince—they can flatten anyone who hassles them on their own.

The **Ward Warehouse**

This shopping center (see p. 214) has a range of restaurants, from practical to semi-chic, all reasonably priced. **Beni Kai** is a Japanese restaurant that's beautifully appointed with a rock garden at the entranceway that continues to the inside. It's bright and airy, neo-Japanese traditional. Prices are reasonable, with set menu dishes like unagi kabayaki for $12.95, or miso-fried fish at $9.25. They have a wide selection of don buri, yakitori, and tempura for around $6. Open Mon.-Sat. 11 a.m.-2 p.m. for lunch, and for dinner from 5 p.m.

Nearby is the opposite side of the coin. A small lunch stand sells *saimin* and *yakitori* for under $4. Mostly you stand and eat, but there are a few tables in the common mall area. Also, for fast foods you'll find **Cookie Kitchen** and **Dave's Ice Cream,** supposedly the favorite of local people who compare it with the much-touted Lappert's. It's locally made and supposedly the best. In the mall you'll find **Harpo's,** your basic pizza parlor, and **The Old Spaghetti Factory,** serving a wide variety of pasta not quite like Mama makes, but passable, and at a reasonable price.

For those into health foods try **Aloha Health Food,** primarily a vitamin and mineral store, but they do have some prepared food and drinks in a cooler. Right across is **Coffee Works,** specializing in gourmet coffee and tea. They have a bakery and sandwiches for under $5, croissants $1.50. So take your vitamins on one side and get jazzed on the other. The **Farmer's Market** is not in the Ward Warehouse but just across the street, at 1020 Auahi, where you can pick up fresh produce and flowers.

Orson's Restaurant is a seafood house on the second floor. It's actually quite elegant considering the location, with a prize-winning sunset view of the small boat harbor at Kewalo Basin across the way. The inside, too, is richly appointed in woods and glass. Prices are $12-15 for fresh catch of the day complimented by an extensive wine list.

The **Chowder House** on the ground floor has fresh-grilled *ahi* for $8.25, snow crab salad ($5.95), Manhattan clam chowder ($2.25), clams and oysters on the half shell ($6), bay shrimp cocktail ($2.95), deep-fried shrimp ($5.85), and daily specials from $5-8.

The Ward Center

This upscale shopping center is directly across the street from Ala Moana Park, and next door to the Ward Warehouse. The following are some of its restaurants and eateries, where you can enjoy not only class, but quality as well.

R. Fields Wine Co. is not really a restaurant, but a purveyor of exquisite food, fine wines, crackers, cookies, cheeses, imported pastas, and caviar. Most of the wines are top shelf from California like King Cellars, Dominus, Opus I, Sutter Home (a fluke, leftover from their catering business), and Robert Mondavi, with a nice vertical of their reserve wines going back to 1968. Also older French wines, as well as German wines.

Chocoholics would rather visit the **Honolulu Chocolate Company** than go to heaven. Mousse truffles, Grand Marnier truffles, chocolate eggs with pistachio or English walnut will all send you into eye-rolling rapture. If you enter, forget any resolve about watching your weight. You're a goner!

For a quick lunch try **Mocha Java** or **Crepe Fever**. Both are yuppie, upscale, counter-service-type places with a few tables. Both have a selection of sandwiches with an emphasis on vegetarian. Crepe Fever has stuffed whole croissants and grain sandwiches. If you want a designer lunch, that's the place to go. For a double-fisted American sandwich with all the trimmings try **Big Ed's**, a deli serving no-nonsense corned beef ($5.35), ham ($4.50), tuna salad ($4.25), or polish sausage. Takeout as well as sit down, actually a good seating area away from the bustle at the south end of the shopping center.

Al Fresco's on the corner in the Ward Center is an upscale semi-deli and restaurant whose tables spill out into a little courtyard. Stay simple with small pizza ($8.95), Caesar salad ($6.95), or move onto smoked chicken with mustard-herb-butter pasta for $13.95, pesto with smoked salmon ($13.95), boneless chicken breast ($14.95). Specials every day like grilled eggplant for $8.95 up to blackened *onaga* ($19.95). This Mediterranean-style cafe is gourmet; while perhaps not designed for an elegant evening, it will give you fine dining at reasonable prices for what you're getting.

The premier, or at least best-known, restaurant in the complex is **Keo's Thai Restaurant**, known for its mouthwatering Thai dishes and for its beautiful decor. The menu is extensive, with plenty of dishes for non-meateaters. Prices range but can be quite reasonable for Thai noodles, chicken, shrimp, or vegetarian ($6.95-8.95), house salad ($4.95), green papaya salad ($4.95), spring rolls (four for $4.95), and tofu, shrimp, or chicken satay for under $9. Try the delicious soups like spicy lemon grass or Thai ginger for $3.75 per serving. Entrees like the Evil Jungle Prince has quite a spicy reputation, or tame down with Asian watercress stir-fried with garlic, yellow bean sauce, and beef, shrimp, or vegies from $6.95-8.95. Keo's has another location, and operates the Mekong I and II, simpler and less expensive restaurants. Keo's is known for its beautiful flower displays of torch ginger, orchids, or plumeria on every table, and you may eat inside or outside.

The **Yum Yum Tree** is an affordable American standard restaurant that features pies and cakes from its bakery, along with homestyle fresh pasta. They have an extensive dining area, quite cheerful with dark wood floors, ferns, hanging greenery, and an open-beam ceiling. Breakfast is 7 a.m.-12 p.m., lunch 11 a.m.-5 p.m., dinner 5 p.m. to midnight, cocktails 7 a.m.-closing. Adjacent is **Compadres Mexican Restaurant,** tel. 523-1307, with the standards of burritos, tostadas, enchiladas, and tacos at reasonable prices. This small chain, with restaurants in California and Australia, also serves fresh fish à la Mexicana, and has one of the largest selections of tequilla in the Pacific

Don't let the name **Andrew's Restaurant,** tel. 523-8677, fool you. It's actually an excellent Italian and European restaurant on the second floor that makes its own pasta. Starters include *calamari fritto* ($6.25), wilted spinach salad ($3.50), and minestrone ($3); entrees are canneloni ($13.95), frogs legs ($16.75), a variety of veal dishes for under $20, and complete dinners with all the trimmings for $17-25.

Upstairs too is **Monterey Bay Canners Seafood Restaurant,** which features all-you-can-eat salad, soup, and hot potato bar for $5.95 from 11 a.m.-3 p.m. They have the cheapest prices in the shopping center. Specials are sautéed tiger prawns, an *ono* sandwich and chowder, Cajun combo, and lobster with black bean sauce, all under $8. From the broiler try Alaskan halibut ($13.95), New York steak and scampi ($19.95), traditional favorites like teriyaki chicken breast ($10.95), and some pastas. Then they have what they call the Fisherman's Choice luncheon entrees like *ono,* halibut, teri chicken, and catfish for $7.95. Entertainment nightly provided by "Carlos." Not bad at all for a small California chain, with other locations at the Outrigger in Waikiki and at Pearlridge Shopping Center.

Restaurant Row

This new-age complex at 500 Ala Moana (across from the Federal Building) points the way to "people-friendly" development in Honolulu's future. It houses shops and businesses, but mostly restaurants, all grouped together around a central courtyard and strolling area. Some restaurants are elegant and excellent, while others are passable and plain. But they are all in a congenial setting, and you can pick your palate and style preference as easily as you'd pick offerings at a buffet. Start at the central fountain area with its multicolored modernistic Lego-inspired tower. Every Saturday at 8 p.m. jazz is offered here overlooking the waterfront.

The **Sunset Grill,** tel. 521-4409, is on the corner. With wraparound windows, a long and open bar, and comfortable maple chairs, it lives up to its name. This is the place to come for a quiet evening drink in the downtown area. The food is prepared in full view on a *kiawe*-fired grill, wood-roasting oven, and Italian rotisserie. Choices include a variety of pasta, gourmet salads, calamari, fresh fish, oysters, chicken, veal, and lamb. Lunch is a wide variety of plump juicy sandwiches of turkey, sausage, beef, fish, or chicken. The chefs at the Sunset aren't afraid to blend East with West using basil, vinaigrette, Gorganzola, salsa, black bean sauce, strawberries, curry, oyster sauce, hollandaise, and tangy peppers in a wide variety of creations. Open daily from 11 a.m., weekends from 9 a.m., with a late-night menu on weekends.

The Rose City Diner will take you to a more innocent America when bobby-soxers sat on the hoods of their boyfriends' Chevys and listened to Buddy Holly on the AM radio. Fabian, Dion, Annette, or Ricky would feel right at home ordering burgers and BLTs from this classic menu, except that they would be better than ever. The roller-skating waitresses wear pink uniforms with white aprons and jaunty hats. The booths, like a cool Elvis outfit, are pink and black. The walls are covered with pictures of five decades of actors and musicians: Satchmo, Jimmy Stewart, Ronald Reagan, Bogart, Elvis, Marlon, Sophia, Rock, Marilyn, Jane, Hitchcock, Lucy, Dezi, Fred, and Ethel—they're all here. Booths have table-top jukeboxes. Try a slider burger with grilled onions, miniburgers served in a basket on French fries, bird on a bun (teriyaki chicken with swiss cheese and Thousand Island dressing), a chili sundae (chili, sour cream, onions, and cherry tomato on top), and wash it down with root beer floats, Cherry Cokes, and frothy malts. Open for breakfast, lunch, and dinner, 24 hours.

One of the simple restaurants is **Marie Callender's,** featuring heartland American pot pies, burgers, pasta, salads, and breakfast specials. The strawberry pie is delicious. Fast-food pawns will be happy to hear that **Burger King** is here too. **R. Fields Wine Co.**, for a do-it-yourself meal, is here with its gourmet wines, crackers, cheeses, escargot, caviar, and paté. **Cheers** is a small bar open 11 a.m.-2 a.m. Stuck in the corner, it tries to live up to its TV namesake by welcoming the local execs and secretaries in for an after-work drink and chat. It's comfortable, friendly, sports-oriented, and smoky.

In the middle of the complex is **The Row,** an outdoor bar with finger food. The **Honolulu Chocolate Co.** is next. Like a smug little devil, it tempts with chocolate truffles, mocha clusters, and fancy nut rolls. So sin! You're on vacation. The **Paradise Bakery Cafe** is a simple counter restaurant with pie, coffee, and donuts.

Trattoria Manzo, tel. 522-1711, owned by Tony Manzo, offers very special Italian dishes from the Abruzzi, a coastal and mountainous region along the Adriatic known for its hearty cooking. Choose an antipasto from Italian cold cuts to clams in red wine sauce for $7 and under. Assorted soups and salads range from $3 to $6 for *insalata calamari.* Select your favorite pasta, and then cover it with one of 20 delectable sauces, all under $10. Chicken, veal, and steak are grilled, simmered in wine sauce, or made into parmigiana, or choose a traditional lasagna, *gnocchi,* or a good old pizza. The interior is sharp with neon strips, and black marble tables and chairs.

The Black Orchid, tel. 521-3111, is the loveliest flower in the "Row." It's an art deco neo-speakeasy arranged perfectly for intimate romance or friendly socializing by interior decorator Meriam Braselle. Waiters are in tuxes, and all the ladies having dinner are offered a rose. Billie Holiday would look sleek in a sequined dress at the black marble bar. Bogie and his mobsters might survey the scene from one of the raised upholstered booths while Fred Astaire glides past reflecting glasswork to a table for two in the corner. The walls, covered in murals by Tamara, suggest this classic nightclubbing era. The restaurant is open for lunch and dinner daily and is extremely popular. Dinner reservations, especially on weekends, are a must. During the evening, both men and women would feel most comfortable in their sharpest evening wear. Jackets are suggested, but collared shirts and dressy slacks will do.

San Francisco-trained, chef Nick Sayada makes a cioppino as delicious as the best found on Fishermen's Wharf. Tom Selleck, one of the owners, loves the black and blue *ahi sashimi,* crisped in fiery Cajun spices. Starters include oyster, clam, and mussel bisque, or warm red cabbage salad with goat cheese. Entrees are rack of lamb in wine sauce, grilled swordfish, veal piccatta, fresh pasta, lobster and more lobster live from Maine, in cream, black bean sauce, or in fettuccini. Molokai sends venison, while the best island beef, fish, and poultry are grilled, sautéed, roasted, and baked in heady sauces and spices. An extensive wine list will add the right smoothness and zest to the gourmet meal. Desserts are handmade ice cream, exquisite flaky pastries, and pies like banana made with vanilla mousse.

The lunch and dinner menu change weekly, the lounge menu is available until 3 a.m., and the morning catch decides the fresh fish of the day. There is daily entertainment in the lounge, with dancing to live music until 4 a.m. Vocalist Azure McCall brightens the evening with a fine selection of jazz and swing numbers, while the contemporary sounds of Norm Compton with Armed and Dangerous keeps you dancing all night. If you are looking for *the* special setting for a night out, pick The Black Orchid.

INEXPENSIVE DINING AROUND TOWN

The following restaurants are located in and around the greater Honolulu area.

The **University of Hawaii,** Manoa Campus, hosts a number of restaurants, ranging from an inexpensive cafeteria to international cuisine at the East-West Center. Inexpensive to moderate restaurants include: **Manoa Gardens,** salad and snacks; **Campus Center Dining Room,** for full meals; and the **International Garden,** at Jefferson Hall in the East-West Center. For a great little lunch in a quiet setting in this area see the Waioli Tea Room p. 195.

At the Hawaii Maritime Center (see p. 183) you'll find **Coasters Restaurant** tucked away in the rear overlooking Honolulu Harbor. American standards with a full complement from the sandwich board. Not great food, but a great setting and away from the bustle of Honolulu. More interesting and definitely more local is **Pier Eight Restaurant** sandwiched under the huge elevated pier area just nearby the Maritime Center. Basic Chinese fast food to go, open daily 10 a.m.-5 p.m.

King's Bakery and Coffee Shop is a favorite of local people, at 1936 S. King St. and Pumehana, tel. 941-5211 (one of three locations). They're open 24 hours, and get very busy around 6 p.m. when they allow only groups of two or more to sit in the few booths; the rest eat at the counter. The menu is American/Hawaiian/Oriental. Full meals are around $5. Not great, but good and wholesome. The bakery has seven-grain bread, whole wheat, but mostly white fluffy stuff with tons of powdered sugar. However, they do offer "tofuti," a soft ice cream-like dessert made from healthful tofu. Their other locations are at the Kaimuki Shopping Center and Eaton Square. Across the street from King's Bakery are two inexpensive eateries, **McCully Chop Suey**, and **Yoshi's Sushi Yakiniku Restaurant.**

Down to Earth Natural Foods, open Mon. to Sat. 10 a.m.-8:30 p.m., Sun. 10 a.m.-6 p.m., at 2525 S. King St., tel. 947-7678, is a kind of "museum of health food stores" serving filling, nutritious healthfood dishes for very reasonable prices. Sandwiches, like a whopping avocado, tofu, and cheese, are under $5. Daily full-meal specials, like vegie stroganoff, eggplant parmigiana, and lasagna are around $4, including salad. There are plenty of items on the menu that will fill you up for under $3. Healthwise, you can't go wrong! Just up the street at 2471 S. King, across from the Star Garden Market, is the tiny **Saimin Bowl Restaurant.** Their name says it all, and you can have a huge steaming bowl of soup for a few dollars.

Kokua Co-op Natural Foods And Grocery Store, at the corner of S. Beretania and Isenberg, tel. 941-1921, is open to the public Mon-Sat. 9 a.m-8 p.m., Sun. 10 a.m.-7 p.m. Full-service store with organic and fresh produce, cheese, milk, juices, bulk foods, and breads.

Sekiya's Restaurant and Deli at 2746 Kaimuki Ave., tel. 732-1656, looks like a set from a 1940s tough-guy movie. The food is well prepared and the strictly local clientele will be amazed that you even know about the place.

Hale Vietnam, 1140 12th Ave. in Kaimuki, tel. 735-7581, is building an excellent reputation for authentic and savory dishes at very moderate prices. It gets the highest praise from local people, who choose it again and again for an inexpensive evening of delicious dining.

For a quick *bento* or sushi to go, try **Matsuri Sushi,** tel. 949-1111, at the corner of Kapiolani Blvd. and McCully. This quick-stop is perfect to pick up lunch on your way out of the Waikiki area.

Suehiro's at 1824 S. King, open daily for lunch and dinner, with takeout service, tel. 949-4584, gets the nod from local Japanese people. The menu here is authentic, the decor strictly Americana, and the food well prepared and moderately priced.

People's Cafe, 1300 Pali Hwy., is open Mon. to Sat. 10 a.m.-7:30 p.m., tel. 536-5789. Two going on three generations of the same Japanese family have been serving the full range of excellent and inexpensive Hawaiian food at this downhome restaurant. It's not fancy, but the food is good and the surroundings clean.

Coco's Coffee House at the corner of Kalakaua and Kapiolani is an American standard that's open all night. It's like a million others in the U.S. where you can order a hot roast beef sandwich for a few bucks, or just sip a coffee into the wee hours, staying out of the weather.

Another of the same is the **Hungry Lion,** tel. 536-0148, at 1613 Nuuanu Avenue. Open 24 hours, it serves everything from Oriental food to steaks. Many local people come here after a night out. Nothing special, but decent wholesome food on formica tables.

M's Coffee Tavern is a favorite with downtown office workers for great lunches, excellent coffee, and cocktails, at 124 Queen St., tel. 531-5739.

Walli Wok, tel. 943-1WOK, is a Chinese Restaurant that delivers, but you must spend a minimum of $8. They'll come to anywhere in the downtown and Waikiki area, and are perfect for condo dinners, or late-night snacks. The food is passable, and the servings ample.

Two inexpensive yet authentic restaurants sit next door to each other at 1679 Kapiolani Blvd., the **Kintoki Japanese Restaurant,** tel. 949-8835, and the **Sukyung Korean Restaurant.** This semi-seedy area has plenty of "girlie bars," but the food is good and authentic, with most items priced below $5.

Penny's Plate Lunches, on the Sand Island Access Rd. next to Dirty Dan's Topless Go-Go Joint, is one of the least expensive and most authentic Hawaiian plate-lunch stands you can find. The most expensive lunch is *lau lau,* pork and butterfish wrapped in a *ti* leaf, at around $3.50. You can also try baseball-sized *manapua* for around $.60. Penny's is out of the way, but definitely worth a stop.

You can't get much cheaper than free, and that's what the **International Society for Krishna Consciousness** offers every Sunday at 5:30 p.m. for its vegetarian smorgasbord. Their two-acre compound is just off the Pali Hwy. at 51 Coelho Way, tel. 595-4913. Of course there're a few chants for dessert. *Hare Krishna!*

Downtown Honolulu

In central Honolulu, mostly along Bishop Street's financial district, you'll find excellent and inexpensive restaurants that cater to the district's lunch crowd. (For restaurants in Chinatown, see p. 220.) One of the best is the **Croissanterie**, tel. 533-3443, at 222 Merchant St., open Mon.-Fri. 6 a.m.-9 p.m., Sat. to 4 p.m., closed Sunday. They serve up gourmet coffee and baskets of croissants stuffed with everything from tuna to strawberries and cream. There're salads, soups, Japanese food, and a pasta table with lasagna

and linguini with salad and garlic bread for under $5. The vintage building, which recently housed a bookstore, has brick walls, hardwood floors, and straight-backed cane chairs, all part of the decor in this sidewalk-style European cafe.

Another good place is **Al's Cafe** in the 1100 block of Bishop, open Mon.-Fri. 6 a.m.-4 p.m., Sat. 7 a.m.-1 p.m. Daily lunch specials like tuna or ham and cheese sandwiches and a medium soft drink or coffee for $3. Fast food in the area is **Jack in the Box, Taco Bell,** and **Pizza Hut** across the street from Woolworth's on Hotel Street. Heading down Hotel toward Chinatown you'll pass **Kathy's Kitchen,** at Bethel and Pauahi, where for around $4 you can get a plate lunch.

Art And The Sandwich

In Honolulu there are a few opportunities to feed your mind and soul along with satiating your appetite.

The **Garden Cafe,** tel. 531-8865, at the Honolulu Academy of Arts, 900 S. Beretania, is a classy place for lunch. Open 11:30 a.m.-1 p.m. Tues. to Fri., Thurs. supper at 6:30 p.m., it's set up in a garden of this excellent museum under a canopy. The cafe serves *different* soups like ice pumpkin soup with parsley, salads such as crunchy pea or orange, and sandwiches of ham with pepper jelly. Desserts run $1.50, with full luncheon at $6.50. The food is delicious, but be aware that the portions are not for the hungry, being designed primarily for patrons of the arts who seem to be wealthy matrons from the fashionable sections of Honolulu who are all watching their waistlines.

Don't let the Porsches, Mercedeses, and BMWs parked vanity plate to vanity plate in the parking lot discourage you from enjoying the **Contemporary Cafe,** tel. 523-3362, at the Contemporary Art Museum, 2411 Makiki Heights Drive. The small but superb menu is as inspired as the art in the museum, and the prices are astonishingly inexpensive. Dine inside or out, or perch on the porch. Appetizers are paté, mussels, escargot, or smoked salmon for under $4. Soups and salads are wilted spinach, chilled chicken breast, Greek salad, and shrimp Louie for $4-6. Sandwiches are a fine selection including smoked breast of turkey, or *ahi* Caesar for under $5. Desserts run from cheesecake to pecan pie, and beverages include homemade lemonade, and cappuccino. For a wonderful cultural outing combined with a memorable lunch, come to the Contemporary Cafe. It's just so . . . contemporary!

Fast Foods And Treats

Fast-food fanciers and fanatics have nothing to fear on Oahu. There're enough quick eateries to feed an army, mainly because there is an Army, plus a Navy and Marine Corps of young men and women on the island, not to mention the army of tourists. If you're after pizza, burgers, shakes, and fries, choose from 36 **McDonald's,** 13 or so **Jacks-in-the-Box,** 24 **Pizza Huts,** 10 or so **Zippy's,** six **Wendy's,** a few **Farrell's** and good old **Dairy Queens.**

For shave ice try the **Waiola Store** on the corner of Paani and Waiola. You can get it in Waikiki, but for the real stuff in its syrupy glory come here. Open Mon.-Sat. 7 a.m.-9 p.m., Sun. 8 a.m.-7:30 p.m. If you go to the Willows just around the corner (see p. 209) this is a great place to come for an authentic island treat.

MODERATE DINING AROUND TOWN

The following listings are for restaurants where two can dine for around $30. This does not include drinks.

Castagnola's Restaurant, tel. 988-2969, in the Manoa Marketplace, is quickly gaining a reputation as an authentic Italian restaurant offering dishes at a reasonable price. Away from the action, they're quiet and cozy. The decor is peasantish, with Chianti bottles, ropes of garlic, and checkered tablecloths. Two could dine on antipasti, soup, pasta, and a glass of wine for $25.

The Hideaway Restaurant at La Mariana Yacht Sailing Club, 50 Sand Island Access Rd. (see p. 197) is the only real restaurant on Sand Island. Henry, for many years a ship's cook, can cook everything well—maybe not great, but well. If a Chinese person came

here and wanted chop suey Henry could do it. If a guy wanted steak and potatoes, you got it! Pasta? Here it is! The Hideaway is an out-of-the-way place, local, and real Hawaiiana. This is where all the yachties come. They serve appetizers, even escargot, for $6.75, chicken wings ($5.25), sautéed mushroom buttons ($5.25). From the broiler, rib-eye steak is $11.50. The most expensive is an eight-ounce filet mignon ($14.95). From the sea, deep-fried scallops ($10.50), shrimp scampi served over linguini ($10.95), *ahi* fresh fillet or steak cut for $10.95. That's the cheapest fresh *ahi* around.

Henry is also known for his onion rings. They're not on the menu; you have to know about them. Now you know. The Sunday brunch is excellent, but basic—eggs, potatoes, a slab of ham, rice, and toast for $3.50. Hard to beat. Inside hang Japanese glass floats that at night are diffused with different colors, providing mood lighting for the cozy black booths and wooden tables with high-backed wicker chairs.

Shiruhachi at 1901 Kapiolani Blvd., tel. 947-4680, is a completely authentic Japanese sushi bar operated by Hiroshi Suzuki. As a matter of fact, until recently 90 percent of the clientele were Japanese, either visiting businessmen or locals in the know, and the menu was only in Japanese. However, everyone is more than welcome. With a beer, you get free *otsumami* (nibbles), with a wide selection of sushi and other finger foods like *yakitori* at about $2 for two skewers. A separate section of the restaurant turns into a cocktail lounge, somewhat like an *akachochin,* a neighborhood Japanese bar where people go to relax. There's taped music and a dance floor. If you're into authentic Japanese, this is a great one.

Auntie Pasto's at 1099 S. Beretania and the corner of Pensacola, tel. 523-8855, is open daily for lunch, dinner, and late nights. The vibe is upbeat pizza parlor, where you can even bring your own wine. Most of the Italian menu is around $6; the specialty is a fish stew loaded with morsels for about $12. Their large salad with garlic bread is cheap, and enough for two. No reservations necessary, quiet, comfortable.

Willows is at 901 Hausten, just behind Kapiolani Blvd. on the north side of the Ala Wai Canal, tel. 946-4808. Like a tiny tropical oasis surrounded by the cement of the city, there's a willow-shaped pool bubbling with uncountable carp. Once inside, the garden opens up, and there are even strolling musicians singing Hawaiian standards. Local people love it, a definite tip-off. The food is Hawaiian/Oriental/American. And the dessert pies are great! It's best known for its Sunday brunch from 10 a.m.-1 p.m., when the huge restaurant is filled with local families. The few minutes' drive from Waikiki keeps most tourists away.

For lunch start with Johnny B's Mushrooms (fresh whole mushrooms seasoned with a special butter) for $4, teriyaki meat sticks ($5), or Puna's Favorite Salad of the Sea (whole gulf shrimp, crab meat, gently poached scallops nestled in a bed of lettuce topped with a fruit garnish) for $11.50. Enter along a covered walkway. The decor is upgraded South Seas with natural wood beams. Basically you're dining outside. The tables are set with pink tablecloths, and the chairs are bent bamboo with red fluffy pillows, many under gay umbrellas. The grounds are an integral part of the decor. All around are exotic plants, some hanging. In the main dining room the ceiling is solid wood, open-beamed with a skylight and ceiling fans. The post and beams are gnarled twisted logs with their natural bark intact. One wall is solid lava, and the effect is very pleasing. This open, breezy, restaurant is basic Hawaiian, at a good price.

TGI Fridays is a raucous singles' bar known for some delectable morsels such as stuffed potatoes, quiches, and the like. It's across the street from the Blaisdel Center at 950 Ward Ave., open daily 11 a.m.-2 p.m., tel. 523-5841. Plenty of swingers and college students keep the joint jumpin'.

Wo Fat's at 115 N. Hotel St., tel. 533-6393, has had a little experience satisfying customers—the oldest eatery in Chinatown, it's been at the same location for over 80 years, and open for business for 100! Besides serving delicious food from a menu with hundreds of Cantonese dishes, the building itself is monumentally ornate. You're entertained just checking out the decor of lanterns, dragons, gilt work, and screens. Most dishes are reasonably priced and start at around $5. This restaurant is highly respected by the people of Chinatown and is part of the Chinatown Tour offered by the Chamber of Commerce. (See p. 113.)

EXPENSIVE DINING AROUND TOWN

Sometimes only the best will do, and Honolulu can match any city for its fine restaurants. More fine dining is found in Waikiki, see p. 249.

Won Kee Seafood Restaurant, 100 N. Beretania, is a splurge joint where you get delicious seafood. Free parking on Mauna Kea Street. This is the place for Honolulu's in-the-know crowd. Tasteful and elegant surroundings.

Fishermen's Wharf Restaurant, Ala Moana Blvd. at Kewalo Basin, tel. 538-3808, serves lunch and dinner, reservations necessary. Tough parking, but free with validation in local lots. The restaurant has two sections: upstairs is the **Captain's Bridge** and downstairs is the **Seafood Grotto.** The greatest thing about this restaurant is its location, right on Fishermen's Wharf with plenty of bobbing boats at anchor and local color just outside the windows. The waitresses wear cutesie-pie sailor suits, the waiters striped jerseys. The service is adequate but not special, mostly due to the number of people served—always packed! For a renowned fish restaurant too many offerings are plain old deep-fried. For example, the shrimp stuffed with cheese and crab meat is merely breaded and popped in the fryer. Good, but not special. The cheapest item on the menu is spaghetti, not linguini, with canned clam sauce. Two can dine for around $30, to say you've been there, but you'll hardly hurry back.

The **Chart House** at 1765 Ala Moana Blvd. near Ala Wai Yacht Harbor, is open daily 4 p.m. (Sun. 5 p.m.) till 2 a.m., tel. 941-6660. They offer a happy hour until 7 p.m., *pu pu* until midnight, and nightly entertainment. Shellfish specialities start at $15, with chicken and beef dishes a few dollars cheaper.

India House, 2632 S. King St., is open daily for lunch and dinner, tel. 955-7552. Extraordinary Indian dishes prepared by chef Ram Arora. A wide selection of curries, vegetarian dishes, special *naan* bread, kabobs, and fish *tikka*. Specialty desserts of homemade ice cream and toppings.

Windows of Hawaii sits atop the Ala Moana Bldg. at 1441 Kapiolana Blvd., serving American and continental. Great views from this revolving restaurant. Lunch (sandwiches) for under $8, and complete dinners from $15. Extremely popular for sunset. Reservations, tel. 941-9138. Champagne brunch Sat. and Sun. 10 a.m.-2 p.m

Keo's Thai Restaurant, 625 Kapahulu, open nightly from 5:30-11 p.m., tel. 737-8240, has become an institution. It serves great Thai food at expensive prices. They pride themselves on the freshest ingredients, spices tuned up or down to suit the customer, and Keo's recipes taught to each chef personally. There's always a line, with a few benches in the parking lot for waiting customers, but no reservations are taken. The eight-page menu offers most of Thailand's delectables, and vegetarians are also catered to. You can save money and still have the same quality food at **Mekong II,** 1726 S. King, lunch and dinner, tel. 941-6184. Owned by Keo's, it's not as fancy.

Nuuanu Onsen, 87 Laimi Rd. (right off the Pali Hwy., just before Queen Emma's Summer Palace), tel. 538-9184, is one of Honolulu's best-kept secrets. This authentic Japanese teahouse serves a gourmet fixed menu. You leave your cares along with your shoes at the entrance, and are escorted by a kimono-clad waitress to your lacquered table, where you sit on *tatami* mats and enjoy the serenity of the garden framed by the *shoji* screens. The hostess plays geisha-like teahouse games if you like. Here, you enjoy the experience as much as the meal.

LUAUS

To have fun at a luau you have to get into the swing of things. Basically a huge banquet, you eat and drink until you're contentedly uncomfortable, somewhat like Thanksgiving on the beach. Entertainment is provided by local performers in what is invariably called a "Polynesian Revue." This includes the tourist's hula, the fast version with swaying hips and dramatic lighting, a few wandering troubadors singing Hawaiian standards, and someone swinging swords or flaming torches. All the Hawaiian standards like *poi, haupia, lomi* salmon, *lau lau,* and *kalua* pig are usually served. If these don't suit your appetite, various Oriental dishes, plus chicken, fish, and roast beef do. If you leave a luau hungry, it's your own fault!

Luaus range in price from $40-50 per person. The price oftentimes includes admission to the theme parks at which many are now presented. The least expensive, most authentic, and best luaus are often put on by local churches or community groups. They are not held on a regular basis, so make sure to peruse the free tourist literature where they advertise. The following luaus are institutions and have been operating for years. If you ask a local person "Which is the best?" you won't get two to agree. It's literally a matter of taste.

The **Royal Hawaiian Luau** on the Ocean Lawn of the Royal Hawaiian Hotel, every Mon. from 6-9 p.m. tel. 923-7311, *is* the classic Hawaiian feast, complete with authentic foods, entertainment, and richly spiced with *aloha*. Authenticity is added by lawn seating on traditional *lau hala* mats (table seating too) while the sun sets on Waikiki Beach and the stars dance over Diamond Head. Entertainment is an hour-long Polynesian extravaganza featuring Tahitian and traditional hula, a Samoan fire dance, bold rhythmic drumming, and singing by Sam Bernard. The buffet is a lavish feast of *kalua* pig, salmon, *mahi mahi,* steak, and sides of *poi, haupia,* and a sinful but scrumptious table of desserts like coconut cake, *lilikoi* chiffon pie, banana bread, and guava chiffon pie. You are presented with a fresh flower lei and welcomed at the open bar for mai tais and other tropical drinks. $49.50 adults, $39.50 children under 12.

Chuck Machado's is open every Tues., Fri., and Sun. at 7 p.m., tel. 836-0249, at the Waikiki Outrigger Hotel. Great show that you can enjoy just by strolling on the nearby beach. **Paradise Park Luau,** Mon., Wed., and Thurs., a full day beginning at 2 p.m. with free transportation and admission to the park, tel. 944-8833.

Germaine's Luau, often claimed by local people to be *the* best, is held at Ewa Beach,

tel. 946-3111. **Paradise Cove Luau** boasts a private beach with a shuttle bus departing Waikiki at 4 p.m. and returning by 10 p.m., tel. 945-3571. The **Great Hawaiian Luau** is held at Makapuu Point, tel. 926-8843.

ENTERTAINMENT

Dancing, Disco, And Lounge Acts

Anna Bannana's, at 2440 S. Beretania, tel. 946-5190, is the "top banana" for letting your hair down and boogieing the night away. It's out by the university just across from Star Market. This dance joint has a laid-back atmosphere, reasonable beer prices, $3 cover which goes to the band, no dress code, and a friendly crowd. Dancing is upstairs, light dining downstairs, and a backyard to cool off between sets. Great place, great fun!

The **Club Jubilee,** at 1007 Dillingham Blvd., tel. 845-1568 sways with Hawaiian music every night but Monday. Listen to hula tunes on traditional and quickly fading slack key guitar. People from the audience, when moved by the music, will take to the dance floor or the stage for an impromptu performance. What they lack in polish they make up for in sincerity. Everybody's welcome. Beer around $2.50, with plenty of *pu pu,* like watercress with mayonnaise and soy sauce, along with regular island munchies.

University of Hawaii students trumpet the mating call at **Moose McGillycuddy's,** at 1035 University Ave., tel. 944-5525, especially every Thursday, which is Ladies Night. Standard but good food priced for the student pocketbook, and plenty of dancing.

The **Black Orchid,** at Restaurant Row, the hottest new nightclub/ restaurant in Honolulu (see p. 205), has live music nightly, fantastic food, and a classic "neo-Bogart" atmosphere.

Studebaker's at Restaurant Row (see p. 204) is a neon-lit, chrome deco bar with two red Studebakers in the window. Daytime it's a restaurant, but in the evening it's a disco and bar. From 4-7 p.m. enjoy the best deal with a one-drink minimum, and $1.50 buffet which can easily be a light dinner. The bartenders and cocktail waitresses climb on

stage every hour and jitterbug for the audience, demonsatrating classic "American Bandstand" routines and steps. One wall of glass bricks diffuses the light, and from the outside makes all the dancers look as if they're in a fishbowl. *Uptown* dress code, male and female peacocks welcome. No one under 23 admitted.

Rumors, in the Ala Moana American Hotel, 410 Atkinson St., tel. 955-4811, is an established disco that cranks up around 9 p.m. and features the newest in dance and rock videos. Also, the restaurant atop the building, Windows of Hawaii, supplements your dinner with an evening lounge act.

Tony Roma's, 98-150 Kaonohi St. in the Westridge Mall, Aiea Town, tel. 487-9911, offers a lounge act Sun. to Fri., and daily happy hour from 4:30-8:30 p.m. with a special *pu pu* menu.

TGI Fridays, 950 Ward Ave., tel. 523-5841, is a lively night spot. Good food, large portions, reasonable prices, and music. **Pecos River Cafe,** at 99-016 Kamehameha Hwy., tel. 487-7980, has country music, featuring Nick Masters and the Mustangs.

Freebies

At **Centerstage,** Ala Moana Center, various shows are presented—mostly music (rock, gospel, jazz, Hawaiian) and hula. Performances usually start at noon. The **Young People's Hula Show,** every Sun. at 9:30 a.m., is fast becoming an institution. Here, hula is being kept alive, with many first-time performers interpreting the ancient movements that they study in their *halau.*

The **Royal Hawaiian Band,** founded over 100 years ago, performs Fri. at noon on the Iolani Palace Bandstand.

Hilo Hattie, 700 Nimitz Highway, the largwith hotel pickup. Up to 80,000 garments are on display in the showroom. It's hard to resist spending: prices and craftsmanship are good, and designs are the most contemporary. Open daily 8:30 a.m.-5 p.m., tel. 537-2926.

The giant pineapple water tower off Iwilei Road guides you to the **Dole Pineapple Factory,** which has been completely refurbished into a mini-mall with distinctive Hawaiian shops and a cafeteria. Here, millions of Hawaii's fruit are canned, juiced, and sliced for shipment around the world. Free samples are available. Least activity is during the winter months, but something fascinating is always going on. In the summertime, at the height of the harvest, this factory can process over three million cans of fruit per day! No reservations needed for small groups. Contact the Dole Company at 650 Iwilei Rd., tel. 536-3411, open 9 a.m. to 3 p.m., small admission.

Girlie Bars And Strip Joints

You'll have no excuse if your maiden Aunt Matilda or local chapter of Friendly Feminists ever catches you going into one of these joints, sonny boy! There's not even a hint of a redeeming social value here, and the only reason they're listed is to let you know where *not to go* if you're offended by raunchy sex shows. Many of these "lounges," as they're called, are strung along the 1600 and 1700 blocks of Kapiolani Blvd., and in the little alleys running off it. Mostly, tough-looking Oriental men own or operate them, and they open and shut quicker than a streetwalker's heart. Inside are two types of women: the dancers and the "lap sitters," and there's definitely a pecking order in these henhouses. (For a full description, see p. 163.) Most patrons are local men or GI types, with only a smattering of tourists. Personal safety is

usually not a problem, but a fool and his money are soon parted in these bars.

Here are some *without* the bad reputations that frequently go along with this type of clip joint. **Misty II Lounge,** operated by a Vietnamese guy named Dean, has been there five years, an eternity in this business; Dean immediately fires any girl with bad vibes. This club is at 1661 Kapiolani Blvd., tel. 944-1745. Just behind it in the little alleyway are the **Orchid, Musume,** and **Winners Club**—all about the same. Two clubs considered to be good ones by their patrons are **Butterfly Lounge,** 903 Keamoku, tel. 947-3012, and the **Stop Lite Lounge,** at 1718 Kapiolani, tel. 941-5838.

Chinatown's **Hotel Street** (see p. 219) has hookers, both male and female, walking the heels off their shoes. They cruise during the day, but the area really comes alive at night. Mostly, these people are down-and-outers who can't make it against the stiff competition along the main areas of Waikiki. The clientele is usually servicemen and hard-core locals. A few clubs in this area offer strippers. Always be prepared for fights and bad vibes in any of these joints. A few that tourists have entered and survived include the **Zig Zag, My Way,** and **Hubba Hubba Club** (see p. 219.)

Dirty Dan's, 205 Sand Island Access Rd., tel. 841-9063, is an old-fashioned topless go-go bar, the same as the famous one in San Diego. It's frequented mostly by GIs and can get pretty rowdy, especially late on weekends. The place is clean and prides itself on giving you a fair shake. It's not at all like the grab joints listed above. The women here are young and beautiful and *not* allowed to fraternize with the clientele. You can look, but you *cannot* touch. This helps to keep away the sleaze element. Draft and bottled beer are reasonably priced.

SHOPPING

If you don't watch the time, you'll spend half your vacation moving from one fascinating store to the next. Luckily, in greater Honolulu the majority of shopping is clustered in malls, with specialty shops scattered around the city, especially in the nooks and crannies of Chinatown (see p. 217). For a general overview of what the island has for sale, along with listings for bookstores, flea markets, sundries, and art shops, see p. 83. For food shopping see p. 130.

Ala Moana Shopping Center

This is the largest shopping center in the state, and if you want to get all of your souvenir hunting and special shopping done in one shot, this is the place. It's on Ala Moana Blvd., just across from the Ala Moana Beach Park, open weekdays from 9:30 a.m.-9 p.m., Sat. 9:30 a.m.-5:30 p.m., Sun. 10 a.m.-5 p.m., tel. 946-2811. Recently, the Ala Moana Shopping Center has taken off its comfortable Hawaiian shirt and shorts and donned designer fashions by Christian Dior and Charles Jordan. Local people are irritated, and they have a point, to a point. The center has plenty of downhome shopping left, but it now caters as much to the "penthouse" as it does to the "one room efficiency." It used to be where the *people* shopped, but now portions are being aimed at the affluent tourist, especially the affluent Japanese tourists who flaunt designer labels like politicians flaunt pretty secretaries. If anything, the shopping has gotten better, but you'll have to look around a bit more for bargains.

Plenty of competition keeps prices down, with more than enough of an array to suit any taste and budget. About 100 stores include all of Hawaii's major department stores like **Sears, Penney's,** and **Liberty House.** Utilitarian shops like shoe makers, eateries, banks, and boutiques feature everything from flowers to swim fins. It's also a great place to see a cross-section of Hawaiian society. Another pleasantry is a free hula show every Sunday at 9:30 a.m. on the **Centerstage** (see p. 211). The **Hawaii Visitors Bureau** maintains an information kiosk just near Centerstage. The following is a mere sampling of what you'll find.

The restaurants in the **Makai Food Court** are exceptional, if not for taste, at least for price, and unbelievable in variety of cuisine. In a huge open area you'll find dishes from Bangkok to Acapulco, from Tokyo to San Francisco. Most of these restaurants are counters for ordering, with tables in a common dining area. Great for people-watching, too!

A good one-stop store with plenty of souvenir-quality items at affordable prices is good old **Woolworth's.** They have all of the same sundries as Mainland stores, but plenty of Hawaiian and Oriental baubles fill the shelves, too. The film prices are some of the best.

House of Music sells records and tapes. This is a good store to shop for those island sounds that'll immediately conjure up images of Hawaii whenever they're played. Ground floor, tel. 949-1051.

The Honolulu Book Shop, tel. 941-2274, has the largest selection of books in the state, especially their Hawaiiana section. Books make inexpensive, easy-to-transport, and long-lasting mementos of your trip to Hawaii. Ground level near Centerstage.

Francis Camera Shop, tel. 946-2879, is a well-stocked camera store with a fine selection of merchandise sure to please the most avid camera buff. If you need something out of the ordinary for your camera bag, this is a good place to come. The staff is friendly and will spend time giving you advice. However, the best place to buy film is at **Sears** (no credit cards). **Woolworth's** and **Longs Drugs** also have good prices, but for cheap and fast developing try **Fromex Photo,** tel. 955-4797, street level, ocean side.

The Crackseed Center, tel. 949-7200, offers the best array of crackseed (spiced nuts, seeds, and fruits) that have been treats for island children for years. There're also dried and spiced scallops at $68 per pound and cuttlefish at $2.50 per pound—such a deal! Prices are inflated here, but their selection can't be beat, and you can educate yourself about these same products in smaller stores around the island. Crackseed is not to everyone's liking, but it does make a unique souvenir. Spirolina hunters can get their organic fix at **Vim and Vigor,** featuring vitamins, supplements, and minerals.

Shirikaya is a Japanese-owned department store between Penney's and Liberty House on the mountain side of the complex. They have a fascinating assortment of gadgetry, knick-knacks, handy items, and nifty stuff that Nippon is so famous for. It's fun just to look around, and the prices are reasonable. Japanese products are also available at **Iida's,** a local store dating back to the turn of the century, featuring garden ornaments and flower-arrangement sets, tel. 946-0888.

Specialty shops in the center include: **The Ritz Department Store,** with high fashions for men and women; **Hawaiian Island Creations, Products of Hawaii,** and **Irene's,** all selling a wide assortment of island-made goods and souvenirs, from cheap to exquisite; **India Imports,** many unique items from the subcontinent, and eelskin products; **Tahiti Imports,** with bikinis, muumuus, and a wide selection of handicrafts from throughout Polynesia; **Jeans Warehouse** for you *aloha* buckaroos; and **San Francisco Rag Co.** for nice rags sewn together well.

The Ward Warehouse

Located just a few blocks west of Ala Moana Center, at 1050 Ala Moana Blvd., open weekdays 10 a.m.-9 p.m., Sat. 10 a.m.-5 p.m., Sun. 11 a.m.-4 p.m., tel. 531-6411. This modern two-story complex lives up to its name as a warehouse, with a motif from bygone days when stout wooden beams were used instead of steel. The wide array of shops here includes an array of inexpensive restaurants (see p. 202), but the emphasis is on arts and crafts, with no less than 10 shops specializing in this field.

Greenhouse Magic is dazzling in silk flowers and plants. **Imports International** has nifty items from around the world—clothing, rugs, knickknacks, wicker baskets, tasteful postcards, jewelry, clothing for women, and shirts for men. Also hand-painted ducks, frogs, and parrots are everything from ties to centerpieces. Next door is **Future Heirlooms Collectibles,** with pottery, baskets,

and ceramics from Asia. Wonderful but expensive ethnic clothing comes from Thailand, Indonesia, and Malaysia. Gaily decorated, they come as vests, pants, coats, and jackets, all 100-percent cotton.

The Art Board is excellent for poster art, with racks of limited editions from which to choose. Postcards by some of the islands' best artists and a good crystal collection keep the vibes positive in this small but jampacked shop. **Ono Gallery** sparkles with jewelry, hanging stained glass, wooden boats, candles, bronzes, and sculpture. Give the tots their first lesson in impulse buying at **Hello Kitty's,** a toy store, or at **Kris Kringle's Den.** Show them how a pro does it at **B.B. Sports, Blue Ginger, Imports Intl., In the Sun,** or **Royal Alima.**

Kids of all ages will love **Neon Leon,** where you can buy masks, flying bats, puppets, a lot of neon, fake buns, and a pineapple head if you've left yours at home. **Books, Comics, and Games** for serious funmakers is on the second floor, while **Waldenbooks** has a tremendous selection of printed material on the first. Repent past gluttonies at **Aloha Health Food,** primarily a vitamin and mineral store. Or dress your feet at **Thongs and Things,** with everything in thongs from spiked golfing thongs to Teva sandals, the best all-around footwear for the island. Upstairs is **Birkenstock Footprints,** with their wonderfully comfortable ugly ducklings.

Perhaps the premier shop in the Warehouse is the **Artists Guild,** with very fine art by local artists. Most work has either a Hawaiian theme or utilizes island materials. Woodworkers, like Allen Wilkenson, fashion beautiful *koa* rocking chairs for $1900 or a table from *koa,* maple, and rosewood for $6800. Less expensive but terrific pieces are handwoven women's blouses by Gwendolyn for about $60 each. Shelves of pottery start from $20, with natural woven baskets from $50. Lynn Walton has been showing her work here for about 10 years. She does acrylic paintings similar to Pegge Hopper's, though she's been painting longer. A slight controversy as to who got it from whom doesn't detract from the beauty of this work. Leighton Lam, a resin artist who makes everything from jewelry to fine arts is well represented. Lucille Cooper works in raku and goes beyond pottery to sculpture. Rick Mills, a professor at the University of Hawaii, shows his glasswork here. Browse, buy, or pick up a memento like hand mirrors, boxes, combs, and earrings for under $15.

Ward Center

Across the street from the Ward Warehouse, this relatively new shopping center is gaining a reputation for some exclusive shops. Open weekdays 10 a.m.-9 p.m., Sat. 10 a.m.-5 p.m., Sun. 11 a.m.-4 p.m., tel. 531-6411. The Ward Center is appointed in light wood and accentuated by brick floors that give the feeling of an intimate inside mall, although much is outside. For the excellent restaurants here see p. 203.

R. Fields showcases fine wines and exquisite foods, crackers, cookies, cheeses, imported pastas, and caviar. **Images International Of Hawaii** is an exclusive art shop where you'd like to become a patron of the arts. They feature Tatsuo Ito, a master of *rimpa,* characterized by the use of 24-karat gold on fans forming a three-piece panel three by six feet. Scenes are traditional Japanese motifs of *sakura,* wisteria, cranes, chrysanthemums, and waves. Contrast this with a remarkable Lucite sculpture by Frederik Hart called *Contemplation.* Another gallery is at the Hyatt Regency in the lobby area, where they feature the work of Hisashi Otsuka.

Ladies will find exclusive fashions at **Pappagallo, Imago,** and **Susan Marie of Honolulu.** Men can outfit themselves in the most stylish fashions at **Ross Sutherland.** Promenade in style with a lid from **The Honolulu Hat Co.,** accented by a diamond stickpin from the **Imperial Collection.**

The Colonnade is a cluster of shops inside the Ward Center. It includes **Regency Shoes, Lady Judith,** and **Art A La Carte.** Just down the way is **Willowdale Galleries,** twinkling with elegant antiques. It's like looking into a giant china closet full of the best place settings and crystal. Stuck back in a remote corner, where mystics feel more at home, is **Sedona,** a metaphysical new-age store. They have oils, crystals, agates,

books, and consciousness-lifting tapes. Recharge your spiritual batteries with psychic readings by Pamela Higa, who gives "self empowerment sessions and intuitive services," tel. 262-9674.

Downtown Shopping

If you're touring the historical sights of downtown Honolulu, take a short stroll over to the corner of Bishop and King streets, as good a place as any to call the center of the financial district. The names atop the buildings, both vintage and new, trace "big business" in Hawaii. There's good food to be enjoyed in the restaurants in this area (see p. 207) along with some shops stuck away in the corners of the big buildings. For Chinatown shopping see p. 218. Also, an enjoyable time can be had at the **Dole Cannery Square,** with shopping in its new mini-mall, see p. 218. **Long's Drugs,** tel. 534-4551, is at 1088 Bishop, and almost next door is **Woolworth's,** tel. 524-8980, for any sundries and necessities.

The full-service **Honolulu Bookshop** is on the corner of Bishop and Hotel, tel. 534-6224. The selections are excellent. **Nautilus Of The Pacific** is at 1141 Bishop, specializing in estate jewelry and Hawaiian heirlooms, with plenty of sculptures and ceramics from Japan and China. **Hawaiian Islands Stamp and Coin,** tel. 531-6251, at 1111 Bishop St., street level in the International Savings Building, displays rare coins, stamps, and paper money of the U.S., Hawaii, and worldwide. **Discount Store,** at 65 S. Hotel St., sells TVs, VCRs, radios, and electronic gear. **Amar's Sporting Goods,** tel. 536-0404, at the corner of Bethel and Pauahi, is one of the bigger sporting goods stores on Oahu.

Bargains And Discounts

For discounts and bargains, try the following: **Crazy Shirts Factory Outlet,** at 99-969 Iwaena St., Aiea, tel. 487-9919, or 470 N. Nimitz Hwy., Honolulu, tel. 521-0855, seconds and discontinued styles, with a minimum savings of 50 percent. **Swimsuit Warehouse,** 870 Kapahulu Ave., Honolulu, tel. 735-0040, has women's swimsuits under $20, plus shorts and tops. **The Muumuu Factory,** 1526 Makaloa St., offers great sales—get there early and bring your helmet and shoulder pads to fight off the crowds. The **Hawaii Fashion Factory** at 1031 Auahi St., 2nd floor, is just between the Ward Center and the Ward Warehouse. Fashions at factory prices, with the public welcome to visit the showrooms. **Goodwill Thrift Shop,** at 83 N. King, tel. 521-3105, displays the same bargains as on the Mainland, but with a wide assortment of alohawear. **Nearly New Thrift Shop,** 1144 Koko Head Ave., tel. 732-3272, has consignment sales of quality merchandise. **Symphony Thrift Shop,** 1923 Pensacola, tel. 524-7157, is a consignment shop for used clothing in excellent condition, and usually name brands. **The Discount Store,** 188 S. Hotel St., tel. 537-4469, boasts excellent prices on tape recorders, tapes, batteries, and electrical equipment. For **flea markets,** see p. 85

Miscellaneous

Everyone, sooner or later, needs a good hardware store. You can't beat the selection at **Kilgo's,** 180 Sand Island Rd., tel. 845-3266. They have it all.

For camera and photo supplies **Central Camera** is a fine store in the downtown area where the salespeople are very helpful. Across from Hawaiian Telephone at 1164 Bishop St., tel. 536-6692. Open 8:30 a.m.-4 p.m. Mon.-Fri. and 8:30-11 a.m. Saturday. (Also see Ala Moana Shopping Center, p. 213). For **sporting goods,** try: **Big 88,** 330 Sand Island Rd., tel. 845-1688, many military items; **Amar Sporting Goods,** 1139 Bethel St., tel. 536-0404, sporting goods, sportswear, and a full range of accessories and equipment.

CHINATOWN

Chinatown has seen ups and downs in the last 130 years, ever since Chinese laborers were lured from Kwangtung Province to work as contract laborers on the pineapple and sugar plantations. They didn't need a fortune cookie to tell them that there was no future in plantation work, so within a decade of their arrival they had established themselves as merchants, mostly in small retail businesses and restaurants. Chinatown is roughly a triangle of downtown Honolulu bordered by Nuuanu Street on the east, N. Beretania Street on the north, and S. King Street forming the hypotenuse. Twice this area has been flattened by fire, once in 1886 and again in 1900. The 1900 fire was deliberately set to burn out rats that had brought bubonic plague to the city. The fire got out of control and burned down virtually the whole district. Some contended that the fire was allowed to engulf the district in order to decimate the growing economic strength of the Chinese. Chinatown reached its heyday in the 1930s when it thrived with tourists coming and going from the main port at the foot of Nuuanu Street.

Today, Chinatown is a mixed bag of upbeat modernization, and run-down sleazy storefronts. Although still strongly Chinese, there are Japanese, Laotians, Vietnamese, and even an Irish pub, O'Toole's, on Nuuanu Avenue. This is Asia come to life: meat markets with hanging ducks, and Chinese, Korean, Japanese, and Vietnamese food with their strange aromatic spices all in a few blocks. The entire district takes only 10 minutes to walk and is a world apart from *tourist* Oahu. Crates, live chickens, incredible shops, down-and-outers, tattoo parlors, and temples are found in this quarter. When Hotel Street meets River Street, with the harbor in the background, it all abruptly ends. This is a different Honolulu, a Pacific port, crusty and exciting.

Around Chinatown
Look for the pagoda roof of **Wo Fat's** on the corner of Hotel and Mauna Kea streets. This is the oldest chop suey house in Honolulu, started in 1886 by Mr. Wo Fat, a baker. It's a good landmark for starting your tour. If you want to clear your head from the hustle and bustle, visit the **Kuan Yin Temple,** where Buddha is always praised with some sweet-smelling incense. For peace and quiet, or to check out some old-timers playing checkers or dominoes, cross the river and enter **Aala Triangle Park.** Treat yourself by walking a few minutes to **Foster Botanical Park** at 180 N. Vineyard for a glimpse of rare and exotic flora from around the world. (See p. 195.)

Chinatown

While walking River Street, bordering Nuuanu Stream, behind the Cultural Plaza, notice what most people think is a temple but is really **Izumo Taisha Jinja,** a Japanese Shinto shrine. All the accouterments of a shrine are here—roof, bell, prayer box. This one houses a male deity. You can tell by the cross on the top. There's a ferrous concrete example of a *torii* gate. **Lum Sai Ho Tong** across the street from the Shinto shrine is a basic Chinese Buddhist temple, very small. Below it is Edwin's Upholstery Shop, part of the temple.

You can easily do Chinatown on your own, but for a different slant and some extremely knowledgeable guides try the **Chinese Chamber of Commerce Tour,** tel. 533-3181, that's been operating as a community service for almost 30 years. They'll guide you around Chinatown for only $4, with an optional $5 lunch at Wo Fat's. Or try the **Hawaiian Heritage Center Tour** from 1026 Nuuanu Ave., tel. 521-2749, every Mon., Wed., and Fri. at 9:30 a.m., for $4, and a lunch at Wo Fat's for $5. An excellent source of general information is the **Hawaii Chinese History Center,** 111 N. King St., Honolulu, HI 96817.

Shopping
For shopping head to the **Cultural Plaza,** on the corner of Mauna Kea and Beretania streets, but note that it has been struggling

lately and shops come and go with regularity. It's more fun to look at than to shop. You'll find **Vin Ching Jade Center,** and **Dragongate Bookstore, Excellent Jewelry Factory,** and **Peninsula Jewelry.** The Cultural Plaza **Moongate Stage** is the centerpiece. Here they perform Chinese dances and plays, and herald in the Chinese New Year. If there is a presentation (free), attend.

Nearby you'll find the **People's Open Market,** a co-operative of open-air stalls selling just about everything that Chinatown has to offer at competitive prices. Follow your nose to the pungent odors of fresh fish at **Oahu Fish Market** on King Street, where ocean delectables can be had for reasonable prices.

Pauahi Nuuanu Gallery, open weekdays 10:30-4, Sat. 9-1, at the corner of Pauahi and Nuuanu streets, is owned and operated by Lorna Dunn. It's small, but so are diamonds, and inside it's loaded with Hawaiian arts and crafts. The most impressive are the wooden bowls—light as a feather and thin as glass, made by Michael Ilipuakea Dunn, Lorna's son. Besides bowls there are little wooden jewelry boxes by Michael. Mythical carvings by Richard Morgan Howell depict Hawaiian legends in wood and stone. Bruce Clark and Rick Mills, an instructor at the University of Hawaii, are glasswork artists. The painters represented are Laka Morton, a Kauai artist, Jianjie Jie, and Douglas Tolantino, a Filipino-

Hawaiian, with heavy oils by Ellen Joseph Gilmore. Expensive prices, but quality work.

Waterfall Galleries, owned by award-winning photographer William Waterfall, are at 1160A Nuuanu St., tel. 521-6863. William runs the gallery, takes the photos, and collects the artwork that's here. The photography is all original. Plenty of the artwork comes from Asia, especially Balinese carvings and celadon pottery from Thailand, which is done in woodburning kilns and signed by the potter. William, while doing travel assignments, buys the artwork and schleps them back. His gallery is full of sculptures, bas-reliefs, and masks from previous trips. So you don't know what you'll get when you come in here, but you can count on it being tasteful and original.

Pegge Hopper Gallery is next door to Waterfall Galleries. Ms. Hopper is one of the three most famous working artists in all of Hawaii. Her original works grace the walls of the most elegant hotels and homes in the islands. If you would like to purchase one of her bold and amazing serigraphs, this shop has the best and widest selection.

Cindy's Flower Shop is just next to Wo Fat's, and they have fresh leis at cheap prices. Located right where S. Beretania turns into N. Beretania, at Smith street across from the Honolulu Towers, are a garland of flower shops like Lita's Leis and Mauna Kea Leis, famous for good products and prices. At River and S. Beretania is an open **people's market** every Monday from 10 a.m.- 11:15 a.m., selling fresh produce from local gardens.

The **Wingon Co.** at 131 Hotel has porcelain ware, but the feature is the big crocks of crackseed. If you want it the way it *was* made, this is it.

Yuan Chai Tong Ltd. Oriental Herbs and **Dr. W.S. Lam** licensed acupuncturist occupy a storefront on the corner of River and N. King. Nearby on Maunakea is **Fook Sau Tong's,** another Chinese herb specialist. Look in the window to see coiled snake skin, a few dried-out snakes, some flat-looking lizards, and who-knows-what. They better be good for you. If you need a bounce put back in your step, maybe some tonics that re-

semble road tar and a few needles in the ear are just what the doctor will order.

Down Smith Street is **Kam Mau Co.,** whose shelves are stacked with every conceivable (and inconceivable) Oriental food. This is a great place to sample authentic crackseed. If your tummy revolts or if you need a quick tonic head next door to **Lai An Tong's** herb shop where some mashed antelope antler or powdered monkey brain will set you straight again.

On the corner of Mauna Kea and Hotel you'll find **New World Fashions,** men and women's wear, quality, value, and low prices.

Chinatown Nights

Chinatown is relatively safe, especially during the daytime, but at night, particularly along infamous Hotel Street, you have to be careful. When the sun sinks, the neon lights and the area fires up. Transvestites and hookers slide down the street, shaking their wares and letting you know that they're open for business. Purchasing might leave you with a few souvenirs that you'd never care to *share* with the folks back home.

Not many tourists come this way. But walking down Hotel Street is really an adventure in and of itself. If you stay on the main drag, right down the middle, you'll be OK. There are a lot of nondescript places like **China Bar,** that open to the street like a wound oozing the odor of stale beer and urine. At Hotel and Nuuanu you'll find the Honolulu Police Department downtown substation. And then the smut begins. It seems as though you get the cops and the smut at the same places.

The **Hubba Hubba Club,** with its live nude shows, no cover, and not too inflated drinks, is the best of Hotel Street. This is not a place for candy-asses, wimps, or missionaries. Simply put, there are naked women in here doing exotic and bizarre acts. The Hubba Hubba is basically a clip joint on the up and up. Inside are flashing lights, a runway, and $3 beers, with only mild pressure as you sit and watch the act. If you invite one of the dancers to sit with you it's $10. The women, for what they get paid (not much), really put a lot into it. They all have costumes and acts

Hotel St. entertainer

and basically they do four songs. They start off in everything from space-age erotica to old-fashioned white gowns and then off they go. Most wear garter belts for tips and perform their act within breathing distance.

As you walk down Hotel Street toward the river it gets sleazier. Next comes the **Zig Zag Club,** which is basically a gin joint. Interspersed is an assortment of peep shows, followed by the **Swing Club,** with disco dancing from 10:30 a.m.-2:30 a.m., and then **Two Jacks Bar** (bar and cabaret). **Elsie's Bar,** at 145 N. Hotel St., open 6 a.m.-2 a.m., looks meaner than a tattooed snake, but it's a safe place. So if you want to have a night of fun and relaxation come in here. They offer Hawaiian music by the Puamana Serenaders along with fairly decent Hawaiian food. A few doors down are steps leading upstairs to the **Original Bath Palace.** The *original* place where drunken fools were taken to the cleaners.

Food

You can eat delicious ethnic food throughout Chinatown. If not Honolulu's best, the entire district, food-wise, is definitely Honolulu's cheapest. On almost every corner you've got places like **Mini Garden Noodle and Rice Shop** and **Cafe Paradise** for breakfast, lunch, and dinner. They're basic and cheap eateries whose ambience is a variation of formica topped- tables and linoleum floors. In almost all, the food is authentic, with most

featuring Oriental foods. You can easily get meals here for $3 to $5. Some eateries appear greasier than the Alaska Pipeline, so you'll have to vibe them out. The local people eat in them regularly, and most are clean enough. An example is **Neon's Filipino Restaurant** on S. Hotel near the Hubba Hubba Club. The sign says "Come in and have a halo halo, consists of many delicious fruits and flavor of canned juices. And by the way order a piece of custard." They serve Filipino dishes like *mongo ampalaya,* shrimp *pinakabet,* and *pancit* Canton for around $5.

Right at the corner of N. Hotel and Mauna Kea, you'll see **Wo Fat's Chinese Chop Suey,** tel. 533-6393, the oldest chop suey house in Hawaii, where you're guaranteed an authentic meal at reasonable prices. A visit to Chinatown is incomplete without lunch at Wo Fat's, or at least a tour of this extremely ornate restaurant. The three floors are covered with paintings of dragons, birds, flowers and a variety of land and sea scapes. Murals, carvings, and hanging lanterns create the mood of "rococo Chinese." The menu is like a small phone book, with literally hundreds of choices of fish, fowl, beef, and vegetarian dishes. It's hard to spend more than $10 per person, with many dishes considerably less.

Doong Kong Lau offers *hakka* cuisine and sizzlers. It's on the river side of the Cultural Plaza, open Mon. 9 a.m.-9:30 p.m., Tues.-Sun. 8 a.m.- 9:30 p.m., tel. 531-8833.

Inside it's utilitarian with leatherette seats and formica tables. You come here for the food. Savories include stir-fried squid with broccoli for $5.95, stir-fried scallops with garlic sauce for $7.95, stir-fried oysters with black beans for $6.95, sizzle plates like seafood combo at $7.95, shark fin with shredded chicken, $16.50. The menu reads, "The chief recommends deep fried shrimp with toast." Who's to argue with the chief! **Wan Kee Seafood Restaurant** is another restaurant in the Cultural Plaza. Locals swear by it, especially the lunch specials for $4.95.

The **Royal Kitchen,** tel. 524-4461, in the Cultural Plaza, is very popular with local families and business people. They're especially known for their takeout baked *manapua,* soft dough with pork and spices, and for their Chinese sausage, *lupcheung.* Open very early in the morning.

And stuck right in the center of Asia, what else would you expect to find but **Eleno's Mexican Restaurant.** Basic Mexican food like tacos, tostadas, enchiladas, and refills of chips and salsa, all around $5.

Pho May Vietnamese Restaurant at 1029 Mauna Kea St., tel. 533-3522, open daily 9-9, is a family-operated restaurant, and it is excellent. There is no ambience, but the food more than makes up for it. Nothing is over $5. Specialties include Vietnamese soups of steak, well-done brisket and flank, tendon and tripe for $3.95, French bread and beef juicy cube for $3.95, and hot-and-sour soup for two bucks. With the soup they give you a stalk of fresh basil that you break up

yourself, a spice that resembles cilantro, and sprouts that you add to the soup. Try shrimp and pork salad ($4), or crab meat fried wonton ($4), and chicken curry ($4). And I had the curry chicken—terrific. For well under $10 you'll waddle away totally satiated

There's a really decent-looking Vietnamese restaurant called **Sau Duong** at 58 N. Hotel, tel. 538-7658. Home-cooked dishes like sour soup with fish ($8), lemon grass-spiced pork chop ($5.50). House specialties like fine sliced papaya salad with shrimp and pork ($3.75). Open for breakfast, lunch, and dinner.

To Chau Vietnamese Restaurant, at 1007 River, tel. 533-4549, and **Ha Bien** next door to "Tattoo Parlor" serve basic Vietnamese fare for under $5 for most dishes. They're around the corner from the action of Hotel Street, and are family-oriented. Ha Bien is open strange hours, Mon. 8 a.m.-4 p.m., open the remainder of the week until 6 p.m.

Another Vietnamese restaurant is **My Canh,** tel. 599-1866, at 164 N. King St., open Mon.-Sat. 9-5, Sun. 9-3. Their menu reads ""you can select one specialty of the heart warming combination of the followings: rare steak well cooked, brisket and tendon, regular is $4, special is $4. BBQ meat spring for roll rice vermicelli is $4.25."

One place that you shouldn't miss is **Shung Chong Yuein,** a Chinese cake shop at 1027 Mauna Kea. Look in to see yellow sugar cakes, black sugar cakes, shredded coconut with eggs, salted mincemeat, Chinese ham with egg, lotus seeds, and steamed buns.

WAIKIKI

Waikiki ("Spouting Water") is like a fresh young starlet from the sticks who went to Hollywood to make it big, and did, though maybe too fast for her own good. Everyone always knew that she had a double-dip of talent and heart, but the fast lane has its heartaches, and she's been banged around a little by life. Even though her figure's fuller, her makeup's a little askew, and her high heels are worn down, she has plenty of chutzpah left, and when the curtain parts and the lights come up, she'll play her heart out for her audience.

Waikiki is a classic study of contradictions. Above all, it is a result of basic American entrepreneurism taken to the nth degree. Along the main strip, high-powered business-people cut multimillion-dollar deals, but on the sidewalks it's a carnival midway with hucksters, handbillers, and street people selling everything decent and indecent under the tropical sun. To get a true feeling for Waikiki, you must put this amazing strip of land into perspective. The area covers only seven-tenths of a square mile, which at a good pace, you can walk in 15 minutes. On any given day, about 110,000 people crowd its beaches and boulevards, making it one of the most densely populated areas on Earth. Sixty thousand of these people are tourists; 30,000 are workers who commute from various towns of Oahu and cater to the tourists, and the remaining 20,000 actually call Waikiki home. The turnover is about 80,000 new tourists per week, and the pace never slackens. To the head shakers, these facts condemn Waikiki as a mega-growth area gone wild. To others, these same figures make Waikiki an energized, fun-filled place to be, where "if you don't have a good time, it's your own fault."

For the naive or the out-of-touch looking for "grass-shack paradise," the closest they'll come to it in Waikiki is painted on a souvenir ashtray. Those drawn to a smorgasbord of activities, who are adept at choosing the best and ignoring the rest, can't go wrong! People and the action are as constant in Waikiki as the ever-rolling surf.

History
The written record of this swampy area began in the late 1790s. The white man, along with his historians, cartographers, artists, and gunpowder, were already an undeniable presence in the islands. Kalanikupule, ranking

chief of Oahu, hijacked the *Jackall,* a small ship commanded by Capt. Brown, with which he intended to spearhead an attack against Kamehameha I. The chief held the *Jackall* for a while, but the sailors regained control just off Diamond Head and sent the Hawaiians swimming for land. The ship then hastened to Kamehameha to report the treachery, and returned with his armada of double-hulled canoes, which beached along Waikiki. The great king then defeated Kalanikupule at the famous battle of Nuuanu Pali, and secured control of the island. Therafter Waikiki, pinpointed by Diamond Head, became a well-known landmark.

Waikiki's interior was low-lying swampland, long known to be good for fishponds, taro, rice, and bananas, but hardly for living. The beach, however, was always blessed with sunshine and perfect waves, especially for surfing, a sport heartily loved by the Hawaiians. The royalty of Hawaii, following Kamehameha, made Honolulu their capital, and kept beach houses at Waikiki. They invited many visiting luminaries to visit them at their private beach. All were impressed. In the 1880s, King Kalakaua was famous for his beach house hospitality. One of his favorite guests was Robert Louis Stevenson, who spent many months here writing one of his novels. By the turn of the 20th century Waikiki had become a highly exclusive vacation spot.

In 1901 the Moana Hotel was built, but immediately a protest was heard because it interfered with the view of Diamond Head. In 1906, Lucius Pinkham, then director of Hawaii's Board of Health, called the mosquito-infested area "dangerous and unsanitary," and proposed to drain the swamp with a canal so that "the whole place can be transformed into a place of unique beauty." By the early 1920s, the Ala Wai Canal was built, its dredgings used to reclaim land, and Waikiki was demarcated. By the end of the 1920s, the Royal Hawaiian Hotel, built on the site previously occupied by the royal beach house, was receiving very wealthy guests who arrived by ocean liner, loaded down with steamer trunks. They ensconced themselves at Waikiki, often staying for the duration of the season.

For about 40 years, Waikiki remained the enchanted domain of Hollywood stars, dignitaries, and millionaires. But for the brief and extraordinary days of WW II, which saw Waikiki barricaded and barb-wired, GIs—regular guys from the Mainland—were given a taste of this "reserved paradise" while on R&R. They brought home tantalizing tales of wonderful Waikiki, whetting the appetite of middle America.

Beginning just before statehood and continuing through the '60s to the mid-'70s, hotels and condos popped up like fertilized weeds, and tourism exploded with the advent of the jumbo jet. Discounted package tours began to haul in droves of economy-class tourists. Businesses catering to the tastes of penny-pinchers and first-timers elbowed their way into every nook and cranny. For the first time Waikiki began to be described as tacky and vulgar. For the old-timers, Waikiki was in decline. The upscale and repeat visitors started to snub Waikiki, heading for hidden resorts on the Neighbor Islands. But Waikiki had spirit and soul, and never gave in. In the last few years, its declining hotels started a campaign to regain their illustrious images. Millions upon millions of dollars have poured into renovations and remodelings. Luxury hotels renting exclusive and expensive rooms have reappeared, and are doing a booming business.

Waikiki Today

The Neighbor Islands are pulling more and more tourists away, and depending on point of view, this is either boon or bust for Waikiki. Direct flights to Maui and the Big Island allow more tourists than ever to bypass Oahu but still a whopping 80 percent of the people visiting the islands spend at least one night in a Waikiki hotel, which offer the lowest room rates in Hawaii. The sublime and the gaudy are neighbors in Waikiki. Exclusive shops are often flanked by buskers selling plastic hula dolls. Burgers and beer mingle their pedestrian odors with those of Parisian cuisine. Though Waikiki in many ways is unique, it can also come off as "Anytown, U.S.A." But most importantly it somehow works, and works well. You may not find "paradise" on Waikiki's streets, but you will find a willing "dancing

WAIKIKI

ALA WAI CANAL
ALA WAI BLVD.

KUHIO AVE.

KALAKAUA AVE.

ALA MOANA

KALIA RD.

TO
ALA MOANA
SHOPPING
CENTER

HILTON
LAGOON

ALA WAI
YACHT HARBOR

FORT DeRUSSY
ARMY MUSEUM

FORT DeRUSSY
BEACH

WAIKIKI
BEACH

KUHIO
BEACH

KALAKAUA AVE.

HONOLULU
ZOO

THE FENCE
(ART)

KAPIOLANI PARK
BANDSTAND

KAPIOLANI PARK

WAIKIKI
SHELL

TO
DIAMOND
HEAD

MONSARRAT AVE.

KAPAHULU AVE.

PAKI ST.

0   0.5 mi

0   0.8 km

NOT ALL HOTELS SHOWN

1. Westin Ilikai	11. Sheraton Waikiki	20. Ilima
2. Travel Lodge	12. Royal Hawaiian	21. Hyatt Regency
3. Hilton Hawaiian	13. Surfrider	22. Aston Honolulu Prince
4. Breakers	14. Outrigger	23. Pacific Monarch
5. Edgewater	15. Beachcomber	24. Kuhio Village
6. Halekulani	16. Sheraton Moana	25. Waikiki Hana
7. Coral Seas	Surfrider	26. Hawaiian Regent
8. Holiday Isle	17. Coral Reef	27. Holiday Inn
9. Hawaiian Monarch	18. Miramar	28. Queen Kapiolani
10. Aloha Towers	19. Island Colony	29. Waikiki Beachside

© MOON PUBLICATIONS, INC.

partner," and if you pay the fiddler, she'll keep the beat.

Non-Americans, especially Japanese, still flock for dream vacations, mostly staying at Waikiki hotels, 25 percent of which are owned by Japanese firms. Mainlanders and locals alike are disgruntled when they see the extent to which Waikiki has become a Japanese town. It's one of the only cities in America where you can have trouble ordering a meal or making a purchase if you don't speak Japanese! The visiting Japanese have been soundly warned by the tour operators before they arrive to never talk to strangers, especially someone on the street. Un-fortunately for them, this means a vacation in which they never really leave Japan. They're herded into Japanese-owned shops and restaurants where prices are grossly inflated, and from which the tour operators get kickbacks. Local shopkeepers, not on the list, are aggravated. They say that the once-timid Japanese visitor will now show irritation if the shopkeeper doesn't speak Japanese, and will indignantly head for the door if there is no one provided to deal with them in their native tongue. Also, these visitors have been taught to bargain with American shopkeepers, who they are told inflate prices. This makes for some rugged interaction when the price is already fair, but the Japanese visitor won't believe it. Although a survey was done that says the Japanese tourist spends an average of $500 per day, as opposed to a Mainlander who spends $100/day, the Japanese really don't spread their money around as much as you would think. The money spent in Japanese shops primarily goes back to Japan. It's an incestuous system that operates in Waikiki.

SIGHTS

To see Waikiki's attractions, you have to do little more than perch on a bench or loll on a beach towel. Its boulevards and beaches are world-class for people-watching. Some of its strollers and sunbathers are *visions,* while others are real *sights.* And if you keep your ears open, it's not hard to hear every American accent and a dozen foreign languages. Some actual sights are intermingled with the hotels, boutiques, bars, and restaurants. Sometimes, too, these very buildings are the sights. Unbelievably, you can even find plenty of quiet spots—in the gardens of Kapiolani Park, and at churches, temples, tearooms, and ancient Hawaiian special places sitting unnoticed amidst the grandiose structures of the 20th century. Also, both the Honolulu Zoo and Waikiki Aquarium are well worth a visit.

Getting Around
By far and away the best way to get around Waikiki is on foot. For one, it's easily walked from one end to the other in less than 20 minutes, and walking will save you hassling with parking and traffic jams. Also, TheBus and taxis are abundant, and along with rental cars, have been covered in the Introduction under "Getting Around." Those who have opted for a rental car should note that many of the agencies operate Waikiki terminals, which for some can be more convenient than dropping your car at the airport on the day of departure. Check to see if it suits you. The following information is specific to Waikiki, and offers some limited alternatives.

In mid-1987, **pedicabs,** for all intents and purposes, were outlawed in Waikiki. There used to be 150-160 pedicabs that offered short taxi rides. They took people shopping, sightseeing, and between hotels, but basically they were a joy ride. Mainstream business people considered them a nuisance, and there were rumors that some drivers dealt drugs, so they were finally outlawed. Now only 10-12 legal pedicabs operate in and around Waikiki. They're not allowed to go along Kalakaua Avenue, pickup or dropoff at hotels, or use any of the main drags. They stay on the back streets or in the park, where they are constantly watched by the police. Charges are a hefty $3 per minute. The main customers are Japanese tourists who marvel at being peddled around town by a muscular *gaijin* in a rickshaw-type conveyance never seen in their own homeland any longer.

The **Waikiki Trolley,** tel. 526-0112, offers tours throughout Waikiki and downtown Honolulu. A day pass costs $10 adults, $5 children, and you can get on and off as much as you like. The trolley is really an open-air bus, but it's well done and plenty of fun.

The most distinctive and fun-filled cars on Oahu are the hotrods available from **Cruisin' Classics,** 2139 Kuhio Ave., tel. 923-6446. They have a fleet of American and European classic cars that have been completely restored. Owner Don Pierce operates the company and has done the majority of the work

Waikiki Trolley

himself on the 1928 Model-A Fords. He has completely reinforced the frame and incorporated a Mustang front suspension, engine, transmission, and rear end. They've all been updated with automatic transmissions, and power steering (easy to drive). All are equipped with AM/FM cassette players and *oouugah* horns. Pick a roadster that'll seat four with the rumble seat, or a four-door convertible touring car, which seats five.

Prices start at $89 up to $250 for a stretch limo. They offer collision damage waiver for additional $14.95, or you can accept full responsibility. Insurance for these particular cars is not automatically covered by your credit card company, which is often the case with normal rental cars. If your hotel is in the Waikiki area they'll fetch you in their stretch limo, and when you return their car, they'll take you back to your hotel.

A reasonable alternative for Waikiki is to rent a bicycle or moped. **Interisland Rentals,** at 535 Royal Hawaiian Ave., tel. 946-0013 has scooters and bicycles. Scooters are normally $12.95 for four hours, from 8 a.m.-6 p.m. $18.95, 24 hours around $25. Bicycles, basically city cruisers with no gears, are $9 for four hours, or $12 for the day. They also have cars and jeeps available, and if you need a helmet they're free. You have to be 18 years or older to rent mopeds or cars. More of the same is available from **Hawaiian Island Cruisers,** at 2139 Kuhio Ave., behind Zorro's Pizza, tel. 926-8725. Brand-new mopeds start at $13.95 for four hours, $15.95 for six, $19.95 for eight, and the 24-hour special is $24.95. If things look slow ask about better prices. They'll deal!

Waikiki does an excellent job of conveying traffic, both auto and pedestrian, along Kalakaua Avenue, the main drag fronting Waikiki. They've installed very clear yet unattractive combinations of stoplights and street names. These are metal L-shaped beams, painted a dull brown, that straddle the roadways, clearly pinpointing your location. Unfortunately, they match the area about as well as work boots match a hula dancer. To give the feeling of an outdoor strolling mall, sidewalks along Kalakaua have been widened and surfaced with red brick.

The **Kapiolani Park Kiosk** is on the corner of Kapahulu and Kalakaua avenues. The kiosk uses vintage photos to give a concise history of Kapiolani Park. An overview map shows all the features of the park. Information is available here concerning events at the Aquarium, Zoo, Waikiki Shell, the Kodak Hula Show, the Art Mart (a collection of island artists selling their creations along the Zoo Fence (see p. 257), and the Kapiolani Bandstand, where you're treated to free concerts by top-name bands and orchestras (see p. 255).

DIAMOND HEAD

If you're not sandwiched in a man-made canyon of skyscrapers, you can look eastward from anywhere in Waikiki and see Diamond Head. Diamond Head *says* Waikiki. Western sailors have used it as a landmark since the earliest days of contact, and the Hawaiians

Diamond Head

beach performers

undoubtedly before that. Ships' artists etched and sketched its motif long before the names of the new-found lands of Hawaii, Waikiki, and Oahu were standardized and appeared on charts as *Owyhee, Whytete,* and *Woohoo.* The Hawaiian name was Leahi ("Brow of the Ahi"); legend says it was named by Hi'iaka, Madame Pele's younger sister, because she saw a resemblance in its silhouette to this yellowfin tuna. The name "Diamond Head" comes from a band of sailors who found calcite crystals on its slopes and thought they'd discovered diamonds. Kamehameha I immediately made the mountain *kapu* until his adviser John Young informed him that what the seamen had found, later known as "Pele's tears," except as souvenirs were worthless. Diamond Head was considered a power spot by the Hawaiians. Previously, Kamehameha had worshipped at a *heiau* located on the western slopes, offering human sacrifice to his bloodthirsty war-god, Ku.

Geologically, the 760-foot monolith is about 350,000 years old, formed in one enormous explosion when seawater came into contact with lava bubbling out of a fissure. No new volcanic activity has been suspected in the last 200,000 years. The huge rock is now Hawaii's state monument and a national natural landmark. Its crater serves as a Hawaii National Guard depot; various hiking trails to the summit bypass installations left over from WW II (see p. 134). Getting there takes only 15 minutes from Waikiki, either by TheBus no. 57 or by car along Diamond Head Road. The southeast *(makai)* face has some of the most exclusive and expensive real estate in the islands. The Kahala Hilton Hotel here is regarded by many to be one of the premier hotels in the world, and nearby is the super-snobbish Waialae Country Club. Many private estates—homes of multimillionaires, Hollywood stars, and high-powered multinational executives—cling to the cliffside, fronting ribbons of beach open to the public by narrow rights-of-way that oftentimes are hemmed in by the walls of the estates.

KAPIOLANI PARK

In the shadow of Diamond Head is Kapiolani Park, a quiet 140-acre oasis of greenery, just a coconut's roll away from the gray cement and flashing lights of Waikiki. It has proved to be one of the best gifts ever received by the people of Honolulu, ever since King Kalakaua donated this section of crown lands to them in 1877, requesting that it be named after his wife, Queen Kapiolani. In times past it was the site of horse and car races, polo matches, and Hawaii's unique *pa'u* riders, fashionable ladies in long flowing skirts riding horses decked out with leis. The park was even the sight of Camp McKinley, the U.S. Army HQ in the islands from 1898 to 1907.

It remains a wonderful place for people to relax and exercise away from the hustle of Waikiki. The park is a mecca for jogging and aerobics, with many groups and classes meeting here throughout the day. It also serves as the starting point for the yearly **Honolulu Marathon,** one of the most prestigious races in the world. The beach part of the park, called Sans Souci, is very popular with local people and those wishing to escape the crowds, just a few beach blanket-lengths away (see p. 232).

Its **Waikiki Shell,** an open-air amphitheater, hosts many visiting musical groups, especially during Aloha Week. The Honolulu Symphony is a regular here, providing free concerts, especially on summer evenings. Nearby, the **Kapiolani Bandstand** hosts the Royal Hawaiian Band on Sunday afternoons. Also, under the shade of the trees toward Waikiki Beach, plenty of street entertainers, including clowns, acrobats, and jugglers, congregate daily to work out their routines to the beat of conga drums and other improvised music supplied by wandering musicians. Families and large groups come here to picnic, barbecue, and play softball. The park grounds are also home to the free **Kodak Hula Show** (see p. 255), Elks Club, prestigious Outrigger Canoe Club founded at the turn of the century, Waikiki Aquarium, and 45-acre Honolulu Zoo.

Just in front of the zoo, by the big banyan, are hundreds and hundreds of pigeons, the "white phantoms of Waikiki." In the morning they are especially beautiful darting through the sunshine like white spirits. Go to the Stop N Go or the ABC Store at the corner of Kapahulu and Kapiolani and buy birdseed. Take a few handfuls and stand among the pigeons. They will perch on your arms, shoulders, and head and peck away. If you're not wearing toed shoes be advised that if you drop seed between your toes, you'll get an instant and free pedicure by the hungry birds. This is great fun and free!

WAIKIKI AQUARIUM

The first Waikiki Aquarium was built in 1904, its entranceway framed by a *torii* gate. Today's aquarium was built and stocked in 1954, and a plan is now underway to rebuild and refurbish it with a new entranceway, "touch tanks," and an opening directly to the sea. The aquarium, located at 2777 Kalakaua Ave. (TheBus # 2), tel. 923-9741, is open daily 9 a.m.-5 p.m., $2.50 donation for adults, children under 16 and seniors free. A self-guiding book describing the marinelife is available for $5, and an audio tour ("magic wand" device) in English and Japanese is $.50.

Although over 300 species of Hawaiian and South Pacific fish, flora, and mammals

Kapiolani Park

live in its sparkling waters, the aquarium is much more than just a big fish tank. The floor plan contains four galleries of differing themes, and a seal tank. The **South Seas Marine Life** exhibit shows fish found in waters from Polynesia to Australia. The tanks hold sharks, turtles, eels, rays, clams, a seahorse, and colorful coral displays. Another exhibit, **Micronesia Reef Builders,** is perhaps the most amazing of all. It contains live coral that seem more like extraterrestrial flowers than specimens from our own seas. Some are long strands of spaghetti with bulbous ends like lima beans, others are mutated roses, or tortured camellias, all moving, floating, and waving their iridescent purples, golds, and greens in a watery bouquet.

When you hear a coach's whistle blow, the seals are about to perform their antics. Watch these natural hams from the side of their newly renovated tank. These Hawaiian monk seals are one of only two species of tropical seals on Earth. Endangered, there are only about 1,500 individuals still surviving. The performances are more of a detailed description of the seals and their dwindling environment. This is a very special opportunity, and extremely worthwhile. (See p. 329).

The aquarium contains a bookshop with a tremendous assortment of titles on fish, birds, reptiles, amphibians, and the flora of Hawaii. Restrooms are behind the bookshop area as you face the main gate. The University of Hawaii offers seminars and field trips through the aquarium, everything from guided reef walks to mini-courses in marine biology; information is available at the aquarium.

Just near the aquarium is the **Waikiki Natatorium,** a saltwater swimming pool built in 1927 as a WW I memorial, allowed to decay over the years until it was closed in 1980. Plans constantly afoot in the House of Representatives call for a restoration.

HONOLULU ZOO

The trumpeting of elephants and chatter of monkeys emanates from the jungle across the street at the Honolulu Zoo, 151 Kapahulu Ave., tel. 923-7723, open daily 8:30 a.m.- 4:30 p.m., with special shows in summer at 6 p.m., admission $3, yearly pass $5. As you walk along or ride the tram, you find the expected animals from around the world: monkeys, giraffes, lions, big cats, a hippo, even a grizzly bear. The Honolulu Zoo has the *only* reptiles in Hawaii—three snakes in the Reptile House. Many islanders love this exhibit, because snakes in Hawaii are so exotic! But the zoo is much more than just a collection of animals. It is an up-close escapade through the jungle of Hawaii, with plants, trees, flowers, and vines all named and described. Moreover, the zoo houses Hawaii's indigenous birdlife, which is fast disappearing from the wild: Hawaiian gallinules, coots, hawks, owls, and the *nene,* the state bird, which is doing well in captivity, with breeding pairs being sent to other zoos around the world. The zoo is also famous for its Manchurian cranes, extremely rare birds from Japan, and for successfully mating the Galapagos turtle. A **petting zoo** of barnyard animals is great for kids. A concession stand serves typical junk food and soft drinks.

FREE SIGHTS AND CURIOSITIES

On the beach near the Surfrider Hotel are the *kahuna* **stones,** a lasting remnant of old Hawaii. The Hawaiians believed these stones were imbued with *mana* by four priests from Tahiti: Kinohi, Kahaloa, Kapuni, and Kapaemahu. They came to visit this Polynesian outpost in ancient times and left these for the people, who have held them in reverence ever since.

The **Urusenke Teahouse** is an authentic teahouse donated to Hawaii by the Urusenke Foundation of Kyoto. It is located at 245 Saratoga Rd, which lies along the Waikiki side of Fort DeRussy. Every Wed. and Fri. from 10 a.m.-12 p.m., teamaster Yoshibuma Ogawa performs the ancient and aesthetic art of *chanoyu* (tea ceremony). The public is invited (free) to partake of the frothy *matcha,* a grass-green tea made from the delicate tips of 400-year-old bushes. To find delight and sanctuary in this centuries-old ritual among

Moana Hotel

the clatter and noise of Waikiki offers a tiny glimpse into the often puzzling duality of the Japanese soul.

As you walk along Kalakaua Avenue, directly across from Waikiki Beach proper is **St. Augustine Catholic Church.** This modernistic building squashed between high-rises is worth a quick look. The interior, serene with the diffused light of stained glass, looks like a series of A-frames.

Believe it or not, you should pass through the McDonald's at the Royal Hawaiian Shopping Center to see a permanent collection of Hawaiian art on display. Among the exhibits are carvings, paintings, macramé, and featherwork. Many of the works are by Rocky Kaiouliokahihikoloehu Jensen, a famous island artist.

If you are fascinated by the military and its history, visit **Battery Randolph** at Fort DeRussy, at the corner of Kalia and Saratoga roads. Plenty of displays and historical artifacts, free guided tour, open Tues. through Sun., 10 a.m.-4:30 p.m., tel. 543-2687. See also p. 193.

Even if you're not a guest at the following hotels, you should at least drop by their lobbies for a quick look. Dramatically different, they serve almost as a visual record of Waikiki's changing history. The **Moana Hotel,** the oldest, dating from 1901, is a permanent reminder of simpler times when its illustrious clientele would dance the night away at an open-air nightclub suspended over the sea. The Moana houses the Banyan Court Room, named after the enormous banyan tree just outside. From here, "Hawaii Calls" beamed Hawaiian music to the Mainland by shortwave for 40 years beginning in 1935. In its heyday, the show was carried by over 700 stations. The hotel's architecture is a classic example of the now quaint "colonial style."

Across the street are the giant, modernistic, twin towers of the **Hyatt Regency.** The lobby, like most Hyatts, is wonderful, with a huge waterfall and a jungle of plants, all stepped down the series of floors, making an effect like the "Hanging Gardens of Babylon." The **Pacific Beach Hotel,** at 2490 Kalakaua Ave., is a first-rate hotel and a great place to stay in its own right. But if you don't, definitely visit the lobby, where the Oceanarium Restaurant has three full floors dedicated to an immense aquarium holding 280,000 gallons of sea water. The old mafia dons used to send their rivals to "sleep with the fishes"; here, you have an opportunity to dine with the fishes. Usually you go snorkeling to watch the fish eat, but in this particular instance the fish watch you eat.

The **Royal Hawaiian Hotel,** built in 1927 on the site of the old royal beach house, once had fresh pineapple juice running in its fountains. Now surrounded by towering hotels, it's like a guppy in a sea of whales. However, it does stand out with its Spanish-Moorish style, painted in distinctive pink. In the old days, only celebrities and luminaries came to stay—who else could afford $3 per day? Although it's younger than the Moana, many consider it the grande dame of Hawaiian hotels. The entranceway is elegantly old-fashioned, with rounded archways, over-stuffed couches, and lowboys. You pass through the lobby on a shocking cerise and green rug. All the rooms are appointed in this trademark pink, with matching towels, sheets, and pillowcases. When you visit the Royal Hawaiian, the most elegant lobby is not where you check in. Rather, turn right from there and follow the long hallway toward the sea. This becomes an open breezeway, with arches and columns in grand style. You'll come to a small circular area in the hotel. Here is the heart, with Diamond Head framed in the distance.

WAIKIKI BEACHES AND PARKS

In the six miles of shoreline from Gray's Beach fronting the Halekulani Hotel in central Waikiki to Wailupe Beach Park in Maunalua Bay just east of the Kahala Hilton, are at least 17 choice spots for enjoying surf activities. Most of the central Waikiki beaches are so close to each other that you can hardly tell where one ends and another begins. All of these are generally gentle, but as you head east the beaches get farther apart and have their own personalities. Sometimes they're rough customers. As always, never take *moana* for granted, especially during periods of high surf. To get information on beaches and their conditions, call Honolulu Water Safety, tel. 922-3888; handicapped people can get information on specialized beach facilities and parks by calling, 523-4182. Now that you've finally arrived at a Waikiki beach, the one thing left to do is kick back and R-E-L-A-X.

Waikiki Beach stretches for two miles, broken into separate areas. A multitude of concession stands offer everything from shave ice to canoe rides. It's not news that this beach is crowded. Sometimes when looking at the rows of glistening bodies, it appears that if one person wants to tan his other side, everybody else has to roll over with him. Anyone looking for seclusion here is just being silly. Take heart—a big part of the fun is the other people.

Umbrella stands set up along Waikiki Beach fronting Kalakaua rent boogie boards, surfboards, paddle boats, and snorkel gear. They're convenient, but their prices are much more ($5 for two hours) than many shops offering the same equipment (see p. 259). The guys by the big banyan tree are slightly cheaper than those set up by the breakwater just before Kapiolani Park. However, all offer decent prices for surfing lessons ($15 per hour including board and lesson, standing

Waikiki

guaranteed), and a $5 ride on an outrigger canoe, which gets you three waves and about 20 minutes of fun. Bargaining is acceptable.

Gray's Beach

This westernmost section's name comes from Gray's-By-The-Sea, a small inn once located here. The narrow white-sand beach lies in front of the Halekulani Hotel that replaced it. Take Lewers Street off Kalakaua Avenue and park along Kalia Road; a right-of-way is between the Reef and Halekulani hotels. The sea is generally mild here and the swimming is always good, with shallow waters and a sandy bottom. Offshore is a good break called **No. 3's,** a favorite with surfers.

Next door is **Royal Moana Beach,** lying between Waikiki's oldest man-made landmarks, the Moana and Royal Hawaiian hotels. Access is unlimited off Kalakaua Avenue. The inshore waters here are gentle and the bottom is sandy and generally free from coral. Offshore are three popular surfing areas, **Popular's, Queen's,** and **Canoes.** Many novices have learned to surf here because of the predictability of the waves, but with so many rookies in the water, and beach activities going on all around, you have to remain alert for runaway boards and speeding canoes.

Waikiki Beach Center
And Prince Kuhio Beach Center

When people say "Waikiki Beach," this is the section to which they're referring. Both beaches front Kalakaua Avenue, and a long sand retaining wall called Slippery Wall fronts both beaches, creating a semi-enclosed saltwater pool. Here, you'll find surfing, canoeing, snorkeiing, and safe year-round swimming along the gently sloping, sandy-bottomed shoreline. There are comfort stations, concession stands, and lifeguards. Be careful of the rough coral bottom at the Diamond Head end of Kuhio Beach. Covered with a coating of oil-slick seaweed, Slippery Wall definitely lives up to its name. Though local youngsters play on the wall, the footing is poor and many knees have been scraped and heads cracked after spills from this ill-advised play. The surf on the seaward side of the wall churns up the bottom and creates deep holes that come up unexpectedly, along with an occasional rip current.

Kapiolani Beach Park

This is the only park along Waikiki with facilities for barbecueing and picnicking. Although it's only a short stroll down the beach from Waikiki, it gets much less use. This is where local families and those in the know come to get away from the crowds. In the park and along the beach are restrooms, volleyball courts, picnic tables, lifeguard towers, a bath house, and concession stand. Activities include surfing, fishing, snorkeling, and year-round safe swimming. Just be careful of the rocky bottom that pops up unexpectedly here and there. Kapiolani Park incorporates **Sans Souci Beach** at the eastern end. This beach, in front of the Colony Surf and Kamaaina hotels, has unlimited access. Changing facilities are found at the deteriorating Honolulu Natatorium, a saltwater pool built in the '20s. Many families with small children come to Sans Souci because it is so gentle.

The **Natatorium** is in a sad state. Battles rage on whether it should be refurbished or torn down. Unless something has been done by the time you arrive, it's better to avoid its murky waters. Be careful of the rocky areas and dangerous dropoffs along the channel, especially in front of the Natatorium. **Kapiolani Park Center** is the beach closest to Waikiki. The swimming is good here, with the best part at the Waikiki end. The beach is at its widest, and the bottom is gently sloping sand. The area called **The Wall** has been designated as a special bodysurfing area. Supposedly, board riders are restricted from this area, but if the surf is good they're guaranteed to break the rules. Experts can handle it, but novices, especially with runaway boards, are a hazard.

Around Diamond Head

Kaluahole Beach is located at the Waikiki side of Diamond Head. The water conditions are safe all year 'round, but the beach is small and lies along a seawall. Once a large beach, it was paved over for building purposes. It has one public right-of-way, poorly marked and sandwiched between private homes. It's almost at the end at 3837 Kalakaua Avenue. The surfing in this area is generally good, and the breaks are known as "Tongg's," named after a local family that lived along this shore.

Diamond Head Beach Park is an unlimited access area along Beach Road (marked). It covers almost two acres of undeveloped shoreline. Unfortunately, the beach is very narrow and surrounded by unfriendly rock and coral. The waters, however, are quite protected and generally safe, except in periods of high surf. This area is good for fishing and finding quiet moments.

Kuilei Cliffs Beach Park lies below Diamond Head Road, with access available from three lookout areas along the road. You must walk down the cliff trails to the beaches below. Here are plenty of secluded pockets of sand for sunbathing, but poor swimming. The surf is generally rough, and the area is always frequented by surfers. Offshore is hazardous with submerged rocks, but this makes it excellent for diving and snorkeling—for experts only! Currents can be fierce, and you can be dashed against the rocks. Whales can sometimes be spotted passing this point, and to add to the mystique, the area is considered a breeding ground for sharks. Most visitors just peer down at the surfers from Diamond Head Road, or choose a spot of beach for peace and quiet.

Farther east is **Kaalawai Beach.** The swimming is good here and generally safe because of a protecting reef. Many locals come to this area to fish, and it is good for bodysurfing and snorkeling. The waters outside the reef are excellent for surfing, and produce some of the biggest waves on this side of the island. Access is by public right-of-way, marked off Kulumanu Place, a small side road running off Kahala Avenue, or by walking along the shoreline from Kuilei Beach.

Kahala Beach, lying along Kahala Avenue, can be reached by a number of marked rights-of-way located between the high fences of estates in the area. The swimming is not particularly good, but there are plenty of pockets of sand and protected areas where you can swim and snorkel. Local people come to fish, and the surfing is good beyond the reef. The Kahala Hilton is located along this beach at the eastern end. The public can use "their" beach by walking from Kahala Beach. The swimming here is always safe and good because the hotel has dredged the area to make it deeper. Concession stands and lifeguards are provided by the hotel.

Wailupe Beach Park lies on the Waikiki side of Wailupe Peninsula in Maunalua Bay, and will be the last beach covered in this chapter. This beach park, clearly marked off the Kalaniana'ole Highway, provides restrooms and picnic facilities. The swimming is safe, but the bottom can have either oozy mud or sharp coral in spots. Be careful of the boat channel surrounding the area because the deep dropoff is very abrupt.

ACCOMMODATIONS

Waikiki is loaded with places to stay: 170 properties holding 34,000 rooms jammed into one square mile. And they come in all categories of hotels and condos, from deluxe to dingy. Your problem won't be finding a place to stay, but choosing from the enormous selection. During "peak season," (Christmas to Easter and again in summer) you'd better have reservations, or you could easily be left out in the *warm*. The good news is that, room for room, Waikiki is the cheapest place to stay in the state. Hotels along the beach tend to be slightly more expensive than their counterparts on a side street or back lane. The beachfront hotels have the surf at the doorstep, but those a block away have a little more peace and quiet. The following listings are not exhaustive. They couldn't be! Here is just the best from all categories which you can use as a barometer to measure what's available.

INEXPENSIVE

Youth Hostels
Waikiki's two youth hostels are within a five-minute walk from each other. Both cater to international travelers who are doing it on an economy budget. Plenty of travelers, especially from Australia and New Zealand, use the hostels. Both hostels are friendly, comparably priced, well maintained, and offer advice on inexpensive dining and activities in and around Waikiki. Jack, the manager of Hale Aloha, is particularly helpful.

Hale Aloha Youth Hostel is located in Waikiki at 2417 Prince Edward St., Honolulu, HI 96815, tel. 926-8313. Walk down Kalakaua until you see the Hyatt Regency. Two streets directly behind is Prince Edward. Directions are also available at the Airport Information Counter. A dorm room bunk is $12. Couples only can rent a studio for $25, which has to be reserved at least two weeks in advance with first night's deposit. No credit cards. The business office is open 8-10 a.m., and 5-9 p.m. The hostel closes at 11 p.m. and all must leave daily from 10 a.m.-5 p.m. Maximum three-day stay, especially during peak

seasons, can sometimes be extended at the discretion of the house parent. Requests must be made before 7:30 p.m. the previous day. Baggage may be left for the day for $1. No key deposits will be returned for keys not returned by 10 a.m. Visitors are not allowed at any time. No alcohol or smoking. Chores are required. Lockers available.

International Club Hostel Waikiki at 2413 Kuhio Ave., tel. 924-2636, has kitchen and laundry facilities and relaxed island-style lounge. Prices: dorm style (five beds in each) $15 per night. Care deposit $10, returned to you when you give back the key. Double rooms, $20, no key deposit. They accept reservations. When the YHs are full try the **Waikiki Prince** just next door to Hale Aloha, at 2431 Prince Edward St., tel. 922-1544. Listed as a hostel, it is about the cheapest in Waikiki at about $25-35/night during low season.

Honolulu's YM/WCAs and official American Youth Hostel are near, but not technically in Waikiki. Find a complete list under "Honolulu—Accommodations," p. 199.

Waikiki Hana Hotel
This hotel at 2424 Koa Ave., Honolulu, HI 96815, tel. 926-8841, (800) 367-5004, sits just behind the massive Hyatt Regency on a quiet side street. The hotel has just 73 rooms, so you don't get lost in the shuffle, and the friendly staff go out of their way to make you feel welcome. The Waikiki Hana is surrounded by high-rise hotels, so there's no view, but the peace and quiet just one block from the heavy action more than makes up for it. Rooms start at a very reasonable $62 and go to $89 for a superior with kitchenette. All rooms have telephone, a/c, color TV, electronic safes, and are gaily appointed with bright bedspreads and drapes. The **Super Chef Restaurant,** on the ground floor of the hotel, is one of the best in Waikiki for atmosphere, food, and very reasonable prices (see p. 246). On-site parking is another good feature in crowded Waikiki. For a quiet, decent but basic hotel in the heart of Waikiki, the Waikiki Hana can't be beat!

Waikiki Beachside Apartment Hotel

This hotel, at 2556 Lemon Rd., Honolulu, HI 96815, tel. 923-9566, is owned and operated by Mr. and Mrs. Wong, who keep a close eye on who they admit, as they run a very decent and clean hotel. They rent weekly and monthly, charging from $250 to $1000, off-season cheaper. Per diem rooms are sometimes available, but you have to speak to Mrs. Wong first. Furnished units have full kitchens and baths with twin beds and a convertible sofa. Up to three people no extra charge. Laundry facilities but no maid service. Reservations reluctantly accepted (they like to see you first). Parking extra.

Outrigger Coral Seas Hotel

The Outrigger Coral Seas, at 250 Lewers St., Honolulu, HI 96815, tel. 923-3881, (800) 367-5170, is an old standby for budget travelers, designed that way by Mr. Pat Kelly, an octogenarian who lives down the street and wanted to provide a good cheap place for people to stay in Waikiki. This is the epitome of the economy tourist hotel and houses Perry's Smorgasbord. It's one of the Outrigger Hotels, and seems to get all the hand-me-downs from the others in the chain. There's a restaurant, cocktail lounge, TV, pool, and parking. Rates are an economical $45 s, $55 d, $15 extra person, and just a few dollars more for a kitchenette. Not to everyone's taste, but with plenty of action and the beach only a few steps away.

Edgewater Hotel

The Edgewater, at 2168 Kalia Rd., tel. 922-6424, is another budget standby in the palpitating heart of Waikiki. Rates begin at a reasonable $45 s, to $110 for a suite, $15 extra person. Facilities include swimming pool, good Italian restaurant, parking, TV, and maid service. Kitchenettes slightly extra.

Royal Grove Hotel

The Royal Grove, at 151 Uluniu Ave., tel. 923-7691, run by the Fong family, gives you a lot for your money. You can't miss its paint-sale pink exterior, but inside it's much more tasteful. The older and cheaper wing is about $35 per room, the newer upgraded wing with a/c is around $45. Most are studios and one-bedroom apartments with full facilities. A tiny pool in the central courtyard offers some peace and quiet away from the street. The Royal Grove passes the basic tests of friendliness and cleanliness. It's used but not abused. During low season, Sept. 1- Dec. 15, they offer reduced weekly and monthly rates.

MODERATE

The **Queen Kapiolani Hotel,** 150 Kapahulu Ave., Honolulu, HI 96815, tel. (800) 367-5004, on Oahu tel. 922-1941. With its off-the-strip location and magnificent views of Diamond Head, this is perhaps the best, and definitely the quietest, hotel for the money in Waikiki. You're only seconds from the beach, and the hotel provides a spacious lobby, parking, restaurant, TV, a/c, shops, and a swimming pool. Rates begin at $72 standard, to $102 for a superior; a few rooms have kitchenettes. The main lobby is being rejuvenated with a $2 million face lift. The stately marble columns have been redone, new wallpaper has been applied, and the shopping area is being upgraded. The overall effect is an open and airy frame with the still life of Diamond Head in the background. Select rooms have been made first-class with new carpeting, draperies, furnishing, and amenities. Most will boast a spectacular view of Diamond Head. Excellent choice for the money; for reservations write directly or to Hawaiian Pacific Resorts, 1150 S. King St., Honolulu, HI 96814, tel. 531-5235. Also, featured in the Peacock Dining Room, is one of the best buffets in Waikiki, (see p. 245).

You can't beat the value at the **Pacific Monarch Hotel/Condo.** Directly behind the Hyatt Regency at 142 Uluniu Ave., Honolulu, HI 96815, tel. 923-9805, (800) 367-6046, it offers some great features for a moderately priced hotel. Fully furnished studios begin at $75, one-bedroom apartments from $110, all a/c, with on-site parking, standard rooms available, too. The rooms are bright and cheery with full bath, living/dining area, and cable TV. End units of each floor are larger, so request one for a large or shared party. The swimming pool, with a relaxing jacuzzi, perches high over Waikiki on the 34th floor of the hotel, offering one of the best city scapes in Honolulu. The lobby is sufficient but small. It's accented with a lava fountain and two giant brass doors. A security key allows guests through the main door to the elevators. Save money and have a great family experience by setting up temporary housekeeping at the Pacific Monarch.

You can capitalize on the off-beach location of The **Honolulu Prince,** at 415 Nahua St., Honolulu, HI 96815, tel. 922-1616, (800) 922-7866, where you'll find a hotel/condo offering remarkably good value for your money. One of the newest editions to Aston Resorts, the hotel/condo invites you into its fully furnished one-and two-bedroom suites. All offer a/c, color cable TV, fully equiped kitchens, and daily maid service. Prices begin at $74 for a standard room, $115 one bedroom, and $130 two bedroom, with substantial discounts during low season. The apartments are oversized, with a huge sitting area that includes a sofa bed for extra guests. The Honolulu Prince is not fancy, but it is clean, decent, and family-oriented. A fine choice for a memorable vacation at affordable prices.

The **Breakers Hotel,** 250 Beach Walk, Honolulu, HI 96815, tel. (800) 426-0494, on Oahu 923-3181, is a family-style hotel. Only minutes from the beach, somehow it keeps the hustle and bustle far away. Every room has a kitchenette and overlooks the shaded courtyard of coconut and banana trees. Facilities include a/c, TV, pool, and parking. Studios begin at $75, one bedroom at $110, all fully furnished.

The **Waikikian Hotel,** 1811 Ala Moana Blvd., Honolulu, HI 96815, tel. 949-5331, or (800) 367-5124, is at the north end of Waikiki near the Ala Moana Boat Harbor and is surrounded by ultra-modern high-rise hotels. This character-laden hotel is only two stories, and is an enclave of peace amidst hustle and bustle. There is a feeling of days gone by as you move down the charming walkway through painstakingly cared-for grounds. Ferns, palms, and flowers line the walk, and at night it is accentuated with lighted torches. If you know what to expect you'll be happy with this hotel. Don't expect luxury, but do

expect a double dip of character. The grounds front the safe Hilton Hawaiian Village Lagoon with a short walk to the waves of Waikiki. Prices are reasonable at $69 with family suites for $135.

Outrigger Hotels have 20 locations in and around Waikiki offering thousands of rooms. Many of the hotels are on quiet side streets, others are on the main drags, while still more perch on Waikiki Beach. Although they're not luxurious, they do offer good accommodations and all have pools, restaurants, a/c, TV, and parking. Rates vary slightly from hotel to hotel: some have kitchen facilities and cost $75 d to $300 for a suite, $10-15 extra person. For information call (800) 367-5170, in Canada (800) 826-6786, or write to central reservations, 2335 Kalakaua Ave., Honolulu, HI 96815.

Ilima Hotel, 445 Nohonai St., Honolulu, HI 96815, tel. (800) 421-0767, on Oahu tel. 923-1877, fronts the Ala Wai Canal overlooking the Ala Wai Golf Course. This condo-style hotel is a few blocks from the beach—quiet atmosphere and budget rates. They have just completed a $1.5 million renovation, featuring waveless waterbeds in their deluxe suites. Studio units begin at a reasonable $45 s, $8 extra person, and one bedroom $75, two bedroom $85. All units have full kitchens, a/c, TV, along with a pool, parking, and maid service. Good value.

Miramar Hotel, 2345 Kuhio Ave., Honolulu, HI 96815, tel. (800) 367-2303, on Oahu tel. 922-2077, is in the heart of Waikiki. The hotel, refurbished and renamed in the last few years, offers generous-size rooms, with lanai, pool, restaurant, a/c, TV, and parking. Rates range from $65 s to $75 d, $15 extra person.

Waikiki Shores Apartments, 2161 Kalia Rd., Honolulu, HI 96815, tel. (800) 367-2353, on Oahu, tel. 926-4733, has studios and one-and two-bedroom apartments, minimum stay three nights. No children under 12, weekly maid service, parking. All units have full kitchens; studios $75, $130-260 for a two-bedroom.

Holiday Inn Waikiki Beach, 2570 Kalakaua Ave., Honolulu, HI 96815, tel. (800) 465-4329, on Oahu tel. 922-2511. No surprises at a good old Holiday Inn offering a/c, TV, pool, parking, restaurants, and maid service. Standard rooms begin at around $95, $120 for deluxe, and $1000 for the penthouse. Extra person $15. The Holiday Inn is at a good location just near Kapiolani Park and away from the heavy bustle.

A reasonably priced accommodation is the **Coconut Plaza Hotel** at 450 Lewers St., tel. 923-8828, (800) 882-9696. Rates are about $100 for a double during peak season. Off-season is cheaper, with a special day rate of $50 for bona fide business travelers. A continental breakfast is free daily in the lobby, with a free mai tai party on Fridays. Fully a/c with a hotel pool.

The **Waikiki Joy** at 320 Lewers St., Honolulu, HI 96815, tel. 923-2300 or (800) 367-8047, ext. 230, used to be an old funky hotel. A Japanese firm recently bought it and refurbished it into yuppie heaven. It has a new facade, and all rooms have been redone in shades of white on white. Amenities include pool, color TV, VCR, and some rooms with private jacuzzi. Rates are from $110 to $250.

DELUXE

Hilton Hawaiian Village

The Hilton, at 2005 Kalia Rd., Honolulu, HI 96815, tel. 949-4321 or (800) 445-8667, is at the far western end of Waikiki, just below Fort DeRussy. This is a glorious first-rate hotel, an oasis of tranquility as it sits in its own quiet corner of Waikiki. Enter along 200 yards of the private hotel driveway, passing the village, a small mall with exclusive shopping and dining. Facing you are the Hilton's "towers," the Tapa, the Diamond Head, the Rainbow, and the prestigious Alii Tower. Rainbow Tower, so called because of the huge multistoried rainbow on the entire side of this building, is, according to the *Guinness Book of World Records,* the tallest ceramic-tile mosaic in the world. Rooms in all are deluxe with magnificent views. Amenities include color TV, a/c, self-service bar, refrigerator, and safe.

The Alii Tower pampers you even more with a private pool with nightly gourmet *pu pu,* turn-down service, fresh flowers, fruit baskets, concierge service, flowers, fitness center, sauna, and bath accessories. Rates are from $140-235 throughout the Village, and from $225-335 in the Alii Tower.

The towers form a semicircle fronting the beach, not a private beach because none can be private, but about as private a public beach as you can get. Few come here unless they're staying at the Hilton. It's dotted with palms—tall royal palms for elegance, shorter palms for shade. The property has three pools. The main pool, surounded by luxuriant tropical growth, is the largest in Waikiki. The lagoon area is the music of water in bubbling rivulets, tiny waterfalls, and reflecting pools. Torches of fire and ginger, banana trees, palms, ferns, and rock gardens are the grounds. The Hilton is a complete destination resort where you can play, relax, shop, dine, dance, and retreat. It's a hotel that knows what it's about and has found its center.

The *action* of Waikiki is out there, of course, just down the driveway, but you don't feel it unless you want to. Relax and enjoy the sunset accompanied by music at anyone of 10 lounges like the **Shell Bar,** or in the main foyer where another small casual bar swings to the tunes of a piano stylist. Exotic and gourmet dining from throughout the Pacific rim is available at the Village's 10 restaurants, especially the hotel's signature **Bali By the Sea** and **Golden Dragon** restaurants (see p. 251). As you pull into the driveway there's a geodesic dome, like a giant stereo speaker, where **Don Ho and his Polynesian Extravaganza** perform nightly (see p. 255). The Hilton Hawaiian Village has everything to keep its temporary "villagers" contented and happy.

Hawaiian Regent Hotel

The Hawaiian Regent, at 2552 Kalakaua Ave., Honolulu, HI 96815, tel. 922-6611, (800) 367-5370, has a long history of treating guests like royalty. The hotel now stands on what was the original site of Queen Liliuokalani's summer cottage. The Regent was the first major Hawaiian project of master designer Chris Hemmeter, famed for his magnificent Westin Kauai and Hyatt Regency Waikaloa hotels. The grand tradition of the hotel is reflected in the open sweeping style that marks a Hemmeter project. After almost two decades, the Regent appears extremely modern becasue its design was so visionary when it was built.

With almost 1,400 units, the hotel ranks as the third-largest hotel in Hawaii after the Hilton Hawaiian Village and the Sheraton Waikiki. Rates are from $110 for a standard room to $350 for a deluxe suite. Children are especially taken care of with the "Keiki K.A.I. Club," a summer program, and honeymooners can choose a junior suite with special amenities for a reduced price. All rooms are oversized and include cable TV, a/c, nightly turn-down service, and in-room safes. You can step across the street to mingle with the fun-seekers on Waikiki Beach, or relax in one of the hotel's two pools. A championship Laykold tennis court is open from sunrise to sunset, with lessons and rackets available.

The hotel offers a variety of exclusive shops in an off-lobby mall area like Shirokiya and Sandcastles for alohawear and evening wear. An on-site beauty shop and Japanese acupressure/massage service are there to revitalize you after a hard day of having fun in the sun. The Regent is renowned for its fine dining, entertainment, and late-night disco. The **Lobby Bar** is perfect spot to perch while listening to relaxing Hawaiian music every evening. **The Cafe Regent,** an open-air restaurant just off the main lobby, is open for a breakfast, buffet, and lunch selections from 6 a.m.-2:30 p.m. The **Tiffany Restaurant,** dinner only, has casual dining in an elegant atmosphere of stained-glass ceiling and shuttered windows (see p. 246). The **Ocean Terrace,** designed for kicking back and watching life go by, is a poolside bar serving sandwiches and hamburgers at very good prices. The premier restaurant of the hotel, and one of Waikiki's consistently best, is the award-winning **The Secret,** previously known as the Third Floor (see p. 250), where you can not only dine in Polynesian splendor, but be treated to a magnificent selection of wines collected by Richard Dean, one of only two *sommeliers* in all of Hawaii.

Enjoy a daily international buffet or spectacular Sunday brunch at **The Summery,** or a traditional Japanese meal at the **Regent Marushin.** You won't be told to hush while you dance or relax to the sounds of live music in **The Library.** And, if you have "dancing feet" head for **The Point After,** one of Waikiki's swingingest high-tech discos that will rock you until the wee hours. Women will enjoy showing the boys how to really hoop and holler as they review the "hunks" in Hawaii's own **All-Male Dance Review** at the Point After nightly Tues.- Saturday. If you're after peace and quiet head for the **Garden Courtyard,** a multipurpose area in the center of the hotel. Sit among flowers and full-grown coconut and bamboo trees. Every Mon., Wed. and Fri. from 10 a.m.-12 p.m. learn lei-making, hula, or even Hawaiian checkers by *kapuna* who come just to share their *aloha.* The Hawaiian Regent is a first-class hotel that really knows how to make you feel like a visiting monarch. Rule with joy!

Sheraton Moana Surfrider Hotel

The Moana, at 2365 Kalakaua Ave., Honolulu, HI 96815, tel. (800) 325-3535, on Oahu tel. 922-3111, is the oldest and most venerable hotel in Waikiki (see p. 230). Now operated by Sheraton Hotels, it has just completed a $50 million upgrade, which has restored the class and beauty for which the Moana has long been famous. More than just recapturing turn-of-the century grandeur, the Moana has surpassed it by integrating all of the modern conveniences. The original Italian Renaissance style is the main architectural theme, but like a fine opera, it joins a variety of architectural themes that blend into a soul-satisfying finale. The restoration has connected the three main buildings, the Moana, Ocean Lanai, and Surfrider, to form an elegant complex of luxury accommodations, gourmet dining, and distinctive shopping. The Moana, filled with memories of times past, is magical. It's as if you stood spellbound before the portrait of a beautiful princess long deceased, when suddenly her radiant look-alike granddaughter, dazzling in jewels and grace, walks into the room.

You arive under the grand columns of a porte cochere where you are greeted by doormen in crisp white uniforms, and hostesses bearing leis and chilled pineapple juice. The lobby is a series of genteel parlor arrangements conducive to very civilized relaxation. Art, urns, chandeliers, sofas, *koa* tables, flowers, vases and pedestaled glass-topped tables wait in attendance. A brass birdcage elevator takes you to the second floor, where a room filled with 80 years of Moana memorabilia whispers names and dates of the Moana's grand past. After a fresh chilled glass of pineapple juice, you are escorted to check-in.

Upstairs, the rooms are simple elegance. Queen-size beds, overstuffed chairs, and fat fluffy pillows and bedspreads extend their waiting arms. All rooms have a/c, a remote-control master keyboard for TV, lights, and music. But this is the Moana! Sachet-scented

the Royal Hawaiian Hotel

closets hold *yukata,* terry slippers, and satin hangers. Fresh coffee with percolator is provided, along with a self-serve mini-bar, and daily newspaper. Bathrooms are tile and marble appointed with huge towels and stocked with fine soaps, shampoos, creams, makeup mirrors, and a bathroom scale which you can hide under the bed.

Being the first hotel built in Waikiki, it sits right on the beach with one of the best views of Diamond Head along the strip. A swimming pool with sundeck is staffed with attentive personnel, and the activities center can book you on a host of activities, including a classic outrigger canoe ride or a sunset sail on a catamaran. Three restaurants, a grand ballroom, snack bar, and two lounges take care of all your dining needs. Rooms in the Moana wing overlook Banyan Court, scene of a nightly entertainment such as a Polynesian revue, or chamber music provided by a pianist or harpist. Open the windows, allowing the breezes to billow the lace curtains while the waves of Waikiki join with the music below in a heavenly serenade. Rooms are $145-170 standard, $235-260 superior. A superb hotel offering old-fashioned service.

Royal Hawaiian Hotel

At 2255 Kalakaua Ave., Honolulu, HI 96815, tel. (800) 325-3535, on Oahu tel. 923-7311, the Royal Hawaiian is second oldest, and it too provides an ongoing experience in turn-of-the-century charm. A basic bedroom starts at around $195 s, with suites ranging from $300 to over $1600. The Moana and Royal Hawaiian are worth a visit even if you don't stay there. (See p. 230)

The Royal Hawaiian has just completed a $25 million restoration, which has recaptured the grand elegance of days past. Doors first opened in 1927, at a cost of $4 million, an unprecedented amount of money in those days for a hotel. The Depression brought a crushing reduction to Hawaiian tourism, bringing the yearly total down from a whopping 22,000 to under 10,000 (today more visitors arrive in one day), and the Royal became a financial loss. During WW II, with Waikiki barb-wired, the Royal was leased to the Navy as an R&R hotel for sailors from the Pacific Fleet. After the war, the hotel reverted to Matson Lines, the original owner, and reopned in 1947 after a $2 million renovation. Sheraton Hotels purchased the Royal in 1959, built the Royal Tower Wing in 1969, sold the hotel in 1975, but remained as operating managers.

Original doors were one solid and one louvered so you could catch the ocean breezes and still have privacy. Today, the hotel is fully air conditioned so the old doors have been removed and new solid rosewood doors carved in the Philippines have been added. Rooms might have four-poster beds, canopies, twins, or kings, depending upon your preference. All rooms have remote-control TV, refrigerators, electronic safes, and computer hookups on telephones for lap-top computers. Furniture is French provincial, with bathrooms fully tiled. Completely renovated rooms in the original section have kept the famous pink motif, but are slightly more pastel. They have a marble tile bathroom, a brass butler, louvered drawers, and a huge bed. The tall ceilings are even more elegant with molded plaster cornices. Guests are treated to banana bread on arrival, daily newspaper, and turn-down service with a complimentary late-night sweet treat. Preferential tee-off times at the Makaha Resort are also offered. Each floor of the original Royal has a pool elevator, so guests in beachwear don't clash with the early evening black-tie set. A Hospitality Suite is provided for early morning check-ins, or late check-outs. It offers guests, at no extra charge, shower facilities, maid service six times during the day, coffee-making facilities, and a sitting and lounging area.

Some of the prestige suites are truly luxurious, costing just under $2000 per night. They feature huge balconies with tiled floors, where a party of 25 could easily be entertained. The tastefully carpeted bedrooms boast a quilt-covered bed heaped with a half dozen pillows. The huge bathrooms overlook the beach and have a small built-in jacuzzi. In the massive Governor's Suite is a formal dining room, two huge bedrooms, two magnificent sitting areas, one a formal parlor, and the other an "informal" rec-room. The Royal

Towers, an addition dating from 1969, are preferred by many guests because every room has an ocean view. From the balcony of most, you look down onto the swimming pool, the beach, palm trees, and Diamond Head in the distance.

If you stay at the Royal Hawaiian, you can dine and sign at the Moana, Surfrider, Sheraton Waikiki, or Princess Kaiulani, all operated by Sheraton Hotels. One of the best features of the Royal, open to guest and non-guest, is the remarkable luau every Monday night (see p. 210), and the extraordinary food and entertainment provided nightly by the Brothers Cazimero in the hotel's famous and elegant Monarch Dining Room (see p. 253).

Hyatt Regency

The Hyatt, at 2424 Kalakaua Ave., Honolulu, HI 96815, tel. (800) 228-9005, on Oahu tel. 922-9292, is magnificent. If the frenetic pace gets to be too much, just head for the peaceful lobby with pine trees and cascading waterfall. The hotel offers a/c, TV, lounges, shops, restaurants, swimming pool, and parking. Basic rooms start at around $130 d, $15 extra person, and go to $1,000 for a suite. An excellent choice for an expensive hotel.

LUXURY

Waikiki is home to two of the finest hotels in the world. The **Halekulani Hotel,** in mid-Waikiki at 2199 Kalia Rd., Honolulu, HI 96815, tel. (800) 367-2343, on Oahu tel. 923-2311, was an experiment in impeccable taste that paid off. A few years ago the hotel was built with the belief that Waikiki could still attract the luxury-class visitor. Since opening, the hotel, recognized as a member of the Leading Hotels of the World, has been constantly filled. It's a hotel that takes care of the smallest details, like cloth hand towels, even in the lobby restrooms. When you arrive you are escorted to your room, where you register. Soon, a bellman appears bearing a silver tray nestling a fine china plate on an embroidered linen cloth which holds an array of chocolates, compliments of the house. Each room, done in seven shades of white, has three telephones, a bathroom as large as many hotel rooms, bath towels the size of parlor rugs, and a private lanai. Each night a little white box tied with silver string is placed on your pillow, and inside is a gift from the management. Prices begin at around $190 d, and go to around $325, suites $650, $35 extra person. If you want to splurge on one night of luxury, the Halekulani is unforgettable.

Long considered one of the finest hotels in the world is the **Kahala Hilton,** 5000 Kahala Ave., Honolulu, HI 96816, tel. (800) 367-2525, on Oahu tel. 734-2211. Technically not in Waikiki, but a few minutes' drive east. The hotel was built almost 30 years ago and is proud that most of its key workers have been there from the first days. A large number of guests return yearly and have formed friendships with the staff. Located away from Waikiki and surrounded by the exclusive Waialae Country Club (not even hotel guests are welcome unless they are members), the hotel gives a true sense of peace and seclusion. It has an excellent formal restaurant, The Maile, a private beach, swimming pools, all water-sport gear available, a saltwater pond holding three porpoises, and a lovely breezy lobby. The rooms, large with sweeping ocean and mountain views, rent for $180-400 d, $495-1700 for a suite. The Kahala obviously isn't for everyone, but there's no doubt that you definitely get all that you pay for.

FOOD

The streets of Waikiki are an international potluck, with over a dozen cuisines spreading their tables. Because of the culinary competition, you can choose restaurants in the same way that you peruse a buffet table, for both quantity and quality. Within a few hundred yards are all-you-can-gorge buffets, luaus, dinner shows, fast foods, ice cream, and jacket-and-tie restaurants. The free tourist literature runs coupons, and placards advertise specials for breakfast, lunch, and dinner. Bars and lounges often give free *pu pu* and finger foods that can easily make a light supper. As with everything in Waikiki, its restaurants are a close-quartered combination of the best and the worst, but with only a little effort it's easy to find great food, great atmosphere, and mouthwatering satisfaction. For a list of luaus in greater Honolulu, including Waikiki see p. 210.

Note: At many of the moderately priced restaurants listed below and at all of the expensive restaurants *reservations are highly recommended.* It's much easier to make a two-minute phone call than it is to have your evening spoiled, so please call ahead. Also, many of the restaurants along the congested Waikiki strip provide valet parking (usually at no charge), or will offer validated parking at a nearby lot. So check when you call to reserve. Attire at most Hawaiian restaurants is casual, but at the better restaurants it is dressy casual, which means close-toed shoes, trousers, and a collared shirt for men, and a simple but stylish dress for women. At some of the very best restaurants you won't feel out of place with a jacket, but ties are not usually worn.

INEXPENSIVE

Eggs And Things, tel. 949-0820, is a late-night institution open from 11 p.m.-2 p.m. the following afternoon, at 1911 Kalakaua Ave. just where it meets McCully. A number of discos like The Wave and Pink Cadillac are just around the corner, so the clientele in the wee hours are partiers and revelers. The decor is wooden floors and formica tables, but the waitresses are top-notch and friendly. The food is absolutely excellent and it's hard to spend over $6. Daily specials are offered from 1-2 a.m., while morning specials from 5-8 a.m. get you three pancakes and two fresh eggs cooked as you like for $1.99. Waffles and pancakes are scrumptious with homemade fresh fruit or coconut syrup. Besides the eggs and omelettes the most popular item is fresh fish, which is usually caught by the owner himself, Mr. Jerry Fukunaga, who goes out almost every day on his own boat. It's prepared Cajun-style, or sautéed in garlic and butter, with two fresh eggs and a choice of pancakes, rice, or home-fried potatoes. Prices vary according to market price from $6.75 to $8. Casual attire acceptable, BYO booze OK.

Around the corner is **The Dynasty Restaurant,** tel. 947-3771, at 1830 Ala Moana Boulevard. They have a large and varied selection of Chinese food that is acceptable but not memorable. They are, however, open 24 hours, which is the main reason for going there.

Da Smokehouse, tel. 946-0233, 470 Ena Rd., open daily from 11:30 a.m. to midnight, is one of those places where the food is excellent, but you wouldn't want to eat there. Why? Because it is primarily a takeout restaurant with only a few booths stuck in the back where *da* smoke and *da* grease from *da* wood-fired smoker is *da* decor. Your choices are smoked beef, pork, chicken and ham all served picnic style, with two choices of home-made potato salad, baked beans, rice, or cole slaw. Price ranges $3.50 to $10 for char-broiled smoked prime rib. The combo plate of all of the above that can easily feed four is only $15. No liquor, so BYO. Free delivery makes Da Smokehouse a perfect alternative to inflated room service prices at surrounding hotels, or for a home-cooked dinner in your condo. You'll love it!

Country Life Restaurant, at 421 Nahua St., is a new, all-natural food restaurant operated by the Seventh-day Adventists. The cuisine is fresh, wholesome, and totally vegetarian, using no animal products whatsover. Meals are a set price of $3.99 to $4.49 per pound, so you can fill your plate with anything on the menu that seems appetizing. Entrees change daily and can be anything from lasagna to pecan loaf with cashew gravy. Desserts are delicious, sugarless, and wholesome including blackberry cobler, and an assortment of whole grains and fruits. The salad bar couldn't be fresher, and is even more delicious with an assortment of home-made spreads.

Ruffage Natural Foods, at 2442 Kuhio, tel. 922-2042, is one of a very few natural food restaurants in Waikiki. They serve non-fish sushi, a wide assortment of tofu sandwiches, natural salads, tofu burgers, and smoothies. Everything is less than $5. It's a small hole-in-the-wall type eatery that's easy to miss. A few tables outside under a portico is the ambience.

Ezogiku is a chain of Japanese restaurants. Open til the wee hours, these no-atmosphere restaurants serve inexpensive hearty bowls of Sapporo *ramen* (renowned as the best), curry rice, and *gyoza*. They have multiple locations in around Waikiki at 2083 Kuhio Ave., 2420 Koa Ave., 2546 Lemon Rd., and 2141 Kalakaua Avenue. Ezogiku is a no-frills kind of place. Small, smoky, counter seating, and totally authentic. They're so authentic that on their dishes they spell *ramen* as *larmen*. You not only eat inexpensively, but you get a very authentic example of what it's like to eat in Japan . . . cheaply. Eat heartily for around $6.

The Jolly Roger is an American standard restaurant with a Hawaiian flair. If you're after good old tuna salad sandwiches, hot roast beef, a tostada even, or just plain soup and salad, this would be your best bet in Waikiki. The Jolly Roger has two locations, at 2244 Kalakaua (always too crowded so the service suffers), and 150 Kaiulani, where it's slightly quieter. Actually the Kaiulani restaurant borders on tasteful with a dark green decor accented with bronze, pleasant booth seating, and a profusion of ferns and hanging plants. Both open from 6:30 a.m.-1 a.m. Breakfasts are waffles, pancakes, omelettes, and meats, but try their orange bread as standard or French toast. Lunch specials are hamburger steak $4.95, with dinners well under $10. Happy hour from 6 a.m.-6 p.m. pours exotics for $1.75, draft beer $1.50, free pu pus from 4-6 p.m. Nightly entertainment in the bar section, especially The Blue Kangaroo at the Kalakaua Avenue Jolly Roger (see p. 253).

Man Lee's Chinese Restaurant, 124 Kapahulu, tel. 922-6005, is a basic Chinese restaurant that offers specials. Breakfast is a bargain with hotcakes, eggs, sausage, and coffee for around $2.99. The atmosphere is quiet since it's around the corner from most of the action. A belly-filler only.

Wong and Wong, at 1023 Maunakea, tel. 521-4492, is a simple and basic Chinese restaurant where you can have a good and filling meal at a reasonable price. Many people who live and work in and around Waikiki choose to go here for Chinese food.

Perry's Smorgy at 2380 Kuhio Ave., tel. 926-9872, and at the Coral Seas Hotel, 250 Lewers St., tel. 923-3881, is the epitome of the budget travelers' "line 'em up, fill' em up, and head 'em out" kind of restaurant. There is no question that you'll waddle away stuffed, but forget about any kind of memorable dining experience. When you arrive, don't be put off by the long lines. They move! First, you run a gauntlet of salads, breads, and potatoes, in the hopes that you'll fill your plate. Try to restrain yourself. Next comes the meat, fish, and chicken. The guys serving up the roast beef are masters of a whole lot of movement and very little action. The carving knife whips around in the air, but does very little damage to the joint of beef. A paper-thin slice is finally cut off and put on your plate with aplomb. The carver then looks at you as if you were Oliver Twist asking for more. Added pressure comes from the long line of tourists behind, who act as if they have just escaped from a Nazi labor camp. The breakfast buffet is actually very good, with all the standard eggs, meats, juices, and rolls, and the food in general, considering the price, is more than acceptable.

Pizzeria Uno at 2256 Kuhio (and Seaside), tel. 926-0646, is part of a small chain that allows each of its locations to be individual, although the deep-dish "Chicago-style" pizza remains the same. Open daily 11 a.m.-midnight, live entertainment Wed.-Sat., express lunch Mon.-Fri. 11-3, with specials including soup or salad. Appetizers like pizza skins, potato- flavored pizza wedges with onions and zesty cheese for $4.75, and individual-size pizzas for $5.95 keep prices down. Large pizzas like "Spinoccoli" are different with spinach, fresh broccoli, a blend of cheeses, and a little garlic for $10.95. Also, burgers and sandwiches, with names like "The Big Frankie," no teenie weanie, mark Pizzeria Uno as a casual fun-filled restaurant. Happy hour, 11 a.m.-6 p.m. is good value with draft beer at $.95, and all tropical drinks for $1.95. Breakfast is a "sunrise special," two golden-brown pancakes, two strips of bacon, and an egg for $1.99 from 6 a.m.-noon. Modern and upbeat

with black and white decor. On the beaten track, but worth a stop.

The **Waikiki Seafood and Pasta Co.,** is at the Outrigger Surf Hotel, 2280 Kuhio Avenue. Dinners are good but not memorable, and range from inexpensive to reasonable. Fresh pasta starts from golden herb pasta for $5.95, pasta of the day ($6.95). Other dishes are calimari marinara ($9.95), veal piccata ($12.95), calimari steak Italiana ($10.95). Specials like vegie lasagna are $6.95 with the most expensive at $14 for veal parmigiana. Good value, and acceptable food. A change from deep-fried *mahi mahi*.

Peking Garden, 307 Royal Hawaiian Ave., tel. 922-3401, is a hole-in- the-wall eatery just behind the Waikiki Medical Center heading *mauka*. They serve Chinese-American food basically in the form of filling plate lunches for around $3.50. A good choice is the Peking fried chicken.

Shorebird Beach Broiler is on the beach behind the Reef Hotel at 2169 Kalia Rd., tel. 922-2887, giving this budget restaurant the best gourmet location in all of Waikiki. Here you'll find a limited but adequate menu of cook-your-own selections for under $12 (discount tickets save you more). Open breakfast, lunch and dinner from 5 p.m. Walk through the lobby to the beach for a remarkable sunset while dining. Included is a good fresh salad bar of vegetables and fruits. Beverages are included, but you pay extra for bread. Nightly there's disco dancing from 9 p.m.-2 a.m. Good value and a pleasing setting.

Ferdinand's in the Coral Reef Hotel, 2299 Kuhio Ave., tel. 923-5581, is a no-nonsense place running specials and discount tickets. Basically it's an American standard restaurant with a Hawaiian flavor. An attempt is made at entertainment, a Don Ho clone singing in the background. The food is decent but not memorable; with discounts two can eat for around $15. Besides inexpensive food, they have inexpensive drinks at happpy hour, beers $1 or $1.25. They also have free *pu pu* from 4-6 p.m. Breakfast special is a choice of two pancakes or toast and jelly and bacon or sausage, or an egg any style for $1.99.

The **Holiday Inn** at 2570 Kalakaua Ave., has very reasonable dining. Breakfast specials for $1.99 gets pancakes, eggs, and bacon. Dinners are specials for $10 and under like roast beef for $8.95. Basic American food in the street-level dining room.

Hamburger Mary's at 2109 Kuhio, tel. 922-6722, has two claims to fame. It serves home-style food at reasonable prices, and has long been famous as a gay and lesbian hangout. The decor, given the open structure of the building facing Kuhio, is actually quite nice. The front is a terrace with a brick floor, round tables, and wrought-iron chairs. The *inside* area has a little grass shack motif, with curios hanging from the ceiling—old glass bottles, chandeliers, a flying angel, even an old surfboard. The back room holds a pool table and a dance floor. Rock and roll is always happening. Breakfasts are served all day long. At lunch they feature salads such as a fresh garden salad for $5.25, or stuff your own (your choice of papaya, avocado, or tomato stuffed with chicken, tuna, cream cheese, or cheddar cheese) for $7.25. Big hearty Hamburger Mary sandwiches are the Mary burger $4.25, avocado burger $6.25, meatless sandwiches like avocado or cheddar cheese for under $6. Soups and sides are plentiful, but try a bowl of homemade beef chili for $3.50. A great people-watching spot with good food at moderate prices.

Waikiki Malia Hotel Restaurant, 2211 Kuhio Ave., tel. 923-7621. Open 24 hours, specials for around $7.95; crisp salad bar and a huge well-done baked potato with dinner. Beverages not included. Good value.

It's Greek To Me, at the Royal Hawaiian Shopping Center, 2201 Kalakaua Ave., tel. 922-2733 is a combination sandwich bar and restaurant serving traditional Greek food such as *falafel, moussaka,* and *souvlaki.* Fat-so sandwiches are about $6.50, while the dinners are generally under $10. Also, pizza, steaks, and some Mediterranean dishes. Open sidewalk cafe perfect for a casual meal right after the beach.

The Islander Coffee House on Lewers St., tel. 923-3233, in the Reef Towers Hotel, has inexpensive breakfasts of two pancakes, eggs, and bacon for $2.29. They also offer steak and eggs Benedict for $3.89, chef salad ($5.65), hamburgers under $5, and specials every day for inexpensive prices. No dining experience whatsoever, but downhome prices in the heart of Waikiki.

The **Mongolian Barbecue** at the Kuhio Mall, 2301 Kuhio Ave., tel. 923-2445, open daily 11 a.m.-10 p.m., would make Genghis Khan smile. He could feed his army for peanuts. There is no decor, but this is a very good and inexpensive place to eat. For $12.95 you get the "Full Mongolian," for which you select your own fresh meats of beef, chicken, pork, and lamb, vegies, sauces, and spices from chilled serving trays. Then you watch them cook your order in the fire pit. Included is rice and a famous homemade sesame bun. If you can handle it, you can go back for a second round. Children under 12 get the same treatment for $7.95. If it sounds like too much, try the "Quick Mongolian" for $5.95, which is the same but the items are selected for you by the servers, and no seconds. The "Mini-Mongolian" for $4.95 is your choice of beef, lamb, chicken, or pork with vegies, served with rice or homemade bun. Limited fish selections as well.

INEXPENSIVE: KAPAHULU AVENUE

Once Kapahulu Avenue crosses Ala Wai Boulevard, it passes excellent inexpensive to moderately priced restaurants, strung one after the other.

The first is **Rainbow Drive-In,** at the corner of Kanaaina Avenue. It's strictly local, with a kids' hangout feel, and the plate lunches are hearty and well-done for under $4. Another of the same, **K C Drive-In** just up the road a few blocks at 1029 Kapahulu, specializes in waffle-dogs, shakes, and even has carhops. Both are excellent stops to pick up plate lunches on your way out of Waikiki heading for the H-1 Freeway.

The first sit-down restaurant on the strip is **Irifune** Japanese Restaurant, at 563 Kapahulu, tel. 737-1141, directly across from **Zippy's,** a fast-food joint. Irifune serves authentic, well-prepared Japanese standards in its small dining room. Most meals begin at $6, with a nightly special for around $8. You're also given a card that is punched every time you eat there; after 20 meals, you get one free.

The next is **Ono Hawaiian Foods,** an institution in downhome Hawaiian cooking. This is the kind of place that a taxi driver sends you to when you ask for the real thing. It's clean, basic, with the decor being photos of local performers hung on the wall. If you want to try *lomi* salmon, poi, or *kalua* pig, this is *da kine place, brah!* Prices are cheap. Open Mon. to Sat. 10:30 a.m.-7:30 p.m., 726 Kapahulu, tel. 737-2275. And, if you have a sweet tooth, just up the road is **Leonard's Bakery** that specializes in *malasadas* and *pao dolce.*

The **Rama Thai Restaurant** is on the corner of Kapahulu and Winam streets, across from New World Chinese Restaurant. Open daily for lunch, and dinner from 5:30-10 p.m., tel. 735-2789. The interior is *uptown* with some track lighting and linen tablecloths, but the prices and food are still *downhome Bangkok.* Wonderful choice is *satay* beef appetizer for $6.95, chicken and ginger soup in coconut milk spicy broth ($6.95), and red Thai curried beef, chicken, or scallops for $6.95. Almost half of the menu is vegetarian. All items are à la carte, so it's not that cheap; a complete meal costs around $15. The fishball soup is out of this world, with plenty for two. The tofu in coconut milk is also a great choice.

To round out the multicultural cuisines of Kapahulu Avenue, try **Plaza Manila,** at 750 Palani Ave. and Kapahulu. Open daily except Mon., from 11 a.m.-10 p.m., tel. 734-0400. Traditional Filipino dishes with many American and Hawaiian standards.

Fast Foods And Snacks

There are enough formica-tabled, orange-colored, golden-arched, belly-up-to-the-window places selling perfected, injected, and inspected ground cow, chicken, and fish to feed an army . . . and a navy, and marine corps too. Those needing a pre-fab meal can choose from the royal **Burger King,** and **Dairy Queen, Jack-in-his-Box, Ronnie McDonald, Pizza Hut-2-3-4, Wendy's,** and dippy **Zippy's Drive-In.** Addicts find your own pushers!

Farrels Restaurant at the International Market Place and the Royal Hawaiian Center serves ice cream and a good selection of sandwiches and soups for decent prices. Along Kalakaua Avenue are **Baskin Robbins,** and **Haagen Dazs.** For cheap Italian try the **Noodle Shop** in the Waikiki Sand Villa Hotel, tel. 922-4744.

Minute Chef, across from the Sheraton Moana Surfrider Hotel, on Kalakaua Ave., has hamburgers for $.99 cents, cheese burgers $1.19, sandwiches $2.50, and roast beef for about $3.99. A change of pace from the styrofoam box-type fast foods. Not bad, for cheap fast food.

Zorro's, with eight or so locations in and around Honolulu (two on Kuhio Ave. in Waikiki), tel. 926-5555, is your basic pizza parlor that includes a limited menu of pasta, sandwiches, and salad. The standard 16-inch pizza ranges from $10.99 to $19.89 depending upon toppings. Pastas are all under $6, and sandwiches under $5. Open from 10 a.m.-4 a.m. with free delivery.

The Patisserie at 2330 Kuhio (about three more scattered around town), tel. 922-9752, offer fresh French pastries, coffee, and sandwiches. They're not bad for this neck of the woods. Fairly decent food at acceptable prices. Good for early mornings if you want just a light breakfast.

Fatty's Chinese Fast Food, 2345 Kuhio, tel. 922-9600, is very inexpensive. For about $3.50 you get a giant plate of Chinese fast food. A belly-filler only, but not bad.

MODERATE

Peacock Dining Room, at the Queen Kapiolani Hotel, 150 Kapahulu, tel. 922-1941, open 5:30-9 p.m., offers one of the most outstanding buffets in Waikiki for both price and quality. Different nights feature different cuisines. All are special but the Japanese buffet on Wednesday and Thursday and the seafood buffet on Friday are extraordinary. All range from $12.95 to $15.95. The room itself is very tasteful with white tablecloths and full service. Every time you return to the buffet just leave your empty plate and it will be taken away for you. Help yourself from an amazing array of entrees that are expertly prepared. The salad bar is extremely varied, and the desserts will make you wish that you saved room. Excellent value.

Tiffany's Steakhouse at the Hawaiian Regent, 2552 Kalakaua, tel. 922-6611, dinner from 6-9:30 p.m., is a casual restaurant featuring thick juicy steaks, a varied and ample salad bar, and a good selection of fresh fish and seafood selections. Evenings are magical because of a stained-glass ceiling illuminated with backlighting. The furnishings are European contemporary that counterpoint louvered windows all around. Tables are set with pink tablecloths and heavy crystal ware while subdued lighting and ceiling fans add comfort and romance to your meal. The menu begins with escargot ($6.95), soups and chowder (under $4), and a seafood bar for $6.95. The house specialties are generous portions of prime rib ($19.95), filet mignon ($21), short rib ($18.50), tempura ($18.50), and seafood Newburg ($17.95). À la carte salad bar is $7.95. Tiffany's is that special blend of elegant and casual where you can dine in style and still be presented with a moderate check.

The **Super Chef Restaurant,** tel. 926-7199, at the Waikiki Hana Hotel 2424 Koa Ave., is a sleeper. It is definitely one of *the* best moderately/inexpensively priced restaurants in Waikiki where you can get an *almost* gourmet meal for a terrific price. Being in a small hotel on a side street keeps the crowds away, so the quality of the food and service never suffers. The restaurant decor is not spectacular, but it is classy with small linen-covered tables and drum-seat chairs in a open and cheery room. The staff is very friendly, and the chefs prepare each meal individually behind a tile counter. Breakfast is from 6:30-10:30 a.m. when they feature buttermilk pancakes, bacon and ham, or Portuguese sausage with a large juice for just $2.25; or choose a *wiki wiki* breakfast of pastry, juice, and Kona coffee for only $1.75. No lunch menu and dinner is from 5-10 p.m. One special is a complete dinner of steak with two lobster tails for only $11.95, or rack of lamb for $8.95. What's the catch? The portions are moderate but definitely not miniscule, and on

top of it the cooking is just a half step below excellent. Definitely worth a try.

Carlos Castaneda wouldn't even notice as he walked past two psychedelic green cactuses into **Pepper's,** at 150 Kaiulani Ave., tel. 926-4374 open daily for lunch from 11:30 a.m.-4 p.m., dinner from 4 p.m.-1:30 a.m.! The interior is Yuppie-Mex with a wraparound rectangular bar with a fat wooden rail, and low ceilings done in a Mexican-style stucco. The specialties of the house are prepared in a smoke-fired oven for that hearty outdoor flavor in the heart of "Rancho Waikiki." Light meals are chicken taco salad for $4.50, the Pepper club ($4.94), and tuna melt ($4.95), with a good selection of salads. But you can get these anywhere so go "south of the border" for burrito madness ($7.50), complete flautas dinner for $7.95, or selections from the mesquite grill like marinated chicken breast ($10.95), baby-back ribs (full slab) for $14.95. You can also pick Mexican favorites like tacos, enchiladas, and fajitas, all served with rice, beans, and Mexican salad. Nothing on the Mexican side is more than $10.95, with most around $7. Interface your face with good food at a decent price at Pepper's, *hombre.*

Eating at **Caffe Guccinni** is like following a Venetian gondolier to his favorite restaurant. It's not fancy but the food is good and plentiful, and the pasta is made fresh daily. The staff is usually a cook and a waiter who seats you at one of a half dozen tables that are mostly outdoors. At 2139 Kuhio Ave., tel. 922-5287, daily from 3-11 p.m., they're easy to miss because they're stuck back off the street, which means a nice and quiet area. Prices are garlic bread ($2), Caesar salad ($5.50), or house specialties (with soup or salad), like eggplant parmigiana ($8.50), pasta contesto ($8.50), spaghetti and meatballs ($9.50), and manicotti ($9.75). The cappuccino and espresso are freshly brewed and extraordinarily good. For dessert have *cannoli,* a flaky pastry stuffed with ricotta and smothered with slivers of almond and chocolate—excellent.

Hernando's Hideaway, at 2139 Kuhio, tel. 922-7758, open daily 11 a.m.-10 p.m., sits well off the street and is a very casual Mexican restaurant where the emphasis is on plenty of good food and having a good time. Tables are mostly outside under an awning and covered with butcher-block paper so you can crayon your heart away and get rid of your anxieties by scribbling all over the table. Every day is a special drink day, and there is live entertainment on Wednesday and Sunday. Happy hour brings $2 margaritas. Throughout the week there're bikini contests, and ladie's night on Wednesdays. All this activity attracts a younger crowd of both resort workers and vacationers. The menu is average Mexican dishes from nachos to tostadas. You can eat until your're as stuffed as a burrito for under $8. Olé!

The **New Orleans Bistro,** at 2139 Kuhio, tel. 926-4444, open from 11 a.m. to midnight, along with its zesty Cajun and creole dining, offers jazz nightly. The chef, from New Orleans, has put together a small but superb sampler menu of the finest in Cajun cooking. The prices are a touch expensive, but if you're bored with the average offerings of *mahi mahi* and teri chicken, you'll be glad that you found the Bistro. They've done the most with this limited location. The tables, covered in pink tablecloths, are arranged so that there is an intimate and romantic feeling, and somehow the hustle and bustle of Kuhio has been minimized. Appetizers begin at $4.95 and sharpen your palate with deep-fried calimari, or oysters Bienville, and Gulf Coast oysters baked on the half shell topped with New Orleans classic cream sauce and laced with shrimp for $10.95. Salads are basically $5 and include beefsteak tomato (Maui Feast) and house salad of hearts of palms ($4.95). Entrees are mesquite-grilled lemon herb chicken $12.95, Louisiana fresh fried catfish ($14.95), blackened fish du jour (seasonal price), or smoked *kalua* shrimp and angel hair pasta ($15.95). If reptiles and amphibians pique your fancy there're frog legs and alligator tenderloins barbecued, blackened, or deep-fried with cocktail sauce, served with Cajun rice and vegies for $19.95. A good choice for a different dining experience.

Bobby McGee's Conglomeration, at the Colony East Hotel, 2885 Kalakaua, tel. 922-1282, open Mon.-Thurs. 5:30-10 p.m., Fri., Sat., and Sun. 5-11 p.m. This is a riproaring fun-filled place for the entire family. One of those rare combinations that caters to all ages and all pocketbooks, and foodwise it won't let you down. The waiters and waitresses are all in costume, so you might be served your meal by Batman or Annie Oakley. The interior has numerous rooms, so you can sit close to the disco dance floor in case you have the overwhelming urge to twist off a few calories, or you can sit in a quiet room well away from the music. Create your own combos by mixing and matching selections like fried clam strips, top sirloin, deviled crab, island chicken. Pick any two for $14.95, any three for $16.95, each additional $3.95. Also traditional dishes are top sirloin for $13.75, *mahi mahi* macadamia for $8.95, or lasagna for $8.25. Children's menu for under $5. Plus an assortment of sandwiches for $5. All entrees come with the salad bar, which is set up in an old bathtub. If you can't make up your mind where to dine, Bobby McGee's is a sure bet.

The Blue Water Cafe, 2350 Kuhio Ave., tel. 926-2191, open from 7 a.m.-10 p.m., dancing from 10 p.m.-4 a.m., is basic and cozy with heavy oak tables, brass rails, and wooden armchairs. With a name like Blue Water you'd think they were big on fish, but they're the home of the "one-pound porterhouse steak" for only $9.95. They also serve Maine lobster with garlic and butter pasta for $19.95, and the chef's specials like strips of tenderloin sautéed with mushrooms and onions ($10.95) and Pacific red snapper ($10.95). Happy hour is 11-7 and 9-midnight, $1.50 for standards in the lounge only. The large-screen TV used nightly in the disco shows Hawaiian activities during the day and evening. So while you're chomping your steak you can be learning about Hawaii too!

Pieces of Eight in the Coral Seas Hotel, tel. 923-6646, open daily 5-11 p.m., happy hour from 4-6 p.m., piano bar nightly. This steak and seafood house has managed to create a comfortable and relaxed atmosphere where they serve up excellent steaks and very good fish dishes at a moderate price. The decor is dark wood and burnished brass in a romantically lit main room. A piano stylist tinkles in the background. It's the perfect combination of restaurant that will match itself to your mood. Come for that special night out or just a casual evening meal. "Early birders" from 5-6:30 p.m. can peck selections like garlic chicken, or fish 'n' chips with salad bar for $5.95. Entrees are 10-ounce top sirloin ($11.95), ground beef sirloin ($8.50), filet mignon ($15.95), *mahi mahi* amandine for $10.95. All dinners include choice of potato, rice, or bread and salad bar at $2.50 extra. A great choice for good food and a pleasant setting at affordable prices.

The House of Hong, 260 Lewers St., tel. 923-0202, open daily 11 a.m.- 10:30 p.m., Sun. from 4 p.m., piano bar nightly except Sunday. Not bad for a standard, no surprises Chinese restaurant. The decor borders on tasteful with some tables outfitted in starchy white tablecloths accented by inlaid murals and painted ceilings of China scenes. The Cantonese lunch special is weekdays from 11 a.m.-3 p.m. for $4.95, with early-bird specials from 4-6 p.m.—dishes like egg flower soup, chicken chow mein, sweet and sour pork, crispy wonton, fried rice, fortune cookie, and Chinese tea for $9.95. Not great, but no complaints except for a *sometimes* pushy doorman who tries to hustle you inside.

The Oceanarium at the Pacific Beach Hotel, 2490 Kalakaua Ave., tel. 922-1233, offers a sundown special from 5-6:30 p.m. for $10-12 including *mahi mahi,* teri steaks and chicken, chicken fettuccini, and barbecued ribs. They even have a seafood sampler for $12.95. Full breakfast and lunch menus. For lunch, try the tropical fruit plate ($7.50) or an entree like Cajun five-spice chicken for $7.50. Dinner appetizers like Cajun calimari begin at $4.25, New York peppercorn steak for $19.95, or special combos like Hawaiian lobster for $21.95. Also fresh island catches at market prices. The Oceanarium is done in elegant muted colors as if you were under water. See p. 230 for a description of the massive 280,000-gallon aquarium that is the decor.

Trattoria, in the Edgewater Hotel, 2168 Kalia Rd., tel. 923-8415, serves savory dishes from Northern Italy. Particularly good are the veal plates with an appropriate bottle of Italian wine.

Benihana of Tokyo at the Hilton Rainbow Bazaar, 2005 Kalia Rd., tel. 955-5955, is a medium-priced Japanese restaurant for those who are jittery about the food and prices. Meals are designed to fit *gaijin* taste, and cooks flash their knives and spatulas at your table—as much a floor show as a dining experience. Good, basic Japanese food, *teppan*-style.

Rascals on Kuhio, at the Kuhio Mall, 2301 Kuhio Ave., tel. 922-5566, is open for dinner only, and doubles as a nightclub with late-night suppers served until 3 a.m. and dancing until 4 a.m. Varied menu of seafood, featuring Cajun-style shrimp soup.

Popo's Margarita Cantina, International Market Place, tel. 923-8373, and Compadres Mexican Bar and Grill, Outrigger Prince Hotel, 2500 Kuhio Ave., tel. 924-4007, offer tacos, enchiladas, chips and salsa, done in a reasonably good Mexican style with good value on the combination plates.

Mandarin Palace, the Miramar Hotel, 2345 Kuhio Ave., tel. 926-1110, for lunch and dinner. Highly rated for its Oriental cuisine in a full-blown Chinese atmosphere.

Seafood Emporium, Royal Hawaiian Shopping Center, 2201 Kalakaua Ave., tel. 922-5477. Moderately priced for seafood, with one of the island's largest selections of domestic and imported fish. A good choice for a reasonable lunch or dinner.

The Great Wok of China, Royal Hawaiian Center, 2201 Kalakaua Ave., tel. 922-5373. Decent food, it's fun to eat here as chefs prepare food at your table in, you guessed it, woks. A good assortment of meat, seafood, and vegetable dishes, guaranteed not to be the steam-table variety.

Spat's, Hyatt Regency, 2424 Kalakaua, tel. 922-9292, is a fun restaurant doubling as a disco, featuring passable Italian cuisine, with decent veal dishes and pasta.

If local people want a buffet they head for Kengos's Buffet, 1529 Kapiolani Blvd, tel. 941-2241, which is a sure sign that you get value for your money. Friday evenings are extremely popular with a special seafood buffet for $14.95. If you're heading for Kengo's go at lunchtime because you get the exact same buffet for $7.50. Every day is slightly different, but you can count on a huge assortment of food that is sure to please.

EXPENSIVE

Sergio's, at the Ilima Hotel, 445 Nohonani, open daily for dinner only from 5:30-11:30 p.m., tel. 926-3388, is one of the finest restaurants over all, and *the* best Italian restaurant in Honolulu. The dishes are culinary masterpieces, painstakingly prepared using only the freshest ingredients that have been imported from around the world. Like the true works of art that they are, the dishes are elegantly presented by a professional and knowledgeable staff. The interior is romantic, subtle, and simple, with a combination of booths and tables. Sergio prepares foods from all regions of Italy, blending and matching hearty peasant soups, fresh salads, and antipasti garnished with aromatic cheeses and spicy prepared meats, pasta dishes, entrees, and desserts. The more than a dozen choices of pasta come with sauces of savory meat, or delicate vegeatbles, and seafood. Entrees are chicken, beef, and fresh fish that make your taste buds rise and shout "Bravo! Sergio! Bravo!"

If food was fine art, and the French definitely regard it as such, the dishes prepared at **Michel's** would deserve their rightful place at the Louvre. Located at the Colony Surf Hotel, 2895 Kalakaua Ave., tel. 923-6552, open daily from 7 a.m.-10 p.m. Michel's is literally on the beach, so your appetite is piqued not only by sumptuous morsels, but by magnificent views of the Waikiki skyline boldly facing the Pacific. The interior is "neo-French elegant," with the dining rooms appointed in soft pastels, velour chairs with armrests, white tablecloths, crystal chandeliers, heavy silver service, and tasteful paintings. The bar is serpentine and of polished koa. Michel's Sunday brunch is legendary. Choose an entree and the remainder of the brunch comes with it. Suggestions are baked avocado with crab meat for $22, or renowned eggs Benedict for $17. You get a choice of broiled fresh grapefruit with sherry, sliced oranges and melon, fresh Hawaiian pineapple slices, Puna papaya with limes, along with a sparkling champagne cocktail, and baskets of banana or blueberry muffins and Kona coffee.

Daily breakfasts are a wild mushroom omelette for $8.50, or breakfast steak and eggs for $14.50, Belgian waffles ($9.50), buttermilk pancakes ($7.50). Lunch is appetizers like baked oysters Michel ($8), or Michel's Reuben sandwich $9. Fruits of the sea are steamed king crab leg for $18, and from the grill come spring lamb chops ($17). Dinner is *magnifique* with fresh Maine lobster on ice ($25), delicate baby coho salmon garnished with shrimp served in its own sauce ($30), or tournedos rossini, a center cut of tenderloin with goose liver and truffles. The dining experience at Michel's is completely satisfying with outstanding food and outstanding service, all in an outstanding setting.

One of the most laudable achievements in the restaurant business is to create an excellent reputation and then to keep it. **Nick's Fishmarket** at the Waikiki Gateway Hotel, 2070 Kalakaua, tel. 955-6333, open nightly for dinner from 6-11:30 p.m., has done just that . . . and keeps doing it. Many gourmets consider Nick's *the* best dining in Waikiki, and it's great fun to find out if they know what they're talking about. Owner Randy Schoch pays personal attention to every detail at Nick's, while executive chef Edward Fernandez creates the culinary magic. Tuxedoed waiters, knowledgeable about every dish and the extensive wine list, add a just- right touch of elegance. Start with fresh-baked clams casino ($8.95), smoked salmon ($9.50), or if you're in the mood how about beluga caviar for only $70. For soup order the Fish Market Chowder, or Chef Fernandez's famous chicken noodle soup. Salads are wonderful too with Nick's special salad, or Caesar salad prepared at your table for $7.50. Seafood and fish entrees are unbeatable. Choose from a wide assortment of island fish like *ono, ahi,* and *opakapaka* that are broiled, baked, seared, or served in a rich Amandine or dill sauce. Fresh Maine lobster, bouillabaisse of lobster, crab, and shrimp, or fresh catfish Cajun style will make you rejoice. Although Nick's is primarily fish, don't overlook the veal, steaks, and chicken with sides of pasta.

An excellent choice is one of Nick's complete dinners featuring entree, soup or salad, vegetables, and hot drink for $26.95. Dancing and listening music happensnightly with No Excuse from 9 p.m.-1:30 a.m. Tues.-Sat., while Leroy Kahuku plays island favorites on his mellow guitar on Sun. and Mondays. If you had only one evening in Waikiki and you wanted to make it memorable, you'd have a hard time doing better than Nick's Fishmarket.

The Secret, previously known as the Third Floor, is the signature restaurant at the Hawaiian Regent, 2552 Kalakaua, tel. 922-6611, open nightly from 6-9:30 p.m. As you enter, you pass an arrangement of cornucopiae holding fresh fruits and fish, while others brim over with gourds, Indian corn, bread turtles and alligators. A wheelbarrow is loaded with nuts. The decor in the main room is high-back, peacock, wicker chairs, where you're wrapped in the arms of bamboo in a booth-like atmosphere. The room is of open-beam construction overlooking Waikiki Beach. In the center is a koi pond with gas torches lit for that extra touch. Hanging from the ceiling are banners that give you the feeling of being at a medieval feast, Polynesian style. Strolling minstrels, The Anacan's, play a seemingly infinite melody of moody contemporary tunes, while a harpist gives an impression of heavenly strains on Monday evenings. Waiters are extremely professional, providing insightful tips to the menu that they have memorized. The Secret is renowned for its fine wines, with over 340 selections that are expertly managed by Richard Dean, one of only two master *sommeliers* in all of Hawaii. Within the restaurant is a wine room that can hold a private party of 12 that may choose from a special menu. As you peruse the menu you are presented with a plate of freshly baked Indian *naan* bread. Select the hors d'oeuvres bar, which has smoked salmon, caviar, and duck paté, enough for a meal for a reasonable $12. Specialties are a *Casserole des fruits de Mer* (lobster, scallops, shrimp, and *opacapaca* in fennel sauce) for $29.50, scampi Provençal ($31.25), rack of spring lamb ($32), and medallions of venison for $29. The Secret has a long and well-deserved reputation as one of the finest eating establishments in Waikiki. A romantic dinner here will long be remembered.

Matteo's, in the Marine Surf Hotel, 364 Seaside, tel. 922-5551, open from 6 p.m.-2 a.m., is a wonderfully romantic Italian restaurant that sets the mood even outside by welcoming you with a red canopy and brass rail that leads to a carved door of *koa* and crystal. Inside is dark and stylish, with high-backed booths, white tablecloths, and marble-top tables. On each is a rose, Matteo's signature. Dinners begin with hot antipasti such as stuffed mushrooms à la Matteo ($6.50), seafood combo ($11.50), or cold antipasto for two for $10.95. Light fare of *ensalada e zuppa* (salad and soup) like special salad ($5.75), heart of romaine lettuce ($6.75), clam soup ($9.50) matched with garlic bread ($1.50) or pizza bread ($2.50), makes an inexpensive but tasty meal. Entree suggestions are chicken *rollatini*, $16.50, veal *rollatini* (rolled veal stuffed with bell peppers, mushrooms, onions, spinach, mozarella) for $20.95, or *bragiola* (rolled beef with mozarella cheese, garlic, fresh basil, and baked with marinara sauce) for $15.95. Complete dinners come with Matteo's special salad, pasta, vegetables, and coffee or tea and include *mahi mahi* Veronica (sautéed fish in lemon sauce and seedless grapes) for $22.95, or veal parmigiana at $23.95. Pastas are very reasonable and dishes include *gnocchi* ($12.95), manicotti à la Matteo ($10.95). An extensive wine list complements the food. If you are out for a special evening of fine dining and romance, Matteo's will set the mood, and the rest is up to you.

Colony Steak House, at the Hyatt Regency, 2424 Kalakaua, tel. 922-9292. As the name implies, they specialize in excellent cuts of steak that you personally choose, as well as fish and a truly superb salad bar. **Bagwell's,** also in the Hyatt Regency, tel. 922-9292, is a superb French restaurant with an imaginative menu and great wine list. The chef is Yves Menoret, formerly of Alexis in San Francisco. The prices are richer than French pastry.

Restaurant Suntory, Royal Hawaiian Shopping Center, tel. 922-5511, is a very handsome restaurant with different rooms specializing in particular styles like *shabu shabu, teppanyaki,* and sushi. The prices used to be worse, but they're still expensive. However, the food preparation and presentation are excellent, and the staff is very attentive.

Furusato Sushi, right next to the Hyatt Regency at 2424 Kalakaua Ave. tel. 922-4991, and **Furusato Tokyo Steak** downstairs are both expensive but top-notch Japanese restaurants. The food and service are authentic, but they are geared toward the Japanese tourist who expects, and almost demands, to pay high prices. In the steakhouse expect steak since very little else is on the menu. Upstairs is sushi. Free valet parking is great for this congested part of Waikiki.

The **Hilton Hawaiian Village** at 2005 Kalia Rd., is one of the finest destination resorts in Hawaii. Its two signature restaurants, both *Travel Holiday* award winners, complement the resort perfectly. **Bali By The Sea,** tel. 941-2254, open daily for dinner from 6-10 p.m., may sound like Indonesian cuisine, but it's more continental than anything else. The setting couldn't be more brilliant. Sit by the open windows so that the sea breezes fan you as you overlook the gorgeous Hilton beach with Diamond Head off to your left. The room is outfitted in a blue paisley carpet, high-backed, armrest-type chairs, white tablecloths, and classical place settings with silver service. Upon ordering, you are presented with a complimentary platter of hors d'oeuvres. Choose appetizers like gratin of oysters with Julienne of duck, or fettuccini with wild mushrooms with prosciutto and sun-dried tomatoes. Soups are bisque of shrimp and lobster or a classic French onion. Entrees are a magnificent selection of fish from Hawaiian waters baked, sautéed, and broiled and then covered in a variety of sauces from fresh basil to mint and tomato vinaigrette. Meat entrees are breast of chicken and lobster, or medallions of venison simmered in pears, cranberry and *poivrade* sauce. The meal ends with a fine presentation of desserts, or a complimentary steaming chocolate Diamond Head. Bali by the Sea is a superb choice for an elegant evening of fine dining.

The **Golden Dragon,** tel. 946-5336, open nightly for dinner from 6-10 p.m., would tempt any knight errant to drop his sword and to pick up chopsticks. This too is a fine restaurant where the walls are decorated with portraits of emperors, and the plates carry the Golden Dragon motif. The interior color scheme is a striking vermilion and black, with the chairs and tables shining with a lacquerware type of patina. The floor is dark *koa*. Outside, the terrace has pagoda-style canopies under which you may dine. Obviously the Golden Dragon isn't your average chop suey house,

the Dragon Room at the Hilton Hawaiian Village

but the menu has all of the standard Chinese fare from lemon chicken to . . . well, chop suey, but it doesn't end there. The food is expertly prepared, and two fine choices are the exotic Imperial Beggar's Chicken (for two), which takes 24 hours' notice to prepare and Chef Dai's Selection (for two), which includes lobster in black bean sauce, shrimp, almond duck, beef in rice wine, duck fried rice, and a special dessert all for only $40. For a first-class restaurant with impeccable food and service, the prices at the Golden Dragon are very, very reasonable.

The **Surf Room,** is in the Royal Hawaiian Hotel, 2259 Kalakaua Ave., tel. 923-7311. The menu is solid but uninspired. However, the setting couldn't be lovelier, and the huge buffet is staggering.

Hy's Steak House, 2440 Kuhio Ave., tel. 922-5555, is one of those rare restaurants that is not only absolutely beautiful, but serves great food as well. Decorated like a Victorian sitting room, its menu offers things other than steaks and chops, but these are the specialties and worth the stiff-upper-lipped price.

ENTERTAINMENT

Waikiki swings, beats, bumps, grinds, sways, laughs, and gets down. If Waikiki has to bear being called a carnival town, it might as well strut its stuff. Dancing (disco and ballroom), happy hours, cocktail shows, cruises, lounge acts, Polynesian extravaganzas, and the street scene provide an endless choice of entertainment. Small-name Hawaiian trios, soloists, pianists, and sultry singers featured in innumerable bars and restaurants woo you in and keep you coming back. Big-name island entertainers and visiting international stars play the big rooms. Free entertainment includes hula shows, ukulele music, street musicians, jugglers, artists, and street-walkers. For a good time, nowhere in Hawaii matches Waikiki. Also see p. 211 for other listings in and around greater Honolulu.

Bars, Happy Hours, And Lounge Acts
Plaza Lounge, tel. 922-6885, in the Waikiki Shopping Plaza, presents Mel Cabang, a fat, bald, and funny-as-hell Filipino singer-comedian. He plays with the audience, like Don Rickles, but he's so *gestalt* that you can't believe it. His risqué repartee, fine guitar-playing, and surprisingly good voice don't quite seem to fit his face. Tuesday to Sat. from 9 p.m., no cover, $2 per drink.

Brother Noland is a local talent who appears around town, but most often performs at the lounge in the Waikiki Sheraton, tel. 922-4422. He's the cutting edge for ethnic Hawaiian groups playing hot reggae, origi-

nals, and plenty of Stevie Wonder, solo or with a group, and shouldn't be missed.

Steve and Theresa are excellent Hawaiian musicians. Their sound is a melodious mixture of traditional and contemporary. Accomplished musicians with beautiful voices, they often appear at La Mex in the Royal Hawaiian Shopping Center, tel. 923-2906.

In the Park Shore Hotel, 2586 Kalakaua Ave., The Bar is a quiet, relaxing place to have a drink. A talented pianist and organist, Andre Branch, plays nightly. Free.

The **Irish Rose Saloon** at 227 Lewers, presents live entertainment nightly with dancing till 4 a.m., and features sporting events on their big-screen TV. Happy hour is from 3-8 p.m. Right across the street from the Outrigger Coral Seas Hotel, just at the entrance of the Al Herrington Show.

A great little homey bar called the **Brass Rail** serves up cold draft beer and deli sandwiches. They're into sports and especially Monday Night Football, which usually begins in Hawaii at 7:30 p.m. Located on the ground floor of the Outrigger Waikiki Hotel, at 2335 Kalakaua.

The **Rose and Crown Pub** in King's Village has a pianist playing sing-along favorites in what is a very close rendition of an English-style pub. They have daily specials; for example, on Saturday if you wear your Rose and Crown hat you have happy hour prices all night long. So drink hearty, and hold on to your hat! The crowd is a good mixture intent on swilling beer and partying. Noisy, raucous, and fun.

Key Largo is a *bar,* and bars are not so easy to find in Waikiki. Stuck away at 142 Uluniu St., it attracts a mostly local crowd, especially Wed.-Sat. when they feature live rock and roll bands. Key Largo doesn't have the vibe of a rough joint, but it is the sort of place where a fool and his teeth can easily be parted.

Jolly Roger Restaurant at the 2244 Kalakaua and 150 Kaiulani (see p. 242) presents a changing mixture of live music nightly in their lounge open until 2 a.m. A good spot for listening to music and enjoying conversation around the bar.

The Grapevine, corner of Prince Edward and Uluniu streets, presents low-key live music. Artists change, but expect a guitarist playing soulful Hawaiian music.

In the International Market Place, the **Cock's Roost Steak House** offers free entertainment, with no minimum or cover. Nearby, the **Crow's Nest,** above the Jolly Roger Restaurant, at 2244 Kalakaua, features local and visiting entertainers. If Blue Kangaroo, a hilarious comedy act, is playing, don't miss them. The entertainers, Mike Drager and Jay Cook, have been singing and playing their guitars and various other stringed instruments together for over 25 years. They first played at the Crow's Nest in 1972, and in their own words "can't believe the sumbitch lasted this long." Their ribald songs are extremely egalitarian . . . they insult all races, creeds, and sexes equally. As the night gets later their humor gets raunchier. Be forewarned, and have a ball.

The Brothers Cazimero have an excellent and well-deserved reputation as one of Hawaii's finest duos, singing a lovely blend of Hawaiian and contemporary music. You can usually catch them at the Royal Hawaiian Hotel's Monarch Room. Dinner and cocktail shows are from 7 p.m. Tues. to Saturday. Alohawear is fine, tel. 923-7311.

Trappers in the Hyatt Regency is an intimate jazz nightclub, with overstuffed chairs and cozy booths; continuous jazz from 5:30 p.m.

Baron's Studio, Waikiki Plaza Hotel, tel. 946-0277, is home to jazz vocalist Azure McCall. Open nightly, quiet drinks, fine background tunes.

The **Polynesian Pub,** 2490 Kalakaua, tel. 923-3683, offers happy hour nightly and contemporary Hawaiian music. Right-priced drinks, no cover.

The Garden Bar, Hilton Hawaiian Village, tel. 949-4321, features John Norris and the New Orleans Jazz Band on Sun. from 2 to 6 p.m.

Discos, Dancing And Nightclubs
Ballroom dancers will enjoy **Tea Dancing at the Royal** in the Monarch Room of the Royal Hawaiian Hotel, featuring the 14-piece Del Courtney Orchestra, Mon. from 5:30-8:30 p.m. The **Maile Lounge** at the Kahala Hilton, tel. 734-2211, offers live music for ballroom dancing nightly.

Nick's Fishmarket at the Gateway Hotel, 2070 Kalakaua (see p. 249), swings with contemporary dance music until 1:30 a.m. A mixed crowd, but mostly a mature crowd who have stayed on to dance after a magnificent meal that Nick's is known for. Music is provided by No Excuse, headliners that make Nick's their home when not on tour.

The **Paradise Lounge** in the Rainbow Tower of the Hilton Hawaiian Village is a jazz nightclub, perfect for a night of relaxing entertainment. They have a pianist nightly and a polished wooden dance floor. Weekends brings a variety of jazz ensembles for your listening and dancing pleasure. Perfect for a romantic evening.

The Wave is a rock 'n' roll and new wave hotspot with live music nightly, 1877 Kalakaua Ave., tel. 941-0424. It has become an institution of late-night fun and dancing. The crowd is mixed, and you can either choose to dance, or perch upstairs in the balcony behind glass where you can check out the dancers below, or have a few drinks and some conversation. The Wave is a sure bet for a night of fun.

Pink Cadillac at 478 Ena is just around the corner from the Wave. Open till 2 a.m., its large dance floors rock with merrymakers ages 18 and up. It's a happening place for younger rockers. Alcohol is served, but if you are under 21 you'll be braceletted, which

the distinctive mural at The Wave

means you can't drink. The cover charge is $10 for ages 18-21, $5 over 21.

The following are disco nightclubs in and around Waikiki. Most have videos, a theme, a dress code of alohawear and shoes, no sandals, and start hopping around 9 p.m. with the energy cut off around 4 a.m.

The **Jazz Cellar,** 205 Lewers St., features mostly live rock and roll and some jazz. The place jumps till 4 a.m. and has plenty of special nights like Thirsty Tuesdays and Ladies' Night. Put on your dancin' shoes, casual attire, tel. 923-9952.

Lewers Street Annex at 270 Lewers is a basic disco dance spot featuring Top-40 tunes. The clientele is mostly young visitors and some local workers who stop in for a late-night drink. A special feature is their "12 o'clock high," basically happy hour prices from 12 noon-12 midnight. Standard drinks $1.50, domestic beers $1.50, margaritas and mai tais $1.50. Good for casual drinking, dancing, and meeting people.

The Infinity at the Sheraton Waikiki presents golden oldies and contemporary live music nightly from 8 p.m. Good dance floor.

The **Blue Water Cafe,** 2350 Kuhio Ave, once the home of live music, now has disco and videos. Distinguished by it's copper and brass appointment, including full copper doors to the restrooms, pillars are covered in copper and the ceiling looks like closely fit barrel staves. Waitresses are particularly good-looking.

The **3-D Ballroom,** 2260 Kuhio, is a crummy little joint two floors up with super-loud music for teeny-boppers and punkers.

The Point After, 2552 Kalakaua Ave., tel. 922-6611. Fatso sofas in this football-theme nightspot. A local favorite with a dress code.

Spats in the Hyatt Regency, tel. 922-9292, is an Italian restaurant that turns into a disco around 9 p.m. The decor is 1920s art deco. Classy, well known, and swinging.

Red Lion Dance Palace, 240 Lewers St., tel. 922-1027, offers high-tech video and disco and a pool bar. Beachwear OK, from 2 p.m.-4 a.m.

Masquerade and **Phaze,** next door to each other at the corner of McCully and Kalakaua avenues, feature a heavy sound system and wild light shows. Cutting-edge videos, great dance floors, and wild tunes till 4 a.m.

Cilly's, 1909 Ala Wai Blvd., tel. 942-2942, **Annabelle's** at the Westin Ilikai, 1777 Ala Moana Blvd., tel. 949-3811, and **Steel Wings,** also at the Westin Ilikai, are well-known discos where you can't help having a good time. All have reputations as swinging nightspots.

Exotic live dancers, like exotic live plants, need a unique atmosphere in which to bloom. Both seem to crave light, one sunlight, the other a spotlight. Most of the flashy fleshy nightspots of Waikiki used to be a few blocks away along Kapiolani Blvd. (see p. 162) but they have been moving ever closer to the heart of Waikiki. Now they are strung along Kuhio Avenue, where they're easily recognizable by their garish neon lights which advertise their wares. The Kuhio Avenue exotic dance spots are supposedly a step up in class from their Kapiolani Boulevard counterparts, but when their dancers strip to the buff, the difference is hardly noticeable . . . or very noticeable, depending upon point of view. The names of the strip joints really don't matter, just look for the signs of "exotic dancers." Usually a $10 cover and $5 for a drink.

Dinner Shows
And Polynesian Extravaganzas
Free tickets to these extravaganzas are handed out by condo time-share outfits stationed in booths along the main drags. For attending their sales presentations, usually 90 minutes, you can get tickets to the Don Ho Show, among others—but they might be the toughest freebies you've ever earned. The presentation is a pressure cooker. The sales people are pros, who try every imaginable technique to get you to sign. If you're really interested in time-sharing, the deals aren't too bad, but if you're there only for the tickets, what a waste of time!

The **Don Ho Show** at the Hilton Hawaiian Village has been attracting huge crowds for years, leaving some thrilled, appalling others. There are some truly dazzling costumes and plenty of glitzy Hawaiian acts, complete with music and dance. Don Ho, a talented vocalist and veteran performer, is either totally relaxed in his role or dulled by its repetition. Some consider his sexual humor in bad taste, but it's no different from what you hear in most nightclubs. After all, the show isn't a prayer meeting. Don Ho plays with the audience, especially the older folks, making pointed jokes about Mainlanders. Of course everyone roars with laughter—blame it on the potent mai tais. There are two shows Sun. through Fri.: the dinner show from 6:30-8:30 p.m. for about $70 per couple, and the cocktail show from 8 p.m. about $35 per couple,

includes one drink. For details and reservations, call 949-4321.

Al Harrington, billed as "The South Pacific Man," has also been attracting crowds for years at the Polynesian Palace in the Reef Towers Hotel on Lewers St., tel. 923-9861. Another wonderfully costumed Polynesian extravaganza takes you on a musical tour through the South Pacific. Personable Harrington takes time to make everyone feel comfortable, and though he too has been doing the show for years, he manages to keep sparkle in his performance. Two dinner shows and two cocktail shows nightly except Saturdays. The buffet dinner is reputed to be exceptional. Prices are about $70 per couple for the dinner show, half that for the cocktail shows.

The Kahala Hilton, tel. 734-2211, presents **An Evening With Danny Kaleikini.** This extraordinary island entertainer has been captivating audiences here for almost 20 years. This show has class; it doesn't draw the large budget-oriented crowds. Two shows nightly except Sun., dinner show at 7 p.m., cocktail show at 9 p.m.

Tavana's Polynesian Spectacular in the Long House of the Hilton Hawaiian Village, tel. 923-0211, combines Polynesian music, song and dance, dramatic effects, and costumes. Two shows nightly: dinner seating at 5:30 and 8:30 p.m., cocktails at 6:30 and 9 p.m.

Dick Jensen, The Hula Hut, 286 Beachwalk, tel. 923-3838, is a dinner show with an all-you-can-eat buffet. Seating at 8 p.m., $30 per person, cocktail show 8:45 p.m., $18 per person, one cocktail included.

Free Entertainment
Check the newpapers and free tourist literature for times to the following events.

The **Royal Hawaiian Band** plays free concerts on Sunday afternoons at the bandstand in Kapiolani Park, oftentimes with singers and hula dancers. Also in the park, free concerts are periodically given by a variety of local and visiting musicians at the Waikiki Shell.

The **Kodak Hula Show** is free, though it's a hassle to get in. The show is held on Tues., Thurs., and Fri. at 10 a.m. in Kapiolani Park.

Extremely popular, people start lining up at 8 a.m.; be there by 9 if you want a seat. You sit on bleachers with 3,000 people, while Hawaiian *tutu* bedecked in muumuus, leis, and smiles play ukuleles and sing for the ti-leaf-skirted dancers. You can buy film and even rent a camera, as befits the show's sponsor, the Eastman Kodak Company—snap away with abandon. The performance dates back to 1937, and some of the original dancers, now in their 80s, still participate. At the finale, the dancers line up on stage with red-lettered placards that spells out H-A-W-A-I-I, so you can take your own photo of the most famous Hawaiian postcard. Then the audience is invited down for a free hula lesson. People who are too hip hate it, *kamaainas* shy away from it, but if you're a good sport, you'll walk away like everyone else with a big smile on your face.

A potpourri of contemporary entertainment is also found in Kapiolani Park on weekends. Just across from the zoo, musicians, jugglers, clowns, unicyclists, and acrobats put on a free, impromptu circus. Some of the best are B.J. Patches, Twinkles, and Jingles from a local troupe called Clown Alley.

The ukulele tree in front of the Reef Hotel, 2169 Kalia Rd., has heard the lovely melodies of Hawaii for 50 years. Every Sun. at 8 p.m. local musicians and sometimes well-known guests come to play and be heard.

The **Royal Hawaiian Shopping Center** provides free entertainment throughout the week: quilting, *lau hala* weaving, pineapple cutting, and free hula lessons every Friday at 10 a.m. with Aunti Maiki Aiu Lake.

Aunty Bella's Leis, 2200 Kalakaua Ave., gives free lei-making classes Mon., Wed., and Fri. at 10:30 a.m. The flowers are free and you keep the lei that you string.

At the Shore Bird Restaurant, 2160 Kalia, a **female bikini beauty** contest is held on Sun. at 4 p.m. You can win $400 for first prize, second prize $150, third $50. All finalists receive dinner for two at the Shore Bird Beach Broiler and much, more.

SHOPPING

The biggest problem concerning shopping in Waikiki is to keep yourself from burning out over the endless array of shops and boutiques. Everywhere you look someone has something for sale, and with the preponderance of street stalls lining the boulevards, much of the merchandise comes out to greet you. The same rule applies to shopping as it does to everything in Waikiki—class next door to junk. Those traveling to the Neighbor Islands should seriously consider a shopping spree in Waikiki, which has the largest selection and most competitive prices in the islands. A great feature about shopping in Waikiki is that most shops are only a minute or two from the beach. This enables your sale-hound companion to hunt while you relax. There's no telling how much money your partner can save you! "Ingrate! This bathing suit could have cost $50, but I got it for $25. See, you saved $25 while you were lying here like a beached whale." Everyone concerned should easily be mollified. Charge!

The Fence
The best place to find an authentic island-made souvenir at a reasonable price is at **The Fence,** located along the fence of the Hono-

lulu Zoo fronting Kapiolani Park. The new offical name is **Artists of Oahu/Sunday Exhibit.** Some of the island's best artists congregate here to display and sell their works on Wednesday and weekends from 10 a.m.-4 p.m. Individual artists are only allowed to display one day a week. The Fence was the good idea of Honolulu's current mayor, Frank Fasi, who decided that Oahu's rich resource of artists shouldn't go untapped. There are plenty of excellent artists whose works are sure to catch your fancy. Here are some of the best.

John Costello does colorful island-inspired paintings in pointillism, many of which have a fantastic, dreamlike quality. **Mary Ann Abel,** whose pen and inks of things Hawaiian, especially children's faces, are inspired. **Daniel Wang,** one of the few practicing deaf artists in the U.S., specializes in a remarkable palm painting technique done on rice paper with Chinese inks and watercolors. **Bob Reeves** works with island woods and specializes in *koa* frames. **Caridad Sumile** does beautiful paintings and portraits in watercolors and acrylics.

Marge Claus has a colorful batik style. **Patrick Doell** has a very realistic, almost picture-postcard style. **Maggie Kobayashi**

Waikiki Bazaar

John Costello, artist

incorporates the female form with nautical suggestions and loves doing mermaids. **"June of Art,"** Hoegler-Reda piles on layers of paint to achieve a three-dimensional quality. **Leonard Wood** loves animals and renders them in quiet pastels.

Cathy Thompson does dreamy, impressionistic lily ponds. **Joe Hunt** loves the "joy of life" and renders lively paintings of color and movement. **Edna Loo** does whimsical vignettes of children in Hawaiian setings. **Dianne Jeanine** paints soft flowing watercolors of flowers, sunsets, and seascapes. **Francine McGee** uses layers of glazing with modern transclucent colors to achieve Old Master-like seascapes. **Theresia Brinsen** is noted for the brilliance of the knife-technique in land- and seascapes. **Peggy Pai Laughlin** does batik and oil on silk and free-stitch embroidery.

Gifts And Souvenirs

If you would really like to return from the islands with a unique gift try **Hawaiian Pillows and Kits,** tel. 734-5032. The pillowcases are excellent renditions of the distinctive style of quilting developed in Hawaii after being introduced by the missionaries of last century. Rose Tam-Hoy, the owner, shows her handiwork at the Sheraton Moana's Banyan Courtyard on Fridays and at various other hotels throughout the week. Rose is a wealth of knowledge on Hawaiin quilting, and is happy to offer demonstrations and lessons.

Another islander demonstrating and selling Polynesian crafts is Faitu Powell of **Powell's Souvenirs,** tel. 926-6797. Faitu also sets up a small display at the Moana on Friday, and across the way at the Princess Kaiulani on Saturdays. She specializes in handmade hula skirts, leis, head bands, *haku,* and a variety of handicrafts. All of her souvenirs are authentic.

Fine Japanese art can be seen and purchased at two outstanding shops in Waikiki's Eaton Square, **Gallery Mikado** and **Gara Kuta-Do.**

ABC Stores scattered throughout Waikiki were founded by a local man, Sid Kosasa, who learned the retail business from his father. This "everything store" sells groceries, sundries, and souvenirs. Prices are good especially on specials like lotions and beach mats. Very convenient.

You can purchase colorful, dramatic **Hawaiian calendars** drawn by Herb Kane, a well-known local artist, at all of the Burger King outlets. Fine mementos, they sell for under $3.

On Kalakaua between Kealohilani and Ohua streets above the ABC Store is **Lowest Factory Prices.** They've got very good prices on all-cotton shirts and muumuus, a rarity. Every price tag offers 10 percent off.

Those who just couldn't return home without a deep Hawaiian tan can be helped by visiting **Waikiki Aloe.** They specialize in skincare products, lotions, and tanning supplies. In the Royal Hawaiian Shopping Center and the Kuhio Mall.

The **Waikiki Business Plaza,** 2270 Kalakaua Ave., houses a number of jewelry stores. In one stop you can get a pretty good idea of prices and availability. Look for jewelry boxes laden with jade, gold, turquoise, pearls, coral, *puka* shells, and eel, snake, and leather goods.

Military Shop of Hawaii has an entire wall dedicated to military patches, along with clothes, memorabilia, and collectibles. At 1921 Kalakaua Ave., tel. 942-3414.

Those with good taste but a limited budget should check out **Hawaiian Wear Unlimited,** liquidators of alohawear from most of Hawaii's big manufacturers. Located at the Royal Hawaiian Shopping Center, daily 9 a.m.-10 p.m. Also, **Robin Claire** "resale boutique" sells used designer clothing. At 1901 Kapiolani Plaza, tel. 941-8666.

Kite Fantasy, 2863 Kalakaua Ave., tel. 922-KITE, is sure to have an aerial toy to tickle your fancy. Kapiolani Park across the road is one of the best spots around to fly a kite, and they give free kite-flying lessons regardless of whether you purchase a kite or not; daily display at 11 a.m. and 2 p.m. Next door to the old Natatorium and the New Otani Hotel, you'll see multicolored kites floating in the breeze. Inside they have the "finest collection of kites, windsocks, and toys" in Hawaii. The phenomenal winds in Hawaii that generate good waves and good windsurfing conditions, also generate excellent kite-flying conditions. Hardly a day goes by that there isn't wind enough to get a kite up. And, because the winds are so gusty and changeable, it makes for some fantastic kite-flying acrobatics. Nearby in the park is what they call the Kite Tree, where kite flyers congregate in the evening. So if you're interested, go fly a kite!

Waikiki Fashion Center, 2310 Kuhio, next door to Zorro's, sells alohawear like plenty of other stores, but the prices are pretty good,

and they even feature an ad for $5 off with a purchase of $20 or more.

For a full range of **photo supplies** at bargain prices try: **Woolworth's,** 2224 Kalakaua Ave.; **Fox Photo** in the International Market Place and the Waikikian and Reef Towers hotels; and **Photo Stores** here and there along Kalakaua, Kuhio, Kalia, and Lewers streets. **Island Camera and Gift Shop,** on Kalakaua across from the Moana Hotel, is a small, but a full-service camera store. Handbillers often give money-saving coupons to a variety of photo stores.

Duty-free goods are always of interest to international visitors. You can find a duty-free store on Royal Hawaiian Ave., just behind Woolworth's. Also, if you want to see a swarm of Japanese jostling for position in a tiny little store trying to feed a buying frenzy, that's the spot.

Waikiki Shopping Centers

The largest credit card oasis is the **Royal Hawaiian Shopping Center.** This massive complex is three stories of nonstop shopping, running for three blocks in front of the Sheraton and Royal Hawaiian hotels. It's open daily 9 a.m.-10 p.m., till 9 p.m. on Sun., tel. 922-0588. This complex provides an excellent mixture of small intimate shops and larger department stores. There's a **post office** on the second-floor "B" building. The second and third floors of this shopping center are pretty quiet. It's off the street so not as many tourists find there way here. It's a good place to do some comparative browsing before making your purchases.

Where the Royal Hawaiian Shopping Plaza ends the **Waikiki Shopping Plaza** begins, but on the other side of the street. Here, you'll find multilevel shopping. The mall's centerpiece is a five-story waterfall, an impressive sculpture of water and plexiglass. Another feature of this mall is *Waikiki Calls,* a free hula show. The plaza is open daily 9 a.m.-11 p.m., tel. 923-1191.

The **International Market Place** is an open-air shopping bazaar that feels like Asia. Its natural canopy is a huge banyan, and the entire complex is across from the Moana

Hotel at 2330 Kalakaua Ave., open daily from 9 a.m. until the vendors get tired at night, tel. 923-9871. Among some fine merchandise and a treasure or two is great junk! If you're after souvenirs like bamboo products, shell-work, hats, mats, lotions, alohawear, and carvings, you can't do better than the International Market Place. The worst thing is that everything starts to look the same, the best is that the vendors will bargain. Make offers. If you successfully work your way through the gauntlet of shops without getting scalped, you may be able to find out what the future may bring by stopping at the Enchanted Tree. Here you can get psychic readings and healings. Mini-readings $10, six-month reading $15, one-year reading $20, family reading $25, and life reading $35. Located under the big banyan.

Directly behind the marketplace is the Kuhio Mall, at 2301 Kuhio Avenue. Basically the same theme with open-air shops: gifts, fashions, food, and handmade artifacts. Enjoy the free Polynesian Show nightly at 7 and 8 p.m. This is a little older, funkier mall, one grade up from what you would find in the International Market Place and Duke's Alley. You'll find among others S.K. Takahashi, jewelry and gifts, and the Waikiki Aloe Center, where you can watch their lab at work. If you wanted a low-key place to discover "treaure junk" this mall is good. It's even better than the International Marketplace because it's more low-key. There aren't nearly as many people here and the salespeople are not as pushy.

Walk to the rear of the mall and go upstairs to what's called the Craft Court. You'll find crafts and plants made or grown in Hawaii sold by a small co-op of shops. Inside are haku lei (flat) that work as a hat band, a butterfly gallery, with specimens gathered from insect breeding farms, silk flower arrangements, and plants certified for export (blooming and nonblooming varieties of anthurium, ginger, plumeria, orchids), and flower bouquets. Judy Vess has a shop here selling hand-blown pyrex glass teardrops. Inside the tear-shaped glass is sterilized ocean water, sands from Hawaii, and five little sea shells from three different islands. An-

other shop sells a replica of a double-hulled canoe that looks very authentic, but is made from rolled newspaper. It's been laquered and shellacked, so it has a realistic brown patina to it, complete with the distinctive crab claw sail. Weaving, and pottery selections are very reasonable. If you want something at Christmas time to remind you of Aloha Santa, they have Christmas wreaths made out of local forest products.

For those who can't stand to waste an opportunity to shop, they can do so while passing through Duke's Alley, a shortcut between Kuhio and Kalakaua avenues. Here you'll find a row of stalls selling basically the same merchandise as in the International Market Place.

The Hyatt Regency Shopping Center, also called the Atrium Shops, is located on the first three floors of the Hyatt Regency Hotel, 2424 Kalakaua Ave., tel. 922-5522, open daily 9 a.m.-11 p.m. The 70 or so shops here are mighty classy: if you're after exclusive fashions or a quality memento, this is the place. There's a continental-style sidewalk cafe, backed by a cascading indoor waterfall. Often free entertainment and fashion shows are put on by the various shops.

Smaller Malls

King's Village, at 131 Kaiulani Ave., just next to the Hyatt Regency, takes its theme from last century, where boardwalks pass 19th-century look-a-like shops, complete with a changing-of-the-guard ceremony nightly at 6:15 p.m. This attractive complex offers free entertainment, and attracts some of the best local street artists who usually set up their stands at night. The Waikiki Trade Center is on the corner of Seaside and Kuhio avenues with some of Waikiki's most elegant shops, featuring sophisticated fashions, exquisite artwork, and fine dining. The Rainbow Bazaar is a unique mall located at the Hilton Hawaiian Hotel, 2005 Kalia Road. Fun just to walk around, shops feature three main themes: Imperial Japan, Honk Kong Alley, and South Pacific Court.

The Waikiki Bazaar is on Kalakaua across from a brand-new building called

A.N.A. Kalakaua Center, a multihued building in pastels. It's beautiful. Reminiscent of newer constructions seen in Japan. The Bazaar is bizarre. Upstairs, and in little booths are an orgy of porno shops. A person who couldn't read Japanese *katakana* wouldn't know that they said "porno." The Bazaar is there expressly for the use of Japanese tourists.

Street Artists And Vendors

You don't have to try to find something to buy in Waikiki—in fact, if you're not careful, the merchandise will come after you! This takes place in the form of street vendors, who have been gaining a lot of attention lately. Some view them as a colorful addition to the beach scene, others as a nuisance. These carnival-type salespeople set up their mobile booths mainly along Kalakaua Avenue, with some on Kuhio Avenue and the side streets in between. In dealing with them you can have a positive experience if you remember two things: they have some pretty nifty junk, and you get what you pay for.

Also, street artists set up their palettes along busy thoroughfares, and especially at the entrances to small shopping malls. Most draw caricatures of patrons in a few minutes for a few dollars—fun souvenirs. An outstanding street artist is Mai Long, a Vietnamese man who sets up in King's Alley and does superb profiles or full face all in color for less than $10.

Right here under the Waikiki banyan is a gentleman named Coco who makes coconut-frond hats, basically a dying art. Just near the canoe rides, you'll see his hats and baskets. Depending on the hat, you can get one for $15 or so. The baskets, good for holding fruit, incidentals, or whatever, are a real souvenir of Hawaii. With Coco making them right before you very eyes, you can't get more authentic than that. Coco says you can still learn how to weave in the Hawaiian tradition. His dad, Uncle Harry Kuikai, weaves at the Royal Hawaiian Shopping Center every Tues. and Thurs. from 9:30- 11:30 a.m. He'll teach you the basics of weaving and you can make your own souvenir (free). For longer-term tourists, there's an eight-week weaving class sponsored by the Kamehameha School. Just call the high school and inquire as to time and fees.

As you walk around Waikiki you'll see plenty of street-side booths offering unbelievable prices like "rent a car for $5, a jeep for $15, Pearl Harbor Cruise $5, Don Ho Show $20". Why so cheap? They're basically an advertising firm that signs you up to listen to a 90-minute spiel on a time-share condo. What happens during and after the 90-minute hard pitch is up to you, but you do get the payoff at the end.

CENTRAL OAHU

For most uninformed visitors, central Oahu is a colorful blur as they speed past in their rental cars en route to the North Shore. Slow down, there are things to see! For island residents, the suburban towns of Aiea, Pearl City, Mililani, and Wahiawa are home. Both routes heading north from Honolulu meet in **Wahiawa,** the island's most central town. The roads cross just near the entrance to **Schofield Barracks,** a warm-up target for Japanese Zeros as they flew on their devastating bombing run over Pearl Harbor.

Wahiawa was of extreme cultural and spiritual importance to the early Hawaiians. In town are **healing stones,** whose mystic vibrations were said to cure the maladies of sufferers. In a field not far from town are the

Kukaniloko, the royal birthing stones, where the ruling *ali'i* labored to give birth to the future noblemen of the islands. While in town you can familiarize yourself with Oahu's flora by visiting the **Wahiawa Botanical Garden,** or take a quick look at a serene Japanese temple.

As you gain the heights of the **Leilehua Plateau,** sandwiched between the Waianae and Koolau ranges, a wide expanse of green is planted in cane and pineapple. Just like on supermarket shelves, Del Monte's **Pineapple Variety Garden** competes with Dole's **Pineapple Pavilion,** a minute up the road. As a traveler's way station, central Oahu blends services, amenities, and just enough historical sites to warrant stretching your legs, but not enough to bog you down for the day.

WAHIAWA AND VICINITY

Wahiawa is like a military jeep: basic, ugly, but indispensable. This is a soldiers' town, with servicemen from Schofield Barracks or nearby Wheeler AFB shuffling along the streets. Most are young, short-haired, short-tempered, and dressed in fatigues. Every-

where you look are cheap bars, burger joints, run-down discos perfumed with sweat and spilled beer, and used-furniture stores. Route 99 turns into Rt. 80 which goes through Wahiawa, crossing California Avenue, the main drag, then rejoins Rt. 99 near the Del Monte

Pineapple Garden. Wahiawa has seemingly little to recommend it, and maybe because of its ugliness, when you do find beauty it shines even brighter.

SIGHTS

Wahiawa Botanical Gardens

In the midst of town is an oasis of beauty, 27 acres of developed woodlands featuring exotic trees, ferns, and flowers gathered from around the world. Located at 1396 California Ave., they're open daily except Christmas and New Year's, from 9 a.m.-4 p.m., admission free. The parking lot is marked by an HVB warrior; walk through the main entranceway and take a pamphlet from the box for a self-guiding tour. When it rains, the cement walkways are treacherously slippery, especially if you're wearing thongs. The nicer paths have been left natural, but they can be muddy. Inside the grounds are trees from the Philippines, Australia, Africa, and a magnificent multihued Mindanao gum from New Guinea. Your senses will be bombarded with fragrant camphor trees from China and Japan, and the rich aroma of cinnamon. Everywhere are natural bouquets of flowering trees, entangled by vines and highlighted by rich green ferns. Most specimens have been growing for a minimum of 40 years, so they're well established.

The Healing Stones

Belief in the healing powers of these stones has been attracting visitors since ancient times. When traveling down Ohai Street (Rt. 80) take a left on California Avenue, and follow it to Kaalalo Place. To glimpse the religion of Hawaii in microcosm, in a few blocks you pass the Riusenji Soto Buddhist Mission, followed by the healing stones, next door to Olive United Methodist Church. If you've never experienced a Buddhist temple, make sure to visit the grounds of **Riusenji Soto Mission.** Usually no one is around, and even if the front doors are locked you can peer in at an extremely ornate altar graced by Buddha, highlighted in black lacquer and gold. On the grounds look for a stone *jizo,*

patron of travelers and children. In Japan he often wears a red woven hat and bib, but here he has on a straw hat and muumuu.

An HVB Warrior marks the stones, just past the Kaalala Elementary School, across the street from a beautiful eucalyptus grove. A humble cinder-block building built in 1947 houses the stones. When you swing open the iron gate it strikes a deep mournful note, as if it were an instrument designed to announce your presence and departure. Inside the building, three stones sit atop rudimentary pedestals. Little scratches mark the stones, and an offertory box is filled with items like oranges, bread, a gin bottle, coins, and candy kisses. A few votive candles flicker before a statue of the Blessed Virgin.

CENTRAL OAHU

N.B. ONLY MAIN ROADS SHOWN

© MOON PUBLICATIONS, INC.

Kukaniloko, The Birthing Stones

Follow Rt. 80 through town for about a mile. At the corner of Whitmore Avenue is a red light: right takes you to Whitmore Village and left puts you on a dirt track that leads to another eucalyptus grove marking the birthing stones. About 40 large boulders are in the middle of a field with a mountain backdrop. One stone looks like the next, but on closer inspection you see that each has a personality. The royal wives would come here, assisted by both men and women of the ruling *ali'i,* to give birth to their exalted offspring. The baby's umbilical cord, a sacred talisman, would be hidden in the cracks and crevices of the stones. Near the largest palm tree is a special stone that appears to be fluted all the way around, with a dip in the middle. It, along with other stones nearby, seem perfectly fitted to accept the torso of a woman in a reclining position. Notice that small fires have been lit in the hollows of these stones, and that they are discolored with soot and ashes.

Schofield Barracks

Stay on Rt. 99, skirt Wahiawa to the west, and go past the entrance to Schofield Barracks. Schofield Barracks dates from the turn of the century, named after Gen. John Schofield, an early proponent of the strategic importance of Pearl Harbor. A sign tells you that it is still the "Home of the Infantry, Tropic Lightning." If you enter here through the McComb Gate, you can visit the **Tropic Lightning Museum** with memorabilia going back to the War of 1812. There are planes from WW II, Chinese rifles from Korea, and deadly *pungi* traps from Vietnam.

The museum has lost many of its exhibits in recent years. They've been taken to the Army Museum in Waikiki. But the base is still interesting to visit and remains one of the prettiest military installations in the world. With permission, you can proceed to the Kolekole Pass, from where you get a sweeping view of inland and coastal Oahu. While heading north on 99 as you pass Scoffield Barracks, notice a few run-down shops about 50 yards past the entrance. Stop here and look behind the shops at a wonderful still life created by the Wahiawa Reservoir (good fishing, see p. 153).

Pineapples

A few minutes past the entrance to Schofield Barracks, Rt. 803 bears left to Waialua, while Rt. 99 goes straight ahead and begins passing rows of pineapple. At the intersection of Rt. 80 is the **Del Monte Variety Garden.**

Kukaniloko, royal birthing stones

Schofield Barracks

You're free to wander about and read the descriptions of the history of pineapple production in Hawaii, and of the genetic progress of the fruit made famous by the islands. This exhibit is much more educational and honest than the **Dole Pineapple Pavilion** just up the road, the one with all the tour buses lined up outside. You too can enter and pay $1.50 for a sad little paper plate half filled with pineapple chunks. Or how about $.60 for a glass of canned pineapple juice from a dispenser that you'd find in any fast-food store. Unless the pineapple harvest has been abundant, you can't even buy a fresh fruit, and when you can, they're no cheaper or fresher than those in any grocery store. The Dole Pineapple Pavilion is firmly entrenched along the tourist route, but as a positive public relations scheme it is a blunder!

PRACTICALITIES

Food And Shopping

Kemoo Farm at 1718 Wilikina Dr., tel. 621-8481, just past the entrance to Schofield Barracks, has been a *kamaaina* favorite since 1935. The restaurant has a soothing bucolic feeling, perched on the banks of man-made Wahiawa Reservoir. Servings are family style with homemade bread, fresh trout, and rich gravies dolloped over roast beef or duck.

Sunday and Wednesday feature a brunch complete with island entertainment. Reservations are necessary for these days, and advisable for the remainder of the week. Dinner and drinks for two runs about $50.

Dot's Restaurant, off California Ave. at 130 Mango St., tel. 622-4115, is a homey restaurant specializing in American-Japanese food that gives a good square meal for your money. The interior is a mixture of Hawaiian/Oriental in dark brown tones. Lunch specials include butterfish, teriyaki chicken, pork, or beef plates all for around $4.50. Miso soup is $2, and simple Japanese dishes go for about $3.50. The most expensive item on the menu is steak and lobster for $15. Dot's is nothing to write home about, but you definitely won't go hungry.

If you're into fast foods, no problem. The streets are lined with **Jack in the Box** elbowing **Ronald McDonald,** who's trying to out-flash the old **Burger King.**

The streets of Wahiawa are lined with stores that cater to residents, not tourists. This means that the prices are right, and if you need supplies or necessities, this would be a good place to stock up. On the corner of California and Oahi streets is a **Cornet Store,** an old-fashioned five and dime, where you can buy anything from suntan lotion to a crock pot. The **Big Way Supermarket** is at the corner of California and Kilani avenues.

AIEA, PEARL CITY, AND VICINITY

The twin cities of Aiea and Pearl City, except for the USS *Arizona* Memorial and perhaps a football game at Aloha Stadium, have little to attract the average tourist. Mainly they are residential areas for greater Honolulu, and for the large numbers of military families throughout this area.

PEARL HARBOR: USS *ARIZONA* MEMORIAL

Even as you approach the pier from which you board a launch to take you to the USS *Arizona,* you know that you're at a shrine. Very few spots in America carry such undeniable emotion so easily passed from one generation to another: here, Valley Forge, Gettysburg, not many more. On that beautiful, cloudless morning of December 7, 1941, at one minute before 8 o'clock, the United States not only entered the war, but lost its innocence forevermore.

The first battle of WW II for the U.S. actually took place about 90 minutes before Pearl Harbor's bombing when the USS *Ward* sank an unidentified submarine sliding into Honolulu. In Pearl Harbor, dredged about 40 years earlier to allow superships to enter, the heavyweight champions of America's Pacific Fleet were lined up flanking the near side of Ford's Island. The naive deployment of this "Battleship Row" prompted a Japanese admiral to remark that never, even in times of maximum world peace, could he dream that the military might of a nation would have its unprotected chin stuck so far out, just begging for a right cross to the jaw. When it came, it was a roundhouse right, whistling through the air, and what a doozy!

Well before the smoke could clear and the last explosion stopped rumbling through the mountains, 3,581 Americans were dead or wounded, six mighty ships had sunk into the ooze of Pearl, 12 others stumbled around battered and punch-drunk, and 347 warplanes were useless heaps of scrap. The Japanese fighters had hardly broken a sweat, and when their fleet, located 200 miles north of Oahu, steamed away, the "east wind" had indeed "rained." But it was only the first squall of the American hurricane that would follow.

Getting There

There are a few options on how to visit Pearl Harbor and the USS *Arizona* Memorial. If you're driving, the entrance is along Rt. 99, the Kamehameha Highway, about a mile south of Aloha Stadium; well-marked signs

Under attack: The Japanese attack on Pearl Harbor set off a chain of events which would make the U.S. the domineering power of the Pacific.

Arizona *Memorial*

direct you to the parking area. If you're on H-1 west, take exit 15A, and follow the signs. You can also take TheBus, numbers 50, 51, and 52 from Ala Moana Center, or # 20 Airport from Waikiki, and be dropped off within a minute's walk of the entrance. Depending upon stops and traffic, this can take well over an hour. **Arizona Memorial Shuttle Bus,** a private operation from Waikiki, takes about 20 minutes and will pick you up at your hotel, tel. 926-4747, about $2.50 one way, reservations necessary. Returning, no reservations are necessary; just buy a ticket from Gloria, the lady selling them under the green umbrella in the parking lot.

The **Arizona Memorial Visitor Center** is a joint venture of the U.S. Park Service and the Navy, and is free! The Park Service runs the theater and museum, and the Navy operates the shuttle boats that take you out to the memorial shrine. The complex is open daily from 8 a.m. to 3 p.m., when you can visit the museum and the theater, and take the shuttle boats out to the memorial. If the weather is stormy, or waves rough, they won't sail so call 422-0561 or 422-2771. As many as 3,000 people visit per day, and your best time to avoid delays is before 9:30 a.m. Also, a number of boats operate out of Kewalo Basin doing **Pearl Harbor Cruises.** Costing about $10 for an extensive tour of Pearl Harbor, they are not allowed to drop passengers off at the memorial itself.

Bookstore And Theater
As you enter, you're handed a numbered ticket. Until it's called, you can visit the bookstore/gift shop and museum. The bookstore specializes in volumes on WW II and Hawaiiana. The museum is primarily a pictorial history, with a strong emphasis on the involvement of Hawaii's Japanese citizens during the war. There are instructions of behavior to "all persons of Japanese ancestry," from when bigotry and fear prevailed early in the war, as well as documentation of the 442nd Batallion, made up of Japanese soldiers, and their heroic exploits in Europe, especially their rescue of Texas's "lost batallion." Preserved newspapers of the day proclaim the "Day of Infamy" in bold headlines.

When your number is called you proceed to the comfortable theater where a 20-minute film includes actual footage of the attack. The film is historically factual, devoid of an overabundance of flag waving and mom's apple pie. After the film you board the launch: no bare feet, no bikinis or bathing suits, but shorts and shirts are fine. Twenty years ago visitors wore suits and dresses as if going to church!

The Memorial
The launch, a large vessel handled and piloted with professional deft, usually by women Naval personnel, heads for the 184-foot-long alabaster memorial straddling the ship

USS Bowfin,
WW II submarine

that still lies on the bottom. Some view the memorial as a tombstone; others see it as a symbolic ship, bent by struggle in the middle, but raised at the ends pointing to glory. The USS *Arizona* became the focus of the memorial because her casualties were so severe. When she exploded, the blast was so violent that it lifted entire ships moored nearby clear out of the water. Less than nine minutes later, with infernos raging and huge hunks of steel whizzing through the air, the *Arizona* was gone. Her crew went with her; nearly 1,100 men were sucked down to the bottom, and only 289 somehow managed to struggle to the surface. To the left and right are a series of black and white moorings with the names of the ships tied to them on the day of the attack.

The deck of the memorial can hold about 200 people; a small museum holds the ship's bell, and a chapel-like area displays a marble tablet with the names of the dead. Into a hole in the center of the memorial, flowers and wreaths are dropped on special occasions. Part of the superstructure of the ship still rises above the waves, but it is slowly being corroded away by wind and sea water. The flag, waving overhead, is attached to a pole anchored to the deck of the sunken ship. Sometimes, on weekends, survivors from the attack are aboard to give firsthand descriptions of what happened that day. Many visitors are

Japanese nationals, who often stop and offer their apologies to these Pearl Harbor survivors, distinguished by special military-style hats. The Navy ordered that any survivor wishing to be buried with his crew members had that right. In 1982 a diver took a stainless-steel container of the ashes of one of the survivors to be laid to rest with his buddies.

Nearby Attractions

The **USS** *Bowfin,* a WW II submarine moored within walking distance of the *Arizona* Memorial Center, has been turned into a self-guiding museum. It's open from 9:30 a.m.-4:30 p.m., admission $3 adults, $1 children ages 6-12. In the little compound leading to the sub is a snack bar with some tables, a few artillery pieces, and a torpedo or two. As you enter, you're handed a telephone-like receiver; a recorded transmitted message explains about different areas on the sub. The deck is made from teak wood, and the deck guns could go fore or aft depending on the skipper's preference. You'll also notice two anchors; one, under a fresh coat of paint, was salvaged from the pink sub used in the film *Operation Petticoat*.

As you descend, you feel as if you are integrated with a machine, a part of its gears and workings. In these cramped quarters of brass and stainless steel lived 90 to 100 men, all volunteers. Fresh water was in short supply, and the only man allowed to shower was the cook. Officers were given a dipper of water to shave with, but all the other men grew beards. With absolutely no place to be alone, the men slept on tiny stacked shelves, and only the officers could control their light switches. The only man to have a miniscule private room was the captain.

Topside, twin 16-cylinder diesels created unbelievable noise and heat. A vent in the passageway to the engine room sucked air with such strength that if you passed under it, you'd be flattened to your knees. When the sub ran on batteries under water, the quiet became maddening. The main bunk room, not much bigger than an average bedroom, slept 36 men. Another 30 or so ran the ship, while another 30 lounged. There was no night and day, just shifts. Coffee was constantly available, as well as fresh fruit, and the best mess in all the services. Subs of the day had the best radar and electronics available. Aboard were 24 high-powered torpedoes, and ammo for the topside gun. Submariners, chosen for their intelligence and psychological ability to take it, knew that a hit from the enemy meant certain death. The USS *Bowfin* is fascinating and definitely worth a visit.

The Navy holds an **open house** on one of its ships berthed at Pearl Harbor on the first Saturday of each month. For information call 474-8139. You must enter through the main Nimitz Gate, and then follow the signs to the ship, which is usually at the Bravo or Mike piers. On your way to the docking area you stop at the Family Services area where you can pick up some snacks or ice cream at a Baskin-Robbins concession. The sailors conducting the tour are polite and knowledgeable, and the tour is free. Those never in the service can always spot the officers—the guys with the white shoes. Take TheBus to the Nimitz Gate, or if you've visited the *Arizona* Memorial, a convenient shuttle connects for only $.50.

The **Pacific Submarine Museum** is also reached through the Nimitz Gate. It's free but you need a pass from the gate. It's open Wed. through Sun. 9:30 a.m.-5 p.m., tel. 471-0632.

BEACHES AND SIGHTS

As you travel up Aiea Heights Road, an exit off H-1, you get a world-class view of Pearl Harbor below. It's not glorious because it is industrialized, but you do ride through suburban sprawl Hawaiian style until you come to the end of the road at **Keaiwa Heiau State Recreation Area.** In the cool heights above Aiea Town, these ancient grounds have a soothing effect the minute you enter. Overnight tent camping is allowed here, with exceptionally large sites (permit needed, see p. 132); for the few other visitors, the gates open at 7 a.m. and close at 6:30 p.m. As you enter the well-maintained park (a caretaker lives on the premises), tall pines to the left give a feeling of alpine coolness. Below, Pearl Harbor lies open, like the shell of a great oyster.

Keaiwa Heiau was a healing temple, surrounded by gardens of medicinal herbs tended by Hawaii's excellent healers, the *kahuna lapaau*. From the gardens, roots, twigs, leaves, and barks were ground into potions and mixed liberally with prayers and love. These potions were amazingly successful in healing Hawaiians before the white man brought his diseases. Walking onto the stone floor of the *heiau*, it's somehow warmer and the winds seem quieter. Toward the center are numerous offerings, simple stones wrapped with a *ti* leaf. Some are old, while others are quite fresh. Follow the park road to the **Aiea Loop Trail,** which heads back 4.5 miles roundtrip onto one of the ridges descending from the Koolaus. Pass through a forest of tall eucalyptus trees, viewing canyons to the left and right. Notice, too, the softness of the "spongy bark" trees growing where the path begins. Allow three hours for the loop.

Blaisdell Beach Park's waters, which can be considered part of Pearl Harbor, are too polluted for swimming. It's sad to think that at the turn of the century it was clear and clean enough to support oysters. Pearl Harbor took its name from Waimomi, "Water of Pearls," which were indeed harvested from the oysters and a certain species of clam growing here. Today, sewage and uncountable oil spills have done their devastation. Recently, oysters from the Mainland's East Coast have been introduced, and are being harvested from the mud flats. Supposedly, they're fit to eat. Facilities include a pay phone, tables, and restrooms. Access is off Rt. 99 just past Aloha Stadium and before you enter Pearl City.

Keehi Lagoon Beach Park is also polluted, but some people do swim here. The park is at the northern tip of Keehi Lagoon, at 465 Lagoon Dr., just past the **Pacific War Memorial** on Rt. 92 (the Nimitz Highway). Here are restrooms, picnic facilities, a pay phone, and local people use the area for pole fishing and crabbing.

PRACTICALITIES

Accommodations
Except for long-term, accommodations are virtually nonexistent in this area. Luckily **bed and breakfast** homes provide some alternatives. One of the most interesting is the home of Corry and Helga Trummel, who reside in Pacific Palasades above Pearl City. What started out as a tract house has become a living museum. Helga has been collecting and inheriting art since she was a little girl in prewar Germany. Every nook and cranny has a curio from Europe, Asia, or Hawaii and Helga loves to share her artwork and the fascinating stories of her youth. The first floor is completely dedicated to the guests. There's a music room, a library with a fine collection of books on WW II and the western states, two bedrooms and a separate cottage in the back. Out here too is a small pool, dry sauna, and an observation platform high on the hill. Inside, as you mount the steps to the second floor you're greeted by a wooden statue of a woman with a bowl on her head, original oil paintings, and a grandfather clock, all from last century. Enter the breakfast nook and suddenly you're in a German hunting lodge. The green and white table and benches painted with flowers are over 100 years old. Gaze around to see a stuffed bear, antique sitar, a mountain goat, stag, stuffed

ducks, a collection of beer steins, a white moose head, pronghorn, and a bar. All in what once was a tract house kitchen! The main house is furnished like a very rich German chocolate cake, maybe not to everyone's taste, but definitely filling. Make reservations by contacting Bed & Breakfast Hawaii (see p. 120 for a full listing).

The **Pepper Tree Apartment Hotel,** at 98-150 Lipoha Pl., Aiea, HI 96701, tel. 488-1993, offers furnished studios and apartments, all with complete kitchens and baths, TV, and phones. A laundromat and swmming pool are also available. Many military personnel use this facility as temporary housing.

Shopping, Dining, And Services
The main shopping center in Aiea is the **Pearlridge Shopping Center,** with hundreds of stores, restaurants, and speciality shops. Prices here are geared toward island residents, not tourists, so you have a good chance of coming away with a bargain.

Buzz's Steak House, 98-751 Kuahao Pl. (at the corner of Moanoloa and Kahumanu), tel. 487-6465, is futuristic, like something a kid would build with an erector set. It'd be perfect if it were down by the sea, where you could see something, but from where it's located you can peer at Pearl Harbor in the distance, or have a world-class view of the freeway. The steakhouse is owned and operated by an old island family whose business grew into a small chain of restaurants from their original location in Kailua. This is one of the remaining three. Buzz's is an institution where islanders go when they want a sure-fire good meal. There's a salad bar and you prepare your own charbroiled steaks and fish. The prices are reasonable.

The **Waimalu Shopping Plaza,** located along Kaahumanu St. between the Kamehameha Hwy. (Rt. 99) and the H-1 Freeway, has a small cluster of shops and restaurants. There's a **Times Supermarket,** open 24 hours with its pharmacy and deli, and the **Good Health Store,** open 9 a.m.-7 p.m., Sat. 11 a.m.-6 p.m., selling food supplements and minerals. In the same complex is **Stuart Anderson's Cattle Co.,** tel. 487-0054, open daily for lunch and dinner, lounge until 2 a.m.

weekends, serving huge steaks and all the trimmings. Here too is **Melnita's Kitchenette,** tel. 487-2467, with basic and inexpensive Filipino food. Melnita's features Pampango cuisine, open for lunch and dinner, takeout, and catering.

Across the road is the **Elephant and Castle Restaurant,** at 98-1247 Kaahumanu, tel. 487-5591, open for breakfast, lunch and dinner. This restaurant has done an excellent job of creating an English-style pub atmosphere. The interior is cool and rich with red velvet, heavy chairs, tapestries, open beams, and a pool table and dart boards in the pub area. Nightly, it's one of the best places for a beer and a chat in the area. The food is good too. For example, try English fish and chips for $4.95, burger platter $5, hot sandwiches $5, soup and sandwich $4.75. Specials on weekends are English prime rib dinner, queen size $10.95, king $14.95, New York steak $14.95, seafood scampi $10.95. Enjoy merry old England Hawaiian style.

The **Pearl City Tavern,** at 905 Kamehameha Hwy. (corner of Waimano Home Dr.) tel. 455-1045, is the best restaurant in the Pearl City/Aiea area. The cuisine is a combination of seafood, steaks, sushi, and main stream Japanese. They're famous for their monkey bar," which features rhesus monkeys behind the bar in a glass cage. After a couple of stiff belts some customers mistakenly think that they're looking into a mirror. There's a fish tank bubbling away and a separate tank for live Maine lobsters, a specialty of the house. Choose a table or romantic booth in the huge dining room appointed with Japanese scrolls, a huge lantern, and *shoji* screens. For lunch try escargot, $5.50, seafood *pu pu,* $2.15, chef salad, $8, shrimp Louie, $7.50, or a bowl of Boston clam chowder for only $1.50. Dinner is delicious with a choice of chicken Oriental salad, $6, prime rib, $15.75, filet of *mahi mahi,* $15, or seafood Newburg, $15.75. Or choose three different entrees for $25 from: soft-shell crab, shrimp and scallops, king crab legs, and roast prime rib. Dinners include won ton soup or salad, potatoes, french bread and butter. Complete Japanese dinners are miso soup and trimmings, rice and tea, and a choice of any three of the following entrees: broiled fish, *sashimi,* beef teriyaki, butterfish *misoyaki,* or chicken teriyaki at $17.25 per person. If you're in the Pearl Ridge/Aiea area and want a special night out, this is the place!

SOUTHEAST OAHU

KOKO HEAD TO WAIMANALO

It's amazing how quickly you can leave the frenzy of Waikiki behind. Once you round the bend past Diamond Head and continue traveling east toward Koko Head, the pace slackens measurably . . . almost by the yard. A minute ago you were in traffic, now you're cruising. It's not that this area is undeveloped; other parts of the island are much more laid-back, but none so close to the action of the city. In the 12 miles you travel from Honolulu to Waimanalo, you pass the natural phenomenon of Koko Crater, a reliable blowhole, the most aquatically active underwater park in the islands, and a string of beaches, each with a different personality.

Man has made his presence felt, too. The area has some of the most exclusive homes on the island, as well as Hawaii Kai, a less exclusive project developed by the visionary businessman Henry Kaiser, who 20 years ago created this harbinger of things to come. There's Sea Life Park, offering a day's outing of fun for the family, plus shopping centers, the mostly Hawaiian town of Waimanalo, and Bellows Air Force Base, unused by the military

and now one of the finest camping beaches on the island. Besides camping, few accommodations are found out here, and few restaurants. This lack of development preserves the area as scenic and recereational, prized attributes that should be taken advantage of before this sunny sandbox gets paved over.

SIGHTS, BEACHES, AND PARKS

The drive out this way accounts for half of the 360 degrees of what is called **The Circle Route.** Start by heading over the Pali Highway down to Kailua, hitting the sights on the way, or come this way first along Diamond Head Road to Rt. 72 as you make the loop back to the city. The only consideration is what part of the day you'd rather stop at the southeast beaches for a dip. For the most part, the beaches of this area *are* the sights, so both are combined in this one section. The road abounds with scenic points and overlooks. This is the part of Oahu that's absolutely beautiful in its undevelopment. It's hard to find a road on any of the Hawaiian islands that's going to be more scenic than this. At first the countryside is dry because this is the leeward side. But, as you approach Waimanalo it gets much more tropical. The road is a serpentine ribbon with one coastal vista after another, a great choice for a joy ride just to soak in the sights. The following listings assume that you follow Rt. 72 from Waikiki to Waimanalo. For beaches between Waikiki and the following, please see pp. 232-233.

Maunalua Bay

Maunalua ("Two Mountain") Bay is a four-mile stretch of sun and surf between Diamond Head and Koko Head, with a beach park about every half mile. The first is **Waialae Beach County Park** in Kahala. Go straight ahead on Kahala Avenue for one

minute instead of going left on Rt. 72 to join H-1 on to Haunauma Bay. This section is the Beverly Hills of Honolulu, as many celebrities like Tom Selleck and Carol Burnett have homes here. The least expensive home in this section would easily be pushing $1 million. Waialae is a popular windsurfing spot, crowded on weekends. It's a small beach park with basic amenities in a beautiful location where Makapuu Head wraps around and gives the impression that there are two islands off in the distance, but it's just the way Oahu bends at this point.

Next comes **Kawaikui Beach Park.** No lifeguard, but the conditions are safe year-round, and the bottom is shallow, muddy, and overgrown with seaweed. In times past, islanders came to the confluence of a nearby spring to harvest special *limu* that grow only

© MOON PUBLICATIONS, INC.

rugged southeast coast

where fresh water meets the ocean. You'll find unlimited access, parking stalls, picnic facilities, and restrooms. Few people use the park, and it's ideal for sunning, but for frolicking in the water, give it a miss.

In quick succession come **Niu and Paiko beaches,** lying along residential areas. Although there is public access, few people take advantage of them because the swimming, with a coral and mud bottom, is less than ideal. Some residents have built a pier at Niu Beach past the mudflats, but it's restricted to their private use. Paiko Lagoon is a state bird sanctuary; binoculars will help with sightings of a variety of coastal birds.

The residential area in the hills behind **Maunalua Bay Beach Park** is Hawaii Kai, built by Henry Kaiser, the aluminum magnate. The controversial development was often denigrated as "suburban blight." Many felt it was the beginning of Oahu's ruination. The park fronts Kuapa Pond, at one time a huge fishpond, later dredged by Kaiser, who used the dredged material to build the park which he donated to the city in 1960. Now, most of the land has been reclaimed except for Koko Marina, whose boat launch constitutes the primary attraction of the park. You'll find a large sandy parking area where **Paradise Jet Skis** (look for a tent) rents self-powered skis, pricey at $40 per hour, tel. 235-1612.

Except for the boat launch (only one on this side of the island), the area is of little recreational use because of the mud or coral bottom. However, swimming is possible and safe, but be careful of the sudden drops created by the dredged boat channels. Two undeveloped parks are located at the end of Poipu Drive, **Kokee and Koko Kai parks.** The currents and beach conditions make both unsuitable for swimming, but they're popular with surfers. Few others come here, but the views of the bay are lovely with glimpses of Molokai floating on the horizon to the south.

Hanauma Bay State Underwater Park

One of the premier beach parks in Hawaii is located in the sea-eroded crater of an extinct volcano just below Koko Head. People flock here to snorkel, scuba, picnic, and swim. During the day, the parking lot at the top of the hill overlooking the crescent bay below looks like a used car lot, jammed with Japanese imports, vans, and tour buses. A shuttle bus ($.50) runs up and down the hill. If you want to avoid the crowds come in the early morning or after 4 p.m. when the sun dips behind the crater, and tourists and buses leave on cue. There's still plenty of daylight, so plan your trip accordingly. The **Hanauma Express** is a red, white, and black bus that cruises Kuhio and Kalakaua avenues. It comes by about once every 15 minutes and stops at all the major hotels. For $1.50 they'll take you to Hanauma Bay so you can avoid the drive and the hassle with parking once at the bay.

The reef protects the bay and sends a maze of coral fingers right up to the shoreline. A large sandy break in the reef, **Keyhole,** is a choice spot for entering the water and for swimming. The entire bay is alive with tropical fish. Many have become so accustomed to snorkelers that they've lost their fear entirely, and willingly accept food from your fingers—some so rudely you had better be careful of getting your fingers nibbled. The county provides lifeguards, restrooms, showers, picnic facilities, pavilion, and food concession.

Before you enter the water, do yourself a favor and read the large bulletin board near the pavilion that describes conditions. It divides the bay into three areas ranging from beginner to expert, and warns of sections to avoid. Be especially careful of **Witches Brew,** a turbulent area on the right at the mouth of the bay that can wash you into the **Molokai Express,** a notoriously dangerous rip current. Follow a path along the left-hand seacliff to **Toilet Bowl,** a natural pool that rises and falls with the tides. If the conditions are right, you can sit in it to float up and down in a phenomenon very similar to a flushing toilet.

You cannot rent snorkel gear at the park. If you haven't rented from a dive shop in Waikiki where the prices are cheapest, try the Aloha Dive Shop, tel. 395-5922, in the nearby Koko Marina Shopping Center. (See p. 146 for more along with excursions to Hanauma Bay.)

For a sweeping view, hike to the summit of **Koko Head,** not to be confused with Koko Crater, another good hike but farther east on Rt. 72. To start your trek, look for a paved road closed off to vehicles by a white metal fence, on the right before the road to the parking lot. A 15-minute hike takes you to the 642-foot summit of Koko ("Blood") Head. This was the last place that young, wandering Madame Pele attempted to dig herself a fiery nest on Oahu; as usual, she was flooded out by her jealous sister. From the summit you get an unobstructed view of Molokai 20 miles across the Kaiwi Channel, the bowl of Hanauma Bay at your feet, and a sweeping panorama of Diamond Head and the Koolau Mountains.

Below are two small extinct craters, Nono'ula and Ihi'ihilauakea.

Koko Crater

Koko Crater's official name is Kohelepelepe ("Fringed Vagina"). Legend says that Pele's sister, Kapo, had a magical flying vagina that she could send anywhere. Kamapua'a, the pig-god, was intent on raping Pele, when Kapo came to her aid. She dispatched her vagina to entice Kamapua'a, and he followed it to Koko Head where it made the crater, and then flew away. Kamapua'a was unsuccessful when taking a flying leap at this illusive vagina.

You can either hike or drive to the crater. To begin the hike, look for the road to the "Hawaii Job Corp Training Center" just across from Hanauma Bay. Follow the road down past a rifle range and park at the job training building. Behind is an overgrown tramway track. The remaining ties provide a rough but adequate stairway to the top. At the 1,208-foot summit is an abandoned powerhouse and tramway station. The wood is rotted and the floors are weak! The crater itself lies 1,000 feet below. An easier but less exciting route is to follow Rt. 72 for two miles to Wawamalu Beach near the Hawaii Kai Golf Course, and then take a left on Kealahou Street. En route you pass **Koko Crater Stables,** tel. 395-2628, which offers guided trail rides into the crater. Park your car here, and nearby is a walking path that leads into the crater. On the floor of Koko Crater is a botanical garden that, due to the unique conditions, specializes in succulents.

Halona Cove

As you round a bend on Rt. 72 you come to the natural lookout of Halona Cove, which means "The Peering Place," an excellent vantage point from which to see whales in season. Just before Halona, a sign will point you to the **Honolulu Japanese Casting Club,** with a stone wall and a monument. The monument at one time was of O Jisan, the Japanese god of protection, destroyed by overzealous patriots during WW II. The current monument was erected after the war, and O Jisan was carved into it. Below is a secluded little beach that's perfect for sunbathing. The only way to it is to scramble down the cliff. Swim only on calm days, or the wave action can pull you out to sea and then suck you into the chamber of the famous **Halona Blowhole** just around the bend. There's a turnout at the blowhole for parking. The blowhole is a lava tube at the perfect height for the waves to be driven into it. The water compresses, and the pressure sends a spume into the air. Be extremely cautious around the blowhole. Those unfortunate enough to fall in face almost certain death.

Sandy Beach Park

Sandy Beach is one of the best bodysurfing beaches on Oahu, and the most rugged of them all. More necks and backs are broken on this beach than on all the other Oahu beaches combined. But because of the east-breaking waves, and bottom, the swells are absolutely perfect for bodysurfing. The lifeguards use a flag system to inform you about conditions. The **red flag** means "stay out." When checking out Sandy Beach, don't be fooled by bodysurfers who make it appear easy. These are experts, intimately familiar with the area, and even they are injured at times. Local people refer to the beach as "Scene Beach" because this is where young people come to strut their stuff. This is where the boys are because this is where the girls are. There are restrooms, a large parking area, and two lifeguard towers. Rip-offs have happened, so don't leave valuables in your car. *Kaukau* wagons park in the area, selling a variety of refreshments.

As the road skirts the coastline, it passes a string of beaches which look inviting but are extremely dangerous because there is no protecting reef. The best known is **Wawamalu,** where people come to sunbathe only. Across the road is **Hawaii Kai Golf Course,** tel. 395-2356. You have a choice of two courses: the Championship, offering a full round of golf with beautiful views, challenging holes, and excellent greens; or the Executive, a shorter par-three course for those with limited time. This is an excellent public course, but the greens fee is high.

The lifeguards do a great job at Sandy Beach.

Makapuu Beach Park

This beach park is below Makapuu ("Bulging Eye") Point, a projection of land marking Oahu's easternmost point, and a favorite launching pad for hang gliding. Makapuu is *the* most famous bodysurfing beach in the entire state, but it can be extremely rugged; more people are rescued here than at any other beach on Oahu (except Sandy Beach). In winter the conditions are hazardous, with much of the beach eroded away, leaving exposed rocks. With no interfering reef, the surf can reach 12 feet—perfect for bodysurfing, if you're an expert. Board riding is prohibited. In summer, the sandy beach reappears, and the wave action is much gentler, allowing recreational swimming. There are restrooms, lifeguard towers with a flag warning system, and picnic facilities.

Offshore is **Manana** ("Rabbit") Island. Curiously, it does resemble a rabbit, but it's so named because rabbits actually live on it. They were released there in the 1880s by a local rancher who wanted to raise them but who was aware that if they ever got loose on Oahu they could ruin much of the crop lands. During the impotent counterrevolution of 1894, designed to reinstate the Hawaiian monarchy, Manana Island was a cache for arms and ammunition buried on its windward side. Nearby is tiny Kaohikaipu ("Turtle") Island that, along with Manana, is reserved as a seabird sanctuary.

Sea Life Park
This is a cluster of landlocked tanks holding an amazing display of marine animals that live freely in the ocean just a few hundred yards away. Offshore is Rabbit Island. Admission is $7.75, children ages 7-12 $5, "behind-the-scenes tour" $9, tel. 259-7933, open daily 9:30 a.m.-5 p.m., Fri. until 10 p.m. The best bus to take is #57 from Ala Moana Center, or #58, which comes straight up Kuhio Avenue. The park hosts a variety of shows by trained seals, whales, dolphins, and the Ocean Science Theater. The Hawaiian Reef Tank is a 300,000-gallon fish bowl where you can see the fish being hand fed; Whaler's Cove is where the park's whales perform acrobatics and other tricks.

Outside the entrance turnstile is a shopping complex and The Galley Restaurant. Also, the **Pacific Whaling Museum** is here and free to the public. It houses one of the largest collections of whaling artifacts and memorabilia in the Pacific. The Whaler's Cove has a replica of a whaling ship called the *Essex Nantucket*. Sea lion food is available, and there's a public feeding daily at 11:30 a.m., 1:30 p.m., and 3:30 p.m., also 5 p.m. on Friday. Sea Life Park is a great learning experience for a family or anyone interested in sealife, especially if you're going to be into snorkeling or scuba.

Kaupo Beach Park
This is the first park that you come to along the southeast coast that is safe for swimming. It is between Sea Life Park and Waimanalo. The park is undeveloped and has no lifeguards, so you must exercise caution. The shore is lined with protective reef or rocks, and the swimming is best beyond the reef. Close to shore, the jutting rocks discourage most swimmers. Surfers frequent Kaupo, especially beginners, lured by the ideal yet gentle wave action.

Kaiona Beach Park
Just before you enter the ethnically Hawaiian town of Waimanalo, you pass **Kaiona Beach Park,** which you can spot because of the semipermanent tents pitched there. Local people are very fond of the area, and use it extensively. Look inland to view some remarkable cliffs and mountains that tumble to the sea. The area was at one time called Pahonu, "Turtle Fence," because a local chief who loved turtle meat erected a large enclosure in the sea into which any turtle that was caught by local fishermen had to be deposited. Parts of the pond fence can still be

Rabbit Island

Bellows Beach

seen. Facilities include restrooms, showers, and a picnic area. Swimming is safe year-round, and tent and trailer camping are allowed with a county permit.

Waimanalo

This small rural town was at one time the center of a thriving sugar plantation owned by the *hapa* Hawaiian nobleman, John Cummins, who was responsible for introducing rabbits to Manana Island. It has fallen on hard times ever since the plantation closed in the late 1940s, and now produces much of Honolulu's bananas, papayas, and anthuriums from small plots and farms. The town sits in the center of Waimanalo Bay, which is the longest (3½ miles) stretch of sand beach on Oahu. To many people, especially those from Oahu, it is also the best. Few but adequate travelers' services are in town (see "Services" below).

The **Olomana Golf Course,** tel. 259-7926, is a 6,000-yard, relatively easy, par-71 course, inexpensive and close to town. You think you're in Waimanalo when you pass a 7-eleven Store and McDonald's in a built-up area, but that isn't it. You keep going about a mile or two and and then you'll come to the older section of town which is Waimanalo proper.

Waimanalo County Beach Park, as you enter town by the 7-eleven and McDonald's, provides camping with a county permit. The beach is well protected and the swimming is safe year-round. Snorkeling is good, and there are picnic tables, restrooms, and recreational facilities, including a ball park and basketball courts. This park is right in town, and not secluded from the road. Although the facilities are good, the setting could be better.

Just outside of town is **Waimanalo Bay State Recreation Area,** which remains largely undeveloped, and is much better situated. The access road is hard to spot, but just after McDonald's look for a tall wire fence with the poorly marked entrance in the center. It is good for picnicking and swimming, which can sometimes be rough. The area, surrounded by a dense ironwood grove, is called "Sherwood Forest," due to many rip-offs by thieves who fancy themselves as Robin Hood, plundering the rich and keeping the loot for themselves. Guess who the rich guys are? Fortunately, this problem of breaking into cars is diminishing, but take necessary precautions. This is the best beach on this section of the island.

Bellows Beach County Park, a one-time active Air Force base, is now one of Oahu's finest beach parks, and there's camping too! As you enter a sign warns that "This military installation is open to the public only on the following days: weekends—12:00 noon Friday to 6:00 a.m. Monday; federal and state holidays—6:00 a.m. to 6:00 a.m. the following day. Camping is authorized in this park by permit from the City and County of Honolulu,

Parks and Recreation Board, only." They mean it! The water is safe for swimming year-round, but lifeguards are on duty only during the above-stated hours. Bodysurfing and board surfing are also excellent in the park, but snorkeling is mediocre. Surfboards are not allowed in the area between the two lifeguard towers. After entering the main gates, follow the road for about two miles to the beach area. You'll find picnic tables, restrooms, and cold-water showers. The combination of shade trees and adjacent beach make a perfect camping area. The park is marked by two freshwater streams, Waimanalo and Puha, at either end.

SERVICES

Except for the excellent camping, you're limited when it comes to accommodations in this area. **Hawaiian Family Inns,** a small cooperative of private homes in and around Hawaii Kai, provides European-style bed and breakfast. Each home differs slightly, but most have a private entrance, bath, yard and beach privileges, and some kitchen facilities. Daily rates are a reasonable $35, less during the off-season, with weekly and monthly discounts available. The three homes involved can be reached by calling 395-3710, 395-4130, or 395-8153.

The first place to pick up supplies as you head east on Rt. 72 is at the **Times Super Market** in the **Niu Valley Shopping Center,** located about halfway between Diamond Head and Koko Head. The store is open until 11 p.m., and they have some of the best food prices on the island. **Dave's Ice Cream** and a small restaurant, **The Swiss Inn,** are about all that's here.

Roy's Restaurant, 6600 Kalanianaole Hwy., tel. 396-7697, just before Hawaiikai Dr., features L.A. *nouvelle cuisine.* The presentation is very Japanese, colorful, and pleasing to the eye. The crab cake, minced with celery and red bell pepper, flash-fried and served with a cream sauce, is out of this world. The lamb in a deep rich gravy is an excellent choice, or try the blackened *ahi* with a *wasabi* mustard sauce. Reasonably expensive.

Koko Marina Shopping Center

Located along the highway in Hawaii Kai, this center is the largest and easiest access shopping center that you'll find on the way to Hanauma Bay. For photo supplies and sundries, try Thrifty Drugs, Ben Franklin's, Clic Photo, and Surfside Camera. There are two banks, a **Waldenbooks** and a satellite city hall for camping permits (tel. 395-4481). **Foodland** provides most supplies for picnics and camping, and you can dine at Chuck's Steak House, McDonald's, Magoo's Pizza, Baskin-Robbins Ice Cream, Sizzler, Kentucky Fried Chicken, and Kozo Sushi. More expensive restaurants include **Stromboli Ristorante,** with fresh pasta, and **Pacific Broiler,** quite picturesque near the waterway, with salads for under $5, fresh fish dishes for $15, and pastas from $12-15.

The **Aloha Dive Shop** at the Koko Marina is a full-service dive shop. You can rent or buy snorkeling and scuba gear. So if you haven't picked up rentals from Waikiki and you're heading out to Hanauma Bay, come here. They have plenty of different dives. They start at $52 for beginners, certified divers for $62, and certification courses (three days) are $295, featuring all-boat diving at Manalua Bay and Koko Head and Diamond Head.

The Japanese own the Koko Marina Center. In the center are thrill-ride (jet-skis, parasails, etc.) booking agencies that will take non-Japanese tourists, but are more for the Japanese tourists who come in here by bus loads and immediately head out on one of these thrill rides. They've already booked in Japan, so it's all set up and off they go.

Upstairs on the water side of the Koko Marina is **American Sports Ltd.,** tel. 395-5319, that offers jet-skiing, snorkeling, and can book you into parasailing and scuba diving as well. Their special deal is jet-skiing, snorkeling, plus lunch for $49. Lunch is a sandwich and French fries, or for Japanese, *bento* if you prefer.

Waimanalo And Vicinity Practacalities

For a tasty and inexpensive lunch try any of a number of *kaukau* wagons around Sandy Beach. Get basics at **Mel's Market,** where you can pick up almost all camping supplies.

Waimanalo town is growing up. As you enter you'll find a **7-eleven** and **McDonald's.** Keep going for a mile or so to find **Waimanalo Shopping Center** in the middle of town. Here are **Jack in the Box** and two gas stations. You can do all your business, pick up lunch and supplies, and to head on down the road or go to the beach. In the shopping center is **visitor information, Woolworth's** and **Waimanalo Market.**

A good little restaurant here is **Waimanalo Cafe,** a downhome place with Naugahyde booths and formica tables selling American standard and Hawaiian foods. The Waimanalo Cafe features an assortment of plate lunches for $5. One of their best, if you're into meat, is an eight-ounce hamburger steak with fried onions, fries, and a salad for $4.95. So you can't beat the prices. The cafe actu-

ally has some atmosphere. Overhead are skylights and peculiar open beams painted green. While waiting for your meal walk up to the bar area. The back wall of the bar is loaded with unique bumper stickers. Have a read and a chuckle while your food is being prepared.

Pine Grove Village is an open-air bazaar where local people come to sell handmade products and produce. The majority of items are authentic and priced well below similar products found in Honolulu. Participants and times vary, but a group is usually selling daily until 6 p.m. Some excellent buys include local fruits and vegetables, leis, shellwork, hand-dipped candles, bikinis, jewelry, and leather goods. Price haggling is the norm; when the seller stops smiling, that's about the right price.

WINDWARD OAHU

Oahu's windward coast never has to turn a shoulder into a harsh and biting wind. The trades do blow, mightily at times, but always tropical warm, perfumed with flowers, balmy and bright. Honolulu is just 12 miles over the hump of the *pali,* but a world apart. When *kamaaina* families talk of going to "the cottage in the country," they're most likely referring to the windward coast. In the southern parts, the suburban towns of **Kailua** and **Kaneohe** are modern in every way, with the lion's share of the services on this side. Kailua has Oahu's best windsurfing beach and a nearby *heiau,* preserved and unvisited, while Kaneohe sits in a huge bay dotted with islands and reef. The coastal **Kamehameha Highway** (Rt. 83) turns inland to the base of the *pali,* passing the **Valley of the Temples,** resplendent with universal houses of worship. At **Kahaluu** starts a string of beaches running north, offering the full range of Oahu's coastal outdoor experience. You can meander side roads into the mountains near the Hawaiian villages of **Waiahole** and **Waiakane,** where the normal way of life is ramshackle cottages on small subsistence farms.

The coast bulges at **Ka'a'awa,** where the **Crouching Lion,** a natural stone formation, seems ready to pounce on the ever-present tour buses that disturb its repose. Nearby is the **Plantation Spa,** an energized retreat where you can have your cosmic batteries recharged. **Punaluu** is famous for **Pat's,** the only resort in the immediate area, and for **Sacred Falls Park,** a short hike to a peak at Oahu's beautiful and natural heart (if it isn't muddy). Suddenly, you're in manicured **Laie** where Hawaii's Mormon community has built a university, a temple perfect in its symmetry, and the **Polynesian Cultural Center,** a sanitized replica of life in the South Seas, Disney style. The northern tip at **Kahuku,** site of one of Oahu's oldest sugar mills, is where the **North Shore** begins. Kahuku Point houses two refuges, one for wildlife, and the other for Oahu's only nudist camp, both protecting endangered species from mankind's prying eyes.

It makes little difference in which direction you travel the windward coast, but the following will be listed from south to north from Kailua to Kahuku. The slight advantage in traveling this direction is that your car is in the right-hand lane, which is better for coastal views. But, as odd as it may seem, this dynamic stretch totally changes its vistas depending upon the direction that you travel. You can come one way and then retrace your steps, easily convincing yourself that you've never seen it before. The road is clearly marked with mile markers. They decrease as you head north from Kaneohe on Rt. 83, the Kamehameha Highway. Also see "Camping and Hiking" (pp. 135-136) for trails in the area.

Beaches And Parks

Over a dozen beaches line the 24 miles of the windward coast from Kailua to Kahuku. The majority offer a wide range of water sports and camping. A few offshore islands, refuges for Hawaiian waterbirds, can be visited and explored. You can walk to these islands during low tide, and even camp there. See "Camping and Hiking" (p. 131) for other state and county parks not along the coast.

KAILUA AND VICINITY

The easiest way into Kailua ("Two Seas") is over the Koolaus on Rt. 61, the Pali Highway. As soon as you pass through a long tunnel just after Nuuanu Pali Lookout (see p. 188) and your eyes adjust to the shocking brilliance of sunshine, look to your right to see Mt. Olomana. Its 1,643-foot peak is believed to be the volcanic origin of Oahu, the first land to emerge from the seas. Below lies Kailua and the Kawainui Marsh, perhaps the oldest inhabited area on this side of the island. Kamehameha I, after conquering Oahu in 1795, gave all this land to his chiefs who had fought for him. The area became a favorite of the ruling *ali'i* until the fall of the monarchy at the turn of this century. The Kawainui Canal drains the marsh and runs through Kailua. A good vantage point from which to observe it is along Kalaheo Ave., the main road running along the coast in Kailua. Kailua has approximately 45,000 people, technically making it the state's largest windward city. It's developed with shopping centers, a hospital, and the *best* sailboarding beach in the state (see below). For a full description of sailboarding activities at Kailua Beach please refer to "Sports," p. 149-150. Four golf courses surround the town, and a satellite city hall dispenses **camping permits.**

SIGHTS

A good touring loop is to continue straight on Rt. 61 until it comes to the coast. Turn on Kalaheo Road, which takes you along the coast to Kailua Beach Park. In the waters offshore will be a spectacle of windsurfers, with their sails puffed out like the proud chests of multicolored birds. To the left of the beach is **Mokapu** ("Sacred Area") **peninsula,** home of the Kaneohe Marine Corps Base. Notice that the rock that separates the peninsula creates a large natural archway navigable by sizable boats. Most of the little islands in the bay are bird sanctuaries. The farthest, **Moku Manu,** is home to terns and man-of-wars, birds famous for leading fishermen to schools of fish. Up on the coastal bluffs is a gray house with a flat roof, the residence of a local woman called the "Birdlady of Kailua." The woman has a reputation for taking care of any sick or injured birds that people bring to her. The entire home is carved from rock, including the chairs and table. Every once in a while tours are offered to the home for a few dollars. They're irregular, so check the local papers, and you may be lucky enough to be there at just the right time.

Aalapapa Drive gains the heights from the beach and takes you through an area of beautiful homes until you come to **Lanikai Beach.** At one time trees came down to the shoreline, but it has steadily eroded away. The Navy attempted to start a retaining reef by dumping bargeloads of white bath tile just offshore. Their efforts were not successful, but many homes in town now have sparkling new white-tiled bathrooms! As Aalapapa Drive loops back to town, it changes names to Mokulua; a pulloff here affords an expan-

WINDWARD OAHU
KAILUA TO KAHUKU

JAMES CAMPBELL
WILDLIFE REFUGE
KII POND

TO
HALEIWA

KAHUKU

MALAEKAHANA BAY

LAIE BEACH PARK
LAIE BAY

LAIE

POLYNESIAN
CULTURAL
CENTER

POUNDERS BEACH
KOKOLOLIO BEACH

HAUULA BEACH PARK

HAUULA

MAKAO BEACH

PUNALUU

PUNALUU BEACH PARK

SACRED FALLS STATE PARK

MAHIE PT

KAHANA BAY
BEACH PARK

MAKAUA BEACH PARK
SWANZY BEACH PARK

KAUHIIMAKAOKALANI
(CROUCHING LION)

KAAAWA

KAAAWA BEACH PARK

MAKAHONU PT.

KAHANA
VALLEY
STATE
PARK

SUGAR MILL
RUINS (1864)

KOOLAU RANGE

CHINAMAN'S HAT

WAIKANE

WAIAHOLE BEACH PARK

WAIAHOLE

KAALAEA

KAPAPA I.

MOKU MANU
SEABIRD SANCTUARY

PYRAMID
ROCK

KANEOHE
MARINE CORPS
AIR STATION

MOKAPU PT.

MOKAPU

MOKAPU PENINSULA

KAHALUU

KANEOHE
BAY

BYODO-IN
TEMPLE

HEEIA

MOKU O LOE
(COCONUT I.)

KAILUA BAY

KANEOHE

KAILUA

KAILUA BEACH PARK

MOKU LUA IS.

KAWAINUI
SWAMP

LANIKAI

LIKELIKE HWY.

NUUANU PALI
STATE PARK

BELLOWS FIELD
BEACH PARK

*WAIMANALO
BAY*

PALI HWY.

HONOLULU

TO
WAIMANALO

KAMEHAMEHA HWY.

KALANIANAOLE HWY.

0   2 mi
0   3 km

© MOON PUBLICATIONS, INC.

Kailua Beach, the sailboarding capital of Oahu

sive panorama of the bay below. By daytime it's enjoyable, but in the evening local kids come here to hang out and drink beer.

Ulupoa Heiau

This *heiau* was dedicated to the Ulu line of *ali'i,* who were responsible for setting up *heiau* dedicated to the sacred birth of chiefs. Oftentimes the umbilical cord was cut just as a drum was sounded, then the cord *(piko)* was placed in a shallow rock depression at a *heiau.* This temple was supposedly built by the legendary *menehune.* The stone craftsmanship is remarkable—measuring 140 feet wide and 30 feet high. Atop the temple is a pathway that you can follow. Notice small stones wrapped in *ti* leaves placed as offerings. To get there, as you approach Kailua on Rt. 61 look for a red light and a 7-eleven store. Turn left onto Uluoa Street, following it to Manu Aloha Street, where you turn right. Follow it to the end and park in the YMCA lot. A small lane leads from here to **Maunawili Falls** (see p. 135).

BEACHES

Along the shoreline of an exclusive residential area, just south of Kailua, sits **Lanikai Beach.** Three clearly marked rights-of-way run off Mokulua Drive, the main thoroughfare. No facilities but good snorkeling and swimming year-round, with generally mild surf and a long, gently sloping, sandy beach. The beach runs south for almost a mile, broken by a series of seawalls designed to hold back erosion. Many small craft use the sandy- bottomed shore to launch and land. Popular with local people, but not visited much by tourists.

Kailua Beach Park is the main beach in the area. In the last few years, it has become the sailboarding capital of Hawaii. Local people complain that at one time the beach was great for family outings, with safe conditions and fine facilities. Now the wind has attracted a daily flotilla of sailboarders, kayak racers, and jet-skiers. The congested and contested waters can be dangerous for the average swimmer. Many sailboarders are beginners, so if you're a swimmer, be careful of being run over. The conditions are similar to out-of-control skiers found on the slopes of many mountains. The sailboarding area is clearly marked with buoys, which recently were moved 100 yards northeastwards, making the area larger.

The park boasts a pavilion, picnic facilities, restrooms, showers, lifeguards, boat ramp, and food concession. The surf is gentle year-round, and the swimming safe. Children should be careful of the sudden dropoffs in the channels formed by the Kaelepulu Canal as it enters the sea in the middle of the beach park. Good surfing and diving are found around Popoi'a Island just offshore. Follow Rt. 61 through Kailua until it meets the coast, and then turn right on S. Kalaheo St. following it to the beach park. For sailboard rentals and instruction see pp. 149-150.

Kalama Beach is reached by making a right onto N. Kalaheo. This beach has no facilities and is inferior to Kailua Beach Park, but the swimming is good, and sections of the beach have been made off-limits to any surf-riding vehicles.

PRACTICALITIES

Accommodations

The **Kailua Beachfront Vacation Homes** offer two completely furnished and ready-to-move-into rental homes with a minimum stay of five days. The one-bedroom home rents for $95-110 up to four persons, the three-bedroom home from $190-220 for up to six persons. Located along S. Kalaheo, 10 properties from Kailua Beach Park. For peak seasons like Christmas and Easter reservations up to a year in advance are not unusual. Normally reserve three to six months in advance. Homes have telephones, color TVs, beach furniture, parking, maid service on request, and BBQs. The three-bedroom has full kitchen with electric stove, a large refrigerator, dishwasher, washer and dryer, and all lanai furniture. The smaller house is complete except for dishwasher. For information and reservations write Kailua Beachfront Vacation Homes, 133 Kailuana Pl., Kailua, HI 96734, tel. 261-3484.

One of the finest guest homes in Kailua is **Sharon's Serenity**. This beautiful property sits on a quiet side street fronting the picturesque Kawainui Canal. Sharon goes out of her way to make you feel comfortable and welcome. The fridge is always filled with cold beer and soft drinks, and the coffee is always fresh-perked. Sharon also takes the time to sit with you, giving advice on where to dine, what to see, and a candid description of activities that are worthwhile. The meticulously clean, and beautifully appointed home features guest rooms with color TV, a spacious family room, swimming pool, lanai, and beautiful views of the *pali,* and the bay. Sha-

ron's Serenity is an excellent choice. To make reservations contact B&B Honolulu Statewide (see p. 121 for details.)

Pacific Hawaii Bed and Breakfast lists private homes in and around Kailua. Rates and homes differ dramatically, but all are guaranteed to be comfortable and accommodating. For information and location, write Pacific Hawaii Bed and Breakfast, 970 N. Kalaheo, Suite A-218, Kailua 96734, tel. (800) 999-6026 or 262-6026.

Food

For a quick snack at a juice bar try **Vim and Vigor,** a small island chain with a half dozen stores. This one's at the corner of Kailua Rd. and Hahani St., tel. 262-9911. Besides normal health food items, including Hain products, they serve sandwiches for under $3, and a variety of exotic smoothies for $1.50. Bread choices are whole grain, nine-grain, and pita. Open Mon. through Sat. 9 a.m.-5 p.m., Sun. 10 a.m.-4 p.m.

The **Kailua Shopping Center,** 540 Kailua Rd., has one of the very best restaurants in Kailua for value in the **Barbecue East,** tel. 262-8457, open Mon.-Sat. 11 a.m.-9 p.m., Sun. 1-9 p.m., last Sun. of the month 5-9 p.m. The prices are terrific, the service friendly, and the food is delicious in this formica and linoleum decor restaurant. It's really an international potpourri that Hawaii is famous for because with every plate you get Korean kimchi, Japanese miso soup, Hawaiian fish, American macaroni salad, and a bit of coleslaw. If that's not all the peoples of Hawaii accounted for, then what is? Specials include *ahi jun* or teriyaki, butterfish, or scallops *jun* for $6.95. The sashimi special is *ahi* sashimi with fried scallop, fried oysters, kalbi beef, barbecued chicken, and sides for $10.75. You can even have a sashimi mixed plate of barbecued chicken and beef, sashimi, and the works for only $7.45. Korean specials are *kalbi* beef, or *pulgogi,* or chicken *mando* and all the trimmings for $8.95. They also serve beer and wine. The best choice for the money in Kailua, but no decor whatsoever.

If you want to save even more, at the other end of the shopping plaza is **Okazu-ya,** just a takeout lunch window, Japanese and

Korean style. In the same small complex is **Chef's Grill** Sandwich and Plate Lunch, and a **Baskin-Robbins** for your sweet tooth.

The 100 block of Hekili Street could be Kailua's version of Honolulu's Restaurant Row. Along this street is the **No Name Bar**, tel. 261-8725, just across from the bowling alley. The No Name Bar is for beer-drinking types who want a good meal as well. They have Sunday morning football at 7:30 a.m., and serious Monday night football at 6:30 p.m. Open Mon.-Fri. 3 p.m.-2 a.m., Sat. 11 a.m.-2 a.m., Sun. 3 p.m.-midnight, happy hour 4-7 p.m., with live entertainment nightly. Choices include salads like cobb salad for $5.50, No-name salad of ham, turkey, Swiss, provolone, eggs, and cukes for $5.95. Mixed plates can be empañadas—fresh-baked pastry filled with chick peas, olives, Cheddar, and spicy Mexican sauce, $4.95, or sausage bread, $4.95 small, $6.50 large. Chili is $2.95., and sandwiches are under $5.

The **Princess Chop Suey** is your basic chop suey joint two doors down from the No Name. Open Mon.-Sat. 10:30 a.m.-9 p.m., Sun. 12-9 p.m., tel. 839-0575. Naugahyde booths and formica tables. Everything under $5.

Next door is **Sisco's Cantina,** tel. 262-7337, featuring complete Mexican cuisine, open 11 a.m.-10 p.m. Sun.-Thurs., 11 a.m.-11 p.m. Fri. and Saturday. Tostadas, tacos, burritos, enchiladas, and chiles rellenos are all under $8. More expensive dishes are shrimp Veracruz $12, fajitas $15.25, for two $18.95. All come with Mexican corn, sautéed Tex-Mex mushrooms and salad. Inside, the south-of-the-border atmosphere is created with hanging piñatas, stucco walls, and blue-tile tables. A minute down the street is **Detroit Italian Deli,** featuring subs and ice cream.

L'Auberge Swiss Restaurant at 117 Hekili St., tel. 262-4835, is *so* continental and one of the finest restaurants on the entire windward coast. Don't miss it. Owned and operated by the Baltzer family, the small dining room is known for crepes stuffed with delicious morsels like crab or mushrooms and garnished with a rich sauce. The fresh fish is excellent, and they sometimes serve Maui rabbit. Appetizers include homemade country paté $6, fresh oysters on the half shell, $7. Soup of the day is $2.50, and salads like hearts of Manoa vinaigrette is $3. The setting is not romantic, but they've done a great job creating a pleasant atmosphere with red and white checkered tablecloths. Dinner is served Tues.-Sat. 6-10 p.m., Sun. 5:30-9:30, p.m.; for reservations call 263-4663 after 2 p.m. They have light Swiss dinners like bratwurst and *rosti* (pan fried veal-pork sausage with sauteed onions and potatoes) for $8.25, or veal and fresh mushrooms cooked in a cream sauce and served in a pastry shell with rice pilaf and fresh vegies for $8.50. Pasta prepared a different way each day varies in price. Swiss cheese fondue is $9.50, veal *scallopini marsala* is $15, and filet mignon Michelle is $16.50. Treat yourself to desserts like *meringue glace* ($2.75) or a chocolate snowball, a large scoop of ice cream dipped in chocolate and nuts and Kahlua-flavored caramel sauce ($3). Their special is Grandmother's Opfelchuechli, apple slices in liquor, fried in beer batter, dipped in cinnamon sugar, and served with vanilla cream sauce for $3.50. L'Auberge is simply fine dining at its best.

If you're interested in two distinctly different types of food you can try the **Sunshine Cafe,** 124 Oneawa St., tel. 261-0353, just across the street from **Taco Bell.** This former health food eatery is now a full-fledged luncheonette but still has a small selection of health food products. Open Tues.-Sat. 11 a.m.-8 p.m. At dinner they usually do several specials, which could be spinach lasagna, eggplant enchiladas, or spaghetti from $5.95-6.95. Cindy, the owner, uses organic ingredients whenever available. Other selections are the King Neptune sandwich—tuna salad, tomato, sprouts ($3.75), smoked salmon ($4.95), garden burger (meatless burger patty made from grains, nuts, and cheeses compacted) for $3.75. Mexican twists like tasty tostadas are $4.50, and vegetarian chili is $1.75 up to $5.95 for an extra large; Pele's plate, chili served with brown rice, salad, and a whole wheat roll is $4.50. Cindy specializes in desserts, whipping up cobblers and deep-dish fruit pies sweetened with honey. A great lunch or light dinner for the health-conscious. Next door is **Ching Lee Chop Suey,** a downhome, inexpensive Chinese restaurant where you can have a complete meal for under $5.

Uluniu Street has inexpensive places to eat, one after the other. After making a left from Kuulei Road (Rt. 61) onto Oneawa, a main thoroughfare, turn right onto Uluniu just at the large Kailua Furniture. First is an authentic hole-in-the-wall Japanese restaurant, **Kailua Okazuya.** They specialize in *donburi,* a bowl of rice smothered with various savories. Try their *o yakodon buri,* chicken and egg with vegetables over rice for under $4. They serve plate lunches and a sushi special that can't be beat which includes fresh fish, shrimp, abalone, and octopus for only $5! Next door is **Insam Korean Restaurant,** with more of the same Korean style, and up the street is the **New Chinese Garden,** a basic Chinese restaurant with decent prices. None of these restaurants are remarkable, but will fill you up with good enough food for a very reasonable price.

The address of **Kolohe Restaurant** (Kolohe means "rascal"), at 415-F Uluniu St., open 11 a.m.-6:30 p.m. Mon.-Fri., tel. 261-3050, won't help you much in finding this authentic Hawaiian food restaurant. Instead look for the McDonald's off Kailua Rd., and walk behind across the municipal parking lot. Except for vintage photos of canoeists and old Hawaiiana on the walls, there is no decor, but that doesn't detract from the excellent and inexpensive cuisine. They offer a fixed menu of *kalua* pig, *pipikaula, lomi* salmon, and one-scoop rice for $4.75, along with a variety of mix-and-match combo plates for under $5. It doesn't sound very Hawaiian, but their chopped steak is absolutely delicious. Don't overlook strange-sounding items like fried *aku* or *ahi* bones, which are a local favorite. Kolohe Restaurant is the genuine article, and if you want real Hawaiian cuisine this is the best in Kailua.

You'll first notice **Someplace Else,** at the corner of Aulike and Kuule Rd., open 11 a.m.-2 a.m., food service till 10 p.m., no breakfast except Sun. brunch from 9 a.m., tel.

262-8833, because of the huge multicolored umbrellas in the outside patio area. This is Kailua's upscale yuppie restaurant. It's a jungle in there with hanging plants, ferns, and flowers in every nook and cranny. The works of a local artist, Jean Myoko Kuboto, who specializes in *gyotaku,* printmaking using a fish which is covered in ink and then stenciled onto paper, adorns the walls. Throughout the week specials are offered, with Tuesday being "*wahine* night" (girl's night), with $1 drinks, 5 p.m.-closing, and Wednesday is "over the hump night"—10 p.m.-midnight all drinks $1.75. Besides a full bar, there is an array of fruit smoothies for $1.75.

Lunch brings a broiled *ono* sandwich for $6.25, chicken almond salad ($5.25), or crab-stuffed tomato for $7.95. The extensive menu continues with omelettes, and appetizers like escargot ($5.95), stuffed mushrooms ($5.95), and clam chowder, French onion, gazpacho, and soup of the day for under $3. South-of-the-border selections are burritos, chimichangas and the like for around $7. The broiler fires up with top New York steak ($14.95), barbecued ribs ($11.95), and chicken marsala for under $10. If you are looking for a place to "do lunch," or an evening of civilized conversation, don't go anywhere until you've tried Someplace Else.

For Italian try **Florence's,** 20 Kainehe St., tel. 261-1987. Florence has cooked up a few pots of spaghetti over the past 30 years that have kept locals and tourist coming back for more. You receive a full dinner, including minestrone, salad, bread, beverage, a side of macaroni, and the entree of the day for $10. Not only inexpensive but *delicioso!* Open for lunch, too, with savory meatball sandwiches a great choice.

Buzz's Original Steakhouse, at 413 Kawailoa Rd., tel. 261-4661, is really *the* original steakhouse of this small island chain owned by the Schneider family. Buzz's is just across the road from Kailua Beach Park, situated along the canal. This restaurant is an institution with local families. It's the kind of place that "if you can't think of where to go, you head for Buzz's." The food is always good, if not extraordinary. They have top sirloin

($12.95), pork chops ($11.95), chicken teri ($10.75), fresh fish usually about $18, and *mahi mahi* ($11.95). Salad bar is included with all entrees, and separately for $6.95. Everything is charbroiled. A can't-go-wrong choice.

Saeng's Thai Cuisine, at 315 Hahani, tel. 263-9727, open Sat.-Sun. 5-9:30 p.m., Mon.-Fri. 11 a.m.-2:30 p.m. and again from 5-9:30, offer spicy Thai food with an emphasis on vegetarian meals. Appetizers and starters are Thai crisp noodles ($4.25), sautéed shrimp ($7.95), salads like green papaya salad $4.25, *yum koong* (shrimp salad) for $6.95, and chicken coconut soup ($5.95). Specialties include spicy stuffed calimari ($8.95), Thai red curry ($6.95), and à la carte beef, pork, and chicken dishes, all under $6. Vegetarians can pick from mixed vegies with yellow bean paste ($4.95), mixed vegies with oyster sauce ($4.95), or zucchini tofu ($4.95). Saeng Thai is a good change of pace at a decent price.

Orson's Bourbon House, along the main drag at five Hoolai St., tel. 262-2306, is just behind the Burger King on a little side street. This Cajun-style restaurant prepares blackened *ahi,* a medium-rare fish, (wonderful as appetizer, but can do as an entree for $7,) fried calimari ($5.95), and *mufaletas* (a sub sandwich New Orleans style). Special of the day could be fresh silver salmon sautéed for $12.50. The decor is fine dining with white starched tablecloths, and fresh flower bouquets, while the bar area is rich with *koa* wood trim. Nightly entertainment is provided by Joel Kerosaki from Mon.-Thurs., and Carol Atkinson from Fri.-Sun., who perform a mixture of Hawaiian, jazz, and contemporary tunes. A good selection for a quiet dinner.

Captain Bob's Picnic Sail, tel. 926-5077, tours Kaneohe Bay daily and features lunch and all you can drink on its three- to four-hour sail for $35. You can work off lunch snorkeling or playing volleyball on the beach. The food is passable, but the setting offshore with the *pali* in the background is world class. Captain Bob also has a good reputation for community spirit, often taking local children's groups out on his boats. For most people desiring to see the waters along the windward coast

while spending a pleasant afternoon, this is the best bet.

Shopping And Services

These two towns of Kailua and Kaneohe have the lion's share of shopping on the windward coast. You can pick up basics in the small towns as you head up the coast, but for any unique or hard-to-find items, Kailua/Kaneohe is your only bet. The area offers a few shopping centers. The **Windward Mall,** at 46-056 Kamehameha Hwy., Kaneohe, tel. 235-1143, open weekdays 9:30 a.m.-9 p.m., Sat. to 5:30 p.m., Sun. 10 a.m.-5 p.m., is the premier, full-service mall on the windward coast. Besides department stores like Liberty House and Sears, there are shops selling everything from shoe to health foods.

The **Kaneohe Bay Mall** across from the Windward Mall is a little more downhome, and features a Longs Drugs, especially good for photo supplies. The **Aikahi Park Shopping Center** along Kaneohe Bay Dr., at the corner of Mokapu Blvd., is a limited shopping center whose main shops are a Safeway and a Sizzler Restaurant. The **Kailua Shopping Center** at 540 Kailua Rd. also has limited shopping that includes a **Time's Supermarket,** open till 10 p.m., and a well-stocked **Honolulu Bookshop,** tel. 261-1996, open Mon.-Fri. 9:30-9, Sat. 9:30-5:30, Sun. till 5 p.m., for a full range of reading material. There's also a **Cornet Store** along Kailua Ave. for sundries, lotions, and notions, and a **Longs Drug.**

Thursday mornings bring a **farmers' market** into town for only one hour from 8:50-9:50 a.m. Those in the know arrive early to get a number at their favorite stalls, which can sell out within minutes of opening. Great for fresh flowers and fruits.

You might pick up an heirloom at **Heritage Antiques,** daily 10-5:30, at the corner of Kailua Rd. and Amakua St., tel. 261-8700, which is overflowing with Oriental, Hawaiian, and Americana antiques. Here too are **jewelers,** H.W. Roberts and J.K. Phillips, who specialize as gemologists as well.

You'll find just about anything at **Holiday Mart** on Hahani Road., or picnic supplies at the landmark **Kalapawai Store,** at the corner of Kailua and Kalaheo roads, which marks the best entrance to Kailua's sailboarding beaches.

Campers can reach the **satellite city hall** for information and permits by calling 261-8575. A **post office** is at the corner of Kailua and Hahani, just across from the Hawaiian National Bank. Medical aid is available from **Castle Medical Center,** tel. 261-0841. A local **colonics therapist,** tel. 261-4511, is Alcyone at 122 Oneawa St., who specializes in detoxification programs and massage, and **Family And Urgent Medical Care** is at 660 Kailua Rd., tel. 263-4433.

KANEOHE AND VICINITY

The bedroom community of Kaneohe ("Kane's Bamboo") lies along Kaneohe Bay, protected by a huge barrier reef. Within the town is **Hoomaluhia Regional Park,** so large that guided hikes are offered on a daily basis. Offshore is Moku o' Loe, commonly called **Coconut Island.** It became famous as the opening shot in the TV show "Gilligan's Island," although the series itself was shot in California. In ancient times, it was kapu and during WW II served as an R&R camp for B-29 crews. Many of the crews felt the island had bad vibes, and reported having a streak of bad luck. In recent times, Frank Fasi, Honolulu's mayor, suggested that Hawaii's gate-crashing guests, Ferdinand and Imelda Marcos, should lease Coconut Island. It never happened.

SIGHTS

In the northern section of town is **He'eia Pier,** launching area for the *Coral Queen,* tel. 247-0375, a glass-bottomed boat that sails throughout the bay. A popular attraction, so make reservations. Fortunately, in recent years, the once crystal-clear bay, which was becoming murky with silt because of development, is clearing again due to conservation efforts.

A sandbar has been building in the center of Kaneohe Bay that has made a perfect anchorage for yachts and powerboats. These boat people drop anchor, jump off, and wade to the bar through waist-deep, clear waters. It has become an unofficial playground where you can fling a Frisbee, drink beer, fly a kite, or just float around. Part of the sand bar rises above the water and some BBQ chefs even bring their hibachis and have a bite to eat. Surrounding you is Kaneohe Bay with Chinaman's Hat floating off to your right, and a perfect view of the *pali* straight ahead. The epitome of *la dolce vita,* Hawaiian style.

Senator Fong's Plantation, at 47-285 Pulama Rd., Kaneohe 96744 (near Kahaluu), tel. 239-6775, open daily 9 a.m.-4 p.m., for guided tram tours, adults $6.50, children $3, under five free. Hawaii's newest attraction is a labor of love created by Senator Hiram Fong, who served as the state senator from 1959 to 1976. Upon retirement he returned to his home, and ever since has been beautifying his gardens started over 35 years ago. The result is 725 acres of natural beauty.

For a fun-filled day on Kaneohe Bay, far from the crowds of Waikiki, try **North Bay Boat Club's** "A Day on the Bay," located on the grounds of Schrader's Windward Marine Resort, 47-039 Lihikai Dr., Kaneohe, tel. 239-5711, ext. 112. "Your day" includes hotel pickup, BBQ lunch, open bar, sailboarding, kayaking, snorkeling, and sailing. Scuba introductory dives and jet-ski rides are also available at extra cost from **Wave Riders of Kaneohe,** tel. 239-5711, who offer a self- propelled tour around the bay on a jet-ski for $40 per hour, or $60 for two people for an hour.

All Hawaii Cruises, tel. 926-5077, features a snorkel/sail with with Captain Bob, who has an excellent reputation with local people. Your adventure includes hotel pickup, BBQ lunch, open bar, a four-hour sail, glass-bottom viewing, and reef walking. This is an excellent opportunity to view the awesome beauty of the windward coast.

KAILUA/KANEOHE

BEACHES

Kaneohe Bay offers **Kaneohe Beach Park, He'eia State Park,** and **Laenani Beach Park,** all accessible off Rt. 836 as it heads northward along the coast. All are better for the views of Kaneohe Bay than for beach activities. They have restrooms and a few picnic tables. The water is safe year-round, but it's murky and lined with mudflats and coral heads. The same conditions hold true for **Waiahole Beach Park** about four miles north, but this area is much less developed, quieter, and good for beachcombing.

Heeia State Park lies along Rt. 836 between Kaneohe and Kahaluu and is designated as an "interpretive park." It sits high on Kealohi Point overlooking He'eia Fishpond below. Kealohi translates as "The Shining," because it was a visible landmark to passing voyagers, but there is a much deeper inter-

pretation. To the Hawaiians this area was a "jumping-off point into the spirit world." It was believed that the souls of the recently departed came to this point and leapt into eternity. The right side, Heeia-kei, was the side of light, while the left side, Heeia-uli, was the domain of darkness. The wise *kahuna* taught that you could actually see the face of God in the brilliant sun as it rises over the point.

On the grounds are a main hall, pavilion, restrooms, and various short walks around the entire area with magnificient views of Kaneohe Bay. The park contains numerous indigenous plants and mature trees, the perfect laboratory for the educational goals set by The Friends of Heeia State Park. As an interpretive park, programs are offered for the community and visitors alike. Bernadette Lono, the Director of Hawaiian Studies, gives personal tours of the area. Her family has been part of this *ahuapua* (ancient land division) for countless generations. Bernadette first acquaints you with the area by asking you to sit Hawaiian style on the grass. The earth or *aina* is fundamental to the Hawaiian belief system, and you should start connected to it. She goes on to explain the symbiotic relationship between inland farmers whose fields stretched to Eolaka, the top of *pali*, and the fishermen who plied the waters of Mokapu on the other side of the peninsula.

Below, He'eia Fishpond is now privately owned by a Mr. Brooks, who has taken over the management of the pond from the Bishop Estates on a 20-year lease. He will raise mullet *(ama)*, the traditional fish raised by the ancient Hawaiians and *kapu* to all except the *ali'i*.

PRACTICALITIES

Accommodations

The **Bayview Apartment Hotel** has fully furnished one- and two-bedroom units at $64 for one bedroom, $82 for two. Three-day minimum stay, but you can stay for one or two if there's room. The hotel is a no-frills cinderblock building that is clean and friendly. There's parking, TV, swimming pool, no in-room phones, but an intercom calls you to the front desk. For reservations and information write Bayview Apartment Hotel, 44-707 Puamohala St., Kaneohe, HI 96744, tel. 247-3635.

The **Schrader's Windward Marine Resort** in Kaneohe has fully furnished apartments. It calls itself "a small rural resort," and although not far from city lights, it's definitely off the beaten track—literally on the edge of Kaneohe Bay, so close that it boasts fishing from the lanai of some apartments. Follow Rt. 836 from Kahaluu for a few minutes until you spot the Pineapple Hut (a tourist trap) and St. John's by the Sea Church. Turn here down Lihikai Drive to the resort.

There are 53 units here, but they differ greatly as they sprawl along the bay. The gray building, a housing project clone along the road front, is part of the place, and oddly enough are some of the most expensive units at $85-100 per night. All units have living rooms, color TV, phones, daily maid service,

refrigerators and air-conditioning, but only 19 have stoves and these rent for $65-200 per night. Least expensive with a full kitchen is $65. The rooms are spotless but old. Because of the age of the building, it's as if you've gone back 30 years to old Hawaii. The resort houses a fair number of TLA people (Temporary Lodging for Military). This is the only place for them to stay on the island.

The best deal for the money is a one-bedroom away from the road and facing the bay. If you call and specify any unit with a lanai you're going to get at least a partial view of the bay. The resort also offers motorboats, kayaks, sailboards, and small sailboats through its sister organization, North Bay Boat Club. Get a break at Wave Runners of Kaneohe (jet-skis) and Twilight Cruise, a narrated cruise of the bay every Tuesday evening on a pontoon boat. Discounts offered on long stays, package deal with Thrifty car rental.

For information write Schrader's Windward Marine Resort, 47-039 Lihikai Dr., Kaneohe, HI 96744, tel. (800) 367-8047, ext. 239, Canada (800) 423-8733, ext. 239, on Oahu 239-5711.

Dining And Nightlife

Fortunately, or unfortunately, Kaneohe is a bit of a wasteland as far as tourist services, nightlife, and eating out are concerned. Most people who live here head for the action in Honolulu. There are a few limited choices. Recently opened **Falia's** serves steak and lobster in their medium-priced dining room. They also offer vintage Hawaiian music with Blah Pahi Nui, who plays excellent slack-key guitar. **Fuji's Delicatessen,** at 45-270 Wm. Henry Rd., tel. 235-3690, is a local favorite known for its downhome Japanese, Korean, and Hawaiian cooking served family style on long communal tables. **Marie Callender's,** a national chain, has a restaurant at 46-056 Kamehameha Hwy., tel. 235-6655, and serves decent food in a pleasant atmosphere. They also feature Kaleo Okalani, three women with rich voices who harmonize beautifully.

If you're looking for a real cultural experience, head for **Bob's Saimin,** at 46-132-A

Kahuhipa St., tel. 247-7878, especially late in the evening where you can get hearty bowls of soup and a selection of barbecued meats for inexpensive prices. The best deal in town is at **Kim Chee One,** at 46-010 Kamehameha

Hwy., tel. 235-5560, which has a few sister restaurants scattered around Oahu. The setting is plain, but you'll have trouble finishing the excellent Korean mixed barbecued plate for $6.95, easily enough for two.

KAHEKILII HIGHWAY

Where Rt. 83 intersects the Likelike Highway on the southern outskirts of Kaneohe, it branches north and changes its name from the Kamehameha Highway to the Kahekilii Highway until it hits the coast at Kahaluu. This four-mile traverse passes two exceptionally beautiful valleys: Haiku Valley and the Valley of the Temples. Neither should be missed.

SIGHTS

Haiku ("Abrupt Break") **Gardens** is a lovely section of commercial area that includes a restaurant (see below) and some quiet condominiums. After you pass a community college, Haiku Road is past two red lights. Turn left here and proceed for about one-half mile until you see the entrance. The gardens date from the mid-1800s, when Hawaiian *ali'i* deeded 16 acres to an English engineer named Baskerville. He developed the area, creating a series of spring-fed lily ponds, a number of estate homes, and planting flowers, fruits, and ornamental trees. Later a restaurant was built, now owned by the Ing family, and the grounds became famous for their beauty, often used for outdoor weddings and special gatherings.

You're welcome to walk through the gardens. Proceed from the restaurant down a grassy area to a pond, where perhaps you'll attract an impromptu entourage of ducks, chickens, and guinea fowl that squawk along looking for handouts. Amidst the lush foliage is a grass shack used for weddings. A path leads around a larger pond whose benches and small pavilions are perfect for contemplation. The path leads under a huge banyan, while a nearby bamboo grove serenades with sonorous music if the wind is blowing.

Valley Of The Temples
The concept of this universal faith cemetery is as beautiful as the sculpted *pali* that serves as its backdrop. A rainy day makes it better. The *pali* explodes with rainbowed waterfalls, and the greens turn a richer emerald, sparkling with dewdrops. Don't miss the Valley of the Temples Memorial Park, 47-200 Kahekili Hwy., tel. 239-8811. Admission is $2 or *kamaaina* rates of $5 per carload, but you have to prove you're from Hawaii. High on a hill sits a Christian chapel, an A-frame topped by a cross. The views can be lovely from up here, but unfortunately the large windows of the chapel perfectly frame some nondescript tract housing, and a Pay 'n' Save supermarket below. Great planning!

The crown jewel of the valley is **Byodo-In Temple** ("Temple of Equality"), a superbly appointed replica of the 900-year-old Byodo-In of Uji, Japan (depicted on the 10-yen coin). This temple dates from June 7, 1968, 100 years to the day when Japanese immigrants first arrived in Hawaii. It was erected through the combined efforts of an American engineering firm headed by Ronald Kawahara in accordance with a plan designed by Kiichi Sano, a famed Kyoto landscape artist. Remove your shoes before entering the temple. A three-ton brass bell, which you're invited to strike after making an offering, creates the right vibrations for meditation, and symbolically spreads the word of Amida Buddha.

The walls hold distinctive emblems of different Buddhist sects. Upstairs wings are roped off, with no entry permitted. Stand on the gravel path opposite the main temple. You'll see a grating with a circle cut in the middle. Stick your face in to see the perfectly framed contemplative visage of Buddha. Cross a half-moon bridge to the left of the temple and follow the path to a small gazebo. Here a rock, perfectly and artistically placed, separates a stream in two, sending the water to the left and right. The pagoda at the top of the path is called the Meditation House. Go to this superbly manicured area to get a sweeping view of the grounds. In front of the Meditation House is a curious tree; pick up one of the fallen leaves, and feel the natural velvet on the backside.

The grounds are alive with sparrows and peacocks, and from time to time you'll hear a curious-sounding "yip, yip, yip" and clapping hands. Follow it to discover Mr. Henry Oda, who will be surrounded by birds taking crumbs from his fingers, and a boiling cauldron of *koi* in the waters below with mouths agape demanding to be fed. He has taken over for the recently retired Mr. Hisayoshi Hirada, the original "Birdman of Byodo-In." Mr. Hirada translates his first name into "long live a good man," and he, well into his 80s, is living proof. Mr. Hirada began training the birds and carp of Byodo-In after his *first* retirement. He would come daily to feed the fish, clapping his hands while he did so. Soon the Pavlovian response took over. Simultaneously, a small and courageous bird, which Hirada-san calls Charlie, began taking crumbs from his fingers.

Mr. Oda does a great job of showing visitors around, but old-timers say that there is no one like Mr. Hirada, and if he happens to be there while you're visiting, you have been blessed by the great Buddha of Byodo-In. A small gift shop selling souvenirs, cards, and some refreshments is to the right of the temple. If you wish to photograph the complex, it's best to come before noon, when the sun is at your back as you frame the red and white temple against the deep green of the *pali*.

Kahaluu

This town is at the convergence of the Kahekilii Highway and the Kamehameha Highway (Rt. 83) heading north. Also, Rt. 836, an extension of the Kamehameha Highway, hugs the coastline heading down to Kailua-Kaneohe. It offers some of the most spectacular views of a decidedly spectacular coast, with very few tourists venturing down

Charlie and the Birdman

this side road. Kahaluu Town is a gas station and a little tourist trap selling junk just in case you didn't get enough in Waikiki. The Hygienic store sells liquor, groceries, soda, and ice, all you'll need for an afternoon lunch. The Waihee Stream, meandering from the *pali*, empties into the bay and deposits fresh water into the ancient **Kahaluu Fish Pond,** a picture-perfect tropical setting. So picture-perfect is the place that it has provided the background scenery to TV and Hollywood productions such as an episode from "Jake and the Fat Man," a setting for *Parent Trap II,* and the famous airport and village scene from *The Karate Kid.* All of the scenery has been torn down, but you can still overlook the fishpond by taking a short walk just behind the bank in town.

WAIAHOLE AND VICINITY

If you want to fall in love with rural, old-time Oahu, go to the northern reaches of Kaneohe Bay around Waihole and Waikane, a Hawaiian grass-roots area that has so far eluded development. Alongside the road are many more fruit stands than in other parts of Oahu. For a glimpse of what's happening look for the Waiahole Elementary School, and turn left up Waiahole Valley Road. The road twists its way into the valley, becoming narrower until it turns into a dirt track. Left and right in homey, ramshackle houses lives downhome Hawaii, complete with taro patches in the backyards. Another road of the same type is about one-half mile up Rt. 83 just before you enter Waikane. If you're staying in Waikiki, compare this area with Kuhio Avenue only 45 minutes away!

Route 83 passes a string of beaches, most with camping. Offshore from Kualoa County Park is Mokoli'i ("Small Reptile") Island, commonly called **Chinaman's Hat** (between mile marker 30 and 31) due to its obvious resemblance to an Oriental chapeau. If the tides are right, you can walk out to it (sneakers advised because of the coral), where you and a few nesting birds have it to yourself. Kualoa Park has undergone extensive renovations. There is an expansive parking area, plenty of picnic tables, and a huge grassy area fronting the beach. The road passes through what was once sugar cane country. Most of the businesses failed last century, but you will see the ruins of the Judd Sugar Works a mile or so before reaching Ka'a'awa. The dilapidated mill stands although it was closed more than a century ago. Entering is not advised!

Kualoa County Regional Park

With the *pali* in the background, Chinaman's Hat Island offshore, and a glistening white strand shaded by swaying palms, Kualoa is one of the finest beach parks on windward Oahu. One of the most sacred areas on Oahu, the *ali'i* brought their children here to be reared and educated, and the area is designated in the National Register of Historic Places. It has a full range of facilities and services, including lifeguards, restrooms, and picnic tables. The park is open daily from 7 a.m.-7 p.m., with overnight camping allowed with a county permit (mandatory). The swimming is safe year-round along the shoreline dotted with pockets of sand and coral. The snorkeling and fishing are good, but the real treat is walking the 500 yards to Chinaman's Hat at low tide. You need appropriate footgear (old sneakers are fine) because of the sharp coral heads. The island is one of the few around offshore Oahu that is not an official bird sanctuary, although many

Chinaman's Hat

shorebirds do use the island and should not be molested.

Because of its exposure to winds, Kualoa is sometimes chilly. Although the park is popular, it is not well marked. It lies along Rt. 83, and if you're heading north, look for a red sign to the Kualoa Ranch. Just past it is an HVB Warrior pointing to the park and Chinaman's Hat. Heading south the entrance is just past the HVB Warrior pointing to the Kualoa Sugar Mill ruins.

PRACTICALITIES

Food And Shopping

The **Haiku Gardens Restaurant,** true to its name, sits surrounded by a fragrant garden in a lovely, secluded valley (see p. 292). The restaurant is undergoing massive renovations and is supposed to open as a Chart House, a chain with an excellent reputation for good food at reasonable prices.

The **Hygienic Store** along Rt. 83 just past the Valley of Temples sells groceries and supplies. It's flanked by stalls selling fruits and shellwork at competitive prices.

Follow the Kahekilii Hwy. to Rt. 83 past Waiahole and Waikane, where you'll find some of the best roadside fruit stands on Oahu. One little stand just near the Waiahole Elementary School (mile marker 34.5) is manned on non-school days by two young sisters, Zalia and Kahea. Their smiles alone are worth a stop. Just up Rt. 83 is another stand that features drinking coconuts. Do yourself a favor and have one. Sip the juice and when it's done, eat the custard-like contents. A real island treat, nutritious and delicious.

KA'A'AWA TOWN AND VICINITY

SIGHTS

When you first zip along the highway through town you get the impression that there isn't much, but there's more than you think. The town stretches back toward the *pali* for a couple of streets. On the ocean side is **Ka'a'awa Beach Park,** a primarily local hangout. Across the road is the post office, and the **Ka'a'awa Country Kitchen,** which serves breakfast and plate lunches, where you can easily eat for $5. They have a few tables, but the best bet is to get your plate lunch and take it across the street to the beach park. Next door is a **7-eleven** with gas and incidentals. Behind the post office is **Pyramid Rock,** obviously named because of its shape.

Oahu's *pali* is unsurpassed anywhere in the islands, and it's particularly beautiful here. Take a walk around. Stroll the dirt roads through the residential areas and keep your eyes peeled for a small white cross on the *pali* just near Pyramid Rock. It marks the spot where a serviceman was killed during the Pearl Harbor invasion. His spirit is still honored by the perpetually maintained bright white cross. While walking you'll be treated to Ka'a'awa's natural choir—wild roosters crowing any time they feel like it, and the din of cheeky parrots high in the trees. A pair of parrots escaped from a nearby home about 10 years ago, and their progeny are joyfully relishing life in the balmy tropics. If you'd like to mimic one of these fancy-free parrots see **The Plantation Spa** (p. 296) for a uniquely revitalizing experience in Ka'a'awa.

As you come around the bend of Mahie Point, staring down at you is a very popular stone formation, the **Crouching Lion.** Undoubtedly a tour bus or two will be sitting in the lot of the Crouching Lion Inn. As with all anatomical rock formations, it helps to have an imagination. Anyway, the inn is much more interesting than the lion. Built by George Larsen in 1928 from rough-hewn lumber from the Pacific Northwest, the huge stones were

excavated from the site itself. The inn went public in 1951 and has been serving tourists ever since (for menu and prices see below).

Ka'a'awa And Kahana Bay Beaches

Three beach parks in as many miles lie between Ka'a'awa Point and Kahana Bay. The first heading north is **Ka'a'awa Beach Park,** a popular camping beach (county permits) with restrooms, lifeguards, and picnic facilities. An offshore reef running the entire length of the park makes swimming safe year-round. There's a dangerous rip at the south end of the park at the break in the reef.

Swanzy County Park, two minutes north, also has camping with a county permit. The sand and rubble beach lies below a long retaining wall, often underwater during high tide. The swimming is safe year-round, but is not favorable because of the poor quality of the beach. Swanzy is one of the best squidding and snorkeling beaches on the windward coast. A break in the offshore reef creates a dangerous rip, and should be avoided.

Kahana Bay County Park is a full-service park with lifeguards, picnic facilities, restrooms, the area's only boat launch, and camping (county permit). Swimming is good year-round, although the waters can be cloudy at times, and a gentle shorebreak makes the area ideal for bodysurfing and beginner board riders. This entire beach area is traditionally excellent for *akule* fishing, with large schools visiting the offshore waters at certain times of year. It once supported a large Hawaiian fishing village; remnants of fishponds can still be seen. On the mountainside is **Kahana Valley State Park** amidst a mixture ironwoods and coconut trees. Here's restrooms, fresh water, and picnic tables. Few visit here, and it's perfectly situated for a quiet picnic.

Huilua Fish Pond lies between Ka'a'awa and Punaluu, not far from the Paniola Cafe (about mile marker 25.8). Look to the mountainside for Trout Farm Road and immediately to your right, on the ocean side, is the fishpond. Spot a small bridge and a great

near Ka'a'awa

launching area for a canoe, kayak, or flotation device. Once in, go left under the traffic bridge. Follow Kahana Stream as it gets narrower and narrower (but passable) as it heads inland. You can even use the overhanging ferns to pull yourself along. It's deep so be aware. If you go to the right, you'll reach the bay. It's fairly safe until you come to open ocean. TheBus stop is directly across from the launching area so you can get off here, enjoy the sights, and then continue on.

PRACTICALITIES

The Plantation Spa

The Plantation Spa is essentially into three-part harmony . . . of body, mind, and spirit. By itself it can't make you sing, but it can provide the perfect space for you to re-attune to your own deep cosmic melody and, perhaps, with effort, to belt out a few glorious chords by the time you leave. Set on seven lovely acres of what once was the summer estate of Mary King, heiress to Schilling Spices, it was originally created as a retreat, and it still is, but now even more so.

The spa began in 1987 when Bodile Anderson, the owner and operator, brought a long-held dream into reality. For years Bodile had led health seminars throughout Hawaii, taking her guests to various resorts. But something wasn't quite right. Bodile felt that she needed her own place, free from outside influences and interruptions because the tune she taught and the tune she sang was very subtle.

Mostly, Bodile shares her clean and sensible lifestyle with you, and claims that the way she lives is the way she was raised in her native Sweden. She's primarily self-taught, even taking excursions to visit Philippine faith healers, but she learned her basic techniques and philosophy from her friend Ebba Weareareland, who, along with her husband Are, were pioneers in the self-health movement begun in Switzerland over 50 years ago.

Bodile is aided by a remarkably knowledgeable, skillful, and diverse staff who have come up with the perfect combination of pampering and working you into shape. In essence they are the *potters* and you are the willing clay. They will create a designer week of exercise (aerobics, hikes, swimming, and more), contemplation, meditation, relaxation, cultural pursuits, and right eating habits. From you they need a desire to show up and some enthusiasm.

The peaceful grounds, kept impeccably by Simaile and Taniella, two Tongan gentlemen, are an ally. You enter off the beach road passing through gates that open onto an expansive lawn that gives a buffer to the outside world. There's an outdoor weight-room, and to the rear of that some change rooms. Here too is a freeform swimming pool

Plantation Spa

to seven days, and you'll be monitored and counseled along the way. Many people have reported a great weight *loss* while experiencing an energy *gain* while on the spa's special fasting program. For others, meals are wholesome vegetarian, prepared with fresh and basic ingredients. All take a hand in preparing their specialties but the main cooks are Gini Maddocks and all-around hand Jeannine Lundgren, who will be your message therapist and fearless leader on morning beach walks.

Your week at the spa begins with reception and orientation at 4 p.m. on Sunday and ends the following Saturday at 10 a.m. The spa can pick you up at the airport, so don't rent a car. You won't be going anywhere else. All the rooms are the same price, $1250 for seven days, six nights, based on double occupancy, or $1550 for single occupancy. Prices include all meals, activities, facilities, and all normal programs. For reservations and information contact the Plantation Spa at 51-550 Kamehameha Hwy., Ka'a'awa, HI 96730, tel. 237-8685 or (800)422-0307.

complete with jacuzzi to untie muscles, and the melody of a small waterfall to unjangle nerves. The grounds rise behind the main house to the second level, where there's a guesthouse with two separate rooms. If you follow still farther up the hill you come to what was the Orchidarium, which is now used for massage and herbal wraps, so that you emerge as fresh as a daisy.

Food, and its relationship to good health, is emphasized at the spa. The purification process begins with what you eat. If you choose, you can fast for anywhere from one

The Crouching Lion Inn

There was a time when *everyone* passing through Ka'a'awa stopped at the Crouching Lion Inn. Now "everyone" has become "too many" ever since the tour buses started packing in here for lunch. The Inn, along Rt. 83 in Ka'a'awa, tel. 237-8511, is beautiful enough to stop at just to have a look, but if you want a reasonably quiet meal, avoid lunchtime and come in the evening. Dinners are pricey and include *mahi mahi* ($12), fisherman's catch ($20), rack of lamb ($19), or Hawaiian chopped steak ($12). If you're not hungry and just wish to enjoy the rustic inn, the cocktail lounge has lost its liquor license, but you can still order a coffee or soft drink.

PUNALUU AND HAUULA

PUNALUU

When islanders say Punaluu ("Coral Diving") they usually combine it into the phrase "Pat's at Punaluu" because of the famous resort that's been delighting local people and visitors for years (at mile marker 23.2). It's a favorite place to come for a drive in the "country." Punaluu is a long and narrow ribbon of land between the sea and the *pali*. Its built-up area is about a mile or so long, but only a hundred yards wide. It has gas, supplies, camping, and some of the cheapest accommodations anywhere on Oahu (see below). The **Punaluu Art Gallery,** operated by Scott Bechtol, famous candle artist, offers distinc-

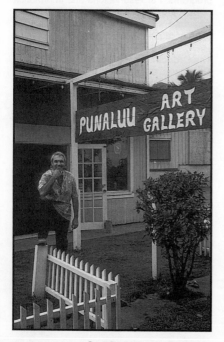

Scott Bechtol

tive island art. On the northern outskirts of town, a sign points to **Sacred Falls,** an excellent hike, weather permitting (see p. 136).

A few hundred yards south of Pat's is **St. Joachim Church.** There's nothing outstanding about it, merely a one-room church meekly sitting on a plot of ground overlooking the sea. But it's real, homegrown, where the people of this district come to worship. Just look and you might understand the simple and basic lifestyle that still persists in this area.

The **Punaluu Art Gallery,** in Punaluu around mile marker 24, tel. 237-8325, open daily 10 a.m.-6 p.m., formerly owned by Dorothy Zoler, is the oldest art gallery on windward Oahu. The new owner, candle artist Scott Bechtol, remains dedicated to showcasing the works of an assortment of the finest artists that the North Shore has to offer. Scott is well known for his wonderful sculpted candles, all made from the finest beeswax. Some are lanterns shaped like a huge pita bread with the top third cut off. The remainder is sculpted with a scene that glows when the candle is lit. Others are huge tikis, dolphins, or flowers, all inspired by the islands. There's even a 10-foot whale! Some of the larger candles are $70, the man-size tiki is about $800, but smaller candles are only $5, and Scott's unique "crying tiki" sells for only $20. Scott creates all of this beautiful glowing art with just one precision carving tool . . . a Buck knife!

Other artists shown are Betty Jenks from Ka'a'awa, who does original miniature oils for $20, that are about the size of a compact mirror. Bill Cupit creates "bananascapes." Bill removes the outer bark from the banana tree, then he tears and cuts it to make a scene of boats or mountains. The result is a three-dimensional piece. Bill's wife is an artist who specializes in seascapes made with seaweed. Other beauty is added by Janet Holiday's silkscreen prints, Bruce Clark's woodcarvings, and Peter Hayward's oil paintings. The Punaluu Art Gallery is a jewel case of man-made beauty surrounded by natural beauty. They harmonize perfectly.

HAUULA

This speck of a town is just past Punaluu between mile markers 21 and 22. The old town center is two soda machines, two gas pumps, and two limited supply stores, Masa's and Ching Jong Leong's. Another store, Segame's, sells cold beer and liquor. At the estuary of a stream is **Aukai Beach Park,** a flat little beach right in the middle of town. A **7-eleven** and a little church up on the hill with the *pali* as a backdrop add the seemingly mandatory finishing touches. Just near the bus stop on the south end, look for a local man who is usually there selling leis. The flowers and vines are fresh-picked from the immediate area, and the prices and authenticity are hard to beat.

Outdoor enthusiasts will love the little-used **Hauula Loop Trails.** These ridge trails head up the valleys gaining height along the way. They offer just about everything that you can expect for a Hawaiian trail, the mountains, the valleys, and vistas of the sea. Built by the CCC during the Depression, the trails are wide, and the footing is great even in rainy periods which can shut down the nearby **Sacred Falls Trail.** (See p. 136 for a complete description). At the north end of town is the **Hauula Kai Center,** a small shopping center where you'll find the Lotus Inn Chop Suey, a Pay 'n' Save, Lindy's Food (a supermarket), the Bethlehem Baking Co., and a post office (See p. 300 for more details.)

BEACHES

Right along the highway is **Punaluu County Beach Park.** Punaluu provides shopping, and the beach park has restrooms, cooking facilities, camping by permit (recently closed, so check), but no lifeguards. The swimming is safe year-round inside the protected reef. Local fishermen, usually older Filipino men who are surfcasting, use this area frequently. They're friendly and a great source of information for anyone trying to land a fish or two. They know the best baits and spots to dunk a line.

Hauula County Beach Park is an improved beach park with lifeguards, picnic facilities, restrooms, pavilion, volleyball court, and camping (permit). Safe swimming year-round inside the coral reef, with good snorkeling, and surfing usually best in the winter months. Rip currents are present at both ends of the beach at breaks in the reef, and deep holes in a brackish pond are formed where Maakua Stream enters the sea. Across the road are the ruins of the historic **Lanakila Church** (1853), partially dismantled at the turn of the century to build a smaller church near Punaluu.

PRACTICALITIES

Accommodations

Two institutions at Punaluu are sure to please. Each is in a different economic and social category, but because they're off the beaten track, both offer great value. **Pat's at Punaluu** (mile marker 23.2) is more famous as a restaurant than as condominium apartments, but you'll be pleased with both. Daily rates are $54-62 cottage, $58-66 one bedroom, $102-120, three-bedroom, same rate up to four persons, extra person $10. At Pat's are a magnificent beach, parking, TV, a fine restaurant, swimming pool, and weekly maid service. They offer a "room 'n' wheels" package, and discounts on long stays. Pat's is off the beaten track, so definitely call ahead to check room availability. Turning up and expecting a room is a foolish maneuver, and remember that this is a condo, not a hotel, so one-night stays are not the norm. Next to the restaurant is a small convenience store that may or may not look open. But inside (separate business) is a small desk, open 8:30 a.m.-1 p.m., where you register. Another rental office on the property is open until 9 p.m., but check-in after that costs extra since someone has to stay around to let you in. For information write Pat's at Punaluu Condo, 53-567 Kamehameha Hwy., Hauula, HI 96717, tel. 293-8111.

The **Countryside Cabins** are a wonderful, inexpensive, and definitely funky place to stay. They're owned and operated by a sparkling older woman, Margaret Naai. The entrance is hard to spot, but it's located *mauka* about halfway between Pat's of Punaluu and the Paniolo Cafe. Look for the small white sign that says "Cabins." You're greeted by a large black dog named Smokey. He's a big baby so don't worry. Margaret comes out with a rolled-up newspaper to fend Smokey off because he jumps on her: Smokey weighs 98 pounds, she only 96. Completely furnished studios are $25 daily, $175 weekly, $475 monthly. Unfurnished rooms are $20 nightly, $140 weekly, $300 monthly. Margaret will reserve a room for you if you send a $10 deposit. She's a peach, but she's getting on in years, so it would be best to send a SASE envelope with your deposit and not count on her to remember. For information and reservations, write Countryside Cabins, 53-224 Kamehameha Hwy., Hauula HI 96717, tel. 237-8169.

Food

An institution along the windward coast, **Pat's of Punaluu** has an extraordinary view of the coast. The interior is quite tasteful with open beams, ceiling fans, high-backed wicker chairs, and a long polished *koa* bar. The feeling is warm, peaceful, and very tropical. There's a little bandstand, some fish tanks, and a large lava rock wall that counterpoints the white stucco. Breakfast for $5 is huge, and a bargain. Lunch is a Pat's burger for $6.25, grilled teri chicken ($6.25), tropical fruit salad for $6.50 (also a lunch buffet on weekdays). Dinner is quite gourmet with offerings of sashimi, escargot, or beer-battered *mahi mahi* for appetizers ($6-8). Soup, like seafood bisque, and a salad of fresh-tossed greens are around $4. Entrees include grilled choice New York steak ($16.95), grilled lamb ($12.75), fresh *opakapaka* ($17.95), and a complete chef dinner for $25, which changes regularly. Open for breakfast 8 a.m., lunch 11 a.m.-2 p.m., dinner from 5-9:30 p.m.

No trip to Pat's is complete without sampling the fresh tarts famous since 1945—your choice of banana, pineapple, or coconut ladled into an oven-fresh tart and mounded with whipped cream. Pat's is also famous for mai tais, made fresh ($5), and so laced with booze that if you intend on driving, only have one!

Pat's presents an authentic hula show Sat. and Sun. at 7 p.m. Contemporary dance music follows. Pat's, long renowned as a good old-fashioned Hawaiian-style restaurant, has been going through transition in the last few years. Luckily, it is definitely back on the right track. The previous owners tried to make it a tourist trap complete with a mediocre cafeteria to cater to the tour-bus crowd. The new owners have reclaimed Pat's and saved it from a fate worse than deep-fried *mahi mahi*. They're restoring Pat's to its old island-style tradition, and doing an admirable job. Pat's is back, and is definitely worth a stop.

What tropical island would be complete without a cowboy cafe serving rattlesnake chili? The **Paniolo Cafe** along the highway in Punaluu (mile marker 23), tel. 237-8521, has a foot-stompin' dance floor with country music and just the right touch of cowboy class. A stuffed longhorn steer glares from one wall, a rattler, as thick as a wrestler's arm, from the other. You'll dine on barbecued beef, ribs, chicken, and an assortment of Mexican food all priced around $9.95. A whopping 12-ounce steak is $16, and the rattlesnake chili at $5 *is* authentic. Try their deep-fried bananas with wild honey for dessert. Or you could broil your own entrees like *mahi mahi*, a small steak, or teri chicken for under $10 including the salad bar.

The Paniolo is friendly and attracts a mixed crowd, along with a regular clientele of local people. No one is going to hassle you, but if you're looking for trouble you'll be served a good old knuckle sandwich, pardner! You can order 16-ounce Mason jars of Miller Light or Bud for $2. Sashay to the tunes of the Bourbon Cowboys on Fri. and Sat. from 9-11:30 p.m. and again on Sunday afternoons. The Paniolo is a great bar, a commodity hard to find on Oahu, and the only one of its kind along the windward shore.

Shopping

The **Hauula Shopping Center** features **Pay 'n' Save** for everything from film to swim fins, and the **Village Food Mart,** open from 9-9 weekdays, 9-5 Sunday for all food needs.

The **Hawaiian-Polynesian Cultural Supply,** tel. 293-1560, open 9:30 a.m.-5 p.m. weekdays, half day Saturday, is a rare and unique hula supply store. They feature fine Polynesian crafts used in the hula like *ip'u* (gourd drums), hula skirts, headdresses, beads, and shell leis. There are other accouterments and art items like *koa* bowls, carved turtles, and mother-of-pearl necklaces. All items are handmade in Tahiti, Samoa, Tonga, and Hawaii, basically from throughout Polynesia. T-shirts, sweatshirts, and suntan oil are also sold. All items offered are authentic, and the storekeepers are friendly and informative regarding the hula. A great store in which to browse and to pick up a unique and *real* souvenir.

LAIE TO KAHUKU

LAIE

The "Saints" came marching into Laie ("Leaf of the *le* Vine") and set about making a perfect Mormon village in paradise. What's more, they succeeded! The town itself is squeaky clean, with well-kept homes and manicured lawns that hint of suburban Midwest America. Dedicated to education, they built a branch of **Brigham Young University** (BYU) that attracts students from all over Polynesia, many of whom work in the nearby Polynesian Cultural Center. The students vow to live a clean life, free of drugs and alcohol, and not to grow beards. God doesn't like beards! In the foyer of the main entrance look for a huge mural depicting Laie's flag-raising ceremony in 1921, which symbolically established the colony. The road leading to and from the university campus is maze-like but easily negotiable.

The first view of the **Mormon Temple,** built in 1919, is very impressive. Square, with simple architectural lines, this house of worship sits pure white against the *pali,* and is further dramatized by a reflecting pool and fountains spewing fine mists. This tranquil, shrine-like church is open daily from 9 a.m.-9 p.m., when a slide show telling the history of the Laie colony is presented, along with a guided tour of the grounds. "Smoking is prohibited, and shirts (no halter tops) must be worn to enter." The temple attracts more visitors than any other Mormon site outside of the main temple in Salt Lake City.

Polynesian Cultural Center

The real showcase is the Polynesian Cultural Center. PCC, as it's called by islanders, began as an experiment in 1963. Smart businessmen said it would never thrive way out in Laie, and tourists didn't come to Hawaii for *culture* anyway. The PCC now rates as one of Oahu's top tourist attractions, luring about one million visitors annually. Miracles do happen! PCC is a nonprofit organization, with proceeds going to the Laie BYU, and to maintaining the center itself.

Covering 42 acres, the primary attractions are seven model villages including examples from Hawaii, Samoa, the Marquesas, Fiji, New Zealand, Tonga, and Tahiti. Guides lead you through the villages either on a walking tour, or by canoe over artesian-fed waterways. A shuttle tram runs outside the center, and will take you on a guided tour to the BYU campus, the Temple, and a short tour of the community. The villages are primarily staffed with people from the representative island homelands. Remember that most are Mormons, whose dogma colors the attitudes and selected presentations of the staffers. Still, all are genuinely interested in dispensing cultural knowledge about their traditional island ways and beliefs, and almost all are characters who engage in lighthearted bantering with their willing audience. The undeniable family spirit and pride at PCC makes you feel welcome, while providing a clean and wholesome experience, with plenty of attention to detail.

The morning begins with the **Fiafia Festival,** a lei greeting that orients you to the Center. Next comes **Music Polynesia,** a historical evolution of island music presented by singers, musicians, and dancers. A brass band plays from 5:30 p.m., touring the different villages, and the **Pageant of Canoes** sails at 2 and 3 p.m. The largest extrava-

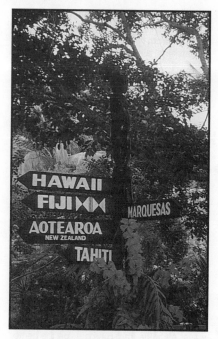

Polynesian Cultural Center

PCC is open daily except Sunday from 12:30 p.m. General admission to the center is $24.95 adult, $9.95 children under 11, under five free. There are also a variety of other packages available including an all-day pass, with dinner buffet and evening show for around $50, children $40. For more information contact PCC at tel. 293-3333. TheBus #52 leaves from Ala Moana to the center and takes about two hours. Most island hotels can arrange a package tour to PCC.

KAHUKU

This village, and it is a village, is where the *workers* of the North Shore live. Kahuku, has little to recommend it, except that it is very real, and a lingering slice of what Hawaii was, not so long ago. Do yourself a favor, and turn off the highway for a two-minute tour of the dirt roads lined by proudly maintained homes that somehow exude the feeling of Asia. Of course there is the Kahuku Superette for supplies, and **Huevos Restaurant,** open daily 7 a.m.-1 p.m., and again on Fri. and Sat. from 5:30-9 p.m., basic Mexican. Huevos is in a dilapidated old building in the center of town (follow signs) and is worth a visit just to soak up the local scene. A little white *kaukau* wagon sits across the roadway from the school. They sell great food that they pick up in Chinatown everyday. They're here only during school hours, when you can pick up a tasty and inexpensive lunch.

Keep a sharp eye out for a truck and a sign featuring fresh shrimp for $5.95 just along the road. Follow it to **Ahi's Kahuku Restaurant,** operated by Roland Ahi and son, open daily 7 a.m.-9 p.m. The shrimp couldn't be fresher as it comes from Pacific Sea Farms, an aquaculture farm just a few minutes away. The longest that these plump babies have been out of the water is 48 hours, so you are definitely getting *the* best. In this no-frills but super-friendly restaurant, you can have your shrimp cooked to order as scampi, deep-fried, tempura, a cocktail, or sautéed. You get about five to seven shrimp, depending on the size. The shrimp is the *pièce de resistance,* but they have basic sandwiches like tuna and

ganza occurs during an evening dinner show called **This is Polynesia.** Beginning at 7:30 p.m., the center's amphitheater hosts about 3,000 spectators for this show of music, dance, and historical drama. The costumes and lighting are dramatic and inspired; it's hard to believe that the performers are not professionals. Soon to open is an *Imax,* a wraparound movie screen, that attempts to give you a real sense of what it's like to take a canoe around the shores of Fiji, or to tramp the mountains of New Zealand.

Food is available from a number of snack bars, or you can dine at the **Gateway,** which serves you a buffet dinner as part of a package including the Polynesian extravaganza. A luau, and a Mission Buffet are offered now and again, usually at 5:30 p.m., so there's plenty of time to eat and then catch the show if you desire.

*Kahuku Mill
Shopping Center*

hamburger, both under $4, and entrees like spaghetti with meat sauce for $4.95, and steak and *mahi mahi* combo for $10.95. Complete meals come with green salad, fresh vegetables, rice, and tea. They also serve beer and wine, and on Saturday nights feature a sing-along *kareoke,* where you can become an instant star.

On the north end of town is **The Mill Shopping Center,** which is really the town's old sugar mill that has been recycled. The interior is dominated by huge gears and machinery, power panels, and crushers that are the backdrop for a string of shops, a restaurant, and the Kahuku Theater. The 10-foot gears and conveyor belts have all been painted with bright colors, and seem like a display of modern art pieces. Outside is a **Circle K** food store and gas station, **Lee's Gifts and Jewelry, Island Snow** for shave ice, **Tropical Memories Jeweler,** and a post office. Inside is the **Country Kitchen,** open 8 a.m. till 10 p.m. This restaurant has utilized the theme perfectly by situating a portion of its tables in an old caboose. They have a full range of sandwiches and burgers for under $5, and dinners like ham and broccoli supreme, $6.05. Country suppers are the likes of fried chicken, $9.45, roast turkey, $9.45, ribeye steak, $11.95, Mexican salad for $5.25, and grilled chicken breakfast salad for $5.75; special prices for seniors and children.

BEACHES

At the north end of Laie, you'll pass **TT Surf Shop,** about the only shop in this neck of the woods offering surfing equipment, boards, or boogie boards.

At the southern end of Laie is **Pounder's Beach,** so named by students of BYU because of the pounding surf. The park area is privately owned, open to the public, with few facilities (a few portable outhouses and picnic tables). This beach experiences heavy surf and dangerous conditions in the winter months, but its excellent shoreline break is perfect for bodysurfing. The remains of an old pier at which inter-island steamers once stopped is still in evidence.

Laie County Park is an unimproved beach park with no facilities, but a one-mile stretch of beach. The shoreline waters are safe for swimming inside the reef, but wintertime produces heavy and potentially dangerous surf. Good snorkeling, fishing, and throw-netting by local fishermen; get there by following the stream from the bridge near the Laie Shopping Mall.

Kakela Beach is a privately owned facility where camping is allowed. Secure a reservation from Zion Securities, 55-510 Kamehameha Hwy., Laie, HI 96762, tel. 293-9201. Or check in with the caretaker if you arrive during daylight hours, when chances are good that you can find a spot without reservations. Camping is $5 per person per night. The area is improved with showers and picnic facilities. No BBQs but you can bring your own camp stove. This facility is private, under-used, and secure. Pitch your tent among the ironwoods overlooking the beach, which has good swimming and bodysurfing.

Malekahana State Recreation Area

This is the premier camping beach along the north section of the windward coast. Separated from the highway by a large stand of shade trees, it offers showers, restrooms, picnic facilities, and camping (state permit). Offshore is Moku'auia, better known as **Goat Island.** You can reach this seabird sanctuary by wading across the reef during low tide. You'll find a beautiful crescent white-sand beach and absolute peace and quiet. The swimming inside the reef is good, and it's amazing how little used this area is for such a beautiful spot. Be aware that there are two entrances to the park. The north entrance, closest to Kahuku, puts you in the day-use area of the park, where there are restrooms and showers. Offshore, about 200-300 yards, is a small island. *You can not wade to this island. It is too far, and the currents are strong.* The entrance to the camping section is south a minute or two (around mile marker 17) and is marked by a steel gate painted brown and a sign welcoming you to Malekahana State Recreation Area. You must be aware that the gates open at 7 a.m. and close at 6:45 p.m. Goat Island is only a stone's throw from shore. Reef walkers or tennis shoes are advised.

PRACTICALITIES

Accommodations

The **Laniloa Lodge Hotel** is just outside the Polynesian Culture Center, and has been recently given a face lift. Rooms are $60 s, $65 d, $70 for a triple, $75 for four, and $120-175 for a suite. They also offer $49 for a double room if you purchase two all-day tickets to the Polynesian Cultural Center. All rooms have a/c, TV, and there's parking, a pool, and a restaurant that closes early on Sundays, but McDonald's is next door. For information write Laniloa Lodge Hotel, 55-109 Laniloa St., Laie, HI 96762, tel. 293-9282 or (800) 526-4562.

Kekeala Hale is a condominium rental fronting Kekeala Beach, at 55-113 Kamehameha Hwy., Laie, HI, 96762 tel. 293-9700. They call themselves "private Polynesia at its best," and being as secluded as they are, they have a point. Cottages are over a thousand square feet with a full kitchen and bath, with one king and four twins beds in each unit. A tennis court on property is featured. Rates for cottages that sleep six to 12 (using foam pads) are $240 daily, $600 for a weekend, $1440 weekly. Rates for a cottage sleeping four to six is $120 daily, $720 weekly. All require a three-day minimum.

Lora Dunn's House is at 55-161 Kamehameha Hwy., Laie, HI 96762, tel. 293-1000 (between mile markers 19 and 20, ocean side). Lora admits people on a first-come first-served basis, but will happily take phone reservations for which she requires a deposit. Chances of turning up and finding a vacancy are poor, so at least call from the airport to check availability. A separate studio for two people is $175, while the downstairs self-contained unit of her home, which is larger and can accommodate four people, runs about $350 per week. Good value in a quiet, if not spectacular, setting.

Food

When you enter Laie you will be greeted by the Stars and Stripes flying over the entrance of the Polynesian Cultural Center. Next door is a whopper of a **McDonald's,** and in keeping with the spirit of Polynesian culture, looks like a Polynesian longhouse. Just next door is the **Laniloa Lodge,** whose restaurant features breakfast specials for under $4, and complete dinners with soup, salad, vegies, and Kona coffee for only $10.95. They're open every day from breakfast until 8 p.m., except Sunday when the restaurant closes at 2 p.m. The food is wholesome but ordinary at the Laniloa Lodge, tel. 293-5888.

A few minutes down the road, the **Haaula Shopping Center** provides a small variety of dining spots. At the **Lotus Inn Chop Suey,** tel. 293-5412, you'll get a tasty and filling meal daily from 10 a.m.-9 p.m. for under $6. A full menu of Cantonese-style food includes ginger chicken, shrimp, and beef. Happy hour runs from 3-7 p.m., when well drinks cost $1.25 and are accompanied by free *pu pu.* **Country Health Food,** specializing in sandwiches and smoothies, is open Mon.-Sat. 9 a.m.-7 p.m., tel 293-2153. They are almost as much of a restaurant, as they are a health food store. Some tasty items are the garden salad $2.50, nachos for $3, and an assortment of freshly made sandwiches like the

Tuna Terrific, $3.25, Avocado Supreme, $3.25, and Texas-style BBQ meat-free burger for $3.50. Energize with a full selection of herbal ice teas, fresh-squeezed orange juice or carrot juice. Smoothies are strawberry, cocobutternut shake, made with nonfat milk, cocoa protein, peanut butter, egg, and banana for $2.75. A great change of pace. The shopping center also features a **Domino's Pizza,** and the **Bethlehem Baking Company,** open daily 6:30 a.m.-6 p.m., with an assortment of yummies including sweet homemade breads of pineapple and coconut.

THE NORTH SHORE

This shallow bowl of coastline stretches from Kaena Point in the west to Turtle Bay in the east. **Mount Kaala,** verdant backdrop to the area, rises 4,020 feet from the Waianae Range, making it the highest peak on Oahu. The entire stretch is a day-tripper's paradise with plenty of sights to keep you entertained. But the North Shore is synonymous with one word: surfing. Thunderous winter waves, often measuring 25 feet (from the rear!) rumble along the North Shore's world-famous surfing beaches lined up one after the other—**Waimea Bay, Ehukai, Sunset, Banzai Pipeline.** They attract highly accomplished athletes who come to compete in prestigious international surfing competitions. In summertime *moana* loses her ferocity and lies down, becoming gentle and safe for anyone.

Haleiwa, at the junction of the Farrington Highway (Rt. 930) heading west along the coast and the Kamehameha Highway (Rt. 83) heading east, is fast becoming the central town along the North Shore. The main street is lined with restaurants, boutiques, art gallerys, small shopping malls, and sports equipment stores. **Waialua,** just west, is a "sugar town" with a few quiet condos for relaxation. Farther west is **Dillingham Airfield,** where you can arrange to fly above it all in a small plane or soar silently in a glider. The road ends for vehicles not far from here, and then your feet have to take you to Kaena Point, where *the* largest waves pound the coast. Heading east, you'll pass a famous *heiau* where human flesh mollified the gods. Then come the great surfing beaches and their incredible waves. Here and there are tidepools rich with discovery, a monument to a real local hero, and **Waimea Falls Park,** the premier tourist attraction of the North Shore.

BEACHES AND SIGHTS

The main attractions of the North Shore are its beaches. Interspersed among them are a few sights definitely worth your time and effort. The listings below run from west to east.

The most-traveled route to the North Shore is from Honolulu along the H-2 freeway, and then directly to the coast along Rt. 99 or Rt. 803. At Weed Circle or Thompson Corner, where these routes reach the coast, turn left along the Farrington Highway, following it to road's end just before Kaena Point, or right along the Kamehameha Highway (Rt. 83), which heads around the coast all the way to Kailua.

Be aware that *all* North Shore beaches experience very heavy surf conditions with dangerous currents from October through April. The waters, at this time of year, are not for the average swimmer. Please heed all warnings. In summertime, leap in!

ALONG THE FARRINGTON HIGHWAY

Waialua

The first town is Waialua ("Two Waters"). Take Waialua Beach Road just off the Weed Traffic Circle coming north on Rt. 99, or follow the signs off the Farrington Highway. At the turn of the century, Waialua, lying at the terminus of a sugar-train railway, was a fashionable beach community complete with hotels and vacation homes. Today, it's hardly ever visited, and it's not uncommon to see as many horses tied up along main street as it is to see parked cars in this real one-horse-

town. Sundays can also attract a rumble of bikers who kick up the dust on their two-wheeled steeds.

The sugar mill, an outrageously ugly mechanical monster, is still operating and is central to the town. Quiet Waialua, with its main street divided by trees running down the middle, *is* rural Oahu. There's a general store for supplies, post office, and snacks at the **Sugar Bar,** a restaurant in the old Bank of Hawaii building. If you're returning to Haleiwa take Haleiwa Road, a back way through residential areas. Look for Paalaa Road on the right and take it past a small Buddhist temple that holds an *o bon* festival honoring the dead, traditionally observed in July.

Mokuleia Beach Park And Dillingham Airfield

Mokuleia is the main public access park along the highway. It provides picnic facilities, restrooms, lifeguards, playground area, and camping (county permit). In summertime, swimming is possible along a few sandy stretches protected by a broken offshore reef. Mokuleia Army Beach, across from the airfield, is a wider strand of sand. It's very private, and the only noise interrupting your

bikers at Waialua

afternoon slumber might be planes taking off from the airfield. A minute farther toward Kaena is an unofficial area with a wide sand beach. During the week you can expect no more than half dozen people on this 300-yard beach. Remember that this is the North Shore and the water can be treacherous. Careful! Five minutes past the airfield, the road ends. This is a good place to check out giant waves.

Across the road is **Dillingham Airfield,** small but modern, with restrooms near the hangars and a new parking area. A public phone is available in hangar G-1. Most days, especially weekends, a few local people sell refreshments from their cars or trucks. The main reason for stopping is to take a small plane or glider ride. **Glider Rides,** tel. 677-3404, take you on a 20- to 30-minute flight for $40 single, $60 double. The owner is Bill Star, who has been flying from here since 1970. They fly seven days a week starting at about 10 a.m. on a first-come, first-served basis. They suggest you bring a camera, and arrive before 5 p.m. to get the best winds. There's always a pilot with you to make sure that your glider ride is a *return* trip. Another glider operation is **Mile High Glider Rides.** They fly for 30 minutes, and they offer a sit-up-front-and-try-the-controls-type ride complete with acrobatics and instruction. They fly out of hangar No. 10, and charge about $80 per ride. **Surf Air Tours,** tel. 637-7003, flies Cess-

na 172s or 206s for a half-hour along the North Shore for $30 per person, or on a longer "circle-island tour" for $50 per person. It's worthwhile, but the glider ride is more exceptional.

In quick succession after Dillingham Airfield come undeveloped **Kealia Beach,** safe during calm periods, and **Mokuleia Army Beach,** improved and open to the public. Local people have erected semipermanent tents in this area and guard it as if it were their own. **Camp Harold Erdman** is next, one of the best-known camps on Oahu. This YMCA facility is named after a famous Hawaiian polo player killed in the '30s. The facility is used as a summer camp for children, throughout the year for special functions, and as a general retreat area by various organizations. Access is limited to official use.

Kaena Point

Kaena Point lies about 2½ miles down the dirt track after the pavement gives out. Count on three hours for a return hike and remember to bring water. The Point can also be reached from road's end above Mahuka on the Waianae (leeward) side of the island. Kaena has *the* largest waves in Hawaii on any given day. In wintertime these giants can reach above 40 feet, and their power, even when viewed safely from the high ground, is truly amazing. Surfers have actually plotted ways of riding these waves, which include being dropped by helicopter with scuba tanks. Reportedly, one surfer named Ace Cool has already done it. For the rest of us mortals . . . "who wants to have that much fun anyway!" Kaena Point is the site of numerous *heiau*. Due to its exposed position, it, like similar sites around the islands, was a jumping-off point for the "souls of the dead." The spirits were believed to wander here after death, and once all worldly commitments were fulfilled, they made their "leap" from earth to heaven. Hopefully, the daredevil surfers will not revive this tradition!

HALEIWA AND VICINITY

Haleiwa ("Home of the Frigate Birds") has become the premier town of the region, mainly because it straddles the main road and has the majority of shopping, dining, and services along the North Shore. **Haleiwa Ali'i Beach Park** is on the western shores of Waialua Bay, which fronts the town. This beach park is improved with restrooms, lifeguard tower, and small boat launch. Lifeguards man the tower throughout the summer, on weekends in winter. The shoreline is rocks and coral with pockets of sand, and although portions can be good for swimming, the park is primarily noted for surfing, in a break simply called "Haleiwa."

Head eastward and cross the **Anahulu River Bridge.** Park for a moment and walk back over the bridge. Look upstream to see homes with tropical character perched on the bank with a bevy of boats tied below. The scene is reminiscent of times gone by.

A much better park is **Haleiwa Beach Park,** clearly marked off the highway on the eastern side of Waialua Bay. Here you'll find pavilions, picnic facilities, lifeguards, restrooms, showers, food concessions, and camping (county permit). The area is good for fishing, surfing, and most importantly, for swimming year-round! It's about the only safe place for the average person to swim along the entire North Shore during winter.

Kawailoa Beach is the general name given to the area stretching all the way from Haleiwa Beach Park to Waimea Bay. A string of beaches, **Papailoa, Laniakea,** and **Chun's Reef,** are just off the road. Cars park where the access is good. None of these beaches is suitable for the recreational swimmer. All are surfing beaches, with the most popular being Chun's Reef.

WAIMEA BAY AND VICINITY

The two-lane highway along the North Shore is pounded by traffic; be especially careful around Waimea Bay. The highway sweeps around till you see the steeple of **St. Peter and Paul Mission** with the bay below. The steeple is actually the remnants of an old rock-crushing plant on the site. **Waimea Bay Beach Park** has the largest rideable waves

typical rural Buddhist temple, outskirts of Haleiwa

in the world. This is the heart of surfers' paradise. The park is improved with a lifeguard tower, restrooms, and a picnic area.

During a big winter swell, the bay is lined with spectators watching the surfers ride the monumental waves. In summertime, the bay is calm as a lake. People inexperienced with the sea should not even walk along the shorebreak in winter. Unexpected waves come up farther than expected, and a murderous rip lurks only a few feet from shore. The area is rife with tales of heroic rescue attempts, many ending in fatalities. A plaque commemorates Eddie Aikau, a local lifeguard credited with making thousands of rescues. In 1978, the *Hokulea,* the Polynesian Sailing Society's double-hulled canoe, capsized in rough seas about 20 miles offshore. Eddie was aboard, and launched his surfboard to swim for help. He never made it, but his selfless courage lives on.

Waimea Falls Park

Look for the well-marked entrance to Waimea Falls Park, mountainside from the bay. You can drive for quite a way into the lush valley before coming to the actual park entrance. As you enter, a local man sells Hawaiian coconut-frond hats. These are the authentic article, priced right at around $6. The park is primarily a botanical garden with a fascinating display of flowers and plants, all labeled for your edification. If you choose not to walk, open-air tour buses take you through the grounds narrating all the way. The highlight is professional diving from the 55-foot rock walls into the pool below Waimea Falls. This event, along with the ancient hula (excellent, and authentic), a display of Hawaiian games, and feeding of wildlife are scheduled four times throughout the day, so whenever you arrive you'll have an opportunity to see them. Nature paths, great for carefree roaming, lead into the valley. Admission is $9.95 adults, $6 juniors, and $2 children, open daily 10 a.m.-5:30 p.m., tel. 638-8511. The **Proud Peacock** (see p. 316) serves dinner until 9 p.m. Monthly (check the free tourist literature), on the Friday night closest to the full moon, beginning at 8:30 p.m., the park offers a free guided moon-viewing tour.

Waimea Falls Park

Pupukea Beach Park

A perfect place to experience marinelife is the large tidepool next to Pupukea Beach Park, the first one north of Waimea Bay, across the street from the Shell gas station. A long retaining wall out to sea forms a large and protected pool at low tide. Wear footgear and check out the pools with a mask. Don't be surprised to find large sea bass. A sign warns against spearing fish, but the local people do it all the time. Be careful not to step on sea urchins, and stay away from the pool during rough winter swells, when it can be treacherous. The beach park has restrooms, picnic facilities, and fair swimming in sandy pockets between coral and rock, but only in summertime. County camping with a permit was allowed in this beach park, and may be available again.

The middle section of the park is called **Shark's Cove,** though no more sharks are here than anywhere else. The area is terrific for snorkeling and scuba in season. Look to the mountains to see **The Mansion** (see below), and next to it the white sculpture of the **World Unity Monument.** If you had to pick a spot from which to view the North Shore sunset, Pupukea Beach Park is hard to beat!

Further down the road, as you pass mile marker nine you can't help noticing a mammoth redwood log that has been carved into a giant statue representing an ancient Hawaiian. Peter Wolfe, the sculptor, has done a symbolic sculpture for every state in the union, this being his 50th. This statue is extremely controversial. Some feel that it looks much more like an American Indian than a Hawaiian, and that the log used should have been a native *koa* instead of an imported redwood from the Pacific Northwest. Others say that its *intention* was to honor the living and the ancient Hawaiians, and that is what's important. Just off to the left a small shop sells plants, towels, and shellwork from the Philippines.

Puu O Mahuka Heiau

Do yourself a favor and drive up the mountain road leading to the *heiau* even if you don't want to visit it. The vast and sweeping views of the coast below are incredible. About one mile past Waimea Bay the highway passes a Foodland on the right. Turn here up Pupukea

Road and follow the signs. Ignore the warning at the beginning of the access road; it's well maintained.

Puu O Mahuka Heiau is large, covering perhaps five acres. Designated as a state historical site, its floorplan is huge steps, with one area leading to another just below. The *heiau* was the site of human sacrifice. People still come to pray as is evidenced by many stones wrapped in *ti* leaves placed on small stone piles lying about the grounds. In the upper section is a raised mound surrounded by stone in what appears to be a central altar area. The *heiau's* stonework shows a high degree of craftsmanship throughout, but especially in the pathways. The lower section of the *heiau* appears to be much older, and is not as well maintained.

Drive past the access road leading to the *heiau* and in a minute or so make a left onto Alapio Road. This takes you through an expensive residential area called **Sunset Hills** and past a home locally called **The Mansion**—look for the English-style boxwood hedge surrounding it. The home was purported to be Elvis Presley's island hideaway. Almost next door are the grounds of the **Nichiren Buddhist Temple,** resplendent with manicured lawns and gardens. This area is a tremendous vantage point from which to view Fourth of July fireworks that light up Waimea Bay far below.

THE GREAT SURFING BEACHES

Sunset Beach runs for two miles, the longest white-sand beach on Oahu. Winter surf erodes the beach, with coral and lava fingers exposed at the shoreline, but in summertime you can expect an uninterrupted beach usually 200-300 feet wide. The entire stretch is technically Sunset Beach, but each world-famous surfing spot warrants its own name though they're not clearly marked and are tough to find . . . exactly. Mainly, look for cars with surfboard racks parked along the road. The beaches are not well maintained either. They're often trashed, and the restrooms, even at Waimea Bay, are atrocious. The reason is politics and money. Efforts all go into

**NORTH SHORE
SURF BEACHES**

SUNSET BEACH

BANZAI PIPELINE

83

SHARKS COVE

FOODLAND

PUPUKEA RD.

RUBBER DUCKIES

BEACH
PARK

"THREE TABLES"

CATHOLIC
CHURCH

PINBALLS

MARIJUANA'S

WAIMEA BAY

TO HALEIWA

NOT TO SCALE

© MOON PUBLICATIONS, INC.

Waikiki, where the tourists are. Who cares about a bunch of crazy surfers on the North Shore? They're just a free curiosity for the tourists' enjoyment!

The **Banzai Pipeline** is probably the best-known surfing beach in the world. Its notoriety dates from *Surf Safari,* an early surfer film made in the 1950s, when it was dubbed "Banzai" by Bruce Brown, maker of the film. The famous tube-like effect of the breaking waves comes from a shallow reef just off-shore which forces the waves to rise dramatically and quickly. This forces the crest forward to create "the Pipeline." A lifeguard tower near the south end of the beach is all that you'll find in the way of improvements. Parking is along the roadway. Look for Sunset Beach Elementary School on the left, and the Pipeline is across the road. You can park in the school's lot on non-school days.

Ehukai Beach Park is the next area north. It has a lifeguard tower and restroom, and provides one of the best vantage points from which to watch the surfing action on the Pipeline and Pupukea, the area to the right.

Don't expect much when you come to **Sunset Beach Park** itself. Except for a lifeguard tower, there is nothing. This beach is the site of yearly international surfing competitions. Almost as famous as the surfing break is the **Sunset Rip,** a notorious current offshore that grabs people every year. Summertime is generally safe, but never take *moana* for granted.

PRACTICALITIES

ACCOMMODATIONS

Places to stay are quite limited along the North Shore. The best deals are renting beach homes or rooms directly from the owners, but this is a hit-and-miss proposition, with no agency handling the details. You have to check the local papers. The homes vary greatly in amenities. Some are palaces, others basic rooms or shacks, perfect for surfers or those who consider lodging as secondary. Check the bulletin boards outside the Surf and Sea Dive Shop in Haleiwa and Foodland supermarket.

Expensive

The **Turtle Bay Hilton** is a first-class resort on Turtle Bay, the northern extremity of the North Shore, Box 187, 57-091 Kamehameha Hwy., Kahuku, HI 96731, tel. 293-8811. Once a Hyatt hotel, it was built as a self-contained destination resort. It's surrounded by sea and surf on Kuilima Point, which offers protected swimming year-round. All are welcomed at the beach, so if you come for a day, park in the hotel parking lot and validate your ticket at one of the hotel restaurants to only pay $1 for parking. TheBus also stops at the hotel. The entrance to the hotel is grand, as it's lined with six-foot-high hibiscus and a formal lawn. The resort is complete with a golf course, tennis courts, pool, full water activities including sailboarding and scuba lessons, horseback riding, shopping, and the fanciest dining on the North Shore. Since the hotel is isolated, you should *always* call ahead to book any of these activities, even for guests staying at the hotel. There's very little shopping in this area, so if you're after film, or basic picnic supplies, stop at the hotel's mini mall. All rooms are ocean view, but not all are oceanfront. Oceanfront is slightly more expensive, but is worth the price, especially from January to April when humpback whales cavort in the waters off the point. Rooms are furnished with full baths, a mini-fridge, dressing room, a large vanity, ample closets, a/c, and cable TV. Junior suites come complete with a li-brary, large bathroom and changing room, two couches, a sitting area, queen-size bed, and a large enclosed lanai. Rates based on double occupancy begin at $135 for a studio, extra person $15, $235 cottage, $300-950 for a suite. Room rates may seem high, but you actually get much more than what you would pay for a mainstream hotel of similar stature. The Hilton family plan allows children free when they stay in a room with their parents. See "Food" below for a full listing of the fine dining offered at the Turtle Bay Hilton.

The most important features of the **Mokuleia Beach Colony,** at 68-615 Farrington Hwy., Waialua, HI 96791, is what's missing . . . hustle, bustle, and noise. This secluded condo, backdropped by mountains, fronted by the sea, and nestled next to a stately white-fenced polo field, is the epitome of serenity, whose colors are

Turtle Bay

emerald green and sky blue, and whose music is the rolling surf. Each privately owned *hale* is split into two 700-square-foot open-floor-plan units that are fully furnished. All have a screened lanai which doubles as a day room, a living room area, modern kitchen, bedroom, and a full bath. Cooling is provided by ceiling fans and shuttered windows and screens that catch the balmy breezes. Tennis courts and a pool are part of the complex. Average prices range from $550-600 weekly. Sundays usually bring sky divers and hang gliders who land in the polo field next door except during polo season, which brings a match every Sunday from March through August. The Colony has formed an association which handles rentals. To book a *hale* contact Bobbie Kane, c/o Kane International, 2828 Paa St., Suite 2130, Honolulu, HI 96819, tel. 833-1600, fax (808) 834-0577.

Ke Iki Hale is a small condo complex operated by Alice Tracy, 59-579 Ke Iki Rd., 96712, tel. 638-8229. Pass the Foodland Supermarket heading north, and look for a school sign. Turn left here to the beach to find the condo. The property has 200 feet of private beach with a sandy bottom that goes out about 300 feet (half that in winter). The condo is quiet with a home-away-from-home atmosphere. Rates are: one-bedroom beachfront, $125 per day, $700 per week, $2400 per month; two-bedroom beachfront $125 per day, $775 per week, $2500 per month. Units on the grounds with no beachfront are about 25 percent less.

Surfer Rentals

The North Shore of Oahu is long famous for its world-class surfing. The area attracts enthusiasts from around the world who are much more concerned with the daily surfing report than they are with deluxe accommodations. The Kamehameha Highway is dotted with surfer rentals from Haleiwa to Turtle Bay. Just outside their doors are the famous surfing breaks of Marijuana's, Rubber Duckies, and Pinballs, all famous and known to world-class surfers. Some of these accommodations are terrific, while others are barely livable. Here's a sample of what's offered.

The **Plantation Village** at 59754 Kam Hwy., Haleiwa 96712, tel. 638-8663, lies across from Three Tables Beach by Shark's Cove, between mile markers 6 and 7. It's on TheBus line and only a five-minute walk from a Safeway store for supplies. The Plantation Village, once a real Filipino working village, has cottages by the sea, secure behind a locked gate, and furnished with cable, stereo, linens, dishes, washers and dryers, ice machines, and cleaning service. There is a full kitchen and even a cook whom you pay separately for preparing your meals if you wish. Many of the fruit trees on the grounds provide the guests with complimentary bananas, papayas, breadfruit, or whatever is happening. Prices are $15 for a shared room and bath with two or three others. Ask for Unit 2, which is the same price, but a tiny private room. The small (300 square feet) private cottages, once the homes of real plantation workers, sleep two and are $50 per night. A $100 per night deluxe cottage sleeps four, and you get a large front lanai, two couches, wicker furniture in a sitting room, cable TV, a/c, fan, full bath with vanity, and kitchen fully furnished with microwave, stove, and fridge. The Plantation Village is geared to long stays and has a one-week minimum policy. They will come to the airport to pick you up for $25, which is great if you have a surfboard and gear. During surfing season the place is booked out. Reserve two months in advance, full deposit during high season (Dec.-Feb.), one-half deposit other months. No refund policy in high season.

The **Vacation Inn and Hostel,** 59-788 Kam Hwy., Haleiwa, HI 96712, tel. 638-7838, specializes in budget accommodations for surfers, backpackers, and families. Owned and operated by the Foo Family, the main building in this small cluster of buildings is at mile marker 6, the fourth driveway past the church tower coming from Waimea Bay. There are a number of facilities and room styles which could put you on the beach or mountainside, depending on availability and your preference. Basic rates are $12 for a bunk in the hostel-style rooms, which includes cooking and laundry facilities, and TV in the communal room. Each room has four bunks, microwaves, shower, and bath. The feeling is definitely not deluxe, but it is adequate. A complex on the beach offers a $65 room which sleeps four, has a complete kitchen, two double beds, a roll-out couch, ceiling fan, and a world-class view of the beach from your lanai. The back house, on the mountainside, is further away from traffic and is amongst the trees. It's on stilts, and has an open ceiling and rustic common area. Rates are $33 for the main rooms (two people), a private loft for $25 (it would be hot up there), or share a bunk for $12. The Vacation Inn has only one rule: use common sense, and clean up after yourself. They provide free boogie boards and snorkeling gear, and will rent you bikes and surfboards. Airport transportation is $5, $25 if it's a special trip. Everyone's friendly and laid-back. Book ahead. A good choice.

Between mile markers 9 and 10 look for a small sign that says "Rooms. In this very basic accommodation you can rent for a night, a week, or a month ($400). There's no name, but call 638-8895 for info. Expect communal cooking facilities, shared bath, and no maid service. This is basically a crash pad for surfers and travelers. Not recommended for anyone interested in anything but basic and cheap.

FOOD

Inexpensive

McDonald's golden arches rise above Haleiwa as you enter town. Historic Haleiwa Theater was torn down so that the world could have another Egg McMuffin. Here too is a **7-eleven** convenience store. Almost next door is **Pizza Hut.** Besides pizza, their salad bar isn't bad.

Between the two, but a culinary world apart, **Celestial Natural Foods,** tel. 637-6729, open weekdays 9 a.m.-6:30 p.m., Sun. 10-6, sells natural and health foods, and vegetarian meals at the snack bar. Smoothies are $2.50; most sandwiches and a variety of salads are under $3.50.

Cafe Haleiwa, a hole-in-the-wall eatery on your left just as you enter town, serves one of the best breakfasts on Oahu. Their "dawn patrol" from 6-7 a.m. includes eggs and whole-wheat pancakes for $2.50. Specials of the house are whole-wheat banana pancakes, French toast, spinach and mushroom quiche, and steaming-hot Kona coffee. One of the partners, Jim Sears, is called "the wizard of eggs" and has built up a local following. The cafe attracts many surfers, so it's a great place to find out about conditions.

If you're tired or just need a pick-me-up head for the North Shore Marketplace (after McDonald's, mountainside) where you'll find the **Coffee Gallery,** open from 5:30 a.m.-9:30 p.m. They pour gourmet coffees and offer a selction of deli sandwiches and salads for under $5. The **China Inn** here serves a variety of inexpensive dishes like sweet and sour pork $3.50, sweet and sour fish $3.25, and hamburgers. Take it out to the shade of the lanai. A minute past is the **Haleiwa Chinese Restaurant,** tel. 637-3533, open daily 10 a.m.-9 p.m. The interior is basic but the food is very good. Their steamed sea bass and *kung pao* chicken are both excellent. A gigantic bowl of tofu soup is $4, while most main courses are under $6. One of the best inexpensive eateries on the North Shore.

You can tell by the tour buses parked outside that **Matsumoto's** is a very famous store on the North Shore. What are all those people after? Shave ice. This is one of the best places on Oahu to try this island treat. Not only do the tourists come here, but local families often take a "Sunday drive" just to get Matsumoto's shave ice. Try the Hawaiian Delight, a mound of ice smothered with banana, pineapple, and mango syrup.

The **Country Drive-In** is across from Haliewa Shopping Center. They have plate lunches (20 varieties), smoothies, and country breakfasts like corned beef hash and fried eggs with breakfast meat for $2.25. Quick and good.

The tiny town of Waialua (see p. 307) is home to **The Sugar Bar,** located in the old Bank of Hawaii Building. They feature an international cuisine, hot dogs from America to bratwurst from Germany. *Magnifique!*

East from town across from Shark's Cove is **Shark's Shack,** a *usually* open lunch wagon that'll fix you a sandwich or rent you snorkeling gear. Next door is **Pupukea Shave Ice** for an island treat. Farther toward

Sunset Beach (around mile marker 9) look for **Diamico's Pizza,** open for breakfast, lunch, and dinner, and the Sunset Beach store, home of Ted's Bakery.

Moderate/Expensive

Steamer's in the Haleiwa Shopping Plaza, tel. 637-5071, is a clean and modern restaurant serving seafood, beef, and chicken. There's plenty of brass, paneled walls, and low lighting. Lunches are especially good with a wide choice of omelettes from $5, including one made from crab, shrimp, and mushrooms; all come with blueberry or French muffins. Whet your appetite with sushi, steamed clams, or have full fish dinners starting at $10. Dining daily 11 a.m.-11 p.m., bar until 2 a.m.

   Rosie's Cantina, also in the plaza, open Sun.-Thurs. 7 a.m.-10 p.m., Fri.-Sat. 7-11 p.m., prepares hearty Mexican dishes for a good price. The inside is "yuppie Mex" with brass rails, painted overhead steam pipes, and elevated booths. Expect to pay $4 for enchiladas and burritos, while meat dishes are $8-9. Order the enchilada stuffed with crab for $9; add a salad and two could easily make this a lunch. **Pizza Bob's** across the way has an excellent local reputation, and its little pub serves up delicious pizza, salad, lasagne, and sandwiches.

   The Proud Peacock, Waimea Falls Park, tel. 638-8531, is open daily for lunch and dinner. It's fun to dine here even if you don't enter the park. From the dining room, you can look into some of the nicest gardens while feeding crumbs to the peacocks. The beautiful mahogany bar was made in Scotland almost 200 years ago. You can have a light soup and salad, but their seafood *pu pu* platter is hard to beat. Roast pork and roast beef are well-prepared favorites here. A Moonlight Buffet from 5-9 p.m. is served to adults for $9.95, children 12 and under $5.95, on two full-moon nights a month. Included are prime rib, chicken, *mahi mahi,* and Hawaiian-style pork. Guided tours begin at 8:30 p.m. sharp.

   Jameson's By the Sea, 62-540 Kamehameha Hwy., tel. 637-4336, is open daily for lunch, dinner, and cocktails. It's at the north end of Haleiwa overlooking the sea. Its outdoor deck is perfect for a romantic sunset dinner while inside the romantic mood is continued with track lighting, *shoji* screens, cane chairs with stuffed pillows, candle with shades, and tables resplendent with fine linen. Appetizers include a salmon plate for $7.95, stuffed mushrooms with escargot $5.50, and fresh oysters $7.95. Chowder and salad are under $4. Try the Yokohama soup, and salad with any of the delicious homemade dressings. Desserts are glorious. Have the lemon macadamia chiffon pie for $3.50. Main dishes like *mahi mahi,* stuffed shrimp, shrimp curry with mango chutney, and sesame chicken range from $14 to $19. The fresh catch is priced daily. The bar is quiet at night and serves a variety of imported beers; try South Pacific, imported from New Guinea. The service is top-notch; the dining room closes at 10 p.m. and the bar an hour later. Reservations highly recommended. Request a window seat for sunset.

   The **Sea View Inn,** 66-011 Kamehameha Hwy., Haleiwa, tel. 637-4165, is a green cinder-block building on the left before you cross the Anahulu River bridge. It's hard to tell if they are open since they have been in a period of transition lately. The word is that the restaurant will become a Chart House, which is a chain known for good food at decent prices.

Classy Dining

If you're looking for gourmet dining in an incredibly beautiful setting head for the Turtle Bay Hilton. **The Cove Restaurant,** open 6-9:30 p.m. (reservations advised), is the signature restaurant at the resort and welcomes you for an evening of fine dining. Slowly stroll a wooden walkway leading past tiny waterfalls and a profusion of plants to the main room that overlooks the manicured grounds and pool. Start with onion soup with provolone, $5.75, Tahitian crab soup, $6, or a variety of fresh island salads for $6. Move on to filet mignon $21.50, veal chops, $22, fresh tiger prawns and lobster, $30, and a choice of fresh catch for $23. Enjoy dessert while peering through floor-to-ceiling windows that frame the living mosaic of Turtle Bay turned brilliant by a legendary North Shore sunset.

The **Seatide Room** is synonymous with Sunday brunch. It enjoys a wonderful reputation, and if friends or family come visiting, islanders take them here to impress. Brunch is buffet style from 9 a.m.-2 p.m. and features mounds of fresh fruits and pastries, fresh-squeezed fruit juices, imported cheeses, eggs Florentine and Benedict, fresh fish, seafood, sashimi, shrimp, crab claws, and flowing champagne. Reservations not taken, $21 adults. Expect a wait, which goes easily as you enjoy the magnificent scenery.

The **Palm Terrace** is the most "ordinary" of the hotel's restaurants, but *good* ordinary. Open from 6:30 a.m.-11 p.m., it serves hearty American favorites from all 50 states. For example you can order a plate of potato *latkas* combined with *lomi* salmon which would put a smile on the face of a Jewish *bubby* from the Bronx, and on the face of a Hawaiian *tutu* from Hilo. The views overlooking Turtle Bay combined with excellent value for money makes the Palm Terrace the best *ordinary* restaurant on the North Shore.
The **Bay View Lounge** is a casual restaurant/nightclub offering a deli-luncheon buffet. It's open 11:30 a.m.-1 a.m. and serves complimentary *pu pu* around sunset, which is a perfect time to drop in. On weekends the Bay View Lounge is the hotspot disco, ID's required after 9 p.m., dress code is collared shirts and close-toed shoes.

SHOPPING AND SERVICES

As you enter Haleiwa from the west, you'll pass a **Shell** gas station and **The North Shore Market Place,** with a full-service **post office.** Across the road is **Excell Wet Suits And Water Sports,** a full-service surf shop that rents snorkeling gear.

Ka'ala Art, open 9 a.m.-6 p.m. daily, tel. 637-7065, as you enter Haleiwa (across from McDonald's), is a perfect place to stop, with some of the best shopping on the North Shore. The brothers Costello, John and Kevin, who own and operate the shop, are knowledgable, longtime residents of the North Shore who don't mind dispensing directions and information. The premiere items are John's original artwork, wonderful paintings that are impressionistic and magical, with many of these unique designs silk-screened onto 100 percent cotton T-shirts or made into inspiring posters. John has also turned his hand to carvings of dolphins and other Hawaiian themes. Also featured are fine carvings from Tonga, Tahiti, and Fiji that John has hand-selected on his travels. Small but wonderful items are tapa cloth made by a Tongan woman named Sella who lives nearby, batiks from Thailand, and jewelry made locally and from Asia. The Costello brothers travel to buy, and they have a keen eye for what's happening and distinctive. When you come in here you'll be in for a treat. It looks as if a rainbow has spilled in a corner

Ka'ala Art

of the shop where 100 percent cotton *pareu* ($12-35) from Hawaii, Tahiti, and Indonesia vibrate in living color. Their "art-clothing" includes a rack of bikinis, locally made in 100 percent cotton for $14-40, hats, tops for women, beach shoes, towels, slippers, and men's batik shirts for $34. Two of the best local artists displayed are Mango and Caridad Sumile. There's a fine postcard selection, candles, and a smidgen of touristy junk just to remind you that you're still on Oahu.

The **North Shore Marketplace,** along the Kam Highway between McDonald's and the Haleiwa Shopping Center, is a small complex with some interesting shops. **The Coffee Gallery,** selling gourmet coffees, is open daily from 5:30 a.m.-9:30 p.m. Next door the **Island Wear Factory Outlet** has inexpensive alohawear. The most interesting shop is **Jungle Gem's,** tel. 637-6609, open 9:30 a.m.-5 p.m., with a metaphysical assortment of crystals, crystal balls, African trading beads, gems, jewelry, and thunder eggs. The owners, Brent Landberg and Kimberely Moore, are knowledgeable gemologists and jewelers who do much of the fine work on display. Shop assistant Darja Cocca is a **licensed massage therapist,** tel. 638-5661, P.O. Box 1237 Haleiwa 96712, whose specialties are Swedish deep-tissue massage and acupressure, which she combines with live food cleanses and yoga therapy. Darja definitely has the "gift of touch," and she will "hand tailor" a program designed for you. Her prices are reasonable, and the experience is extraordinary.

Next door is another fine shop, **More Or Less Beach Wear,** tel. 638-6859, open 9 a.m.-6 p.m. daily, where they make custom bathing suits and sell hand-painted T-shirts by local artists. The owner and chief designer, Lucinda Vaughen, will take a personal hand in fitting and designing just the right suit for you. **Raging Isle Sports,** tel. 637-7707, 10 a.m.-6 p.m. daily, is primarily a surf shop and manufacturer of Barnfield's Raging Isle Boards, but they rent and sell bikes, and you can pick up items from a pair of shorts to a tennis racket. The bikes are an assortment of beach cruisers and mountain bikes that rent from $10-20 daily, and $55-115 weekly. They also service and repair bikes.

Haleiwa

As you move down the Kamehameha Highway from west to east you'll pass in rapid succession the **Haleiwa Flower Shop** on the left selling leis and fresh-cut flowers. Next comes **Oogenesis Boutique,** with original fashions for women, and almost next door is **Haleiwa Acupuncture Clinic**, tel. 637-4449, with Richard Himmelmann, in cooperation with Healing Touching Massage by Brenda McKinnon, and chiropractic care by Dr. Edward Bowles, who will make house calls. Next to the clinic **Race Hawaii,** tel. 637-SURF, open 9 a.m.-6 p.m. daily, 8 a.m.-7 p.m. during top season, is a famous surfboard design shop owned by Scott Bucknall, who has patented the x-fin scag design. They rent boards during the surf season and sell bathing suits, biking pants, and T-shirts bearing their logo. On the right is **A Guy Selling Shells.** He specializes in hanging baskets, made from bubble shells and cowrie. Prices range from $50 down to $5, with most coming from the Philipines.

Proceeding along you'll come to **Hawaii Surf And Sail,** open 8:30 a.m.-7:30 p.m., tel. 637-5373. They have surfboards (rental $10 /day), sailboards, and accessories. The **Consignment Shop,** behind the Country Kitchen, sells well-chosen junk and previously owned ladies' apparel and accessories, artwork, clothing, and towels. Nearby look for a sign to **Fantasy Cycles,** open 10 a.m.-7 p.m., Sun 10 a.m.-3 p.m., owned by Bob Frattin. He rents bikes for $10 day or $45/week. Bob will start off entry-level riders with a map and riding pointers. Bob will also take riders on trail tours that include lunch. Must be experienced, not for the beginner or couch potato. **Ila Ila Gallery** is across the street from the Protestant church, founded in 1892, and next door to Aoki's Shave Ice. This co-op shows the efforts of local artists who have been juried in order to place their artwork on consignment. Featured are the fine candle sculptures of **Scott Bechtol** (see p. 298).

Past Matsumoto's Store look for the **Fetig Art Gallery,** tel. 637-4933. Most of the work is by Beverly Fetig, who has been painting the islands for a quarter century. For the last few years she's been painting European scenes, which occupy a room by themselves. The gallery is the oldest on the North Shore, and most of the artists are well-known. Prices for original works start at $45 and go up to around $4000. Only a few prints, by well-known artists and numbered, start at around $175. Even if you can't afford paintings from the Fetig Gallery, it's a good place to see the state of the arts on the North Shore.

The **Haleiwa Shopping Center** provides all the necessities in one-stop shopping: boutiques, pharmacy, photo store, and general food and merchandise. It's in the center of Haleiwa, tel. 622-5179. Some shops are: **Rix** with jewelry, women's fashions, and alohawear; **Flavormania,** a gourmet ice cream palace; **Et Cetera's,** a tiny but jampacked souvenir store with woodcarvings, teas, alohawear, and shells; **Space And Lace** sells hats, slippers, shoes, towels, and sunglasses; **Liquor Galley**, open daily 9 a.m.-midnight is a full-service liquor store; and **Haliewa Family Health Center,** a walk-in clinic, tel. 524-2527, open 8 a.m.-5 p.m. daily, closed Sunday.

Wyland Gallery, across the street from the shopping plaza, is open daily 9 a.m.-6 p.m., tel. 637-7498. Wyland is a famous environmental artist known for his huge whale and marinelife murals, in addition to watercolors and fine oil paintings. The gallery is large, spacious, and well lit. Everything has a Hawaiian or sea theme, and there's even a huge fish tank filled with tropical fish. Delight at the magnificent bronze sculptures by Dale Evers, depicting whales and manta rays in sublime frozen movement. There're modern sepia-tone photos by Kim Taylor Reese, watercolors of Hawaiian maidens by Janet Stewart, lithographs by Roy Tabora of palms trees and cliffs with Michelangelo skies, bronze dolphins by Christopher Bell, wood sculptures by Kerry Sweet, Margaret Keene's lithographs of children with big eyes, and Sue Phillipson's oils of island flowers. You can walk away with a limited-edition lithograph by Wyland with original watercolor mark framed in *koa* for $940. If the original artwork is too expensive, there're posters, mini-prints, and postcards. Wyland's gold jewelry sculpture is beautiful, distinctive, and affordable.

For food and picnic supplies try the **Haleiwa IGA,** tel. 637-5004, or **Foodland,** along the highway past Waimea Bay, tel. 638-8081.

For a full range of surfing, snorkeling, and diving equipment try **Surf and Sea** near the Union 76 gas station in Haleiwa. They've got boogie boards, masks and fins, tanks, weights, surfboards, and sailboards. They can even arange flights from Dillingham Airfield.

The best source of general **information** for the North Shore is to peruse the bulletin boards outside of Surf and Sea and the Foodland Supermarket.

". . . but a diversion, the most common is upon the water . . . the men lay themselves flat upon an oval piece of plank . . . they wait the time for the greatest swell that sets on shore, and altogether push forward with their arms to keep on its top, it sends them in with a most astonishing velocity . . ."

James King, c. 1779

THE LEEWARD COAST

The Waianae ("Mullet Waters") Coast, the leeward face of Oahu, is separated physically from the rest of the island by the Waianae Range. Spiritually, culturally, and economically, the separation is even more profound. This area is Oahu's last stand for ethnic Hawaiians, and for that phenomenal cultural blending of people called *locals*. The idea of "us against them" permeates the consciousness of the area. Guidebooks, government pamphlets, and word of mouth warn tourists against going to Waianae because "the natives are restless." If you follow this poor advice, you not only miss the last of undeveloped coastal Oahu, but the absolute pleasure of meeting people who will treat you with genuine *aloha*. Along the coast are magnificent beaches long known for their surf, new condos and developments nestled in secure valleys, prime golfing, and inland, roads that'll take you to the roof of Oahu. Waianae is the home of small farms, run-down shacks, and families that hold luaus on festive occasions, where the food and entertainment are the real article. Anyone lucky enough to be invited into this quickly disappearing world will be blessed with one of the last remaining authentic cultural experiences in Hawaii.

The possibility of hassles shouldn't be minimized because they do happen, but every aggressor needs a victim. The biggest problem is thievery, of the sneak-thief variety. You're marked as a tourist because of your new rental car. If you leave valuables in it, or lying unattended on the beach, they have a good chance of disappearing. But who does silly things like this *anywhere* in the U.S.? You won't be accosted, or held up at gunpoint, but if you bother a bunch of local guys drinking beer, you're asking for trouble. Moreover, the toughness of Waianae is self-perpetuating, and frankly the locals *like* the hard reputation. A few years back a feature writer reported that when he visited Waianae some toughs threw rocks at him. No one had ever reported this before, but after a big stink was made about it, more and more people had rocks thrown at them when they visited here. In recent years *pakalolo* has had a tremendous effect on the area. Local guys began growing and smoking it. This brought some money back into the depressed region, and it changed the outlook of some of the residents. They felt a camaraderie with other counter-culture people, many of whom happened to be *haole*. They could relax and not feel so threatened with pursuing an often elusive materialistic path. Many became more content with their laid-back lifestyle, and genuinely less interested with the materialistic trip all the way around.

In truth, *we* shouldn't be warned about *them,* but vice versa. The people of Waianae are the ones being infringed upon, and it is they who, in the final analysis, will be hassled, ripped off, and ultimately dispossessed. Recent articles by Oahu's Development Conference strongly state that future development will center on the island's northwestern shore ... the Waianae Coast! A few rocks are poor weapons against developmental progress, which is defined by the big boys with the big dreams and the big bucks to back them up.

BEACHES AND SIGHTS

The Waianae Coast is very accessible. One road takes you there. Simply follow the H-1 freeway from Honolulu until it joins the Farrington Hwy. (Rt. 93). It runs north, opening up the entire coast. A handful of side roads lead into the interior, and that's about it! A strange recommendation, but sensible on this heavily trafficked road, is to drive north to the end of the line and then stop at the scenic sights on your way back south. This puts you on the ocean side of the highway where you won't have to worry about cutting across two lines of traffic, which can be a steady stream making it tough to navigate. TheBus #51 runs the entire Waianae Coast, and stops at all of the following beaches.

Note: Many of the beach parks along this coast offer **camping,** but their status periodically changes to **no camping** without notice. Many of the other campers are local people in semipermanent structures; the reason that the status changes quickly is to prevent these people from squatting. Also, remember that this is the leeward coast, which gets plenty of sunshine. Many of the beach parks do not have shade trees, so be prepared. June is the prettiest month because all the flowers are in bloom, but it's one of the worst times for sunburn. The entire coast is great for snorkeling, with plenty of reef fish. However, keep your eyes on the swells, and always stay out during rough seas, when waves can batter you against the rocks. The parks listed below run from south to north.

HEADING NORTH

Barber's Point Beach Park
The first beach is Barbers Point Beach Park, at the end of Kalaeloa Boulevard. Turn down it where H-1 and the Farrington Hwy. join. The

Waianae Coast

Point was named after Capt. Henry Barber, who was shipwrecked here in 1795. Few people, even island residents, visit this beach park. It's in an industrial area and the shoreline is rocky. One pocket of white-sand beach is open to the public, though it fronts a private residence. The swimming is safe only in summer, and you'll find picnic facilities, restrooms, and camping (county permit).

Kahe And Hawaiian Electric Beach Park

Kahe and Hawaiian Electric beach parks are just where the Farrington Hwy. curves north along the coast. They're the first two *real* Waianae beaches, and they're symbolic. You come around the bend to be treated to an absolutely pristine view of the coast with the rolling sea, white-sand beach, cove, and the most hideous power plant you've ever seen. Kahe Beach Park offers restrooms, pavilion, and picnic facilities. The beach is poor except for a section just east of the improved park. Swimming is dangerous except on calm summer days. The Hawaiian Electric Beach Park, across from the power plant, is known as "Tracks" to island surfers because of the railroad tracks that run along the shore here. Facilities include picnic tables, pavilion, restrooms, showers, and parking along the highway. The white-sand beach is wide, and the swimming generally safe. The mild waves are perfect for learning how to surf. If you keep your eyes trained out to sea, the area is beautiful. Don't look inland!

Nanakuli Beach Park

Nanakuli Beach Park is on the southern outskirts of Nanakuli ("Pretend To Be Deaf") Town, which is the first real town of the Waianae Coast. If you get to the red light you've gone a little too far. The beach park is community-oriented, with recreational buildings, basketball courts, baseball diamond, and kiddies' play area. Camping has been permitted with a county permit. Lifeguards work on a daily basis, and the swimming is generally safe except during periods of high winter surf. The northern end of the beach, called Kalanianaole, is generally calmer than the southern end. They're divided by a housing project, but connected by a walkway. The southern section is fronted by a cliff with a small cove below. During periods of calm surf, the waters are crystal clear and perfect for snorkeling.

Ulehawa Beach Park

Ulehawa Beach Park, just north of Nanakuli, offers restrooms, picnic facilities, lifeguards, and sometimes camping. The best swimming is in a sandy pocket near the lifeguard tower. Surf conditions make for good bodysurfing. Most of the park, along a rocky cliff, is undeveloped. Here you'll find unlimited fishing spots. A shallow lagoon is generally safe for swimming year-round. As always, it's best to check with the local people on the beach.

Maili Beach Park

Maili Beach Park is at the southern end of Maili ("Many Small Stones") Town. It lies between two streams coming down from the mountains. Amenities include restrooms, picnic facilities, lifeguard tower, and camping . . . sometimes! The best swimming is in front of the lifeguard tower. The beach is broken into three parts by a housing development. In wintertime the beach disappears, but it returns wide and sandy for the summer. Most of the park is undeveloped. In town is a **7-eleven** and gas stations. As you drive through town notice a giant outcropping, Maili Point, which meets the sea like a giant fist. It has the same dominant presence as Diamond Head. When you go through town you'll see what's been happening around here since development has come to Waianae. Pull off at Maili Beach Park, and to your right are the modest homes of local people. Look up the coast to where the mountains come down to the sea. Out on that headland you can see a giant resort and on the bending backbone leading up to it modest homes of the local people. The beach is at least 300 yards long, and family-oriented. Plenty of coral pockets offer good snorkeling. Don't just jump in. Ask the locals or swing by the lifeguard tower to make sure that it's safe.

Lualualei Beach Park

Lualualei Beach Park has restrooms, camping sometimes, and picnic facilities. The entire park is largely undeveloped and lies along low cliffs and raised coral reef. Swimming is almost impossible. It's primarily good for fishing and looking.

Pokai Beach Park

Pokai Beach Park is one of the nicest along the Waianae Coast, located just south of Waianae Town. It provides restrooms, camping sometimes, lifeguards, and boat ramp, which brings plenty of small craft into the area. Don't be surprised to see a replica of a double-hulled canoe, often used for publicity purposes. It last appeared in a beer commercial. The park is clean, well maintained, reasonably secure, and family-oriented. There's surfing, snorkeling, and safe swimming year-round. If you're heading for one beach along Waianae, this is a top choice.

To get a look at a small working harbor or to hire a fishing boat, visit **Waianae Boat Harbor** as you head north from town. Huge installed stones form an impressive man-made harbor, with everything from luxury yachts to aluminum fishing boats. To head inland take **Waianae Valley Road.** You quickly gain the heights of the Waianae Range, and eventually come to a sentry box with a soldier inside. From here Kolekole Road is closed to the public, but if you stop and identify yourself, you'll be given permission to go to **Kolekole Pass.** The awesome view is well worth the trip.

Makaha Beach Park

Makaha Beach Park is famous for surfing, and as you approach, you can't help spotting a dominant headland called **Lahi Lahi,** which was a one-time island. Called "Black Rock" by the local fishermen, and used as a landmark, it still marks Makaha. Surfing competitions have been held here since the Makaha International Surfing Competition began in 1952. In recent years, a local lifeguard named Richard "Buffalo" Keaulana, known to all who've come here, has begun the Annual Buffalo Big Board Riding Championship. Paul Strauch Jr., inventor of the "hang five," comes to Makaha whenever he has a chance, along with Buffalo's sons and other pro surfers, many of whom live in the area. The swimming can be dangerous during high surf, but excel-

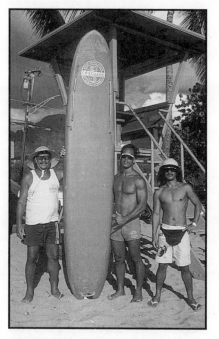

Buffalo at Makaha Beach

lent on calm days. Winter brings some of the biggest surf in Hawaii. Always pay heed to the warnings of the lifeguards.

The meaning of Makaha doesn't help its image. It translates as "Fierce," relating to a bunch of bandits who lived in the surrounding hills and terrorized the region. They would wait for small bands of people walking the road, then swoop down and relieve them of their earthly goods. If you follow Makaha Valley Road inland, you pass condos and high-rises clinging to the arid walls of this leeward valley. Surrounded by an artificial oasis of green, this developed resort area provides golfing and all the amenities of a destination resort. Stop in at the Sheraton Makaha to ask permission to visit the **Kaneaki Heiau,** a 17th-century temple restored by the resort under the direction of the Bishop Museum. This temple was dedicated to Lono, the benevolent god of harvest and fertility. The grass and thatched huts used as prayer

and meditation chambers, along with a spirit tower, have all been replicated.

Once past Makaha, the road gets rugged, with plenty of private places to pull off. This crab claw of land, which ends at Kaena Point, forms a bay. The seascape demands attention but look into the interior. The mountains seem naturally terraced as they form dry, deep valleys. All are micro-habitats, each different from the other. On top of one notice a gigantic golf ball, really a radar tracking station, that lets you know that you're coming to the end of the passable road.

Keaau Beach Park

Keaau Beach Park has restrooms, picnic facilities, and camping (county permit). The improved part of the park has a sandy beach, but mostly the park is fronted by coral and lava, and is frequented mostly by fishermen and campers. The unimproved section is not good for swimming, but it does attract a few surfers, and is good for snorkeling and scuba but only during calm periods. The improved section is a flat grassy area with picnic tables, shade trees, and pavilions.

Yokohama Bay

Yokohama Bay is the end of the line. The pavement ends here, and if you're headed for Kaena Point (see p. 308) you'll have to walk. Yokohama Bay is a long stretch of sandy beach that is mostly unimproved. A lava-rock bathhouse is on the right, just after the entrance. The area was named because of the multitude of Japanese fishermen who came to this lonely site to fish. It's still great for fishing! The swimming can be hazardous because of the strong wave action and rough bottom, but the snorkeling is superb. Mostly the area is used by surfers and local people, including youngsters who dive off the large lava rocks. This is inadvisable for people unfamiliar with the area. Yokohama is a great place to come if you're after a secluded beach. Weekdays, you'll have it to yourself, with a slightly greater number of people on the weekends. Definitely bring cold drinks, and remember that there are no shade trees, so a hat or beach umbrella is a necessity. Many camp here unofficially.

Notice a rugged beach area, marked by dumped household appliances, just south of Yokohama Bay. Notice broken-down vans and makeshift tents of ripped tarps put up by local people who have staked out this area and who live here semipermanently. If you're looking for trouble, you've found the right spot.

Kaneana Cave is a few minutes south on your left as you head back down the coast. You probably didn't notice it on your way north because of the peculiar land formation that conceals the mouth in that direction. Unfortunately, people have come here with spray cans and trashed the cave. If you can overlook that, it's a phenomenon—a big one. You can spot it by looking for three cement blocks, like road dividers, right in front of the entrance. It's at the foot of a 200-foot outcropping of stone. When you see local people defacing the natural beauty like this, it's hard to believe that the Hawaiians had such a spirit bond with the *aina.*

PRACTICALITIES

ACCOMMODATIONS

Except for camping, there are no inexpensive places to stay along the Waianae Coast. Some local people let rooms for a good rate, but there is no way to find this out in advance. Your best bet is to check out the **bulletin board** at the Food Giant Supermarket in Waianae. Accommodations range from moderate to expensive, with Makaha Valley being the most developed resort area of Oahu outside of Waikiki. Except for the Sheraton Makaha Resort, all are condos and require a minimum stay of seven days.

The **Maili Cove** rents one-bedroom apartments for $350-450 per week. They have a swimming pool, parking, TV, along with a few hotel units. Located at 87-561 Farrington Hwy., Waianae, HI 96792, tel. 696-4447.

The **Makaha Beach Cabanas** are in Makaha along the beach just past the high school. All units have a lanai overlooking the water. They're not fancy but are spotlessly clean and serviceable. All units are fully furnished with complete kitchens; from $350 per week. Contact the Makaha Beach Cabanas, 84-965 Farrington Hwy., tel. 696-7227.

The **Makaha Shores** are privately owned units that overlook a beautiful white-sand beach and provide great viewing of the surfers challenging the waves below. All units are fully furnished with weekly rates of $290 studio, $400 one-bedroom, and $500 two-bedroom. Contact the condo at 84-265 Farrington Hwy., Makaha 96792, tel. 696-7121.

The least expensive accommodations are at the **Makaha Surfside.** The beach is rocky near the condo, but it makes up for this with two pools and a sauna. All units are individually owned and fully furnished. Weekly rates begin at $290 studio to $400-475 for a one-bedroom. Daily rates range from $40 to $55. For information write Makaha Surfside, 85-175 Farrington Hwy., Makaha 96792, tel. 696-2105.

Makaha Valley Towers rise dramatically from Makaha Valley, but they don't fit in. They're either a testament to man's achievement or ignorance, depending on your point of view. In keeping with the idea of security, you drive up to a gate manned by two guards. You're stopped, asked your business, and sent unsmilingly on your way. The condo provides fully furnished units, a/c, TV, and pool. Weekly rates are $365 studio, $400-500 one-bedroom. If you're staying in this ill-fitting high-rise, at least try to get a top floor where you can take advantage of the remarkable view. For rates and information: Makaha Valley Towers, 84-740 Kili Dr., Makaha 96792, tel. 695-9055.

The **Sheraton Makaha Resort** is famous for its hideaway golf course, among the top five on Oahu. The 6,400-foot par-72 course is relatively flat and costs $15 guest, $40 non-guest, plus $10 for a mandatory cart. The Sheraton has done an exemplary job with the units, some of the nicest on the island. This is a true destination resort with a complete list of activities, including horseback riding, tennis, two swimming pools, and a full comple-

typical camping beach, Leeward Coast

ment of hotel-sponsored beach and water activities (although the ocean is a few miles away). Rooms begin at $85 d to $250 for a suite. For information and reservations, write Sheraton Makaha Resort, Box 896, Waianae, HI 96792, tel. (800) 325-3535, on Oahu 695-9511.

FOOD

For anyone with an urge to eat a two-scoop plate lunch, no problem. Little drive-in lunch counters are found in almost every Waianae town. Each serves hearty island food such as teriyaki chicken, pork, or *mahi mahi* for under $5. A good one is the **Nanakuli Drive-In** in the middle of town. **Makaha Drive-In** is more of the same. Another popular spot is **Red Baron Pizza** in the Waianae Shopping Center, tel. 696-2396.

You also see plenty of fruit sellers parked along the road. Their produce couldn't be fresher, and stopping provides you not only with the perfect complement to a picnic lunch but with a good chance to meet some local people.

For your shopping and dining needs in Nanakuli, try the **Pacific Shopping Mall** where you'll find the **Nanakuli Chop Suey Restaurant,** open 10 a.m.-8:30 p.m., tel. 668-8006, serving standard Chinese fare at local downhome prices (chicken dishes under $5, beef or pork to $4.75.) Just behind McDon-

ald's is the **Eden BBQ Lounge** with sit-down and takeout Korean food at moderate prices, tel. 668-2722, open 10-9 daily. In town is **Big Daddy's Plate Lunch,** where you can dine on island standards with a mandatory two-scoop rice for around $5.

The **Waianae Mall** is a complete shopping facility. Don't worry about bringing supplies or food if you're on a day excursion. You'll find all that you need at the mall, which includes Cathay Deli, Red Baron Pizza, Subway Sandwiches, Woolworth's, Big-Way Supermarket, and Pay 'n' Save Drugs. Have no fear if you're addicted to fast foods. Some major franchises have decided that your trip to leeward Oahu wouldn't be complete without something processed in a styrofoam box. **Burger King** is in the mall, and in town **McDonald's** golden arches rise alongside the highway just across from **Taco Bell**. If you're looking for ethnic flavor try the **Bayside Drive-In** for a plate lunch, or the local **Tamura Supermarket**. You'll spot a number of gas stations in the middle of town, along with a **Domino's Pizza, Circle K,** and a **7-eleven** convenience store.

Makaha has **Makaha Drive-In,** a plate lunch stand, **Woolworth's,** and a shopping basket of neighborhood markets.

The **Fogcutter** is a semicasual place offering steaks and seafood, at 84-111 Orange St., Makaha, tel. 695-9404. Prices are reasonable and the food is good. To pinpoint the Fog Cutter, one of the only sit-down places to eat at in Makaha, look for the Cornet Store on the right as you head north through town. The first right past it is Orange Street, where you're welcomed by two old smokestacks. The restaurant offers lunch, dinner, and cocktails. Prepared beef is priced at $1.45 per ounce (pick your own size), with chicken dishes at $10. The Captain's seafood mix (shrimp, *mahi,* scallops, and crab) is priced right at $12.25. All dinners include salad bar and homemade clam chowder or Portuguese bean soup. Hours 11-2 lunch, 6-10 dinner. The bar is friendly with a nautical theme highlighted by captains' chairs, charts, a ship's compass, and sailing paraphernalia.

The **Rusty Harpoon** is between Waianae and Maili overlooking the sea. It probably serves the best food for the money along the coast. In keeping with the name the airy interior is rustically nautical, complete with hurricane lamps and of course a few harpoons. The menu is chicken, fish, and beef, but the best deals are the Hawaiian plates. Lunch prices are excellent at around $5, but expect double that for the dinner menu.

The **Sheraton Makaha** has a number of restaurants ranging from sandwich bars to elegant dining. The Kaala Room features an impressive menu of fresh fish, steaks, and continental cuisine. Get a table with a long sweeping view of the valley, wonderful at sunset. Daily for dinner, tel. 695-9511. The hotel's Pikake Cafe serves breakfast, lunch, and dinner with an assortment of sandwiches and international dishes.

The **Food Giant** grocery store in Waianae has a good selection of Oriental and Hawaiian food. To know what's happening along the Waianae Coast check out the bulletin board in front. The **Waianae Hawaiian Cultural and Art Center** offers workshops in lei-making, *lau hala* weaving, hula, and the Hawaiian language. They welcome people either to observe or participate in their programs. For times and schedules contact the **State Foundation of Culture and Arts,** tel. 548-4145.

Pokai Pottery on Pokai St., Waianae, is owned and operated by Bunkie Eakutis. His studio is attached to his home, where he makes ceramics sold around the island through the Artists' Guild.

THE NORTHWESTERN ISLANDS

Like tiny gems of a broken necklace, the Northwestern Hawaiian Islands spill across the vast Pacific. Popularly called the **Leewards,** most were discovered last century, oftentimes by hapless ships that ground to a sickening halt on their treacherous, half-submerged reefs. Their captains left their names: Lisianski, Kure, French Frigates, Hermes, and Pearl. Even today, craft equipped with the most modern navigational devices must be wary in these waters. They remain among the loneliest outposts on the face of the Earth.

Land And Climate
The Leewards are the oldest islands of the Hawaiian chain, believed to have emerged from the sea at least six million years ago; some experts say 25 million years! Slowly they floated northward past the suboceanic hotspot as the other islands were built. Measured from **Nihoa Island,** about 100 miles off

the northern tip of Kauai, they stretch for just under 1,100 miles to **Kure Atoll,** last of the **Midway Islands.** There are 13 islets, shoals, and half-submerged reefs in the chain. Most have been eroded flat by the sea and wind, but a few tough volcanic cores endure. Together they make up a land mass of approximately 3,400 acres, the largest being the Midways at 1,280 acres, and the smallest the **Gardner Pinnacles** at just over 2½ acres. The climate is similar to that of the main islands with a slightly larger variance. Temperatures sometimes dip as low as 50 degrees and climb as high as 90 degrees.

Administration And History
Politically, the Leewards are administered by the city and county of Honolulu, except for the Midway Islands, which are under federal jurisdiction. None are permanently inhabited, except for some lonely military and wildlife

field stations on Midway, Kure, and the French Frigate Shoals. All are part of the **Hawaiian Islands National Wildlife Refuge,** established at the turn of the century by Theodore Roosevelt. In pre-contact times, some of the islands supported a Tahitian culture markedly different from the one that emerged on the main Hawaiian islands. Necker Island, for example, was the only island in the entire Hawaiian archipelago on which the inhabitants carved stone figures with a complete head and torso. On many of the others, remnants of *heiau* and agricultural terracing attribute to their colonization by pre-contact Hawaiians. Over the years, natives as well as Westerners have exploited the islands for feathers, fertilizer, seals, and fish.

The islands are closely monitored by the U.S. Fish and Wildlife Agency. Permission to land on them is granted only under special circumstances. Studies are underway to determine if the waters around the islands can support some commercial fishing, while leaving a plentiful supply of food for the unique wildlife of these lonely islands.

Wildlife

Millions of seabirds of various species have found permanent sanctuary on the Leewards, using them as giant floating nests and rookeries. Today the populations are stable and growing, but it hasn't always been so. On Laysan, at the turn of the century, egg hunters came to gather uncountable albatross eggs, selling the albumen to companies making photographic paper. They brought their families along, and their children's pets, which included rabbits. The rabbits escaped and multiplied wildly. In no time they invaded the territories of the **Laysan honeycreeper, rail,** and **millerbird,** rendering them extinct. Laysan has recovered and is refuge to over six million birds, including the rare and indigenous **Laysan teal** and **finch.**

An amazing bird using the rookeries is the **frigate bird.** The male can blow up its chest in a mating ritual like a giant red heart-shaped balloon. Also known as **man-of-war birds,** they oftentimes pirate the catches of other birds, devour chicks, and even cannibalize their own offspring.

Some of the most prolific birds of the Leewards are terns, both the delicate all-white **fairy tern** and its darker relative, the **sooty tern.** Other distinctive species include a variety of boobies, and the **Laysan albatross,** which has a wingspan of 10-12 feet, the world's largest.

Besides birds, the islands are home to the **Hawaiian monk seal,** one of only two spe-

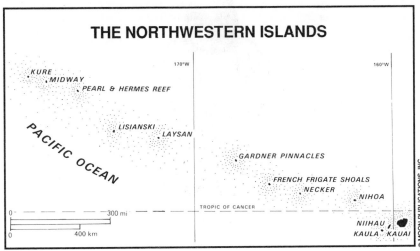

THE NORTHWESTERN ISLANDS

KURE
MIDWAY
PEARL & HERMES REEF

170°W   160°W

PACIFIC OCEAN

LISIANSKI
LAYSAN

GARDNER PINNACLES

FRENCH FRIGATE SHOALS
NECKER
NIHOA

TROPIC OF CANCER

0 — 300 mi
0 — 400 km

NIIHAU
KAULA · KAUAI

© MOON PUBLICATIONS, INC.

monk seal

cies of indigenous Hawaiian mammals. These beautiful and sleek animals were hunted to near extinction for their skins. Man encroached on their territory more and more, but now they are protected as an endangered species. About 1,000 individuals still cling to existence on various islands.

The **green turtle** is another species that has found a haven here. They were hunted to near extinction for their meat and leather, and of the few colonies around the world, the largest in the U.S., is on the French Frigate Shoals.

*unique figurine of
Necker Island*

MUSEUMS, LIBRARIES, ZOOS, GALLERIES, AND GARDENS

Aloha Tower and Maritime Museum, at Ala Moana Blvd. and Bishop St., Honolulu 96813, tel. 536-6373 or 548-5713. A landmark that said "Hawaii" to all who arrived by sea before planes took over. Great harbor and city views from top of tower. Visit Hawaii Maritime Center on 9th floor and famous double-hulled canoe *Hokule'a* and tall-masted *Falls of Clyde,* berthed just next door at Pier 7.

Army Museum, Fort DeRussy, Box 8064, Honolulu 96815, tel. 543-2639. Official records, private papers, and photos documenting activities of the U.S. Army in east Asia and the Pacific islands. Access to holdings is by appointment.

Bishop Museum and Planetarium, 1525 Bernice St., Honolulu 96819, tel. 847-3511. Open daily 9 a.m.-5 p.m., $4.75 for adults, $2.50 ages 6 to 17, under 6 free. The best collection in the world on Polynesia in general and Hawaii specifically. A true cultural treat. Should not be missed.

Children's Museum of Natural History, 1201 Ala Moana Blvd., Honolulu 96814, Mon.-Fri. 9 a.m.-4 p.m., Sat. 9 a.m.-noon. Natural history and science exhibits.

Contemporary Museum of Art, under the direction of Fritz Frauchinger, at 2411 Makiki Heights Rd., tel. 526-1322, open Mon.-Sat. 10 a.m.-4 p.m., noon-4 p.m. Sun., closed Tues., admission $3. The focus is on exhibitions, not collections, although works by David Hockney are on permanent display. Changing exhibits reflect different themes in contemporary art.

East-West Center, Burns Hall 4076, 1777 East-West Rd., University of Hawaii, Honolulu 96848, tel. 948-8006. Cultural institute bringing together the peoples, art, history, and ways of East and West.

Episcopal Church in Hawaii, Queen Emma Square, Honolulu 96813, tel. 536-7776. Records and photos of church ministry in Hawaii from 1862.

Foster Botanical Garden, 50 N. Vineyard Blvd. Open daily 9 a.m.-4 p.m., tel. 531-1939. Nine-acre oasis of exotic trees and rare plants.

Friends of Waipahu Cultural Garden Park, Box 103, Waipahu 96797, tel. 677-0110. Recreation of plantation village in the style of a living museum.

Hawaii Chinese Historical Center, 111 N. King St. Room 410, Honolulu 96813, tel. 536-9302. Open 12 hours per week. Rare books, oral histories, and photos concerning the history of Chinese in Hawaii.

Hawaiian Historical Society, 560 Kawaiahao St., Honolulu 96813, tel. 537-6271. Open Mon.-Fri. 10 a.m.-4 p.m. Extensive collection of 19th-century materials on Hawaiian Islands. 3,000 photos, 10,000 books, maps, microfilm. Adjacent to Hawaiian Mission Children's Society. Should be seen together. Should not be missed.

Hawaii Medical Library, Inc., 1221 Punchbowl St., Honolulu 96813, tel. 536-9302. History of medicine in Hawaii.

Hawaii Maritime Center at Pier 7, Honolulu Harbor, 96813, tel. 523-6151. Open daily 9 a.m.-5 p.m., admission, $6. A museum chronicling the exploration and exploitation of Hawaii by the seafarers that have come to its shores.

Hawaiian Mission Children's Society, 553 S. King St., Honolulu 96813, tel. 531-0481. Open Mon.-Fri., 10 a.m.-4 p.m. Admission: $1.50 adults, $.75 children. Records, personal journals, letters and photos of early

19th-century Congregational missionaries to the Hawaiian Islands; archive of the Congregational Church in the Pacific. Shouldn't be missed.

Hawaii Pacific College Library. College information call 544-0200.

Hawaiian State Archives, Iolani Palace Grounds, Honolulu 96813, tel. 547-2355. Open Mon.-Fri. 7:45 a.m.-4:30 p.m. Archives of the government of Hawaii. Private papers of Hawaiian royalty and government officials, photos, illustrations, etchings recording Hawaiian history. For anyone seriously interested in Hawaii. Shouldn't be missed.

Honolulu Academy of Arts, 900 S. Beretania St., Honolulu 96814, tel. 538-3693. Object is to collect, preserve, and exhibit works of art (to conduct a public art education program related to the collection). Permanent and special exhibitions. Tours, classes, lectures, and films.

Honolulu Botanical Gardens, 50 N. Vine Yard Blvd., Honolulu 96817, tel. 533-3406. See Foster Botanical Gardens.

Honolulu Zoo, 151 Kapahulu Ave., tel. 521-3487. Open daily 9 a.m.-5 p.m. Quiet respite from hustle of Waikiki. Includes a collection of tropical birds as well as pandas, zebras, and gibbon apes. Great for kids of all ages.

Iolani Palace, Box 2259, Honolulu 96804, tel. 536-3552. Iolani Palace Grounds. Performs all aspects of historic research, restoration, and refurbishing of palace. The only royal palace in the U.S. Vintage artwork, antiques.

Kamehameha Schools, Kapalma Heights Rd., Honolulu 96813, tel. 842-8620. Open Mon.-Fri. 7:30 a.m.-4 p.m. Traditional school for children of Hawaiian descent. Rare books, periodicals, slides on Hawaiiana.

Libraries. Oahu has more than a dozen libraries all over the island. The Central Administration number is 988-2194. Library for the Blind and physically handicapped is at 402 Kapahulu Ave., tel. 732-7767.

Paradise Park, 3737 Manoa Rd., Honolulu 96822, tel. 988-2141. Exotic birds displayed in a tropical forest setting; includes trained birds in performance.

Punahou School, 1601 Punahou St., Honolulu 96822, tel. 944-5823. Collection available by special arrangement. Institutional archives of the oldest private school in Hawaii.

Queen Emma Summer Palace, 2913 Pali Hwy., Honolulu 96817, tel. 595-3167. Restored historic home, built about 1848. Furniture and mementos of Queen Emma and her family. Some items belong to other members of royal family.

Sea Life Park, Makapuu Point, Waimanalo 96795, tel. 259-7933. Varieties of Pacific marine plant and animal life, including several species of dolphins and whales. Feeding pool, Kaupa Village, turtle lagoon, restaurant, gift shop.

USS *Arizona* Memorial and Submarine Museum, Arizona Memorial Dr., Pearl Harbor 96818, tel. 422-2771. A free tour of the sleek 184-foot white concrete structure that spans the sunken USS *Arizona*. Free Navy launches take you on the tour of "Battleship Row." Open Tues.-Sun. 8 a.m.-3 p.m. No reservations, first-come, first-served. Launches every 15 minutes. Visitor center offers graphic materials and film, reflecting events of the Pearl Harbor attack.

USS *Bowfin,* 11 Arizona Memorial Drive. Open daily 9:30 a.m.-4:30 p.m., tel. 423-1341. Fully restored WW II submarine. Insight into the underwater war. Self-guided tours. Fascinating. Next door to *Arizona* Memorial.

BOOKLIST

INTRODUCTORY

Aloha, The Magazine of Hawaii and the Pacific. Honolulu, Hl.: Davick Publications. Subscription, P.O. Box 27810, San Diego, CA. 92128. This excellent bimonthly magazine is much more than just slick and glossy photography. Special features may focus on sports, the arts, history, flora and fauna, or just pure island adventure. *Aloha* is equally useful as a "dream book" for those who wish that they could visit Hawaii, and as a current resource for those actually going. One of the best for an overall view of Hawaii, and well worth the subscription price.

Barrow, Terrence. *Incredible Hawaii.* Rutland, VT.: Tuttle, 1974. Illustrated by Ray Lanternman. A pocket-sized compilation of oddities, little-known facts, trivia, and superlatives regarding the Hawaiian Islands. Fun, easy reading, and informative.

Cohen, David, and Rick Smolan. *A Day in the Life of Hawaii.* New York: Workman, 1984. On December 2, 1983, 50 of the world's top photojournalists were invited to Hawaii to photograph a variety of normal-life incidents occurring on that day. The photos are excellently reproduced, and are accompanied by a minimum of text.

Day, A.G., and C. Stroven. *A Hawaiian Reader.* New York: Appleton, Century, Crofts, 1959. A poignant compilation of essays, diary entries, and fictitious writings that takes you from the death of Captain Cook through the "statehood services."

Emphasis International. *On the Hana Coast.* Honolulu: Emphasis International Ltd., 1983. Text by Ron Youngblood. Sketches of the people, land, legends, and history of Maui's northeast coast. Beautifully illustrated with line drawings, vintage photos, and modern color work. Expresses true feeling and insight into people and things Hawaiian by letting them talk for themselves. An excellent book capturing what's different and what's universal about the people of the Hana District.

Friends of the Earth. *Maui, The Last Hawaiian Place.* New York: Friends of the Earth, 1970. A pictorial capturing the spirit of Maui in 61 contemporary color plates along with a handful of historical illustrations. A highly informative as well as beautiful book printed in Italy.

Hawaii Magazine, P.O. Box 485, Mt. Morris, IL 61054 covers the Hawaiian islands like a tropical breeze. Feature articles on all aspects of life in the islands with special departments on travel, happenings, exhibits, and restaurant reviews. Up to the minute information, and a fine read.

Island Heritage Limited. *The Hawaiians.* Norfolk Island, Australia: Island Heritage Ltd., 1970. Text by Gavan Daws and Ed Sheehan. Primarily a "coffee table" picture book that lets the camera do the talking with limited yet informative text.

Hopkins, Jerry. *The Hula.* Edited by Rebecca Crockett-Hopkins. Hong Kong: APA Productions, 1982. Page after page of this beautifully illustrated book sways with the dynamic vibrancy of ancient Hawaii's surviving artform. Hopkins leads you from dances performed and remembered only through legends to those of past and present masters captured in vintage and classic photos. For anyone interested in the history and the spirit of Hawaii portrayed in its own unique style of expressive motion.

Judd, Gerritt P., comp. *A Hawaiian Anthology.* New York: MacMillan, 1967. A potpourri of observations from literati such as Twain and Stevenson who have visited the islands over the years. Also, excerpts from ordinary people's journals and missionary letters from early times down to a gleeful report of the day that Hawaii became a state.

Krauss, Bob. *Here's Hawaii*. New York: Coward, McCann Inc., 1960. Social commentary in a series of humorous anecdotes excerpted from this newspaperman's column from the late '60s. Dated, but in essence still useful because people and values obviously change very little.

Lueras, Leonard. *Surfing, The Ultimate Pleasure*. New York: Workman Publishing, 1984. An absolutely outstanding pictorial account of Hawaii's own sport—surfing. Vintage and contemporary photos are surrounded by well-researched and written text. Bound to become a classic.

McBride, L.R. *Practical Folk Medicine of Hawaii*. Hilo, HI.: Petroglyph Press, 1975. An illustrated guide to Hawaii's medicinal plants as used by the *kahuna lapa'au* (medical healers). Includes a thorough section on ailments, diagnosis, and the proper folk remedy to employ. Illustrated by the author, a renowned botanical researcher and former ranger at Volcanoes National Park.

Michener, James A. *Hawaii*. New York: Random House, 1959. Michener's fictionalized historical novel has done more to inform *and* misinform readers about Hawaii than any other book ever written. A great tale with plenty of local color and information that should be read for pleasure and not considered fact.

Naturist Society Magazine. P.O. Box 132, Oshkosh, WI 54920. This excellent magazine not only *uncovers* bathing-suit-optional beaches throughout the islands, giving tips for naturalists visiting Hawaii, but also reports on local politics, environment, and conservation measures from the health conscious nudist point of view. A fine publication.

Piercy, LaRue. *Hawaii, This and That*. Hilo, Hi.: Petroglyph Press, 1981. Illustrated by Scot Ebanez. A 60-page book filled with one-sentence facts and oddities about all manner of things Hawaiian. Informative, amazing, and fun to read.

Rose, Roger G. *Hawaii: The Royal Isles*. Honolulu: Bishop Museum Press, 1980. Photographs, Seth Joel. A pictorial mixture of artifacts and luminaries from Hawaii's past. Includes a mixture of Hawaiian and Western art depicting island ways. Beautifully photographed with highly descriptive accompanying text.

Wilkerson, James A., M.D., ed. *Medicine for Mountaineering*. 3rd ed. Seattle: The Mountaineers, 1985. Don't let the title fool you. Although the book focuses on specific health problems that may be encountered while mountaineering, it is the best first-aid and general health guide available today. Written by doctors for the layman to use until help arrives, it is jampacked with easily understandable techniques and procedures. For those intending extended treks, it is a must.

HISTORY/POLITICAL SCIENCE

Albertini, Jim, et al. *The Dark Side of Paradise, Hawaii in a Nuclear War*. Honolulu: cAtholic Action of Hawaii. Well-documented research outlining Hawaii's role and vulnerability in a nuclear world. This book presents the anti-nuclear and anti-military side of the political issue in Hawaii.

Apple, Russell A. *Trails: From Steppingstones to Kerbstones*. Honolulu: Bishop Museum Press, 1965. This "Special Publication #53" is a special-interest archaeological survey focusing on the trails, roadways, footpaths, and highways and how they were designed and maintained throughout the years. Many "royal highways" from pre-contact Hawaii are cited.

Ashdown, Inez MacPhee. *Old Lahaina*. Honolulu: Hawaiian Service Inc., 1976. A small pamphlet-type book listing most of the historical attractions of Lahaina Town, past and present. Ashdown is a life-long resident of Hawaii and gathered her information firsthand by listening to and recording stories of ethnic Hawaiians and old *kamaaina* families.

————. *Ke Alaloa o Maui*. Wailuku, HI.: Kamaaina Historians Inc., 1971. A compilation of the history and legends of sites on the island of Maui. Ashdown was at one time a "lady in waiting" for Queen Liliuokalani and has since been proclaimed Maui's "Historian Emeritus."

Bell, Roger. *Last Among Equals: Hawaiian Statehood and American Politics*. Honolulu: University of Hawaii, 1984. Documents Hawaii's long and rocky road to statehood, tracing political partisanship, racism, and social change.

Cameron, Roderick. *The Golden Haze*. New York: World Publishing, 1964. An account of Captain James Cook's voyages of discovery throughout the South Seas. Uses original diaries and journals for an "on the spot" reconstruction of this great seafaring adventure.

Daws, Gavan. *Shoal of Time, A History of the Hawaiian Islands*. Honolulu: University of Hawaii Press, 1968. A highly readable history of Hawaii dating from its "discovery" by the Western world down to its acceptance as the 50th state. Good insight into the psychological makeup of the influential characters that formed Hawaii's past.

Department of Geography, University of Hawaii. *Atlas of Hawaii*. 2nd ed. Honolulu: University of Hawaii Press, 1983. Much more than an atlas filled with reference maps, it also contains commentary on the natural environment, culture, sociology, a gazetteer, and statistical tables. Actually a mini-encyclopedia.

Feher, Joseph. *Hawaii: A Pictorial History*. Honolulu: Bishop Museum Press, 1969. Text by Edward Joesting and O.A. Bushnell. An oversized tome laden with annotated historical and contemporary photos, prints, and paintings. Seems like a big "school book," but extremely well done. If you are going to read one survey about Hawaii's historical, social, and cultural past, this is the one.

Fuchs, Lawrence. *Hawaii Pono*. New York: Harcourt, Brace and World, 1961. A detailed, scholarly work presenting an overview of Hawaii's history, based upon psychological and sociological interpretations. Encompasses most socio-ethnological groups from native Hawaiians to modern entrepreneurs. A must for social historical background.

Handy, E.S., and Elizabeth Handy. *Native Planters in Old Hawaii*. Honolulu: Bishop Museum Press, 1972. A superbly written, easily understandable scholarly work on the intimate relationship of pre-contact Hawaiians and the *aina* (land). Much more than its title implies, should be read by anyone seriously interested in Polynesian Hawaii.

The Hawaii Book. Chicago: J.G. Ferguson, 1961. Insightful selections of short stories, essays, and historical and political commentaries by experts specializing in Hawaii. Good choice of photos and illustrations.

Hawaiian Children's Mission Society. *Missionary Album*. Honolulu: Mission Society, 1969. Firsthand accounts of the New England missionaries sent to Hawaii and instrumental in its conversion to Christianity. Downhome stories of daily life's ups and downs.

Heyerdahl, Thor. *American Indians in the Pacific*. London: Allen and Unwin Ltd., 1952. Theoretical and anthropological accounts of the influence on Polynesia of the Indians along the Pacific coast of North and South America. Fascinating reading, with unsubstantiated yet intriguing theories presented.

Ii, John Papa. *Fragments of Hawaiian History.* Honolulu: Bishop Museum, 1959. Hawaii's history under Kamehameha I as told by a Hawaiian who actually experienced it.

Joesting, Edward. *Hawaii: An Uncommon History.* New York: W.W. Norton Co., 1972. A truly uncommon history told in a series of vignettes relating to the lives and personalities of the first white men in Hawaii, Hawaiian nobility, sea captains, writers, and adventurers. Brings history to life. Absolutely excellent!

Lee, William S. *The Islands.* New York: Holt, Rinehart, 1966. A socio-historical set of stories concerning *malihini* (newcomers) and how they influenced and molded the Hawaii of today.

Liliuokalani. *Hawaii's Story By Hawaii's Queen.* Rutland, VT.: Tuttle, 1964. A moving personal account of Hawaii's inevitable move from monarchy to U.S. Territory by its last queen, Liliuokalani. The facts can be found in other histories, but none provides the emotion or point of view as expressed by Hawaii's deposed monarch. A "must" read to get the whole picture.

Nickerson, Roy. *Lahaina, Royal Capital of Hawaii.* Honolulu: Hawaiian Service, 1978. The story of Lahaina from whaling days to present, spiced with ample photographs.

Smith, Richard A., et al., eds. *The Frontier States.* New York: Time-Life Books, 1968. Short and concise comparisons of the two newest states: Hawaii and Alaska. Dated information, but good social commentary and an excellent appendix suggesting tours, museums, and local festivals.

Takaki, Ronald. *Plantation Life and Labor in Hawaii, 1835-1920.* Honolulu: University of Hawaii Press, 1983. A perspective of plantation life in Hawaii from a multi-ethnic viewpoint. Written by a nationally known island scholar.

MYTHOLOGY AND LEGENDS

Beckwith, Martha. *Hawaiian Mythology.* Honolulu: University of Hawaii Press, 1970. Forty-five years after its original printing, this work remains *the* definitive text on Hawaiian mythology. Ms. Beckwith compiled this book from many sources, giving exhaustive cross-references to genealogies and legends expressed in the oral tradition. If you are going to read one book on Hawaii's folklore, this should be it.

Colum, Padraic. *Legends of Hawaii.* New Haven: Yale University Press, 1937. Selected legends of old Hawaii reinterpreted, but closely based upon the originals.

Elbert, S., comp. *Hawaiian Antiquities and Folklore.* Honolulu: Univerity of Hawaii Press, 1959. Illustrated by Jean Charlot. A selection of the main legends from Abraham Fornander's great work, *The Polynesian Race.*

Melville, Leinanai. *Children of the Rainbow.* Wheaton, Ill.: Theosophical Publishing, 1969. A book on higher spiritual consciousness attuned to nature, which was the basic belief of pre-Christian Hawaii. The appendix contains illustrations of mystical symbols used by the *kahuna.* An enlightening book in many ways.

Thrum, Thomas. *Hawaiian Folk Tales.* Chicago: McClurg and Co., 1907. A collection of Hawaiian tales from the oral tradition as told to the author from various sources.

Westervelt, W.D. *Hawaiian Legends of Volcanoes.* Boston: Ellis Press, 1916. A small book concerning the volcanic legends of Hawaii and how they related to the fledgling field of volcanism at the turn of the century. The vintage photos alone are worth a look.

NATURAL SCIENCES

Abbott, Agatin, Gordon MacDonald, and Frank Peterson. *Volcanoes in the Sea*. Honolulu: University of Hawaii Press, 1983. A simplified yet comprehensive text covering the geology and volcanism of the Hawaiian Islands. Focuses upon the forces of nature (wind, rain, and surf) that shape the islands.

Boom, Robert. *Hawaiian Seashells*. Honolulu: Waikiki Aquarium, 1972. Photos, Jerry Kringle. A collection of 137 seashells found in Hawaiian waters, featuring many found nowhere else on Earth. Broken into categories with accompanying text including common and scientific names, physical descriptions, and likely habitats. A must for shell collectors.

Brock, Vernon, and W.A. Gosline. *Handbook of Hawaiian Fishes*. Honolulu: University of Hawaii Press, 1960. A detailed guide to most of the fishes occurring in Hawaiian waters.

Carlquist, Sherwin. *Hawaii: A Natural History*. New York: Doubleday, 1970. Definitive account of Hawaii's natural history.

Carpenter, Blyth, and Russell Carpenter. *Fish Watching in Hawaii*. San Mateo, Ca.: Natural World Press, 1981. A color guide to many of the reef fish found in Hawaii and often spotted by snorkelers. If you're interested in the fish that you'll be looking at, this guide will be very helpful.

Fielding, Ann, and Ed Robinson. *An Underwater Guide to Hawaii*. Honolulu: University of Hawaii Press, 1987. If you've ever had a desire to snorkel/scuba the living reef waters of Hawaii and to be familiar with what you're seeing, get this small but fact-packed book. The amazing array of marinelife found throughout the archipelago is captured in glossy photos with accompaning informative text. Both the scientific and common names of specimens are given. This book will enrich your underwater experience, and serve as an easily understood reference guide for many years.

Hamaishi, Amy, and Doug Wallin. *Flowers of Hawaii*. Honolulu: World Wide Distributors, 1975. Close-up color photos of many of the most common flowers spotted in Hawaii.

Hawaii Audubon Society. *Hawaii's Birds*. Honolulu: Hawaii Audubon Society, 1981. A field guide to Hawaii's birds, listing the endangered indigenous species, migrants, and introduced species that are now quite common. Color photos with text listing distribution, description, voice, and habits. Excellent field guide.

Hosaka, Edward. *Shore Fishing in Hawaii*. Hilo, HI.: Petroglyph Press, 1984. Known as the best book on Hawaiian fishing since 1944. Receives the highest praise because it has born and bred many Hawaiian fishermen.

Hubbard, Douglass, and Gordon MacDonald. *Volcanoes of the National Parks of Hawaii*. Volcanoes, HI.: Hawaii Natural History Assoc., 1982. The volcanology of Hawaii, documenting the major lava flows and their geological effect on the state.

Island Heritage Limited. *Hawaii's Flowering Trees*. Honolulu: Island Heritage Press. A concise field guide to many of Hawaii's most common flowering trees. All color photos with accompanying descriptive text.

Kay, E. Alison, comp. *A Natural History of the Hawaiian Islands*. Honolulu: University of Hawaii Press, 1972. A selection of concise articles by experts in the fields of volcanism, oceanography, meteorology, and biology. An excellent reference source.

Kuck, Lorraine, and Richard Togg. *Hawaiian Flowers and Flowering Trees*. Rutland, VT.: Tuttle, 1960. A classic field guide to tropical and subtropical flora illustrated in watercolor. A "to the point" description of Hawaiian plants and flowers with a brief history of their places of origin and their introduction to Hawaii.

Merlin, Mark D. *Hawaiian Forest Plants, A Hiker's Guide.* Honolulu: Oriental Publishing, 1980. A companion guide to trekkers into Hawaii's interior. Full-color plates identify and describe the most common forest plants encountered.

————. *Hawaiian Coastal Plants.* Honolulu: Oriental Publishing, 1980. Color photos and botanical descriptions of many of the plants and flowers found growing along Hawaii's varied shorelines.

Merrill, Elmer. *Plant Life of the Pacific World.* Rutland, VT.: Tuttle, 1983. The definitive book for anyone planning a botanical tour to the entire Pacific Basin. Originally published in the 1930s, it remains a tremendous work.

Nickerson, Roy. *Brother Whale, A Pacific Whalewatcher's Log.* San Francisco: Chronicle Books, 1977. Introduces the average person to the life of Earth's greatest mammals. Provides historical accounts, photos, and tips on whale-watching. Well written, descriptive, and the best "first time" book on whales.

Sohmer, S. H., and R. Gustafson. *Plants and Flowers of Hawaii.* Honolulu: University of Hawaii Press, 1987. Sohmer and Gustafson range the vegetation zones of Hawaii, from mountains to coast, introducing you to the wide and varied floral biology of the islands. They give a good introduction to the history, and the uniqueness of the evolution of Hawaiian plantlife. Beautiful color plates are accompanied by clear and concise plant descriptions, with the scientific and common Hawaiian names listed.

Stearns, Harold T. *Road Guide to Points of Geological Interest in the Hawaiian Islands.* Palo Alto, CA.: Pacific Books, 1966. The title is almost as long as this handy little book that lets you know what forces of nature formed the scenery that you see in the islands.

van Riper, Charles, and Sandra van Riper. *A Field Guide to the Mammals of Hawaii.* Honolulu: Oriental Publishing. A guide to the surprising number of mammals introduced into Hawaii. Full-color pages document description, uses, tendencies, and habitat. Small and thin, makes a worthwhile addition to any serious trekker's backpack.

TRAVEL

Birnbaum, Stephen, et al., eds. *Hawaii 1984.* Boston: Houghton Mifflin, 1983. Well-researched, informative writing, with good background material. Focuses primarily on known tourist spots with only perfunctory coverage of out-of-the-way places. Lacking in full-coverage maps.

Bone, Robert W. *The Maverick Guide to Hawaii.* Gretna, LA.: Pelican, 1983. Adequate, personalized writing style.

Fodor, Eugene, comp. *Fodor's Hawaii.* New York: Fodor's Guides, 1983. Great coverage on the clichés, but short on out-of-the-way places.

Great Expeditions Magazine, P.O. Box 8000-411, Sumas, WA 98295. A must for any serious adventurer, this magazine covers unique destinations, far-flung treks, cultural discoveries, and money-saving tips. Back issues available to almost every corner of the Earth.

Hammel, Faye, and Sylvan Levy. *Frommer's Hawaii on $35 a Day.* New York: Frommer, Pasmantier, 1984. Hammel and Levy are good writers, but the book is top-heavy with info on Honolulu and Oahu and skimps on the rest.

Riegert, Ray. *Hidden Hawaii.* Berkeley, CA.: And/Or Press, 1982. Ray offers a "user-friendly" guide to the islands.

Rizzuto, Shirley. *Hawaiian Camping.* Berkeley, CA.: Wilderness Press, 1979. Adequate coverage of the "nuts and bolts" of camping in Hawaii. Slightly conservative in approach and geared toward the family.

Smith, Robert. *Hawaii's Best Hiking Trails*. Also, *Hiking Kauai, Hiking Maui, Hiking Oahu*, and *Hiking Hawaii*. Berkeley: Wilderness Press, 1977 to 1982. Smith's books are specialized, detailed trekker's guides to Hawaii's outdoors. Complete with useful maps, historical references, official procedures, and plants and animals encountered along the way. If you're focused on hiking, these are the best to take along.

Stanley, David. *South Pacific Handbook*. 4th ed. Chico, CA.: Moon Publications, 1989. The model upon which all travel guides should be based. Simply the best book in the world for travel throughout the South Pacific.

Sutton, Horace. *Aloha Hawaii*. New York: Doubleday, 1967. A dated but still excellent guide to Hawaii providing sociological, historical, and cultural insight. Horace Sutton's literary style is the best in the travel guide field. Entertaining reading.

Thorne, Chuck. *The Diver's Guide to Maui*. Kahului, Hl.: Maui Dive Guide, 1984. A no-nonsense snorkelers' and divers' guide to Maui waters. Extensive maps, descriptions, and "straight from the shoulder" advice by one of Maui's best and most experienced divers. A must for all levels of divers and snorkelers.

Thorne, Chuck, and Lou Zitnik. *A Divers' Guide to Hawaii*. Kihei, Hl.: Hawaii's Diver's Guide, 1984. An expanded divers' and snorkelers' guide to the waters of the six main Hawaiian islands. Complete list of maps with full descriptions, tips, and ability levels. A must for all levels of snorkelers and divers.

Wurman, Richard. *Hawaii Access*. Los Angeles: Access Press, 1983. The "fast food" publishers of travel guides. The packaging is colorful and bright like a burger in a styrofoam box, but there's little of substance inside.

COOKING

Alexander, Agnes. *How to Use Hawaiian Fruit*. Hilo, Hl.: Petroglyph Press, 1984. A full range of recipes using delicious and different Hawaiian fruits.

Fitzgerald, Donald, et al., eds. *The Pacific House Hawaii Cookbook*. Pacific House, 1968. A full range of Hawaiian cuisine, including recipes from traditional Chinese, Japanese, Portuguese, New England, and Filipino dishes.

Gibbons, Euell. *Beachcombers Handbook*. New York: McKay Co., 1967. An autobiographical account of this world-famous naturalist as a young man living "off the land" in Hawaii. Great tips on spotting and gathering naturally occurring foods, survival advice, and recipes. Unfortunately the lifestyle described is long outdated.

Margah, Irish, and Elvira Monroe. *Hawaii, Cooking with Aloha*. San Carlos, CA.: Wide World, 1984. Island recipes including *kalua* pig, *lomi* salmon, and hints on decor.

LANGUAGE

Boom, Robert, and Chris Christensen. *Important Hawaiian Place Names*. Honolulu: Boom Enterprises, 1978. A handy pocket-sized book listing most of the major island place names and their translations.

Elbert, Samuel. *Spoken Hawaiian*. Honolulu: University of Hawaii Press, 1970. Progressive conversational lessons.

Elbert, Samuel, and Mary Pukui. *Hawaiian Dictionary*. Honolulu: University of Hawaii, 1971. The best dictionary available on the Hawaiian language. The *Pocket Hawaiian Dictionary* is a condensed version of this dictionary, which is less expensive and adequate for most travelers with a general interest in the language.

GLOSSARY

Words marked with an asterisk (*) are used commonly throughout the islands.

a'a*—rough clinker lava. *A'a* has become the correct geological term to describe this type of lava found anywhere in the world.

ahuapua—pie-shaped land divisions running from mountain to sea that were governed by konohiki, local *ali'i* who owed their allegiance to a reigning chief

aikane—friend; pal; buddy

aina—land; the binding spirit to all Hawaiians. Love of the land is paramount in traditional Hawaiian beliefs.

akamai—smart; clever; wise

akua—a god, or simply "divine." You'll hear people speak of their family or personal *amakua* (ancestral spirit). A favorite is the shark or the *pueo* (Hawaiian owl).

ali'i*—a Hawaiian chief or nobleman

aloha*—the most common greeting in the islands; Can mean both hello or goodbye, welcome or farewell. It also can mean romantic love, affection, or best wishes.

amakua—a personal or family spirit, usually an ancestral spirit

aole—no

auwe—alas; ouch! When a great chief or loved one died, it was a traditional wail of mourning.

halakahiki—pineapple

hale*—house or building. Often combined with other words to name a specific place

such as Haleakala ("House of the Sun") or Hale Pai ("printing house")

hana*—work; combined with *pau* means end of work or quitting time

hanai—literally "to feed." Part of the true *aloha* spirit. A *hanai* is a permanent guest, or an adopted family member, usually an old person or a child. This is an enduring cultural phenomenon in Hawaii, in which a child from one family (perhaps that of a brother or sister, and quite often one's grandchild) is raised as one's own without formal adoption.

haole*—a word that at one time meant foreigner, but which now means a white person or Caucasian. Many etymological definitions have been put forth, but none satisfies everyone. Some feel that it signified a person without a background, because the first white men could not chant their genealogies, as was common with Hawaiians.

hapa*—half, as in a mixed-blooded person being referred to as *hapa haole*

hapai*—pregnant; used by all ethnic groups when a *keiki* is on the way

haupia*—a coconut custard dessert often served at luaus

heiau*—a traditional Hawaiian temple. A platform made of skillfully fitted rocks, upon which structures were built and offerings made to the gods.

holomuu*—an ankle-length dress that is much more fitted than a muumuu, and which is often worn on formal occasions

hono—bay, as in Honolulu ("Sheltered Bay")

ho'oilo—traditional Hawaiian winter that began in November *hoolaulea*—any happy event, but especially a family outing or picnic

hoomalimali*—sweet talk; flattery

huhu*—angry; irritated

hui*—a group; meeting; society. Often used to refer to Chinese businessmen or family members who pool their money to get businesses started.

hukilau—traditional shoreline fish-gathering in which everyone lends a hand to *huki* (pull) the huge net. Anyone taking part shares in the *lau* (food). It is much more like a party than hard work, and if you're lucky you'll be able to take part in one.

hula*—a native Hawaiian dance in which the rhythm of the islands is captured by swaying hips and stories told by lyrically moving hands. A *halau* is a group or school of hula.

huli huli—barbecue, as in *huli huli* chicken

i'a—fish in general. *I'a maka* is raw fish.

imu*—underground oven filled with hot rocks and used for baking. The main cooking feature at luaus, used to steam-bake the pork and other succulent dishes. Traditionally the tending of the *imu* was for men only.

ipo—sweetheart; lover; girlfriend or boyfriend

kahili—a tall pole topped with feathers, resembling a huge feather duster. It was used by an *ali'i* to announce his presence.

kahuna*—priest; sorcerer; doctor; skillful person. *Kahuna* had tremendous power in old Hawaii which they used for both good and evil. The *kahuna ana'ana* was a feared individual because he practiced "black magic" and could pray a person to death, while the *kahuna lapa'au* was a medical practitioner bringing aid and comfort to the people.

kai—the sea. Many businesses and hotels employ *kai* as part of their name.

kalua—roasted underground in an *imu*. A favorite island food is *kalua* pork.

kamaaina*—a child of the land; an old-timer; a longtime island resident of any ethnic background; a resident of Hawaii or native son. Oftentimes hotels and airlines offer discounts called "*kamaaina* rates" to anyone who can prove island residency.

kanaka—man or commoner; later used to distinguish a Hawaiian from other races. Tone of voice can make it a derisive expression.

kane*—means man, but actually used to signify a relationship such as husband or boyfriend. Written on a door it means "Men's Room."

kaola*—any food that has been broiled or barbecued

kapu*—forbidden; taboo; keep out; do not touch

kapuna—a grandparent or old-timer; usually means someone who has gained wisdom. The statewide school system now invites *kapuna* to talk to the children about the old ways and methods.

kaukau*—slang word meaning food or chow; grub. Some of the best food in Hawaii comes from the "*kaukau* wagons," trucks that sell plate lunches and other morsels.

kauwa—a landless, untouchable caste that was confined to living on reservations. Members of this caste were often used as human sacrifice at *heiau*. Calling someone *kauwa* is still considered a grave insult.

kava—a mildly intoxicating traditional drink made from the juice of chewed awaroot, spat into a bowl, and used in religious ceremonies.

*keiki**—child or children; used by all ethnic groups. "Have you hugged your *keiki* today?"

kiawe—an algaroba tree from S. America commonly found in Hawaii along the shore. It grows a nasty long thorn that can easily puncture a tire. Legend has it that the trees were introduced to the islands by a misguided missionary who hoped the thorns would coerce natives into wearing shoes. Actually, they are good for fuel, as fodder for hogs and cattle, and for reforestation, none of which you'll appreciate if you step on one of their thorns, or flatten a tire on your rental car!

kokua—help. As in "Your *kokua* is needed to keep Hawaii free from litter."

kona wind**—a muggy subtropical wind that blows from the south and hits the leeward side of the islands. It usually brings sticky hot weather, and is one of the few times when air-conditioning will be appreciated.

konane—a traditional Hawaiian game, similar to checkers, played with pebbles on a large flat stone used as a board

koolau—windward side of the island

kukui—a candlenut tree whose pods are polished and then strung together to make a beautiful lei. Traditionally the oil-rich nuts were strung on the rib of a coconut leaf and used as a candle.

kuleana—homesite; the old homestead; small farms. Especially used to describe the small spreads on Hawaiian Homes Lands on Molokai.

*Kumulipo**—ancient Hawaiian genealogical chant that records the pantheon of gods, creation, and the beginning of mankind

la—the sun. Often combined with other words to be more descriptive, such as *La*-haina ("Merciless Sun") or Haleaka*la* ("House of the Sun").

*lanai**—veranda or porch. You'll pay more for a hotel room if it has a lanai with an ocean view.

lani—sky or the heavens

*lau hala**—traditional Hawaiian weaving of mats, hats, etc., from the prepared fronds of the pandanus (screw pine)

*lei**—a traditional garland of flowers or vines. One of Hawaii's most beautiful customs. Given at any auspicious occasion, but especially when arriving or leaving Hawaii.

lele—the stone altar at a *heiau*

limu—edible seaweed of various types. Gathered from the shoreline, it makes an excellent salad. It's used to garnish many island dishes and is a favorite at luaus.

lomi lomi—traditional Hawaiian massage; also, raw salmon made up into a vinegared salad with chopped onion and spices

*lua**—the toilet; the head; the bathroom

luakini—a human sacrifice temple. Introduced to Hawaii in the 13th C. at Wahaula Heiau on the Big Island.

*luau**—a Hawaiian feast featuring poi, *imu*-baked pork, and other traditional foods. Good ones provide some of the best gastronomical delights in the world.

luna—foreman or overseer in the plantation fields. They were often mounted on horseback and were renowned either for their fairness or cruelty. They represented the middle class, and served as a buffer between the plantation workers and the white plantation owners.

*mahalo**—thank you. *Mahalo nui* means "big thanks" or "thank you very much."

mahele—division. The "Great Mahele" of 1848 changed Hawaii forever when the traditional common lands were broken up into privately owned plots.

*mahi mahi**—a favorite eating fish. Often called a dolphin, but a *mahi mahi* is a true fish, not a cetacean.

mahu—a homosexual; often used derisively like "fag" or "queer"

maile—a fragrant vine used in traditional leis. It looks ordinary but smells delightful.

makaainana—a commoner; a person "belonging" to the *aina* (land), who supported the *ali'i* by fishing, farming, and as a warrior

*makai**—toward the sea; used by most islanders when giving directions

make—dead; deceased

*malihini**—newcomer; tenderfoot; a recent arrival

malo—the native Hawaiian loincloth. Never worn anymore except at festivals or pageants.

*mana**—power from the spirit world; innate energy of all things animate or inanimate; the grace of god. Mana could be passed on from one person to another, or even stolen. Great care was taken to protect the *ali'i* from having their mana defiled. Commoners were required to lie flat on the ground and cover their faces whenever a great *ali'i* approached. *Kahuna* were often employed in the regaining or transference of mana.

manauahi—free; gratis; extra

manini—stingy; tight. A Hawaiianized word taken from the name of Don Francisco *Marin,* who was instrumental in bringing many fruits and plants to Hawaii. He was known for never sharing any of the bounty from his substantial gardens on Vineyard Street in Honolulu.

*mauka**—toward the mountains; used by most islanders when giving directions

mauna—mountain. Often combined with other words to be more descriptive, such as Mauna Kea ("White Mountain").

mele—a song or chant in the Hawaiian oral tradition that records the history and genealogies of the *ali'i*

menehune—the legendary "little people" of Hawaii. Like leprechauns, they are said to have shunned mankind and possessed magical powers. Stone walls said to have been completed in one night are often attributed to them. Some historians argue that they actually existed and were the aboriginals of Hawaii, inhabiting the islands before the coming of the Polynesians.

moa—chicken; fowl

*moana**—the ocean; the sea. Many businesses and hotels as well as places have *moana* as part of their name.

moe—sleep

moolelo—ancient tales kept alive by the oral tradition and recited only by day

*muumuu**—a "Mother Hubbard," an ankle-length dress with a high neckline introduced by the missionaries to cover the nakedness of the Hawaiians. It has become fashionable attire for almost any occasion in Hawaii.

nani—beautiful

nui—big; great; large; as in *mahalo nui* (thank you very much)

ohana—a family; the fundamental social division; extended family. Now used to denote a social organization with grass-roots overtones, as in the "Protect Kahoolawe Ohana."

okolehau—literally "iron bottom"; a traditional booze made from ti root; okole means your "rear end" and hau means "iron," which was descriptive of the huge blubber pots that it was made in. Also, if you drink too much it'll surely knock you on your okole.

ono*—delicious; delightful; the best. Ono ono means "extra or absolutely delicious."

opihi—a shellfish or limpet that clings to rocks and is gathered as one of the islands' favorite pu pu. Custom dictates that you never remove all of the opihi from a rock; some are always left to grow for future generations.

opu—belly; stomach

pa'hoehoe*—smooth ropey lava that looks like burnt pancake batter. Pa'hoehoe is now the correct geological term used to describe this type of lava found anywhere in the world.

pake—a Chinese person. Can be derisive, depending on tone in which it is used. It is a bastardization of the Chinese word meaning "uncle."

pali*—a cliff; precipice. Hawaii's geology makes them quite common. The most famous are the pali of Oahu where a major battle was fought.

paniolo*—a Hawaiian cowboy. Derived from the Spanish espaniola. The first cowboys brought to Hawaii during the early 19th century were Mexicans from California.

papale—hat. Except for the feathered helmets of the ali'i warriors of old Hawaii, hats were generally not worn. However, once the islanders saw their practical uses and how fashionable they were, they began weaving them from various materials and quickly became experts at manufacture and design.

pau*—finished; done; completed. Often combined into pau hana, which means end of work or quitting time.

pa'u—long split skirt often worn by women when horseback riding. Last century, an island treat was when pa'u riders would turn out in their beautiful dresses at Kapiolani Park in Honolulu. The tradition is carried on today at many of Hawaii's rodeos.

pilau—stink; bad smell; stench

pilikia—trouble of any kind, big or small; bad times

poi*—a glutinous paste made from the pounded corn of taro which ferments slightly and has a light sour taste. Purplish in color, it's a staple at luaus, where it is called "one-, two-, or three-finger" poi, depending upon its thickness.

pono—righteous or excellent

pua—flower

puka*—a hole of any size. Puka is used by all island residents, whether talking about a pinhole in a rubber boat or a tunnel through a mountain.

punalua—the tradition of sharing mates in practice before the missionaries came. Western seamen took advantage of it, and this led to the spreading of contagious diseases and eventually to the ultimate demise of the Hawaiian people.

punee*—bed; narrow couch. Used by all ethnic groups. To recline on a punee on a breezy lanai is a true island treat.

pu pu*—an appetizer; a snack; hors d'oeuvres; can be anything from cheese and crackers to sushi. Oftentimes, bars or nightclubs offer them free.

pupule—crazy; nuts; out of your mind

pu'u—hill, as in Pu'u Ulaula ("Red Hill")

tapa*—a traditional paper cloth made from beaten bark. Intricate designs were stamped in using beaters, and natural dyes added color. The tradition was lost for many years, but is now making a comeback, and provides some of the most beautiful folk art in the islands.

taro*—the staple of old Hawaii. A plant with a distinctive broad leaf that produces a starchy root. It was brought by the first Polynesians and was grown on magnificently irrigated plantations. According to the oral tradition, the life-giving properties of taro hold mystical significance for Hawaiians, since it was created by the gods at about the same time as mankind.

ti—a broad green-leafed plant that was used for many purposes, from plates to hula skirts (never grass), and especially used to wrap religious offerings presented at the *heiau*.

tutu*—grandmother; granny; older woman. Used by all as a term of respect and endearment.

ukulele*—*uku* means "flea" and *lele* means "jumping," so literally "jumping flea"—the way the Hawaiians perceived the quick finger movements on the banjo-like Portuguese folk instrument called a *cavaquinho*. The ukulele quickly became synonymous with the islands.

wahine*—young woman; female; girl; wife. Used by all ethnic groups. When written on a door it means "Women's Room."

wai—fresh water; drinking water

wela—hot. *Wela kahao* is a "hot time" or "making whoopee."

wiki*—quickly; fast; in a hurry. Often seen as *wiki wiki* (very fast), as in "Wiki Wiki Messenger Service."

INDEX

Italicized page numbers indicate information in captions, call-outs, charts, illustrations, or maps.
Boldface page numbers offer the primary reference to a given topic.

HOTEL INDEX

RESTAURANT INDEX

ABOUT THE AUTHOR

Joe Bisignani is a fortunate man because he makes his living doing the two things that he likes best: traveling and writing. Joe has been with Moon Publications since 1979 and is the author of *Japan Handbook, Kauai Handbook, Hawaii Handbook,* and *Maui Handbook.* When not traveling, he makes his home in Northern California.

ABOUT THE ILLUSTRATORS

Mary Ann Abel was born and raised in a small town in West Virginia. She uses this background to infuse her work with what she values most: family and nature. Mary Ann is a member of the Sunday Art Mart in Honolulu, where she sells her artwork. She also displays at various "juried shows" in and around Honolulu, and currently, her work can be seen at the Myonghee Art Gallery in Waikiki. Mary Ann lives in Honolulu with her husband Richard and her daughters Robin and Nicole. Her illustrations appear on pages 256 and 271.

Brian Bardwell pages 131, 222, and 281.

Sue Strangio Everett was born and raised in Chico, California, where she attended Chico State University, majoring in Fine Art. For the past 12 years she has refined and developed her skills, working primarily as a graphic artist. Sue is also accomplished in pottery design and glazing, silk screening, weaving, etching, stained-glass work, and pen and ink. She drew the illustrations on pages 86, 166, and 169.

Debra Fau is a born artist. She can't help it . . . she's French. Deb lives in Chico where she sings with a rock 'n' roll band, does batik, tie-dye, and paintings. She keeps the wolf from the door by cocktail waitressing, where she's renowned for carrying the best tray in town. Her drawings appear on pages 328 and 330.

Richard Fields, born in Whittier, California, grew up in an art environment. His father was a film animator. With the encouragement and support of his parents, his talents blossomed and his skills grew to include oil painting, sculpture, and ceramics. Having received an impressive succession of awards throughout his adolescence, he was, at 18, shown at the Laguna Festival of Arts and the Pageant of Masters. His already distinctively styled California landscapes found an appreciative market among Southern California collectors. An amateur botanist and an avid hiker, Richard takes every available opportunity to sketch on locale. He incorporates a mixed media of airbrush, acrylics, colored pencils, India ink, and stencils into his original artwork. His painting appears on the cover.

Louise Foote lives on an experimental urban commune in Chico. She works as an archaeologist, renovates homes, and builds custom furniture. Sometimes, she turns her hand to illustrating, and her work appears on pages 12, 13, 14, 16, 18, 44, 48, 72, 83, 127, 144, 145, 154, 155, 156, 173, 280, and 327.

Diana Lasich Harper has been a contributing artist to several Moon books. After receiving a degree in Art at San Jose State University, California, she moved to Hawaii where she lived for four years. Much of her time there was spent cycling, hiking, and *always* drawing. From

Hawaii, Diana moved to Japan where she lived for two years and studied woodblock printing, *sumie,* and *kimono* painting. Her illustrations appear on pages 5, 11, 15, 37, 38, 69, 70, 77, 79, 122, 123, 124, 125, 139, 147, 168, 201, 216, 261, and 305.

Bob Race taught Fine Arts at Butte Community College near Chico for 14 years. He now manages the Illustration and Cartography departments at Moon Publications. His drawings appear on pages 1, 131, 139, 174, 217, 222, 262, 272, 281, 306, and 320.

Pathways.

Over one thousand years ago, Polynesians in outrigger canoes crossed the vast ocean with determination, skill and the strong commitment of the people.

Today, Hawaiian Airlines has pathways to the east and west. East to Los Angeles, San Francisco, Seattle, Portland, Las Vegas and Anchorage. West to American Samoa, Western Samoa and the Kingdom of Tonga. And in Hawaii, we still connect these lovely islands just as we've done for the past 60 years. And our deep Polynesian roots make hospitality second nature and every guest first in our heart.

Our spirit is unique. We are Hawaiian.

HAWAIIAN.®
The Colors of Paradise.

U.S. Toll Free 1-800-367-5320, Statewide Toll Free 1-800-882-8811.
Call Hawaiian or your travel agent.

Moon Handbooks—The Ideal Traveling Companions

Open a Moon Handbook and you're opening your eyes and heart to the world. Thoughtful, sensitive, provocative, and highly informative, Moon Handbooks encourage an intimate understanding of a region, from its rich culture and history to essential practicalities. Fun to read and packed with valuable information on accommodations, dining, recreation, plus indispensable travel tips, detailed maps, charts, illustrations, photos, glossaries, and indexes, Moon Handbooks are ideal traveling companions: informative, entertaining, and highly practical.

TO ORDER BY PHONE: (800) 345-5473 • Monday-Friday • 9 a.m.-5 p.m. PST

The Pacific/Asia Series

BALI HANDBOOK by Bill Dalton
Detailed travel information on the most famous island in the world. 12 color pages, 29 b/w photos, 68 illustrations, 42 maps, 7 charts, glossary, booklist, index. 428 pages. **$12.95**

INDONESIA HANDBOOK by Bill Dalton
This one-volume encyclopedia explores island by island the many facets of this sprawling, kaleidoscopic island nation. 30 b/w photos, 143 illustrations, 250 maps, 17 charts, booklist, extensive Indonesian vocabulary, index. 1,050 pages. **$17.95**

SOUTH KOREA HANDBOOK by Robert Nilsen
Whether you're visiting on business or searching for adventure, *South Korea Handbook* is an invaluable companion. 8 color pages, 78 b/w photos, 93 illustrations, 109 maps, 10 charts, Korean glossary with useful notes on speaking and reading the language, booklist, index. 548 pages. **$14.95**

SOUTHEAST ASIA HANDBOOK by Carl Parkes
Helps the enlightened traveler to travel with wide eyes and an open mind to discover the real Southeast Asia. 16 color pages, 75 b/w photos, 11 illustrations, 169 maps, 140 charts, vocabularies and suggested readings, index. 873 pages. **$16.95**

JAPAN HANDBOOK by J.D. Bisignani
An indispensable tool for understanding and enjoying one of the world's most complex and intriguing countries. 8 color pages, 200 b/w photos, 92 illustrations, 112 maps and town plans, 29 charts, appendix on the Japanese language, booklist, glossary, index. 504 pages. **$12.95**

OAHU HANDBOOK by J.D. Bisignani
A handy guide to Honolulu, renowned surfing beaches, and Oahu's countless other diversions. Color and b/w photos, illustrations, 18 maps, charts, booklist, glossary, index. 350 pages. **$11.95**

HAWAII HANDBOOK by J.D. Bisignani
Winner of the 1989 Hawaii Visitors Bureau's Best Guide Book Award and Grand Award for Excellence in Travel Journalism, this guide takes you beyond the glitz and high-priced hype and leads you to a genuine Hawaiian experience. 12 color pages, 318 b/w photos, 132 illustrations, 74 maps, 43 graphs and charts, Hawaiian and pidgin glossaries, appendix, booklist, index. 788 pages. **$15.95**

KAUAI HANDBOOK by J.D. Bisignani
Kauai Handbook is the perfect antidote to the workaday world. 8 color pages, 36 b/w photos, 48 illustrations, 19 maps, 10 tables and charts, Hawaiian and pidgin glossaries, booklist, index. 236 pages. **$9.95**

MAUI HANDBOOK: Including Molokai and Lanai by J.D. Bisignani
"No fool-'round" advice on accommodations, eateries, and recreation, plus a comprehensive introduction to island ways, geography, and history. 8 color pages, 60 b/w photos, 72 illustrations, 34 maps, 19 charts, booklist, glossary, index. 350 pages. **$10.95**

SOUTH PACIFIC HANDBOOK by David Stanley
The original comprehensive guide to the 16 territories in the South Pacific. 20 color pages, 195 b/w photos, 121 illustrations, 35 charts, 138 maps, booklist, glossary, index. 740 pages. **$15.95**

MICRONESIA HANDBOOK:
Guide to the Caroline, Gilbert, Mariana, and Marshall Islands by David Stanley
Micronesia Handbook guides you on a real Pacific adventure all your own. 8 color pages, 77 b/w photos, 68 illustrations, 69 maps, 18 tables and charts, index. 287 pages. **$9.95**

FIJI ISLANDS HANDBOOK by David Stanley
The first and still the best source of information on travel around this 322-island archipelago. 8 color pages, 35 b/w photos, 78 illustrations, 26 maps, 3 charts, Fijian glossary, booklist, index. 198 pages. **$8.95**

TAHITI-POLYNESIA HANDBOOK by David Stanley
All five French-Polynesian archipelagoes are covered in this comprehensive guide by Oceania's best-known travel writer. 12 color pages, 45 b/w photos, 64 illustrations, 33 maps, 7 charts, booklist, glossary, index. 225 pages. **$9.95**

NEW ZEALAND HANDBOOK by Jane King
Introduces you to the people, places, history, and culture of this extraordinary land. 8 color pages, 99 b/w photos, 146 illustrations, 82 maps, booklist, index. 546 pages. **$14.95**

BLUEPRINT FOR PARADISE: How to Live on a Tropic Island by Ross Norgrove
This one-of-a-kind guide has everything you need to know about moving to and living comfortably on a tropical island. 8 color pages, 40 b/w photos, 3 maps, 14 charts, appendices, index. 212 pages. **$14.95**

The Americas Series

NORTHERN CALIFORNIA HANDBOOK by Kim Weir
An outstanding companion for imaginative travel in the territory north of the Tehachapis. Color and b/w photos, 69 maps, illustrations, booklist, index. Approximately 850 pages. **$16.95**

NEVADA HANDBOOK by Deke Castleman
Nevada Handbook puts the Silver State into perspective and makes it manageable and affordable. 34 b/w photos, 43 illustrations, 37 maps, 17 charts, booklist, index. 301 pages. **$10.95**

NEW MEXICO HANDBOOK by Stephen Metzger
A close-up and complete look at every aspect of this wondrous state. 8 color pages, 85 b/w photos, 63 illustrations, 50 maps, 10 charts, booklist, index. 350 pages. **$11.95**

TEXAS HANDBOOK by Joe Cummings
Seasoned travel writer Joe Cummings brings an insider's perspective to his home state. 12 color pages, b/w photos, maps, illustrations, charts, booklist, index. Approximately 400 pages. **$11.95**

ARIZONA TRAVELER'S HANDBOOK by Bill Weir
This meticulously researched guide contains everything necessary to make Arizona accessible and enjoyable. 8 color pages, 194 b/w photos, 74 illustrations, 53 maps, 6 charts, booklist, index. 505 pages. **$13.95**

UTAH HANDBOOK by Bill Weir
Weir gives you all the carefully researched facts and background to make your visit a success. 8 color pages, 102 b/w photos, 61 illustrations, 30 maps, 9 charts, booklist, index. 450 pages. **$11.95**

ALASKA-YUKON HANDBOOK by Deke Castleman, Don Pitcher, and David Stanley
The inside story, with plenty of well-seasoned advice to help you cover more miles on less money. 8 color pages, 26 b/w photos, 92 illustrations, 90 maps, 6 charts, booklist, glossary, index. 384 pages. **$11.95**

WASHINGTON HANDBOOK by Dianne J. Boulerice Lyons
Covers sights, shopping, services, transportation, and outdoor recreation, and has complete listings for restaurants and accommodations. 8 color pages, 92 b/w photos, 24 illustrations, 81 maps, 8 charts, booklist, index. 400 pages. **$11.95**

BRITISH COLUMBIA HANDBOOK by Jane King
With an emphasis on outdoor adventures, this guide covers mainland British Columbia, Vancouver Island, the Queen Charlotte Islands, and the Canadian Rockies. 8 color pages, 56 b/w photos, 45 illustrations, 66 maps, 4 charts, booklist, index. 396 pages. **$11.95**

GUIDE TO CATALINA: and California's Channel Islands by Chicki Mallan
A complete guide to these remarkable islands, from the windy solitude of the Channel Islands National Marine Sanctuary to bustling Avalon. 8 color pages, 105 b/w photos, 65 illustrations, 40 maps, 32 charts, booklist, index. 262 pages. **$9.95**

GUIDE TO THE YUCATAN PENINSULA: Including Belize by Chicki Mallan
All the information you'll need to guide you into every corner of this exotic land. 8 color pages, 154 b/w photos, 55 illustrations, 57 maps, 70 charts, appendix, booklist, Mayan and Spanish glossaries, index. 391 pages. **$11.95**

CANCUN HANDBOOK: and Mexico's Caribbean Coast by Chicki Mallan
Covers the city's luxury scene as well as more modest attractions, plus many side trips to unspoiled beaches and Mayan ruins. Color and b/w photos, illustrations, over 30 maps, Spanish glossary, booklist, index. 257 pages. **$9.95**

The International Series

EGYPT HANDBOOK by Kathy Hansen
An invaluable resource for intelligent travel in Egypt. 8 color pages, 20 b/w photos, 150 illustrations, 80 detailed maps and plans to museums and archaeological sites, Arabic glossary, booklist, index. 510 pages. **$14.95**

PAKISTAN HANDBOOK by Isobel Shaw
For armchair travelers and trekkers alike, the most detailed and authoritative guide to Pakistan ever published. 28 color pages, 86 maps, appendices, Urdu glossary, booklist, index. 478 pages. **$15.95**

IMPORTANT ORDERING INFORMATION

TO ORDER BY PHONE: (800) 345-5473 · Monday-Friday · 9 a.m.-5 p.m. PST

PRICES: All prices are subject to change. We always ship the most current edition. We will let you know if there is a price increase on the book you ordered.

SHIPPING & HANDLING OPTIONS:
1) Domestic UPS or USPS 1st class (allow 10 working days for delivery):
$3.50 for the 1st item, 50 cents for each additional item.

Exceptions:
- **Moonbelt** shipping is $1.50 for one, 50 cents for each additional belt.
- Add $2.00 for same-day handling.
2) UPS 2nd Day Air or Printed Airmail requires a special quote.
3) International Surface Bookrate (8-12 weeks delivery):
$3.00 for the 1st item, $1.00 for each additional item.

FOREIGN ORDERS: All orders which originate outside the U.S.A. must be paid for with either an International Money Order or a check in U.S. currency drawn on a major U.S. bank based in the U.S.A.

TELEPHONE ORDERS: We accept Visa or MasterCard payments. Minimum order is US$15.00. Call in your order: 1-(800) 345-5473. 9 a.m.-5 p.m. Pacific Standard Time.

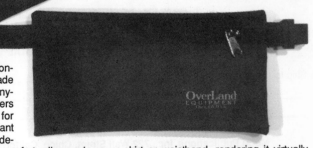

MOONBELTS. A new concept in moneybelts. Made of heavy-duty Cordura nylon, the **Moonbelt** offers maximum protection for your money and important papers. This pouch, designed for all-weather comfort, slips under your shirt or waistband, rendering it virtually undetectable and inaccessible to pickpockets. Many thoughtful features: 1-inch-wide nylon webbing, heavy-duty zipper, and a 1-inch high-test quick-release buckle. No more fumbling around for the strap or repeated adjustments, this handy plastic buckle opens and closes with a touch, but won't come undone until you want it to. Accommodates travelers cheques, passport, cash, photos. Size 5 x 9 inches. Available in black only.　**$8.95**

ORDER FORM

FOR FASTER SERVICE ORDER BY PHONE: (800) 345-5473 · 9 a.m.-5 p.m. PST
(See important ordering information on preceding page)

Name:_____ Date:_____

Street:_____

City:_____

State or Country:_____ Zip Code:_____

Daytime Phone:_____

Quantity	Title	Price

Taxable Total	
Sales Tax (6.25%) for California Residents	
Shipping & Handling	
TOTAL	

Ship to: ☐ address above   ☐ other_____

_____

_____

Make checks payable to:
Moon Publications, Inc., 722 Wall Street, Chico, California 95928, USA
We Accept Visa and MasterCard
To Order: Call in your Visa or MasterCard number, or send a written order with your Visa or MasterCard number and expiration date clearly written.

Card Number: ☐ **Visa**   ☐ **MasterCard**

☐☐☐☐ ☐☐☐☐ ☐☐☐☐ ☐☐☐☐

expiration date:_____

Exact Name on Card: ☐ same as above

☐ other_____

signature_____